REVIEWS OF UNITED KINGDOM
STATISTICAL SOURCES

VOLUME XX

RELIGION

Recurrent Christian Sources

Non-recurrent Christian Data

Judaism

Other Religions

REVIEWS OF UNITED KINGDOM STATISTICAL SOURCES

Editor: W. F. Maunder

Assistant Editor: M. C. Fleming

REVIEWS OF UNITED KINGDOM STATISTICAL SOURCES

Edited by W. F. Maunder

Professor Emeritus of Economic and Social Statistics, University of Exeter

Assisted by M. C. Fleming

Reader in Economics, Loughborough University

VOLUME XX

RELIGION

Recurrent Christian Sources

by

L. M. BARLEY
Bible Society, Swindon

Non-recurrent Christian Data

by

C. D. FIELD
John Rylands University Library, Manchester

Judaism

by

B. A. KOSMIN
North American Jewish Data Bank, New York

Other Religions

by

J. S. NIELSEN
*Centre for the Study of Islamic and Christian-Muslim Religions,
Birmingham*

Published for
The Royal Statistical Society and
Economic and Social Research Council

by

PERGAMON PRESS

OXFORD · NEW YORK · BEIJING · FRANKFURT
SÃO PAULO · SYDNEY · TOKYO · TORONTO

U.K.	Pergamon Press, Headington Hill Hall, Oxford OX3 0BW, England
U.S.A.	Pergamon Press, Maxwell House, Fairview Park, Elmsford, New York 10523, U.S.A.
PEOPLE'S REPUBLIC OF CHINA	Pergamon Press, Qianmen Hotel, Beijing, People's Republic of China
FEDERAL REPUBLIC OF GERMANY	Pergamon Press, Hammerweg 6, D-6242 Kronberg, Federal Republic of Germany
BRAZIL	Pergamon Editora, Rua Eça de Queiros, 346, CEP 04011, São Paulo, Brazil
AUSTRALIA	Pergamon Press Australia, P.O. Box 544, Potts Point, N.S.W. 2011, Australia
JAPAN	Pergamon Press, 8th Floor, Matsuoka Central Building, 1-7-1 Nishishinjuku, Shinjuku-ku, Tokyo 160, Japan
CANADA	Pergamon Press Canada, Suite 104, 150 Consumers Road, Willowdale, Ontario M2J 1P9, Canada

First edition 1987

Library of Congress Cataloging-in-Publication Data
Religion
(Reviews of United Kingdom statistical sources; v. 20)
Includes indexes.
Contents: Recurrent Christian sources /
by L. M. Barley — Non-recurrent Christian data /
by C. D. Field — Judaism / by B. A. Kosmin — [etc.]
1. Great Britain—Religion—Statistical services.
2. Great Britain—Religion—Statistics. I. Royal
Statistical Society (Great Britain) II. Economic
and Social Research Council (Great Britain)
III. Series
BL980.G7R45   1987   200'.941   87–2325

British Library Cataloguing in Publication Data
Religion —(Reviews of United
Kingdom statistical sources; v. 20).
1. Great Britain — Religion — Statistical services
I. Barley, L. M. II. Royal Statistical
Society III. Economic and Social Research
Council IV. Series
306'.6   BR759
ISBN 0-08-034778-9

Printed in Great Britain by A. Wheaton & Co. Ltd., Exeter

CONTENTS OF VOLUME XX

FOREWORD

The Sources and Nature of the Statistics of the United Kingdom, produced under the auspices of the Royal Statistical Society and edited by Maurice Kendall, filled a notable gap on the library shelves when it made its appearance in the early post-war years.Through a series of critical reviews by many of the foremost national experts, it constituted a valuable contemporary guide to statisticians working in many fields as well as a bench-mark to which historians of the development of Statistics in this country are likely to return again and again. The Social Science Research Council* and the Society were both delighted when Professor Maunder came forward with the proposal that a revised version should be produced, indicating as well his willingness to take on the onerous task of editor. The two bodies were more than happy to act as co-sponsors of the project and to help in its planning through a joint steering committee. The result, we are confident, will be judged a worthy successor to the previous volumes by the very much larger "statistics public' that has come into being in the intervening years.

Mrs SUZANNE REEVE
Secretary
Economic and Social Research Council

Mrs E.J.SNELL
Honorary Secretary
Royal Statistical Society

August 1986

August 1986

* SSRC is now the Economic and Social Research Council (ESRC).

MEMBERSHIP OF THE JOINT STEERING COMMITTEE

(May 1986)

Chairman: Miss S. V. Cunliffe

Representing the Royal Statistical Society:

Mr M. C. Fessey

Dr S. Rosenbaum

Mrs E. J. Snell

Representing the Economic and Social Research Council:

Professor J. P. Burman

Mr I. Maclean

Miss J. Morris

Secretary: Mr D. E. Allen

INTRODUCTION TO VOLUME XX

Statistical sources on religion are not highly developed in either method or concept nor are they profuse in the quantitiy of recurrent data generated. Perhaps this situation should not be surprising since their economic importance is minimal, their social significance is remarkeably little explored given the widespread conviction of the link between religious belief and actual behaviour, while their use to the churches at even a purely administrative level is not widely appreciated. Clearly a statistician must regard this state of affairs as regrettable and although it can hardly be expected that this volume will bring a revolution to either ecclesiastical or sociological thinking it may be hoped at least that it may contribute to a gradual process of enlightenment.

By far the larger part of the available data naturally relates to the Christian churches and this is suffsuiciently extensive to require a split between serial or recurrent sources on the one hand and ad hoc survey data on the other. The former are the subject of Lynda Barley's review for which she undertook a special enquiry to over 100 church agencies seeking up to date information on all their available data. Returns required at least every 10 years are regarded as recurrent. Dr.Clive Field completes the coverage of Christian data by an extensive examination of non-recurrent material, that is primarily survey results, of which there is an astonishing wealth. In the third review Dr. Barry Kosmin sets out the available Jewish data which comprise the best recorded and the most extensive of the sources in the non-Christian sector. The statistical sources on the remaining religions practised in the UK are brought together by Dr. Jorgen Nielsen in the final review of the volume.

This entire work is greatly indebted to a contributor who appears wonly modestly as the author of a prologue, namely Peter W. Brierley. In fact, he played a key role in the formative stages of the project which provided the 'lift-off' not forthcoming from any other quarter. It was his enthusiastic and energetic response to my appeal that made the whole thing possible and a great deal ov his time went in organizing tht preparatory meetings which mapped out the programme for this volume. In addition, he gave detailed guidance on the preparation of the first review on recurrent Christian sources.

The expected termination of ESRC support for the series has now been decided and this will, of course, complete a long period of sponsorship which has entailed the entire financial burden. Hence, unless some other sponsor comes forward to assume the role, the series must end when the present contents of the pipeline are exhausted. Although reviews in progress still represent a substantial programme, it means inevitably that the project will have failed to achieve the aim with which it started of providing a complete coverage of sources in the whole economic and social field. Not only have several reviews fallen by the wayside (which is scarcely surprising in that the main incentive for contributors is the warm glow of satisfaction that comes from the fulfillment of such a necessary professional task) but topics in other areas have not yet been commissioned while several already publ ished now require updating. The project has accummulated a wealth of experience in its task and while it is a going concern it would need only a relatively modest grant to keep it in business but to start *de novo* or even to revive it after a lapse

The primary aim of this series is to act as a work of reference to the sources of statistical material of all kinds, both official and unofficial. It seeks to enable the user to discover what data are available on the subject in which he is interested, from where they may be obtained, and what the limitations are to their use. Data are regarded as available not only if published in the normal printed format but also if they are likely to be released to a *bona fide* enquirer in any other form, such as duplicated documents, computer print-out or even magnetic tape. On the other hand, no reference is made to material which, even if it is known to exist, is not accessible to the general run of potential users. The distinction, of course, is not clear-cut and mention of a source is not to be regarded as a guarantee that data will be released; in particular cases it may very well be a matter for negotiation. The latter caution applies with particular force to the question of obtaining computer print-outs of custom specified tabulations. Where original records are held on magnetic tape it might appear that there should be no insuperable problem, apart from confidentiality, in obtaining any feasible analysis at a cost; in practice, it may well turn out that there are capacity restraints which override any simple cost calculation. Thus, what is requested might make demands on computer and programming resources to such an extent that the routine work of the agency concerned would be intolerably affected.

The intention is that the source for each topic should be reviewed in detail, and the brief supplied to authors has called for comprehensive coverage at the level of 'national interest'. This term does not denote any necessary restriction to statistics collected on a national basis (still less, of course, to national aggregates) but it means that sources of a purely local character, without wider interest in either content or methodology, are excluded. Indeed, the mere task of identifying all material of this latter kind is an impossibility. The interpretation of the brief has obviously involved discretion and it is up to the users of these reviews to say what unreasonable gaps become apparent to them. They are cordially invited to do so by communicating with me.

To facilitate the use of the series as a work of reference, certain features have been incorporated which warrant a word or two of explanation. First, the text of each review is designed, in so far as varying subject matter permits, to follow a standard form of arrangement so that users may expect a similar pattern to be followed throughout the series. The starting point is a brief summary of the activity concerned and its organisation, in order to give a clear background understanding of how data are collected, what is being measured, the stage at which measurements are made, what the reporting units are, the channels through which returns are routed and where they are processed. As a further part of this introductory material, there is a discussion of the specific problems of definition and measurement to which the topic gives rise. The core sections on available sources which follow are arranged at the author's discretion – by origin, by subject subdivision, or by type of data; there is too much heterogeneity between topics to permit any imposition of complete uniformity on all authors. The final section is devoted to a discussion of general shortcomings and possibly desirable improvements. In case a contrary expectation should be aroused, it should be said that authors have not been asked to produce a comprehensive plan for the reform of statistical reporting in the whole of their field. However, a review of existing sources is a natural opportunity to make some suggestions for future policy on the collection and publication of statistics within the scope concerned and authors have been encouraged to take full advantage of it.

Secondly, detailed factual information about statistical series and other data is given in a Quick Reference List (QRL). The exact nature of the entries is best seen by glancing at the list and accordingly they are not described here. Again, the ordering is not prescribed except that entries are not classified by publication source since it is presumed that it is this which is unknown to the reader. In general, the routine type of information which is given in the QRL is not repeated verbally in the text; the former, however, serves as a search route to the latter in that a reference (by section number) is shown against a QRL entry when there is a related discussion in the text.

Third, a subject index to each review acts as a more or less conventional line of enquiry on textual references; it is a computerised system and, for an individual review, the only advantage is the possibility of easily permuting entries. The object at this level is merely to facilitate search by giving as many variants as possible. In addition, however, it also makes possible selective searches by keyword over any combination of reviews and a printout of the entries found may then be prepared.

Fourth, each review contains two listings of publications. The QRL Key gives full details of the publications shown as sources and text references to them are made in the form [QRL serial number]; this list is confined essentially to data publications. The other listing is a general bibliography of works discussing wider aspects; text references in this case are made in the form [B serial number].

Finally, an attempt is made to reproduce the more important returns or forms used in data collection so that it may be seen what tabulations it is possible to make as well as helping to clarify the basis of those actually available. Unfortunately, there are severe practical limitations on the number of such forms that it is possible to append to a review and authors perforce have to be highly selective.

If all or any of these features succeed in their intention of increasing the value of the series in its basic function as a work of reference it will be gratifying; the extent to which the purpose is achieved, however, will be difficult to assess without 'feedback' from the readership. Users, therefore, will be rendering an essential service if they will send me a note of specific instances where, in consulting a review, they have failed to find the information sought.

As editor, I must express my very grateful thanks to all the members of the Joint Steering Committee of the Royal Statistical Society and the Economic and Social Research Council. It would be unfair to saddle them with any responsibility for shortcomings in execution but they have directed the overall strategy with as admirable a mixture of guidance and forbearance as any editor of such a series could desire. Especial thanks are due to the Secretary of the Committee who is an unfailing source of help even when sorely pressed by the more urgent demands of his other offices.

The authors joins me in thanking all those who gave up their time to attend the seminar held to discuss the first draft of the reviews and which contributed materially to improving the final versions.

We are most grateful to Pergamon Press Ltd. for their continued support and in particular to Grace Belfiore, the Behavioral Sciences section head, and to the Production Department who put all the pieces together. The subject index entries have been compiled by Mrs. Marian Guest who has also acted as editorial assistant throughout. Special thanks are due to Mr.Ray Burnley who again has masterminded our use of the Lasercomp System at Oxford University Computer Service and to the latter for the use of this facility. Finally, we also wish to record our appreciation of the permission granted us to reproduce certain copyright material by the Controller of Her Majesty's Stationery Office.

W.F. Maunder

University of Exeter

August 1986

33: RECURRENT CHRISTIAN DATA

LINDA BARLEY

With a Prologue by Peter Brierly

REFERENCE DATE OF SOURCES REVIEWED

This review is believed to represent the position at March 1985, although the bulk of the research was carried out in 1983. Amendments and additional material have been incorporated where appropriate up to the proof-reading stage of September 1985.

LIST OF ABBREVIATIONS

BARB	Broadcasters Audience Research Board
CIO	Church Information Office
DES	Department of Education and Science
FCFC	Free Church Federal Council
FEBA	Far East Broadcasting Association
FIEC	Fellowship of Independent Evangelical Churches
ISIS	Independent Schools Information Service
NYI	Nazarene Youth International
OMF	Overseas Missionary Fellowship
SHRE	Society for Research into Higher Education
UCCF	Universities and Colleges Christian Fellowship

ACKNOWLEDGEMENTS

I am indebted to Mr Peter W. Brierley, MARC Europe, for his guidance and suggestions, and to Mr Alan Jesson of the Bible Society, for his correction of the final script. Thanks are also due to Rev. Dr Leslie Francis and Ms Judith Muskett, Culham College Institute, for their advice concerning the schools section.

CONTENTS OF REVIEW 33

PROLOGUE

By Peter Brierley

Religious statistics are intrinsically fascinating. They are more than a codifying of an interesting sociological phenomenon. They reflect in numerical terms a complex pattern of human behaviour, belief and understanding. This book seeks to identify the sources of all those salient items which make up the richly covered tapestry, so that those wishing to see part or all of the picture may be helped in their task.

0.1 What is Included?

One of the most obvious problems of this particular volume is that of defining the key word in its title - *religious*, which in this context is tantamount to defining *religion*. The New Oxford Illustrated Dictionary defines *religion* as the "human recognition of a super-human controlling power and especially from a personal God or gods entitled to obedience and worship". The predominant religion in the United Kingdom is Christianity and the three broad historical streams of the Christian faith are seen in this country - Protestantism, Catholicism, and the Orthodox Church. There are two established churches, the Church of England and the Church of Scotland, which are two of the many autonomous denominations in the Protestant group. Even the Catholic group has several components, from the dominant Roman Catholic Church to the smaller groups like the Old Catholics, or the Ukrainian Catholic Church. Likewise there are a number of distinct national groups within the Orthodox Church.

The Christian faith is not the only religious faith in this country. Hinduism, Islam, Buddhism, Sikhism are all present, as are more modern developments of these ancient creeds, like the Ahmadiyya Movement of the Muslims, and the Rastafarians. Also present in the United Kingdom, though growing less quickly in the eighties than they did in the seventies are those religions which have some relationship to Christianity but which have departed from the fundamental tenets of traditional Christianity. The most common of these is to say that Jesus is not the Son of God. This so-called *non-Trinitarian* group includes the Jehovah's Witnesses, Mormons, Christadelphians, Christian Scientists, Theosophists, Church of Scientology, Unification Church (Moonies), Worldwide Church of God and so on. As this volume indicates, there are very few non-Christian or extra-Christian groups, outside the Jews, publishing statistics relating to their activities.

Other elements of religiousness, the so-called *common* or *intrinsic* religion, general religiosity or superstition, have not been included. This is for the pragmatic reason of

9

definition (for there are few widely accepted in this broad area) and because in practice there are very few data available. Some references to religiosity where they are pertinent are found in the section of non-recurrent data.

0.2 How are the reviews organized?

The bulk of available statistical detail relates to the Christian faith. This corpus is too large to be treated as a unit, and has therefore been divided into two reviews. The first deals with recurrent data, that is to say, data which are or have been regularly published, and at the time of writing (March 1983) were generally available. Recurrent or regular has been defined, somewhat arbitrarily, as sources of data published at least once every ten years. In fact the very large majority of items in this heading are published much more frequently. The reviewer, Mrs Lynda Barlcy, has generally confined herself to material published since World War II.

The second review relating to Christian statistics, deals with non-recurrent data, that is, the *ad hoc* material of surveys, theses, and other frequently one-off studies undertaken by numerous bodies or individuals over the years. Whilst the major relevant historical items pre-dating 1945 are indicated, Dr Clive Field's massive study has been mainly confined to the mass of data produced since the late 1940s when market survey research began in earnest in the United Kingdom.

Of the non-Christian religions, the Jews produce the greatest volume of statistics, They therefore have been described in a separate review most ably by Dr Barry Kosmin, with attention confined largely to the years after 1930. All other data for religions in the UK other than Christianity are brought together in the fourth and final review. Inevitably this review is more heterogeneous than the others, though Dr Jorgen Nielsen has brought some homogeneity into his review by focussing on salient social and demographic factors.

Although a prime aim has been to make these reviews *user friendly*, it has not been easy to decide in which section certain groups should be placed, like the Unification Church or the Church of Scientology. Where a group uses the word *church* in its title (as do the Moonies with their *Unification Church*) that group has been included in the Christian sections, since the etymology of the word *church* is Christian. The recurrent Christian section does however break its data into two broad categories within each section - Trinitarian and non-Trinitarian. This is to aid the reader who frequently will know if he or she is wanting information about one of the mainstream, orthodox Christian groups and can therefore look them up under *Trinitarian*, or about one of those outside this broad area, and can find them under *non-Trinitarian*. The Trinity referred to in this division is that of traditional Christianity, of God the Father, God the Son and God the Holy Spirit in one Essence. Some of the *non-Trinitarian* churches do in fact have their own alternative formulation of the Trinity.

0.3 Collection of the Data

The Jewish and Other Religions sections have been written by experts in their respective fields, who have utilised both desk research and extensive contacts with appropriate bodies. Whilst Dr Clive Field was able to draw on his extensive earlier work, he also made numerous additional enquiries, involving hundreds of letters, making many visits and the copying of relevant articles. This did not however use any structured form for collection of material, and may thus be considered as extended desk research.

Mrs Barley used a simple questionnaire when writing to over 100 headquarters of Christian churches in the UK. The results are shown in the detailed listings she gives. A full response was ultimately achieved since those who did not reply in writing were followed up by telephone, in some instances on numerous occasions. A list of the addresses of the groups she approached is given in the *United Kingdom Christian Handbook*, 1983 edition, [QRL.2].

In all cases extreme care has been taken to ensure accuracy, and the follow-up of enquiries and queries through letter and telephone has been vigorously pursued. Whilst no author would wish to be excused the responsibility for any statement in his manuscript, nevertheless the material presented can in the final analysis only be as good as that obtained in answer to specific enquiries or through personal verification. The drafts of each author have been scrutinised by all, and the whole collectively subjected to comment by a wider caucus of qualified people. All suggestions made have been considered and incorporated whenever possible. The work largely took place over the years 1981 and 1982, and has been updated as much as possible as the book has passed through the press.

0.4 The Structure of the Churches Data Collection System

Each church body is totally autonomous, and what data it collects, and when, is entirely within its own purview and own authority structure. Needless to say this varies from one body to another. An indication of the historical background and organisational structure of many of the major denominations, as well as several smaller groups, is given is the book *International Church Index (Doctrinal)* [B.2] and is not therefore repeated here.

The basis of all published data on individual churches is a form completed annually by the minister or priest and sent to the appropriate headquarters. These forms vary considerably in the information requested. and in time of completion. The Anglicans and Roman Catholics gross up for non-response and although the description of the method used is not published it is available on request from the Anglican Church. The method used, based on the population living in the area for which no return has been received, is perhaps particularly questionable in those inner city areas where church attendance is normally particularly low. Others, such as the Baptist Union of Great Britain and Ireland, only publish the information actually received, repeating data of earlier years when no new information has been received. The Grace Baptist Group publish figures of those churches who return the form, and no attempt is made to gross up for all the churches in that particular group. Only the Methodist Church ensures that one year's return balances exactly with the previous year. They will not publish their figures until the gains and losses experienced over a particular year match the difference between the total of one year and the year before. Only the Anglican, Roman Catholic, Church of Scotland and Methodist data systems were computerised at the time of writing. Little external verification of the data supplied is undertaken. Most years most denominations approach all their churches, but the Anglicans are increasingly using samples. Grossing- up problems vary accordingly.

This is but the structural element of the problems of understanding what the data really indicate. The difficulty of defining religion at all leads to a second problem very familiar with social researchers. This is the conflict between beliefs, attitudes and behaviour. The New Testament, for example, defines *pure* religion in a behavioural dimension, that is, the visiting of "orphans and widows in their affliction" and "keeping oneself unstained from the world". But can such behaviour actually be measured? The merits and demerits of qualitative research in measuring perceived actual behaviour will not be discussed here, but one observation may be pertinent. It is that quantitative assessments of church-going in this country must not be confused with attitudes towards the deity. There are essentially two elements, one of which is concerned with, simplistically, the number of people who say "I believe in God", and the other which is concerned with the behavioural manifestation of that belief. Thus, one cannot infer the true religious following in Britain from market research studies that ask people simply the frequency with which they attend church. Expressed belief, church membership, church-going and other behavioural dimensions may all differ widely.

0.5 Problems of Data Measurement

0.5.1 *Diversity of terminology*

Terminology is a major problem, apparent from the descriptions given in individual sections. One of the most important words has unfortunately one of the greatest varieties of meaning - that is church membership. There is little agreement amongst the main Christian churches or non-Christian religions as to what this is. For example, some in the Church of England equate it with a person being on their *Electoral Roll* (not to be confused with the local authority Electoral Roll). Any baptised adult (aged 16 or over) who has been to a particular church over the previous six months may ask to be put on it; if one should go to more than one Anglican church it is possible for that person to be on more than one Electoral Roll. The Roman Catholics define membership as the Catholic population, that is those who were baptised in the Catholic Church as infants. Baptist Church members, on the other hand, are those who have been baptised as adults, and certain West Indian churches prefer the speaking of tongues before admitting a baptised person into membership. The theological overtones implicit in many such definitions make it extremely unlikely for any quick resolution of this problem.

It is particularly unfortunate that the term *membership* is often used as a proxy for indicating church attendance. It was apparent from the publication *Prospects for the Eighties* that church attendance and church membership in England are two different phenomena. That publication showed clearly that not all members attend church, though undoubtedly many do. The third logical element - attenders who are not members - also exists, sometimes in large numbers (as with the West Indian churches). The same phenomenon exists outside the main Christian churches. The Unification Church has few members but many attenders; the Jehovah's Witnesses regularly have more attending their meetings than belong to the movement. On the other hand, hundreds of Muslims and Hindus never go to a mosque or temple, and there are scores of Jews who rarely if ever attend a synagogue.

Ascertaining the denomination of church-goers is beginning to become a problem, especially for younger people. Some attend, say, a Methodist church on a Sunday morning and a Pentecostal church in the evening. But the question "What is your denomination?" assumes a singular answer! Others, particularly perhaps those attending House Churches or charismatic or Free Fellowships, find their movement insufficiently well classified for them to articulate a recognisable denomination-like title. Some, too, do not wish, for psychological reasons, to join any group with a specific title.

A further example of problems of terminology, seen in the use of the word *church*, is naturally of particular importance when dealing with religious statistics. The majority of churches are specially built structures in use regularly for worship of God, but there are about 5,000 groups, most of whom have left other churches, who meet every Sunday in an ordinary house to worship God, which are usually called *house churches*. These are autonomous, self-governing churches but have no obvious external sign of their existence. Hence, even counting the number of churches in a particular locality is not straightforward, and the same is true of the buildings used by Buddhists, Hindus and others.

0.5.2 *Diversity in timing*

The larger denominations all collect statistics from their churches on a regular basis, but the time when these figures are counted varies from one church to another. Roman Catholics count their mass attendance in the month of May, the Methodists count their membership in October, and the Baptists quote their membership figures for the year ending in December. The Church of England counts its electoral roll numbers every November, though occasionally (as in 1975) it omits a year.

0.5.3 *Differing periodicities*

The Methodists count their church membership every year, but church attendance figures only every third year. The Church of England has a major electoral roll revision every six years (this practice began in 1972, and was repeated in 1978 and 1984). At these revisions, all on the Electoral Roll *have* to sign on afresh. Inevitably the first count after the revision shows a drop from the previous count since those who have died or moved out of the parish are excluded.

0.5.4 *Lack of continuity*

These problems are compounded by a fourth - the lack of continuity. Dr Currie's monumental work *Churches and Church-Goers* [QRL.4] gives virtually all the available national statistics on church membership from the earliest dates of collection up to 1970. This book is a massive collection of historical religious data and is important to any serious student of long term trends. Its usefulness is however hindered by gaps at certain times, and of course the different definitions used make it impossible to compare truly across denominations, though within-denominational comparisons are more valid.

0.5.5 *Non-professional data collection*

The type of evaluation given by church headquarters administrators of forms requesting church statistics varies from one church to another, but it is frequently undertaken without professional assistance. Thus published data are not always as accurate, comprehensive or robust as researchers and others might wish.

0.5.6 *Absence of crucial data*

Certain types of information of major interest to researchers are rarely if ever collected in the macro, and thus geographical analyses, for example, are virtually inhibited. The age and sex of those going to church were only collected on a geographically uniform basis throughout all England in recent times, in 1979 (with the results published in *Prospects for the Eighties* [B.8]), in Wales in 1982, and in Scotland in 1984. The socio-economic category of church-goers, often thought to be mainly middle class, has only been explored in sample surveys; likewise the ethnic origin of church members and their political viewpoint. What kinds of job do church members have? What is their marital status? How many families go to church? Do church families have more children on average than non-church families? When church members move, do they continue their church membership? How far do they change denominations? All these are questions of concern, with varying answers in the massive sociological literature which we are fortunate to possess in this country. Some answers naturally tend to be only for one or two groups, or in one particular locality. This is not to castigate in any way the excellence of the steady stream of topical research that is undertaken, but emphasises the need for the background building studies against which smaller elements may be suitably interpreted and verified. The exception is Northern Ireland, where the religious persuasion of individuals, collected as part of the population census, is published in a separate volume, and analyses church affiliation by some of these variables.

0.6 Data Utilisation

Underlying all these mechanical or socio-political features is one which is absolutely fundamental, which if corrected might contain the seeds which would allow the plant of better statistics to grow. This is simply the fact that many clergy do not feel that numerate data are of use to them in their ministry, or, believing they would feel threatened by such, tend to ignore them. Thus there is little use of statistical information by those who might naturally expect to apply it.

However, the situation is perhaps changing from the 1972 church leaders conference in Birmingham where it was stated that "a fresh approach to the collection and use of statistical information is the basic pre-requisite of any realistic planning" (*Stand Up and Be Counted* [B.9]). The proportion of sources in the Bibliographic Section with a publication date of the 1970s or later indicates that this problem is in the process of being rectified.

A.T.Pierson wrote in 1886, "Facts are the fingers of God. To know the facts ...is the necessary condition of intelligent interest. Knowledge does not always kindle zeal, but zeal is 'according to knowledge' and will not exist without it." It is hoped that this volume may in some small way help feed that knowledge and stimulate that interest and zeal.

CHAPTER 1

INTRODUCTION

This review of United Kingdom recurrent Christian data seeks to represent a comprehensive guide to statistics generally available in March 1983, the time of writing. All regularly collected or non *ad-hoc* statistical data have been incorporated in this section. Whilst historical references are included where beneficial to the reader, this section does not include a detailed analysis of all historical Christian data. The review has been restricted by considerations of space, to provide coverage of sources of statistics which were either published or have been generally available since the Second World War. Government, church, and other independent sources of Christian statistics are included. This review does not describe in detail the various data collection methods employed by different sources or how these methods change over time. The reader should refer to the data source concerned.

For ease of analysis only, Christian Churches have been split into two broad categories, namely Trinitarian and Non-Trinitarian. Those in the former category formally adhere to the historic description of the "Trinity" as God the Father, God the Son and God the Holy Spirit. These churches might also be described as the orthodox, main-line denominations. Those in the latter category do not accept this formula, generally because they consider that Jesus Christ is not an equal part of the Godhead. A full list of the United Kingdom Christian Churches covered in this review is given in chapter 3. Various denominational groups have by necessity been employed within the Trinitarian category and these are also detailed there. No theological or sociological framework for Christian Churches is provided; the reader is asked to refer to the individual Churches for such information. The *UK Christian Handbook* [QRL.2] provides the necessary points of contact, while [B.2] and [B.5] give useful doctrinal outlines for many of the major Churches. The denominational grouping to which the Church of England has been assigned is strictly known as Episcopal (excluding Roman Catholic) and consequently is referred to in this way in the Quick Reference List. However, the major denominations in this group are part of the Anglican Church and within the text are frequently also referred to by this title. Non-Conformist churches strictly are those whose forbears did not follow the seventeenth century worship legislation, but the term has come to include all the Protestant denominations outside the Anglican Communion. Today most of the Non-Conformist churches prefer the term Free Churches, which is the phrase used in this review.

The recurrent data on Christian Churches have been divided into three broad areas. "Church People" has been taken to include all statistics gathered on church members, attenders, manpower and other people affiliated in some way to the Christian Churches in the United Kingdom. "Church Plant" refers to all data recorded on church buildings, schools and other places of education, attendance and staffing at these places of education also being included. The final area of Christian statistics concerns "Church Programme". Financial data, rites of passage (baptisms, marriages and funerals), religious publishing, broadcasting and other agencies are dealt with here.

As this review seeks to detail all relevant Christian data published or available since 1945, it may be assumed that where individual churches are not mentioned in the Quick Reference List, the relevant data is not collected by or on behalf of the church in question. Some churches, for example, the House Church movement, West Indian Churches, the Church of God and Brethren Churches collect little if any data regularly and consequently there are few references to them. For details of the House Church movement the reader is referred to Joyce Thurman's book [B.6] and in the case of the African/West Indian Churches, Roswith Gerloff's thesis [B.3] may be of assistance.

To compile this volume the headquarters of all known Christian churches in the United Kingdom were contacted with regard to any external or internal statistics maintained on a regular basis. These Churches were sent a simple postal questionnaire. All the major Churches responded and most of the smaller ones. The reader is referred to the *UK Christian Handbook* [QRL.2] for a comprehensive list of all United Kingdom Christian Churches and their headquarter offices. The nine largest missionary societies, other large Christian agencies, several theological colleges and other places of training and the two national broadcasting companies were also contacted, most of whom replied. In total, a response was received from 74% of the organisations contacted and the remainder were followed up by telephone. Government, other collective and non-denominational sources were traced using desk research methods while the final draft scripts were sent to fifteen or so denominational representatives for verification.

CHAPTER 2

DEFINITION AND MEASUREMENT

The major problem in the interpretation of Christian recurrent data lies in the different definitions and methods of measurement utilised by the different Churches. For a detailed understanding of the terminology and practices employed by individual Churches the reader is advised to contact each church or denomination concerned see *UK Christian Handbook* [QRL.2]. Brief outlines of selected individual Churches are provided in a few published volumes, for example, [B.2], [B.5] and *Free Church* [QRL.59]. In recent years many Churches have sought to improve the precision of the statistics gathered within the Church. In 1958 the Church of England and the Roman Catholic Church made substantial definition revisions with consequential advances in this area. However, most Churches collect their statistical information through the minister, secretary or other person in charge of each local church. These clergy or leaders are often far from objective observers and the quality of the data supplied can reflect this. One might suppose that most statistics of membership for example would be over-estimates of the actual situation but where these figures are used within a Church for financial purposes (such as providing the basis of remitting funds to central headquarters) they may in fact be under-estimates. Whilst data definitions may be precise, the collection mechanisms are not and this, alongside the diversity in terminology, presents any researcher with serious problems.

2.2 Church Members

Churches define membership in very different ways. Church of England members are strictly those who are registered on the Electoral Roll of a local Church of England church. To be registered an individual has to be 16 years of age or over, baptised as an Anglican, and have habitually attended public worship in the parish or resided in the parish for a period of 6 months prior to the enrolment. However, some observers regard all those baptised into the Church of England as members irrespective of present attendance, analogous to the Roman Catholic population. Most Free Churches regard members as baptised adults, though some have additional or alternative requirements such as making a "profession of faith" or "speaking in tongues". For the purpose of this review definitions of membership have been taken as those operated by each denomination or Church concerned. The following types of statistics are therefore to be found within the "Church People – Members" section: a) Anglican Electoral Roll, confirmation and communicant figures. b) Roman Catholic population (adult and child), reception, conversion and confirmation figures. c) Methodist membership. d) Baptist membership and baptismal (adult) figures. e) Other Churches membership, communicant and baptisms (where infant baptism is not practiced).

Confirmation, communicant attendance and adult baptism (where infant baptism is not practiced) are included where they are seen as indicating membership commitment.

2.3 Church Community

Within every Christian denomination or church there are those who, while affiliated in some way to the Church in question, are not actual members of it. They may or may not regularly attend the Church in question. Whilst the Northern Ireland decennial census monitors religious affiliation among that population, generally such data gathering is left to individual churches. People who are loosely connected with particular Churches what have may be termed "religious allegiance" or "affiliation", or be part of "religious communities". Those churches which collect data on religious affiliation in the population do so in many different ways. The Methodist Church refers to its Community Roll while smaller Churches count the number of adherents or families.

Many Churches gather information on the number of congregations or communities in various geographical areas. The Anglican and Catholic Churches collect data on parishes (i.e. areas of pastoral oversight) which may contain more than one congregation or place of worship.

2.4 Church Attenders

Churches endeavour to monitor "usual Sunday services attendance" or "average attendance" but this relies heavily on the timing of the count and the judgement of the minister or person in charge in assessing the actual number. Some Churches count the attenders at individual services or special services, for example, Easter or Christmas. Neither of these measures is entirely satisfactory. Aggregating attenders at individual services inevitably means that some people are counted twice or more while some habitual attenders are omitted (through sickness etc.). Monitoring attendance at festival services usually but not necessarily, over-estimates the normal attendance because of the inclusion of worshippers who only come on these special occasions, and visitors or holiday-makers present due to the effect of increased population mobility at these times. Usually church attendance is taken to include only adults but the Catholic Church, for example, counts the number of adults and children at Mass.

Children may attend church by participating in normal church worship or attending Sunday Schools organised alongside adult services. All references to child attendance at worship, Sunday Schools and other youth organisations have been included in this section.

2.5 Church Professional Manpower

Church members can be broadly divided into two categories:
(1) ministers, clergy and other professional church workers or leaders (not all of whom will be ordained) and
(2) lay members, that is all other members.
It is the first group which is covered under this section, whether they are full-time or part-time. The training of such workers is dealt with separately under "Professional Manpower Training" and overseas workers or missionaries have also been categorised separately.

Professional manpower in Christian churches takes many forms. Full-time ministry encompasses clergy, ministers, pastors, preachers, chaplains, deacons (Catholic and Anglican), parish workers, lay workers, deaconesses, members of religious communities, sisters and other offices. Church workers have different roles and status in different churches and the reader is advised to gather such information from individual churches prior to any detailed data analysis. Deacons, for example, form assistant clergy in Anglican and Catholic churches whereas in many Free Churches it is a position of part-time lay leadership (usually in assistance to the minister). Other positions of part-time, lay leadership include elders, lay leaders, lay or local preachers and lay pastors. All these are treated here as Professional Manpower.

2.6 Church Building

Church buildings include churches, chapels, cathedrals, mission halls, places of worship, church halls, rectories, vicarages, convents and other associated church buildings. In many Churches congregations meet in public places of worship, so that any count of the number of congregations provides a reasonable estimate of the number of churches or places of worship. In such Churches monitoring of congregations (assemblies, fellowships etc.) is included in this section (as well as in "Church Community"). Other Churches meet in the homes of members and sometimes do not have any specific church buildings. Consequently the interpretation of buildings and congregation data must be undertaken with care, allowing for differences in religious practice.

Many churches organise church buildings or congregations into administrative areas usually under the oversight of a senior minister, bishop etc. In Anglican and Catholic Churches individual churches are grouped into parishes, dioceses and provinces. Free Church areas include circuits (Methodist), associations (Baptist), presbyteries (Presbyterians) and districts (Congregational). Non-Trinitarian administrative areas include Area Councils (New Church) and District Councils (Spiritualists). The boundaries of these areas are generally not coterminous with regional or county boundaries, but maps showing the relationship between denominational and government adminstrative areas for four major denominations in England are included in [B.8]. Certain forms of Church buildings are given specific coverage in this volume. Schools and places of higher education (including Colleges of Education) are listed in the sections with these titles while theological colleges and other places of training for church workers are itemised under Professional Manpower Training.

2.7 Rites of Passage

Rites of Passage have been taken for the purposes of this review as baptisms or christenings (in Churches which practice infant baptism), marriages and funerals. Confirmations together with adult baptisms in Churches which do not practice infant baptism have been included under "Church Members" as these rites present an admission to committed or participatory membership (in some sense). Ordinations and admission into the ministry are regarded as the culmination of "Professional Manpower Training". Many Churches which practice infant baptism are becoming more restrictive in their use of this rite. The Church of England, for example, has authorised the use of the alternative service of thanksgiving. No statistics are currently kept in this area but such practices no doubt contribute to the decreasing baptism figures.

CHAPTER 3

CHURCH CATEGORIES

This chapter lists all the United Kingdom Christian Churches covered by this review. To facilitate easy access to this review, Christian Church data has been classified for statistical purposes into categories (see 1.2). The categories used are listed below and serve only for ease of analysis, no theological or sociological statement is intended by this arbitrary classification system. The categories are employed in the Quick Reference List as well as in the main text.

3.2 Trinitarian Denominations

Episcopal (excluding Roman Catholic)
Church of England
Church of Wales
Scottish Episcopal Church
Church of Ireland
Free Church of England
Moravian Church in Great Britain and Ireland
Methodist
Methodist Church in Great Britain
Methodist Church of Ireland
Wesleyan Reform Union
Independant Methodist churches
Free Methodist Church
Baptist
Baptist Union of Great Britain & Northern Ireland
Baptist Union of Wales
Baptist Union of Scotland
Baptist Union of Ireland
Old Baptist Union
Grace Baptist Assembly (formerly some Strict Baptist Churches)
Gospel Standard Strict Baptist
Presbyterian
Presbyterian Church of Wales
Church of Scotland
Presbyterian Church of Ireland
Presbyterian Church of England
Free Church of Scotland
United Free Church of Scotland

Free Presbyterian Church of Scotland
Reformed Presbyterian Church in Scotland
Reformed Presbyterian Church in Ireland
Non-Subscribing Presbyterian Church in Ireland
Evangelical Presbyterian Church in Ireland
Free Presbyterian Church of Ulster
Congregational
United Reformed Church
Fellowship of Churches of Christ
Congregational Federation
Evangelical Fellowship of Congregational Churches
Union of Welsh Independants
Congregational Union of Scotland
Congregational Union of Ireland
Pentecostal/Holiness (including African/West Indian)
Assemblies of God
Apostolic Church
Elim Pentecostal Church
Church of the Nazarene
Emmanuel Holiness Church
African/West Indian:
    Aladura International Church
    Church of Cherabim and Seraphim
    Church of God of Prophecy
    New Testament Church of God
    Wesleyan Holiness Church
Roman Catholic
Church in England and Wales
Church in Scotland
Church in Northern Ireland
Old Roman Catholic
Liberal Catholic
Churches for Overseas Nationals:
    Croation
    German
    Hungarian
    Latvian
    Lithuanian
    Slovene
    Ukrainian
Orthodox
Assyrian Church of the East
Coptic Orthodox
Ethiopian Orthodox
Greek Orthodox Archdiocese
Latvian Orthodox
Oriental Orthodox

Polish Orthodox
Rumanian Orthodox
Russian Orthodox in Exile
Byelorussian
Serbian Orthodox
Orthodox Syrian
Ukrainian Orthodox
Other Trinitarian
Christian Brethren
Darby Brethren
Fellowship of Independent Evangelical Churches
Countess of Huntingdon's Connexion
Religious Society of Friends (Quakers)
Salvation Army
Seventh-Day Adventist Churches
Union of Evangelical Churches
Evangelical Lutheran
Lutheran Church in Ireland
Polish Evangelical Lutheran Church in Exile
Latvian Evangelical Lutheran
Estonian Evangelical Lutheran Church
Churches for Overseas Nationals:
    Chinese
    Danish
    Dutch
    Finnish
    French Protestant
    German Christ Church
    Greek Evangelical
    Hungarian Reformed
    Italian Pentecostal
    Japanese Christian
    Evangelical Mennonites
    Norwegian Seamen's
    Spanish Evangelical
    Swedish
    Swiss
    Swiss Reformed
    Urdu and Punjabi

3.3 Non-Trinitarian Churches

Christadelphians
Church of Christ, Scientist
Jehovah's Witnesses
Church of Jesus Christ of Latter-Day Saints (Mormons)
New Church

Church of Scientology
Spiritualists
Theophists
Unification Church (Moonies)
Unitarian and Free Christian Churches
The Way
Worldwide Church of God

CHAPTER 4

TRINITARIAN CHURCH PEOPLE

4.1 Community

4.1.1 *Data Collection*

It is often desirable to quantify church affiliation or attachment even at the vaguest level without the more rigorous definitions associated with church membership figures. Many people would align themselves with a particular denomination (for example, on hospital admittance) but would not wish to be called members or regular attenders. Denominations officially linked to the State tend to embrace a large number of such people but other denominations are not exempt from this phenomenon.

It is in this area of religious affiliation that independent data sources often concentrate whereas denominational sources do not collect data of this nature to any significant extent. The only denominations which specifically count those who are loosely affiliated to their church are the Methodist and some Presbyterian, Congregational or Pentecostal denominations. The Church of England has published general population densities or composition and the number of baptised persons (obtained from government sources). However, this denomination has no specific criterion for affiliation and has now decided not to publish any such data for years beyond 1979. Although the Roman Catholic population figures and the Church of England Electoral Roll are referred to as the churches membership, they may also in certain circumstances be appropriate as a measure of Church affiliation.

The only government monitor of religious affiliation is carried out in Northern Ireland. A decennial census is conducted which includes questions of religion for the whole population *Census of Population– Religious Tables* [QRL.36]. Censuses are also carried out in the United Kingdom Armed Forces and Prison service where religious adherence is monitored usually on a quinquennial and annual basis respectively. Hospitals do not collate any such data though it is recorded on patients records. Only three other non-denominational sources remain: *World Christian Encyclopaedia* [QRL.1] is an independent source covering religious adherence on an extremely detailed worldwide basis, while the other two *World Christian Handbook* [QRL.3] (now replaced by [QRL.1]) and *Churches and Church-Goers* [QRL.4], are collective rather than primary sources.

Statistics are also kept on groups of adherents in certain geographical areas. Specific denominations tend to collect such figures, for example, Congregational denominations monitor the number of congregations while Anglican and Roman Catholic denominations record the population of their parishes. Descriptions of data relating to such measures are included in this section.

Ad hoc statistics relating to denominational community sizes are sometimes known on a local basis but not recorded collectively. Individual church ministers and priests often know their congregation or community size for pastoral purposes but no attempt may be made regularly to record these figures. Only centrally recorded data is referred to in this volume.

4.1.2 *Data Limitations*

The main problem with data on religious affiliation is one of definition. Different denominations define denominational affiliation in different ways. It is in the final analysis a subjective judgement and figures should be interpreted as estimates or approximations for the actual size of a religious community.

Different definitions of religious affiliation may be appropriate for different study or research purposes. The prospective researcher, is advised to consider most carefully the definition most relevant to each individual study. When comparisons are made between denominations the definitions and the methods of data collection used must be compatible.

Geographical patterns of denominational affiliation do not directly reflect active denominational strength in particular areas of the United Kingdom. State denominations necessarily have a high following or degree of affiliation among the population but such people may not have a deep commitment to the particular denomination in question (as reflected by, for example, membership figures). Indeed such commitment may be highly nominal and may be easily transferable to other denominations and religions. Affiliation does not convey any information as to its intensity, consequently denominational community figures must be interpreted alongside statistics on membership and attendance.

Figures reported by different sources for denominational affiliation may differ for various reasons. Underlying these reasons are different compilation methods but the motives of the data collators must also be taken into account. Denominations themselves may want to inflate figures to present a large religious community and other sources may have similar aims. However, where figures are used for financial calculations it may in fact be desirable to under-estimate community figures. Independent sources are usually more objective in their approach. Where definitions are inexact, (as in this area of religious affiliation), and subjective judgements are required by those collecting the data, it is easy for figures to reflect those subjective judgements (see 2.1).

4.1.3 *Terminology*

People loosely attached to particular Churches or religions may be referred to by terms such as religious community (e.g. Methodists), religious adherents (e.g. Congregational Federation), religious affiliation or population religion. Different denominations employ different terminology and various forms of measurement. Many rely on the subjective judgement of local ministers (see 4.1.2.4).

Anglican and Roman Catholic churches, for example refer to parishes, congregations and benefices to describe groups of adherents. Ecclesiastical parishes vary between these two churches. Although each has a legal status they are different to local government Electoral Register parishes. An ecclesiastical parish is the area under the pastoral care of local clergy or ministers; often the population of a parish is referred to. A congregation is usually the term used to describe the group of people worshipping in a certain church or parish. Sometimes a congregation may be loosely referred to as a church but usually this term is reserved for the church building. A benefice is the area for which one minister or clergyman is responsible and may include several parishes.

4.1.4 *Trends*

Statistics concerning religious adherence are usually slow to change. In Northern Ireland the government collects decennial data to reveal long-term trends in religious adherence, while individual denominations in Great Britain collect relevant data annually. In recent years religious adherence in the United Kingdom has steadily decreased and in view of the fact that long-term trends are usually required in the area of religious affiliation quinquennial or decennial figures frequently suffice.

Parish populations and local congregations may be subject to rapid increase or decrease in size in these days of high population mobility. If figures are required relating to certain areas of the United Kingdom then annual data are preferable at least for preliminary assessment.

4.1.5 *Related Data*

Many families who send their children to denominational schools or places of higher education regard themselves as religious adherents. Data referring to the number of people involved is to be found in the relevant sections under "Church Plant". Sunday School attenders may also in some denominations more appropriately be regarded as religious adherents rather than commited church members or attenders. Data involving Sunday School rolls (i.e. those attending, however irregularly) come into this category (see 4.3.2.5). All Sunday School figures are, however, dealt with alongside other data involving Adult and Child Attenders.

4.2 Members

4.2.1 *Data Collection*

Membership of a Church can mean a variety of things depending on the denomination concerned (see 4.2.3). It can be interpreted as sacramental membership (for example the Catholic population) or participatory membership (for example Baptist membership). Membership of the Anglican and Roman Catholic Churches involves christening or baptism, usually as an infant. In the Anglican Church those baptised as infants have to wait until 16 years or over (recently changed from 17 or over) before being eligible for membership i.e. inclusion on the Electoral Roll (see 4.2.2.4). Membership of most Free Church denominations requires adult baptism or "profession of faith" for acceptance into the church. (A few smaller denominations have still stricter requirements).

In addition to formal membership statistics there are also confirmation and commuicant statistics for some denominations (e.g. Presbyterian Churches) and these are included in this section. Confirmation data together with figures on adult baptisms (for denominations which do not practice infant baptism) are listed here as reflecting additions to the number of committed or participatory members. Communicant figures are included where they reflect committed or practicing membership (see 4.3.3.1).

There are numerous collective sources for denominational statistics on church membership but there is no regularly maintained independent record ([B.8] being a recent possible exception). Collective sources rely on individual denominations themselves to supply figures. As each denomination has its own definition of membership interdenominational comparisons are difficult to interpret. Collective sources endeavour to cope with this problem, but the reader is advised to discover which denominational statistics have been utilised as 'membership' in each of the sources.

Government does not currently collect any statistics on church membership; such sources e.g. *Social Trends* [QRL.104] derive their figures from other sources and consequently comparisons of government data for different time periods must be made with care.

4.2.2 *Data Limitations*

The major limitations of church membership data are the diversity of terminology employed and the variety of definitional interpretations. This is explained in more detail below. Any comparison of denominational membership figures must take into account the particular definitions used by each of the denominations in question (see 4.2.3). For instance in some denominations the majority of members are adults, (for example, the Church of England) whereas in other denominations members can be of any age (for example the Roman Catholic Church).

Some observers consider that Anglican communicant figures (reflecting participatory membership) make a better comparison than Electoral Roll figures (reflecting formal membership) with membership statistics for the Free Church denominations. Often Easter Week communicants are taken as these services are central to the Anglican faith, though such attenders may go to their Anglican churches less frequently than their Free Church peers. Other Festival services tend to attract visitors while Sunday communion services are for various reasons more variable in their attendance figures.

The inclusion of children in membership statistics for some denominations and not for others prevents direct denominational comparisons. Catholic attendance at Mass (reflecting participatory rather than sacramental membership) forms a reasonable comparison with Free Church membership when such denominational comparisons are required. However, the inclusion of children in the Catholic but not the Free Church figures requires the application of an estimation procedure.

Every six years from 1972 the Church of England undertakes a major revision of its Electoral Roll. During each six year period members are added to the roll and the parish priest removes all those who die, move away or no longer wish to remain members. At the end of the six year period the roll is revised through a specific signature by all those who wish to remain members; this resulted in a sudden decrease in 1972 and 1978 which built up again over the next six year period. Although this procedure does ensure a more accurate measure of Anglican membership, the resulting six year cycle should be smoothed before comparisons are made with other statistics.

Despite the problems mentioned above membership statistics remain a useful means of comparing denominational strength in the United Kingdom. It is advisable to consider them alongside attendance figures but these are more subject to wide variations over shorter periods than membership.

4.2.3 *Terminology*

Each denomination has its own definition for church membership together with its own terminology. Only the major denominations will be covered here (see 2.2).

Anglican and Catholic Churches practice infant baptism and accept this as the criterion for church sacramental membership (see 4.2.2.1). In the Catholic Church this is referred to as the Catholic population and consists of children (any age) and adults. In the Church of England baptised people are accepted as members at 16 years of age when their name becomes eligible for placement on the Electoral Roll. Confirmation is not a required condition for membership in either denomination though it is expected of all commited or participatory members.

Other denominations (for example, the Methodist Church) practice infant baptism but do not consider such children as members, nor allow this criterion alone to qualify for adult membership. An adult profession of faith or acceptance into the church is required. Denominations such as Baptists and some Independent Churches often require adult baptism by immersion or a "profession of faith" as their condition of membership.

Confirmation is strictly required in, for example, the Church of England, Methodist and Presbyterian denominations before a person can take communion. (In the Church of England communicant statistics are collected regularly while this is not so in the Methodist and Presbyterian Churches). In Anglican Churches confirmation usually occurs during the early teens while in Free Churches it may be delayed until "adulthood" has been reached. Children in the Catholic Church however, may take Communion from age 7 and are confirmed when aged about 11 years or over. Although children may participate in Anglican communion services they do not usually take communion until confirmed.

4.2.4 *Trends*

By comparison with attendance figures church membership series are generally much smoother and not subject, to the same extent, to short term fluctuations. This makes them ideal for monitoring long term trends.

Most denominations produce membership figures annually and these present the best initial way to determine any major changes. However, as the number of members varies little from year to year triennial data may suffice. Indeed the Methodist Church only publishes annual membership every three years while the Church of England supplements its biennial/triennial census with sample survey results.

Confirmation and relevant adult baptism series are fairly small in magnitude and any fluctuations are quite significant, annual data is therefore necessary. Annual data is also desirable for communicant figures although the timing (i.e. the particular Sunday or services at which the numbers are recorded) is crucial for the interpretation of the data (see 4.3.2.3).

Researching trends over time must necessarily take note of mergers between denominations. In 1972, for example, the Congregational Churches and the Presbyterian Church of England merged to make the United Reformed Church, which absorbed all the Presbyterians, but some Congregational Churches remained outside this union. Most of the latter are now members of either the Congregational Federation or the Evangelical Fellowship of Congregational Churches. In September 1981 some members of the Association of the Churches of Christ merged with the United Reformed Church, those not joining either became members of the Fellowship of Churches of Christ or totally independent churches. Many other merger schemes have been debated in the last decade but none have succeeded. The Anglicans and Methodists failed to agree to unite in 1977 and failed to covenant together in 1982. Talks are under way concerning the Presbyterian Church of Wales and the Methodist Church in Wales.

4.3 Attenders

4.3.1 *Data Collection*
Church attenders are usually considered under two separate headings namely adult attenders, and children and young people. Consequently, the Quick Reference List has been divided into these two categories. As it is almost impossible to monitor individual attenders, statistics usually refer to attendances, the difference being that an individual attender may make more than one attendance at church services on a particular Sunday (going both morning and evening, for example). In one source however [B.1], estimates are made to link attendance with the number of attenders by publishing the percentage of adult church-goers attending more than one service on a Sunday. Only the Roman Catholic Church considers total attendance (i.e. adult and child) and does not have any specific count of its children and young people.

Attendance (adult and child) at church is not regularly monitored by the government; any government statistics published, for example *Social Trends* [QRL.104], have in fact been obtained from separate sources, usually surveys. Individual denominations keep their own records of church attendance (which are not always published) but the form this data takes varies from one denomination to another. There are several sources which seek to collate this denominational data and some which analyse various survey results e.g. *World Christian Encyclopaedia* [QRL.1].

Data dealing with attendance at the usual form of church worship (as indicated by each denomination) are included in this section. Consequently, measures of "usual attendance" and "average attendance" are included alongside the Catholic "attendance at Mass" (see 4.3.3.1). Church attendance on specific occasions (for example Christmas) are also included but data relating to specific forms of worship (for example, Anglican Holy Communion, baptisms and funerals) are to be found elsewhere in this review (see 4.3.5).

Sunday Schools were in the past places of basic education (reading, writing and arithmetic) but in modern times they have become closely associated with individual denominations and are now places of religious education on a denominational basis. Sunday School attenders are now regarded as the children in church rather than scholars; the Methodist and Congregational Churches made this change of definition in the 1960's, and the Roman Catholic and Anglican Churches in 1958. Data concerning Sunday Schools (child attendance, teachers etc.) has therefore been included in this section alongside other information relating to Children and Young People.

4.3.2 *Data Limitations*

Adult attendance is monitored by the various denominations in a variety of ways. It may refer to attendance at particular services (e.g. Methodist Church), average attendance per year (Reformed Presbyterian Church of Ireland), usual total Sunday attendance (Church of England) or attendance at Mass on a particular Sunday (Roman Catholic) or weekly attendance (Moravian Church). Into all these measures comes the question of the number of people who attend more than once on a Sunday or in a week. There is no denominational data which sheds any light on this problem although it is generally agreed that the number of people involved is decreasing. The size of this problem varies from one denomination to another. It is largest in the Free Churches but has been estimated in England to be about 13% of church attendance overall. Studies are currently underway to ascertain the extent of this phenomenon in Wales and Scotland [B.1]. Readers should bear in mind the magnitude of this multiple attendance problem when interpreting data.

Patterns of church attendance vary a great deal depending on the denomination concerned. Anglicans, for example, tend to attend church less frequently than their Catholic or Free Church counterparts. Practicing Catholics are expected to attend Mass at least once a week while Anglicans are much less strict, confirmed members are only required to communicate three times a year, one of which must be Easter. It is advisable to interpret attendance figures alongside those of membership and in the light of individual denominational practices.

Data concerning adult and child church attendance is measured by different denominations at different times of the year, each trying to find an "average" or "normal" period. Attendance usually varies according to the time of the year and therefore the collection time point is crucial to the interpretation of such data. In some denominations (e.g. Catholic Churches) these fluctuations are less noticable than in others. During the summer months, for example, attendance may be low while on special occasions, for example, Easter, Christmas, Harvest, Mothering Sunday, Feast days or Church Anniversaries attendance will be high. National or local events or even the weather may influence attendance from one week to another. Likewise attendance at particular services varies. Evening services, for example, are attended less in winter months or may not be held at all. The pattern of church-going has changed over time as has the timing of its measurement by denominations. The Roman Catholic Church, for example, began in 1974 to monitor attendance in October of each year rather than April as had formerly been the case.

Sunday School attendance is usually comparable between different denominations, although many now include their children in church services rather than separate Sunday Schools. Sunday Schools cater for children of varying ages depending on the denomination concerned. Statistics concerning children associated with particular denominations may count them as Sunday School or as part of church attendance. Most Roman Catholic churches do not run Sunday Schools and consequently children are included in the figures for total attendance at Mass.

Attendance at Sunday Schools or young peoples groups can be measured in several ways. The school or group "roll" will usually consist of all those associated in any way with the Sunday School or group. The number who attend will in general be less then the number on the roll and the number present on any particular Sunday will be even less.

Published data on attendance is comparatively sparse. Even when augmented by published information on membership, frequently an incomplete picture emerges owing to nonavailability of collective data on certain groups (for example, the House Church Movement). Estimates of religious practice are given in [QRL.1] and [QRL.2], but the lack of direct sources for these should be noted.

4.3.3 *Terminology*
Various descriptions of adult church attendance have been given above in section 4.3.2.1. In addition there are certain services which are considered central to denominational belief. Such services are usually called Holy Communion, the Eucharist, the Lord's Supper or the Mass. In Catholic churches the Mass is said or sung in the majority of services. Practicing Catholics are obliged to attend Sunday Mass (fulfilled by Saturday evening Mass in certain places) and therefore any measure of Catholic attendance at Mass will be high, uniform (i.e. few random fluctuations) and a fair representation of the number of practicing Catholics. These data have therefore been included in the section on church attendance. In Anglican churches attendance at Holy Communion or the Eucharist is not recorded although the number of communcants is. This figure tends to reflect the number of confirmed members attending the service in question and may fluctuate considerably. Anglican communicant data has been included in this review alongside Church membership statistics. Free Churches record attendance at Holy Communion or the Lord's Supper in addition to attendance at other more usual services. Participation in these "special" services is often restricted to members only and therefore this data has also been categorised under Church Members.

Children and young peoples' attendance at church may be measured by reference to Sunday Schools, Bible Classes, Youth groups; Youth organisations etc. In some Free Churches, children may be referred to as Sunday School scholars or pupils.

4.3.4 *Trends*
Both child and adult church attendance varies from year to year and annual data is therefore generally preferable. Some denominations (for example, the Methodist

Church) do not monitor their church attendance this frequently and in these cases additional data of a different nature (for example, membership) may help in the interpretation of short term variations. The Church of England while only running a census every two or three years usually carries out annual surveys in other years.

Attendance statistics reflect short-term changes in religious behaviour better than membership figures. When considering long-term trends it is advisable to smooth church attendance series to allow for "random" fluctuations between years (see 4.3.2.3).

4.3.5 *Related Data*

Some denominations maintain records of adult and child attendance at specific midweek church-based meetings i.e. other than church services. Meetings involving adults include Bible Studies, Prayer Meetings, Womens Meetings etc. and are included in this section alongside data dealing with Adult Attenders. Young people may be catered for at youth organisations (for example, Girls and Boys Brigades), youth fellowships, youth clubs or Bible Classes and for the purposes of this review are included within "Children and Young People".

Many denominations which run Sunday Schools or other youth activities maintain records of the manpower and resources involved, for example, Sunday School teachers, youth leaders, meeting places and expenses. These are also included in the Quick Reference List within the section concerning Children and Young People.

Data relating to "special" forms of church services are not covered in this section. As explained in 4.3.3.1, Anglican and Free Church communion statistics are included with figures on confirmations alongside Church membership statistics. Baptism, marriage and funeral data are described under "Rites of Passage" while ordination statistics are detailed under "Professional Manpower Training".

4.4 Professional Manpower

4.4.1 *Data Collection*

Nearly all denominations (with the exception of, for example, the Quakers) incorporate some role of individual leadership and many have full-time positions responsible for a variety of functions. In Anglican, Roman Catholic and many Free Churches there are positions for full-time and part-time ministers, priests and other workers and also for voluntary but ordained persons working as "non-stipendiary ministers". There are also numerous positions of lay leadership (full-time and part-time) but little data is kept on this. The main exceptions are the offices of lay preacher, local preacher, reader and lay pastor which are designed to assist the full-time ministry in various ways depending on the denomination concerned. Data relating to these offices is available from individual denominations, for example the *Church of England Yearbook* [QRL.42].

Statistics on church manpower are maintained by individual denominations in various ways. The only current central or government source is the decennial Census of Population [QRL.35] which contains detailed data on religious professions.

These records are maintained from 1841 and refer since 1861 to England and Wales. Figures are available by clergy status and various administrative geographical areas but only the Church of England and Roman Catholic churches are distinguished separately and only then irregularly. The Church of England maintain very detailed records including analyses by clergy status, geographical movements, ministerial gains and losses, retirements and pensioners. Other denominations tend to keep records solely by ministerial status and geographical location. Where a central payment system operates for clergy such information will be maintained but not necessarily published. Collective sources e.g. *World Christian Encyclopaedia* [QRL.1], *UK Christian Handbook* [QRL.2], *Whitackers' Almanac* [QRL.110] exist which seek to collate such denominational data.

Data on full-time ministry normally refers to men only. This is particularly so in Anglican and Roman Catholic Churches where women are not allowed into the priesthood (although the Church of England does allow women into the diaconate). Where Free Churches fully allow women ministers (as in the United Reformed Church) they are included in the basic data.

Most positions of leadership (ministerial and lay, full-time and part-time) relate to the local church or to a group of churches. However, in the major denominations chaplains (full-time or part-time ministers or deaconesses) are assigned to hospitals, prisons, places of higher education, schools, industry, the Armed Forces and other areas of religious activity. Those concerned with education are dealt with in the relevant sections under Church Plant while the remainder are described here. Chaplains may or may not be devoted full-time to their particular areas of ministry. Some denominations will in certain circumstances ask a chaplain to undertake additional pastoral work in a local church.

The Anglican and Roman Catholic churches run communities for people engaged in certain forms of full-time ministry, for example, religious houses and convents. Usually the communities are linked to a particular religious order or foundation rather than local churches, and are concerned with school teaching, social work, prayer or religious learning. In contrast to the situation portrayed in 4.4.1.3, these religious communities admit men and women equally although individual communities usually only cater for either men or women. Data concerning these communities can be found in this section and in the chapter on "Church Buildings." Some convents and schools may also be found under Church Schools.

4.4.2 *Data Limitations*

In general, positions of leadership have different status and fulfil different functions in different denominations. The ordained ministry, for example, is regarded slightly differently in Anglican and Roman Catholic Churches while amongst Free Churches the status of a minister varies even more. In particular lay workers undertake varying roles in different denominations. Any comparison of denominational manpower statistics must take into account the various forms of ministry operating in different denominations. The widely differing systems of church government also have some bearing on the role of the church ministers and other church workers.

4.4.3 *Terminology*

Every denomination has its own terminology for the various forms of ministry it embraces. It is advisable to refer to each denomination concerned for guidance on manpower terminology employed prior to any denominational comparisons or analysis of manpower statistics. Distinctions between lay and ordained forms of ministry vary a great deal between denominations and are particularly prone to misinterpretation. A full list of denominational head offices can be found in *UK Christian Handbook* [QRL.2].

Full-time ministry in the Church of England involves ordained clergy (priests, vicars, bishops, chaplains, rectors etc.), trainee clergy (i.e. deacons), parish workers, lady workers, deaconesses, members of religious communities etc. In the Roman Catholic Church positions exist for priests, assistant priests, deacons, chaplains, members of religious communties, bishops, sisters etc. Among Free Churches there are ministers, pastors, preachers, chaplains, lady workers, deaconesses, probationers etc., each with different areas of responsibility.

Lay (mainly part-time) ministry in the Church of England usually consists of readers and other office-bearers while Free Churches involve elders, deacons, local or lay preachers, lay pastors and other officers. The Roman Catholic Church embraces little lay ministry but this is changing with growing numbers of other servers and catechists. Although some of the positions listed in 4.4.3.2 are known as "lay" positions of ministry (for example,deaconesses), they are often full-time posts and are therefore listed alongside the ordained ministry.

4.4.4 *Trends*

The number of ministers, clergy, elders etc. in any denomination varies from year to year and consequently it is advisable to consider annual data where possible. The number of entrants to the full-time ministry is a case where annual data is particularly appropriate as the series usually consists of relatively small numbers and can fluctuate a great deal.

The extent and importance of lay ministry has increased in recent years in all the major denominations. The growth in such figures needs to be related to the apparent decline in entrants to the full-time ordained ministry. Neither the ordained nor the lay ministry should be analysed in total isolation.

4.4.5 *Related Data*

Certain denominations (usually Protestant rather than Catholic) publish the income and expense levels of their ministries. These have been included in the Quick Reference List relating to this section. Only the Church of England maintains data dealing with aspects of manpower provision other than total manpower levels. For example, it monitors in some detail clergy retirements and deaths see *Church of England Yearbook* [QRL.42] and *Facts and Figures about the Church of England* [QRL.55].

4.5 Professional Manpower Training

4.5.1 *Data Collection*

Professional Manpower Training is taken here to mean the training of ministers, priests, and other professional church workers. In any denomination training is given to lay members for part-time lay offices, for example, Readers and Lay Preachers, but very few relevant records are published. Candidates for full-time or part-time ministry can train at theological colleges, Seminaries, Bible Colleges and other centres of Christian Studies. Not every student who successfully completes a suitable course is accepted into the ministry but in most denominations ministers and other professional staff must have undergone some form of theological training. However, a few denominations, for example, the Baptists, accept ministers in certain circumstances without formal theological training.

The majority of denominations have their own recognised courses of theological training end some run their own training centres for example, the Church of England, the Roman Catholic Church, the Salvation Army, the Baptists, the Methodist Church and the Seventh-Day Adventist Church. Training for full-time work is almost always a full-time occupation and many training colleges are residential in a similar manner to colleges of higher education. However, unlike colleges of higher education, theological training can be pursued at any age and many colleges provide married or family accommodation if necessary. There is an increasing tendency for men and women to enter professional church work as mature students. This has meant an increase not only in the number of courses suitable for married students but also an increase in the number of part-time non-residential training courses which allow the student to continue in employment while training for full-time or part-time positions of leadership.

Data on manpower training is almost exclusively maintained by the particular denomination concerned, there being only one collective source [QRL.2]. Institutions of training vary as to the extent to which statistics are kept. Denominational training centres tend to rely on their particular denomination to maintain comparative records from year to year. However, some interdenominational colleges, for example, Bible Schools, do collate regular statistics or are able on request to do this from existing records. Training centres not covered by the Quick Reference List may still be able to compile any required statistics. Their exclusion from the Quick Reference List merely means that appropriate data are not published or collated ready for release to interested parties. Many colleges will willingly compile data according to the researcher's specification or allow the researcher access to appropriate records.

Data on ministerial training is generally concerned with the number of students or candidates in training, the number of ordinations, probationary ministers or ministerial candidates and the number of theological colleges, Seminaries, Bible Schools or other places of training. A few colleges like Selly Oak Colleges, William Booth Training College (Salvation Army) and Newbold College (Seventh-Day Adventist) keep records of the academic staff involved while the Church of England compiles figures as to the overall cost of its ministerial training. Catholic records of training for the priesthood are also well maintained and available on request.

4.5.2 *Data Limitations*

Ministers, priests and other professional staff play different roles in different denominations and consequently their pattern of training is usually quite different. Training may take anything from one to five years; it may involve a large amount of practical experience or it may only involve a little. Denominational training facilities cannot be compared without taking such things into consideration. Statistics on ministerial training are consequently not very meaningful in isolation; they should at least be employed in conjunction with figures on members and ministers etc.

Many denominations have staff who fulfil different roles and who therefore have different forms of training. This is particularly so in the case of ordained/ministerial and lay positions. In order to investigate a denomination's provisions for the training of its workers the wide variety of manpower positions available needs to be taken into consideration though little data is available in the area of lay training.

4.5.3 *Terminology*

The status of different places of manpower training varies for different denominations. Catholic priests usually undergo full-time (academic) training at a seminary (or possibly theological college). Anglican men and women must train at theological colleges or undertake similar courses, whereas Free Churches will accept theological training at theological colleges or Bible colleges. Ministers, priests and other ordained workers (mainly full-time) usually undergo more rigorous training than lay (often part-time) staff who may only undertake evening teaching courses.

People in training for church work may be called cadets (Salvation Army), deacons (Church of England), ordination candidates, probationary ministers, preachers-on-trial, student ministers, theological students or Bible students depending on the particular denomination and the stage reached in the training procedure. Deacons, probationary ministers and preachers-on-trial have completed the majority of their formal training and are employed by the Church while they gain experience of the work involved. Where more appropriate, references to probationary ministers, deacons and preachers on trial have been included in the previous section on Professional Manpower. The reader is asked to refer to both sections when investigating this area.

4.5.4 *Trends*

Student and candidate numbers can vary a great deal from year to year even though individual Theological Colleges and Bible Schools endeavour to keep numbers at a constant level. It remains advisable to consult annual data in most cases. In recent years increasing numbers of women and older candidates have embarked on courses of training leading to professional positions in the Church. Any analysis of such data will need annual details.

The number of places available for manpower training at the various colleges, seminaries etc. remains fairly static from year to year; quinquennial figures are adequate here and are given for each college in [QRL.2].

4.5.5 *Related Data*

Several denominations train teachers for their schools and therefore have their own colleges of education. Whilst this could be regarded as manpower training, such training is usually (though not exclusively) undertaken immediately after school or further education. Consequently, the training of primary and secondary school teachers has been included in the sections dealing with places of higher education.

4.6 Missionaries

4.6.1 *Data Collection*

Church workers serving abroad are generally referred to as missionaries. They may be involved in church leadership, church foundation, childrens work, literacy or radio programmes, teaching and training, building and agricultural programmes, Bible translation work, medical facilities, evangelism and numerous other religious or church related activities. In the past missionaries tended to serve in general capacities and were trained with this in mind. In modern times, however, missionaries from the United Kingdom are increasingly sent to provide specific assistance on a short-term basis, often in association with national churches in the recipient country and have undergone specialised forms of training, for example, in agriculture or medicine.

The number of missionaries serving abroad from the United Kingdom has decreased in the last decade, see *UK Christian Handbook* [QRL.2]. Overseas countries and churches are increasingly becoming more self-sufficient and consequently missionaries often serve in specialist positions sometimes under the local church.

Overseas missionaries are commissioned either by their denomination, religious order, relief organisation or missionary society and most receive some financial support from their local church. Religious orders and some societies have denominational affiliations and in these cases they have been listed in the Quick Reference List under the denomination concerned.

The majority of missionary or relief societies and religious orders produce figures relating to the number of workers abroad, on furlough or on leave and these are available on request. A comprehensive list of the relevant societies and orders has not been included here; only the largest organisations and those producing additional data have been listed in the Quick Reference List. For a complete list of relevant organisations together with a breakdown of their missionary, office and other personnel the reader is requested to refer to [QRL.2]. Details of the annual income of many missionary societies is also given there, as well as a total estimate for all societies.

The most comprehensive collective source of missionary statistics is [QRL.2] although there are several less detailed collective sources. There is, however, no independent data collection and ultimately the researcher must rely on individual denominations, religious orders and missionary societies for the provision of necessary data.

In recent years many overseas Churches have begun to send missionaries to the United Kingdom, for example, the Seventh- Day Adventist Church. Data concerning such missionary activity is difficult to trace but one source comprehensively collates the number of missionaries from North America the *Mission Handbook* [QRL.9], another gives world wide collective data [QRL.1] and some data are also supplied in [QRL.2].

4.6.2 *Data Limitations*

Missionary statistics are not particularly meaningful in isolation. They should be interpreted against background knowledge of the country, society, religious order or denomination involved. They do not directly reflect the size of the organisation or denomination concerned but alongside other data (e.g. finance) they may help to do this.

Very little data on missionary activity is produced regularly but individual organisations and denominations often maintain detailed records for their own use. Researchers may find data particular to their enquiry kept in a different form and requiring the necessary collation. For example, lists of missionaries with their years of service in a particular society would probably provide (if suitably analysed) details of marital status, sex, whether they were ordained or lay missionaries, their length of service and area of responsibility. Many individual enquiries can often be satisfactorily answered from internal records not publicly available.

4.6.3 *Terminology*

Church workers serving overseas may be lay workers, ordained ministers, members of religious orders, congregations or societies. Some denominations make a clear distinction between some of these categories. In the Methodist Church, for example, lay overseas workers are often referred to as missionaries while ministers, chaplains, priests etc. retain their specific titles.

Missionaries serve abroad for periods of varying length. Some make a lifelong commitment, while for others the period of service may be only two to four years. Missionaries who return after a period of leave or "furlough" for a second term of service are called "career" missionaries while others who only complete one term of service are called "short-term" missionaries. Missionary organisations and individual denominations vary as to the proportion of personnel falling into these two categories see [QRL.2]. Members of missionary religious orders tend to regard their service abroad as a long-term commitment while relief agencies may sponsor an overseas worker for less than five years service. The training, country and field of service often vary according to the length of service envisaged. Some organisations and denominations, for example, the Church Missionary Society, refer to missionaries serving for less than two or three years as "volunteers" while long-serving overseas personnel are termed "missionaries".

4.6.4 *Trends*

The number of missionaries or other workers serving in a particular country can alter quickly when there is a sudden political change in the country concerned. Recent examples of this have occured in Uganda, Ethiopia and Iran where missionaries were expelled suddenly or withdrawn by the home society following the change in government. Normally, the number of missionaries serving abroad or in any particular country changes little over short periods of time. When global statistics or those covering a large number of countries are required triennial or quinquennial figures are usually sufficient. However, annual data may be necessary for certain individual countries.

4.6.5 *Related Data*

Missionary organisation staff operating in the United Kingdom (such as office staff and home field staff) have been included in this section. References to data concerning overseas churches operated by United Kingdom missionary personnel have also been placed in the Quick Reference List under this section.

Missionaries particularly long-term, lay missionaries usually undergo specific forms of training. Such training is often provided by the religious order itself or at Bible Schools and other places of "Professional Manpower Training". The reader is advised to refer to this section for guidance on such data.

CHAPTER 5

TRINITARIAN CHURCH PLANT

5.1 Church Buildings

5.1.1 *Data Collection*

Church buildings may include churches, chapels, cathedrals, missions, church halls, meeting places, parsonages, monasteries, convents etc. Very little data is available for the various denominations in the United Kingdom on anything but the numbers of churches and other places of worship.

Local authorities maintain records of church buildings which are used by members of the public. These records are available on request but are not collated in any way, nor is there any complete central government source for the whole of the United Kingdom. However, one government publication *Marriage and Divorce Statistics* [QRL.76] does attempt to record the number of certified places of worship excluding churches and chapels of the Church of England and the Church in Wales. Only individual denominations systematically monitor their buildings and even then with varying degrees of rigour. Comparative sources of statistics on church buildings draw their data from the denominations themselves as there is no available complete and independent source (excluding [B.7]). Volumes which, to varying extents, collate the available statistics on the different places of worship include *UK Christian Handbook* [QRL.2], *World Christian Handbook* [QRL.3] and *Geography of Religion in England* [QRL.6].

5.1.2 *Data Limitations*

The size or number of church buildings does not necessarily reflect the size of denominational allegiance see [QRL.6]. This is particularly true among the larger denominations where church buildings support congregations of varying sizes over a period of years. Statistics concerning the number of church buildings are therefore of limited value in isolation, except in regard to the trends which they display over time. The size of church buildings as well as their number need to be viewed alongside measures of congregation size and vitality.

Among the smaller denominations where congregation sizes are more uniform; comparisons of denominational building statistics are more valid. Indeed where interest is solely in the geographical pattern of allegiance to the smaller denominations the use of building data is often adequate.

5.1.2.3 A few published volumes examine the geographical variation of the provision of churches in the United Kingdom (for example, [QRL.6] and [B.8]). One would expect that where the population is small the number of churches would also be small, the provision of church buildings to a certain extent reflecting the size of the surrounding population. However, in rural areas with small populations this is often not the case. Many rural areas with small populations support numerous churches and inner city areas often find themselves in the reverse situation. If in a given area (for example, a developing urban area) the population size changes over a period then the number of churches may not match the revised population.

Church redundancy procedures vary a great deal between different denominations. In the Church of England, for example, a carefully detailed procedure has to be followed before a church can be closed down. This results in many large churches with small congregations. Among the majority of Free Church denominations, churches may be closed when the local worshipping community can no longer financially support the building (for example, upon death of a major benefactor), or, as with the Methodist Church, when central funds can no longer support a rural church.

The procedure for the establishment of new churches also varies greatly between different denominations. The building of new churches is carefully controlled in the larger denominations but not so in the smaller groups where local financial support is again the crucial factor.

5.1.3 *Terminology*

The term "church" is one which can be applied to a group of worshipping people or to the building in which they worship. Some Free Church denominations do not have places specifically put aside for meeting or worshipping together. The use of the term "church" needs to be interpreted within the denomination in which it is used. Where it can be taken to mean "congregation" rather than "place of worship" (for example, in the House Church movement) it applies more correctly to the section entitled Church Community. However, where "congregation" implies a "place of worship" and *vice versa* the reference is given both in this section and "Church Community" (for example, the Presbyterian Church in Ireland). Terms such as "fellowship", "assembly" or "citadel" are also used by certain denominations to mean church building.

Some larger denominations use terms to refer to a group of one or more congregations or churches. Catholic and Episcopal denominations use the term "parish", "diocese" and "province"; Baptist churches use the term "association"; Methodist churches use the term "circuit"; while other denominations refer to "districts", "provinces" and "presbyteries". These terms are usually employed for administrative convenience and rarely do these area boundaries coincide with local authority county boundaries. An indication of the relative configuration of local authority and church administrative boundaries for four large denominations is given in [B.8].

5.1.4 *Trends*

As explained above, the extent to which church buildings are opened and closed, varies with each particular denomination. In general, however, the number of church buildings for each denomination varies very little over short periods of time, for example, from one year to the next. It is more beneficial to look at medium to long term changes in the numbers of buildings maintained. Indeed some denominations only publish a list of their churches every two years for this reason (see for example *Assemblies of God* [QRL.17] and the entries for the Apostolic Church and the Evangelical Fellowship of Congregational Churches in the Appendix of *Directories*). Quinquennial figures are given in *Churches and Church-goers* [QRL.4] and *UK Christian Handbook* [QRL.2].

5.1.5 *Related Data*
Alongside data on the number of church buildings, isolated denominations maintain records of other related data. The seating capacity of individual churches is recorded by five denominations (the Church of England, the Independent Methodist Churches, the Scottish Episcopal Church, the Baptist Union of Great Britain and Ireland and the Baptist Union of Ireland). The value of church buildings was in the past monitored by the Central Statistical Office in the National Accounts, but this is now only done by the Church Commissioners in their *Report and Accounts* [QRL.39] and a few individual churches.

5.1.5.2 Data on Convents and Religious Houses has been included both in the Quick Reference List in this section under "Other Buildings" and in the section covering Church Professional Manpower.

5.2 Schools

5.2.1 *Data Collection*
Some schools in the United Kingdom were founded by religious bodies. Today these schools are operated either as idependent schools or as voluntary schools within the state maintained sector. The numbers of schools, teachers and pupils in these schools is recorded, and related data, such as teacher/pupil ratios and education costs, are also kept, see, for example, *Scottish Education Statistics* [QRL.101], *Church of England Yearbook* [QRL.42].

Central government records cover all schools in the United Kingdom, particularly maintained schools. It is through the Department of Education and Science, the Scottish Education Department and the Welsh Office, that these statistics are made available in *Statistics of Education* [QRL.105] and *Scottish Education Statistics* [QRL.101]. No denominationally based statistics on schools or education are kept by the Northern Ireland Department of Education and Science. Throughout the United Kingdom individual denominations maintain records of their own schools. The Independent Schools Information Service (ISIS) makes available data on its registered schools (see Appendix on *Directories*).

Most of the voluntary and independent schools were founded by the major denominations, mainly the Church of England, the Roman Catholic Church and the Methodist Church. The majority of voluntary maintained primary schools are Church of England founded, while the majority of voluntary maintained secondary schools are Roman Catholic ones. It should be noted however, that there are far more voluntary maintained primary schools than voluntary maintained secondary schools. The independent sector includes preparatory and secondary schools of which some are residential. Over half of the schools in the independent sector are registered with ISIS, and these schools have three-quarters of the independent school pupils. The majority of ISIS schools are for pupils aged between eight and eighteen years.

It is the Church of England which has the majority of voluntary maintained schools: of the total Church of England voluntary maintained schools about two in every five are of aided status while just less than three are controlled. Nearly all jointly run maintained voluntary schools are aided.

Middle schools and independent schools can be classified for statistical purposes as either primary or secondary, depending on their age range. Consequently, the Quick Reference List refers to data within either primary or secondary categories.

5.2.2 Data Limitations

The number of schools run by each denomination does not directly reflect the strength of that denomination in the United Kingdom. However, the main denominations (Church of England, Roman Catholic and Methodist) do assist with the majority of denominationally based schools.

The degree of religious influence in these Church schools strictly depends on the school governing body, but will vary between the different denominations. Roman Catholic schools will encourage adherence to Catholic religious practices for pupils and their parents. The Church of England schools do not always make similar requests. The neighbourhood churches play different roles in the life of the denominational schools: ministers and priests sometimes but not always, participate in school life.

Data on the religious allegiance of teachers and pupils in denominational schools is produced. However, it cannot be assumed that all teachers and pupils in a denominational school will declare themselves to be members of that denomination. This point is illustrated by figures produced by the Catholic Education Council where approximately 1 in 13 pupils and 1 in 3 teachers in Catholic schools are non-Catholics.

Any investigation into the numbers of denominational schools needs to take into account the size of the schools concerned. The Department of Education and Science has information on school sizes. A survey in January 1963, see *Facts and Figures about the Church of England* [QRL.55], revealed that the Roman Catholic Church had few schools with less than a hundred pupils, while the Church of England operated most of its schools with under one hundred pupils.

Data on religious education is no longer published *Statistics of Education* [QRL.105], but the information is available on request. The researcher needs to be aware of the effect of category changes in the data for example, prior to 1978 figures produced by the Department of Education and Science covered England and Wales; in that year the Welsh Office published separate information on Welsh schools. Prior to 1953 there was not a denominational breakdown of secondary schools in the data, and prior to 1968 aided and controlled schools' data were aggregated.

5.2.3 *Terminology*

Schools run by the Local Education Authority are termed maintained schools - they may be voluntary or county schools. Voluntary schools are either "controlled", "aided" or of "special agreement" status. These terms describe how much influence the Church has on the running of the school. In a controlled school the Foundation Governors are in the minority and all running and maintainance costs are met by the Local Education Authority. In aided schools the Church Foundation has the majority of the Governors who oversee the general running of the school: the Church Foundation is also responsible for external maintainance, and receives a government grant towards the costs incurred. In special agreement schools the Church has the majority number of Governors, but the Local Education Authority has more control than it does in an aided school.

The nature of the state education system has changed radically over the years. Primary (Junior, Infant) and Secondary schools have been replaced in certain areas by Primary, Middle and Secondary schools while Grammar and Secondary Modern have been replaced by Comprehensive Secondary schools. The reader who wishes to cover historical data should bear these revisions in mind [QRL.105].

The only non-maintained schools in the education system now are the independent schools, which do not receive governement grants: until recently there were direct grant schools which did receive government financial aid. Direct grant schools have now been absorbed into either the maintained or independent sectors. Independent schools include preparatory (up to 11/13 years of age) and secondary (over 11/13) pupils. Whilst schools in these categories cannot strictly be classified as either primary or secondary, they have been allocated to the most appropriate category in the Quick Reference List.

5.2.4 *Trends*

The figures for the number of teachers and pupils in denominational schools will vary more from year to year than the figures for the numbers of schools. It may be preferable to use annual data for teachers and pupils but not for the number of schools.

5.2.5 *Related Data*

Since the First World War, when Sunday Schools attracted their peak attendance, their role has altered considerably. These schools used to meet during the week to teach the basic "three R's", but now usually meet once a week, on Sundays, to practice denominational teaching, sometimes in conjunction with Church services/worship. Consequently data dealing with Sunday schools is mentioned in the sections dealing with Church Attenders.

Teachers at schools in the United Kingdom undergo a period of training at either college or university – see 5.3.

5.3 Places of Higher Education

5.3.1 *Data Collection*
Only a few denominations run institutions of higher education. Such institutions are mostly colleges of education i.e. for the purpose of training primary and secondary teachers. The denominations most involved in higher education are the Church of England, the Roman Catholic Church and the Methodist Church. For a comprehensive summary of religious places of higher education the reader is referred to [B.4]. Data is available from individual denominations on the number of colleges under their administration and the number of students involved. During the period up to the 1960's the number of religious colleges of education increased (alongside general growth in higher education) but since this time the Churches involvement has declined.

All the major denominations allocate staff (chaplains) to the oversight of young people at (non-denominational) universities, polytechnics and colleges of education. There are also lay individuals involved in ministry among students but only the Universities and Colleges Christian Fellowship (UCCF) maintains any statistics [QRL.241]. Chaplains are assigned to individual places of higher education but may also be involved with nearby churches. In, for example, the Baptist Union of Great Britain and Ireland, chaplains are given oversight of all Baptist students in a certain town attending places of higher education and are also ministers in charge of a nearby church. Catholic chaplains, however, are usually only involved with students of the particular colleges of higher education assigned to them.

5.3.2 *Data Limitations*
The involvement of individual denominations in the provision of higher education whether measured by the number of institutions, the number of students involved or the number of chaplains provided to the higher education establishments does not strictly indicate the degree of denominational allegiance in the country or in a particular area. Only the major denominations participate in higher education which to a certain extent reflects denominational strength. However, no more detailed results than this can be deduced from the denominational data on higher education establishments. Of those colleges of higher education which have any denominational allegiance, the majority are Anglican (perhaps inevitably as this is the established religion).

5.3.3 *Trends*

The number of colleges of higher education has in recent years declined steadily from year to year. Most available data is collected annually and during more stable periods the researcher may find that a longer time period, for example, quinquennial, will suffice for analytical purposes. Similar trends exist for the number of students and chaplains at colleges of higher education. Quinquennial figures may suffice for long-term analysis but annual figures are recommended for recent years.

5.3.4 *Related Data*

Nearly all denominations employ trained ministers or workers. These staff are often trained at places of higher education by each particular denomination. Places of ministerial training for example, Theological Colleges, Seminaries, Bible Colleges etc. are dealt with under "Professional Manpower Training".

CHAPTER 6

TRINITARIAN CHURCH PROGRAMME

6.1 Finance

6.1.1 *Data Collection*

All Christian denominations maintain central accounts but there is no collective documentary source available to enquirers. Many denominations publish annual accounts in their yearbook or associated publication, for example, the Church of England, the Baptist Union of Great Britain and Northern Ireland, the Scottish Episcopal Church, the Presbyterian Church of Wales, the Congregational Federation and the Religious Society of Friends. Some denominations, such as the Salvation Army, make their accounts available on request from the denominational head office, while other denominational accounts, for example, those of the Old Catholic Church are only available on request from the Charity Commission. Central denominational accounts have not been individually listed in the Quick Reference List. The reader is advised to contact individual denominational head offices. A comprehensive list of these is found in the *UK Christian Handbook* [QRL.2]. In addition, the Church of England maintains accounts for each of its dioceses. These can be obtained directly from the headquarters in the form of their annual report and statement of account.

In addition to annual accounts many denominations maintain other financial records, for example, voluntary contributions, subscriptions, legacies, investments, church contributions to central funds (sometimes called the "quota" in Anglican circles) and missionary giving. It is these financial items which have been listed in the Quick Reference List. Only centrally recorded information is listed as although individual churches and denominational administrative areas maintain their own records, these are too numerous and diverse to be catered for here.

Many denominations encompass organisations, funds, societies, divisions or committees which draw finance from the central denominational funds, for example, the Methodist Church and the Scottish Episcopal Church. Training colleges, administrative funds, missionary funds, childrens' homes, education and youth divisions, stewardship councils and parsonages boards are just some of the organisations dependent on denominational central funds. Financial records of such subsidiary organisations have not been recorded in detail in the Quick Reference List; the reader is referred to the individual denomination concerned.

6.1.2 *Data Limitations*

As we have observed in previous chapters, terminology and administrative practices employed by the denominations vary a great deal. This variety is clearly reflected in their financial statistics and in the different financial definitions adopted by individual denominations. Missionary giving, for example, may involve only the denomination's work overseas or it may include certain Home Missions. Legacies and bequests may be considered part of "giving", "contributions", "donations" or form a separate category within "income". When comparing financial quantities between different denominations the reader must take care to interpret apparently similar data in the light of individual denominational practices and terminology.

The Free Churches are more able and/or willing than others to supply details of the financial state of their operations. Other denominations do not maintain financial records in a form easily usable for comparative financial purposes. There is currently a great paucity of published financial information about the Roman Catholic Church in the United Kingdom, little being available even to *bona fide* researchers.

6.1.3 *Trends*

It is common practice to consider financial statistics on an annual basis and religious groups are no exception. All denominations record financial matters annually, though some work on a calendar year basis, others on a financial year basis and still others on their own individual church year.

It is advisable when comparing data for different years to adjust financial figures according to the rate of inflation operative for the period when the figures were initially collected. Usually, the Government Retail Prices Index is appropriate and sufficiently accurate for this purpose, but when considering, for example, investment other measures may be more suitable. The Church of England publishes several of its financial series at current prices and constant prices (that is adjusted by the Retail Prices Index though this is not the only or even the most appropriate method of depreciating property). Once figures have been inflation adjusted it is possible to observe medium to long-term trends. Two or three yearly intervals may be appropriate here as, for example, is practiced by the Church of England ...see the *Church of England Yearbook* [QRL.42].

Certain denominations keep central records of the financial value of all property owned or maintained by the denomination concerned, (for example, the Church of the Nazarene). Denominations vary in the manner in which these records are kept. Property values may or may not have been depreciated over time and the reader is advised to explore any method used with the individual denomination concerned prior to any trend analysis over time. Details of statistics relating to the value of church buildings are to be found in the section on Church Buildings.

6.1.4 *Related Data*

Financial data is also available from Religious Agencies and Publishers. The reader is requested to refer to the chapters dealing with these aspects of Church Programme.

Church staff, for example, ministers and clergy receive salaries or stipends from local congregations or from central denominational funds. Where detailed information is required on this particular aspect of church finance, the reader is referred to the chapter dealing with Professional Church Manpower. Aggregate figures will be found in denominational central accounts where appropriate and on occasions (as in, for example, the Church of Scotland) in specific funds designed for this purpose.

6.2 Rites of Passage

6.2.1 *Data Collection*
This chapter covers the religious ceremonies associated with baptism or christening (in denominations which practice infant baptism), marriage and funerals. Each of these statistical areas is dealt with separately in the Quick Reference List.

Only certain denominations, for example, Anglican Churches, the Methodist Church, the United Reformed Church and the Catholic Church practice infant baptism. This religious practice became popular when infant mortality rates were high. Today it is a declining practice and the Church of England, for example, has introduced an alternative service of thanksgiving. However, no statistics were being kept in this area at the time of writing.

Baptism figures are only recorded by individual denominations and the reader is generally advised to consult particular denominations when such information is sought. One government publication *Social Trends* [QRL.104] produces some baptism statistics irregularly but only denominational sources are used in this collation exercise. A comprehensive collation of baptism statistics is available in *Churches and Church-goers* [QRL.4] but the data terminates in 1970 and has again been drawn from denominational sources.

Marriages are mainly legalised in registered churches, chapels or buildings before a registrar or authorised person except in the case of the Religious Society of Friends and the Jews. The ministers of State churches are generally suitably authorised whereas other denominations do not always register their buildings or their ministers. Consequently some marriages are solemnized with a civic ceremony to be followed by a religious service of "blessing", which does not have a legal status.

Statistics of marriages solemnized by religious ceremonies are, in contrast to baptism statistics, generally available from government collective sources, for example, *Marriage and Divorce Statistics* [QRL.76], *Annual Report of the Registrar General for Scotland* [QRL.14], and *Annual Report of the Registrar General for Northern Ireland* [QRL.13]. With the exception of Catholic Churches *Catholic Directory* [QRL.32] and *The Catholic Directory for Scotland* [QRL.33] very little data is obtainable from denominational sources. Central government comprehensively monitors wedding ceremonies and categorises the data according to the type of ceremony conducted, the age and marital status of the bride and groom. In addition, registered buildings and divorces are counted by manner of solemnization [QRL.76], [QRL.14]. A few collective sources of religious marriage statistics also exist but these draw on the government data referred to above.

6.2.2 *Data Limitations*

Statistics concerning rites of passage do not necessarily reflect Church membership strengths in the United Kingdom. This is due to different denominational practices together with different membership age profiles of various denominations. Low baptism and marriage figures may simply reflect large numbers of older people belonging to certain denominations.

Figures for the rites of passage in the larger denominations usually reflect church adherence or community rather than membership. This is particularly true in the established Churches. Many Church of England adherents, for example, marry in church and have their children baptised without becoming church members or regular attenders.

Although most baptisms referred to in this chapter involve infants some refer to adults e.g. *Church of England Yearbook* [QRL.42]. The form and purpose of the ceremony remains very similar and consequently such data has been included here. Denominations to which this applies usually practice infant baptism but will baptise adults on request, for example, prior to confirmation into the Church of England.

In recent years there has been a steady increase in the number of second or subsequent marriages. Trinitarian denominations differ in their willingness to marry someone for a second time and this is reflected in statistics for marriages with religious ceremonies. The number of marriages solemnized with a religious ceremony decreased sharply in the 1960's and 1970's and is now just under half of the total number of marriages. This decrease is due to the increasing number of divorced people re-marrying. The number of first-time marriages for both partners with a religious ceremony remains about three times those solemnized in other ceremonies, (see *Population Trends* [QRL.86], Winter 1980 edition). The Free Churches appear to have a more liberal policy towards second and subsequent marriages than the established and Roman Catholic Churches. Remarriage of divorced persons is permitted in Free Churches, including possibly, divorced persons belonging to other denominations.

6.2.3 *Trends*

Government sources monitor marriage statistics annually and given the current rate of change in these figures data is essential, at least, annually. Pre-1960, when marriage trends were almost static, less frequent statistics may be sufficient.

Baptism figures have steadily decreased since the first quarter of the twentieth century, the decrease accelerating in recent years. Annual data is advisable although this may not always be obtainable. The Church of England, for example, have only published either biennial or triennial figures between 1947 and 1978.

Trends in funeral statistics vary greatly between denominations and consequently initial analysis should be based on annual or biennial data.

6.2.4 *Related Data*

Baptisms are also carried out by many denominations (usually Free Churches) which do not practice infant baptism, for example, Baptist Churches. As such baptisms involve adults only and serve as a "profession of faith" or "admission into membership" the section on Church Members deals with these statistics. The Anglican and Roman Catholic Churches do also baptise adults from time to time, these numbers are included in this section for convenience.

Confirmation and ordination statistics are sometimes regarded as "Rites of Passage". However, for the purpose of this review data on confirmations are included under "Church Members" while ordinations are covered within "Professional Manpower Training".

6.3 Religious Agencies

6.3.1 *Data Collection*

Religious agencies include social service organisations, missionary organisations, benefit funds, insurance companies, musical services, Council of Churches training centres, Bookshops, Radio and Television Programme Producers and many other service agencies. The field is almost too wide for a totally comprehensive coverage. Many individual denominations have affiliated funds, committees, boards or divisions. The United Reformed Church, for example, oversees the United Reformed Church Insurance Company Limited, the United Reformed Church History Society and the United Reformed Church Retired Ministers Housing Association (which is not in fact just for retired clergy). Other denominations have orphan funds, social funds, pastoral committees, housing associations, overseas divisions etc. Such closely affiliated denominational agencies are not included in the Quick Reference List. The reader should refer to the relevant denominational handbook or head office. Agencies of independent foundation, although they may be aligned with a particular denomination are included in the Quick Reference List. A full list of such agencies is also to be found in *UK Christian Handbook* [QRL.2].

Data concerning religious agencies is available from collective independent sources and from denominational sources. It provides information on the number of organisations, the number of staff and various financial records. The most detailed source is [QRL.2] where individual Christian agencies are listed and analysed according to the type of agency. The Charity Commission keep records of all Christian charities and these may be appropriate for certain research purposes. Only United Kingdom religious agencies have been included in this review. Other agencies which operate in the United Kingdom or use United Kingdom personnel but are not based in the United Kingdom are not collated in this section (although they are given in [QRL.2]).

All religious agencies maintain annual accounts of income and expenditure together with an annual balance sheet. Sometimes these are available in handbooks, for example, the British Council of Churches publish their annual accounts in [QRL.26]. However, while not being published, many are available from the agency head office. A comprehensive list of these head offices can also be found in [QRL.2].

6.3.2 *Data Limitations*

Statistics on religious agencies are not on their own suitable for denominational comparisons. Many other factors, for example, different denominational practices and deployment of manpower need to be taken into consideration. Their main use is in an analysis of the areas of interest in which religious agencies work and the relative strengths of these areas. For example, there are many conference centres, guest houses, hostels and hotels but few training centres; there are many bookshops but few radio programme producers.

Available figures on the work of religious agencies are recorded by individual agencies in different ways and some are estimated by the head office in answer to particular enquiries. This is frequently true for figures of, for example, office staff. Such data is rarely systematically and accurately recorded from one year to the next. The reader must distinguish between regularly published and accurately collated figures and estimates often produced as required. In general there is very little regularly kept and well recorded data on Church agencies. Consequently trends prove hard to detect and still more difficult to interpret.

Data on religious agencies does not present a complete picture of this aspect of Church Programme. This is because many agencies operate on a local basis and do not have recognised national head offices. Such local agencies, for example, old peoples' centres and interdenominational schemes are not covered in this review but add appreciably to the areas in which religious agencies collectively operate.

6.3.3 *Related Data*

Missionary organisations publish statistics on missionary personnel, office staff and finance. For completeness all statistics on missionary organisations have been listed in the sections dealing with Church Missionaries. Annual accounts have not been individually listed as these are generally available on request from all missionary organisations.

Religious publishing and broadcasting, while strictly being part of this section on religious agencies, have been covered separately under Church Programme. Data concerning these areas of religious activity are dealt with in the following two chapters.

6.4 Religious Publishing

6.4.1 *Data Collection*

Religious publishing is mostly conducted by independent Christian and secular companies rather than denominationally based ones. Consequently the majority of data concerning religious publishing is available from collective sources. Whitaker, for example, periodically publishes compilations and analyses in the *Bookseller*. Some denominations, however, have their own publishing company. The Church of England (through Church Information Office Publishing), the Methodists (through Epworth Press) and the United Reformed Church are examples here. Details of such publishing companies are to be obtained from denominational head offices or individual denominational handbooks. A few religious publishers particularly handle the work of one denomination for example, Paternoster Press handles Christian Brethren titles. Only those who make data available detailing their operation have been included in the Quick Reference List.

Data on religious publishing covers the number of religious publishing agencies, the number of religious books and periodicals published, the quantity (and value) of Scripture distributed and various financial accounts. However, very little data is in fact produced, which makes this area difficult to quantify.

All publishers produce annual accounts. Scripture Gift Mission make these available in their annual *Report* [QRL.94], the United Society for Christian Literature produces a leaflet containing their annual accounts while other publishers will make accounts available on request. Individual references to annual accounts have not been made in the Quick Reference List; the reader is requested to consult individual publishers. A list of Christian book publishers can be found in [QRL.2] and the Publishers Association also produces a list of religious publishing houses.

Most publishers of religious books distribute their products through the book trade, few use direct mail. There are only one or two Christian book clubs. These trade outlets, including the so-called religious bookshops shops, are difficult to quantify exactly as many secular bookshops have religious departments and many religious bookshops sell secular books. There are no regularly produced figures on the readership or sales of religious publications.

6.4.2 *Data Limitations*

It is difficult to obtain a complete picture of religious publishing because many denominations produce handbooks, leaflets etc. not registered as book publications. The area of book or periodical publishing is the easiest to quantify although data remains hard to trace even in these fields.

Publishers' output is a difficult quantity to interpret. For different purposes the reader may want to include or exclude reprints and new editions. Publishers have different policies concerning the printing of a new edition and this is reflected in the figures. Foreign books may be classified as translations or new editions. (For a more detailed guide to this problem see the forthcoming Review in this series on Printing and Publishing by W.D. McClelland). The reader should be clear as to the practical collection process involved before using any publishing statistics.

The value of statistics concerned with religious publishing is primarily the overall picture which collectively they create. Denominational differences will be almost insignificant but the total religious and secular publishing volume of religious materials (books, periodicals etc.) renders interesting comparisons over different years.

6.5 Religious Broadcasting

6.5.1 *Data Collection*

Religious broadcasting is carried out on both national and local radio and television by non-denominational organisations. In the field of radio broadcasting there are several religious companies which produce programmes. Their programmes together with religious programmes produced by secular sources are broadcast through independent United Kingdom radio networks. The only exception to this is the Far East Broadcasting Association. (FEBA) Although a Christian, United Kingdom based organisation it is concerned with religious broadcasts overseas to Africa, Europe and Asia, and operates from a broadcasting station in the Seychelles.

Religious television programmes are almost always produced by existing secular television companies and broadcast by independent television companies or the British Broadcasting Corporation. However, in 1981 the first Christian television programme production organisation was set up under the name of LELLA Productions sponsored by the Trinity Trust.

Only one source [QRL.2] monitors the number of religious programme production organisations and these numbers continue to be very small. Broadcasting companies keep detailed information concerning all their programmes but do not make the information available to the general public. However, they are usually very willing to assist serious researchers who are asked to apply in writing. Times and lengths of programmes are usually available and in the case of the British Broadcasting Corporation and the Independent Broadcasting Authority, audience figures are also kept, see [QRL.202], [QRL.205].

Both the British Broadcasting Corporation and Independent Broadcasting Authority monitor the size of audience to individual programmes through a daily (panel) survey. Qualitative audience reactions are also studied for a selection of programmes. In 1981 the Broadcasters Audience Research Board (BARB) was set up as an independent monitor of television audiences. This board now conducts daily surveys on the size of television programme audiences, publishes weekly top ten ratings and makes the detailed figures available to the British Broadcasting Corporation and Independent Broadcasting Authority. The Broadcasters Audience Research Board itself does not maintain any historic data; data is kept for six months and is then passed to the British Library.

6.5.2 *Data Limitations*

Religious radio and television broadcasting does not reflect religious allegiance or church membership in the United Kingdom except perhaps in its general trends. That is, religious allegiance in the United Kingdom is decreasing while the number of religious programmes is also decreasing. However, many individual religious programmes are maintaining high audience figures despite the decrease in church attendance and membership. There are many factors operating here, for example, a number of people claim to be religious but disillusioned with church-based religion and to many (particularly old people) television is much more "convenient" than church.

Individual denominations are involved in religious broadcasting to various extents. The Roman Catholic Church, for example, has priests with specific responsibilities in this field and several other denominations also assist broadcasting companies in advisory capacities, (for example, on religious advisory panels). However, activity in the field of broadcasting while reflecting denominational interest in such "outreach" does not reflect denominational following in the country at large.

CHAPTER 7

NON-TRINITARIAN CHURCH PEOPLE

7.1 Membership and Attendance

7.1.1 *Data Collection*

The number of people associated with an individual Church can be measured in various ways. Figures are usually based on Church membership, Church attendance or Church adherence (see 4.1.1.1), although data on congregations, ministers and other manpower are also applicable. This chapter on Church People encompasses Church community (adherence), Church membership, Church attendance (adult and child including Sunday Schools), professional manpower and missionaries.

The only central government source on religious allegiance is the Northern Ireland General Office. Figures are compiled from the decennial Census of Northern Ireland and details of religious adherence are published in tabular form *Census of Population – Religious Tables* [QRL.36]. No such coverage is maintained in the similar Census exercises in Great Britain. However, the Home Office maintains records of religious registration in its annual census of Prison Department establishments *Report of the Work of the Prison Department* [QRL.97] and the Ministry of Defence keeps similar records of the religious denominations of Armed Forces. No government records exist relating to church members or attenders.

Some of these Churches keep records of those people associated with them. This is usually measured by membership, attendance or congregational strength. Churches which do not keep regular records of their following within the general population are sometimes able to give approximate figures on request, for example, the Worldwide Church of God, but others, such as the Churches of God (also called Family of Love) cannot or will not. Several comparative sources on religious allegiance exist, [QRL.4], [QRL.2], [QRL.3], [QRL.6] which all in turn employ Church sources. Some Churches (for example, the Jehovah's Witnesses) monitor attendance at memorial services of Jesus' death or the Last Supper. These are included alongside statistics on membership (see 4.3.3.1).

Among these Churches very little data is kept on child attendance or ministerial training. Only the New Church records child attendance at Sunday School while only the Unitarian Church maintains data on ministerial students. The lack of data on ministerial training reflects the fact that in several Churches there is no specialised ministerial role e.g. Christian Science Churches and Theosophist Groups.

Non-Trinitarian Christian Churches based in the United Kingdom rarely engage in Missionary activity outside the United Kingdom. However, some Churches send missionaries to the United Kingdom (for example, the Unification Church and the Mormons) and these have been included in the Quick Reference List under "Missionaries".

7.1.2 *Data Limitations*

Religious allegiance can be measured in different ways, each having different meanings. Only the Northern Ireland Census measures Church adherents i.e. those who would align themselves with each of the individual Churches. The resulting figures over-estimate the number actively involved with each Church. However, in the absence of other data this gives the best indication which is available of where the population sympathies lie.

Most Churches measure the extent of their following among the population by maintaining a record of attendance at their meetings or services. However, a few also count their membership (for example, the Mormons). In most cases figures for the membership of a Church are greater than the average attendance. Different Churches have different criteria of membership, but these figures generally give an indication of those in touch or associated with particular Churches. Membership figures may in fact under-estimate total interest or adherence while over-estimating those actively participating in Churches. Attendance figures serve as a proxy for the number of people actively supporting a Church, but these may be an over-estimate (due to irregular attenders) or an under-estimate (because of, for example, non-attendance due to illness). In a few Churches, for example, the Jehovah's Witnesses, attendance exceeds membership as the latter is regarded as reflecting active commitment and regular participation in the life of the Church.

The Jehovah's Witnesses and the Unitarian Church both produce data on the number of congregations in their Church. Such data is very limited in use as it says nothing about the relative sizes of the congregations. Church allegiance cannot be compared by referring solely to data on the number of congregations. Similarly, allegiance to the Mormon Church cannot be deduced from the data on Mormon Communities without reference to their relative sizes. Some Church congregations or communities may have their own buildings while others may not. In the absence of figures on Church congregations/communities the reader is advised to consult available data on Church buildings or places of worship (see 8.1.4).

Data on congregations, communities (and buildings) can serve a worthwhile function in locating geographical areas in which individual Churches are active. One comparative source attempts to do this *Geography of Religion in England* [QRL.6].

7.1.3 *Terminology*

Churches employ their own terms for what, to the layman, are very similar items; so that people loosely associated with a Church may be called adherents, communities, congregations or have a particular Church affiliation or allegiance (see 4.1.3.1). Congregations in turn may be referred to as, for example, churches, societies (Christian Science) or communities (Mormon). Professional Church Manpower may be called by various names such as overseas ministry or overseas ministers (i.e. missionary activities), lay pastors (Unitarian), practitioners (Christian Scientists), or publishers (Jehovah's Witnesses).

7.1.4 *Trends*

Most data on "Church People" are produced annually. As Church attendance patterns are currently changing quite rapidly, annual examination of available data is worthwhile. However, membership, adherents, manpower and congregations change more slowly and triennial or quinquennial figures may suffice here. Only decennial figures on religious adherents are, in fact, collated through the Northern Ireland Census.

7.1.5 *Related Data*

Churches vary as to the conditions specified for membership. Jehovah's Witnesses, for example, require adult baptism while other Churches accept profession of faith. Such statistics are included in the Quick Reference List under Church Members. A few Churches, for example, the General Conference of the New Church, practice infant baptism and baptisms in these Churches have been included in the section dealing with Rites of Passage (Church Programme).

CHAPTER 8

NON-TRINITARIAN CHURCH PLANT

8.1 Total Property Data

8.1.1 *Data Collection*

Almost the only data available on Non-Trinitarian Church Plant relates to church buildings, (information on Sunday Schools and ministerial training colleges being dealt with under Church People). The General Conference of the New Church gives information on buildings other than the main meeting place - in this case ministers' residences and Sunday School rooms *The General Conference of the New Church Yearbook* [QRL.66].

The researcher must in practice rely almost solely on individual church sources, there being no independent source. Only two volumes attempt to collate the data on Church Plant for these Churches. One only achieves partial Church coverage [QRL.6] while the other gives only quinquennial figures from 1970 [QRL.2].

8.1.2 *Data Limitations*

The size or number of church buildings does not necessarily reflect the size of Church allegiance. Churches do not always meet in specific Church buildings, which makes any comparison of statistics on Church buildings of doubtful validity. Some Churches rely on the use of members' houses for meetings. The largest Church in this category in the United Kingdom, the Mormons, has under two hundred church buildings while the smaller number of Jehovah's Witnesses utilise some eleven hundred churches. The use of data on church congregations can sometimes be useful for such comparisons (see 7.1.2).

The geographical location of the various Churches can be investigated by examining the location of their church buildings, see [QRL.6]. This is almost the only worthwhile use of buildings data in isolation but it still does not provide coverage of all the Churches.

Some Churches finance their buildings from central funds while others rely on the local members to support their own building. Different Church structures and finance procedures can affect the number of church buildings. Such factors should be borne in mind when examining data on buildings.

8.1.3 *Terminology*

The term "church" may refer to a meeting place or the group of people meeting together. Where it refers to the latter (i.e. the "congregation") it has been included under "Church Community" (see 7.1.2). Not all congregations have church buildings hence the disparity evident when comparing such figures (see 4.1.3). Church buildings may be referred to by different Churches as ecclesias (Christadelphians), churches (Mormons), societies (Christian Science), lodges (Theosophists), chapels or meeting houses (Unitarians).

For administrative reasons the larger Churches categorise their churches into groups. Terms such as Area Councils (the New Church) or District Council (the Spiritualists) may be used when describing data categorisations.

8.1.4 *Trends*

As remarked in previous references to church buildings it is more beneficial to look at medium to long-term fluctuations in the numbers of buildings maintained. Although the Mormons and Jehovah's Witnesses are currently growing quite fast quinquennial figures remain adequate, for observing changes over time [QRL.2].

CHAPTER 9

NON-TRINITARIAN CHURCH PROGRAMME

9.1 Rites of Passage

9.1.1 *Data Collection*
There is very little Non-Trinitarian data available on Church Programme. Individual Churches maintain financial records usually on an annual basis while central government records the number of Church weddings. A small amount of data is also kept by individual Churches on rites of passage, publications and agencies but a comprehensive coverage in these areas of all the Churches is not possible. In the latter two cases this is because only a few Churches have affiliated publications or agencies. The Charity Commission keep records of all Christian charities and these may be appropriate for certain research purposes. The scarcity of data on Rites of Passage arises because infant baptism is not applicable to all Churches while marriage and death statistics are not always collected.

Nearly all Churches maintain annual accounts. These have not been individually listed in the Quick Reference List but can be obtained from Church Annual Reports (for example, the *Annual Report of the General Assembly* [QRL.12] for the Unitarian Church) or on request from the Church headquarters. A comprehensive list of these headquarters is given in [QRL.2]. Only the Unitarian Church publishes any other financial data, namely individual congregational contributions [QRL.12].

9.1.2 *Data Limitations*

Not all Churches provide figures on Church programme and consequently Church comparisons in this area are often not possible, the areas of finance and marriage being possible exceptions to this. Such statistics serve, however, alongside other data to ascertain the strengths of the various Churches. They are of limited value in isolation.

9.1.3 *Trends*

Non-Trinitarian Churches have considerably increased in strength in the United Kingdom during recent years. These increases are reflected in Church programme statistics. Individual Churches may also be relatively new to the United Kingdom and this produces noticeable trends in statistics concerned with Church programme. Annual data are consequently needed if trends are to be closely observed.

9.1.4 *Related Data*

Baptisms within Churches which practice infant baptism are documented in this chapter but some Churches practice adult baptism only. The Jehovah's Witnesses are one such Church where adult baptism is a requirement for membership. Statistics concerning the practice of (adult) baptism by such Churches are included under the review of Church Members.

CHAPTER 10

IMPROVEMENTS AND FUTURE DEVELOPMENTS

Various problems of data collection, measurement and definition have been examined elsewhere in this review (see Chapter 2 and Peter Brierley's Prologue). This section provides the author with an opportunity to suggest possible ways in which these problems might be solved or lessened.

There is a serious paucity of data concerning Church People from independent, non-denominational sources. Only the Northern Ireland government regularly collects information on church affiliation although the British government has made abortive attempts in this area. Most regular information detailing Church allegiance in the United Kingdom is collected and made available by individual denominations and Churches. As discussed elsewhere in this review this has resulted in inconsistent data, of poor quality for comparison purposes. An independent source of religious statistics is needed, operating in co-operation with the Christian Churches while maintaining a separate existence and respected both within and outside the Churches. Such an independent source of information would be beneficial to both the Churches and external religious observers/researchers. More rigorous and unbiased collection of data would be possible together with superior resources for professional analysis and interpretation. Better facilities for Church comparisons would also benefit all users of religious statistics. Churches would be able to reduce the funds currently reserved for monitoring religious statistics for their own internal purposes.

Individual Churches recognise different measures of religious allegiance as indicating their strength or following in the population. Even identical terms (e.g. membership) are defined differently in many Churches. This situation not only presents a very diverse picture to the religious observer but often confuses those participating in church life. Some measures of Church allegiance (for example the Church of England Electoral Roll) have become outdated and limited in their usefulness both within the church and outside it. Moves to update, streamline and equate terminology employed in the field of religious allegiance are long overdue. The present situation causes the religious researcher to refer to a wide variety of measures, often compiling some form of *ad hoc*, combined statistic for practical purposes (e.g. some weighted average of membership and attendance). Currently Church attendance perhaps presents the most easily interpretable measure of religious allegiance but even this statistic varies in definitional terms in different Churches.

Many measures of Church allegiance are restricted in their applications because of poor or variable means of collection for example variability in the time interval between observations and changes in the basis of collection. Not only do these variations exist between different denominations and Churches but over periods of

65

time changes may occur within a denomination or Church. The Roman Catholic Church for example collected attendance figures in April of each year but in 1974 this timing was altered to the month of October. The method of collection of Catholic information has also changed in recent years and is now more heavily dependent on the parish priest. Many Churches depend on local staff to report information and the success of this approach varies a great deal. Local response to such requests from Church headquarters is often poor and the judgements made to estimate the required statistics subjective. Some Churches employ estimation methods to compensate for poor response or inconsistent information. These methods vary considerably using historical information, local population demographics, sampling procedures, information on other local churches etc. The diversity and subjectivity in methods of data collection prevents a great deal of meaningful analysis and interpretation. Churches could significantly increase and improve the applications of data collected if more attention was given to the mechanism by which such information is supplied.

Most Churches or denominations divide their constituency into areas for administrative purposes and rarely do these areas coincide with regional, county or local authority areas. Consequently few Churches are able to employ government or local authority population statistics to assist with data interpretations or comparisons. In addition, individual Churches have over the years devised their own administrative boundaries which greatly hinders any inter-Church comparisons. More extensive use of existing data could be made if Churches were to streamline their administrative boundaries bearing in mind other geographical boundaries in current use.

Local authorities monitor (often only on an informal basis) the provision and use of buildings by individual Churches or denominations. However, this information is not collated either on a local or national level. Such statistics on church buildings have to be obtained from the individual denomination or Church concerned using the administrative boundaries appropriate to each. Regional religious research or monitoring would be greatly assisted if government were to regularly collate the information already available concerning local church buildings. The interpretation of, for example, marriage statistics would also be improved.

In all regularly collected religious statistics there is a lack of detail which restricts the applications of those statistics. Churches and external observers would both benefit if some estimation of the composition of the Christian constituency was made. Very little information is known concerning, for example, the age and sex profile of congregations in different Churches or even their levels of occupation, education etc. The knowledge of these factors would influence not only the approach of Church leaders to their congregations but their relationships with people outside the Churches.

There is also a serious lack of regular information concerning religious activity as it occurs in or on behalf of the Christian Churches. Only the increasing monitoring of attendance at Sunday services could be described as significantly contributing to this field. Considerable religious activity exists outside formal Christian worship, for example, in midweek activities, meetings etc. and in services, facilities etc. provided to the community. Religious activity in the media, for example in publishing, music and video is also only recorded on a very limited basis. The importance of the

Christian faith in the United Kingdom today cannot only be measured on the basis of Church membership, formal attendance at worship etc. Other measures of religious activity are long overdue as contributions to the overall representation of church life.

Many of the above recommendations for the improvement of recurrent Christian statistics could be implemented more easily and used more widely if methods of computerisation were more prevalent than at present. Existing information would also be more widely applicable if computer usage was more common. Data analysis and collection would improve to the benefit of both religious observers and researchers from within the Churches and outside them. Far from being an unjustifiable expense, computer facilities would provide an efficient, more cost-effective method for data handling and interpretation.

NOTES TO THE QUICK REFERENCE LIST

1. *Area of coverage* All recurrent Christian statistics are listed in the Quick Reference List in similar order to that employed within the text. The list itemises all data known to be available as at March 1983. A detailed explanation of the ordering employed is given below. All known published sources of United Kingdom recurrent Christian Statistics are listed in the Quick Reference List Key to Publications.

2. *Groupings employed* - Sources of religious data as well as references to data have been categorised into collective and church/denomination categories. Where a source or item of data only refers to an individual church or denomination it has been placed within the appropriate category. A list of denominational and church groupings employed is given in Chapter 3. Where a source or item of data refers to more than one denomination or church it will be found within the "collective" category.

3. *Ordering of data* - a. Collective - Country order (ie United Kingdom, Great Britain, England, Wales, Scotland, Northern Ireland). b. Denominational - Protestant, Catholic and other Trinitarian sources in order of the size of each denominational grouping (ref Chapter 3) followed by the sources for the non-Trinitarian Churches. c. Within each - 1 Major denominations in order of country. d. Denominational grouping: 2 Smaller denominations in order of country. 3 Denominational agencies and missionary organisations.

4. *Secondary sources* - Where references to sources are given in round brackets ie ([QRL.3]) the source is a secondary one, the previously listed source forming the major reference.

5. *Data details* - Possible breakdowns for each piece of data are given in the column headed "Breakdown". The following example serves to illustrate the notation employed within this column. a. "Ministers/lay preachers" - the given data are broken down into two distinct categories namely ministers and lay preachers. b. "Ministers/lay preachers by sex" - ministers and lay preachers are each separately categorised into male and female totals. c. "Ministers and lay preachers by sex" means that the data are available for ministers and lay preachers (aggregate) broken down into male and female categories. d. "Ministers/lay preachers by sex; age" - ministers and lay preachers are each split into male and female but the data to which this this breakdown refers are also available for various age categories in aggregate.

6. *The QRL Key to Publications* - is arranged alphabetically first by authors where one exists and then by title for the remainder.

7. *Directories* - and similar publications giving only lists from which numeral counts must be made by the user are referenced in an annexe to the Key to Publications.

QUICK REFERENCE LIST - TABLE OF CONTENTS

QUICK REFERENCE LIST

Type of data	Breakdown	Area	Frequency or Date	QRL reference	Text Reference and Remarks
COMMUNITY					
Collective Data					
Christian community sizes	Denomination	Great Britain and Ireland	1949, 1952, 1957, 1962, 1967	[QRL.3]	General ref: 4.1 - 7. 4.1.1.3 - 7.1.3
Approximate community sizes	Major denominations	United Kingdom	1975, 1980	[QRL.2]	Compiled from denominational sources. 1985 estimated. 7.1.3
Religious adherents	Professing; nominal; affiliated; practising; non-practising Christians by denominational groups	United Kingdom	1900, 1970, 1975, 1980	[QRL.60]	Forecasts for the year 2000 given
Number of denominational congregations (places of regular worship)	Denomination	United Kingdom	1970, 1975, 1980	[QRL.1]	4.1.1.3 Total number of denominations also given
Religious allegiance in Great Britain and Ireland expressed in percentages	Denomination by area	United Kingdom	1978, 1980, 1983	[QRL.8]	
Religious affiliation	Major denominations	Northern Ireland	Decennial from 1861	[QRL.4]	4.1.1.3 - 7.1.3 Taken from Northern Ireland census
Religious adherents for denominations with 10 or more adherents	Sex by denomination	Northern Ireland	Decennial from 1861	[QRL.36]	4.1.1.3 - 7.1.2
Religious adherence of the population	Major denominations by district council and region	Northern Ireland	Decennial from 1961	[QRL.36]	

Households by religion of head	Major denominations by size of household by persons per room; major denominations by tenure by person per room; major denominations by tenure by amenities; major denominations by size of household by number of rooms occupied.	Northern Ireland	Decennial from 1861	[QRL.36]	Number of households and people given
Economically active persons	Major denominations by sex by occupation and status	Northern Ireland	Decennial from 1861	[QRL.36]	Population aged 15 and over
Persons in employment	Major denominations by sex by industry	Northern Ireland	Decennial from 1861	[QRL.36]	
Population aged 18-69 years	Major denominations by sex by educational attainment	Northern Ireland	Decennial from 1861	[QRL.36]	
Population by religion	Major denominations by sex by age by marital condition; major denominations by age by sex by district councils and regions	Northern Ireland	Decennial from 1861	[QRL.36]	
Denominational allegiance in the Royal Navy; Royal Marines	Denomination by Officers; Ratings by Royal Navy; Royal Marines; Womens Royal Navy Service	United Kingdom	1939, quinquennial from 1946 to 1976	[QRL.222]	4.1.1.3 Quinquennial census held until 1976; now held "as required".
Total strength in the Army	Major denominations	United Kingdom	Annual from 1975	[QRL.222]	Annual data from 1860 to 1937 available from [QRL.65]. 1861 to 1913 given in [QRL.5]
Total strength in the Royal Air Force	Denomination	United Kingdom	1963, 1969, 1971, 1974, annual from 1977	[QRL.222]	
Religious registration of Prison Department establishments	Denomination by sex	England and Wales	Annual from 1962 except for 1980	[QRL.97]	15 years and upwards. 7.1.2

Episcopal Data

Allegiance to the Church of England	County	England	1603	[QRL.6]	
General population	Diocese	England	1963	[QRL.6]	

Type of data	Breakdown	Area	Frequency or Date	QRL reference	Text Reference and Remarks
Church of England diocesan population	Age by sex by diocese	England	Annual	[QRL.42]	Few data kept during Second World War. Regular figures from 1958. Components of change examined. Dioceses related to standard regions.
Persons baptised in the Church of England	Total number	England	Biennial	[QRL.42]	Irregular in recent years. Measured at 30 June. Compared with home population.
Church of England: number of benefices	Held by incumbents; not filled; held by incumbents in plurality	England	Annual	[QRL.39]	
Parochial livings in the Church of England	Occupied; vacant by diocese and size of population	England	1957, 1960, 1963	[QRL.55]	
Home population of Church of England	Urban; rural by diocese	England	1957, 1961, 1963	[QRL.55]	
Church of England: number of ecclesiastical parishes	Population size of diocese	England	Decennial	[QRL.55]	Original data from Registrar General
Church of England: number of parishes	Diocese	England	1957, 1960, 1963	[QRL.55]	

Church of England: number of parishes	Archdeanery; diocese	England	Annual or biennial	[QRL.41]	Parish populations sometimes supplied. Also availabe from [QRL.209].
Scottish Episcopal Church: number of church organizations	Diocese	Scotland	Annual	[QRL.111]	Refers to church based organizations such as Mothers Unions, Scouts etc.
Methodist Data					
Methodist Church community roll	Total number on roll	Great Britain	1969	[QRL.59]	
Methodist Church community roll	District	Great Britain	Annual	[QRL.77]	
Methodist Church in Ireland: adherents	Junior; senior by circuit	Ireland	Annual	[QRL.78]	
Primitive Methodist Church: adherents	Total number	Great Britain	Annual 1880 to 1932	[QRL.4]	Adherents are people associated with the church excluding members
Presbyterian Data					
Geographical location of Presbyterians	County	England	1877, 1963	[QRL.6]	
Presbyterian Church of Wales: number of congregations	Total number	Wales	Annual 1895 to 1968	[QRL.4]	Includes members, adherents and children
Church of Scotland: number of congregations	Presbytery; synod	Scotland	Annual	[QRL.95]	
Presbyterian Church in Ireland: number of families	Presbytery; congregation	Ireland	Annual	[QRL.53]	

Type of data	Breakdown	Area	Frequency or Date	QRL reference	Text Reference and Remarks
Presbyterian Church in Ireland: number of congregations	Presbytery	Ireland	Annual	[QRL.53]	
Free Church of Scotland: number of congregations	Presbytery	Scotland	Annual	[QRL.62]	
United Free Church of Scotland: number of congregations and groups	Total number	Scotland	Annual	[QRL.69]	
Free Presbyterian Church of Scotland: number of congregations	Total number	Scotland	Monthly	[QRL.98]	
Reformed Presbyterian Church in Scotland: adherents, number of families, total number contacted	Individual church	Scotland	Annual from 1960	[QRL.81]	
Reformed Presbyterian Church of Ireland: number of families	Presbytery; congregation	Ireland	Annual	[QRL.80]	
Congregational Data					
Congregational Federation: adherents	Individual Church; area	Great Britain	Annual from 1973	[QRL.49]	
Congregational Union of Scotland: adherents	District	Scotland	Annual from 1900	[QRL.75]	
Pentecostal and Holiness Data					
Apostolic Church: adherents	Total number	United Kingdom	Irregular	[QRL.200]	
The New Testament Church of God: number of congregations	Total number	England	1966, 1968, 1970	[QRL.22]	Total number of administrative districts also given
Roman Catholic data					

Geographic location of Roman Catholics	County	England	1603	[QRL.6]	Also listed individually
Number of Roman Catholic parishes	Diocese	England and Wales	Annual	[QRL.31]	
Number of Roman Catholic parishes	Diocese	Scotland	Annual	[QRL.33]	
Number of Roman Catholic parishes	Diocese	Ireland	Annual	[QRL.71]	
Non-Trinitarian churches					
Jehovah's Witnesses: number of congregations		Great Britain and Ireland	Annual	[QRL.73]	7.1.1
Mormons: number of communities	Size of community	England	1967	[QRL.6]	7.1.2
Unitarian Church: number of congregations	Total number	United Kingdom	Quinquennial 1801 to 1966	[QRL.4]	Eire included after partition
MEMBERS					
Collective Data					
Church membership	Denomination; country	United Kingdom	1970, 1975, 1980	[QRL.2]	General ref: 4.2 - 7. 4.2.1.3 - Some estimation. Members per church and estimates for 1985 given.
Church membership and communicants	Denomination	United Kingdom	1767 to 1970	[QRL.4]	Years covered varies for different dioceses
Church membership and communicants	Denomination	United Kingdom	Annual 1900 to 1979	[QRL.7]	County variation also given for 1979 in [B.8]
Church membership	Major denomination	United Kingdom	Annual	[QRL.25]	
Free Church membership	Major denominations of the FCFC	United Kingdom	Annual	[QRL.60]	

Type of data	Breakdown	Area	Frequency or Date	QRL reference	Text Reference and Remarks
Denominational affiliation and adult membership	Adult members by denomination; total members (community)	United Kingdom	1970, 1975, 1980	[QRL.1]	Total number of denominations also given
Church members	Denominations	Great Britain and Ireland	Annual	[QRL.110]	
Communicants and full members	Diocese	Great Britain and Ireland	1949, 1952, 1957, 1962, 1967	[QRL.3]	
Baptisms and confirmations in selected churches	Major denominations	Great Britain	Irregular	[QRL.104]	4.2.1.4 Appears in full in 1983 edition
Church membership	Selected denominations	Great Britain	1970; 71	[QRL.59]	
Episcopal Data					
Church of England confirmations	Total number	England	Annual 1872 to 1970	[QRL.4]	4.2.3.2
Church of England: number of Easter communicants	Diocese	England	1962	[QRL.6]	4.3.2.2
Church of England: number of confirmations	Diocese	England	1961 to 1963	[QRL.6]	
Church of England: number on electoral rolls	Diocese	England	Annual	[QRL.42] [QRL.45]	4.2.2.4 - few data for second world war. Regular figures since 1958.
Church of England: confirmations	Sex by diocese	England	Annual	[QRL.42] [QRL.45]	Age breakdown given by majority of dioceses

Church of England: parochial communicants	Easter day; Easter week; Christmas day; normal Sunday by diocese	England	Biennial	[QRL.42] [QRL.45]	Also per 1,000 population aged 15 and over. Normal Sunday communicants, 1976 onwards
Church of England: confirmed members	total number	England	Biennial	[QRL.42] [QRL.45]	Irregular in recent years. As at 30 June
Church of England: number on electoral roll	Parish	England	Annual or biennial	[QRL.41]	
Church in Wales: number of Easter communicants	Parish (benefice) diocese	Wales	Annual from 1921	[QRL.40]	
Church in Wales: number of confirmations	Parish (benefice) diocese	Wales	Annual from 1921	[QRL.40]	Llandaff diocese gives breakdown by sex
Church in Wales: number on electoral rolls	Parish (benefice) diocese	Wales	Annual from 1921	[QRL.40]	Llandaff and Bangor dioceses only
Scottish Episcopal Church: number of permanent members	Charge; diocese	Scotland	Annual from 1875	[QRL.15], ([QRL.111])	Defined as adherents i.e. persons definitely attached
Scottish Episcopal Church: number of communicants	Charge; diocese	Scotland	Annual from 1875	[QRL.15], ([QRL.111])	Defined as number of members communicating each year. Number of Eastertide communicants also kept.
Scottish Episcopal Church: number of confirmed persons	Total number	Scotland	Annual	[QRL.231]	

Type of data	Breakdown	Area	Frequency or Date	QRL reference	Text Reference and Remarks
Moravian Church in Great Britain and Ireland: number of members	Total number	United Kingdom	Annual from 1900	[QRL.225]	Incomplete data in nineteenth century. Calculated from average weekly communicants, child attendance and adherents.
Free Church of England: number of confirmations	Diocese	England	Annual	[QRL.61]	
Methodist Data					
Methodist Church: membership roll	New members; transfers; restored members; deaths; lapsed members; total members by district.	Great Britain	Annual	[QRL.77]	4.2.3.3 - As at October - November
Methodist Church: members	Members per church; members per minister (deaconess) by district	Great Britain	Triennial	[QRL.77]	Analysis given in [B.8a]
Methodist Church: membership gains and losses	Categories of gains and losses	Great Britain	Annual 1857 to 1970	[QRL.4]	Data covers United Methodist Free Churches, United Methodist Church, Weslyan Methodist Church, the Methodist Church
Geographical distribution of Methodist members		England	1961	[QRL.6]	Percentage change from 1951 to 1961 also given

Methodist Church in Ireland: members of society	Total members; junior members by circuit; new members; transfers; deaths; losses by district.	Ireland	Annual	[QRL.78]	Annual increase or decrease also given
Weslyan Reform Union: number of members	Junior members; senior members by church and by circuit	England and Scotland	Annual	[QRL.108]	
Independent Methodist Churches: number of members	Adult/junior by church and by circuit; increase/decrease by church and by circuit	England and Wales	Annual	[QRL.29]	1981 members also analysed by age groups. Adult members are aged 18 and over.
Baptist Data					
Baptist Union of Great Britain and Ireland: number of members	Association; county group before 1972	Great Britain	Annual	[QRL.18], ([QRL.19])	4.2.1.1 Prior to 1972 all Baptist churches in England and Wales covered. Members by church given in [QRL.19].
Baptist Union of Great Britain and Ireland: number of baptisms	Association; county group before 1972	Great Britain	Annual	[QRL.18], ([QRL.19])	4.2.3.3
Baptist Churches: membership	By area	England and Wales	Quinquennial 1952 to 1977	[QRL.103]	Membership of Baptist Union churches in England also given
Baptist Churches: baptisms	Total number	England and Wales	Annual 1952 to 1978	[QRL.103]	From 1972 only Baptist Union churches included
Baptist membership	By area	England	1965	[QRL.6]	
Baptist Union of Wales: number of members	Church; association; method of membership	Wales	Annual	[QRL.21]	
Baptist Union of Wales: number of baptisms	Church; association	Wales	Annual	[QRL.21]	

R–D

Type of data	Breakdown	Area	Frequency or Date	QRL reference	Text Reference and Remarks
Baptist Union of Scotland: membership	District association; church; reporting/non-reporting churches	Scotland	Annual	[QRL.100]	Total membership in non-Union churches also given.
Baptist Union of Scotland: number of churches with increasing; decreasing; unchanged membership	Total numbers	Scotland	Annual	[QRL.100]	
Baptist Union of Scotland: number of admissions	Baptisms; transfers; professions of faith by church	Scotland	Annual	[QRL.100]	Total number baptised but not in membership also given
Baptist Union of Ireland: membership	Church	Ireland	Annual from 1865	[QRL.20]	
Baptist Union of Ireland: number of baptisms	Church	Ireland	Annual	[QRL.20]	
Strict Baptist Churches: number of members	Baptisms; additions; losses; members by church	Great Britain	Annual until 1980	[QRL.68]	
Old Baptist Union: membership	Total number	England and Wales	Annual from 1960	[QRL.226]	
Presbyterian Data					
Presbyterians: membership per 10000 of the population	By area	England	1963	[QRL.6]	4.2.1.2
Presbyterian Church of Wales: membership gains and losses	Categories of gain and loss	Wales	Annual 1895 to 1970	[QRL.4]	
Presbyterian Church of Wales: communicants	Presbytery	England and Wales	Annual	[QRL.88]	

Presbyterian Church of Wales: members gained and lost	Categories of reception and loss by presbytery	England and Wales	Annual	[QRL.88]	
Church of Scotland: membership admissions and removals	Categories of admission and removal	Scotland	Annual 1884 to 1970	[QRL.4]	Communicants admitted to and removed from membership rolls
Church of Scotland: number of communicants	Categories of removal and admission by presbytery and by synod	Scotland	Annual	[QRL.95]	Totals given by parish in [QRL.44]
Church of Scotland: number communicating at least once in each year; annual increase in communicants	Presbytery; synod	Scotland	Annual	[QRL.95]	
Presbyterian Church in Ireland: communicants; number attending at least one communion; new communicants	Congregation; presbytery	Ireland	Annual	[QRL.53]	
Presbyterian Church of England: membership gains and losses	Categories of gains and losses	England	Annual 1876 to 1970	[QRL.4]	
United Free Church of Scotland: membership	Church	Scotland	Annual from 1929	[QRL.69]	Total number of communicants also given
Reformed Presbyterian Church in Scotland: total membership	Communicant; baptised; adult male; retired; increase by church; categories of additions and losses by church.	Scotland	Annual from 1960	[QRL.81]	
Reformed Presbyterian Church of Ireland: communicants; average attendance at Lord's Table	Congregation; presbytery	Ireland	Annual	[QRL.53]	

Type of data	Breakdown	Area	Frequency or Date	QRL reference	Text Reference and Remarks
Non-Subscribing Presbyterian Church of Ireland: number of members	Congregation	Ireland	Annual from 1910	[QRL.79]	
Congregational Data					
Congregationalists: membership per 10000 population	By area	England	1964	[QRL.6]	
Congregational Federation: number of members	Church; area	Great Britain	Annual from 1973	[QRL.49]	4.2.4.4
United Reformed Church: number of members	Church; district	England and Wales	Annual	[QRL.107]	
Union of Welsh Independents: number of members	Association	England and Wales	Annual from 1942	[QRL.238]	Available in Financial Report
Congregational Union of Scotland: number of members	District	Scotland	Annual from 1900	[QRL.75]	
Congregational Union of Ireland: number of members	Church	Ireland	Annual	[QRL.48]	
Pentecostal and Holiness Data					
Apostolic Church: number of members	Total number	United Kingdom	Irregular	[QRL.200]	
Church of the Nazarene: number of members	Categories of gain and loss by church and by district	Great Britain and Ireland	Annual	[QRL.74]	
New Testament Church of God: number of members	Baptised; total sect membership	England	1966, 1968, 1970	[QRL.22]	
Roman Catholic Data					

Roman Catholic population	Diocese	World	Annual	[QRL.16]	4.2.3.2 Comparison made with total population
Estimated Roman Catholic population	Diocese	England and Wales	Annual	[QRL.32]	
Estimated Roman Catholic population	Parish; diocese	England and Wales	Annual	[QRL.31]	
Estimated Roman Catholic child population	Age	England and Wales	Annual 1947 to 1974	[QRL.34]	Measured at 31 December. Ages 5 to 14 years covered.
Adult conversions	Ages 7-13/14 and over	England and Wales	Annual 1911 to 1968	[QRL.4]	
Roman Catholic receptions	Diocese	England and Wales	Annual	[QRL.32]	
Roman Catholic converts	Parish; diocese	England and Wales	Annual	[QRL.31]	
Estimated Roman Catholic population	Church; parish; diocese	Scotland	Annual	[QRL.33]	
Estimated Roman Catholic population	County	Scotland	1851, 1951, 1971	[QRL.82]	
Roman Catholic diocesan populations	Diocese	Scotland	1878, decennial 1891 to 1951, 1948, 1971, 1977	[QRL.82]	Diocesan boundaries changed in 1948
Roman Catholic population of Scotland	District; region	Scotland	1977	[QRL.82]	
Scottish Roman Catholic population; net loss/gain per decade	Total numbers	Scotland	Decennial 1901 to 1971, 1976	[QRL.82]	
Roman Catholic: confirmations	Church; parish; diocese	Scotland	Annual	[QRL.33]	
Roman Catholic population	Diocese	Ireland	Annual	[QRL.71]	Comparison made with total population

Type of data	Breakdown	Area	Frequency or Date	QRL reference	Text Reference and Remarks
Old Roman Catholic Church: number of members	Over/under 17 years; born/converted	United Kingdom	Annual from 1908	[QRL.227]	
Liberal Catholic Church: number of members	Total number	Great Britain and Ireland	Annual	[QRL.217]	
Other Trinitarian Denominational Data					
Churches of Christ: number of members; gains and losses	Categories of gains and losses by church and by district	Great Britain and Ireland	Annual 1842 to 1980	[QRL.45]	Average attendance at Communion also given
Fellowship of Churches of Christ: number of members; gains and losses	Categories of gains and losses by church and by district	Great Britain and Ireland	Annual from 1980	[QRL.56]	4.2.4.4 - Average attendance at communion also given
Countess of Huntingdon's Connexion: number of members	Adult; child	England	Annual from 1940	[QRL.210]	
Fellowship of the Independent Evangelical Churches: number of members	Total number	United Kingdom	Biennial	[QRL.214]	Available for serious research
Religious Society of Friends: number of members	Under/over 16 years by sex by county groupings; categories of gains and losses by county groupings	Great Britain	Annual	[QRL.91]	
Religious Society of Friends: increase/decrease in membership	County groupings	Great Britain	Annual	[QRL.91]	
Religious Society of Friends: number of members	Meeting	Great Britain and Ireland	Annual	[QRL.23]	
Salvation Army: number of members(soldiers)	Total number	United Kingdom	Annual from 1945	[QRL.230]	

British Union of Seventh-Day Adventists: number of members	By area	Great Britain and Ireland	Annual from 1900	[QRL.102]	Special research report with age breakdown available on request
Finnish Seaman's Mission: number of members	Adult/child	United Kingdom	Annual from 1965	[QRL.58]	
French Protestant Church: number of members	Adult; catechumenes	London	Annual from 1925	[QRL.215]	Irregular data before 1925. Postal request. London given separately.
Swedish Church: number of members	Total number	England	Annual from 1837	[QRL.235]	
Non-Trinitarian Churches					
Jehovah's Witnesses: number baptised	By area	Great Britain and Ireland	Annual	[QRL.73]	7.2.2
Jehovah's Witnesses: attendance at annual memorial of Jesus's death	By area	Great Britain and Ireland	Annual	[QRL.73]	
Church of Jesus Christ of Latter-Day Saints: number of members	Total number	Great Britain	Annual	[QRL.37]	Membership also available from [QRL.204]
General Conference of the New Church: number of members	Individual society	Great Britain	Annual	[QRL.66]	Number of non-residents, new members, deaths and removals also given
General Conference of the New Church: average attendance at Holy Supper	Individual society	Great Britain	Annual	[QRL.66]	Number of administrations also given
Church of Scientology: number of members	Total number	United Kingdom	Annual	[QRL.109]	Worldwide figures also given
Theosophical Society: number of members	Total number	England	Annual 1907 to 1970	[QRL.4]	

Type of data	Breakdown	Area	Frequency or Date	QRL reference	Text Reference and Remarks
Unification Church: number of members	Total number	United Kingdom	Annual	[QRL.236]	Members are fulltime workers.
ADULT ATTENDERS					
Collective Data					
Proportion of population attending church	Frequency of attendance	United Kingdom	1938, 1947, 1960, 1968, 1969, 1970	[QRL.1]	General ref: 4.3 - 7. 4.3.1.2 Comparison of survey results for Great Britain and Northern Ireland
Percentage of members attending church	Denomination	United Kingdom	1980	[QRL.2]	4.3.2.6 - 7.1.3
Number of church attendants	Denomination by England and Wales; Scotland	Great Britain	1851	[QRL.4]	7.1.3
Church attendance	Selected denominations	Great Britain	Annual 1966 to 1978	[QRL.7]	County variations also given for 1979 in [B.8]
Estimated adult attendances at Christian churches	Denominational groupings	England	Irregular	[QRL.104]	1979 figures broken down by age and sex
Geographical variation in church attendance	By area	England	1851	[QRL.6]	
Attendance at Nonconformist churches	By area	England	1851	[QRL.6]	
Episcopal Data					
Church of England attendance	By area	England	1851	[QRL.6]	General ref: 4.3.2.2. 4.3.3.1
Church of England: usual Sunday service attendance number and per 1000 population	Diocese	England	Biennial from 1976	[QRL.42]	Includes children. Census and survey results.

Moravian Church in Great Britain and Ireland: average weekly attendance	Adult; child	United Kingdom	Annual from 1900	[QRL.223]	Incomplete data for nineteenth century also available

Methodist Data

Methodist Churches: attendance	Denomination by county	England	1851	[QRL.6]	
Methodist Churches: attendance at worship number and percent of membership	Morning; afternoon; evening; principal service; total by district	Great Britain	Triennal	[QRL.77]	Collected in October - November

Baptist Data

Baptist Churches: attendance	By area	England	1851	[QRL.6]	4.3.2.1 Earlier period also covered

Presbyterian Data

Presbyterian Churches: attendance	By area	England	1851	[QRL.6]	4.3.2.1
Reformed Presbyterian Church in Scotland: attendance	Morning; evening service by church	Scotland	Annual from 1960	[QRL.81]	
Reformed Presbyterian Church of Ireland: average attendance	Morning; evening service by congregation and by presbytery	Ireland	Annual	[QRL.53]	

Congregational Data

Congregationalist Churches: attendance	By area	England	1851	[QRL.6]	4.3.2.1

Pentecostal and Holiness Data

Assemblies of God: church attendance	Total number	Great Britain and Ireland	1969, irregular from 1979	[QRL.201]	Estimated attendance over 12 years of age
Elim Pentecostal Church: attendance	Morning; evening service	Great Britain	Irregular from 1952, annual from 1977	[QRL.212]	Available on request for March and October of each year

Type of data	Breakdown	Area	Frequency or Date	QRL reference	Text Reference and Remarks
New Testament Church of God: adherents in regular attendance	Total number	England	1966, 1968, 1970	[QRL.22]	
Roman Catholic Data					
Roman Catholic attendance at mass	By area	England	1851, 1962	[QRL.6]	General ref: 4.3.2.2. Adult and child - 4.3.3.1
Roman Catholic attendance at mass	Parish; diocese	England and Wales	Annual	[QRL.31]	In 1974 collection altered from April to October. Adult and child.
Liberal Catholic Church: attendance	Total number	Great Britain and Ireland	Annual	[QRL.220]	4.3.2.1
Other Trinitarian Denominational Data					
Fellowship of Churches of Christ: average attendance at Gospel services	Church; district	Great Britain and Ireland	Annual from 1981	[QRL.56]	4.3.2.1
Fellowship of Independent Evangelical Churches: attendance	Total number	United Kingdom	Biennial	[QRL.214]	Available on request for serious research
Religious Society of Friends: recognised attenders at meetings	County groupings	Great Britain	Annual	[QRL.91]	Attenders not in membership
Salvation Army: church attendance	Total number	United Kingdom	Annual from 1945	[QRL.230]	
British Union of Seventh-Day Adventists: church attendance	Age groups by area	Great Britain and Ireland	Annual 1945 to 1979	[QRL.234]	Available from research report

French Protestant Church: congregation size	Total number	London	Weekly from 1865	[QRL.215]	Available on request by post
Non-Trinitarian Churches					
Mormons: attendance per 1000 total population	By area	England	1851	[QRL.6]	General ref: 7.2.2. 7.1.3
Church of Jesus Christ of Latter-Day Saints: attendance	Total number	Great Britain	Monthly	[QRL.204]	
General Conference of the New Church: average church attendance	Individual society	Great Britain	Annual	[QRL.66]	Morning and afternoon attendance given
Unification Church: attenders	Total number	United Kingdom	Annual	[QRL.236]	
Unitarians: attendance as percent of total Unitarian following	County groups	England	1851	[QRL.6]	7.1.3
Unitarians: attendance	By area	England	1851	[QRL.6]	
Related Adult Attendance Data					
Wesleyan Reform Union: number of Sunday School teachers; number of devotional meetings; number of devotional meeting members; number of Women's Auxiliary	Circuit or church	England and Scotland	Annual	[QRL.108]	4.3.5
Independent Methodist Churches: numbers of teachers, officers and auxiliary members	Type of organization by church and by circuit	England and Wales	Annual	[QRL.29]	
Church of Scotland: membership of Women's Guild	Parish	Scotland	Annual	[QRL.44]	

Type of data	Breakdown	Area	Frequency or Date	QRL reference	Text Reference and Remarks
United Free Church of Scotland: number of adult week-night societies and number of members	Total numbers	Scotland	Annual	[QRL.69]	
Reformed Presbyterian Church in Scotland: attendance at Bible studies and women's meetings	Church	Scotland	Annual from 1960	[QRL.81]	
Reformed Presbyterian Church of Ireland: average attendance at prayer meetings	Congregation; Presbytery	Ireland	Annual	[QRL.80]	
Church of the Nazarene: adult attendance and enrolement at Sunday School and other adult classes	Church; district	Great Britain and Ireland	Annual	[QRL.74]	
Elim Pentecostal Church: average attendance at weeknight meetings	Total number	Great Britain	Irregular from 1952, annual from 1977	[QRL.214]	Available on request for March and October
Church of Christ: times of services	Church	Great Britain and Ireland	Annual	[QRL.45]	
CHILDREN AND YOUNG PEOPLE *Collective Data*					
Free Church children and young people	Member denominations of the FCFC	United Kingdom	Annual	[QRL.60]	General ref: 4.3.1.4 - 4.3.2.4. 4.3.2.5
Organizations for young people: membership	Organization	United Kingdom	Irregular from 1950, annual from 1973	[QRL.104]	Church affiliated organizations included

Church Sunday School scholars	Denomination	Great Britain	Annual 1951 to 1970	[QRL.4]	4.3.2.4
Christian churches: child attendance	Denominational grouping	England	Irregular	[QRL.104]	1979 data analysed by sex
Episcopal Data					
Church of England Sunday School scholars	Total number	England	Annual 1872 to 1960	[QRL.4]	Aged 3 to 14 years
Church of England: children on Sunday School registers	Age; sex groups by diocese	England	1958, 1960	[QRL.55]	
Church of England: members of youth organizations	Age by sex by diocese	England	1958, 1960	[QRL.55]	
Scottish Episcopal Church: young people and Sunday School children	Type of group by diocese	Scotland	Annual	[QRL.111]	
Methodist Data					
Methodist Sunday School scholars	Total number	Great Britain	Annual 1857 to 1966	[QRL.4]	Data cover United Methodist Free Churches, United Methodist Church, Wesleyan Methodist Church, the Methodist Church
Methodist Church: Sunday School attendance; number of young people in youth clubs	District	Great Britain	Triennial	[QRL.77]	Collected in October

Type of data	Breakdown	Area	Frequency or Date	QRL reference	Text Reference and Remarks
Methodist Church: number of Sunday Schools and youth clubs	District	Great Britain	Triennial	[QRL.77]	
Wesleyan Reform Union: number of Sunday School scholars and members of youth organizations	Total numbers	England and Scotland	Annual	[QRL.108]	
Independent Methodist Churches: number of scholars and youth	Scholars under; over 21, by church and by circuit; youth organization, by church and by circuit.	England and Wales	Annual	[QRL.29]	
Baptist Data					
Baptist Union of Great Britain and Ireland: number of children; number of young people	Association	Great Britain	Annual	[QRL.18, ([QRL.19])	Number by church given in [QRL.19]. Children up to 14 years, young people 14 to 18 years.
Baptist Churches: children and young people	Total number	England	Quinquennial 1952 to 1972	[QRL.103]	Annual figures for Union churches given for 1973 to 1978
Baptist Union of Wales: Sunday School children	Association	Wales	Annual	[QRL.21]	
Baptist Union of Scotland: number of pupils	Under 13 years; over 13 including adults by church	Scotland	Annual	[QRL.100]	

					Number of Sunday School teachers also given
Baptist Union of Ireland: Sunday School scholars; membership of young people's societies; membership of uniformed organizations	Church	Ireland	Annual	[QRL.20]	
Strict Baptist Churches: number of Sunday School scholars	Church	Great Britain	Annual until 1980	[QRL.68]	
Presbyterian Data					
Presbyterian Scottish and Irish Sunday School scholars	Denomination	Scotland and Ireland	Annual 1851 to 1970	[QRL.4]	
Presbyterian Church of Wales: number of children	Presbytery	England and Wales	Annual	[QRL.88]	
Presbyterian Church of Wales: Sunday School scholars	Total number	Wales	Annual 1895 to 1967	[QRL.4]	
Presbyterian Church of Wales: Sunday School membership	Presbytery	England and Wales	Annual	[QRL.88]	
Church of Scotland: Sunday School scholars	Denomination	Scotland	Annual 1876 to 1970	[QRL.4]	
Church of Scotland: number of Sunday School scholars and Bible class pupils	Parish	Scotland	Annual	[QRL.44]	
Church of Scotland: number of Sunday School scholars, and young people	Sunday School scholars, Bible class pupils; uniformed organizations; youth clubs, youth fellowships by sex.	Scotland	Annual	[QRL.95]	
Presbyterian Church in Ireland: Sundays School pupils and number on Bible class rolls	Congregation; presbytery	Ireland	Annual	[QRL.53]	

Type of data	Breakdown	Area	Frequency or Date	QRL reference	Text Reference and Remarks
Reformed Presbyterian Church of Ireland: number of Sabbath School scholars and young people	Congregation; presbytery	Ireland	Annual	[QRL.80]	
Presbyterian Church of England: Sunday School scholars	Total number	England	Annual 1876 to 1970	[QRL.4]	
United Free Church of Scotland: Sundays School scholars and membership of Bible classes, juvenile organisations and youth groups	Scholars by church; total numbers only for others	Scotland	Annual from 1929	[QRL.69]	
Reformed Presbyterian Church in Scotland: Sabbath School and youth societies' attendances	Church	Scotland	Annual from 1960	[QRL.81]	
Congregational Data					
Congregational Federation: number of children	Church; area	Great Britain	Annual from 1973	[QRL.49]	
United Reformed Churches: number of children	Church	England and Wales	Annual	[QRL.88]	
Congregational Union of Scotland: number of Sunday School scholars and members of youth groups and uniformed organizations	District	Scotland	Annual	[QRL.75]	

Pentecostal and Holiness Data

Elim Pentecostal Church: Sunday School and youth meeting attendance	Total numbers	Great Britain	Irregular from 1952, annual from 1977	[QRL.212]	Available on request for March and October of each year
Church of the Nazarene: child, youth enrolement, average weekly child, youth attendance, cradle roll, caravan members, NYI members	Church; district	Great Britain and Ireland	Annual	[QRL.74]	
New Testament Church of God: children and young people	Total number	England	1966, 1968, 1970	[QRL.22]	

Other Trinitarian Denominational Data

Churches of Christ: average Sunday School attendance and number involved in youth activities	Church; district	Great Britain and Ireland	Annual 1842 to 1980	[QRL.45]	
Churches of Christ: Sunday School scholars and Fellowship of Youth members	Age groups by church and by district	Great Britain and Ireland	Annual from 1980	[QRL.56]	
Religious Society of Friends: children	County groupings	Great Britain	Annual	[QRL.91]	Children not in membership
Salvation Army youth	Total number	United Kingdom	Annual	[QRL.230]	
General Conference of the New Church: Sunday School roll and average attendance	Individual society	Great Britain	Annual	[QRL.66]	Children only

Related Children and Young People Data

Type of data	Breakdown	Area	Frequency or Date	QRL reference	Text Reference and Remarks
Church of England: Sunday School teachers	Sex by diocese	England	1958, 1960	[QRL.45]	4.3.5.2
Strict Baptist Churches: number of Sunday School teachers	Church	Great Britain	Annual until 1980	[QRL.68]	
Church of Scotland: Sunday School staff; Bible class teachers	Total numbers	Scotland	Annual	[QRL.95]	
United Free Church of Scotland: number of Bible classes, juvenile organizations, youth groups and Sunday Schools	Total numbers	Scotland	Annual	[QRL.69]	
United Free Church of Scotland: number of Sunday School teachers	Total number	Scotland	Annual	[QRL.69]	
Reformed Presbyterian Church of Ireland: number of Sabbath school teachers	Congregation; presbytery	Ireland	Annual	[QRL.53]	
United Reformed Church: teachers	Church	England and Wales	Annual from 1972	[QRL.107]	Prior to 1972 this information was recorded in [QRL.48]
Church of the Nazarene: officers and teachers	Church; district	Great Britain and Ireland	Annual	[QRL.74]	
Fellowship of Churches of Christ: number of Sunday School teachers and departments	Church; district	Great Britain and Ireland	Annual from 1980	[QRL.56]	

PROFESSIONAL MANPOWER

Collective Data

Religious professions: clergy, ministers, members of religious orders	Status by geographical area (regions, counties, boroughs etc)	England and Wales	Decennial 1841 onwards; 1941 omitted.	[QRL.35]	General ref: 4.4 - 7.1.1 4.4.1.2 1841, 1951 refer to Great Britain; Church of England, Roman Catholic given separately on an irregular basis.
Church ministers	Denomination; country	United Kingdom	1970, 1975, 1980	[QRL.2]	4.4.1.2 Some estimation used. Ministers per church and estimates given for 1985.
Number of clergy and ministers	Denomination	Great Britain and Ireland	Annual	[QRL.110]	4.4.1.2
Number of Christian professionals	Status by denomination	United Kingdom	Irregular 1807 to 1971	[QRL.4]	Later data annual. No data during Second World War.
Staff of churches or missions	Denomination	Great Britain and Ireland	1949, 1952, 1957, 1962, 1967	[QRL.3]	
Christian personnel, full time workers	Nationality	United Kingdom	1973 to 1978	[QRL.1]	4.4.1.2
Free Churches: number of ministers, local and lay preachers	Denomination of the FCFC	United Kingdom	Annual	[QRL.60]	
Chaplaincy staff at Prison Department establishments	Denomination by full-/part-time staff	England and Wales	Occasional from 1960	[QRL.97]	All chaplains working in penal establishments and head office
Geographical location of Puritan ministers	By county	England	1603	[QRL.6]	

Episcopal Data

Type of data	Breakdown	Area	Frequency or Date	QRL reference	Text Reference and Remarks
Church of England					
Church of England: deployment of the clergy	Age by diocese; status by diocese	England	Annual	[QRL.42]	4.4.1.1 Full-time diocesan clergymen. Biennally in [QRL.96].
Church of England: inter-diocesan movements of full-time diocesan stipendiary clergymen	Age by diocese	England	Annual	[QRL.42]	
Church of England: entry and losses of clergymen into full-time diocesan appointments	Age by diocese	England	Annual	[QRL.42]	
Church of England: clergy retirements	Age	England	Annual	[QRL.42]	
Church of England: authorised church workers	Categories by diocese	England	Annual	[QRL.42]	Includes non-stipendiary ministry
Church of England: number of pensioners	Clergy; widows	England	Annual	[QRL.39]	
Church of England: clergymen of incumbent status serving in parishes	Incumbents; team vicars; priests in charge	England	Annual	[QRL.39]	Main source [QRL.42]
Church of England: parochial incumbents	Number of benefices by diocese	England	1957, 1960, 1963	[QRL.55]	
Church of England: parochial livings	Occupied/vacant by diocese and by population size	England	1957, 1960, 1963	[QRL.55]	
Church of England: number of clergymen	Status by diocese	England	1957, 1960, 1963	[QRL.55]	
Church of England: age of all the clergy	Status by age	England	1957, 1960, 1963	[QRL.55]	

Church of England: clergymen in the home area	Age	England	Decennial	[QRL.55]	
Church of England: natural increase in the full-time ordained ministry	Entrants; losses	England	Annual	[QRL.55]	
Church of England: full-time clergymen	Status by length of service; status by age at ordination	England	1957, 1960, 1963	[QRL.55]	
Church of England: number of ecclesiastical dignitaries	Status by age; status by duration of service	England	1957, 1960, 1963	[QRL.55]	
Church of England: deployment of the parochial and cathedral clergy	Livings; assistant clergymen by number of parishes by population size	England	1957, 1960, 1963	[QRL.55]	
Church of England: parochial clergymen in livings	Incumbents; assistant clergymen by population size by diocese	England	1957, 1967, 1963	[QRL.55]	Projections also given
Church of England: ages of parochial incumbents	Age by population size; age by diocese	England	Annual	[QRL.55]	
Church of England: ages of parochial assistant clergymen	Age by population size; age by diocese	England	Annual	[QRL.55]	
Church of England: number of parochial incumbents	Duration of service in livings by diocese; length of service by diocese; age at ordination by diocese	England	Annual	[QRL.55]	
Church of England: number of parochial assistant clergymen	Duration of service in present curacy by diocese; length of service by diocese	England	Annual	[QRL.55]	
Church of England: number of non-parochial clergymen	Appointments by diocese; occupations by diocese	England	1957, 1960, 1963	[QRL.55]	
Church of England: number of clergymen ordained abroad	Appointments by age and by country of ordination	England	1957, 1960, 1963	[QRL.55]	

Type of data	Breakdown	Area	Frequency or Date	QRL reference	Text Reference and Remarks
Church of England: number of clergymen working abroad	Years of ordination; duration of service abroad (for those ordained in England)	England	1957, 1960, 1963	[QRL.55]	
Church of England: number of retired clergymen	Ordained at home; abroad by diocese and by age at retirement and by age	England	1957, 1960, 1963	[QRL.55]	
Church of England: ages at death of clergymen	Before; after retirement by age	England	Annual	[QRL.55]	
Church of England: losses from full-time ordained ministry	Retirement; deaths before retirement; departures abroad by age	England	Annual	[QRL.55]	
Church of England: number of authorized church workers	Sex by appointment by diocese	England	1957, 1960, 1963	[QRL.55]	
Church of England: members of religious communities	Sex, by appointment, by diocese	England	1957, 1960, 1963	[QRL.55]	
Church of England: numbers of clergy, members of religious communities, chaplains, lay ministers, readers	Diocese	England	Annual or biennial	[QRL.41]	Ministerial staff listed by parish where appropriate
Church of England: numbers of General Synod members, suffragan bishops, deans and archdeacons	Total numbers	England	Annual	[QRL.42]	Senior staff listed. Dignatories also listed by diocese.
Methodist Data					
Methodist Church: numbers of ministers and deaconesses in pastoral charge; number of local preachers on trial	District	Great Britain	Triennial	[QRL.77]	4.4.3.2 Collected in October

Methodist Church: number of deaconesses	District	Great Britain	Annual	[QRL.77]	
Methodist Church: number of ministers with special appointments	National Childrens Home chaplains; student chaplains; prison chaplains; homes for the aged chaplains by district	Great Britain	Annual	[QRL.77]	
Methodist Church of Ireland: number of leaders and local preachers	Leaders; local preachers in active work; local preachers on trial by district	Ireland	Annual	[QRL.78]	Ministers, preachers on trial and chaplains also listed
Independent Methodist Churches: number of ministers	Church by circuit	England and Wales	Annual	[QRL.29]	1981 figures analysed by age groups
Baptist Data					
Baptist Union of Great Britain and Ireland: numbers of ministers and pastors in charge	Church; association; area of service	Great Britain	Annual	[QRL.18], ([QRL.19])	In [QRL.19] ministers listed by church and area of service. Includes deaconesses.
Baptist Union of Great Britain and Ireland: number of lay preachers	Lay preachers association	Great Britain	Annual	[QRL.19]	
Baptist Union of Wales: number of ministers and pastors	Church association	Wales	Annual	[QRL.21]	Retired ministers and preachers also given
Baptist Union of Ireland: number of pastors	Church	Ireland	Annual	[QRL.20]	Number of elders and deacons also given. Ministers and lady workers listed.
Old Baptist Union: number of serving ministers	Total number	England and Wales	Annual from 1960	[QRL.226]	
Presbyterian Data					

Type of data	Breakdown	Area	Frequency or Date	QRL reference	Text Reference and Remarks
Presbyterian Church of Wales: numbers of ministers and elders	Ministers in; not in pastoral charge by presbytery; elders by presbytery	England and Wales	Annual	[QRL.88]	Ministers also listed individually
Church of Scotland: numbers of ministers, probationers and office bearers	Category by presbytery and by synod	Scotland	Annual	[QRL.95]	
Church of Scotland: numbers of ministers and elders	Ministers; elders by parish; chaplains; other ministers	Scotland	Annual	[QRL.44]	Ministers also listed individually
Presbyterian Church of Ireland: numbers of ministers and elders	Congregation; presbytery	Ireland	Annual	[QRL.53]	Also gives number of hospital chaplains by presbytery
United Free Church of Scotland: numbers of ministers and office bearers	Ministers in pastorate; retired ministers; male elders; female elders; deacons and managers	Scotland	Annual from 1929	[QRL.69]	
Reformed Presbyterian Church in Scotland: numbers of ministers and office bearers	Ministers; elders; managers and deacons by church	Scotland	Annual from 1960	[QRL.81]	Ministers also listed individually
Reformed Presbyterian Church of Ireland: numbers of ministers and elders	Ministers; elders; deacons by congregation and by presbytery; total number of chaplains	Ireland	Annual	[QRL.80]	Ministers also listed individually
Congregational Data United Reformed Church: numbers of ministers and local preachers	Field of service	England and Wales	Annual	[QRL.107]	General ref: 4.4.1.3 Ministers with pastoral oversight also listed by church

Congregational Union of Scotland: numbers of ministers, lay pastors and lay preachers	Ministers in full pastoral charge; in other charges; without pastoral charge; retired by district; Lay preachers; pastors by district; ministers and pastors	Scotland	Annual from 1960	[QRL.75]	
Pentecostal and Holiness Data					
Church of the Nazarene: number of ministers	Elders; ministers by district; pastors; office bearers by church and by district.	Great Britain and Ireland	Annual	[QRL.74]	
New Testament Church of God: number of full-time ministers	Total number	England	1966, 1968, 1970	[QRL.22]	
Roman Catholic Data					
Number of priests, sisters and members of religious orders	Diocese	World	Annual	[QRL.16]	General ref: 4.4.3.2. 4.4.3.3
Roman Catholic: number of priests	Diocesan priests by area of work by diocese; religious order by diocese; permanent deacons by diocese	England and Wales	Annual	[QRL.32] [QRL.31]	Priests also listed individually. In [QRL.31] listed by parish
Roman Catholic: number of members of religious orders, congregations, societies etc.	Priests; brothers by religious order	England and Wales	Annual	[QRL.31] [QRL.32]	Men only
Roman Catholic: priests in dioceses	Secular; regular by diocese	Scotland	Annual	[QRL.33]	
Roman Catholic: brothers and sisters	Brothers; sisters by diocese	Scotland	Annual	[QRL.33]	
Roman Catholic: number of priests	Diocese	Scotland	1878	[QRL.82]	
Roman Catholic: number of diocesan clergy	Status by diocese	Ireland	Annual	[QRL.71]	Priests also listed individually by parish
Roman Catholic: number of members of religious communities	Priests; brothers by diocese	Ireland	Annual	[QRL.71]	Clergy also listed individually by religious order and diocese

Type of data	Breakdown	Area	Frequency or Date	QRL reference	Text Reference and Remarks
Old Roman Catholic: number of clergy	Active; retired; deaths	United Kingdom	Irregular	[QRL.227]	Academic qualifications and date of birth also recorded.
Orthodox Data					
Greek Orthodox Church: number of clergy	Total number	United Kingdom	Annual from 1926	[QRL.67]	
Russian Orthodox Church in Exile: number of clergy	Priests; deacons; monastics	England and Ireland	Annual from 1978	[QRL.229]	Before 1978 information only kept irregularly in Worldwide Yearbook and registers.
Other Trinitarian Denominational Data					
Churches of Christ: ministerial and lay manpower	Church	Great Britain and Ireland	Annual to 1980	[QRL.45]	
Fellowship of Churches of Christ: number of ministers	Church	Great Britain and Ireland	Annual from 1981	[QRL.56]	
Countess of Huntingdons's Connexion: number of ministers	With; without pastoral charge	England	Annual from 1940	[QRL.50]	Listed individually by church where appropriate
Religious Society of Friends: number of elders and overseers	Elders/overseers by sex by county groupings	Great Britain	Annual	[QRL.91]	
Salvation Army: number of officers, cadets and employees	Officers (active/retired); cadets (first/second year); employees	United Kingdom	Annual	[QRL.99]	

	Division		Frequency	Reference	Notes
Salvation Army: number of officers overseeing corps, outposts, societies and institutions	Division	United Kingdom	Annual	[QRL.230]	
British Union of Seventh-Day Adventists: number of ministers and other workers	Ordained ministers; licensed ministers; literature evangelists by geographical area	Great Britain and Ireland	Annual from 1945	[QRL.234]	Also listed individually in [QRL.102]
Non-Trinitarian Churches					
Christian Science Practitioners: number	Major towns and cities	England	1967	[QRL.6]	7.1.3
Jehovah's Witnesses: numbers of Publishers and Pioneers	Great Britain; Ireland	Great Britain	Annual	[QRL.73]	Publishers are ministers or 'preachers of the good news'. Total hours preached also given.
General Conference of the New Church: ministers and lay preachers	Total number	Great Britain	Annual	[QRL.66]	Ministers also listed by society
Church of Scientology: number of staff	Church; mission staff	United Kingdom	Annual	[QRL.109]	Worldwide figures also available
Unitarian ministers	Total number	United Kingdom	Annual	[QRL.110]	
Related Data					
Church of England: cost of ministry	Stipends; working expenses; housing; pensions	England	Biennial	[QRL.96]	4.4.5
Church of England: clergy stipends	Population size; source of income	England	Annual	[QRL.55]	
Church in Wales: clergy stipends	Parish	Wales	Annual	[QRL.40]	
Scottish Episcopal Church: clergy stipends	Parish	Scotland	Annual	[QRL.15]	

Type of data	Breakdown	Area	Frequency or Date	QRL reference	Text Reference and Remarks
Presbyterian Church of Ireland: expenses and stipends paid to ministers	Expenses; stipend; income; allowances by congregation	Ireland	Annual	[QRL.53]	
Reformed Presbyterian Church in Scotland: expenses and income paid to ministers	Church	Scotland	Annual from 1960	[QRL.81]	
Reformed Presbyterian Church of Ireland: ministerial income	Salary; total income by congregation and by presbytery	Ireland	Annual	[QRL.80]	
Non-Subscribing Presbyterian Church of Ireland: stipend contributions and ministerial income	Congregation	Ireland	Annual	[QRL.79]	
Church of the Nazarene: pastors salaries	Pastor; assistant pastor by church and by district	Great Britain and Ireland	Annual	[QRL.74]	
Roman Catholic: number of convents of religious women	Diocese	England and Wales	Annual	[QRL.32]	
Roman Catholic: number of religious houses	Sex by diocese	Scotland	Annual	[QRL.33]	
Roman Catholic: number of convents	Diocese	Ireland	Annual	[QRL.71]	Also listed individually

PROFESSIONAL MANPOWER TRAINING

Collective Data

Students at theological colleges and Bible schools	Number of places by sex by institution	United Kingdom	1972, 1976, 1980, 1982, 1984	[QRL.2]	General ref: 4.5 - 7.1.4 4.5.1.3 - Residential and non-residential given with length of course and course fees
Birmingham Bible Institute: number of students	Examination achievement	(Students mostly from Europe)	Annual from 1958	[QRL.64]	
Capernwray Bible Schools: number of students	Total number	(Students mostly from Europe)	Annual	[QRL.207]	
London Bible College: number of students	Resident/non-resident	(Students mostly from Europe)	Annual	[QRL.218]	
Selley Oak Colleges: number of students	Subjects; courses	(Students from Asia, Africa, America and Europe)	Annual	[QRL.232]	Sponsored by various protestant churches.
Episcopal Data					
Church of England: deacons ordained	Graduate; non-graduate by diocese	England	Annual	[QRL.42]	4.5.3.2
Church of England: ordination candidates	by diocese	England	Annual	[QRL.42]	
Church of England: allocation of ordinands	Theological college	England	Annual	[QRL.42]	
Church of England: candidates for Holy Orders	Education by diocese; occupation by diocese; age (for those recommended for training)	England	Annual	[QRL.55]	
Church of England: deacons ordained	Graduates/non-graduates; age by diocese	England	Annual	[QRL.55]	Distribution at end of ordination year also given

Type of data	Breakdown	Area	Frequency or Date	QRL reference	Text Reference and Remarks
Church of England: entrants to the full-time ordained ministry	Previous status	England	Annual	[QRL.55]	Ordained, from abroad, from retirement, from the Roman Catholic Church
Methodist Data					
Methodist candidates for the ministry	District	Great Britain	Annual	[QRL.220]	4.5.3.1
Methodist theological colleges: number of students	Sex; residential; non-residential	England	Annual	[QRL.220]	
Independent Methodist Churches: number of student ministers	Church by circuit	England and Wales	Annual	[QRL.29]	
Baptist Data					
Baptist Union of Wales: number of students at theological colleges	Association; college	Wales	Annual	[QRL.21]	
Presbyterian Data					
Presbyterian Church of Wales: candidates for the ministry	Presbytery	England and Wales	Annual	[QRL.88]	
Church of Scotland: ministrial students completing their courses	College	Scotland	Annual	[QRL.95]	
Church of Scotland: number attending elders' courses	Total number	Scotland	Annual	[QRL.95]	
Edinburgh Free Church College: number of students	Year of study	Scotland	Annual	[QRL.89]	

United Free Church of Scotland: number of students and probationers	Total number	Scotland	Annual from 1929	[QRL.69]	
Congregational Data					
Congregation Union for Scotland: number of students in training for the ministry	Year of study	Scotland	Annual from 1900	[QRL.75]	
Pentecostal and Holiness Data					
Elim Bible College: number of students	Total number	England	Annual	[QRL.211]	
Roman Catholic Data					
Roman Catholic: number of candidates for priesthood	Diocese	England and Wales	Annual	[QRL.32]	Number of deacons
Roman Catholic: number of students in seminaries	Major; minor seminaries by diocese	Scotland	Annual	[QRL.33]	4.5.3.1
Roman Catholic: number of seminary students and ordinations to the priesthood	Major; minor seminaries (yearly average students); Irish; Scottish; other colleges (ordination 5 year totals)	Scotland	Quinquennial 1901 to 1975	[QRL.82]	
Roman Catholic: number of ordinations	Irish; foreign dioceses; religious orders; missionary societies: (ordained for)	Ireland	Annual	[QRL.71]	Also listed individually by seminary order or society
Other Trinitarian Denominational Data					
Salvation Army: cadets at training college	Year of study	United Kingdom	Annual	[QRL.99]	4.5.3.2
Episcopal Training Places					
Church of England: theological colleges	College	England	Annual	[QRL.42]	4.5.3.1

Type of data	Breakdown	Area	Frequency or Date	QRL reference	Text Reference and Remarks
Church of Ireland: colleges of theological study	College	Ireland	Annual	[QRL.40]	
Roman Catholic Training Places					
Number of major seminaries	Diocese	Ireland	Annual	[QRL.71]	Also listed individually
Related Data					
Cost and length of average course at theological colleges and Bible schools	Institution	United Kingdom	1972, 1976, 1980, 1982, 1984	[QRL.2]	4.5.1.4
Selley Oak Colleges: number of academic staff	Subject; ordained; lay	England	Annual from 1960	[QRL.232]	
Church of England: cost of ministry training	Total	England	Biennial	[QRL.96]	
Salvation Army: college staff	Officers; employees	United Kingdom	Annual	[QRL.99]	
Seventh Day Adventist: staff of educational institutions	Training college	Great Britain	Annual	[QRL.102]	
MISSIONARIES					
Collective Data					
Collective non-denominational data					
United Kingdom missionaries by continent	Short-term/career/associate by sex, by country of service by missionary society	World	1972, 1976, 1980, 1982, 1984	[QRL.2]	General ref: 4.6 - 7.1.5. 4.6.1.2 Trends analysed by country and continent, sex, status, missionary society

Subject	Detail	Area	Years	Reference	Notes
Number of missionaries	Selected denominations	World	1970; 71	[QRL.59]	Source: [QRL.2]
United Kingdom missionaries by continent	Continent of service	World	1976, 1980	[QRL.104]	
Missionaries from other countries or churches	Ordained/lay workers by country of work by denomination or mission	Africa, America, Asia	1949, 1952, 1957, 1962, 1968	[QRL.3]	Fulltime missionaries
Number of United Kingdom missionaries	Ten United Kingdom missionary societies sending most missionaries; ten countries with largest number of United Kingdom missionaries	World	Annual from 1979	[QRL.84]	Source: [QRL.2]
Number of missions and missionaries serving across the world	Country of sevice	World	1978, 1980, 1983	[QRL.8]	
International sharing of personnel	Nationals sent abroad; nationals from abroad by major denominational group	United Kingdom	Twentieth century	[QRL.1]	4.6.1.6 Nationals from the west communist world and third world also given
Missionaries from Wales	Country of service; missionary society	World	1970, 1973	[QRL.70]	Up to date information available on request. Missionaries listed.
North American Protestant missionary personnel serving in the United Kingdom	Organization	United Kingdom	Biennial	[QRL.9]	4.6.1.6 - Related churches also given
Individual non-denominational missionary organizations					
Overseas Missionary Fellowship: number of full and associate members	Country of service; nationality; full; associate members by on furlough; overseas; home; leave of absence and by sex	World	Annual	[QRL.83]	Irregular statistics kept since 1865

Type of data	Breakdown	Area	Frequency or Date	QRL reference	Text Reference and Remarks
Worldwide Evangelisation Crusade: membership	Country of service	World	Biennial	[QRL.87]	
Bible and Medical Missionary Fellowship: number of members	Country of service	Asia and United Kingdom	Annual	[QRL.203]	
Wycliffe Bible Translators: number of members	Country of service; in training; senior; junior	World	Annual	[QRL.11]	
Episcopal Data					
Scottish Episcopal Church: clergy serving in overseas missions	Total number	World	Annual	[QRL.111]	
United Society for the Propogation of the Gospel: number of overseas missionaries	Geographical; lay; ordained	World	Quarterly	[QRL.90]	Irregular records kept from eighteenth century. Central Africa statistics kept annually to 1965
Baptist Data					
Baptist Missionary Society personnel	Country of service	World	Annual	[QRL.10]	
Presbyterian Data					
Church of Scotland: number of ministers serving abroad	Total number	World	Annual	[QRL.95]	Listed individually in [QRL.44]
Free Church of Scotland: number of missionaries	Country of service	World	Annual	[QRL.63]	
United Free Church of Scotland: number of missionaries	Ordained; unordained	World	Annual from 1929	[QRL.69]	

					Survey results
Presbyterian Church of Ireland: missionaries of the General Assembly	Country of service	World	Annual	[QRL.53]	
Reformed Presbyterian Church of Ireland: number of missionaries	Irish/foreign mission workers	World	Annual	[QRL.80]	
Congregational Data					
Union of Welsh Independents: number of missionaries	Home/foreign	World	Annual	[QRL.237]	
Roman Catholic Data					
Roman Catholic missionary societies: number of members	Missionary society	United Kingdom and the world	Annual from 1979	[QRL.84]	
Roman Catholic missionaries	Sex by religious order, by country of service; sex by lay status by country of service	World	Annual from 1979	[QRL.84]	
Roman Catholic missionary diocesan priests	Overseas; home by diocese	World	Annual from 1979	[QRL.84]	
Roman Catholic missionary priests, brothers and sisters	Priests; brothers; sisters by diocese of origin by country of service	World	Annual from 1979	[QRL.84]	
Roman Catholic home based missionary personnel	Occupation by missionary society	England and Wales	Annual from 1979	[QRL.84]	
Roman Catholic United Kingdom missionaries: number	England and Wales; Scotland by ten Catholic societies sending most missionaries. Ten countries with largest number of Catholic missionaries.	Great Britain	Annual from 1979	[QRL.84]	
Distribution of Irish missionary personnel	Qualification by country by missionary society or order; qualification by status; occupation by country, by missionary society or order, occupation by status	Africa, Asia, Latin America	1965, 1968, 1970	[QRL.72]	
Other Trinitarian Denominational Data					

Type of data	Breakdown	Area	Frequency or Date	QRL reference	Text Reference and Remarks
Echoes of Service: analysis of number of missionaries	Marital status; country of commendation; decade of commencement of full-time service	Asia, Europe, Africa, America, Oceania	Annual	[QRL.51]	Brethren missionaries. Retired and widowed missionaries listed. Serving missionaries listed by country of service.
Non-Trinitarian Churches					
Churches of Christ: number of missionaries	Country of service	Siam, Burma, India, Malawi	Annual 1980 to 1982	[QRL.45]	
Salvation Army: number of workers overseas	Officers; cadets; employees by country of service	World	Annual	[QRL.99]	All nationalities included
Church of Jesus Christ of Latter-Day Saints: number of missionaries	Total number	British Isles	Annual	[QRL.37]	Updates monthly. Also available from [QRL.204]
Related Data					
Missionary society personnel	Status by size of society	United Kingdom	1972, 1976, 1980, 1982, 1984	[QRL.2]	4.6.5.1 Status includes executive and office staff on furlough, abroad and retired
Income of missionary societies	Total	United Kingdom	1976, 1980, 1982, 1984	[QRL.2]	4.6.1.4
Society for the Propogation of the Gospel: number of members of churches	Sex; geographical	Africa, India, Far East	Annual late nineteenth to early twentieth century	[QRL.239]	

Item		Area	Date	Reference	Notes
Church Missionary Society: number of field staff	Diocese	England and Wales	Annual	[QRL.46]	Missionaries - volunteers also listed
Salvation Army: number of corps and institutions overseas	Corps; outposts; institutions; schools by country of service	World	Annual	[QRL.99]	
Salvation Army: overseas service funds	Country	World	Annual	[QRL.99]	
CHURCH BUILDINGS					
Collective Data					
Churches	Denomination; "Total Christian" for England, Wales, Scotland, Northern Ireland	United Kingdom	1970, 1975, 1980	[QRL.2]	General ref: 5.1 - 8. 5.1.1.2 - Church buildings and communities. Parochial churches only for Church of England and Roman Catholic. Some estimation used. Estimates given for 1985.
Churches	Major Free Church denominations	United Kingdom	1970; 71	[QRL.59]	
Places of Regular Worship	Denominations: Great Britain; Ireland	United Kingdom	1949, 1952, 1957, 1962, 1968	[QRL.3]	5.1.1.2
Churches, chapels and places of worship	Selected denominations	United Kingdom	Annual	[QRL.110]	
Number of churches related to United Kingdom missionary organizations with North American personnel	Organization	United Kingdom	Irregular	[QRL.9]	

Type of data	Breakdown	Area	Frequency or Date	QRL reference	Text Reference and Remarks
Denominational congregations (places of worship)	Denomination	United Kingdom	Annual 1970 t0 1980	[QRL.1]	Total number of worship centres in 1970 also given
Number of church buildings	Major denominations; England; Scotland; Wales	Great Britain	Quinquennial 1801 to 1971	[QRL.4]	1851 Census details also given: number of places of worship by denomination and county.
Types of building: number of certified places of worship	Standard regions by major denominations; metropolitan; non-metropolitan counties by major denominations	England and Wales	Annual	[QRL.76]	5.1.1.2 Excludes Church of England and Church in Wales
Total provision of church accommodation: number of seats as a percentage of the population	County	England	1851	[QRL.6]	5.1.2.3

Episcopal Data

Type of data	Breakdown	Area	Frequency or Date	QRL reference	Text Reference and Remarks
Church of England: parochial churches and chapels	Diocese	England	Annual	[QRL.42] up to the 1970's, [QRL.209]	Churches etc. serving specific parishes. Biennial census.
Church of England: parochial churches and chapels	Type of building by diocese; number of churches per parochial living by diocese	England	1957, 1960, 1963	[QRL.55]	Also listed individually in some Church of England diocesan yearbooks

Church of England: extra-parochial churches and chapels	Diocese by type of establishment using them	England	1957, 1960, 1963	[QRL.55]	Churches etc. not serving specific parishes. Includes cathedrals etc.
Scottish Episcopal Church: church buildings	Diocese	Scotland	Annual	[QRL.111], [QRL.15]	Includes missions, chapels and cathedrals. Only churches listed after 1976.
Church of Ireland: churches	Diocese	Northern Ireland	Annual	[QRL.216]	
Moravian Church in Great Britain and Ireland: church buildings and other properties	Type of building	United Kingdom	Occasional	[QRL.223]	
Methodist Data					
Methodist churches	District by size of membership; district by percentage increase in membership	Great Britain	Annual	[QRL.77]	More information available on request than published
Methodist Church: chapels and other preaching places	Frequency of meetings by district	Ireland	Annual	[QRL.78]	
Methodist: provision of chapels	County	England	1851	[QRL.6]	
Independent Methodist Churches: churches and missions	Circuit	England	Annual	[QRL.29]	
Baptist Data					
Baptist Union of Great Britain and Ireland: churches	Associations in England, Wales, Scotland	Great Britain	Annual	[QRL.21] ([QRL.19])	

Type of data	Breakdown	Area	Frequency or Date	QRL reference	Text Reference and Remarks
Baptist Union of Scotland: churches, special ministries and fellowships	Association	Scotland	Annual	[QRL.100]	
Particular Baptist: changes in distribution of churches	By area	England	1689 to 1798	[QRL.6]	
Presbyterian Data					
Geographical location of Presbyterian churches	By area	England	1964	[QRL.6]	
Presbyterian Church of Wales: number of churches	Presbytery; association	England and Wales	Annual	[QRL.88]	
Free United Church of Scotland: number of churches	Presbytery	Scotland	Annual	[QRL.69]	Number of other buildings (e.g. manses) available on request
Congregational Data					
Congregational Federation: number of churches	11 geographical areas	Great Britain	Annual	[QRL.49]	Churches also listed individually
United Reformed Church: number of churches	District; province	England and Wales	Annual	[QRL.107]	
United Reformed Church: number of places of worship	Province	England and Wales	Annual	[QRL.107]	Some churches use more than one place of worship
Congregational Union of Scotland: number of churches	District	Scotland	Annual	[QRL.75]	

Pentecostal and Holiness Data					
New Testament Church of God: number of premises	Owned; rented	England	1966, 1968, 1970	[QRL.22]	
Roman Catholic Data					
Number of Roman Catholic churches	Diocese	World	Annual	[QRL.16]	
Roman Catholic Church: number of churches	Parish; other churches and chapels by diocese	England and Wales	Annual	[QRL.32]	
Roman Catholic Church: number of churches and missions	Churches; missions by diocese	Scotland	1879	[QRL.82]	
Roman Catholic Church: number of churches	Diocese	Ireland	Annual	[QRL.71]	
Liberal Catholic Church: number of places of worship	Total number	Great Britain and Ireland	Annual	[QRL.217]	
Orthodox Data					
Greek Orthodox Church: church buildings	Total number	United Kingdom	Annual	[QRL.67]	
Russian Orthodox Church in Exile: number of church buildings	Total number	England and Northern Ireland	Occasional	[QRL.231]	
Other Trinitarian Denominational Data					
Countess of Huntingdons's Connexion: number of churches and mission stations	Total number	England	Annual	[QRL.50]	Churches also listed individually
Fellowship of Independent Evangelical Churches: number of churches and missions affiliated	Total number	Great Britain	Biennial	[QRL.57]	Churches also listed individually

R–E*

Type of data	Breakdown	Area	Frequency or Date	QRL reference	Text Reference and Remarks
Religious Society of Friends: number of meeting houses	By area	United Kingdom	Annual	[QRL.91]	Meeting places listed in [QRL.23]
Salvation Army: number of centres of work	Division	United Kingdom	Annual	[QRL.99]	Centres of work include corps, outposts, societies and institutions. Further information available on request.
Seventh-Day Adventist Church: number of churches	By area	United Kingdom	Biennial	[QRL.102]	Counties where the denomination is active are also given
Non-Trinitarian Churches					
Christian Science Churches and Societies	Total number	Great Britain	Quinquennial from 1901	[QRL.4]	8.2.2 Figures taken from [QRL.110]
Christian Science buildings:number	Total number	England	1967	[QRL.6]	
Church of Jesus Christ of Latter Day Saints:churches	Total number	British Isles	Annual	[QRL.37]	Figures available monthly. Also available from [QRL.204].
Mormon Churches	Total number	England	1967	[QRL.6]	8.1.4
Church of Scientology: number of churches and missions	Churches; missions	United Kingdom	Annual	[QRL.109]	Worldwide figures also given
Unitarian Churches *Other Buildings*	Total number	England	1966	[QRL.6]	

Church of England: new and redundant parsonages	Total number	England	Annual	[QRL.39]	
Non-Subscribing Presbyterian Church of Ireland: value of manse (or glebe)	Manse	Ireland	Annual	[QRL.79]	
Roman Catholic convents of religious women: number	Diocese	England and Wales	Annual	[QRL.32]	
Roman Catholic religious houses: number	Sex by diocese	Scotland	Annual	[QRL.33]	
Roman Catholic convents: number	Diocese	Ireland	Annual	[QRL.71]	Also listed individually

Redundant Churches

Church of England: number of redundant churches	Future useage	England	Total for 1969-1980	[QRL.39]	

Church Interiors

Church accomodation: seating	Denomination by region	Great Britain	1851	[QRL.4]	5.1.5.1
Church of England: number of seats in parochial churches and chapels, rate per 100 population	Fixed; movable by diocese; rate by diocese	England	1960	[QRL.55]	Not collected after 1960.
Scottish Episcopal Church: church seating	Church	Scotland	Annual	[QRL.111]	Only available up to 1976
Methodist Church of worship: seating and ancillary accommodation	Places of worship	Great Britain	1940, decennial from 1960	[QRL.221]	
Independent Methodist Churches: seating capacity	Church	England	Annual	[QRL.29]	
Baptist Union of Great Britain and Ireland: church seating	Church	England and Wales	Annual	[QRL.19]	

Type of data	Breakdown	Area	Frequency or Date	QRL reference	Text Reference and Remarks
Baptist Union of Ireland: church seats	Church	Northern Ireland	Annual	[QRL.20]	

Value of Church Buildings

Type of data	Breakdown	Area	Frequency or Date	QRL reference	Text Reference and Remarks
Value of Church Commissioners' property	Commercial; residential agricultural; mineral	England	Annual	[QRL.39]	5.1.5.1 Church of England. Excluding churches, chapels, parsonages etc.
Church of England: total cost of buildings	Clergy housing; churches; church buildings	England	Biennial	[QRL.96]	
Independent Methodist churches: value of church property	Church	England	Annual	[QRL.29]	
Non-Subscribing Presbyterian Church of Ireland: value of manse or glebe	Manse	Ireland	Annual	[QRL.79]	
Church of the Nazarene: value of churches and parsonages	District	Great Britain	Annual	[QRL.74]	
Roman Catholic land values as a percentage of the Land Tax assessment	County	England	1715 to 1720	[QRL.6]	

SCHOOLS

Number of Primary Schools

Collective Data

Number of county and voluntary primary schools and departments	Denomination by type; status by type	England	Annual (January census)	[QRL.105]	General ref: 5.2. 5.2.1.2 - 5.2.2.5 Current data not published but available on request. Maintained primary and middle schools only. Categories and breakdowns alter over time. Prior to 1978 data applies to England and Wales
Number of all-age junior and infant primary schools	Status by denomination	England	Annual	[QRL.55]	Compiled from figures supplied by the DES. Maintained schools only.
Number of all-age junior and infant primary schools or departments maintained by local authorities	Status by denomination by size of pupil register	England	1957, 1960, 1963	[QRL.55]	Compiled from figures supplied by the DES. Excluding nursery and special schools.
Number of county and voluntary primary schools	Denomination by type; status by type	England and Wales	Annual to 1978	[QRL.42]	Taken from [QRL.105]
Number of county and voluntary primary schools or departments	Denomination by type; status by type	Wales	Annual	[QRL.242]	Prior to 1978 figures for England and Wales published by DES.
Number of Education authority primary schools	Denomination by region	Scotland	Annual	[QRL.101]	5.2.1.2 Excludes nursery schools

Type of data	Breakdown	Area	Frequency or Date	QRL reference	Text Reference and Remarks
Roman Catholic Data					
Roman Catholic maintained and independent primary schools: number	Type by diocese	England and Wales	Annual	[QRL.34]	5.2.2.3 Includes those run by religious institutions e.g. convents
Roman Catholic voluntary primary schools: number	Status by diocese; type by diocese	England and Wales	Annual	[QRL.32]	Includes those run by religious institutions e.g. convents
Roman Catholic primary schools: number	Diocese	Ireland	Annual	[QRL.71]	Includes those run by religious institutions e.g.convents. Maintained schools only.
Other Trinitarian Denominational Data					
Church of England: preparatory schools	Total number	England	Annual	[QRL.242]	
Methodist schools	voluntary aided	England	Annual	[QRL.219]	Maintained schools only
Methodist and joint Church of England	Voluntary controlled	England	Annual	[QRL.220]	Maintained schools only
Moravian primary schools	Total number	England	Annual	[QRL.52] from nineteenth century	Eighteenth century onwards available on request. Independent schools.

Number of Secondary Schools
Collective Data

Item	Breakdown	Area	Frequency	Reference	Notes
Number of county and voluntary secondary schools and departments	Denomination by type; status by type	England	Annual from 1953	[QRL.105]	5.2.1.2 - 5.2.2.5 - Maintained middle and secondary schools only. Categories and breakdown alter over time. Prior to 1978 data apply to England and Wales.
Number of secondary schools	Status; denomination	England	Annual	[QRL.55]	Compiled from figures supplied by DES
Number of secondary schools or departments maintained by local authorities	Status by pupil register size; denomination by pupil register size	England	1957, 1960, 1963	[QRL.55]	Excluding special schools
Number of county and voluntary secondary schools	Denomination; status; type	England and Wales	Annual to 1978	[QRL.42]	Taken from [QRL.105]
Number of county and voluntary secondary schools	Denomination by type; status by type	Wales	Annual	[QRL.242]	Prior to 1978 figures for England and Wales published by DES
Number of Education authority secondary schools	Denomination by region	Scotland	Annual	[QRL.101]	5.2.1.2 - In 1974; 75 the annual school census was changed from January to September

Roman Catholic Data

Type of data	Breakdown	Area	Frequency or Date	QRL reference	Text Reference and Remarks
Roman Catholic maintained and independent secondary schools: number	Type by diocese	England and Wales	Annual	[QRL.34]	Includes those run by religious institutions e.g. convents
Roman Catholic voluntary secondary schools: number	Status by diocese; type by diocese	England and Wales	Annual	[QRL.32]	Includes those run by religious institutions e.g.convents
Roman Catholic secondary schools: number	Regions; divisions	Scotland	Annual from 1970	[QRL.208]	Maintained schools only.
Roman Catholic independent secondary schools: number	Total number	Scotland	Annual from 1970	[QRL.208]	
Roman Catholic secondary schools: number	Diocese	Ireland	Annual	[QRL.71]	Maintained schools only.
Other Trinitarian Denominational Data					
Church of England: number of independent schools	Total number	England	Annual	[QRL.242]	
Methodist residential secondary schools: number	Total number	United Kingdom	Annual	[QRL.219]	Schools listed individually in [QRL.77]. Independent schools only.
Number of Primary and Secondary Schools					
Roman Catholic Data					
Roman Catholic schools: number	Diocese	World	Annual	[QRL.16]	5.2.2.4

Roman Catholic direct grant, independent, special and approved schools: number	Status by diocese; type by diocese	England and Wales	Annual	[QRL.32]	Includes those run by religious institutions e.g.convents
Roman Catholic approved and special schools: number	Type by diocese	England and Wales	Annual	[QRL.34]	
Roman Catholic vocational, community and comprehensive schools: number	Diocese	Ireland	Annual	[QRL.71]	Includes those run by religious institutions e.g. convents

Teachers in Primary Schools
Collective Data

Teachers in county and voluntary primary schools: number	Denomination by type; status by type	England	Annual (January census)	[QRL.105]	5.2.2.5 - Fulltime equivalent teachers. Categories and data breakdowns alter over time. Prior to 1978 data apply to England and Wales.
Teachers in all-age junior and infant primary schools	Status; denomination	England	Annual	[QRL.55]	Compiled from figures supplied by the DES. Maintained schools only.
Teachers in county and voluntary primary schools: number	Denomination by type; status by type	Wales	Annual	[QRL.242]	Prior to 1976 figures for England and Wales published by DES.
Teachers in county and voluntary primary schools: number	Denomination; status; type	England and Wales	Annual to 1978	[QRL.42]	Taken from [QRL.105]

Type of data	Breakdown	Area	Frequency or Date	QRL reference	Text Reference and Remarks
Teachers in education authority primary schools: number	Remedial; full-time equivalent; visiting teachers by region by denomination	Scotland	Annual	[QRL.101]	Excludes nursery schools
Teachers in education authority primary schools and departments: number	Age by region, by denomination; sex by region, by denomination; mode of employment by region, by denomination; type of employment by region, by denomination; qualifications by region, by denomination	Scotland	Annual	[QRL.101]	In 1974; 75 the annual census was changed from January to September
Full-time teachers in education authority primary schools and departments: number	Source of recruitment by region by denomination	Scotland	Annual	[QRL.101]	
Teachers on first appointment to full-time posts in education authority primary schools: number	College of education by region by denomination	Scotland	Annual	[QRL.101]	
Roman Catholic Data					
Fulltime teachers in Roman Catholic primary schools: number	Graduate; non-graduate by religious status by type of school	England and Wales	Annual (January census)	[QRL.34]	5.2.2.3 - Independent and maintained schools
Other Trinitarian Denominational Data					
Teachers in Moravian primary schools: number	School	England	Occasional from eighteenth century	[QRL.223]	Independent schools only.
Teachers in Secondary Schools					
Collective Data					

Teachers in county and voluntary secondary schools: number	Denomination by type; status by type	England	Annual	[QRL.105]	5.2.2.5 - Full-time equivalent teachers. Categories and breakdown alter over time. Prior to 1978 data apply to England and Wales.
Teachers in secondary schools: number	Status; denomination	England	Annual	[QRL.55]	Compiled from figures supplied by the DES. Maintained schools only.
Teachers in county and voluntary secondary schools: number	Denomination by type; status by type	Wales	Annual	[QRL.242]	Prior to 1978 figures for England and Wales published by the DES.
Teachers in county and voluntary secondary schools: number	Denomination; status; type	England and Wales	Annual to 1978	[QRL.42]	Taken from [QRL.105]
Teachers in education authority secondary schools: number	Denomination by region	Scotland	Annual	[QRL.101]	Full-time equivalent including visiting teachers
Full-time teachers in education authority secondary schools: number	Source of recruitment by region by denomination	Scotland	Annual	[QRL.101]	

Type of data	Breakdown	Area	Frequency or Date	QRL reference	Text Reference and Remarks
Teachers in education authority secondary schools: number	Age by region, by denomination; sex by region, by denomination; mode of employment, by region, by denomination; type of employment by region, by denomination; qualifications by region, by denomination.	Scotland	Annual	[QRL.101]	
Teachers in education authority secondary schools: number	Subject responsibility by region by denomination	Scotland	Annual	[QRL.101]	
Teachers on first appointment to full-time posts in education authority secondary schools: number	College of education by region by denomination	Scotland	Annual	[QRL.101]	
Roman Catholic Data					
Fulltime teachers in Roman Catholic secondary schools: number	Graduate; non-graduate by religious status by type of school	England and Wales	Annual (January census)	[QRL.34]	5.2.2.3 - Independent and maintained schools
Teachers in Roman Catholic schools: number	Catholic; non-Catholic by subject by region or division	Scotland	Annual from 1970	[QRL.208]	Maintained schools only.
Teachers in Roman Catholic independent secondary schools: number	Catholic; non-Catholic by subject	Scotland	Annual from 1970	[QRL.208]	
Non-Catholic teachers in Roman Catholic secondary schools: number	Region or division	Scotland	Annual 1975 to 1978	[QRL.82]	
Primary and Secondary Schools					
Roman Catholic Data					

Full-time teachers in Roman Catholic direct grant, independent, special and approved schools: number	Religious status by graduate; non-graduate by type of school	England and Wales	Annual (January census)	[QRL.34]	5.2.2.3
Other Trinitarian Denominational Data					
Teachers in Greek Orthodox Schools: number	School	United Kingdom	Annual 1926 onwards	[QRL.67]	Independent schools only
Pupils in Primary Schools					
Collective Data					
Pupils in denominational primary schools	Denomination	England	1971, 1979, 1980	[QRL.104]	First available in 1981 edition. Source: DES. Maintained schools only.
Number of pupils in county and voluntary primary schools	Denomination by type; status by type	England	Annual (January census)	[QRL.105]	5.2.2.5 - Current data available on request from DES. Each part-time pupil counted as 0,5 full-time pupil. Categories and breakdown alter over time. Prior
Number of pupils in all-age junior and infant primary schools.	Status; denomination of school	England	Annual	[QRL.55]	Compiled from figures supplied by the DES. Maintained schools only.

Type of data	Breakdown	Area	Frequency or Date	QRL reference	Text Reference and Remarks
Average number of pupils per full-time teacher at all-age junior and infant primary schools or departments maintained by local authorities	Status; denomination of school	England	1957, 1960, 1963	[QRL.55]	Excluding nursery and special schools
Number of pupils in county and voluntary primary schools	Denomination of school by type; status by type	Wales	Annual	[QRL.242]	Prior to 1978 figures for England and Wales published by DES.
Number of pupils in county and voluntary primary schools	Denomination; status; type of school	England and Wales	Annual to 1978	[QRL.42]	Taken from [QRL.105]
Average number of pupils per teacher in county and voluntary primary schools	Denomination; type of school	England and Wales	Annual to 1978	[QRL.42]	Taken from [QRL.105]
Number of pupils in education authority primary schools	Denomination by region	Scotland	Annual	[QRL.101]	Excludes nursery schools
Average roll in education authority primary schools	Denomination by region	Scotland	Annual	[QRL.101]	Excludes nursery schools
Pupil-teacher ratios in primary schools	Denomination; full-time equivalent including; excluding visitors and remedial teachers; region	Scotland	Annual	[QRL.101]	5.2.1.1 - Excludes nursery schools

Roman Catholic Data

Type of data	Breakdown	Area	Frequency or Date	QRL reference	Text Reference and Remarks
Number of pupils in Roman Catholic voluntary primary schools	Status by diocese; type of schools by diocese	England and Wales	Annual	[QRL.32]	

Number of pupils in Roman Catholic maintained primary schools	Roman Catholic; non-Roman Catholic by sex; by type of school	England and Wales	Annual (January census)	[QRL.34]	5.2.2.3
Number of pupils in Roman Catholic maintained primary schools	Age by type of school	England and Wales	Annual (January census)	[QRL.34]	Age categories in individual years
Number of pupils in Roman Catholic maintained primary schools	Type of school by diocese	England and Wales	Annual (January census)	[QRL.34]	Also listed by individual school
Pupils attending Education authority Roman Catholic schools: number and percentage of all pupils	Education authority	Scotland	1971	[QRL.82]	
Pupils attending education authority Roman Catholic schools: number and percentage of all pupils	Region or division	Scotland	1977	[QRL.82]	
Number of pupils in Roman Catholic primary schools	Diocese	Ireland	Annual	[QRL.71]	Maintained schools. Figures sometimes estimated and not given by every diocese.

Other Trinitarian Denomination Data

Number of pupils in Church of England preparatory schools	School	England	Annual	[QRL.242]	
Number of boys and girls at Methodist day schools	Total number	England	Annual	[QRL.219]	Maintained schools only.

Type of data	Breakdown	Area	Frequency or Date	QRL reference	Text Reference and Remarks
Number of pupils at Moravian primary schools	School	England	Occasional from eighteenth century	[QRL.223]	Independent schools only.
Pupils in Secondary Schools					
Collective Data					
Pupils in denominational secondary schools	Denomination	England	1971, 1979, 1980	[QRL.104]	5.2.1.5 First available in 1981 edition. Source: DES. Maintained schools only.
Number of pupils in county and voluntary secondary schools	Denomination by type of school; status by type	England	Annual (January census)	[QRL.105]	Current data not published but available on request from DES. Each part-time pupil counted as 0,5 full-time pupil. Categories and breakdown alter over time.
Number of pupils in secondary schools	Status; denomination of school	England	Annual	[QRL.55]	Compiled from figures supplied by the DES. Maintained schools only.

Subject	Breakdown	Area	Period	Reference	Remarks
Average number of pupils per full-time teacher in local authority maintained secondary schools or departments	Status; denomination	England	1957, 1960, 1963	[QRL.55]	Excluding special schools
Number of pupils in county and voluntary secondary schools	Denomination of school by type; status by type	Wales	Annual	[QRL.242]	Prior to 1978 figures for England and Wales published by DES.
Number of pupils in county and voluntary secondary schools	Denomination of school; status; type	England and Wales	Annual to 1978	[QRL.42]	Taken from [QRL.105]
Average number of pupils per teacher in county and voluntary secondary schools	Denomination of school; type	England and Wales	Annual to 1978	[QRL.42]	Taken from [QRL.105]
Number of pupils in education authority secondary schools	Denomination by region	Scotland	Annual	[QRL.101]	In 1974; 75 the annual school census was changed from January to September.
Average roll in education authority secondary schools	Denomination	Scotland	Annual	[QRL.101]	
Pupil-teacher ratios in education authority secondary schools	Denomination by region	Scotland	Annual	[QRL.101]	5.2.1.1 - Full-time equivalent including visiting teachers

Roman Catholic Data

Subject	Breakdown	Area	Period	Reference	Remarks
Number of pupils in Catholic Voluntary Secondary Schools	Status of school by diocese; type by diocese	England and Wales	Annual	[QRL.32]	

Type of data	Breakdown	Area	Frequency or Date	QRL reference	Text Reference and Remarks
Number of pupils in Roman Catholic maintained secondary schools	Roman Catholic; non-Roman Catholic by sex by type of school	England and Wales	Annual (January census)	[QRL.34]	5.2.2.3
Number of pupils in Roman Catholic maintained secondary schools	Age by type of school	England and Wales	Annual (January census)	[QRL.34]	Age categories in individual years
Number of pupils in Roman Catholic maintained secondary schools	Type of school by diocese	England and Wales	Annual	[QRL.34]	Also listed by individual schools
Pupils attending Education authority Roman Catholic schools: number and percent of all pupils	Education authority; region or division	Scotland	1971, 1977	[QRL.82]	
Number of pupils in Roman Catholic secondary schools	Diocese	Ireland	Annual	[QRL.71]	Maintained schools only. Figures sometimes estimated and not given by every diocese.
Other Trinitarian Denomination Data					
Number of pupils in Church of England independent schools	School	England	Annual	[QRL.242]	
Number of boys and girls in Methodist secondary schools	Total number	United Kingdom	Annual	[QRL.219]	Independent schools only.

Boarders and day scholars at schools of the Society of Friends	School	England and Ireland	Annual	[QRL.91]	Independent schools only. Pamphlet [QRL.92] also available.
Pupils in Primary and secondary schools *Roman Catholic Data* Number of pupils in Roman Catholic direct grant, independent special approved schools	Status of school by diocese; type by diocese	England and Wales	Annual	[QRL.32]	
Number of pupils in Roman Catholic direct grant, independent, special and approved schools	Roman Catholic; non-Roman Catholic by sex by type of school	England and Wales	Annual (January census)	[QRL.34]	
Number of pupils in Roman Catholic schools	Age by diocese	England and Wales	Annual (January census)	[QRL.34]	Age categories in individual years. Independent and maintained schools.
Number of Roman Catholic pupils in Roman Catholic schools	Age by diocese	England and Wales	Annual (January census)	[QRL.34]	Age categories in individual years. Independent and maintained schools.
Number of Roman Catholic pupils in maintained Roman Catholic schools	Age by diocese	England and Wales	Annual (January census)	[QRL.34]	Age categories in individual years
Number of pupils in Roman Catholic direct grant, independent, special and approved schools	Age by type of school	England and Wales	Annual (January census)	[QRL.34]	Age categories in individual years

Type of data	Breakdown	Area	Frequency or Date	QRL reference	Text Reference and Remarks
Number of pupils in Roman Catholic direct grant, independent, special and approved schools	Type of school by diocese	England and Wales	Annual (January census)	[QRL.34]	Also listed by individual school
Pupils attending Scottish Roman Catholic schools	Diocese	Scotland	Decennial 1891 to 1951	[QRL.82]	
Number of pupils in Roman Catholic vocational, community and comprehensive schools	Diocese	Ireland	Annual	[QRL.71]	Figures sometimes estimated and not given by every diocese
Other Trinitarian Denominational Data					
Number of school places provided by the Church of England	Voluntary aided; special agreement	England	Biennial	[QRL.96]	
Number of pupils in Greek Orthodox Schools Related Data	School	United Kingdom	Annual 1926 onwards	[QRL.67]	Independent schools only
Church of England clergy in schools	Total number	England	Biennial	[QRL.96]	Also listed individually in [QRL.41]
Church of England clergy in schools	Diocese	England	1957, 1960, 1963	[QRL.55]	
Cost to Church of England of providing educational facilities	Church schools; voluntary education	England	Biennial	[QRL.96]	5.2.1.1
Grants and expenditure on Scottish Episcopal Church schools	Total amount	Scotland	Annual	[QRL.15]	Primary education only

Number of Scottish Episcopal Church chaplains to schools	Total number	Scotland	Annual	[QRL.15]	Primary education
Financial assistance given to Friends in Society of Friends schools	School	England	Annual	[QRL.91]	

PLACES OF HIGHER EDUCATION

Number of Colleges

Church of Ireland colleges of education	Total number	Ireland	Annual	[QRL.43]	5.3
Seventh Day Adventists education institutions	Total number	United Kingdom	Annual	[QRL.102]	Post secondary education colleges

Number of students

University Christian unions:membership	University	United Kingdom	Annual	[QRL.240]	5.3.1.1 University unions affiliated to UCCF. Attendance is greater than membership.
Number of students at Methodist colleges	Total number	England	Annual	[QRL.220]	
Number of students at Roman Catholic colleges of education	College	England and Wales	Annual (January census)	[QRL.34]	
Number of Roman Catholic students in Scottish colleges of education due to complete training for primary and secondary school teaching per year	Course of study; college or university	Scotland	Annual 1970 onwards	[QRL.208]	

Number of Chaplains etc.

Type of data	Breakdown	Area	Frequency or Date	QRL reference	Text Reference and Remarks
Number of travelling secretaries of Universities and Colleges Christian Fellowship of Evangelical Unions	Regional groupings	Great Britain and Ireland	Annual	[QRL.240]	5.3.1.2
Church of England chaplains in higher education	Universities; polytechnics	England	Annual	[QRL.42]	Chaplains listed individually. Also in [QRL.41]
Church of England clergy in higher education	Universities; colleges of education by diocese	England	1957, 1960, 1963	[QRL.55]	
Number of United Reformed Church chaplains in establishments of higher education	Total number	England and Wales	Irregular	[QRL.238]	
Number of Campus Crusade for Christ full-time Christian workers and evangelists in places of higher education	Total number	United Kingdom	Annual	[QRL.206]	
Number of Navigators full-time Christian workers in universities	Total number	Great Britain	Annual	[QRL.224]	
Related Data					
Higher education costs in the Church of England	Total amount	England	Biennial	[QRL.96]	5.3.4
FINANCE					
Episcopal Data					
Finances of the Church of England	Categories of income and expenditure	England	Biennial	[QRL.96]	6.1 Forecasts also given

Description	Subject	Area	Years	Reference	Notes
Income of Church of England parochial church councils: weekly average per subscriber and Electoral Roll member	Covenanted; uncovenanted giving; collections; voluntary contributions; other income by diocese	England	Biennial	[QRL.42]	6.1.3.2 - Also adjusted by the Retail Price Index
Expenditure by Church of England parochial church councils	Ministry and diocese; church and services; other expenditure by diocese	England	Biennial	[QRL.42]	
Church of England General Synod fund and training for ministry	Training for ministry; General Synod Fund contributions by diocese	England	Biennial	[QRL.42]	Parochial income and diocesan income given annually
Parochial benefice income in the Church of England: livings distributed by total income	Income categories by population size	England	1956, 1959, 1962	[QRL.55]	
Sources of income of parochial church councils of the Church of England	Income groups by diocese	England	1956, 1959, 1962	[QRL.55]	
Comparative standards of contributions to Church of England parochial church councils: distribution of churches by income from giving	Income groups by diocese	England	1956, 1959, 1962	[QRL.55]	
Objects of expenditure by parochial church councils of the Church of England	Expenditure categories by diocese	England	1956, 1959, 1962	[QRL.55]	
Percentage analyses of total income and expenditure of parochial church councils of the Church of England	Categories of income or expenditure by diocese	England	1956, 1959, 1962	[QRL.55]	

Type of data	Breakdown	Area	Frequency or Date	QRL reference	Text Reference and Remarks
Percentages of Church of England parochial church councils' annual incomes given outside the parish	Non-parochial objects; church overseas, by diocese	England	1956, 1959, 1962	[QRL.55]	
Comparative analyses of expenditure of Church of England parochial church councils	Expenditure categories	England	Annual 1922 to 1962	[QRL.55]	
Number and amount of legacies and bequests received by Church of England parochial church councils	Diocese	England	1956, 1959, 1962	[QRL.55]	Number of parishes also given
Church of England parochial quota assessments	Diocese	England	1957, 1960, 1963	[QRL.55]	Also related to parochial church council income
Expenditure of Church of England Assembly Fund	Categories of expenditure; diocesan apportionments	England	1960, 1963, 1966	[QRL.55]	Also related to parochial church council income
Income and expenditure of the Church Commissioners	Catgories of income or expenditure	England	Annual	[QRL.39]	Balance sheet giving income and expenditure categories also examined in more detail
Church in Wales quota contributions	Church; benefice; diocese	Wales	Annual	[QRL.40]	6.1.1.2
Scottish Episcopal Church income	Congregational income; investments; endowments; church contributions to funds by diocese	Scotland	Annual	[QRL.15]	Legacies, donations, contributions, provincial budget, quota allocations given

					6.1.2.2
Contributions to the Moravian Church	Offerings; contributions to specific projects	England and Northern Ireland	Annual from 1900	[QRL.223]	
Methodist Data					
Methodist Church in Ireland: contributions to missions	Home missions; orphans fund; overseas mission by circuit and by district	Ireland	Annual	[QRL.78]	
Methodist Church in Ireland: contributions to central budget	Circuit; district	Ireland	Annual	[QRL.78]	
Statement of income to the Wesleyan Reform Union	Individual contribution	England	Annual	[QRL.108]	
Baptist Data					
Number of legacies received by the Baptist Union of Great Britain and Ireland	Total number	Great Britain	Annual	[QRL.18]	
Baptist Union of Scotland: subscriptions and donations	Church	Scotland	Annual	[QRL.100]	
Baptist Union of Ireland: subscriptions	Individual fund by church	Ireland	Annual	[QRL.20]	
Presbyterian Data					
Presbyterian Church of Wales: financial statement	Receipts; payments; debts; investments by presbytery	Wales	Annual	[QRL.88]	
Church of Scotland: contributuons from congregations	Mission and service ministers' stipend; parish	Scotland	Annual	[QRL.44]	
Presbyterian Church in Ireland: income and expenditure	Organisation; ministerial expenses by congregation	Ireland	Annual	[QRL.53]	
Free Church of Scotland: income and expenditure	Categories of income or expenditure	Scotland	Annual	[QRL.89]	

R-F

Type of data	Breakdown	Area	Frequency or Date	QRL reference	Text Reference and Remarks
United Free Church of Scotland: income and expenditure	Congregation	Scotland	Annual from 1929	[QRL.106]	
Reformed Presbyterian Church in Scotland: congregational giving and expenses	Collections; legacies; ministerial income and expenses	Scotland	Annual	[QRL.95]	
Reformed Presbyterian Church of Ireland: congregational finances, investment income, aid, ministers' salaries	Congregation	Ireland	Annual	[QRL.80]	
Non-Subscribing Presbyterian Church of Ireland: congregational finances, collections, investments and rents, donations, other incomes, grants, ministers' stipends.	Congregation	Ireland	Annual	[QRL.79]	
Pentecostal and Holiness Data					
Church of the Nazarene: church finances	Paid on local; district; college general interests by church	Great Britain	Annual	[QRL.74]	6.1.3.3
Non-Trinitarian Churches					
Unitarian Church: congregational contributuons	Congregation	United Kingdom	Annual	[QRL.12]	9.1.2

RITES OF PASSAGE

Baptisms

Collective Data

	Major denomination		Frequency	Reference	Remarks
Baptisms in selected churches	Major denomination	Great Britain	Irregular	[QRL.104]	General ref: 6.2, 6.2.1.2. 6.2.1.3. - Appears in full in 1982 edition
Baptisms	Church of England; Church of Scotland; Roman Catholic; other selected denominations	Great Britain and Ireland	Annual to 1970	[QRL.4]	
Episcopal Data Church of England: number of baptisms and infant baptism rate per 1000 live births	Infants; other persons by diocese	England	Biennial from 1981, irregular from 1941 to 1948	[QRL.42]	6.2.2.3 - From 1978 infants defined as under 1 year of age Receptions also given for isolated years.
Church of England: number of baptisms and infant baptism rate per 1000 live births	Infant baptisms; baptisms of persons of riper years. Some years by diocese.	England	Annual from 1902	[QRL.55]	
Church in Wales: number of baptisms	Church; benefice; diocese	Wales	Annual	[QRL.40]	
Moravian Church: number of baptisms	Total number	England and Northern Ireland	Annual from 1750	[QRL.223]	
Methodist Data Methodist Church: number of baptisms	District	Great Britain	Annual	[QRL.77]	
Presbyterian Data Presbyterian Church of Wales: number of baptisms	Presbytery	Wales	Annual	[QRL.88]	
Church of Scotland: number of baptisms	Infant; adult by presbytery and by synod	Scotland	Annual from 1882	[QRL.95]	
Presbyterian Church of Ireland: number of baptisms	Congregation; presbytery	Ireland	Annual from 1886	[QRL.53]	Early data irregular
Reformed Presbyterian Church in Scotland: number of baptisms	Congregation	Scotland	Annual	[QRL.81]	

Type of data	Breakdown	Area	Frequency or Date	QRL reference	Text Reference and Remarks
Reformed Presbyterian Church of Ireland: number of baptisms	Congregation	Ireland	Annual	[QRL.80]	
Non-Subscribing Presbyterian Church of Ireland: number of baptisms	Congregation	Ireland	Annual from 1910	[QRL.225]	
Pentecostal and Holiness Data					
Church of the Nazarene: candle roll enrolment	Church	Great Britain	Annual	[QRL.74]	
Roman Catholic Data					
Roman Catholic baptisms	Diocese	World	Annual	[QRL.16]	
Roman Catholic baptisms	Diocese	England and Wales	Annual from 1911	[QRL.32]	Under 7 years of age
Roman Catholic baptisms	Parish	England and Wales	Annual	[QRL.31]	Under 7 years of age
Roman Catholic infant baptisms: number and as percent of live births	Diocese; age groups	England and Wales	Annual 1938 to 1957	[QRL.34] 1961 edition	Source: [QRL.32]
Roman Catholic infant baptisms: number and as percent of live births	Total number	England and Wales	Annual from 1911 to 1957	[QRL.34] 1961 edition	Forecasts to 1961 given
Roman Catholic baptisms	Church; parish; diocese	Scotland	Annual from 1911	[QRL.33]	
Roman Catholic baptisms	Total number	Scotland	Quinquennial 1901 to 1975	[QRL.82]	Figures taken from [QRL.33] and compared with number of Scottish births

Roman Catholic baptisms: number and as percent of live births	Region; district	Scotland	1977	[QRL.82]	
Orthodox Data					
Serbian Orthodox Church births	Church	Great Britain	Annual	[QRL.233]	
Other Trinitarian Denominational Data					
Churches of Christ: number of baptisms	Church	Great Britain and Ireland	Annual from 1980	[QRL.17]	
Fellowship of Churches of Christ	Church	Great Britain and Ireland	Annual from 1981	[QRL.56]	
Finnish Seamen's Mission: number of baptisms	Total number	United Kingdom	Annual from 1920	[QRL.58]	
French Protestant Church: number of baptisms	Total number	London	Annual from 1753	[QRL.215]	
Swedish Church: number of baptisms	By geographical region	England	Annual from 1723	[QRL.235]	
Non-Trinitarian Churches					
Church of Jesus Christ of Latter-Day Saints: baptisms	Total number	Great Britain	Monthly	[QRL.204]	9.4
General Conference of the New Church: number of baptisms	Individual society	Great Britain	Annual	[QRL.66]	
Marriages					
Collective Data					
Marriage: religious and civil ceremonies	First; second; subsequent marriage by manner of solemnisation	Great Britain	Annual	[QRL.104]	General ref: 6.2.1.4, 6.2.1.5. Major denominations only
Marital status of bride and groom before marriage	Previous marital status by manner of solemnisation	England and Wales	1979	[QRL.104]	Major denominations only

Type of data	Breakdown	Area	Frequency or Date	QRL reference	Text Reference and Remarks
Marriages solemnised with a religious ceremony: proportion of all marriages	Total	England and Wales	Annual 1914 to 1979	[QRL.86]	6.2.2.4 - Winter 1980 edition
Manner of solemnisation of marriage with religious ceremonies: proportion of religious marriage	Major denominations	England and Wales	Annual 1909 to 1979	[QRL.86]	Winter 1980 edition
Marital status of bride and groom before marriage	Previous marital status by manner of solemnisation	England and Wales	1978	[QRL.86]	Winter 1980 edition. Major denominations only.
Marriages with a religious ceremony	Previous marital status	England and Wales	Annual 1970 to 1978	[QRL.86]	Winter 1980 edition
Age at marriage of brides and bridegrooms	Manner of solemnisation	England and Wales	1978	[QRL.86]	Winter 1980 edition. Major denominations only.
Median age at marriage of brides and grooms	Marital status by manner of solemnisation	England and Wales	1975, 1978	[QRL.86]	Winter 1980 edition. Major denominations only.
Marriages solemnised in church: proportion of all marriages and as index of the national proportion	Church of England and Church in Wales; Roman Catholic by county	England and Wales	1978	[QRL.86]	Winter 1980 edition. Greater London analysed in more detail.
Manner of solemnisation of marriages	Previous marital condition by age of bride by Church of England and Church in Wales; other denominations	England and Wales	Quarterly	[QRL.76]	
Manner of solemnisation of marriages	Age of bride by age of groom by major denominations	England and Wales	Annual	[QRL.76]	

				Notes
Manner of solemnisations of marriages	Previous marital condition by major denominations	England and Wales	Annual	[QRL.76]	
Manner of solemnisation of marriages: totals and proportions	Standard regions Metropolitan; non metropolitan counties by major denominations	England and Wales	Annual	[QRL.76]	
Manner of solemnisation of marriages: types of preliminaries	Standard regions Metropolitan; non metropolitan counties by Church of England and Church in Wales; other denominations	England and Wales	Annual	[QRL.76]	
Manner of solemnisation of marriages: marriages in registered buildings solemnised before a registrar or authorised person	Standard regions metropolitan; non metropolitan counties by major denominations	England and Wales	Annual	[QRL.76]	
Age at occurence of marriage: total number of civil and religious ceremonies	Metropolitan; non-metropolitan counties; registration districts	England and Wales	Annual	[QRL.76]	
Number of marriages / Marriages registered according to forms of celebration	Denomination / Major denominations	Scotland / Northern Ireland	Annual / Annual	[QRL.14] / [QRL.13]	
Method of celebration: number of marriages registered	Major denominations by district council	Northern Ireland	Annual	[QRL.13]	
Marriages per 1000 total marriages with religious ceremonies	Church of England; Methodist; Roman Catholic by county	England	1962	[QRL.6]	Roman Catholic figures also given for 1851
Marriages by manner of solemnisation	Major denominations	England and Wales	Annual 1838 to 1914, quinquennial 1919 to 1972	[QRL.4]	
Marriages per 1000 total marriages	Church of England and Church in Wales; Roman Catholic; other Christian; Jews; civil ceremonies	England and Wales	Quinquennial from 1844	[QRL.55]	

Type of data	Breakdown	Area	Frequency or Date	QRL reference	Text Reference and Remarks
Marriages by type of solemnisation as percent of all marriages	Major denominations	England and Wales	Quinquennial 1904 to 1962	[QRL.38]	No figures for war years
Marriages in Scotland: number	Method of celebration	Scotland	Decennial 1855 to 1977	[QRL.82]	
Marriages by manner of solemnisation	Major denominations	Scotland	Annual 1855 to 1970	[QRL.4]	
Marriages by manner of solemnisation	Major denominations	Ireland	Annual 1846 to 1970	[QRL.4]	Northern Ireland given separately from 1920
Episcopal Data Marriages in the Moravian Church	Total number	England and Northern Ireland	Annual from 1750	[QRL.223]	
Presbyterian Data Non-Subscribing Presbyterian Church of Ireland: number of marriages	Congregation	Ireland	Annual from 1910	[QRL.225]	
Roman Catholic Data Roman Catholic marriages: number	Diocese	England and Wales	Annual	[QRL.32]	Includes mixed denominational marriages
Roman Catholic marriages; number	Parish	England and Wales	Annual	[QRL.31]	
Roman Catholic marriages: number	Church; parish; diocese	Scotland	Annual	[QRL.33]	
Mixed marriages: percent of all Roman Catholic marriages	Diocese	Scotland	Annual 1966 to 1977	[QRL.82]	Compared to England and Wales
Roman Catholic marriages: number and percent of all marriages	Region or district	Scotland	1977	[QRL.82]	

Orthodox Data					
Serbian Orthodox Church: number of marriages	Church	Great Britain	Annual	[QRL.233]	
Other Trinitarian Denominational Data					
Religious Society of Friends: number of marriages	Both parties members; mixed marriages by number of marriages in meeting houses; number of members married by county groupings	Great Britain	Annual	[QRL.91]	
Finnish Seamen's Mission: number of marriages	Total number	United Kingdom	Annual 1753 onwards	[QRL.58]	
French Protestant Church: number of marriages	Total number	London	Annual 1862 onwards	[QRL.215]	
Swedish Church: number of marriages	By geographical region	England	Annual 1730 onwards	[QRL.235]	
Non-Trinitarian Churches					
Church of Jesus Christ of Latter-Day Saints: marriages	Total number	Great Britain	Monthly	[QRL.204]	9.1.1
General Conference of the New Church: marriages	Individual society	Great Britain	Annual	[QRL.66]	
Other Related Data					
Types of building: number of churches, chapels and registered buildings in which marriages may be solemnised	Standard regions metropolitan; non metropolitan counties by major denominations	England and Wales	Annual	[QRL.76]	6.2.1.5
Divorces by method of celebration of marriage	Major denomination by age of husband by age of wife at divorce	Scotland	Annual	[QRL.14]	
Divorces by method of celebration of marriage	Major denominations by pursuer by grounds for divorce	Scotland	Annual	[QRL.14]	

R-F*

Type of data	Breakdown	Area	Frequency or Date	QRL reference	Text Reference and Remarks
Divorces by method of celebration of marriage	Major denominations by duration of marriage	Scotland	Annual	[QRL.14]	
Roman Catholic divorces: number	Method of celebration of marriage	Scotland	Annual 1971 to 1977	[QRL.82]	
Funerals					
Collective Data					
Membership losses by death	Church of Scotland; Methodist; other selected denominations	Great Britain	Annual to 1970	[QRL.4]	6.2.1.1
Episcopal Data					
Funerals in Moravian Church	Total number	England and Northern Ireland	Annual from 1970	[QRL.223]	
Methodist Data					
Deaths of members of the Methodist Church	District	Great Britain	Annual from 1933	[QRL.77]	
Deaths of members of the Methodist Church in Ireland	District	Ireland	Annual	[QRL.78]	
Presbyterian Data					
Presbyterian Church of Wales: losses by death	Total number	Wales	Annual 1895 to 1970	[QRL.4]	
Church of Scotland: removals by death	Total number	Scotland	Annual 1888 to 1970	[QRL.4]	
Presbyterian Church of England: losses by death	Total number	England	Annual 1876 to 1970	[QRL.4]	
Non-subscribing Presbyterian Church of Ireland: deaths	Congregation	Ireland	Annual from 1910	[QRL.227]	
Roman Catholic Data					

					Comparison with total number of cremations and deaths
Roman Catholic recorded cremations	Crematoria by county	United Kingdom	Annual from 1885	[QRL.85]	
Roman Catholic deaths	Parish	England and Wales	Annual	[QRL.31]	
Roman Catholic deaths	Total number	Scotland	Decennial 1901 to 1976	[QRL.82]	Estimated
Orthodox Data					
Serbian Orthodox deaths	Church	Great Britain	Annual	[QRL.233]	
Other Trinitarian Denominational Data					
Church of Christ: losses by death	Church	Great Britain	Annual until 1980	[QRL.45]	6.2.4
Fellowship of Churches of Christ: losses by death	Church	Great Britain	Annual from 1981	[QRL.56]	
Religious Society of Friends: funerals	Total number	Great Britain	Annual	[QRL.228]	
Finnish Seamen's Mission: funerals	Total number	United Kingdom	Annual from 1920	[QRL.58]	
Swedish Church: funerals	By geographical region	England	Annual 1724 onwards	[QRL.235]	
Non-Trinitarian Churches					
General Conference of the New Church: deceased members	Individual society	Great Britain	Annual	[QRL.66]	9.1.1
CHRISTIAN AGENCIES					
Collective Data					
Funds administered by the Conference of Missionary Societies in Great Britain and Ireland	Project	World	Annual	[QRL.26], [QRL.47]	6.3

Type of data	Breakdown	Area	Frequency or Date	QRL reference	Text Reference and Remarks
Number of Christian agencies	Date of foundation by type of agency; religious affiliation by type of agency	United Kingdom	1980, 1982, 1984	[QRL.2]	Agencies also listed. Annual income and number of full-time staff given.
Major Christian institutions and parachurch institutions	Christian institutions; parachurch agencies	United Kingdom	Annual 1973 to 1978	[QRL.1]	
Christian home missions: total staff	Staff status by type of society	United Kingdom	1977	[QRL.2]	Also listed and number of societies given
Selected charities: income and expenditure	Income and expenditure categories by charity	United Kingdom	Annual	[QRL.104]	Charities ranked by size of voluntary income. Source: Christian Aid Foundation.
Contributions from member churches of the British Council of Churches	Church	Great Britain and Ireland	Annual	[QRL.26]	
Contributions from societies to co-operative finance of the Conference of World Missions	Individual societies	Great Britain	Annual	[QRL.26], [QRL.47]	
Roman Catholic Data					
Number of Roman Catholic convents	Diocese	England and Wales	Annual	[QRL.32]	
Number of Roman Catholic convents	Diocese	Ireland	Annual	[QRL.71]	
Old Roman Catholic charities	Total number	United Kingdom	Annual from 1966	[QRL.227]	

Other Trinitarian Denominational Data

Seventh Day Adventists: number of health-care institutions	Total number	United Kingdom	Annual	[QRL.102]	
Non-Trinitarian Churches					
Church of Scientology: number of social service groups	Categories of social service	United Kingdom	Annual	[QRL.109]	9.1.1 Worldwide figures also available
Unitarian holiday centres	Total number	United Kingdom	Annual	[QRL.12]	Accounts also given
RELIGIOUS PUBLISHING *Collective Data*					
Scriptures distributed by Scripture Gift Mission	Bibles; New Testaments; Gospels; booklets etc	World	Annual	[QRL.94]	General ref: 6.4, 6.4.1.1 Languages used and countries circulated also listed
Number of Christian publishing agencies	Date of foundation by type of agency	United Kingdom	1980, 1982, 1984	[QRL.2]	Also listed individually. Books produced and number of full-time staff given
Number of new titles classified under religion and theology	Reprint and new editions; translations; limited editions	United Kingdom	Quarterly, annual	[QRL.24]	6.4.2.2
Sales and receipts of United Kingdom general printers and publishers	Hardback Bibles by United Kingdom sales; exports	United Kingdom	Quarterly	[QRL.30]	Results of institutions responding to government enquiry. Measured in £ thousands.

Type of data	Breakdown	Area	Frequency or Date	QRL reference	Text Reference and Remarks
Number of religious books in print	Subject area	United Kingdom	1974	[QRL.93]	Contains a list of religious book publishers
Christian literature: number of books, periodicals and libraries	Annual new book titles (all subjects); annual new religious book titles; Christian periodicals; major religious libraries	United Kingdom	1982	[QRL.1]	
Number of new British books	Subject area	Great Britain	Four monthly, annual	[QRL.27]	Listed individually weekly. Cumulations available every four months.
Frequency and number of magazines	Type of society by publication frequency	United Kingdom	1977	[QRL.2]	Number of societies also given
Number of religious bookshops	Size of bookshop by turnover by number of titles stocked	United Kingdom	1980, 1982, 1984	[QRL.2]	Also listed individually
Scripture distribution	Bibles; New Testament by form of distribution; portions; selections	United Kingdom	1975	[QRL.1]	Selected items also given for 1900, 1950, 1960, 1970
Scripture circulation	Bibles; New Testaments; portions; selections by country	Great Britain and Ireland	Annual	[QRL.28]	United Bible Societies data: contributions to World Service budget also given

Other Trinitarian Denominational Data

Type of data	Breakdown	Area	Frequency or Date	QRL reference	Text Reference and Remarks
Salvation Army: level of publishing and supplies	Books; music; recordings; periodicals	Great Britain and Ireland	Annual	[QRL.99]	Includes Campfield Press. Number of staff also given.

Non-Trinitarian Churches					
Unitarian publications	Total number	United Kingdom	Annual	[QRL.54]	9.1.1 Lindsay Press
RELIGIOUS BROADCASTING					
Number of Christian radio and TV programme producers	Date of foundation	United Kingdom	1980, 1982, 1984	[QRL.2]	General ref: 6.5. 6.5.1.3 Also listed individually. Income and number of full-time staff also given
Estimates of listening and viewing audiences: percentages	Individual religious programme	United Kingdom	Annual 1940 to 1970	[QRL.4]	Derived from BBC daily surveys
Independent Television weekly audience reports	Type of religious programme	United Kingdom	Annual 1957 to 1970	[QRL.4]	Average percentages
Regular audience for Christian broadcasting stations	Total number	United Kingdom	1982	[QRL.1]	Compared to audiences for secular broadcasting stations

Type of data	Breakdown	Area	Frequency or Date	QRL reference	Text Reference and Remarks
Size of audience to religious broadcasts on radio	Individual programmes	United Kingdom	Daily from 1955 to mid-August 1981. Averaged data for regular programmes from mid-August 1981 onwards.	[QRL.205]	Population aged 16+ 1955-59. Population aged 5+ 1960 to mid-August 1980. Population 4+ thereafter. Pre-1955 data may be available from archives. Audience re.1 Size of audience to religious broadcasts on BBC television
	Individual programmes	United Kingdom	Daily from 1951	[QRL.205]	6.5.1.4 - 1955 to 1959 Daily Survey of Population aged 16+; 1960 to 2 August 1981 Daily Survey of Population aged 5+; 3 August 1981 onwards metered sets and.1 Size of audience to religious broadcasts on Independent Television

Individual programme		United Kingdom	Daily from late 1950's	[QRL.202]	6.5.1.4 Population aged 4+. Results of daily survey now conducted by BARB. Audience reactions also available for selected programmes.
Number of Far East Broadcasting Association broadcasts	Language; time; frequency; area of individual broadcasts	United Kingdom originating	Half yearly from 1970	[QRL.213]	6.5.1.1

QUICK REFERENCE LIST KEY TO PUBLICATIONS

Reference	Author or Organisation	Title	Publisher	Frequency or Date	Remarks
[QRL.1]	Barrett, David B.	*World Christian Encyclopaedia*	Oxford University Press	1982	Intended to replace [QRL.3]
[QRL.2]	Brierley, Peter W.	*United Kingdom Christian Handbook (formerly United Kingdom Protestant Handbook)*	Evangelical Alliance, British and Foreign Bible Society and MARC Europe	Vol 1 1973, 1976, 1980 - Vol 2 1977 - Vol 3 1980 - Vol 4 1980 combined Volume 1982	
[QRL.3]	Coxhill and Grubb	*World Christian Handbook*	Lutterworth Press	1949, 1952, 1957, 1962, 1967 1984	Replaced by [QRL.1]
[QRL.4]	Currie, Gilbert and Horsley	*Churches and Church-Goers - Patterns of Church Growth in the British Isles from 1700*	Clarendon Press, Oxford	1977	
[QRL.5]	Foot, M.R.D. (Ed.)	*War and Society*	Elek Books Ltd	1973	
[QRL.6]	Gay, John D.	*Geography of Religion in England*	G Duckworth and Co Ltd	1971	
[QRL.7]	Gibbs, Rev. E.	*I Believe in Church Growth*	Hodder and Stoughton	1981	
[QRL.8]	Johnstone, P. J.	*Operation World*	Send The Light Trust	1978, 1980, 1983	
[QRL.9]	Wilson, Samuel (Ed.)	*Mission Handbook*	Missions Advanced Research and Communications Centre, Monrovia, California	Biennial	Available through MARC Europe

Ref	Organization	Publication	Publisher	Frequency	Notes
[QRL.10]	Baptist Missionary Society	*Annual Report*	Baptist Missionary Society	Annual	
[QRL.11]	Wycliffe Bible Translators	*Annual Report*	Wycliffe Bible Translators	Annual	
[QRL.12]	The General Assembly of Unitarian and Free Christian Churches	*Annual Report of the General Assembly*	Unitarian Headquarters	Annual	
[QRL.13]	General Register Office, Northern Ireland	*Annual Report of the Registrar General for Northern Ireland*	HMSO, Belfast	Annual	
[QRL.14]	General Register Office, Scotland	*Annual Report of the Registrar General for Scotland*	HMSO	Annual	
[QRL.15]	Representative Church Council of the Scottish Episcopal Church	*Annual Report of the Representative Church Council of the Scottish Episcopal Church*	Scottish Episcopal Church	Annual	
[QRL.16]	Holy See, Rome	*Annuario Pontiflo*	Holy See, Rome	Annual	Official world directory of the Catholic Church
[QRL.17]	Assemblies of God	*Assemblies of God in Great Britain and Ireland Yearbook and Constitutional Minutes*	Assemblies of God	Biennial	
[QRL.18]	Baptist Union of Great Britain and Ireland	*Baptist Union Annual Report*	Baptist Union of Great Britain and Ireland	Annual	
[QRL.19]	The Council of the Baptist Union of Great Britain and Ireland	*The Baptist Union Directory*	The Baptist Union of Great Britain and Ireland	Annual	
[QRL.20]	Baptist Union of Ireland	*Baptist Union of Ireland Assembly Yearbook*	Baptist Union of Ireland	Annual	
[QRL.21]	Baptist Union of Wales	*Baptist Union of Wales Diary and Handbook*	Baptist Union of Wales	Annual	

Reference	Author or Organisation	Title	Publisher	Frequency or Date	Remarks
[QRL.22]	Hill, Clifford	Black Churches - West Indian and African Sects in Britain	Community and Race Relations Unit of the British Council of Churches	1971	
[QRL.23]	Religious Society of Friends	Book of Meetings	Religious Society of Friends	Annual	
[QRL.24]	Whitaker	The Bookseller	J Whitaker and Son	Monthly	Statistics only published in the last month of every quarter and at the beginning of each year
[QRL.25]	Central Office of Information, London	Britain: An Official Handbook	HMSO	Annual	
[QRL.26]	The British Council of Churches	The British Council of Churches Handbook	The British Council of Churches	Annual	
[QRL.27]	The British Library	British National Bibliography	British Library, Bibliography Division	Weekly	
[QRL.28]	United Bible Societies	Bulletin: World Annual Report	United Bible Societies	Annual	
[QRL.29]	Independent Methodist Churches	Business Handbook of the Annual Meeting of Independent Methodist Churches	Independent Methodist Churches	Annual	

[QRL.30]	Business Statistics office	*Business Monitor PQ489: General Printing and Publishing*	HMSO	Quarterly	With effect from 1983 published as PQ4753 "Printing and Publishing of Books" and PQ4754
[QRL.31]	Individual Catholic Diocesan Offices	*Catholic Diocesan Directories and Yearbooks*	Diocesan Offices	Irregular	
[QRL.32]	Catholic Church in England and Wales	*Catholic Directory*	The Universe, Associated Catholic Publications Ltd	Annual	
[QRL.33]	Catholic Church in Scotland	*The Catholic Directory for Scotland*	Burns and Sons, Glasgow	Annual	
[QRL.34]	The Catholic Education Council in England and Wales	*Catholic Education - A Handbook*	The Catholic Education Council in England and Wales	Biennial	
[QRL.35]	Office of Population Censuses and Surveys	*Census of Population: Economic Activity Tables*	HMSO	Decennial 1831 onwards	Until 1961 referred to as Occupation Tables/Abstracts
[QRL.36]	General Register Office, Northern Ireland	*Census of Population: Religious Tables*	HMSO, Belfast	Decennial from 1861	
[QRL.37]	Church of Jesus Christ of Latter-Day Saints (Mormons)	*Church Almanac*	Deseret News, USA	Annual	
[QRL.38]	Central Board of Finance of the Church of England	*Church and State*	CIO Publishing	1970	
[QRL.39]	The Church Commissioners for England	*Church Commissioners' Reports and Accounts*	Church Commissioners	Annual	

Reference	Author or Organisation	Title	Publisher	Frequency or Date	Remarks
[QRL.40]	Representative Body of the Church in Wales	*Church in Wales Diocesan Handbooks*	Representative Body of the Church in Wales	Annual	
[QRL.41]	Individual Church of England Diocesan Offices	*Church of England Diocesan Yearbooks and Directories*	Diocesan Offices	Biennial or Annual	Each Diocese selects and publishes its own material
[QRL.42]	Central Board of Finance	*Church of England Yearbook*	CIO Publishing	Annual	Some data held on computer. From 1978 annual Statistical Supplement available from biennial census and samples
[QRL.43]	General Synod of the Church of Ireland	*Church of Ireland Directory*	General Synod of the Church of Ireland	Annual	
[QRL.44]	Church of Scotland	*The Church of Scotland Yearbook*	St Andrews Press, Edinburgh	Annual	
[QRL.45]	Churches of Christ in Great Britain and Ireland	*Churches of Christ Yearbook*	Churches of Christ in Great Britain and Ireland	Annual to 1980	
[QRL.46]	Church Missionary Society	*Church Missionary Society Directory*	Church Missionary Society	Annual	Replaces *Together in Mission*

[QRL.47]	Conference for World Mission	*Conference for World Mission Handbook*	Conference for World Mission	Annual
[QRL.48]	Congregational Union of Ireland	*Congregational Register*	Congregational Union of Ireland	Annual
[QRL.49]	The Congregational Federation	*The Congregational Yearbook*	The Congregational Federation	Annual
[QRL.50]	The Countess of Huntingdon's Connexion	*The Countess of Huntingdon's Connexion Annual Report*	The Countess of Huntingdon's Connexion	Annual
[QRL.51]	Echoes of Service	*Daily Prayer Report*	Echoes of Service	Annual
[QRL.52]	Moravian Church of Great Britain and Ireland	*Daily Watchwords*	Moravian Church of Great Britain and Ireland	Annual
[QRL.53]	Presbyterian Church in Ireland	*Directory and Statistics*	Presbyterian Church in Ireland	Annual
[QRL.54]	The General Assembly of Unitarian and Free Christian Churches	*Directory of the Unitarian and Free Christian Churches*	Unitarian Headquarters	Annual
[QRL.55]	Central Board of Finance of the Church of England	*Facts and Figures about the Church of England*	CIO Publishing	1959, 1962, 1965
[QRL.56]	Fellowship of the Churches of Christ in Great Britain and Ireland	*Fellowship of the Churches of Christ Yearbook*	Fellowship of the Churches of Christ in Great Britain and Ireland	Annual from 1981
[QRL.57]	The Fellowship of Independent Evangelical Churches	*FIEC Handbook*	The Fellowship of Independent Evangelical Churches	Biennial
[QRL.58]	Finnish Seamen's Mission	*Finnish Seamen's Mission Magazine*	Finnish Seamen's Mission	Annual
[QRL.59]	Not stated	*Free Church*	Crown House Publications	1970/71
[QRL.60]	Free Church Federal Council	*Free Church Federal Council Annual Report and Directory*	Free Church Federal Council	Annual

Reference	Author or Organisation	Title	Publisher	Frequency or Date	Remarks
[QRL.61]	Free Church of England	*Free Church of England Yearbook*	Free Church of England	Annual	Very little statistical information
[QRL.62]	Free Church of Scotland	*Free Church of Scotland Yearbook*	Free Church of Scotland	Annual	
[QRL.63]	Free Church of Scotland	*From the Frontiers*	Free Church of Scotland	Annual	
[QRL.64]	Birmingham Bible Institute	*Gateway*	Birmingham Bible Institute	Twice yearly	Magazine
[QRL.65]	British Army	*General Annual Return of the Army*	Ministry of Defence	Annual from 1860 to 1937	Available from Stats (M) 1, Ministry of Defence
[QRL.66]	The General Conference of the New Church	*The General Conference of the New Church Yearbook*	The General Conference of the New Church	Annual	
[QRL.67]	Greek Orthodox Church	*Greek Orthodox Archdiocese Yearbook*	Greek Orthodox Arch diocese, London	Annual	Information mostly in Greek
[QRL.68]	National Strict Baptist Assembly	*Handbook of the Metropolitan Association of Strict Baptist Churches*	National Strict Baptist Churches	Annual until 1980	Assembly dissolved in 1981, replaced by Grace Baptist Assembly
[QRL.69]	United Free Church of Scotland	*Handbook of the United Free Church of Scotland*	United Free Church of Scotland	Annual	
[QRL.70]	Evangelical Movement of Wales	*Into All the World-Missionaries from Wales Report*	Evangelical Movement of Wales	1970,1973	

[QRL.71]	Catholic Church in Ireland	*Irish Catholic Directory*	The Universe, Associated Catholic Publications Ltd	Annual	
[QRL.72]	The Irish Missionary Union	*Irish Missionary Personnel Around the World*	The Irish Missionary Union	1972	
[QRL.73]	Jehovah's Witnesses	*Jehovah's Witnesses Yearbook*	Watch Tower Bible and Tract Society of Pensylvania and the Watchtower Bible and Tract Society of New York	Annual	Data also given in January issue of *The Watchtower*
[QRL.74]	Church of the Nazarene	*Journals of the Proceedings of the Annual Assembly of the British Isles, North and South Districts*	Church of the Nazarene	Annual	
[QRL.75]	Congregational Union of Scotland	*Manual of the Congregational Union of Scotland*	Congregational Union of Scotland	Annual	
[QRL.76]	Office of Population Censuses and Surveys	*Marriage and Divorce Statistics*	HMSO	Annual	
[QRL.77]	Methodist Church in Great Britain	*Minutes and Yearbook of the Methodist Conference*	Methodist Church in Great Britain	Annual	Summary data only published every three years but majority collected and available annually. Data held on computer
[QRL.78]	Methodist Church in Ireland	*Minutes of the Annual Conference*	Methodist Church in Ireland	Annual	

Reference	Author or Organisation	Title	Publisher	Frequency or Date	Remarks
[QRL.79]	Synod of the Non-Subscribing Presbyterian Church of Ireland	*Minutes of the Annual Meeting*	Synod of the Non-Subscribing Presbyterian Church of Ireland	Annual	
[QRL.80]	Synod of the Reformed Presbyterian Church of Ireland	*Minutes of the Annual Meeting*	Synod of the Reformed Presbyterian Church of Ireland	Annual	
[QRL.81]	Reformed Presbyterian Church of Scotland	*Minutes of the Synod*	Reformed Presbyterian Church of Scotland	Annual	
[QRL.82]	Roberts, David Mc. (Ed.)	*Modern Scottish Catholicism 1878-1978*	Scottish Catholic Historical Association	1979	
[QRL.83]	Overseas Missionary Fellowship	*OMF Prayer Directory*	OMF Publications	Annual	
[QRL.84]	Roman Catholic Missionary Education Centre	*Our Missionaries*	Roman Catholic Missionary Education Centre	Annual from 1979	
[QRL.85]	The Cremation Society of Great Britain and the International Cremation Federation	*Pharos*	The Cremation Society of Great Britain and the International Cremation Federation	Quarterly	
[QRL.86]	Central Statistical Office	*Population Trends*	HMSO	Quarterly	
[QRL.87]	World Evangelisation Crusade	*Praying Always*	World Evangelisation Crusade	Biennial	
[QRL.88]	Presbyterian Church of Wales	*Presbyterian Church of Wales Yearbook*	Presbyterian Church of Wales	Annual	

[QRL.89]	Free Church of Scotland	*The Principal Acts of Assembly with Minutes and Reports*	Free Church of Scotland	Annual
[QRL.90]	United Society for the Propagation of the Gospel	*Proceedings of the Committees of the Council*	United Society for the Propagation of the Gospel	Quarterly
[QRL.91]	Religious Society of Friends	*Quaker Work - Annual Report*	Religious Society of Friends	Annual
[QRL.92]	Religious Society of Friends	*The Quaker Schools*	Religious Society of Friends	Occasional
[QRL.93]	Whitakers	*Religious Books in Print*	J Whitaker and Son	1974
[QRL.94]	Scripture Gift Mission	*Report of Council*	Scripture Gift Mission	Annual
[QRL.95]	Church of Scotland	*Report of the General Assembly of the Church of Scotland*	Church of Scotland	Annual
[QRL.96]	Central Board of Finance and the Church Commissioners	*Report on the Finances of the Church of England*	CIO Publishing	Biennial	*1978: A Resourceful Church? - 1980: A Giving Church? - 1982: A Responding Church ?*
[QRL.97]	Home Office	*Report on the Work of the Prison Department*	HMSO	Annual
[QRL.98]	Free Presbyterian Church of Scotland	*Reports of Standing Committees of Synod and Accounts*	Free Presbyterian Church of Scotland	Annual
[QRL.99]	Salvation Army	*The Salvation Army Handbook*	Salvationist Publishing and Supplies Ltd	Annual
[QRL.100]	Council of the Baptist Union of Scotland	*The Scottish Baptist Yearbook*	Council of the Baptist Union of Scotland	Annual
[QRL.101]	Scottish Education Department	*Scottish Education Statistics*	HMSO	Annual

Reference	Author or Organisation	Title	Publisher	Frequency or Date	Remarks
[QRL.102]	General Conference of Seventh-Day Adventists	*Seventh-Day Adventists Yearbook*	Review and Herald Publishing Association	Annual	
[QRL.103]	The Council of the Baptist Union of Great Britain and Ireland	*Signs of Hope*	The Baptist Union of Great Britain and Ireland	1979	
[QRL.104]	Central Statistical Office	*Social Trends*	HMSO	Annual	
[QRL.105]	Department of Education and Science	*Statistics of Education Volume 1: Schools*	HMSO	Annual until 1979	No longer published but data available on request to DES, Elizabeth House, 39 York Road, SE1 7PH
[QRL.106]	United Free Church of Scotland	*United Free Church of Scotland Volume of Reports*	United Free Church of Scotland	Annual	
[QRL.107]	The United Reformed Church in England and Wales	*The United Reformed Church Yearbook*	The United Reformed Church in England and Wales	Annual from 1973	
[QRL.108]	Wesleyan Reform Union	*Wesleyan Reform Union Yearbook*	Wesleyan Reform Church House	Annual	
[QRL.109]	The Church of Scientology	*What is Scientology?*	Church of Scientology of California	Annual from 1950	
[QRL.110]	Whitaker	*Whitaker's Almanack*	J Whitaker and Son	Annual	

| [QRL.111] | Representative Church Council of the Scottish Episcopal Church | Yearbook and Directory of the Scottish Episcopal Church | Scottish Episcopal Church | Annual | Data published until 1976 only but figures from 1975 to current time available on request |

SOURCE ADDRESSES

[QRL.200] **Apostolic Church**
Off Bryncwar Road
Penygroes
Llanelli
Dyfed SA14 7PA

[QRL.201] **Assemblies of God**
106-114 Talbot Street
Nottingham NG1 5GH

[QRL.202] **Audience Research Department IBA**
70, Brompton Road
London SW3

[QRL.203] **BMMF International (UK)**
Whitfield House
186, Kennington Park Road
London SE11 4BT

[QRL.204] **Church of Jesus Christ of Latter-Day Saints**
Church Offices
751, Warwick Road
Solihull
West Midlands B91 3DQ

[QRL.205] **Broadcasting Research Dept. BBC**
Broadcasting House
London W1A 1AA

[QRL.206] **Campus Crusade for Christ**
103, Friar Street
Reading
Berks RG1 1EP

[QRL.207] **Capernwray Bible School**
Capernwray Hall
Carnforth
Lancs LA6 1AG

[QRL.208] **Catholic Education Commission**
43, Greenhill Road
Rutherglen
Glasgow
Strathclyde G73 2SW

[QRL.209] **Central Board of Finance of the Church of England**
Church House
Dean's Yard
Westminster
London SW1P 3NZ

[QRL.210] **Countess of Huntingdon's Connexion**
Huntingdon Hall
85, De la Warr Road
East Grinstead
West Sussex RH19 3BS

[QRL.211] **Elim Bible College**
Grenehurst Park
Capel
Dorking
Surrey RH5 5JE

[QRL.212] **Elim Pentecostal Church**
PO Box 38
Cheltenham
Glos GL50 3HN

[QRL.213] **Far East Broadcasting Association**
45, High Street
Addlestone
Weybridge
Surrey KT15 1TJ

[QRL.214] **Fellowship of Independent Evangelical Churches**
136, Rosendale Road
London SE21 8LG

[QRL.215] **French Protestant Church of London**
8/9 Soho Square
London W1V 5DD

[QRL.216] **General Synod of the Church of Ireland**
Church of Ireland House
Church Avenue
Rathmines,
Dublin 6

[QRL.217] **Liberal Catholic Church**
Drayton House
30, Gordon Street
London WC1H 0AN

[QRL.218] **London Bible College**
Green Lane
Northwood
Middlesex HA6 2UW

[QRL.219] **Methodist Church, Education and Youth Division**
2, Chapter House
Pages Lane
London N10 1PR

[QRL.220] **Methodist Church, Ministries Division**
1, Central Buildings
Westminster
London SW1H 9NH

[QRL.221] **Methodist Church, Property Division**
Central Buildings
Oldham Street
Manchester M1 1JQ

[QRL.222] **Ministry of Defence**
Northumberland House
Northumberland Avenue
London WC2N 5BP

[QRL.223] **Moravian Church in Great Britain and Ireland**
Moravian Church House
5, Muswell Hill
London N10 3TJ

[QRL.224] **The Navigators**
Tregaron House
27, High Street
New Malden
Surrey KT3 4BY

[QRL.225] **Non-Subscribing Presbyterian Church of Ireland**
Clerk to the General Synod
21, Cough Moss Park
Camy Duff
Belfast BT8 8PD

[QRL.226] **Old Baptist Union**
The Christian Centre
77-79 Reginald Street
Luton
Beds LU2 7RB

[QRL.227] **Old Roman Catholic Church**
Priory of Our Lady of Port-Royal
10, Barnmead Road
Beckenham
Kent BH3 1JE

[QRL.228] **Religious Society of Friends**
Friends House
Euston Road
London NW1 2BJ

[QRL.229] **Russian Orthodox Church in Exile**
Church House
14, St Dunstan's Road
London W6 8RB

[QRL.230] **Salvation Army**
International Headquarters
PO Box 249
101 Queen Victoria Street
London EC4P 4EP

[QRL.231] **Scottish Episcopal Church** (Address missing)

[QRL.232] **Selly Oak Colleges**
Central House
Birmingham B29 6LQ

[QRL.233] **Serbian Orthodox Church**
89, Lancaster Road
London W11 1QQ

[QRL.234] **Seventh-Day Adventist Church**
Stanborough Park
Watford
Herts WD2 6JP

[QRL.235] **Swedish Church**
6, Harcourt Street
London W1H 2BD

[QRL.236] **Unification Church**
43/44 Lancaster Gate
London W2 3NA

[QRL.237] **Union of Welsh Independents**
Ty John Penry
11, St Helen's Road
Swansea
West Glamorgan SA1 4AL

[QRL.238] **United Reformed Church**
Church Life Department
86, Tavistock Place
London WC1H 9RT

[QRL.239] **United Society for the Propagation of the Gospels**
15, Tufton Street
London SW1P 3QQ

[QRL.240] **Universities and Colleges Christian Fellowship**
38, De Montfort Street
Leicester LE1 7GP

[QRL.241] **Welsh Office**
Gwydyr House
Whitehall
London SW1

[QRL.242] **Woodward Corporation/The Allied Schools**
1, The Sanctuary
London SW1P 3JT

DIRECTORIES AND SIMILAR PUBLICATIONS

The works referenced here contain lists from which counts may be made of such items as the number of parishes, ministers, theological colleges, missionaries, church buildings, church schools, religious publications and similar matters for particular sects. As they do not contain statistical material of direct interest they have not been included in the QRL. Note that some publications covered by the QRL, and hence listed in the QRL Key to Publications, may also contain individual lists, and in some cases this has been noted in the 'Remarks' column of the QRL.

No.	Title	Publisher	Date	Remarks
No. 1	*Annual Report & Directory*	The Mission to Seamen	Annual	
No. 2	*The Apostolic Church Yearbook*	Apostolic Church	Biennial	
No. 3	*The Christian Science Journal*	The Christian Science Publishing Society, Boston, USA	Monthly	
No. 4	*Crockford's Clerical Directory*	Oxford University Press	1858 to 1983 Biennial/ Triennial in recent years	
No. 5	*Directory of Chinese Churches Fellowship in the UK and Europe*	Chinese Overseas Christian Mission	Biennial	
No. 6	*Directory of the Evangelical Fellowship of Congregational Churches*	EFCC	Biennial	
No. 7	*Directory of Religious Orders, Congregations and Societies of Great Britain & Ireland*	John S. Burns & Sons, Glasgow	Biennial	
No. 8	*Elim Pentecostal Church Yearbook*	Elim Pentecostal Church	Annual from 1948	

No.	Title	Publisher	Date	Remarks
No. 9	*The Free Presbyterian Magazine*	Synod Committee of the Free Presbyterian Church of Scotland	Monthly	
No. 10	*Grace Magazine Directory of Churches*	Grace Baptist Assembly	Annual from 1981	
No. 11	*Handbook of the Afro-West Indian United Council of Churches*	Centre for Caribbean Studies	Annual	
No. 12	*Official Handbook of the Presbyterian Church of England*	Presbyterian Church of England	Annual to 1972	
No. 13	*Operation Mobilisation Worldwide Prayer Directory*	Operation Mobilisation	Annual from 1982	
No. 14	*Prayer Manual*	Methodist Church Overseas Division	Annual	
No. 15	*Region Handbooks*	Independent Schools Information Service	Annual	Summary statistics in "Independent Schools- The Facts".
No. 16	*Religious Books and Serials in Print*	R R Bowker Company	Biennial	
No. 17	*The Spiritualists' National Union Diary*	The Spiritualists' National Union	1972 Annual	
No. 18	*Turning the World Upside Down* ·	Echoes of Service	1972	
No. 19	*Yearbook*	Church of Scotland Overseas Council	Annual	
No. 20	*Yearbook of the Union of Welsh Independents*	Union of Welsh Independents	Annual	

BIBLIOGRAPHY

[B.1] Evans, Byron and Peter W. Brierley. *Prospects for Wales* Tonbridge: MARC Europe, London: Bible Society, 1983

[B.2] Facey, Roy A. (Ed.) *International Church Index (doctrinal)*. Plymouth, Index Publications, 1981

[B.3] Gerloff, Roswith. *Directory of Black Churches in Britain* (to be published)

[B.4] Gray, John D. 'Religious bias in British education', in Warren-Piper, D. (Ed.) *Is Higher Education Fair?*, SHRE, Guildford, 1981

[B.5] Highet, John *The Scottish Churches*. Skeffington, 1960

[B.6] Thurman, Joyce V. *New Wineskins: A Study of the House Church Movement*, unpublished MA thesis, University of Birmingham

[B.7] Great Britain: General Register Office, *The Census of Great Britain 1851: Religious Worship in England and Wales*, HMSO.

[B.8] Nationwide Initiative in Evangelism. *Prospects for the Eighties* volume 1. Bible Society, 1980. Nationwide Initiative in Evangelism. *Prospects for the Eighties* volume 2. Bible Society, 1983.

[B.9] *Counting to some Purposes*, Methodist Church Home Division, 1979

[B.10] *Stand Up and Be Counted*, British Council of Churches Committee on Mission, September 1972, (duplicated pamphlet)

SUBJECT INDEX

Computers, 10
Confirmation data, 2.2; 2.7; 4.2.1.2; 4.2.3.2;
    4.2.3.4; 4.2.4.3; 6.2.4.2
Congregational Church, 4.1.1.2; 4.2.4.4;
    4.3.1.4
Congregational Churches, Evangical
    Fellowship of, 4.2.4.4; 5.1.4
Congregational districts, 2.6; 4.1.3.1
Congregational Federation, 4.2.4.4; 6.1.1.1
Congregations, 4.1.3.2; 7.1.3; 7.1.4; 8.1.2; 10
Contact addresses, 1.2; 1.5
Convents, 2.2; 2.6
Convents - see religious communities,
Costs, Staff, 6.1.4.2

Data collectors, Clergy as, 2.1; 2.4; 4.1.1.5;
    4.1.3.1
Data processing, 10
Data source, Independent, 10
Deacons, 2.5
Death statistics, 9.1.1
Deaths, Clergy, 4.4.5
Denominational mergers, 4.2.4.4
Department of Education and Science,
    5.2.1.2; 5.2.2.4; 5.2.2.5
Dioceses, 2.6; 5.1.3.2
District Councils, Spiritualist, 2.6; 8.1.3
Districts, Congregational, 2.6; 4.1.3.1
Doctrinal outlines, 1.2

Easter services, 2.4; 4.2.2.2; 4.3.2.2; 4.3.2.3
Ecclesias, 8.1.3
Educational establishments, 2.6; 4.4.1.4;
    4.5.5; 5.3
Electoral Register, 4.1.3.2
Electoral Roll, 2.2; 4.1.1.2; 4.2.1.1; 4.2.2.2;
    4.2.2.4; 4.2.3.2
Episcopal church, 1.2
Episcopal Church, Scottish, 5.1.5.1; 6.1.1.1;
    6.1.1.3
Epworth Press, 6.4.1.1
Ethiopia, 4.6.4
Evangical Fellowship of Congregational
    Churches, 4.2.4.4; 5.1.4

Faith, Profession of, 2.2; 4.2.1.1; 4.2.3.3;
    7.1.4
Far East Broadcasting Association, 6.5.1.1
Feast days, 4.3.2.3
Fellowship of the Churches of Christ, 4.2.4.4
Financial data, 1.3; 4.4.5; 6.1; 6.3.1.2;
    6.3.1.3; 6.3.3.1; 9.1.1; 9.1.2
Free churches, 1.2; 2.2; 4.2.1.1; 4.2.2.2;
    4.2.2.3; 4.2.3.4; 4.3.2.1; 4.3.2.2; 4.3.3.1;
    4.4.2; 4.4.3.2; 4.5.3.2; 6.1.2.2; 6.2.2.4
Funerals, 1.3; 2.7; 4.3.1.3; 6.2.3.3

Geographical areas, 4.1.1.4; 4.1.2.3; 5.1.2.2;
    5.1.2.3; 7.1.2; 8.1.2
Government sources, 4.3.1.2; 5.1.1.2; 6.2.3.1

Holy Communion, 4.3.1.3
Homes, Old peoples, 6.3.2.3
Hospitals, 4.1.1.3; 4.4.1.4
House Church movement, 1.4; 4.3.2.6;
    5.1.3.1

IBA, 6.5.1.3; 6.5.1.4
Independent data source, 10
Independent Schools Information Service,
    5.2.1.2
Iran, 4.6.4
Ireland, Baptist Union of, 5.1.5.1
Ireland, Presbyterian Church in, 5.1.3.1;
    6.1.1.1
Ireland, Reformed Presbyterian Church of,
    4.3.2.1

Jehovah's Witnesses, 7.1.1; 7.1.2; 7.1.3; 7.1.4;
    8.1.2; 8.1.4; 9.1.4
Jesus Christ, 1.2
Jews, 6.2.1.4

Lay staff, 2.5; 4.4.1.1; 4.4.3.3; 4.4.4.2; 4.5.1.1
LELLA Productions, 6.5.1.2
Local authorities, 5.1.1.2; 10
Local Education authorities, 5.2.3.1
Lord's Supper - see communicant data,

Manpower, 1.3; 2.5; 4.3.5.2; 4.4; 5.3.4;
    6.1.4.2; 7.1.3; 7.1.4
Manpower and training, 2.6; 4.5; 4.6.5.2
Marriages, 1.3; 2.7; 6.2.1.4; 6.2.1.5; 9.1.1;
    9.1.2; 10
Marriages, Second, 6.2.2.4
Mass - see communicant data,
Meetings, Religious, 4.3.5
Members, Church, 1.3; 2.1; 2.2; 4.2; 6.2.2.1;
    6.2.2.2; 7.1.1; 7.1.2; 7.1.3; 7.1.4; 7.1.5; 10
Mergers, Denominational, 4.2.4.4
Methodist Church, 2.3; 4.1.1.2; 4.1.3.1;
    4.2.3.3; 4.2.3.4; 4.2.4.2; 4.3.1.4; 4.3.2.1;
    4.3.4.1; 4.5.1.2; 4.6.3.1; 5.1.5.1; 5.2.2.1;
    6.1.1.3; 6.4.1.1
Methodist Church of Wales, 4.2.4.4
Methodist circuits, 2.6; 5.1.3.2
Methodologies, 1.1; 2.1; 4.1.2.2; 4.1.2.4;
    4.2.4.3; 4.5.4.1; 4.5.4.2; 10
Ministry of Defence, 7.1.1
Mission halls, 2.6; 5.1
Missionaries in UK, 4.6.1.6; 7.1.1
Missionary activity, 1.5; 4.6; 6.3.3.1; 7.1.3

34: NON-RECURRENT CHRISTIAN DATA

Dr CLIVE DOUGLAS FIELD

John Rylands University Library, Manchester

REFERENCE DATE OF SOURCES REVIEWED

This review is believed to represent the position, broadly speaking, as it obtained during the period April-June 1983. The addendum has been inserted at the proof reading stage, March-May 1984, February-April 1985 and January-February 1986, taking account, as far as possible, of any major changes in the situation.

ACKNOWLEDGEMENTS

Financially, I am deeply indebted to the Economic and Social Research Council not only for co-sponsoring the actual production of this review in 1981-85 but also for the award of a postgraduate studentship in 1971-74 and of a post-doctoral fellowship in 1975-77 during which, as it has turned out, much essential preparatory work was undertaken. It is also a pleasure to express my thanks to the British Academy which made an allocation from its Small Grants Research Fund in the Humanities during 1979-80 so that I could explore the religious potential of opinion poll data.

On a more personal level, I am grateful to Pat Thompson and Dr John Walsh of the University of Oxford for steering a novice researcher in the right direction a decade or more ago; to Dr Wallis Taylor, late of the University of Manchester, for encouraging me to embark upon this work; to Emeritus Professor Derek Maunder of the University of Exeter who so readily agreed to my suggestion that a volume on the sources of religious statistics be included in this series and who has proved a most skilful and patient editor ever since; to the panel of experts who, at a seminar held in London in December 1982, subjected the first draft of my text to such constructive criticism; to Dr Michael Pegg and Dr Dorothy Clayton, colleagues at the John Rylands University Library of Manchester, for much needed stimulus and practical assistance; and to the several hundred individuals, far too numerous to mention by name, who, since 1975, have cheerfully answered my queries and positively responded to my requests for relevant documentation.

In the final analysis, as is the case with so many authors, it has only been through the unwavering support of my family that I have succeeded in staying the full course. My parents took a tremendous interest in this enterprise from the outset and helped its progress in every way that they could; sadly, my mother has not lived to see the finished product. Verena and James, for their part, have accepted, entirely without question, the ever increasing inroads of scholarship on our domestic life. For their enthusiasm, self-sacrifice and involvement no words of praise or appreciation could ever be sufficient.

ADDENDUM ON RECENT DEVELOPMENTS

This addendum takes account of major new data sources which have been released, as well as of a few older ones which have come to light, between the spring of 1983 and the late autumn of 1985. In format, it mirrors exactly the section order of the main text, although, for the sake of speed and brevity, each survey is mentioned once only (under the heading which has seemed most appropriate), and no supplementary QRL has been compiled. Additional publication references are gathered together in a separate alphabetical list at the end; they are serially numbered and prefixed with the letter 'A' in order to distinguish them from standard 'QRL' and 'B' entries.

2.1.1. Area studies, cross-national surveys: 1603 census.
An interim listing of the primary documentation for this census, recently published by D.M. Palliser and L.J. Jones [A.47], indicates that diocesan summaries of the results may be found in Bodleian Library, Lincoln College Ms. (e) Lat.124 as well as in British Library, Harleian Ms.280, and that detailed returns survive for part or all of the sees of Bangor, Chichester, Gloucester, Lincoln, Norwich, Winchester and York.

2.1.2. Area studies, cross-national surveys: Compton census, 1676
David Edwards [A.14] has compared the Compton census returns and the 1662-64 hearth tax assessments for Derbyshire in an attempt to determine whether the 1676 basic population figures represented adult males, all adults or total inhabitants, whilst Christopher Buckingham [A.11] has examined the two hundred and twenty extant parochial schedules for the Diocese of Canterbury and concluded that 'incumbents were generally far more cognisant of the various dissenting sects than of popish recusants or persons suspected of such recusancy'.

2.1.4. Area studies, cross-national surveys: opinion polls
Analysis of the data gathered in the EVSSG study, the United Kingdom fieldwork for which was conducted in March 1981, is now entering its final phase. Key religious statistics for Great Britain and eight other countries have already been included in the overall European summary by Jean Stoetzel [A.53], whilst the main British report is scheduled for publication by Macmillan during 1985. As yet, however, there are still no plans for a separate account of the Northern Ireland material.

A major poll on the subject of 'Standards in life' was carried out by the Harris Research Centre (JN 48403) on behalf of London Weekend Television's 'Credo' programme between 30 March and 4 April 1984. The quota sample of 820 adult Britons were asked a total of forty-three questions of which eighteen are immediately relevant to the scope of this review; these chiefly relate to self-assessed religiosity, belief in God, the divinity of Christ, judgement after death, private prayer, denominational affiliation, attendance at public worship, the influence of religion over the nation, the contribution of faith in shaping a moral outlook, the involvement of the Church in politics, disestablishment, contact with the local clergy and perception of the most important task which they had to fulfil. Preliminary findings have appeared in [QRL.47], 1 June 1984, [QRL.5O], 1 June 1984, [QRL.119], 2 June 1984 and [QRL.123], 28 May 1984.

A study of Britain '20 years on' was undertaken by Gallup (JN S.2528), with funding from Abbey Life, in connection with the Television South feature series of that name transmitted during the summer of 1985. Of the one hundred questions put to a national cross-section of 909 people aged sixteen and over, five related to perceived religiosity, belief in God, a soul, sin, the Devil, life after death, heaven, hell, reincarnation, astrology and transcendental meditation, confessional allegiance, frequency of church-going, the role of organised religion in moulding the country's future, Sunday observance, and the trustworthiness of clergymen. All enquiries regarding access to the data should be directed to TVS Production, Television Centre, Southampton, SO9 5HZ.

2.2.1. Area studies, England: national surveys

A second volume of *Prospects for the Eighties*, based upon the census of English places of worship undertaken by the NIE in November 1979 (2.2.1.5- 2.2.1.9), was published in September 1983 [A.80]. Representing the joint effort of Nancy Nason-Clark, who systematically re-examined the 14,725 original questionnaires in 1981-82, and of Peter Brierley, who rearranged and edited her findings into their final form, the core of the work (fifty out of eighty-one pages) consists of a series of tables and histograms illustrating, both for England as a whole and for each of its forty-eight counties, averages and frequency distributions for adult congregational size with disaggregations by the occurrence or absence of growth between 1975 and 1979 as well as by major ecclesiastical types; other features comprise two introductory articles offering a synoptic interpretation of the statistics of attendance and midweek meetings from a sociological and evangelistic perspective and an assessment of their implications for future research and outreach, a miscellany of methodological apparatus, seven maps indicating the geographical spread of 'the unchurched' and the administrative boundaries adopted by the Anglican, Methodist, Baptist, United Reformed and Roman Catholic denominations, and a breakdown of the Greater London figures from volume one by inner and outer borough areas. The report's usefulness as a quantitative tool is severely limited by imperfections in the data set from which it has been compiled (arising both from a low initial response rate and from the inferior quality of such information as was supplied) and by deficiencies in the actual process of secondary analysis (including the application of several contentious or obscure mathematical procedures and the making of extravagant or misleading deductions from the returns) - criticisms which the present author has developed at greater length in a book review that appeared in the Spring 1984 issue of *Church Growth Digest*.

The most comprehensive religious opinion poll to have been undertaken across England alone since December 1963-January 1964 (2.2.1.4) was conducted by Gallup (JN S.2220) in October-November 1982 on behalf of the BS with the intention of taking the spiritual pulse of the English people before the commencement of major evangelistic initiatives by Luis Palau in London in 1983 and by Billy Graham in the provinces in 1984. A quota sample of 1,136 adults aged sixteen and over were interviewed by means of an unusually sophisticated research instrument comprising twenty-nine individual questions and scales designed to measure, amongst other things, the importance of God in their lives, their ownership, use and evaluation of the Bible, denominational affiliation, attendance at public worship both for normal services as well as at Christmas and Easter, ecclesiastical office-holding, and attitudes towards the Church. The computer tabulations for this study [A.65] extend to 239 pages but Jan Harrison [A.27] has prepared a most competent digest of the principal results, highlighting age, sex, social class, regional, urban/rural and religious differences, which, in turn, has attracted considerable coverage and comment in the national press [QRL.44], 21 July 1983; [QRL.50], 15 July 1983; [QRL.51], 15 July 1983; [QRL.53], 8 July 1983; [QRL.55], 8 July 1983; [QRL.57], 8 July 1983; [QRL.67], 8 July 1983; [QRL.72], 14 July 1983; [QRL.123], 8 July 1983.

2.2.2. Area studies, England: community studies

Paul Beasley-Murray [A.3] has now published a brief account of the more than two thousand three hundred replies obtained to the religious questionnaire administered to people in the Altrincham area as part of the 'Faith for to-day' mission held during the first half of September 1977 (2.2.2.15).

Important documentation has been released relating to the interviews with a random sample of 1,630 electors which formed part of the 'Conventional religion and common religion in Leeds' project (2.2.2.18). This includes a full description of the methodology and conduct of the fieldwork in September-October 1982 [A.74] and a copy of the complex 85 page, 183 question survey instrument annotated with a breakdown of the replies received both in terms of actual numbers and percentages [A.36]. Amongst the topics covered in the enquiry were self-assessed spirituality, religious experience, belief in, and images of, God, Jesus Christ, life after death and the paranormal, prayer, religious television programmes, confessional affiliation, church attendance, and the Pope's visit to Britain. The data set is preserved at the ESRC DA as SN 1988.

Nigel Sharp has summarised the results obtained from two recent studies carried out in rural and urban districts of four western counties on behalf of the Swindon based *Evening Advertiser* and BBC Radio Bristol. The first involved personal interviews with 'a proper cross section' of 1,800 men and women aged sixteen to seventy-five who had not attended public worship more than three times a year during the previous quinquennium; they were asked a total of thirteen questions concerning belief in God, Jesus, an afterlife and the divine inspiration of the Bible, denominational preference, reasons for not frequenting services, and attitudes towards the Church [A.49]. The sample recruited for the second investigation comprised 800 regular worshippers who aired their thoughts about the relevance of the Gospel message in the contemporary world, the causes of organised religion's failure and the possible means of its revival, ecumenism, ecclesiastical entanglement in political or trade union affairs, the role of the clergy, liturgical change, and the path to Christian discipleship [A.50].

An unpublished analysis of opinions concerning God and the Church expressed by 1,697 shoppers and other passers-by interviewed at Exeter Guildhall Centre between 8 and 11 June 1983 may be obtained from Ian Marlow, 40 Oxford Road, St. James, Exeter, EX4 6QX.

A socio-religious survey of the inhabitants of the Sea Mills estate in Bristol was undertaken by an ecumenical team between 13 and 24 June 1983. Contact was established with 711 or 34.5% of the 2,063 households, and a brief questionnaire (including four items relating to God and the work of the local churches) was completed by 651 or 15.0% of the 4,347 adult residents. Only 33.0$ of the 528 respondents whose sex is known were men, a figure which is 13.1% below the one recorded at the 1981 civil census and which clearly reflects the fact that all the visits were carried out during the daytime. Data from the enquiry have not been published but are available upon application to K.R. Barrett, 98 Greystoke Avenue, Southmead, Bristol, BS1O 6AH.

Another exercise in doorstep evangelism at Buckhurst Hill, Essex between June and September 1983 has resulted in 2,007 people (41% male and 59% female) giving information about nine aspects of their spiritual condition. Some statistics have been quoted in [QRL.44], 7 June 1984, whilst full particulars may be requested from the minister of the local Baptist Church in Palmerston Road whose members organised the research.

2.3.1. Area studies, Wales: national surveys

Replies to the questions on religious affiliation and worship which were included in the 'Welsh Election Study' of May-September 1979 (see the QRL for methodological details) have been tabulated in [A.2].

A sixty-three page report on the census of membership and attendance of Wales's 5,772 churches, undertaken by the BS on behalf of WfC in May 1982 (2.3.1.6), was published, in separate English and Welsh text editions, in August 1983 [A.8]. Based upon an overall response rate of 70%, ranging from 55% in South Glamorgan to 82% in Dyfed and from 36% with the Christian Brethren to 103% with the Methodists (whose returns were augmented from central administrative records), the following spread of information is presented, through a combination of tables, histograms and pie diagrams, in absolute number (No) or percentage (%) form and with disaggregations by county (Co), seven major denominational groupings (De), the incidence of growth from 1978 to 1982 (Gr) and language of worship (La) as indicated in Table 2.3.1

Also included in the booklet are an indispensable essay by Peter Brierley describing the methodology of the survey and thirteen other brief articles, of variable but generally indifferent quality, commenting upon the results from

Table 2.3.1

Data	Form	Year	Breakdown
Ministers	No	1982	Co, De
Churches	No	1982	Co, De
Churches with midweek meetings	%	1982	Co, De
Time of service	%	1982	Co, De
Language of Service	%	1982	Co, De
Members	No	1978, 1982	Co, De, La
Membership change	%	1978-82	Co, De, La
Members in adult population	%	1982	Co, De
Child attenders	No	1978, 1982	Co, De, La
Change in child attenders	%	1978-82	Co, De, La
Children under 15 attending Sunday School	%	1982	De
Adult attenders	No	1978, 1982	Co, De, La
Change in adult attenders	%	1978-82	Co, De, La
Adult attenders in adult population	%	1982	Co, De
Adult attenders by language of service	%	1982	Co
Adults attending two services	%	1982	Co, De
Age/sex of church attenders	%	1982	Co, De
Growing churches	%	1978-82	Co, De, La
Adult attenders per church: frequency distribution	%	1982	Co, De, Gr
Adult attenders per church: average	No	1982	Co, De, Gr

particular geographical, demographic and ecclesiastical perspectives. The data set has been computerised, so, subject to the guarantees on confidentiality which were given to individual congregations, it is to be hoped that further analysis of the findings may be possible in due course; all enquiries should be directed in the first instance to MARC Europe, Cosmos House, 6 Homesdale Road, Bromley, BR2 9EX.

2.4.1. Area studies, Scotland: national surveys

Two additional opinion polls (2.4.1.7) require to be noted. The first, conducted by RSL (JN J.5342) at the request of the Royal Commission on Local Government in September-October 1967, obtained information on religious organisation membership and churchgoing from a random sample of 1,446 Scots aged twenty-one and above [A.71]. The second, jointly sponsored by the BBC and the *Sunday Standard* and carried out by System Three (JN SOS.283) in February-March 1983, put seventeen relevant questions to a cross-section of 1,044 Scottish adults of fifteen and over; amongst the topics covered were belief in God, Jesus and an afterlife, denominational affiliation, the most recent attendance at public worship other than for a rite of passage and the amount which was contributed to the collection on that occasion, the extent to which Scotland could be regarded as a Christian country, ecumenical co-operation, Roman Catholic rules on interfaith marriage, the provision of ecclesiastical weddings for divorcees, the involvement of the Church in socio-political issues, religious education in state schools, and the role of the clergy within the local community [A.61] [A.64].

2.5.1. *Area studies, Northern Ireland: national surveys*

Further analysis of two of the major sources mentioned in paragraph 2.5.1.1, the surveys of 2,416 males aged eighteen to sixty-four in August 1973-July 1974 and of 1,277 electors in June-November 1978, has been published by Ian McAllister [A.38] and Edward Moxon-Browne [A.43] respectively. The latter's work is particularly notable, containing detailed accounts of the data on self-assessed spirituality, confessional allegiance, churchgoing and the importance of religion in the lives of Ulster's people, of the responses to the various Likert and other measures of socio-political attitudes disaggregated by denomination, and of interviewers' perceptions of the relative difficulty and/or hesitation displayed by informants in answering questions about religion, class and politics.

2.5.2. *Area studies, Northern Ireland: community studies*

Research undertaken by John Hickey [A.28] [B.170] in a small country town in the northern part of the province during the course of 1977 involved interviews with a random sample of 297 adults on a wide range of issues including several, such as frequency of attendance at a place of worship and the desirability/feasibility of unifying the Protestant and Catholic Churches, which were of a specifically religious nature.

Particulars of a major study of 'Protestants and social Change in the Belfast Area', conducted by Frederick Boal, John Campbell and David Livingstone of the Department of Geography, Queen's University of Belfast between April 1982 and May 1984, may be found in ESRC Research Report G/00/23/0025 which is available through the BLLD. Using a variety of techniques and approaches, the most important of them being a special questionnaire survey of 1,400 churchgoers from nine different religious traditions, the aim of the project was to explore the socio-geographical parameters of 'Protestant space' at the denominational, congregational and individual levels and their bearing upon Ulster's political, economic and community problems.

3.1.1. *Denominational studies, national Churches: Church of England*

Several additional sources are now to hand. First, David Wasdell [A.60] has scrutinised the performance of two large churches, one with a strong liturgical ethos situated on the north-west fringe of the London area and the other with a very much 'lower' tradition at the centre of a northern city, in terms of their recurrent records of communicants and giving and the composition of the membership in 1977 by sex, age and residence. Secondly, Peter Brierley [A.6] has constructed a sociological and spiritual profile of the congregation at All Souls, Langham Place, London on the basis of forms completed by 1,624 persons present at morning and/or evening service on Sunday, 22 November 1981; unfortunately, the church is too atypical on account of its size (it is reputed to be the best frequented Anglican place of worship in the whole of England), ultra-evangelical stance and disproportionately high recruitment from the ranks of students and visitors/tourists for the results of the survey to have anything other than purely local significance. Thirdly, William Purcell [A.48] has summarised the replies received from male and female readers of *The Sign*, an inset for parish magazines with a monthly circulation of 350,000 copies, to a short questionnaire appearing in the January 1983 issue concerning attitudes towards infant baptism, the Ten Commandments, compulsory religious instruction in schools, the ordination of women, and modern language services; approximately three quarters of the unspecified number of respondents were aged over fifty and nine tenths were regular communicants. Fourthly, Gallup has undertaken two discrete but overlapping studies of the views on key doctrinal, political and other topics held by samples of 408 non-Anglicans, 575 lay members, 530 full-time or retired clergymen and 43 diocesan, suffragan or assistant bishops contacted, in person or by post, on behalf of Church Society in October-November 1984 [QRL.50], 14 December 1984; [QRL.51], 14 December 1984; [QRL.57], 11 December 1984; [QRL.64], January 1985; [QRL.123], 10-11 December 1984 and by 1,170 professing Anglicans interviewed for the *Sunday Telegraph* in March 1985 [QRL.50], 12 April 1985; [QRL.51], 12 April 1985; [QRL.57], 8 April 1985; [QRL.64], April 1985; [QRL.112], 7 April 1985.

3.2.2. Denominational studies, Free Churches and sects: Baptists
During the early months of 1982 Bryan Gilbert [A.23] of One Step Forward Ministries convened a series of midweek gatherings for the 1,719 members of fourteen Baptist churches situated in urban and rural areas of Derbyshire, Leicestershire, Nottinghamshire and Warwickshire. Some 459 or 26.7% of them, seemingly 'the more faithful, enthusiastic believers', attended and complied with a request to assess, by means of a ten point scale, both their own spiritual commitment and that of their fellowship as a whole in terms of agape love, prayer life, worship, pastoral care, financial giving, interest in overseas missionary work, graciousness, evangelistic witness, Scripture use, and concern for the maintenance of ecclesiastical plant.

Details of the 'caring activities' (essentially all those other than Sunday services or schools and meetings for prayer, Bible study and administration) carried out both on and off their premises by 1,036 of the 2,003 British churches affiliated to the Baptist Union of Great Britain and Ireland were collected by Enid Bichard [A.4] in May 1983.

3.2.4. Denominational studies, Free Churches and sects: Methodists
Two more of the sociological surveys of ten Methodist churches in the London North-East District undertaken by David Wasdell between 1978 and 1981 (3.2.4.4)

have now been published [A.58] [A.59], whilst tabulations for the remaining six (Aveley, East Ham, Elm Park, Goodmayes, Grange Hill and Seven Kings) may be obtained on application to the Unit for Research into Changing Institutions, 115 Poplar High Street, London, E14 OAE.

A twenty-four point questionnaire sent by Michael Hall [A.26] to a non-random but allegedly 'representative' sample of 138 members and adherents of Quinton Methodist Church, Birmingham in the autumn of 1982 elicited 111 replies and provided valuable information concerning their sex, age, marital status, employment, housing, place of residence and secular leisure time pursuits as well as about the extent of, and reasons for, their involvement in the public services, weekday activities and government of this particular congregation.

In September 1983, as part of his preparations for his year as President of the Methodist Conference, the Reverend Gordon E. Barritt (c/o National Children's Home, Highbury Park, London, N5 1UD) wrote to some 2,700 of his co-religionists in an attempt to measure the level of satisfaction with the worshipping and caring life of the Church. Only 816 replies were received, a partial analysis of which appeared in [QRL.72], 5 July 1984.

3.2.5. Denominational studies, Free Churches and sects: other bodies

M.L. Anthony's *Unto the perfect Day: a Survey of Church Growth among Seventh-Day Adventists in the United Kingdom and Eire during the Period 1940-1980* [A.1] makes effective use of both serial data and three major non-recurrent sources: a breakdown of 1,450 baptismal candidates in 1978 and 1979 by age and ethnic origin, an analysis of the racial background and regional distribution of 11,406 attenders and 14,120 members as at 31 December 1980, and an attitudinal study undertaken during the first quarter of 1981 amongst 203 eleven to thirty year olds from the assemblies at Stanborough Park, Camp Hill in Birmingham, and South Manchester.

3.3.1. Denominational studies, Roman Catholicism: early work

An edition of the 1767 papist returns (3.3.1.3) for the Diocese of Canterbury has been produced by Edward Worrall [A.63].

3.3.5. Denominational studies, Roman Catholicism: local studies

During the course of 1983, as a consultation exercise in connection with the preparation of a diocesan pastoral plan, the Bishop of Galloway (of Candida Casa, 8 Corsehill Road, Ayr, KA7 2ST) authorised the distribution of a thirteen point questionnaire, chiefly designed to measure the level of involvement in and satisfaction with various facets of local church life, to every parishioner over the age of fourteen. The 7,772 replies received were fairly representative of the total Catholic population of 50,000 so far as sex, age and employment groups were concerned, but the proportion of regular mass-goers (81%) was almost twice the norm for the see (43%).

4.1.2. Group studies, children: recent research
Leslie Francis, currently engaged as Research Officer at the Culham College
Institute for Church Related Education in Abingdon, has now conducted his twin
surveys of primary and secondary pupils from Essex, Cambridgeshire and Suffolk
(4.1.2.3) for a third time, but as yet neither the results from this latest (1982) nor the
preceding (1978) replication have been published. He has also collaborated with
Paul Pearson and William Kay in exploring, through multiple regression techniques,
the relationship between religiosity on the one hand and two key personality traits,
introversion and neuroticism, on the other amongst samples of 1,088 fifteen to
sixteen year old [A.18] [A.19] [B.123] [B.124] and 1,715 eleven to seventeen year old
[A.17] [A.20] English schoolchildren.

An enquiry carried out amongst ten to fifteen year olds and their mothers in
France, Great Britain (n = 1,500), Japan, Korea and Thailand in September- October
1979 included questions on the importance of being a believer of religion, the role of
divine providence in determining human success or failure, the desire to become a
monk, priest, nun or clergyman, and the performance of various religious rituals
[QRL.7O], 1979-80, whilst a poll of 1,064 Britons aged eight to fifteen undertaken
by NOP from 14-20 March 1984 on behalf of *The Mail on Sunday* [A.85] covered,
amongst many other topics, belief in God and church attendance.

4.2.1. Group studies, young adults: general surveys
A further and very much fuller account of the survey of the religious faith and
practice, moral, social and political opinions, leisure pursuits and psychological
well-being of 1,328 thirteen to twenty year olds who frequented ninety different
Anglican, Nonconformist and Roman Catholic places of worship in the Clitheroe,
Lancaster, Morecambe, Preston and Skelmersdale areas during the period
November 1979-April 1980 (4.2.1.18) has now been prepared by Leslie Francis
[A.16].

The data contained in a Government report on *Young People in the 80's* [A.86],
issued in July 1983, derive from a self-completion questionnaire administered
between December 1981 and February 1982 to a national quota sample of 635
fourteen to nineteen year olds which included a deliberate overrepresentation of the
unemployed (32%) and Asians/West Indians (30%). Amongst the subjects covered in
the enquiry were attitudes towards the retention of religious instruction in schools
and the extent of, and reasons for, participation in activities connected with
churches, temples or synagogues.

The third in a series of surveys of young people aged eighteen to twenty-four
sponsored by the Youth Bureau of the Office of the Prime Minister of Japan was
conducted by Gallup and affiliates in Great Britain (n = 1,035) and ten other
countries between February and June 1983 [QRL.70], 1983-84. Respondents were
asked about the role of religion in life as a whole and, more particularly, as a source
of family disagreements and an object of national pride.

Information on denominational affiliation and views concerning organised
religion were sought in a poll of 748 Britons aged fifteen to twenty-two which was
commissioned by BBC Television's 'ORS 84' programme and conducted by Martin
Hamblin Research Limited from 10-21 December 1983. Details are given in an

unpublished BBC Broadcasting Research Special Report (reference SP83/56/83/100) which is available from 254 The Langham, Portland Place, London, W1A 1AA.

Towards the end of 1982 the Alister Hardy Research Centre (formerly RERU) at Manchester College, Oxford initiated a project, in association with the Christian Education Movement, which was designed 'to investigate those experiences, ideas, feelings and beliefs which young people in the 16-19 age range feel to be of most personal importance to them and have most influence on the formation of their values'. Questionnaires are being distributed, somewhat haphazardly, through the good offices of teachers and youth workers by which means, it is hoped, a large and reasonably representative sample of adolescents will have been assembled from across the whole United Kingdom by the time the study finishes in September 1985.

4.2.3. Group studies, young adults: higher education students
Three major interview based surveys of undergraduate opinions have become available since the compilation of the main text. The first and most sophisticated was undertaken at the University of Leeds in November 1982 (n=212) as part of the 'Conventional religion and common religion in Leeds' project (2.2.2.18); the research instrument was virtually identical to the one employed with the city's electors (see the addendum to Section 2.2.2), and copies of it, annotated with a breakdown of the replies received, can be obtained from the Department of Sociology, University of Leeds. The second and third, which were conceived less from academic than evangelistic motives, were carried out by the Navigators of Great Britain at the Universities of Reading in January-March 1983 (n=144) and Sheffield in January-March 1985 (n=160) and have been summarised in two unpublished papers which may be purchased from John Mulholland of 5 Southbourne Road, Broomhill, Sheffield, S10 2QN; views were canvassed about the nature and purpose of human existence, God, Jesus, an afterlife and a variety of moral topics, and the results were calculated both in terms of percentages for individual questions and as an overall secularisation score extending from 0 (indicative of a purely worldly orientation) at one extreme to 90/100 (reflecting an entirely biblical outlook) at the other.

4.3.1. Group studies, other groups: women
Martin Johnson [A.32] has recently examined the values held by 176 student nurses, overwhelmingly female (96.6%), aged 18-22 (94.9%), of British origin (94.3%) and single (92.6%), who were undergoing training for the register at three schools of nursing situated within a ten mile radius of a large city in the North-West of England. A self-completion questionnaire was used, the key element of which comprised a list of fifty-seven general and nursing-related behaviour patterns and goals, amongst them six specifically religious ones, to which respondents were invited to express their approval or disapproval by ticking one of five Likert style answers. Basic frequency distributions were computed for each of these items, but they were also merged to form sixteen distinct value scales, two of them being of 'religiousness', with median scores on these disaggregated by denominational affiliation, social class, educational achievement and several nursing variables.

As part of a research programme linked to the 1984 'Mission to London' campaign, 1,372 women in the Blackheath, Clapham, Highbury Fields, Newham, Walthamstow and Wimbledon districts of the capital were asked about the most difficult problems, including 'indifference towards God', which they encountered in their everyday lives [A.12].

The importance attached to belief in God and to the influence of the Church was monitored in connection with the 'Woman Study' which Marplan (JN R.53335) conducted during the spring of 1985 with a quota sample of 1,000 female Britons aged eighteen to sixty-five. Results may be obtained by contacting McCann-Erickson Advertising Ltd., the sponsoring body, at 36 Howland Street, London, W1A 1AT.

4.3.2. Group studies, other groups: old people

Confessional allegiance, attendance at church or religious meetings, and the receipt of house visits from vicars, priests or rabbis were amongst the subjects covered in a survey of the experiences of a random sample of 361 widowed individuals, 82% of them aged sixty-five and over, who were interviewed across eight areas of England in May-October 1979 on behalf of the Institute for Social Studies in Medical Care. Some statistics have been published in [A.5], whilst the data set for the enquiry is now available at the ESRC DA (SN 1786).

An investigation of *The residential Life of old People* [A.62] was conducted by NOP in a representative group of one hundred local authority homes throughout England in July and November 1980. 999 residents, 81.6% of whom were aged seventy-five and above, were questioned in all, and the 497 of them who ever left the grounds of their home were asked whether they went to church at any time and, if not, whether this was because they did not want to attend or would like to go but were unable to do so.

Samples of the elderly population, apparently aged sixty and over, of France, Great Britain (n = 1,047), Japan, Thailand and the United States of America were interviewed in January 1981 about the importance of their faith, belief in a life after death, denominational affiliation, participation in religious activity, close friendships formed at a place of worship, and their willingness to consult a priest, minister or monk over a personal problem [QRL.7O], 1981-82 and 1983-84.

4.3.3. Group studies, other groups: coloured people

A survey of the extent to which members of the various ethnic minorities are sharing in the life of the Methodist Church in England and Wales has been carried out by a working group appointed by the President's Council, a 71.1% response being obtained to an initial mailing of 755 congregational questionnaires. Publication of the results is expected during the course of 1985.

5.1.1 Beliefs, overall religiosity: general indicators

Additional self-assessed religiosity data for the United Kingdom have been gathered in connection with Eurobarometers 18 (October 1982; n = 1,335; ESRC DA, SN 1832), 19 (March-April 1983; n = 1,349; ESRC DA, SN 1938) and 20 (October

1983; n = 1,276; ESRC DA, SN 1969), whilst those contained in Eurobarometer 17 of March-April 1982 (5.1.1.2; ESRC DA, SN 1792) have been analysed by Jean-Francois Tchernia [A.55] so as to highlight differences between fifteen to twenty-four year olds and the rest of the adult population.

'Is religion an important element in your life?' was one of the questions included in the 'Planning for social change' study which Millward Brown Market Research (JN 1291) conducted in 1981 amongst a sample of Britons aged sixteen to sixty-four; the sponsoring body, to whom requests for access to the material should be addressed, was the Henley Centre for Forecasting, 2 Tudor Street, Blackfriars, London, EC4Y OAA. A similar enquiry was also put during the course of Eurobarometer 21 of March-April 1984 (n = 1,356; ESRC DA, SN 1999).

5.1.2. Beliefs, overall religiosity: religious experience
Ann Morisy [A.42], in presenting an initial report on the survey carried out amongst a random sample of 172 electors from the city of Nottingham and immediately adjacent county wards in 1976-78 (5.1.2.2), has paid particular attention to the degree of publicity given to their religious experience by the 123 interviewees who claimed to have had one; almost fifty tables of results were prepared, with disaggregations by no fewer than thirteen separate demographic and spiritual variables. Gallup [QRL.64], May 1985 conducted a similar enquiry at the national level from 1-6 May 1985 (n = 1,030, JN CQ.964), whilst investigations of the broader phenomenon of transcendental experience have been completed by Michael Paffard [A.46] in 1973 (n = 200 sixth formers and 200 undergraduates) and by Grahame Miles [A.41] in 1983 (n = 137 sixth formers).

5.2.5. Beliefs, specific beliefs: other beliefs
A post-war investigation of the incidence of superstitious beliefs and practices in the British population has been replicated by Gallup [QRL.64], December 1984 on 14-19 November 1984 (n = 947, JN CQ.942).

6.1.2. Practices, private practices: the Bible
John Alwyn Jones [A.33] [A.34] has administered four Thurstone type scales to 185 College of Education students, 62 males and 123 females, both at the beginning and end of their three year course in order to measure changes in attitudes towards the religious, literary and historical significance of the Bible.

6.1.3. Practices, private practices: religious broadcasting
The Independent Television Authority [A.81] commissioned a poll of seven hundred Britons aged sixteen and over during the early summer of 1961 with the primary intention of monitoring public support for the general principle of religious broadcasting and a 'closed period' on the one hand as well as the audience for and appreciation of specific ITV programmes such as 'About Religion' and the 'Epilogue' on the other. However, the opportunity was also taken to gather some

data of wider relevance, especially relating to the degree of interest shown by respondents in matters of faith, the frequency of church attendance, and the habit of sending children to Sunday school.

6.1.4. Practices, private practices: observance of Christian festivals

The importance attached to the religious dimension of Christmas has been assessed in nation-wide investigations conducted by NOP (n=970, JN 4699) on behalf of BBC TV's 'Breakfast Time' on 7-8 December 1984 [QRL.80], December 1984 and by Gallup for the *Sunday Telegraph* (n=906, JN CQ. 946B) on 10-17 December 1984 [QRL.64], January 1985; [QRL.112], 23 December 1984 and for F.W.Woolworth PLC (n=1,000) during the late summer of 1985 [QRL.53], 28 November 1985.

6.2.2. Practices, public practices: denominational affiliation

Anthony Spencer [A.52] has performed an immensely valuable service in tabulating the proportion of British and, where possible, English, Welsh and Scottish adults identifying themselves as Catholic in thirty-two commercial sample surveys or sets of surveys, including several dating from the early 1960s not previously available to the present writer, undertaken, mostly by Gallup, during the period 1947-81. Unfortunately, he is on far less certain ground when he converts and inflates these rough percentages into absolute numbers, supplements them with an estimate for children and adolescents calculated according to the baptismally based Archer-Dean-Cox crude cohort method, and compares the resulting figures for total Catholic population with denominational census data for Northern and Southern Ireland in order to chart geographical shifts in the allegiance to the Roman Church within the home archipelago between 1948 and 1980.

Further archival evidence has recently been reported by M.E.J. Wadsworth and S.R. Freeman [A.57]. With funding from the Medical Research Council, the health and development of a cohort of 5,362 Britons has been monitored at intervals since their birth during the week 3-9 March 1946, and in 1972 such members as could still be contacted, apparently numbering at least 3,743, were additionally questioned about their faith of upbringing, current confessional attachment and strength of religious beliefs. Quantification of temporal change in the pattern of denominational commitment was thereby facilitated as was the extent to which this was linked with sex, education and other variables.

Rather more up-to-date longitudinal statistics may be extracted from the first in a series of annual 'Social report' studies [A.69], modelled on the widely acclaimed surveys carried out in the United States of America for more than a decade by the National Opinion Research Center, the data for which have been deposited at the ESRC DA (SN 1935). Fieldwork was conducted by SCPR (JN P.705) at 114 randomly selected sampling points throughout Great Britain during March and April 1983, and the 1,761 elector-informants supplied details of their religion both at the time of interview and when they had been aged about sixteen and of the frequency of their attendance at services or meetings connected with it.

6.2.3. Practices, public practices: church membership

The process of preparation and admission of new communicants within the Church of Scotland has been described by David Thomson [A.76] on the basis of one hundred and twenty replies to a questionnaire sent out, during the second half of the 1960s, to two hundred parochial ministers representing a diversity of ages, types and theological outlooks.

A twenty-five page duplicated report on membership in the Religious Society of Friends, the product of eight years' work by a specially appointed Review Committee, was received by Meeting for Sufferings on 3 December 1983. The document contained an analysis of the age, sex and reasons for joining or leaving the Quakers of 229 persons who had been added 'by convincement' in 1976 and of 249 who had resigned in 1978 as well as of the demographic characteristics and level of involvement of all individuals attached to twenty-five local meetings across Great Britain in 1980. Further information may be obtained by writing to the Assistant Recording Clerk at Friends House, Euston Road, London, NW1 2BJ.

6.2.4. Practices, public practices: religious organisations

Data relative to the extent of public participation in voluntary work connected with churches and other religious agencies have been gathered as part of the Government's *General Household Survey, 1981* [A.77], in the course of which 23,289 Britons aged sixteen and over were interviewed, and of polls of 1,886 British electors and 1,349 United Kingdom adults undertaken by SCPR on behalf of the Volunteer Centre in March-May 1981 [A.31] and by Gallup for the Commission of the European Communities from 26 March to 27 April 1983 (ESRC DA, SN 1938).

7.1.2. Church attendance, censuses of attendance: 1979 and 1982 Bible Society censuses

MARC Europe (of Cosmos House, 6 Homesdale Road, Bromley, BR2 9EX) mounted an interesting follow-up study to these censuses during April 1984, a set of questionnaires being sent to a random selection of nearly 6,400 local ministers and ecclesiastical leaders throughout England and Wales inviting their co-operation in recording the location, strength, sex, age, occupational and religious composition of the major 'ethnic/linguistic', 'social/community' or 'occasional' groups of people who did not regularly attend church. The intention was less to conduct a comprehensive survey than to assemble a miscellany of facts from which a report could be quickly compiled and published, in October 1984, to 'act as a resource tool to stimulate evangelistic strategies, endeavour and concern for the non-Christians in our land'.

7.1.3. Church attendance, censuses of attendance: local censuses

Enumerations of attendance at Sunday worship were made at Colne in June 1882 and March 1892 [A.70], at Darwen in March 1896 [A.79], at Washington, Tyne and Wear by the local Council of Churches on 29 May and 5 June 1983, and at Hastings and St. Leonards in October 1983 [A.45]; in the latter case the returns were broken down by sex and age as well as by denomination.

7.2.1. Church attendance, opinion polls: basic attendance
Between 19 and 23 November 1969 LHR asked a sample of 2,519 Britons aged
sixteen and above when they had last been to church on Christmas Day. The
results, disaggregated by sex, social class and region, were published in [QRL.53], 20
December 1969.

7.2.2 *Church attendance, opinion polls: other matters*
Changes in church-going habits over a five year period were monitored by Gallup
(JN CQ.962A) on the basis of a sample of 1,067 adult Britons interviewed from
17-22 April 1985 [QRL.64], April 1985.

8.1.1. Attitudes, religious attitudes: religious influences on national life
Public esteem for the role which the Church and other institutions played in the life
of the nation was gauged in the 'Planning for social change' studies which Millward
Brown Market Research carried out in 1982 (JN 1751/B) and 1983 (JN J2246) on
behalf of the Henley Centre for Forecasting as well as by Gallup [QRL.64], March,
May 1985 from 10-17 December 1984 (n = 945, JN CQ.946B) and 14-19 February
1985 (n = 1,042, JN CQ.953B).

8.1.2. Attitudes, religious attitudes: ecumenism
A further piece of research relative to the Anglican-Methodist Conversations of
1956-72 has come to light since paragraph 8.1.2.2 was written. Consequent upon the
failure of the Convocations of Canterbury and York to endorse the unity scheme by
the required 75% majority in July 1969, John Gore mailed a questionnaire to 124
Anglican and 54 Methodist ministers, randomly selected from every diocese or
district of England, in May 1970 with the intention of documenting the reactions of
local congregations to the vote, the progress which was then being made in fostering
practical co-operation between the two Churches (especially with regard to shared
worship and outreach), and the likelihood of, and interest in, future ecumenical
advance. He received replies from 89 (or 71.8%) and 43 (or 79.6%) of his contacts
respectively, and these were analysed in a Mid-Service Clergy Course project report
[A.24] submitted to, and still available from, St. George's House, Windsor Castle,
SL4 1NJ.
   A survey of Quaker involvement in local ecumenical councils and activities was
undertaken by Friends' Committee on Christian Relationships in January 1983, two
page questionnaires being completed by 319 of the 440 or so meetings across Great
Britain. Val Ferguson and Tony Brown have written an article [A.15] outlining the
main findings of the enquiry, whilst additional data may be requested from the
Assistant Recording Clerk at Friends House, Euston Road, London, NW1 2BJ.

8.1.3. Attitudes, religious attitudes: religious prejudices
A twelfth opinion poll linked to Pope John Paul II's historic pastoral tour of Great
Britain (8.1.3.2) was conducted by NOP (JN 7994) on behalf of *The Observer* [A.68]

between 2 and 5 April 1982 amongst a quota sample of 1,104 adults aged eighteen and over. They were asked a total of twenty-one questions concerning their approval of the visit, the difference which it was likely to make to the domestic ecumenical scene, their attitude towards the reunification of the Roman and Anglican Churches, the success of the pontiff as a religious and world leader, their agreement with papal and Catholic teaching on politics, worker participation, trade unions, birth control, abortion, clerical celibacy, female ordination, inter-faith marriage and divorce, their denominational affiliation and frequency of public worship.

Gallup interviewed two separate groups of adult Britons from 9 to 14 November 1983 (n= 1,066) and 16 to 22 May 1984 (n= 971) in an attempt to discover, amongst other things, whether they considered that discrimination on the grounds of religion actually occurs in this country and whether, as a matter of principle, it should or should not be illegal for it to do so. Results, without any disaggregation by demographics, appear in [QRL.64], November 1983, June 1984 and [QRL.70], 1983-84.

8.2.2. Attitudes, moral attitudes: sexual questions

The relationship between religion of upbringing and the age at which childbearing begins has been explored by Kathleen Kiernan and I. Diamond [A.35] on the basis of data collected in 1977-78 from 3,744 members of the cohort who, since their birth during the week 3-9 March 1946, have formed the subject of the Medical Research Council's National Survey of Health and Development.

Public confidence in the ability of homosexuals to be good members of the Christian, Jewish or other faiths and approval of their recruitment as ministers of religion have been tested for a fourth time by Gallup [QRL.64], March 1985 from 20-25 March 1985 (n=983, JN CQ.958A).

8.2.3. Attitudes, moral attitudes: marriage and divorce

The results of a varied programme of local research undertaken in 1981 on the theme of 'Marriage in the contemporary family' have been described by Catherine Guy [A.25]. Although none of the constituent studies could be considered to be methodologically outstanding, interesting data were obtained, from samples of both young single persons and married couples, concerning, first, the desirability of having a church wedding (n=26 in Newbury, n=58 in Sunderland, n=30 in Walsall, n=129 in York) and, secondly, the likely or actual role of shared religious beliefs in promoting stable conjugal relationships (n=75 in Dorset, n=183 in Kingston-upon-Thames, n=452 in Middlesex).

A self-completion questionnaire published in the early autumn 1982 issue of *Wedding Day & First Home* magazine attracted replies from 645 brides-to-be, 98% of them marrying for the first time, with a mean age of twenty-two years and drawn from all parts of the United Kingdom. They supplied information, analysed in [A.13] and [QRL.123], 26 July 1983, regarding, amongst many other things, their own and their fiance's denominational affiliation as well as the type of ceremony, religious or civil, which they were having and the reasons for their choice.

The decision of the Anglican General Synod in July 1983 to allow divorced persons to remarry in church subject to a three tier vetting process known as 'Option G' was put to the test at a series of consultations held by the bishops in January 1984 with their parochial clergy and, in a few instances, representatives of the laity; so far as can be determined from reports appearing in the religious press [QRL.5O], 20-27 January 1984; [QRL.51], 20 January-3 February 1984, thirty-six of the forty-three English dioceses took a direct vote on the desirability and/or practicality of adopting 'Option G', the outcome of which was so wholly negative that the scheme was subsequently withdrawn, whilst twenty also expressed a view on the overall principle of ecclesiastical remarriage. The opinions of a quota sample of 509 British electors on the self-same principle were canvassed in a NOP telephone poll of 13-14 February 1984 [QRL.55], 16 February 1984; [QRL.80], April 1984.

8.3.1. Attitudes, political attitudes: general surveys
During the course of the first weekend in November 1955 pollsters for the *Daily Express* [QRL.53], 8 November 1955 asked a cross-section of British adults whether or not they favoured the disestablishment of the Church of England.

Between 11 March and 6 April 1983 Research Partners interviewed representative samples of 259 churchgoers and 212 non-churchgoers across Great Britain with the intention of comparing their attitudes to a range of political issues (including blood sports, capital punishment, trade union power, immigration, the monarchy, Northern Ireland, the Common Market, nuclear weapons, the Falklands and overseas aid) as well as their awareness of, and support for, the work of charitable agencies. Only a few results, mostly qualitative, have been released as yet [QRL.44], 10 November 1983; [QRL.51], 4 November 1983; [QRL.72], 3 November 1983, and readers interested in obtaining further data should contact Christian Aid, which commissioned the study, at P.O. Box No.1, London, SW9 8BH.

8.3.2. Attitudes, political attitudes: Sunday observance
Public support for a general liberalisation of the laws relating to Sunday observance was gauged in surveys of the readerships of the *Daily Mirror* [A.67] and *Daily Sketch* [A.66] during January 1953.

Plebiscites on the Sunday opening of cinemas were held in a large number of English towns and urban districts during the years 1932-39 and 1945-50 in accordance with local option arrangements which were introduced by the act 22 and 23 Geo.V, c.51 of 1932 and which, although suspended for the duration of the Second World War, remained on the statute book until the passage by Parliament of 1972, c.19. A provisional list of places where such referenda were conducted, drawn up from reports appearing in the national press, is given in the Supplementary Appendix.

Equity members were balloted about Sunday theatrical performances in March 1943 [QRL.57], 20 March 1943; [QRL.67], 20 March 1943; [QRL.123], 20 March 1943 as well as in February 1963 (8.3.2.2).

Popular attitudes towards the extension of Sunday licensing hours were monitored by Gallup (JN CQ.939A, n=973) from 24 to 29 October 1984 [QRL.64], November 1984.

The National Consumer Council [A.75] has reprinted the results of the November-December 1981 and September 1982 MORI polls on Sunday shopping and also analysed 2,912 Sunday trading advertisements which were placed in local newspapers throughout England, Wales and Scotland over a four week period from mid-October to mid-November 1983. New attitudinal data on the subject have been collected, from country-wide samples of adults, by Millward Brown Market Research (JN J2246) on behalf of the Henley Centre for Forecasting in 1983, by MORI for the Federation of Multiple DIY Retailers in September 1983 (n = 2,045)[QRL.70], 1983-84; [QRL.88], February 1984, Neighbourhood Stores PLC in November 1983 (n = 1,892), the Institute for Fiscal Studies from 4-10 April 1984 (n = 1,964, JN 2431) and the National Consumer Council from 16-22 August 1984 (n = 2,045, JN 2542)[QRL.67], 4 October 1984; [QRL.88], October 1984, 6-10 December 1984 (n = 1,814, JN 2650) and November 1985 (n = 1,800)[QRL.67], 30 December 1985; [QRL.113], 1 December 1985; [QRL.123], 30 December 1985, by NOP for *The Mail on Sunday* on 8 March 1984 (n = 1,048, JN 3479)[QRL.80], April 1984; [A.83] and Aims of Industry on 24-29 October 1985 (n = 1,856, JN 5804)[QRL.50], 29 November 1985; [QRL.51], 29 November 1985, by Gallup on 14-18 November 1985 [QRL.64], December 1985, and by Research Bureau Ltd for the Co-operative Union on 16-30 November 1985 (n = 600 Co-op customers, JN 65377)[QRL.67], 21 January 1986; [QRL.123], 21 January 1986.

Enquiries into the ways in which people spend their Sundays have been undertaken by the BBC Broadcasting Research Department (ESRC DA, SN 2027) across the United Kingdom from 11 June to 6 July 1983 and 9 February to 1 March 1984 (n = 2,986), by MORI throughout Great Britain on behalf of Flymo on 6-10 September 1984 (n = 2,006, JN 2556) and the Federation of Multiple DIY Retailers [QRL.123], 31 October 1985 on 3-8 September 1985 (n = 2,343), and by Audience Selection for Capital Radio [QRL.50], 23 November 1984 in London on 26-28 October 1984 (n = 2.010).

8.3.3. *Attitudes, political attitudes: religious education*

Eight additional surveys on this topic have recently become available. General reports on the state of religious education in English inner-city primary and secondary schools and in Welsh secondary schools have been prepared by, respectively, John Nicholson [A.44] and by Rheinallt Thomas and John Summerwill [A.56] [QRL.124], 25 May 1984. Reviews of morning assembly arrangements have been undertaken by Patrick Souper and William Kay in 202 British independent day schools [A.51] [QRL.124], 13 January 1984, by the BBC's 'Panorama' programme in 3,871 primary and secondary schools [QRL.123], 17 December 1984; [QRL.124], 14 December 1984, and by *The Times Educational Supplement* in 371 maintained and independent secondary schools [QRL.124], 20 December 1985. The provision made for the training of RE teachers at the universities, polytechnics and colleges of England and Wales during the 1983-84 academic session was investigated by Brian Gates [A.22]. Attitudes towards the retention of religious instruction in the curriculum were tested throughout Great Britain by Audience Selection for *TV Times Magazine* from 12-17 May 1983 on the basis of quota samples of 215 secondary pupils, 426 parents and 204 teachers [A.21] [A.73], and by Gallup (JN

CQ.947A) on behalf of the *Daily Telegraph* from 4-8 January 1985 by means of interviews with 845 adults [QRL.57], 21 January 1985; [QRL.64], January 1985.

9.1.2. The Institutional Church, resources: clergy, general surveys
Additional information has been gathered from five separate quota or probability samples of the adult population of Great Britain. The reputation for truthfulness of clergymen and other groups was explored by MORI on 16 December 1983 (n = 1,082, JN 2362)[QRL.70], 1983-84; [QRL.88], January 1984; [QRL.113], 8 January 1984 and on 4-9 June 1985 (n = 1,824, JN 2807)[QRL.88], September 1985. Attitudes towards the ordination of women priests were investigated by Gallup (n = 972, JN CQ. 911) from 11-16 April 1984 [QRL.47], 27 April 1984; [QRL.57], 23 April 1984; [QRL.64], May 1984; [QRL.112], 22 April 1984 and by NOP (n = 1,993, JN 4213) from 18-23 October 1984 [QRL.50], 16 November 1984; [QRL.80], December 1984; [QRL.123], 8 November 1984. The perceived value of vicars and ministers to the community was reviewed by Gallup (n = 955, JN CQ.977A) from 31 July-5 August 1985 [QRL.64], August 1985.

9.1.3. The institutional Church, resources: clergy, denominational surveys
The data set for ORC's telephone poll of Anglican clergymen's views on the Church and politics, referred to in paragraph 9.1.3.1, has now been deposited at the ESRC DA (SN 1826). Two new postal surveys of incumbents have also been completed; one by Hugh Marshall [A.40] in 1979 monitored the degree of satisfaction with the parochial appointments system displayed by men in three contrasting areas who had been in their current post for less than twelve months (n = 78) or for eight years or more (n = 189), the other by Ernie Stroud [A.54] in 1982 investigated the incidence of stress amongst 191 ministers in the Diocese of Chelmsford.

9.2.1. The institutional Church, modernisation: structural change
The results of Michael Hornsby-Smith's study of the socio-demographic characteristics and religious attitudes and practices of delegates to the National Pastoral Congress (9.2.1.2) have been reported in two journal articles [QRL.119], 8-15 May 1982 and a sixty page pamphlet [A.30]; 1,276 usable replies were received, equivalent to a response rate of some 65%, and the analysis focussed on the 89% of them which came from lay persons and priests and on comparisons which could be drawn with the findings of the more general 'Roman Catholic opinion' project of February-March 1978 (3.3.4.4). Instant reactions to fifty-three key recommendations of the Congress were also registered by a self-selecting sample of 2,305 readers of *The Universe* in May-June 1980 [QRL.125], 1 August 1980.

9.2.2. The institutional Church, modernisation: liturgical change
Andrew Bryant [A.9] [A.10] interviewed seventy of the seventy-five adult members of an Anglican congregation in Birmingham in 1980 with a view to examining 'attitudes to and perceptions of Series 3 in terms of the liturgy itself, participation in

tasks, and existential effects and involvement in the related decision-making process', whilst Berkeley Hill [A.29] has described the more dynamic side of Anglican choral life on the basis of postal questionnaires completed, during the period May-August 1982, by 1,223 of the 5,490 parochial choirs which were affiliated to the Royal School of Church Music.

9.3.1. *The institutional Church, outreach: Sunday schools*
Thirty-seven places of worship in Gloucester, fifteen Anglican, twenty Nonconformist or sectarian and two Roman Catholic, contributed to a brief survey of the extent, nature and effectiveness of church work with children which provided background material for a programme in Radio 4's 'Soundings' series on 20 August 1983; application to see the results should be made to the Religious Broadcasting Organiser, BBC, Pebble Mill Road, Birmingham, B5 7QQ. Copies of reports on the condition of Methodist Sunday schools in the Leeds District in 1983 and the Chester and Stoke-on-Trent District in 1984, based upon returns from 74% and 44% of societies, may be obtained respectively from Dr Ivan Reid of the University of Bradford and Mrs Pat Dickinson of 35 High Street, Wolstanton, Newcastle-under-Lyme, Staffordshire, ST5 0SA.

9.3.2. *The institutional Church, outreach: evangelism*
Statistical appraisals have been published of the Billy Graham North of England crusade held at Maine Road stadium, Manchester in May-June 1961 [A.72], of the 'Way to life' outreach to Edinburgh in August 1983 [A.39], and of the inaugural phase of Luis Palau's 'Mission to London' in September-October 1983 [A.7]. In the first case, twenty-three evangelical places of worship supplied details in 1965 of the churchgoing history and persistence in the Christian faith of the 325 persons who had been referred to them four years earlier. In the second, data were gathered on the sex and age of 291 people who registered a first time acceptance of Jesus as Saviour and of 167 other enquirers, and assessments of their spiritual progress after three months were made for 101 and 43 of them respectively. In the third, a comprehensive record was kept of attendances and response rates at the meetings and of the demographic, occupational, geographical and denominational backgrounds of most of the 7,372 individuals who came forward for counselling.

It is pleasing to note that the hoped-for programme of research to accompany the 'Mission England' initiative (10.1.2.4) has now begun to materialise. Important short-term work was accomplished by the Gallup organisation which interviewed samples of the adult population in and around Bristol [QRL.51], 18 May 1984; [QRL.72], 17 May 1984 from 5 to 8 May 1984 (n=458), Sunderland [QRL.50], 1 June 1984 from 18 to 22 May 1984 (n=578) and Liverpool from 28 June to 3 July 1984 (n=613) as well as nationally from 23 to 28 May 1984 (n=1,036) and 6 to 10 August 1984 (n=1,015). In the longer run MARC Europe is attempting to produce a quantitative profile of the 'converts' recorded at each of the six campaign centres, whilst in the South West and South Wales a post-nurture survey is under way to assess the permanency of their commitment (an interim account of this appeared in [QRL.112], 30 December 1984).

R–H

The degree of financial support given by thirty-one of the fifty-eight member congregations of the Milton Keynes Ecumenical Assembly to overseas mission and Christian development agencies has been examined in an unpublished paper of September 1985 by John Nightingale (available through the Board for Mission and Unity, Church House, Dean's Yard, London, SW1P 3NZ) which is summarised in [QRL.44], 16 January 1986.

10.1.1. Future needs and prospects, content: survey populations
Although a definitive investigation of male religiosity is still not in prospect, it is interesting to note that a Marplan poll of 997 British men aged eighteen to sixty-four in October 1983 included two attitudinal questions concerning the importance of the Church and belief in God. Further particulars are available from McCann-Erickson Advertising Ltd., the survey's sponsors, at 36 Howland Street, London, W1A 1AT.

ADDITIONAL REFERENCES

[A.1] Anthony, M.L., *Unto the perfect Day: a Survey of Church Growth among Seventh-Day Adventists in the United Kingdom and Eire during the Period 1940-1980*, (British Union Conference of Seventh-Day Adventists, Watford, 1981).

[A.2] Balsom, Denis, Madgwick, Peter James & Van Mechelen, Denis, *The Political Consequences of Welsh Identity*, Studies in Public Policy no.97, Centre for the Study of Public Policy, University of Strathclyde, Glasgow, 1982.

[A.3] Beasley-Murray, Paul, 'Practices and beliefs', *Church Growth Digest*, Winter 1981/1982, pp.1O-1, 15.

[A.4] Bichard, Enid, *Bridge the Gap*, Department of Mission, Baptist Union of Great Britain and Ireland, London, 1984.

[A.5] Bowling, Ann & Cartwright, Ann, *Life after a Death: a Study of the elderly widowed*, Tavistock Publications, London, 1982.

[A.6] Brierley, Peter, *Growth by Fellowship & Evangelism at All Souls Church, Langham Place: November 1981 Attendance Survey Report*, Bible Society, London, (1982).

[A.7] Brierley, Peter, *Mission to London, Phase 1: who responded?*, MARC Europe, London, 1984.

[A.8] Brierley, Peter & Evans, Byron, *Prospects for Wales: Report of the 1982 Census of the Churches*, Bible Society/MARC Europe, London, 1983.

[A.9] Bryant, Andrew W., 'Lay communicants' attitudes to the eucharist in relation to liturgical change in the Church of England', *Liturgy and Change*, ed. Denise Newton, University of Birmingham Institute for the Study of Worship and Religious Architecture, Birmingham, 1983, pp.75-97.

[A.10] Bryant, Andrew W., 'A Study of lay Attitudes to the Eucharist in relation to liturgical Change within a Birmingham Parish', University of Birmingham M.A. thesis, 1981.

[A.11] Buckingham, Christopher, 'Where have all the papists gone? Or, the Catholics of Kent assessed in the Compton census of 1676', *Kent Recusant History*, no.1, Spring 1979, pp.5-12.

[A.12] Butcher, Andy, 'Women under attack', *Family*, June 1984, pp.22-3.

[A.13] De Bono, Gillian, 'Marriage in the '80s', *Wedding Day & First Home*, Early Autumn 1983, pp.35-7, 75, Late Autumn 1983, pp.12-3, 76.

[A.14] Edwards, David G., 'Population in Derbyshire in the reign of King Charles II: the use of hearth-tax assessments and the Compton census', *Derbyshire Archaeological Journal*, vol. CII, 1982, pp.106-17.

[A.15] Ferguson, Val & Brown, Tony, 'Coal face Christians', *The Friend*, vol.141, 1983, pp.877-8.

[A.16] Francis, Leslie John, *Teenagers and the Church: a Profile of church-going Youth in the 1980's*, Collins, London, 1984.

[A.17] Francis, Leslie John, Pearson, Paul R. & Kay, William K., 'Are introverts still more religious?', *Personality and Individual Differences*, vol.4, 1983, pp.211-2.

[A.18] Francis, Leslie John, Pearson, Paul R. & Kay, William K., 'Are religious children bigger liars?', *Psychological Reports*, vol.52, 1983, pp.551-4.

[A.19] Francis, Leslie John, Pearson, Paul R. & Kay, William K., 'Eysenck's personality quadrants and religiosity', *British Journal of Social Psychology*, vol.21, 1982, pp.262-4.

[A.20] Francis, Leslie John, Pearson, Paul R. & Kay, William K., 'Neuroticism and religiosity among English schoolchildren', *Journal of Social Psychology*, vol.121, 1983, pp.149-50.

[A.21] Furness, Adrian, 'What you think of our schools', *TV Times Magazine*, 18-24 June 1983.

[A.22] Gates, Brian E., 'Towards an adequate staffing base for religious and moral education', *Religious Education Provision, 1984*, Religious Education Council, Lancaster, 1984, pp.3-16.

[A.23] Gilbert, Bryan, 'Baptists & commitment', *Church Growth Digest*, Year 4, Issue 4, Summer 1983, pp.6-8.

[A.24] Gore, John, 'A Study of Actions and Reactions of Anglicans and Methodists since the Vote of Summer 1969, and the Way ahead within the Context of the whole ecumenical Movement', St. George's House, Windsor Castle Mid-Service Clergy Course Research Project, 1970.

[A.25] Guy, Catherine, *Asking about Marriage*, National Marriage Guidance Council, Rugby, 1983.

[A.26] Hall, Michael, '"Who knows but it may continue?" (A History of Methodism in Quinton from 1781 to 1981)', University of Birmingham M.A. thesis, 1983.

[A.27] Harrison, Janet, *Attitudes to Bible, God, Church: Research Report*, Bible Society, London, 1983.

[A.28] Hickey, John, *Religion and the Northern Ireland Problem*, Gill and Macmillan, Dublin, 1984.

[A.29] Hill, Berkeley, *A Survey of Church Music, 1982: the Report of a postal Survey in May 1982 of Churches affiliated to the Royal School of Church Music*, (Royal School of Church Music, Croydon), 1983.

[A.30] Hornsby-Smith, Michael Peter & Cordingley, Elizabeth S., *Catholic Elites: a Study of the Delegates to the National Pastoral Congress*, Occasional Paper no.3, Department of Sociology, University of Surrey, (Guildford, 1983).

[A.31] Humble, Stephen, *Voluntary Action in the 1980s: a Summary of the Findings of a national Survey*, Volunteer Centre, Berkhamsted, 1982.

[A.32] Johnson, Martin, 'Nurses' Values and Nurse Training: a Pilot Survey of the Values of Student Nurses', University of Manchester M.Sc. thesis, 1983.

[A.33] Jones, John Alwyn, 'Student teachers' attitudes to the Bible', *British Journal of Religious Education*, vol.5, 1982-83, pp.139-42.

[A.34] Jones, John Alwyn, 'A Study of the Changes in the Attitudes of Students in a College of Education to the Bible', University of Wales (Cardiff) Ph.D. thesis, 1974.

[A.35] Kiernan, Kathleen E. & Diamond, I., 'The age at which childbearing starts: a longitudinal study', *Population Studies*, vol.37, 1983, pp.363-80.

[A.36] Krarup, Helen, *'Conventional Religion and common Religion in Leeds' Interview Schedule: basic Frequencies by Question*, Religious Research Papers 12, Department of Sociology, University of Leeds, Leeds, (1983).

[A.37] Layton, Geoffrey, 'Religion', *The Navy*, vol.Lll, 1947, pp.147-8.

[A.38] McAllister, Ian, 'Religious commitment and social attitudes in Ireland', *Review of Religious Research*, vol.25, 1983-84, pp.3-20.

[A.39] McInnes, Bennet, 'Counselling', *Church Growth Digest*, Year 5, Issue 2, Winter 1983/4, pp.8-11.

[A.40] Marshall, Hugh, 'Pegs and Holes: Reactions to the Methods of appointing Clergy at Incumbent Level in the parochial Ministry', St. George's House, Windsor Castle Mid-Service Clergy Course Research Project, 1980.

[A.41] Miles, Grahame Banbury, 'A critical and experimental Study of Adolescents' Attitudes to and Understanding of transcendental Experience', University of Leeds Ph.D. thesis, 2 vol., 1983.

[A.42] Morisy, Ann M., 'The Problems of a sociological Definition of religious Experience', University of Nottingham M.Phil. thesis, 1980.

[A.43] Moxon-Browne, Edward P., *Nation, Class and Creed in Northern Ireland*, Gower, Aldershot, 1983.

[A.44] Nicholson, John, *Religious and moral Education in inner City Schools*, Christian Education Movement, London, 1983.

[A.45] Osborne, Barry, *Hastings Church Attendance Survey, October 1983*, Mission for Christ, Hastings, 1984.

[A.46] Paffard, Michael, *Inglorious Wordsworths: a Study of some transcendental Experiences in Childhood and Adolescence*, Hodder and Stoughton, London, 1973.

[A.47] Palliser, David Michael & Jones, L.J., 'The diocesan population returns for 1563 and 1603', *Local Population Studies*, no.30, Spring 1983, pp.55-8.

[A.48] Purcell, William, 'The Sign opinion poll', *The Sign*, no.943, June 1983, p.2.

[A.49] Sharp, Nigel, 'A media man looks at the Church: part I, the non-church goer and the Church', *Church Growth Digest*, Spring 1982, pp.4-7.

[A.50] Sharp, Nigel, 'A media man looks at the Church: part II, the church goer and the Church', *Church Growth Digest*, Summer 1982, pp.3-6.

[A.51] Souper, Patrick C. & Kay, William K., *Worship in the independent Day School*, School Assembly Project Working Paper Three, Department of Education, University of Southampton, Southampton, 1983.

[A.52] Spencer, Anthony E.C.W., 'Catholics in Britain and Ireland: regional contrasts', *Demography of Immigrants and minority Groups in the United Kingdom: Proceedings of the eighteenth annual Symposium of the Eugenics Society, London, 1981*, ed. David A. Coleman, Academic Press, London, 1982, pp.213-43.

[A.53] Stoetzel, Jean, *Les Valeurs du Temps present: une Enquete*, Presses Universitaires de France, Paris, 1983.

[A.54] Stroud, Ernie, 'Stress and Conflict: Chelmsford Clergy', St. George's House, Windsor Castle Mid-Service Clergy Course Research Project, 1983.

[A.55] Tchernia, Jean-Francois, *Young Europeans: an exploratory Study o 15-24 Year olds in E.E.C. Countries*, Commission of the European Communities, Brussels, 1982.

[A.56] Thomas, Rheinallt A. & Summerwill, John S., *RE 11-18 in Wales: Report of a Survey conducted by the Welsh National Centre for Religious Education*, Welsh National Centre for Religious Education, University College of North Wales, Bangor, 1984.

[A.57] Wadsworth, Michael Edwin John & Freeman, S.R., 'Generation differences in beliefs: a cohort study of stability and change in religious beliefs', *British Journal of Sociology*, vol.XXXIV, 1983, pp.416-37.

[A.58] Wasdell, David, *A Profile of Havering Road Methodist Church*, Unit for Research into Changing Institutions, London, 1983.

[A.59] Wasdell, David, *A Profile of the Methodist Church, Barkingside*, Unit for Research into Changing Institutions, London, (1983).

[A.60] Wasdell, David, *Tools for the Task, Number 1: Growth in Context*, Urban Church Project, London, (1979).

[A.61] Webster, Jack, 'Keeping the faith', *Sunday Standard*, 24 April 1983.

[A.62] Willcocks, Dianne M., Peace, Sheila M., Kellaher, Leonie A. & Ring, James, *The residential Life of old People: a Study in 100 Local Authority Homes*, Research Report no.12 and 13, Survey Research Unit, Polytechnic of North London, London, 2 vol., 1982.

[A.63] Worrall, Edward Stanislaus, 'Catholics in the Canterbury Diocese in 1767', *Kent Recusant History*. no.1, Spring 1979, pp.13-9.

[A.64] System Three Scotland, *Attitudes towards religious Issues in Scotland*, System Three Scotland, Edinburgh, 1983.

[A.65] Social Surveys (Gallup Poll) Ltd., *Bible Study, November 1982*, Social Surveys (Gallup Poll) Ltd., London, 1982.

[A.66] 'Brighter Sunday: 96 p.c. say no', *Daily Sketch*, 30 January 1953.

[A.67] 'Brighter Sundays: 59% say no!', *Daily Mirror*, 29 January 1953.

[A.68] 'British cool to unity under Pope', *The Observer*, 11 April 1982.

[A.69] *British social Attitudes: the 1984 Report*, ed. Roger Jowell & Colin Airey, Gower, Aldershot, 1984.

[A.70] *Burnley Guardian*, 1 July 1882 and 25 March 1892.

[A.71] Research Services Limited, *Community Survey, Scotland: prepared for the Government Social Survey by Research Services Limited*, Royal Commission on Local Government in Scotland Research Studies 2, H.M.S.O., Edinburgh, 1969.

[A.72] 'Does it last?', *Crusade*, vol.12, no.1, January 1966, pp.15-7.

[A.73] Audience Selection, *Education in Britain: prepared for 'TV Times'*, Audience Selection, (London), 1983.

[A.74] *End of Year Report, January 1982-January 1983: conventional Religion and common Religion in Leeds (HR 7720)*, Religious Research Papers 10, Department of Sociology, University of Leeds, Leeds, (1983).

[A.75] National Consumer Council, *Evidence to the Committee of Inquiry into proposals to amend the Shops Act*, National Consumer Council, (London), 1983.

[A.76] *First Communion: the Preparation and Admission of new Communicants - Report and Comment by 120 Ministers of the Church of Scotland*, ed. David Patrick Thomson, The Research Unit, Crieff, 1969.

[A.77] Office of Population Censuses and Surveys Social Survey Division, *General Household Survey, 1981: an inter-departmental Survey sponsored by the Central Statistical Office*, H.M.S.O., London, 1983.

[A.78] 'Majority 407'. *Daily Herald*, 13 July 1948.

[A.79] *Preston Herald*, 1 April 1896.

[A.80] *Prospects for the Eighties, Volume Two: from a Census of the Churches in 1979 undertaken by the Nationwide Initiative in Evangelism*, MARC Europe, London, 1983.

[A.81] Independent Television Authority, *Religious Programmes on Independent Television*, Independent Television Authority, (London), 1962.

[A.82] 'Sunday cinemas win poll', *Sunday Express*, 17 February 1946.

[A.83] 'Sunday: let the shops open up says 78 pc of Britain', *The Mail on Sunday*, 11 March 1984.

[A.84] 'Town turns down Sunday cinemas', *Sunday Express*, 16 November 1947.

[A.85] 'The truth about our children', *The Mail on Sunday*, 22 April 1984.

[A.86] Department of Education and Science, *Young People in the 80's: a Survey*, H.M.S.O., London, 1983.

SUPPLEMENTARY APPENDIX

Local plebiscites on the Sunday opening of cinemas in England, 1932-50

Town or District	Date of Poll	Approx. turn-out of electors	source
Acton	2/2/1933	?	[QRL.123], 3/2/1933
Audenshaw	2/1948	10%	[QRL.123], 17/2/1948
Barking	4/1933	?	[QRL.123], 10/4/1933
Barnes	11/3/1933	25%	[QRL.67], 13/3/1933
			[QRL.123], 13/3/1933
Barrow-in-Furness	12/1946	30%	[QRL.123], 23/12/1946
Batley	7/12/1946	26%	[QRL.67], 9/12/1946
			[QRL.123], 9/12/1946
Bishop's Stortford	15/11/1947	?	[A.84]
Blackburn	5/1946	44%	[QRL.57], 10/5/1946
Bolton	12/1946	38%	[QRL.67], 11/12/1946
Bournemouth	22/1/1934	50%	[QRL.123], 23/1/1934
Brentwood	20/5/1939	?	[QRL.123], 22/5/1939
Bristol	3/1947	17%	[QRL.123], 15/3/1947
Broadstairs and St. Peter's	3/1938	?	[QRL.123], 24/3/1938
Bromley	22/2/1933	37%	[QRL.123], 23/2/1933
Bury	17/12/1946	?	[QRL.67], 18/12/1946
Cambridge	3/1947	24%	[QRL.123], 13/3/1947
Canterbury	8/1946	25%	[QRL.123], 9/8/1946
Caterham and Warlington	3/11/1934	42%	[QRL.123], 5/11/1934
Chertsey	31/1/1948	?	[QRL.123], 2/2/1948
Chester	11/1946	?	[QRL.123], 23/11/1946
Croydon	29/11/1932	50%	[QRL.67], 30/11/1932
			[QRL.123], 30/11/1932
Dagenham	18/2/1933	?	[QRL.123], 20/2/1933
Dartford	14/11/1932	?	[QRL.67], 15/11/1932
			[QRL.123], 15/11/1932
East Barnet	13/5/1933	?	None
Eastbourne	14/2/1947	?	[QRL.123], 15/2/1947
Edmonton	4/2/1933	27%	[QRL.123], 6/2/1933

Town or District	Date of Poll	Approx. turn-out of electors	source
Egham	14/4/1934	?	[QRL.123], 16/4/1934
Epping	11/2/1933	50%	[QRL.67], 13/2/1933 [QRL.123], 13/2/1933
Gerrard's Cross	3/1939	?	[QRL.123], 30/3/1939
Glossop	11/3/1947	?	[QRL.67], 12/3/1947
Grays	11/3/1933	60%	[QRL.123], 13/3/1933
Harrow	26/1/1935	?	[QRL.123], 28/1/1935
Hayes and Harlington	21/1/1933	?	[QRL.67], 23/1/1933 [QRL.123], 23/1/1933
Herne Bay	21/11/1932	?	[QRL.67], 22/11/1932
Huddersfield	1/2/1947	?	[QRL.123], 3/2/1947
Hull	5/1947	?	[QRL.67], 22/5/1947
Ilford	1/2/1946	20%	[QRL.53], 2/2/1946 [QRL.57], 2/2/1946 [QRL.74], 2/2/1946 [QRL.123], 2/2/1946
King's Lynn	2/10/1946	?	None
Kingston-on-Thames	14/3/1933	43%	[QRL.123], 15/3/1933
Leeds	9/3/1950	?	[QRL.67], 10/3/1950
Leicester	4/1947	?	[QRL.57], 26/4/1947
Leyton	14/1/1933	27%	[QRL.67], 16/1/1933 [QRL.123], 16/1/1933
Liverpool	21/5/1947	25%	[QRL.67], 22/5/1947 [QRL.123], 22/5/1947
Luton	16/2/1946	30%	[QRL.123], 18/2/1946 [A.82]
Maidstone	19/10/1932	30%	[QRL.67], 20/10/1932 [QRL.123], 20/10/1932
Malvern	10/1946	?	[QRL.57], 9/10/1946
Manchester	8/5/1947	?	[QRL.67], 9/5/1947
Margate	3/1933	?	[QRL.123], 24/3/1933
Merton and Morden	28/1/1933	?	[QRL.123], 24/3/1933 [QRL.67], 30/1/1933
Newbury	8/1946	?	[QRL.57], 15/8/1946
Oldham	21/12/1932	24%	[QRL.67], 22/12/1932 [QRL.123], 22/12/1932
Oldham	13/5/1947	?	[QRL.67], 14/5/1947
Ormskirk	3/10/1949	30%	[QRL.67], 4/10/1949
Orpington	31/1/1948	?	[QRL.123], 2/2/1948
Oxford	12/1946	?	[QRL.123], 16/12/1946
Penge	21/1/1933	25%	[QRL.67], 23/1/1933 [QRL.123], 23/1/1933
Plymouth	17/2/1947	15%	[QRL.74], 19/2/1947 [QRL.123], 19/2/1947

Portsmouth	2/1933	?	[QRL.123], 18/2/1933
Ramsgate	7/1937	?	[QRL.123], 9/7/1937
Richmond	1/3/1933	35%	[QRL.123], 2/3/1933
Rochdale	13/1/1933	28%	[QRL.67], 14/1/1933
			[QRL.123], 14/1/1933
Rochester	9/3/1933	24%	[QRL.123], 10/3/1933
Romford	10/1933	?	[QRL.123], 30/10/1933
Salford	9/8/1946	20%	[QRL.67], 10/8/1946
Sheffield	7/2/1947	?	[QRL.123], 8/2/1947
Sidcup	17/12/1932	44%	[QRL.67], 19/12/1932
			[QRL.123], 19/12/1932
Slough	6/7/1936	20%	[QRL.123], 7/7/1936
Southgate	12/7/1948	?	[A.78]
Stockport	10/1945	25%	[QRL.67], 29/10/1945
Teignmouth	3/1946	?	None
Torquay	28/5/1946	?	[QRL.123], 29/5/1946
Tottenham	12/1/1933	24%	[QRL.67], 13/1/1933
			[QRL.123], 13/1/1933
Twickenham	20/3/1933	27%	[QRL.67], 21/3/1933
			[QRL.123], 22/3/1933
Urmston	8/3/1947	?	[QRL.67], 10/3/1947
Uxbridge	20/5/1933	?	[QRl.123], 22/5/1933
Wallasey	25/5/1933	40%	[QRL.67], 26/5/1933
			[QRL.123], 26/5/1933
Walthamstow	3/12/1932	43%	[QRL.55], 5/12/1932
			[QRL.67], 5/12/1932
			[QRL.123], 5/12/1932
Wanstead and Woodford	15/6/1935	?	[QRL.123], 17/6/1935
Wanstead and Woodford	5/1947	?	[QRL.123], 20/5/1947
Warrington	17/5/1947	33%	[QRL.67], 19/5/1947
Wembley	12/4/1933	25%	[QRL.67], 13/4/1933
			[QRL.123], 13/4/1933
Whitby	16/11/1946	25%	[QRL.67], 18/11/1946
Whitley Bay	6/1933	?	[QRL.123], 12/6/1933
Willesden	13/4/1933	?	[QRL.123], 15/4/1933
Wimbledon	15/6/1935	?	[QRL.123], 17/6/1935
Wood Green	7/1937	?	[QRL.123], 3/7/1937
Worcester	7/2/1947	?	[QRL.123], 8/2/1947

LIST OF ABBREVIATIONS USED IN THE TEXT

BLLD	British Library Lending Division
BMRB	British Market Research Bureau
BS	Bible Society
DA	Data Archive
EA	Evangelical Alliance
ESRC	Economic and Social Research Council
EVSSG	European Value Systems Study Group
GSS	Government Social Survey
JN	Job Number
LHR	Louis Harris Research
MO	Mass-Observation
MORI	Market & Opinion Research International
NDS	Newman Demographic Survey
NIE	Nationwide Initiative in Evangelism
NOP	NOP Market Research (formerly National Opinion Polls)
OPCS	Office of Population Censuses and Surveys
ORC	Opinion Research Centre
QRL	Quick Reference List
RERU	Religious Experience Research Unit, Manchester College, Oxford
RSL	Research Services Limited
SCPR	Social and Community Planning Research
SN	Study Number
URC	United Reformed Church
WfC	Wales for Christ

CONTENTS OF REVIEW 34

CHAPTER 1

INTRODUCTION

1.1 Scope of the Review

1.1.1 *Subject matter*
1.1.1.1 This review attempts to describe non-recurrent, primary sources of Christian religious statistics, both of a personal and institutional nature, gathered within the constituent parts of the United Kingdom, mainly in the period since the Second World War, by the Government, the Churches, commercial market research agencies, and by other independent investigators.

1.1.1.2 Non-recurrent data are defined as those which are compiled on an entirely *ad-hoc* basis, offering little or no potential for the construction of time series, or which have a frequency of collection of less than once in ten years.

1.1.1.3 Attention is focussed on primary data and on publications in which they were either initially reported or subsequently reprinted, whether in whole or in part. Secondary analyses of original data sets and other derivative tabulations are not generally discussed.

1.1.1.4 The term 'Christian' is used in a fairly loose sense. Whilst, organisationally, the main emphasis has been upon denominations which are either in full or associate membership of the British Council of Churches (BCC) or which have obvious theological affinities to BCC member bodies, some reference is occasionally made (for example, 3.2.5.6) to fringe sects and cults whose claims to be Christian may be thought to be less clear-cut. Ideologically too, it has seemed prudent to present the whole spectrum of folk religious beliefs, even to the extent of including cursory treatment of superstitions and the paranormal (5.2.5).

1.1.1.5 Personal and institutional data are equally considered but with some limitations. At the individual level, analysis is biased towards the beliefs and practices of adults, normally, although not always, reckoned to be people of sixteen years and above; surveys of children over the age of eight or so are dealt with on a much more selective basis, principally in Section 4.1. Organisationally, it has not proved possible to take adequate account of the hundreds of sub- and inter-denominational associations which enrich the ecclesiastical scene; names, descriptions, addresses, telephone numbers and other information relating to many of these are given in *A Directory of Christian Communities and Groups* [B.465], the *Directory of Evangelists and evangelistic Organisations* [B.466], the *UK Christian Handbook* [B.561], the *World Christian Encyclopedia* [B.572] or in parallel guides, and readers desiring particular statistics in this field are advised to contact the relevant body directly.

1.1.1.6 The geographical framework is the United Kingdom of Great Britain and Northern Ireland. In the case of Ulster it has been necessary to make a rigid distinction between overtly spiritual data on the one hand and manifestations of the sectarian tribalism which has been such a marked feature of the political troubles on the other; thus, the many opinion polls conducted in the province whose sole religious content is a vague classification of respondents into 'Protestants' and 'Catholics' have been omitted from the discussion. Islands in the British Seas fall within the review's terms of reference, but, in practice, other than the censuses carried out by the Government in 1851 (2.4.1.4) and by the Nationwide Initiative in Evangelism (NIE) in 1979 (2.2.1.5 - 2.2.1.9), there is little to note in this area. Local materials and community studies for the mainland are examined, albeit selectively, provided that they have a wider regional or national importance.

1.1.1.7 Chronologically, the main emphasis is on the period since the end of the Second World War. Significant historical sources of the seventeenth to twentieth centuries, however, are not ignored, and treatment of these will be found chiefly in chapters 2 and 3. Chapter 7 includes a systematic attempt to list all nineteenth and twentieth century censuses of church attendance, an effort justified on the grounds that participation in public worship is the most outward act of religious observance and the one which involves the fewest definitional problems in making comparisons between denominations and over time and space.

1.1.1.8 Although a particularly vigorous attempt has been made to record data collected on a national basis by commercial polling agencies, surveys emanating from other quarters have by no means been neglected. Official figures, the mainstay of so many other reviews in this series, are only occasionally helpful in the present context since, outside of Northern Ireland (where there is a decennial enumeration of religious profession), successive governments, mindful of the political and ecclesiastical controversies which surrounded the taking of the 1851 census of worship [B.101], have been somewhat wary of gathering information on spiritual matters. Within the Churches, the degree of interest and involvement in the data collection process varies enormously; some, like the Methodists (3.2.4), are very statistically conscious, yet many Christians, especially those whose allegiance is to one of the sectarian groups, are deeply suspicious of facts and figures, instancing David's sin in numbering the people of Israel (2 Samuel, 24; 1 Chronicles, 21) by way of vindication of their position. Enquiries by academics and other independent investigators also receive due treatment; postgraduate research theses, for example, are a fundamental source in certain cases, notably in the field of religious education as is evident from a helpful compilation by John Daines [B.92].

1.1.2 *Quality control*
1.1.2.1 With only rare exceptions, the discussion is restricted to surveys for which the original data set and/or some other documentation, whether published,

mimeographed or manuscript, is available either in copyright and other large libraries, in record offices, at the Economic and Social Research Council (ESRC) Data Archive (DA), University of Essex, with sponsoring bodies, with the appropriate collection agency or, in the last resort, with the author of this review. Many additional and potentially relevant studies are known to have been conducted over the years for which neither figures nor even the barest methodological details are now extant. Market research firms are particularly notorious offenders in this regard, opinion polls often being, by their very nature, essentially ephemeral affairs, undertaken for immediate consumption as news rather than for systematic preservation as historical or sociological source materials.

1.1.2.2 Data which are deemed to be methodologically suspect, deriving perhaps from surveys in which informants were not selected according to recognised quota/random principles or which registered dramatically low response rates, are not considered unless they have a special intrinsic interest or there exists a possibility of easily correcting for in-built bias. Investigations involving a base of fewer than one hundred individuals are also ignored in the main.

1.2 Plan of the Review

1.2.1 *Main text*
1.2.1.1 Although it is customary to preface these reviews with an account of the structure of the organisation concerned, it has not been found necessary to include such a discussion on this occasion since the ground is already covered to some limited extent in Lynda Barley's preceding study of Christian serial data but more especially in recent contributions to the secondary literature. With regard to the latter, John Gay's *The Geography of Religion in England* [B.129] and *Churches and Churchgoers* by Robert Currie, Alan Gilbert and Lee Horsley [B.89] offer the longest time perspectives and are most soundly rooted in the empirical evidence. Gilbert's *The Making of post-Christian Britain* [B.131] and a symposium, edited by Rupert Davies, on *The Testing of the Churches, 1932-1982* [B.559] concentrate on the more immediate past. David Martin's *A Sociology of English Religion* [B.258] and Joan Brothers's *Religious Institutions* [B.43] are the most lucid and compact sociological introductions. David Perman's *Change and the Churches* [B.300] and James Bentley's *Cry God for England* [B.17] are examples of the more journalistic approach to the contemporary religious scene.

1.2.1.2 The core of the text is divided into two main sections dealing respectively with general (chapters 2-4) and particular (chapters 5-9) data sources. The most significant cross-national (in other words, covering two or more of the four constituent countries of the United Kingdom), national and sub-national area studies are discussed in chapter 2. Chapter 3 examines multi-topic material relating to individual denominations, and Chapter 4 considers enquiries which are confined to various age cohorts or to other special groups. Data on the specific personal religious beliefs, practices and attitudes of, in the main, the overall adult population are analysed in chapters 5-8, whilst chapter 9 is concerned with statistics illustrative of the work of the institutional Church. Subject cross references are provided wherever appropriate and practicable.

1.2.1.3 Chapter 10 completes the body of the text by offering some concluding reflections on the data sources which are currently available and making a number of modest and cost effective proposals about ways in which the collection of Christian statistics could be improved in the immediate future.

1.2.2 *Appended material*

1.2.2.1 Although the Quick Reference List (QRL) is an invaluable instrument for the recording of serial data, it is somewhat less suitable in the case of a review which derives, as does this one, from many hundreds of *ad-hoc* enquiries. In order to produce a guide which can be readily understood and speedily consulted, it has been found necessary to restrict the QRL to a register of national sample surveys, representative of the entire adult population, and conducted along methodologically similar lines. Other studies are discussed in the main text, and publications arising from them are incorporated in the general bibliography.

1.2.2.2 Again, because of the immense number of investigations which are being considered, it has not proved feasible to provide the comprehensive appendix of specimen forms which is usual in these reviews. The only schedules which are reprinted here are those for the three most important national ecclesiastical censuses conducted by the Government in 1851 (2.1.3, 2.4.1.4), the NIE in 1979 (2.2.1.5 - 2.2.1.9), and by the Bible Society (BS) in conjunction with Wales for Christ (WfC) in 1982 (2.3.1.6). For the rest, copies of questionnaires appear in many of the works cited in the QRL Key to Publications or may be obtained, at cost, from the ESRC DA in the case of data sets which are lodged there.

CHAPTER 2

GENERAL SOURCES: AREA STUDIES

2.1 Cross-National Surveys

2.1.1 *1603 census*
2.1.1.1 The first proper ecclesiastical census took place in 1603 when, at the command of the Privy Council, a return was made by the Anglican clergy of the number of communicants, non-communicants and popish recusants throughout the Provinces of Canterbury (which, at that time, included all of Wales) and York. Diocesan summaries of the results are given in British Library Harleian Ms.280 which has been published on several occasions, most recently by Thomas Hollingsworth [B.185], whilst other primary documentation is in the process of being listed by D.M. Palliser and L.J. Jones of the Department of Economic and Social History, University of Birmingham.

2.1.1.2 The statistics gathered in 1603 are, methodologically, far from satisfactory. First, there was a considerable amount of under-registration; E.A. Wrigley and Roger Schofield [B.433] argue, on the basis of their back projection techniques, that between a fifth and a quarter of all adults may have been missed. Secondly, the digest extant in Harleian Ms.280 appears to have been assembled in great haste and with consequent arithmetical error; for the Diocese of Winchester, for example, it records a total of just 59,105 persons as compared with one of 93,892 derived from an aggregation of the actual parochial schedules. Thirdly, most incumbents did not attempt to distinguish between papists and nonconformists. Fourthly, the number of recusants seems to have been deliberately understated by clergy anxious to project a picture of orthodoxy in their parishes; John Bossy [B.29] suggests that the real figure for adult recusants may have been about three times the officially reported one of 8,590.

2.1.2 *Compton census, 1676*
2.1.2.1 The Compton census was undertaken early in the year 1676 by Bishop Compton of London acting on behalf of Archbishop Sheldon of Canterbury. Local ministers were asked to submit, through their archdeacons and diocesans, the numbers of 'persons... by common account and estimation inhabiting within each parish', 'of popish recusants or persons suspected for such recusancy', and 'of other disenters... of what sect soever which either obstinately refuse or wholly absent themselves from the communion of the Church of England at such times as by law they are required'.

2.1.2.2 The most complete statement of the returns for the Province of Canterbury is to be found in Salt Ms. 33 at the Staffordshire Record Office, a critical edition of which is being prepared for publication by Anne Whiteman [B.413] of Lady Margaret Hall, Oxford, whilst material for individual dioceses survives in Lambeth Palace Library Ms.639 as well as in the Leicestershire, Northamptonshire and other County Record Offices. No comprehensive account for the Province of York is known to exist, although parochial data for the sees of Carlisle and York are in Bodleian Library Tanner Mss. 144 and 150. A reasonably full bibliography of primary sources has been compiled by David Wykes [B.434], the only significant contribution which he misses being that of Mary Dobson [B.99].

2.1.2.3 The Compton data are neither absolutely comprehensive (in Shropshire, for instance, 19% of parishes appear to have failed to participate) nor very easy to interpret. This is especially true of the answers to the first of the three questions, relating to overall population, where the vagueness of episcopal instructions was reflected in major inconsistencies in the basis of calculation not only between different areas of the country but even within the same dioceses or deaneries. Some incumbents recorded total inhabitants including children, many more confined themselves to people over the age of sixteen years, others enumerated communicants or conformists, a few listed families or households, and several seem to have counted just adult males. Scarcely surprising, therefore, that E.A. Wrigley and Roger Schofield [B.433], in comparing, for two separate groups of settlements, the Compton figures with those taken from the census of 1603 and the protestation returns of 1641-42 or with estimates derived from baptismal, marriage and burial registers, could find 'plausible' 1676 statistics for only 56% of parishes in one sample and 53% in the other.

2.1.2.4 Roman Catholic data for the Province of Canterbury are usually held to be fairly reliable in the aggregate, such errors as did occur working in opposite directions and probably tending to cancel each other out; thus, on the one hand, it appears likely that some Church papists may have been classified as conformists, whilst, on the other, there is evidence to indicate that individuals were often wrongly suspected of recusancy. The absence of a detailed picture for the Province of York is a serious deficiency since it was here that Catholicism had its greatest strength; John Miller [B.272] goes so far as to suggest a total of twenty-four to thirty thousand adherents in the northern dioceses *circa* 1680.

2.1.2.5 The number of Dissenters recorded in 1676 was generally much lower than might have been expected from an examination of prosecutions for Nonconformity in the civil and ecclesiastical courts and of other contemporary sources. There are probably four reasons for this. First, some schismatics will have been frightened into submission by the prospect of a new wave of persecution against the sects which the census was widely thought to herald; indeed, in the Diocese of Canterbury, it was openly admitted that 'sending for the present enquiries has caused many to frequent the Church'. Secondly, the substantial body of Dissenters, especially Presbyterians, who, whether from genuine preference or from a baser desire to escape legal sanctions, conformed occasionally by attending 'the communion of the Church of

England at such times as by law they are required' would have been reckoned as Anglicans. Thirdly, there are grounds for suspecting that certain incumbents deliberately understated the total of sectaries in order to create a favourable impression with their religious superiors. Fourthly, given the immense rural base of Dissent at this period, it is likely that smaller and geographically remote groups of Nonconformists may have been overlooked quite unintentionally.

2.1.3 *1851 religious census*

2.1.3.1 In 1851, for the first and last time, the Government included an enquiry into religion as part of the decennial population census of Great Britain. The initiative for doing so seems to have come from Sir George Lewis, Under Secretary at the Home Office, whilst the actual form of the investigation (a schedule completed by the minister or other responsible official of each place of worship requesting information about the name, situation, date of consecration/erection and accommodation of their churches together with details of the attendance at services both on 30 March and during the preceding twelve months) was suggested by George Graham, the Registrar General. The organisation was entrusted to Horace Mann, a twenty-seven year old barrister, Assistant Commissioner for the census from October 1850 to June 1854 and subsequently Secretary to the Civil Service Commission.

2.1.3.2 For the purposes of the survey, England and Wales were divided into 30,610 separate districts each of which was the sphere of an enumerator answerable to one of the 2,190 Registrars of Births and Deaths. During the week ending 29 March the enumerators identified and listed the places of worship in their respective districts and delivered a copy of Form A (for the Established Church) or B (for all other bodies) to the clergyman or official in charge. These forms and the accompanying instructions are reproduced in Appendix 1. The completed schedules were collected on 31 March and, after initial checks for consistency and accuracy, were passed to the local registrars before 8 April. The registrars compared the returns with the enumerators' lists, endeavoured to obtain replies from those churches which had failed to respond, and submitted the documents by 22 April to the Census Office in London where twenty to thirty clerks were employed on the work of analysis. Here the returns were numbered in parochial order and collected into books. Renewed attempts were then made, either by direct correspondence with the individual place of worship or, in the last resort, through the local registrars, to remedy outstanding deficiencies in the schedules. These efforts can be shown to have continued until at least October 1852. Arrangements adopted in Scotland differed from the above in several important respects, and, accordingly, the Scottish enquiry has been given separate consideration later in this chapter (2.4.1.4).

2.1.3.3 The vast majority of the manuscript enumeration returns for England and Wales are preserved in the Public Record Office as Home Office Papers 129 (Halifax, Stockport, Torquay and the city centre of Bristol are amongst the places for which documents have not survived); those for Bedfordshire [B.446], Lincolnshire [B.494] and the Welsh counties [B.522] are also available in print. Mann's own report appeared, in both octavo and folio format, as a Parliamentary Paper on 9 December

1853 [B.450]; it contained a lengthy introduction and a mass of tables with disaggregation of data to registration district or poor law union level. A heavily abridged version, only a third of the size of the original and designed for popular consumption, was issued by Routledge, with the authority of the Registrar General, on 5 January 1854 [B.451]; according to Earl Granville, speaking in the House of Lords on 11 July 1854, this sold twenty-one thousand copies 'almost as soon as published'. Also relevant are Mann's lecture to the Statistical Society of London on 18 December 1854 [B.252] and his detailed letter to *The Times* printed on 11 July 1860 which defended the census against the criticisms then being made of its accuracy.

2.1.3.4 The value of this unique census is somewhat diminished by defects in its methodology and analysis. Highly specific problems encountered in using the data on church attendance and plant are examined in Sections 7.1.1 and 9.1.1.1 respectively, but three more general sources of error require consideration here. First, the enquiry was entirely a voluntary one, a circumstance arising from the fact that the religious questions were not distinctly authorised by the original Census Act (13 & 14 Victoria *cap* 53) but were included as an afterthought under the terms of a clause empowering the Secretary of State to seek information about such further particulars as seemed desirable. Faced with opposition inside and outside Parliament, the Government was obliged to refer the matter to the Law Officers of the Crown whose opinion was that the religious survey could not be enforced under penalty. This decision meant that there could be no legal guarantee against untruthfulness in the completion of the returns (although the character of the persons supplying the statistics, ministers of the Gospel for the most part, might be thought to be security enough), and that some degree of non-response would be inevitable. In practice, the latter was surprisingly low in the end, data on sittings being wanting from only 7.3% of the enumerated churches and estimates of attendance from 4.0% (Church of England 6.7%, all other bodies 2.2%).

2.1.3.5 Secondly, it seems certain that some places of worship were missed by the enumerators. Comparison of the census figures with other contemporary sources, and especially with the evidence submitted by Edward Baines to the Select Committee on Church Rates in July 1851 [B.532], would suggest that, whilst Mann had obtained a fairly full statement of Anglican churches, the number of non-established meetings was underestimated by at least 7%, the most serious omissions occurring with the Primitive Methodists, Baptists, Congregationalists and Unitarians. As far as can be deduced, however, chapels which were overlooked were smaller in size and influence than those which were recorded in the census, so the total percentage error involved for sittings and attendances cannot be very great.

2.1.3.6 Thirdly, various clerical mistakes were made at the processing stage and are reflected in the published tabulations. Many schedules, for example, were assigned to the wrong enumeration or registration district, Welsh place names in particular causing tremendous confusion. Frequent misunderstandings occurred in the denominational classification of churches, the Wesleyans being credited with buildings which were actually occupied by the Wesleyan Reformers, the Israelites being incorrectly identified as Jewish, and so forth. Insufficient care was taken to eliminate duplicated returns, especially numerous with the Methodists whose forms were often completed by the superintendent minister of the circuit as well as by a local chapel official. Arithmetical errors, misprints and the transposition of data were also common. Although, at a national or regional level, the cumulative effect of these mistakes was probably marginal, their impact on the results for an individual community could be quite substantial as George Patterson [B.291] has shown for South Shields.

2.1.3.7 Additional information about the conduct and findings of the census can be obtained in the articles by Kenneth Inglis [B.205], William Pickering [B.302], and David Thompson [B.383] [B.384]. Clive Field [B.109] has provided a reasonably comprehensive bibliography of primary and secondary materials, whilst Michael Drake [B.101] illuminates the political controversies which surrounded the enquiry and the reasons why the experiment was never repeated.

2.1.4 *Opinion polls*
2.1.4.1 So far as can be ascertained, the number of polls of the adult population of the United Kingdom or, more usually, Great Britain conducted since November 1937 and containing at least some questions on religious themes now exceeds three hundred and continues to grow at the rate of about a dozen a year. This total includes seventeen major investigations undertaken in mid-1947 [QRL.75], 23 0ctober - 13 November 1947, July 1948 [QRL.54] 10-11 August 1948, December 1954 [QRL.97], February 1957 [QRL.12] [QRL.74] 15-17 April 1957, February 1968 [QRL.94], May 1968 [QRL.62]; [QRL.64], August 1968, April 1970 [QRL.53], 13 May 1970; [QRL.100], June 1970 [QRL.101], September 1972 [QRL.113], 22 April 1973, August 1974 [QRL.108], May-June 1975 [QRL.12] [QRL.64], June 1975, March 1979 [QRL.25]; [QRL.64], May 1979; [QRL.112], 15 April 1979, July 1979 [QRL.79], 21 December 1979; [QRL.93], September-October 1979 [QRL.92], March 1981 [QRL.16] [QRL.70], 1982-83, April 1981 [QRL.64], April 1981, [QRL.112], 19 April 1981 and March 1982 [QRL.42], [QRL.64], April 1982. Full details of these and all the remaining studies are given in the QRL as well as throughout the text of chapters 5-9, and it is not proposed to repeat them here. Some more general remarks about the background to and interpretation of these materials, however, would seem to be appropriate.

2.1.4.2 The advantages of opinion poll data for our present purposes are threefold. First, they make it possible to collect national figures more quickly, more efficiently, more economically and at more frequent intervals than is feasible by other research methods. Secondly, they enable us to probe the realms of personal beliefs, practices and attitudes which cannot be easily reached by conventional, institutionally based sources. Thirdly, within the undeniable constraints imposed by sample size, they lend themselves to far more intensive statistical analysis than do certain other types of evidence, whether through disaggregation by age, sex, marital status, social class, region and other background variables or by the cross-tabulation of replies to individual questions.

2.1.4.3 The disadvantages of such data are rather less obvious to the casual user and certainly tend to be ignored entirely in media presentations of results. Some of these difficulties (sampling error, for instance) are common to all polls regardless of subject, but four others are more specific to enquiries on religion or, at least, arise in an exacerbated form in such investigations.

2.1.4.4 An initial complication is that large numbers of adults view their faith as far too intimate a matter to be freely discussed with a complete stranger and may well decline to answer questions about it. Geoffrey Nelson and Rosemary Clews, for example, report a 25% refusal rate for their study of *Mobility and religious commitment* [B.284] at Dawley in 1969 as compared with one of under 10% for other social surveys carried out in the town at that time.

2.1.4.5 Secondly, even when people do consent to being interviewed, it is clear that a substantial proportion of them, especially in the lower income groups, have neither interest in nor real understanding of spiritual affairs. Religion is not a subject which impinges regularly on their daily lives, they are unfamiliar with the relevant concepts and terminology, they have rarely explored their own innermost convictions and attitudes, and so, when confronted by a researcher, they find themselves singularly ill-equipped to provide answers to his enquiries. Under these circumstances, a respondent can do one of two things. Either he may consult the range of options offered and select that which he finds the most immediately attractive or, perhaps, the least uncongenial, in which case his reply can hardly be considered meaningful or durable; this is a course of action which is likely to be favoured in omnibus studies where spiritual concerns are but a brief interlude in a bewildering bombardment of questions extending, as did NOP's belief in God investigation of April-May 1964 (ESRC DA, SN 64009), from cake baking to party political preferences. Alternatively, the informant can decline to choose altogether and be registered as undecided; the abnormally large size of the 'don't know' contingent, often in the region of 20% or 30%, is a marked feature of religious opinion polls in Great Britain which, as Gallup discovered in May 1968 [QRL.64], August 1968, invariably tops the league of western nations in this respect.

2.1.4.6 Thirdly, there would seem to be an unfortunate tendency in religious surveys for people to exaggerate both the frequency with which they perform specified acts and the intensity with which they hold particular beliefs or attitudes. Such distortion may be in part unintentional, arising perhaps from a simple misremembering of events, but usually the suspicion is that it is deliberate. Whatever the ravages of secularisation, religion remains very much a 'prestige' issue, and many individuals are still unwilling to forfeit social respectability by appearing to reject or disregard it.

2.1.4.7 Fourthly, allowance has to be made for methodological imperfections on the part of the agency undertaking the fieldwork. Many of the questions asked are vague, lacking precise definitions of key concepts such as 'God', 'reincarnation' or 'the Church', and a few are so badly formulated as to be almost meaningless. Others are far from neutral in their actual wording; thus, 'what is your religion?' implies that the interviewee does have a faith and inevitably produces a higher affirmative response than a 'would you say you have any religion?' type of enquiry. The relatively greater cost of posing, recording and classifying open-ended questions has meant that most investigations use tightly structured research instruments, presenting a range of options, commonly only 'yes', 'no' and 'don't know', which is too limited to accommodate the wealth of answers that are theoretically possible in such an intellectually complex area; even the inclusion of a simple 'don't care' category can make all the difference to the pattern of results achieved.

2.1.5 *Other studies*

2.1.5.1 The Survey Application Trust made an important contribution to the gathering of global religious statistics by preparing five editions of a *World Christian Handbook* in 1949, 1952, 1957, 1962 and 1967, the data being collected primarily through questionnaires completed by the various Churches or derived from their regular publications. The last volume in the series [B.573] included details, for most of the British denominations, of places of worship, full time manpower (ordained and lay), membership and total Christian community. Population figures only were given for the Roman Catholics and Jews, whilst the Irish material is difficult to use because there are no separate returns for the Republic and for Ulster.

2.1.5.2 The Ecumenism Research Agency of 9641 Appaloosa Drive, Sun City, Arizona, 85373 compiles, at triennial intervals, a major microfilm programme illustrating 'The State of the Churches in Great Britain, Ireland, Australia & New Zealand'. Collections for 1974, 1977, 1980 and 1983 are now available and reproduce yearbooks, reports, magazines, pamphlets and manuscript letters which contain miscellaneous quantitative data of both a serial and non-recurrent nature. The value of this resource is somewhat diminished by the fact that approximately one third of all religious bodies approached, notably sectarian and foreign groups, do not participate in the project.

2.1.5.3 The *World Christian Encyclopedia* [B.572], published by Oxford University Press in 1982 under the editorial direction of David Barrett of Nairobi, is a quite monumental work which incorporates a wealth of statistics derived from questionnaire and field surveys, interviews, correspondence and secondary research undertaken between 1965 and 1976. Particular attention is drawn to two standard tables prepared for the Channel Islands, the Isle of Man, the United Kingdom and for a further two hundred and twenty countries presenting, first, national estimates/forecasts of the number of professing, affiliated and practising Christians and adherents of other faiths in the years 1900, 1970, 1975, 1980 and 2000, and, secondly, recent (apparently dating from the early 1970s) denominational totals for places of worship, adult members and overall constituency. Unfortunately, absolutely no indication is given as to the source for individual figures, some of which seem to be, at best, no more than intelligent guesses and, at worst, entirely spurious.

2.2 England

2.2.1 *National surveys*

2.2.1.1 The first specifically English enquiry was undertaken by the Congregational Union in 1834 with a view to obtaining accurate information about the relative strength of the Anglican Church on the one hand and the voluntary religious bodies on the other. Local correspondents in six agricultural and six manufacturing regions were asked to ascertain the number of places of worship, hearers, communicants and Sunday scholars connected with the various denominations in their towns and villages, and, in the end, usable figures were submitted for 1,180 churches in 202 individual communities and on the entire island of Jersey. Geographically, these replies were not well distributed, four counties (Essex, Kent, Lancashire and Yorkshire) alone accounting for 63% of the places surveyed, and only six major urban centres (Bradford, Hull, Liverpool, Nottingham, Sheffield and York) being included. A 50% sample of the data as printed in [B.459] also casts doubt on the care with which they were compiled; statistics of communicants and of scholars were missing in 35% and 26% of cases respectively, whilst just 6% of the returns of hearers were not rounded at all, with 68% being given to the nearest fifty, hundred or thousand. No manuscript documentation for this investigation appears to have survived.

2.2.1.2 During the summer of 1926 readers of two politically Liberal journals were invited to complete an identical fourteen point questionnaire regarding their church membership and attendance and their beliefs in a personal God, a life force, the divinity of Jesus, immortality, the historicity of the first chapter of Genesis, the inspiration of the Bible, the Apostles' Creed, transubstantiation, and the tenets of any branch of Christianity. One of these publications, the *Daily News*, received no fewer than 15,168 replies, equivalent to about one fortieth of its circulation, which were summarised in the issue dated 16 September 1926; the other, the weekly *Nation and Athenaeum*, was sent 1,849, corresponding to roughly one sixth of its net sale, which were discussed in its columns on 16 October 1926. Both sets of data are also conveniently tabulated in Richard Braithwaite's book [B.36].

2.2.1.3 A similar type of investigation was conducted by Geoffrey Gorer some quarter of a century later. His *Exploring English Character* [QRL.15] drew heavily upon the answers given by 4,983 of the more than ten thousand individuals who had responded to his appeal for volunteers inserted in the *People*, Britain's second best-selling Sunday newspaper, on 31 December 1950. This sample fairly reflected the marital, geographic and economic structure of the country, but it was distorted so far as sex (56% men, 44% women) and age (too many persons in the 18-34 year cohort, far too few pensioners) were concerned. The specifically religious data, comprehensively disaggregated by seven socio-demographic variables, related to belief in an afterlife, the Devil, hell and the paranormal, the habit of private prayer, denominational affiliation, church-going, and Sunday school attendance by informants' children. Original schedules are preserved at the Tom Harrisson Mass-Observation (MO) Archive, University of Sussex.

2.2.1.4 Of the opinion polls, the most significant was carried out by Gallup throughout the London, Midlands and Northern Independent Television Areas in December 1963 and January 1964. The 2,211 interviewees were asked a total of seventy-two questions of which twenty-five dealt with spiritual and moral attitudes, twenty-one with aspects of religious broadcasting, thirteen with particular beliefs or practices, and the rest with more secular matters. Full details of this study are given in [QRL.120] and [QRL.121], whilst the actual data set is archived at the ESRC DA, University of Essex.

2.2.1.5 An attempt to survey all thirty-nine thousand Christian churches in England, the Channel Islands, the Isle of Man and the Isle of Wight was made in 1979 by the NIE, a home missionary agency supported by all the leading denominations, with assistance from the BS. Ambitious in its design, this census was rather less than perfect in its actual execution, the methodology being determined by the need to have figures ready for presentation at the NIE National Assembly in September 1980. As Alan Isaacson, research officer for the project, was later to comment in an exceptionally candid technical memorandum (available on request from the BS, Stonehill Green, Westlea, Swindon, SN5 7DG): 'the finite time available for completing the report resulted in rushed work and therefore inaccuracies at each stage'.

2.2.1.6 After a pilot study in July, the investigation proper began in September and October with the creation of a central register of places of worship; although this was fairly comprehensive as such, including many of the isolated and unattached communities which are so notoriously difficult to locate, full postal addresses were often lacking. A brief questionnaire (the Anglican version of which is reproduced in Appendix 1) requesting information on membership and attendance levels in 1975 and 1979 was mailed to the minister or secretary of each meeting at the beginning of November. Reminders were sent out in December, and a further, somewhat ineffective, follow-up by telephone and local chasing was undertaken early in the New Year. Replies were eventually received from just 39% of all congregations and from a mere 18% of Orthodox, 13% of independent and 3% of African or West Indian ones; almost half of this 39%, moreover, failed to supply, either in whole or in part, details of the age and sex of their church-goers.

2.2.1.7 The data base was augmented to 74% by extracting figures relative to non-responding Anglican, Methodist, Baptist and Roman Catholic places of worship from records maintained by the appropriate denominational headquarters. Not all the requisite facts could be obtained in this way, nor did those which were available always correspond to the NIE years of 1975 and 1979. In the latter case, linear change was assumed and the statistics extrapolated.

2.2.1.8 Two major criticisms can be made of the final analysis stage. First, the decision to process the data manually rather than by computer inevitably occasioned human error ('of the 163 returned Anglican questionnaires in the Suffolk file, on recent inspection there were found to be five from Essex and six from Norfolk') as well as preventing disaggregation of the findings beyond ten broad ecclesiastical groupings and the administrative county level. Secondly, to quote Alan Isaacson, 'the scaling of membership and attendance figures' for consistency with those deriving from other sources 'may have added credence to mistaken previous results... A detailed investigation of the non-responding churches would have been preferable'.

2.2.1.9 The summary statistics of the NIE survey as published in *Prospects for the Eighties* [B.517] and in the secular and religious press during the week commencing 12 September 1980 must, therefore, be treated with some caution. Fortunately, however, all the original schedules have been preserved at the BS, and, subject to the guarantees of confidentiality given to informants, they are to be open for secondary analysis. It is very much to be hoped that they can be properly sorted and converted to machine readable format so that a fuller and more reliable picture of the whole exercise may be obtained.

2.2.2 *Community studies*
2.2.2.1 The earliest attempts to gather local religious data in anything like a scientific manner were made during the 1830s and 1840s in connection with the multitude of broader community studies then being undertaken by apostles of the so-called 'statistical movement' on the one hand and by ecclesiastics anxious to measure the market for aggressive home missionary enterprise on the other. Sometimes, as with the surveys of Penzance and Madron by Richard Edmonds in 1838 [B.102] and of Malton by William Charles Copperthwaite in 1841 [B.497], these took the form of returns of the number of sittings, services, communicants, members, average attendances and Sunday scholars supplied by the minister or lay representative of each place of worship. On other occasions, as with Abraham Hume's investigation of the Vauxhall and St. Stephen's districts of Liverpool in 1848 [B.200], house-to-house interviews were conducted in working class areas of the main conurbations with a view to collecting information on denominational affiliation, frequency of church-going, Bible ownership and so forth.

2.2.2.2 Although the sheer amount of local religious research increased considerably during the second half of the nineteenth century, most of it was directed to the measurement of progress or decline in the fields of attendance at worship (7.1.3.2 - 7.1.3.9) and plant (9.1.1.1). For the rest, statistics gathered as a result of massive Free Church domestic visitation campaigns in cities such as Bradford in 1892 [B.486], Birmingham in 1893, Lincoln in 1896, south Manchester in 1899-1900 and Liverpool in 1911, were neither properly analysed nor preserved, whilst Charles Booth's monumental and wide-ranging account of spiritual influences on London life and labour, published in seven volumes in 1902 [B.28], failed to yield any significant body of quantitative data at all.

2.2.2.3 The situation was not really to improve until 1944-45 when MO carried out a major enquiry in the London Borough of Hammersmith on behalf of the Ethical Union. This derived from interviews held with a random sample of five hundred adults aged sixteen and over, the schedule covering, *inter alia*, belief in God, life after death, Christ and the Virgin birth, prayer, confessional allegiance, attendance at public worship, membership of church organisations, attitudes to the Ten Commandments and to religious education in day schools. Results are reported in [QRL.51], 24 August 1945 and [B.518]. The poll was replicated in the same area in August 1960 [QRL.19].

2.2.2.4 Theodore Cauter and John Downham [B.70] presented the findings of a survey of 1,205 sixteen to sixty-nine year olds contacted across Greater Derby in February - April 1953 at the request of the Reader's Digest Association. Topics covered included Bible ownership and use, the extent of listening to religious services on the radio, denominational affiliation, attendance at worship and at other church centred functions, ecclesiastical office-holding, and enrolment of informants' children at Sunday school.

2.2.2.5 William Pickering's exhaustive and undeservedly neglected study of 'The Place of Religion in the social structure of two English industrial towns' [B.303] was based upon research undertaken in Rawmarsh, Yorkshire and Scunthorpe, Lincolnshire between 1953 and 1956. The principal quantitative data derived from censuses of public worship conducted on three consecutive Sundays over the Easter period, spiritual life histories contributed by a random sample of 379 active members of the various Christian bodies [B.304] [B.305], and questionnaires completed by 666 ten to eleven year old day school pupils [B.301].

2.2.2.6 Equally interesting, if rather less detailed, were the two investigations of religious conditions in the Billingham-on-Tees Urban District, County Durham which Peter Kaim-Caudle directed in 1957-59 [B.224] and 1966 [B.223]. Statistics were collected, on each occasion, relative to ecclesiastical manpower, plant and finance, the observance of rites of passage, and the size of congregations both on Easter Day and on an ordinary Sunday a fortnight later.

2.2.2.7 The largest known local opinion poll incorporating religious data was carried out in the Associated Rediffusion Television Area, a region substantially wider than that of Greater London, in 1960 under the supervision of the late David Glass. No fewer than 7,205 adults aged twenty-two and over were questioned about their confessional allegiance, frequency of worship, belief in God, and the importance of religion in their lives. Although the results of this enquiry were never published and the schedules and computer tapes have long since been destroyed, the present author did succeed in obtaining from Professor Glass, some while before his death in 1978, extracts from a typescript book which contained several of the more significant tabulations.

2.2.2.8 A rather less scientific survey was undertaken at Huddersfield the following year by a team of twenty-two students operating from the Queen Street Methodist Mission. They toured public houses, clubs and coffee bars throughout the town and quizzed 1,273 teenagers and grown-ups about their degree of interest in religion, claims to be Christians, belief in God and an afterlife, and past and present connections with the Church. A brief account of the findings appeared in [B.560].

2.2.2.9 The first full-scale investigation of the religious situation in rural areas was conducted by Peter Varney [B.396] in south Norfolk in 1962. This agricultural district, comprising seventy-nine civil parishes with a total population of some forty-five thousand, contained 154 places of worship from which were obtained details of the number of clergy, lay workers, voluntary officials and members together with average attendances at services on Sundays and festivals and at the various weekday cultural and social activities. Two representative communities, one a village with 685 inhabitants, the other a small market town with 1,242, were also selected for intensive study, interviews being attempted with ten per cent samples of their electorates regarding their beliefs and public and private devotions.

2.2.2.10 An ecclesiastical survey of the Birmingham suburb of 'Brookton' was made by Kofi Busia [B.57] in 1963-64 under the auspices of the World Council of Churches, the Selly Oak Colleges and the city's Council of Christian Churches. Although essentially a qualitative enquiry in the Charles Booth mould, some quantitative data were collected, from fourteen of the nineteen congregations, relative to attendances at services and other meetings during part or whole of a thirty-four week period, the occupations of members and the distances travelled to worship.

2.2.2.11 Further research in Birmingham was carried out by Robin Hinings during the summer and autumn of 1965 on the basis of samples of 102 electors and 65 active Anglicans from the affluent district of Hodge Hill [B.182] and of 135 white residents from the redevelopment area of Balsall Heath [B.181]. The questionnaire, which concentrated on informants' religious practices and perceptions of the Church's role within the local community, was subsequently (Easter vacation, 1968) applied to the Clun Valley of Shropshire [B.183].

2.2.2.12 Yet another part of Birmingham, the predominantly middle class suburb of Hall Green, was examined by Cyril Rodd [B.332] [B.333] in January 1966. Comparison was made between 179 Anglican, 153 Methodist and 141 Roman Catholic members with respect to sex, age, marital status, education, socio-economic class, political allegiance, denominational ancestry, attendance at services and other religious meetings, ecclesiastical office-holding, and attitudes to drink, gambling, divorce, family planning, industrial relations and racial issues. Some data were also obtained from a random sample of 309 electors and from a sub-group of 133 non-church individuals.

2.2.2.13 An important review of *Christian Unity in Sheffield* [B.319], co-ordinated by Martin Reardon and sponsored by the local Council of Churches, was completed in 1967. Two main types of evidence were used. First, statistics relative to sittings, communicants, attendances at services, Sunday schools and weekday meetings, magazine distribution, and inter-denominational activities were gathered from the clergy and other officials of the 194 Anglican, Baptist, Congregational, Methodist, Presbyterian, Quaker, Salvation Army and Wesleyan Reform places of worship in the city. Secondly, questionnaires exploring opinions about ecumenical co-operation and mission were returned by some eight hundred lay participants, Catholic as well as Protestant, in the 'People Next Door Programme' which was running at this time.

2.2.2.14 Interviews with a random sample (n = 327, equivalent to a response rate of just 50%) of the adult population of Dawley, Shropshire during the summer of 1969 form the basis of both a report [B.284] and an article [B.283] by Geoffrey Nelson and Rosemary Clews. The enquiry was chiefly designed to measure the effects of social and spatial mobility on levels of belief (in God, Jesus, miracles, the devil, life after death and superstitions) and practice (prayer, grace at meals, religious broadcasts, baptism, denominational affiliation, church membership and attendance).

2.2.2.15 During the first half of September 1977, a team based at Altrincham Baptist Church visited some six thousand homes in Altrincham, Broadheath, Hale, Bowdon Vale, Wellgreen and Timperley as part of a 'Faith for to-day' mission. They obtained replies from over two thousand three hundred persons, 66.3% of them women and 65.5% aged between twenty-one and sixty, to a short questionnaire covering ideas about God, Jesus and life after death, Bible reading, attendance at worship, and the process of becoming a Christian. Details of the results are available from Alan Wilkinson of the Manchester Business School (Booth Street West, Manchester, M15 6PB.) or from the present writer.

2.2.2.16 Opinion Research Centre (ORC) conducted a poll amongst a quota sample of 502 adults aged sixteen and above throughout Greater London on behalf of the Independent Broadcasting Authority in February and March 1978. The theme of the investigation was 'Lonely people and the media', and the interview schedule contained items relating to the value and necessity of faith, self-assessed spirituality, belief in God, and the identification, consumption and impact of religious broadcasts. Complete tabulations are given in [B.496], whilst summary data may be found in Ian Haldane's paper [B.156].

2.2.2.17 In the four weeks leading up to Palm Sunday, 1978, Queen's Road Baptist Church, Coventry embarked on a survey and gospel distribution amongst two thousand homes situated in its immediate neighbourhood. Some 972 individuals, 56,4% of them women and 62.8% aged between twenty-one and sixty, answered questions about their religiosity, belief in God, the Resurrection of Jesus and the afterlife, prayer, Bible reading and ownership, and attendance at divine service. A few figures are quoted in Veronica Zundel's article [QRL.44], 11 May 1978, and others may be requested from the present writer.

2.2.2.18 Robert Towler and Richard Toon have been directing a wide-ranging enquiry into the role of 'conventional' and 'common' religion within contemporary Leeds since November 1979. The first part of this work, which entailed the listing of all places of worship together with estimates of membership and community sizes, the mapping of this information against standard social variables, the creation of a bibliography of relevant publications and of a data archive of original source materials, was concluded in December 1980. The second stage, scheduled for completion in September 1983, has involved the administration of a complex, structured questionnaire to samples of one thousand six hundred electors and two hundred university students. The third phase, initiated in January 1982, is designed to monitor both the religious output of television, radio and the press and its public reception. News of the project, as well as copies of the various research papers arising from it, can be obtained from the Department of Sociology, University of Leeds.

2.3 Wales

2.3.1 *National surveys*
2.3.1.1 What appears to be the first specifically Welsh religious census was undertaken early in 1847 by the Cambrian Educational Society as part of its campaign to resist the spread of day schools and training institutions run on purely Anglican principles. A list of 'trustworthy persons', presumably Dissenters, was drawn up for some three quarters of the parishes in the Principality, and circulars were sent inviting them to arrange for the enumeration of attendances at morning, afternoon and evening services and at morning and afternoon Sunday school in each place of worship therein. Returns were eventually secured from 392 localities distributed across all twelve Welsh counties and incorporating 47% of their total population. The original schedules do not seem to have survived, but aggregate figures were published in the *Congregational Calendar* for 1848 [B.458].

2.3.1.2 Nearly sixty years later, on 21 June 1906, the Government appointed a Royal Commission 'to inquire into the origin, nature, amount and application of the temporalities, endowments and other properties of the Church of England in Wales and Monmouthshire; and into the provisions made, and the work done, by the Churches of all denominations... for the spiritual welfare of the people, and the extent to which people avail themselves of such provision'. In pursuance of this brief, the Commission's Central Evidence Committee amassed a wealth of statistics relating especially to the number of buildings, sittings, members and adherents of the various religious bodies, and these were reproduced in sections V, VI and VII of the final eight volume report [B.537].

2.3.1.3 The value of the Royal Commission's work is seriously reduced by three factors. First, its proceedings were conducted in an atmosphere of unparalleled sectarian rancour which was far from conducive to numerical accuracy; with the possible disestablishment of the Church of England in Wales at stake, it was in the interests of both Anglicans and Nonconformists to maximise their own returns and to discredit the reliability of their opponents'. Secondly, there was a complete failure to reach any agreed definition of such key categories as 'communicant', 'member' or 'adherent', with consequent variation in the basis of the data supplied not only between denominations but even from district to district within the same denomination; in particular, it was claimed, 'the column of adherents... became a hopeless medley of figures' which it was 'useless to add up even for the roughest of estimates'. Thirdly, the statistics related to the year 1905 when Dissenting strength was swollen by the effects of the great Welsh religious revival of 1904-05. These soon wore off, and a review of the position a decade or so later would have left an altogether different impression.

2.3.1.4 A more selective picture was created by an army of reporters from the *Western Mail & South Wales News* who, on Sunday, 10 June 1951, visited 'scores' of 'representative' Anglican and Free Churches in towns and cities, industrial valleys, rural areas and seaside resorts situated in the southern, central and western parts of the country. Information was collected, from ministerial and lay respondents, concerning seating accommodation, membership and the number and ages of worshippers both absolutely and in relation to the position forty to fifty years earlier. A brief analysis of the returns, prepared by the Reverend Ivor Cassam, was published in [QRL.126], 10-12 January 1952.

2.3.1.5 A decade later, in 1961, the Council for Wales and Monmouthshire carried out a fairly rapid and superficial survey of Anglican, Methodist, Baptist, Independent, Welsh Presbyterian and Roman Catholic congregations with a view to determining the approximate total of members, regular attenders and Sunday scholars and the extent of the use of the Welsh language in the public services, teaching and administrative work of these bodies. The material is summarised on pages 80-3 of [B.540].

2.3.1.6 The most recent data derive from a census of membership and attendance which has been undertaken by WfC and the BS along the lines of the 1979 NIE enquiry in England (2.2.1.5 - 2.2.1.9). A questionnaire, the Presbyterian Church of Wales version of which is reproduced in Appendix 1, was sent to each of the principality's six thousand places of worship in April 1982 with a request that it be returned before 25 May; just over 55 % of them did so with a further 10% participating eventually in response to a telephoned reminder. The results, analysed by computer, are expected to be published by the BS and MARC Europe towards the end of 1983.

2.3.2 *Community studies*
2.3.2.1 One of the earliest local surveys was of the village of Glan-Llyn, Merioneth (population 948) conducted by Trefor Owen [B.289] during the late 1940s. Statistics were gathered concerning, *inter alia*, religious profession, church attendance, the representation of families at Sunday school, and denominational intermarriage.

2.3.2.2 Colin Rosser and Christopher Harris [B.334] present the findings of research carried out amongst a random sample of 1,962 Swansea electors in May and June 1960. Respondents were asked about their own confessional affiliation and that of their spouse, parents and children, frequency of worship, membership of religious guilds, place of marriage (church, chapel or registry office), and attitude to the Sunday opening of public houses.

2.3.2.3 An interesting but less scientific investigation was made by Arthur Bird, a Methodist minister, during 1966 [B.21]. He visited fourteen working men's clubs, six public houses and two bingo halls in the mid-Rhondda Valley and secured over 1,180 replies to a questionnaire dealing with attendance at worship, past Sunday school enrolment, criticisms of the Church, and opinions about the conduct of religious services in places of entertainment.

2.3.2.4 The latest and most comprehensive statistics derive from Graham Day's study of 'Religion and community in mid-Wales', completed in 1975, which examined developments in Machynlleth and Newtown, Montgomeryshire. Church membership lists and a census of worship on two consecutive Sundays provided some of the evidence, but the majority came from interviews with 535 adults aged eighteen and over which were held in September 1974. Respondents were asked a total of ninety-three questions of which twenty-nine dealt with purely religious themes such as self-assessed spirituality, the qualities essential to be a good Christian, family devotions, membership and attendance at various stages of the life cycle, place of marriage, attitudes to the Sunday opening of public houses and to the involvement of the Church in local issues or national politics. The data set for this poll is preserved at the ESRC DA, University of Essex (SN 714), whilst additional information relating to the entire project is given in ESRC Research Report HR 2235, available through the British Library Lending Division (BLLD), and in an article by Day and Martin Fitton [B.97].

2.4 Scotland

2.4.1 *National surveys*
2.4.1.1 Scotland's first population census, organised by the Reverend Alexander Webster in 1755, included a classification of the inhabitants into Protestants and Catholics. The returns, made by ministers or elders of the Scottish Church and tabulated on a parochial basis, survive in a manuscript located at the National Library of Scotland and subsequently printed in [B.544]. Webster was enabled to secure a high response to his enquiry by virtue of the fact that he had Government backing for it, that he could call upon his own authority as Moderator of the General Assembly of the Kirk, and that the Society for the Propagation of Christian Knowledge in the Highlands and Islands insisted on the compliance of clergy of presbyteries where it had erected charity schools on pain of withdrawal of those schools.

2.4.1.2 *The statistical Account of Scotland* [B.352] which Sir John Sinclair, the eminent agriculturalist, supervised in the 1790s was also prepared within the framework of the Established Church. A questionnaire covering over one hundred and sixty items relative to social conditions was addressed to each local minister, and detailed descriptions of 938 parishes were eventually obtained. Although ecclesiastical material was collected in some abundance, it was rarely quantified; this was in keeping with Sinclair's definition of statistics, not as a numerical concept, but as an 'inquiry into the state of a country for the purpose of ascertaining the... happiness enjoyed by its inhabitants and the means to its future improvement'. *The new statistical Account of Scotland* [B.508], directed by a committee of the Society for the Benefit of the Sons and Daughters of the Clergy and issued as a series of county volumes in 1845, suffered from a similar limitation.

2.4.1.3 In 1835 the Government appointed a Royal Commission to examine 'the opportunities of public religious worship, and means of religious instruction, and the pastoral superintendence, afforded to the people of Scotland'. Confining their investigations to the 552 parishes (just over half the total) where a deficiency of church accommodation was both alleged and considered by the local clergy actually to exist, the Commissioners gathered a wealth of figures relative to the denominational composition of the population and to the membership, average attendance, sittings and revenues of individual congregations of all the religious bodies. These were presented, with little attempt at aggregation, in nine reports published in 1837-39 [B.535].

2.4.1.4 As we have already noted (2.1.3.2), the 1851 ecclesiastical census was conducted in Scotland as well as in England and Wales. Although the range of information collected was identical in each case, the Scottish data cause the greater problems for the historian and statistician. First, as Horace Mann himself admitted, enumerators north of the border were less careful than their English counterparts in the initial distribution of forms and consequently overlooked a larger proportion of places of worship. Secondly, there was no system of civil registration in Scotland until later in the 1850s, and so the Census Office had no machinery with which to make good any deficiencies in the returns; this was reflected in the high level of non-response, affecting 14.2% of all congregations contacted and 23.6% of those in the Established Church, and in missing data amongst those schedules which were completed (attendance figures, for example, were omitted from 8.3% of them). Thirdly, the official report for religion and education in Scotland, the Isle of Man, Jersey, Guernsey and other islands in the British Seas, released on 3 May 1854 [B.449], was, in Mann's words, both 'brief and hurried', its appearance having been advanced to satisfy the needs of the country's Members of Parliament for evidence to use in the debates on the Scottish Parochial Schools Bill. Fourthly, the original manuscript returns for Scotland have not survived, thereby limiting the possibilities of secondary analysis. Further details about the conduct and results of the enquiry are given in Donald Withrington's article [B.422].

2.4.1.5 At least four distinct attempts were made during the last quarter of the nineteenth century to quantify the extent of allegiance to, or rather disaffection from, organised Christianity in Scotland. James Johnston, a Glasgow minister, led the way in 1874 with *The ecclesiastical and religious Statistics of Scotland* [B.216], whilst *The Distribution & Statistics of the Scottish Churches*, published in 1886 [B.467], was chiefly concerned with the Established, Free and United Presbyterian denominations. Robert Howie's *The Churches and the Churchless in Scotland* [B.196] reviewed available facts about congregations, membership, attendance, Sunday scholars and finance for the 1851-91 period but was marred by sectarian bias, methodological errors, inadequate source references and by its failure to differentiate adequately between real and extrapolated figures. Finally, the Church of Scotland's Commission on the Religious Condition of the People, which reported to the General Assembly of the Kirk from 1891-98, collected a great deal of relevant material, some of which, despite the Commissioners' obvious reservations about the value of such data, was vaguely numerical in its nature.

2.4.1.6 Fifty years were to pass before the next significant contributions to the literature, John Highet's books on *The Churches in Scotland to-day* [B.172] and *The Scottish Churches* [B.173] which analysed the situation in, respectively, 1947-48 and 1958-59. Use was made of a wide range of statistical evidence including, in the case of the second work, questionnaires answered by a random sample of over four hundred clergymen from the Established, Free, United Free, Episcopal, Baptist, Congregational, Methodist and Roman Catholic Churches and by representatives from the smaller Christian denominations which provided valuable information concerning the number and socio-demographic composition of worshippers.

2.4.1.7 Opinion polls constitute the most important source for the last decade or so, particularly relevant being the reviews of public attitudes towards the Church, Sunday activities and the Christmas story which have been conducted in August 1976 [QRL.66], 11-12 October 1976; [QRL.103], September-October 1980 [QRL.66], 27 October 1980; [QRL.102] and November 1981 [QRL.88], October-December 1981; [QRL.104], 21 December 1981. More general investigations, such as the 'Scottish Mobility Study' of May 1974 -September 1975 (ESRC DA, SN981) or the election surveys of October 1974-January 1975 and May-October 1979 (ESRC DA, SN 681 and SN 1604), also contain some religious data.

2.4.2 *Community studies*

2.4.2.1 From the ecclesiastical point of view, the only major contribution to *The third statistical Account of Scotland* to date has been a chapter in the Glasgow volume written by John Highet [B.171]. This described the spiritual condition of the city during the mid-1950s on the basis of, first, figures obtained from twenty-three denominations regarding plant, members, Sunday school, Bible class and other youth work, ministerial stipends, congregational giving, baptisms and so forth, secondly, censuses of church attendance on nine separate Sundays, and, thirdly, a special study, involving some degree of quantification, of evangelistic campaigns and parish missions.

2.4.2.2 A survey of the religious observances, beliefs and attitudes of the people of Falkirk was undertaken by the Departments of Social Anthropology and Christian Ethics and Practical Theology, University of Edinburgh between September 1968 and August 1970. Data derived from returns of church and organisation membership made by twenty-three of the burgh's thirty-nine places of worship, from short questionnaires completed by 258 High School pupils, 1,115 persons present at divine service in September 1969, 169 lay leaders and 290 adults drawn at random from the entire population, and from lengthy interviews with 201 church members and 35 non-members. Full details of both the methodology and results of the project are given in Peter Sissons's final report [B.354], a summary of which appeared in [QRL.73], 16 May 1974.

2.4.2.3 Most recently of all, in 1977, Charles Piggott [B.306] has examined the geographical dimensions of religious commitment on the basis of samples of 661 members from twenty-one Protestant congregations situated in a transect running from Selkirk in the south-east to the coastal district of Ardnamurchan in the north-west and of mass attenders at three Catholic churches in the centre of Edinburgh.

2.5 Northern Ireland

2.5.1 *National surveys*

2.5.1.1 The principal non-recurrent sources comprise four polls of the adult population conducted for Professor Richard Rose in March-August 1968 [QRL.26], the Independent Television Authority and other clients in December 1968 and January 1969 [QRL.94] [QRL.95], the Department of Political Science, Queen's University of Belfast in June-November 1978 [QRL.24], and, by Gallup, for the European Value Systems Study Group (EVSSG) in March 1981 [QRL.70], 1982-3; the content of these is analysed in detail throughout the text of chapters 5-9 and in the QRL. Also relevant is a random sample survey of 2,416 males aged eighteen to sixty-four which was undertaken between August 1973 and July 1974 and included measures of self-assessed religiosity, belief in a devil/hell in afterlife and in the Bible miracles, agreement with the proposition that 'everything that happens must be accepted as God's will', denominational affiliation, attendance at public worship and Holy Communion [B.243].

2.5.2 *Community studies*

2.5.2.1 Little genuinely religious research appears to have been carried out, the main preoccupation being with investigations, both qualitative [B.125] [B.165] and quantitative [B.170] [B.310], of the signs and symptoms of sectarian conflict within everyday life and social relationships.

CHAPTER 3

GENERAL SOURCES: DENOMINATIONAL STUDIES

3.1 National Churches

3.1.1 *Church of England*

3.1.1.1 There are three main sources of Anglican statistics prior to the commencement of systematic, centralised data collection in 1891. First, on the national plane, the Government, acting principally through the Ecclesiastical Commission which it had created in 1835, gathered a wealth of material relative to the manpower, property and revenues of the Church which was published in the official sequence of Parliamentary Papers. Secondly, at a diocesan level, episcopal visitation returns from the early eighteenth century onwards contain information, albeit rather approximate and often seriously incomplete, on services, communicants, average congregations, the religious instruction of children and the like provided by the incumbents of the various parishes; these survive mainly in manuscript form in the appropriate local record offices, but aggregate figures are also usually available after *circa* 1830 in printed visitation charges, most impressively perhaps in those of Bishop Edward Glyn of Peterborough [B.136] [B.137]. Thirdly, there were a number of detailed, *ad hoc* enquiries undertaken in particular places as, for example, by the clergy of a district of the Diocese of Lincoln in 1799 [B.531] or by Alexander Dallas at Wonston, Hampshire in 1829-32 [B.93], the latter survey being notable for its attempts to analyse the results according to age, sex and social class.

3.1.1.2 Twentieth century materials have mostly been of a serial nature, but there are also some more occasional contributions to the literature which are worthy of mention. Nationally, the most significant and original data are furnished by opinion polls, particularly by the exhaustive NOP study of professed and former members of the Church of England sponsored by the *Daily Mail* in March 1960 [QRL.55] 4-8 April 1960 and the briefer Gallup investigation of attitudes to liturgical reform conducted on behalf of Professor David Martin in April-May 1980 (9.2.2.1). Of lesser relevance, being largely derivative from existing recurrent sources, are the reviews of membership, manpower, plant and money prepared by the Central Board of Finance's Statistical Unit in 1959, 1962 and 1965 [B.473], by the Lambeth Conference in 1968 [B.493], and by the Anglican Consultative Council in 1973 [B.499].

3.1.1.3 The only dioceses to have been examined in any detail of recent years are those of Southwark, where a Department of Religious Sociology under the direction of the Reverend Leslie Harman existed from 1963 to 1969, and, more importantly, Blackburn where operational researchers from the University of Lancaster carried out a two stage project during the late 1960s and early 1970s. The first phase of the survey, reported by Alan Mercer, Jennifer O'Neil and Alan Shepherd [B.269], involved the collection of affiliation and confirmation data from a one in nine sample of households in Preston as well as the completion of socio-demographic schedules by those present at services held in the town's twenty-four Anglican places of worship on each of four Sundays. The second stage entailed the creation of a computerised information bank for the entire bishopric based upon the biennial parochial returns to the Central Board of Finance, the Church Commissioners' register of clergy stipends, and on the results of a special form of enquiry sent to all 269 parishes [B.232].

3.1.1.4 More localised studies of the backgrounds, practices or beliefs of active Anglicans have been undertaken by Richard Thompson [B.385] with four Birmingham congregations during the mid-1950s (n=352), by R.E. Hawksley [B.167] at a suburban church in Liverpool in 1959 (n=219), by Trevor Beeson [B.294] on the Roseworth Estate, Stockton-on-Tees in 1960, by Barbara Wollaston [B.425] at St.Mary's, Woolwich in 1965 (n=206), by Robin Hinings [B.182] at Hodge Hill in 1965 (n=65), by Cyril Rodd (2.2.2.12) at Hall Green in 1966 (n=179), by Geoffrey Nelson (of the Department of Sociology, City of Birmingham Polytechnic) at St. Martin's-in-the-Bull-Ring in 1967 (n=109), by David Wasdell at St. Thomas' Crookes, Sheffield [B.405] [B.406] in 1977 (n=315) and St. Oswald's, Preesall [B.409] in 1979 (n=311), and by David Attfield [QRL.123], 19 April 1982; [B.6] at East Hull in 1981 (n=626).

3.1.2 *Church in Wales*
3.1.2.1 The principal non-recurrent source, a six year study of the Diocese of Bangor completed in 1973, is discussed at length by Christopher Harris [B.162]. In response to three separate enquiries, 97 of the 116 parishes provided details of their services, organisations, finances, ecumenical and community contacts, 96 furnished a statement of the number of ministers and places of worship of each denomination within their boundaries, and 37, seemingly those with the highest rates of Anglican affiliation, participated in a general population survey in which a total of two and a half thousand persons aged twenty and over were questioned about, amongst other things, their religious profession and frequency of church attendance.

3.1.3 *Church of Scotland*
3.1.3.1 The Scottish Church has produced serial statistics since the late 1870s and has also commissioned several *ad hoc* investigations. Two major initiatives during the 1970s were the formation of a Committee of Forty under the convenorship of Professor Robin Barbour in 1971 'to interpret... the purpose towards which God is calling His people in Scotland, to...assess... resources...in persons and property for the fulfilment of this purpose, and to make recommendations for the re-shaping of the life and structure of the Church' and of an Economic Survey which was located at the University of Edinburgh from 1972 to 1977. The former group reported to the General Assembly of the Kirk in 1975, and the latter gave birth to a substantial

volume by James Wolfe and Michael Pickford [B.423] which incorporates a wealth of quantitative data, by no means exclusively financial in character, much of it deriving from a reappraisal of already available facts and the remainder being supplied by various small random samples of congregations. Other interesting work has been conducted on a more localised basis, prime examples of this being the theses by John Fraser Kirk [B.233], D.A. Stewart [B.374] and Gillian Watson [B.411] on the Edinburgh situation.

3.2 Free Churches and Sects

3.2.1 *General surveys*

3.2.1.1 After the episcopal returns of 1669 [B.512] and 1676 (2.1.2), the earliest statistical record of Nonconformity is contained in the Reverend Dr.John Evans's 'List of Dissenting Congregations and Ministers in England and Wales, 1715-29' which is preserved as Ms. 38.4 at Dr. Williams's Library, London and gives details of the location, names of pastors, number and quality of 'hearers' (total worshipping constituency, apparently including children) and of voters for Presbyterian, Independent and Baptist meetings. Evans, acting on behalf of the Committee of the Three Denominations of which he was Secretary, obtained his information, mainly in 1716, 1717 and the early part of 1718, from a network of Presbyterian and Independent correspondents up and down the country in order to strengthen the campaign then being waged to secure the repeal of the 1714 Schism Act. The manuscript has never been printed in its entirety, despite the fact that the Baptist data were extracted for publication as long ago as 1910-11 [B.445], but it has been the subject of frequent secondary analysis, most recently by James Bradley [B.35] and Michael Watts [B.412].

3.2.1.2 The Evans list is not wholly free from interpretative difficulties. First, although the mapping of Presbyterian and Independent causes seems to have been fairly comprehensive, research by W.T. Whitley and others would indicate that perhaps a quarter or more of Baptist ones were overlooked. Secondly, approximately one third of meetings, including all of those in Derbyshire, Dorset, Middlesex and Norfolk, provided no estimates of their hearers, whilst some, especially in Wales, returned figures which cannot easily be reconciled with other contemporary evidence. Thirdly, little importance should be attached to the relative statistics of Presbyterians on the one hand and Independents on the other; far from being a rigid distinction between the two bodies at this time, there was, in fact, a considerable degree of interchange, both of ministers and even complete societies, between them.

3.2.1.3 Also preserved at Dr. Williams's Library (Ms. 38.5 and 38.6) are two copies of a 'List of Dissenting Congregations in England and Wales, 1772-3' drawn up by Josiah Thompson, a retired Baptist pastor living in London, with the help of a team of Presbyterian, Independent and Baptist correspondents. Besides the location of meetings, there are notes on the origin, history and present condition of various churches together with the names of ministers in each county who had either signed or otherwise expressed support for petitions to relieve Nonconformist clergy from the modified subscription to the Thirty-Nine Articles which was required under the Toleration Act; numbers of auditors are only occasionally given. The manuscript has been printed, with some omissions, in [B.564].

3.2.1.4 Some half a century later, in June 1829, the House of Commons called upon the Secretary of State for the Home Department to procure a return of 'places of worship not of the Church of England in each parish; distinguishing, as far as possible, of what sect or persuasion, and the total number of each sect in England and Wales'. Results for Lancashire are given in a Parliamentary Paper of July 1830 [B.541], whilst original documentation for Buckinghamshire, Derbyshire, Essex, Hertfordshire, Kent, Leicestershire, Lincolnshire, Norfolk, Northumberland, Nottinghamshire, Suffolk, Sussex, Wiltshire, Worcestershire and the North Riding of Yorkshire survives in local record offices; schedules for all other areas appear to have perished in the fire which ravaged the Palace of Westminster in 1834. The usefulness of the extant data is affected by non-response (in Lancashire, for instance, there are no figures for forty-two settlements containing some 9.4% of the county's entire population), by the failure to achieve an agreed definition of 'place of worship', house meetings being included in some districts but not in others, and by variations in the criteria adopted for calculating the size of congregations.

3.2.1.5 Subsequent research has tended to be of a more localised nature, invariably linked, since the 1890s, with the Free Church Council movement. One notable example was the report on the state of evangelical Dissent in Liverpool which Wilfrid Rowland [B.335] prepared in 1908 on the basis of interviews, questionnaires and a special census of attendance. A more recent case is Gregory Stevenson's survey of Nonconformist allegiance in Greater Swindon in January 1966 which has been reproduced by Kenneth Hudson [B.197].

3.2.2 *Baptists*

3.2.2.1 There is surprisingly little to report before November 1977 when the Baptist Union Council established a Denominational Enquiry Group to examine the causes of, and possible remedies for, numerical and spiritual decline within the Church. The Group sent a questionnaire relating to location, membership, ministry, leadership, activities, pastoral care, young people's work, outreach, worship, finance and ecumenical contacts to a non-random but allegedly representative sample of two hundred and five English and Welsh congregations of whom one hundred and sixty replied. The first hundred returns to be received were analysed statistically in Appendix II of *Signs of Hope* [B.549] which was presented to the Council in March 1979.

3.2.2.2 A parallel but less official investigation, undertaken in 1978 by the Reverend Paul Beasley-Murray of Altrincham and Alan Wilkinson of the Manchester Business School, was designed to evaluate 'the major tenets of the Church Growth Movement... in a British setting'. The 106 item research instrument was completed by a total of 327 English fellowships, 58% of the 561 approached, of which 195 were actually increasing in size and 132 were not but had memberships in excess of fifty. Results are described in *Turning the Tide* [B.11]

3.2.3 *United Reformed Church*
3.2.3.1 There have been two main studies of the former Congregational Church, one conducted by Luke Beaumont [B.12] at ninety-one places of worship in the North-Western Province in 1929-31, the other carried out by Peter Sissons [B.353] throughout Greater Manchester in 1966-67 and incorporating a demographic profile of 3,862 members and 440 deacons as well as special enumerations of attendance at divine service. Barbara Wollaston [B.424] was responsible for the only important survey of the former Presbyterian Church of England, an analysis of the characteristics, practices and opinions of ninety-three of the ninety-nine members of St. Andrew's, Woolwich during the winter of 1966.

3.2.3.2 The United Reformed Church (URC), created by the merger of these denominations in 1972, has sponsored two limited but interesting pieces of quantitative research. The first, summarised in an unpublished report of December 1978 available from the URC Education Committee, monitored the experience of forty-three thriving causes. The second, accomplished in the autumn of 1979 by an *ad hoc* Priorities and Resources Group [B.475], examined membership and attendance patterns for a more random selection of seventy-six societies.

3.2.4 *Methodists*
3.2.4.1 Methodism has a statistical tradition which is quite unrivalled in the history of British religion; annual returns have been made continuously since the 1760s, and there have also been a good many non-recurrent surveys at connexional, district, circuit and chapel levels. Nationally, perhaps the most wide-ranging enquiries were those undertaken by the Primitive Methodist General Missionary Quarterly Committee during the mid-1890s [B.533] and by the Wesleyan Spiritual Advance Committee towards the end of the First World War [B.553]. More specialised studies include two reviews of the plight of the rural Church, one prepared in 1958 on the basis of some forty-five thousand facts relative to manpower, plant, finance, congregations and organisations derived from a sample of 198 circuits [B.543], the other compiled in 1970 and paying particular attention to membership trends and the supply of lay preachers [B.460], and an investigation of work among young adults in 1978 which is briefly referred to in David Winwood's *Before it's too late* [B.421].

3.2.4.2 Some of the earliest regional research was conducted by the Wesleyans throughout Yorkshire in 1830 [B.155] and by the Primitive Methodists across London in 1906 [B.515] and 1918 [B.516]. Of later years, the state of societies within the Liverpool District has been examined in 1966 [B.290] and 1976 [B.538], whilst the life of the Leeds District has been portrayed with the help of lengthy questionnaires answered by 342 members in 1968 [B.393] [B.394] and of censuses of congregational activities and outreach in 1969 and 1971 [B.468] [B.554].

3.2.4.3 Surveys at the circuit level seem to have originated with a sketch of the *Agency and Progress of Wesleyan-Methodism* [B.437] in West Sheffield in May 1845. More recently, major studies of membership, adherence, attendance, organisations, buildings and finance have been completed in the York (Wesley), South Shields and Durham and Deerness Valley circuits in 1967, 1970 and 1974 respectively; documentation for these is held by the present writer.

3.2.4.4 Many instances of chapel based enquiries could be cited, but most are of no more than passing interest. One exception to the rule is Lewis Burton's analysis [B.55] [B.56] of the social stratification of the congregations at Low Hill and Beckminster, Wolverhampton in 1962-65. Another is the series of ten sociological profiles which David Wasdell, Director of the Urban Church Project from 1974 to 1981, has been commissioned to produce in the London North-East District; two of these, dealing with Methodism in Billericay [B.407] and Barking [B.410], have already appeared.

3.2.5 *Other bodies*
3.2.5.1 Censuses of Unitarian places of worship across Great Britain have been published in 1832 [B.562], 1946 [B.571] and 1967 [B.63] [B.453]. The third and by far the most important of these was carried out by the Foy Society Survey Group in 1964-66, data about members, supporters, worshippers, religious societies, plant, manpower, finance, denominational awareness and the like being obtained from 238 out of a total of 258 meetings.

3.2.5.2 The regular collection of Quaker statistics, commenced in 1860, was preceded by various *ad hoc* enumerations of which the most notable was a national return of members, disaggregated by age and sex, procured by the editors of the *Annual Monitor* in June 1847 [B.439]. More topically, Kathleen Slack [B.357] has examined the socio-economic backgrounds and religious commitment of 898 Friends from seventeen centres scattered across England, Wales and Scotland in 1964-65, whilst Richard Errington (of 42 Wrensfield, Hemel Hempstead, HP1 1RP.) is writing up the findings of a demographic and opinion survey conducted amongst attenders at the 1982 Yearly Meeting.

3.2.5.3 The only quantitative sources relating to the Salvation Army are two studies of the general public's knowledge of and attitudes towards its work which were undertaken at London, Bolton and Chester in 1942 and at London, Bristol and Preston in 1946. Several hundred adults were interviewed on each occasion, the results being tabulated in File Reports 1421 and 2387 at the Tom Harrisson MO Archive, University of Sussex.

3.2.5.4 The Lutheran Council of Great Britain (of 8 Collingham Gardens, London, SW5 OHW.) promoted a 'sociological self-study' of eighty-nine churches from its Estonian, German, Hungarian, Latvian and United Synods during the course of 1965-66. Statistics were collected concerning various aspects of congregational life and the age, sex, marital status, occupation, national origin, present citizenship and other characteristics of 8,902 members.

3.2.5.5 Surveys of the activities and evangelistic effectiveness of the 'open' wing of the Christian Brethren movement have been carried out by Graham Brown [B.45] in 1966 (n = 75 assemblies) and by Brown and Brian Mills [B.46] in 1978 (n = 249). Longitudinal data for the twenty-eight fellowships which participated in both enquiries are discussed in *The Harvester* for September 1981 [B.44].

3.2.5.6 Figures relating to other sectarian bodies have nearly all been gathered by means of questionnaires administered by independent academic researchers. Notable examples comprise investigations by Robert Buckle [B.51] of Mormons in Hereford, by James Beckford [B.13] of 180 Jehovah's Witnesses from ten congregations in 1969, by Robin Theobald [B.382] of 274 of the 592 nominal members in eight churches attached to the British Union Conference of Seventh-Day Adventists in 1977, and by Eileen Barker [B.8] of 226 Moonies in 1978.

3.3 Roman Catholicism

3.3.1 *Early work*
3.3.1.1 For some three hundred years between the Reformation and the passage of the Emancipation Act of 1829 the Catholic community of England and Wales was judged a threat to the security of both the Constitution and the Established Church and was subjected to repeated official enumeration. Apart from the general ecclesiastical censuses of 1603 (2.1.1) and 1676 (2.1.2), perhaps the best known and most significant of these papist returns were those undertaken by the Anglican clergy at various dates during the eighteenth century.

3.3.1.2 The first of these surveys, which gave the numbers and often the names and employments of Catholics in 1705-06, failed to achieve national coverage. Manuscript summaries for the Bishoprics of Bangor, Canterbury, Carlisle, Chester, Exeter, Gloucester, Hereford, Lincoln, St. Asaph, Salisbury and York as well as the original incumbents' reports for Durham and Lichfield and Coventry are preserved at the House of Lords Record Office (Main Papers, 1 March 1706), and further documents are known to survive in county or diocesan archives. The schedules for Devon and Cornwall have been edited and published by Kevin MacGrath [B.245], those for Essex by Philip Coverdale [B.84], for Hertfordshire and Middlesex by E.S. Worrall [B.427] [B.426], for London by Margaret Hine [B.180], for Oxfordshire by W.O. Hassall [B.166], for Shropshire by N.Mutton [B.281], and for Staffordshire by Michael Greenslade [B.145].

3.3.1.3 The second investigation, which took place between July and October 1767, sought details of the sex, age, occupation and length of residence of every Catholic in England and Wales. The House of Lords Record Office holds parochial returns for the sees of Chester and Durham and abridged tabulations for all remaining districts (Main Papers, 21 December 1767), whilst incumbents' replies for an additional eleven bishoprics have been traced in local depositories. The Catholic Record Society has published the complete documentation relating to the Diocese of Chester [B.542], and, funds permitting, it intends to issue a second volume covering the rest of the country which would supersede the various printed editions now existing for Devon and Cornwall [B.244], Shropshire [B.281] [B.282], Staffordshire [B.144] and other areas. The most comprehensive modern account of the methodology and results of the census is provided by Jean-Alain Lesourd [B.239] who concludes that the number of papists was probably underestimated by some five per cent; John Bossy [B.29], on the basis of research into rural Northumberland, is inclined to opt for a higher figure of fifteen per cent.

3.3.1.4 The third and last major enquiry in the series was carried out towards the end of 1780. Summaries for all English and Welsh sees are available at the House of Lords Record Office (Main Papers, 5 March 1781), whilst original clerical reports are preserved at the Bodleian Library, Oxford, the Salisbury Diocesan Registry, the Borthwick Institute, York and elsewhere. Undercounting would appear to be a fairly critical problem in the utilisation of these data, many of the parishes replying in 1767 either failing to do so at all thirteen years later or recording an identical or similar figure to the one they had submitted on the former occasion.

3.3.1.5 State endeavour gave way to a process of self-enumeration which was at once less ambitious in its design and far from satisfactory in its actual execution. Indeed, the first major internal survey, made by the four English Vicars Apostolic in 1773 for transmission to the Congregation de Propaganda Fide in Rome and recently reproduced by John Whyte [B.415], set a pattern for vagueness and lack of methodological rigour which was to distinguish much of the Church's statistical effort throughout the nineteenth century and beyond. Investigations of substance and precision, such as Archbishop Vaughan's census of the Diocese of Westminster in 1893-94, are a comparative rarity.

3.3.2 *Newman Demographic Survey*
3.3.2.1 The establishment of the Newman Demographic Survey (NDS) in December 1953 brought about a rapid change for the better [B.365] [B.366]. Under the energetic direction of Anthony Spencer, now of the Department of Social Studies, Queen's University of Belfast, the NDS developed sociological and quantitative research of the highest standards in almost every sphere of the Church's work. Particularly impressive were its school and pastoral statistics programmes, evolved in conjunction with the Catholic Education Council, and the parish census service which operated from 1961 to 1964 and generated a wealth of data on the backgrounds and religious behaviour of the laity [B.342] [B.363] [B.364].

3.3.2.2 Rarely free from staffing and financial difficulties, and never quite enjoying the whole-hearted support of the ecclesiastical hierarchy, the NDS finally collapsed early in 1964. Spencer, not a man to be easily daunted, proceeded to divert his talents to the foundation of a Pastoral Research Centre at Harrow whose most original and significant achievement was the production of two statistical profiles of

Scottish Roman Catholicism in 1967 and 1969. These included figures of estimated population, infant baptisms, adult conversions, confirmations, marriages, deaths, mass attendance, communicants and confessions, all suitably disaggregated by county or burgh, diocese and region [B.368] [B.369].

3.3.3 *Catholic Herald surveys*

3.3.3.1 The *Catholic Herald*, a London weekly newspaper circulating throughout England and Wales, has made three attempts to enlist the co-operation of its readership in the completion and return of questionnaires appearing in its columns. The first, reported in the issue of 5 December 1958, was essentially a piece of market research, the three and a half thousand contributors simply providing information about their personal backgrounds and consumption patterns. The second, which attracted nearly four thousand replies and was published on 12 July 1968, covered similar ground but also probed attitudes to the Vatican Council, the Latin mass, Friday abstinence and Christian unity. The third, launched in January 1977, achieved no fewer than 9,341 responses to a thirty-nine point schedule focussing especially upon liturgical, organisational and other changes in the life of the Church; parallel enquiries were also made in Scotland and Ireland by the *Scottish Catholic Observer* (n = 4,398) and the Dublin *Catholic Standard* (n = 5,774), results appearing in the editions of all three papers for 25 March, 1 and 8 April 1977, with additional analysis in [QRL.47], 12-19 August 1977.

3.3.3.2 Interesting though these data undoubtedly are, the self-selecting samples from which they derive cannot be regarded as representative of the Catholic community at large. Clear demonstration of this fact is afforded by a comparison of the 1977 study with the findings of a truly random survey which was carried out at exactly the same time (3.3.4.2). This reveals the *Herald* informants to have been, in the words of one commentator, 'disproportionately male, single, middle aged, in small households, converts, middle class, politically conservative and from the South-East'.

3.3.4 *Opinion polls*

3.3.4.1 The Gallup Poll has been responsible for four general studies of the beliefs and attitudes of professing Roman Catholic adults. The first, conducted from 18-20 March 1967 on behalf of the *Sunday Telegraph*, involved interviews with four hundred persons distributed across thirty-seven sampling points throughout Great Britain. The twenty-three questions dealt with the authority of the Church, lay participation in ecclesiastical affairs, the leadership of Cardinal Heenan, Christian unity, birth control, abortion, divorce, inter-faith marriage, clerical celibacy, liturgical change, denominational schooling, mass attendance and standard demographic variables. Results are given in [QRL.23]; [QRL.112], 26 March 1967; [B.478].

3.3.4.2 The second investigation took place from 2-28 February 1977 when 368 British Catholics were asked about their backgrounds, frequency of worship, confessional habits, the Latin mass, democracy in the Church, the work of the Vatican Council, ecumenism, the Northern Ireland problem, religious education, contraception and the celibacy of priests. The research was commissioned by the *Catholic Herald* as a check on the accuracy of its own readership profile (3.3.3.1), and the data are summarised in the issues of that paper for 25 March 1977 and 15 September 1978 as well as in [QRL.64], April 1977.

3.3.4.3 Fieldwork for the third study was carried out in Scotland from December 1977 to February 1978 with financial support from the Archdiocese of Glasgow and the Diocese of Motherwell. Interviews of sixty to ninety minutes duration were held with a representative group of 989 Catholics aged fifteen and over, the one hundred and eighty item schedule embracing upbringing, socio-demographic characteristics, religious beliefs and practices, reactions to ecclesiastical modernisation, perceptions of the priesthood, moral attitudes and the role of the Catholic school system. Gallup's computer tabulations for this enquiry extend to four volumes comprising over a thousand pages, but only a fraction of these figures have so far been made public, principally in [QRL.119], 28 April 1979 and [B.569].

3.3.4.4 Hard on the heels of the Scottish survey came a comparable one for England and Wales. Funded by an anonymous trust and directed by Michael Hornsby-Smith and Raymond Lee of the Department of Sociology, University of Surrey, this derived from a quota sample of 1,023 Catholics contacted at one hundred and five points in February-March 1978 and weighted according to mass attendance and occupational distributions revealed in the omnibus *Religion study* [QRL.96] of February-April 1978. The one hundred and fifty-six questions were particularly designed to test 'hypotheses relating to the "effectiveness" of Catholic schools in terms of the religious attitudes, beliefs, behaviour and commitment of their former pupils'. Methodology and key findings are discussed at some length in [B.190] which formed the basis of numerous articles in the secular and ecclesiastical press during the week commencing 29 January 1980, of a major series in *The Tablet* [QRL.119], 2-23 February 1980, and of a pamphlet by David Gerard [B.130]; further analysis has since appeared in [B.192] and [B.193], whilst the data set has now been deposited at the ESRC DA, University of Essex (SN 1570).

3.3.5 *Local studies*
3.3.5.1 The NDS's parish census service (3.3.2.1) was foreshadowed by a number of localised enquiries which were the product of more individual initiatives. Amongst these may be mentioned those by Eugene Langdale [B.236] at Eastcote, Middlesex in December 1954 (n=482 respondents), by Reine Goldstein [B.138] [B.139] at Shildon, County Durham in March 1955 (n=192) and November 1957 (n=150) and in a residential district of London in March 1960 (n=401), by 'Parochus' [B.513] in a northern town towards the end of 1956 (n=485), by Conor Ward [B.402] [B.403] in 'St Catherine's', Liverpool in 1957 (n=96), and by Vanni Bressan [B.38] at the Holy Ghost and St Stephen, Shepherd's Bush.

3.3.5.2 Subsequent work is exemplified by the investigation of 'Tradition and change in the Roman Catholic community in England' which was carried out in four contrasting parishes (two in Preston, two in London, two inner city, two suburban) in 1974-77 by Michael Hornsby-Smith, Raymond Lee and Peter Reilly of the University of Surrey. The first stage of the project employed structured interviewing techniques to compare the educational and occupational backgrounds, religious identification, beliefs and practices, attitudes to a range of social, political and moral issues of randomly selected samples of 267 Catholics and 1,189 other electors. The second phase consisted of in-depth and generally tape-recorded conversations with 183 of these 267 faithful, focussing especially upon 'religious socialisation' and values as well as on reactions to changes in the Church and the implementation of these at the parochial level. Additional methodological information may be found in ESRC Research Report HR 3444, available through the BLLD, whilst the actual data set has now been archived at the ESRC DA (SN 1572).

CHAPTER 4

GENERAL SOURCES: GROUP STUDIES

4.1 Children

4.1.1 *Pioneer work*

4.1.1.1 Numerous studies of children's religious thought and behaviour have been conducted during the last four decades, the majority of them by educationalists employing attitude scales based upon the techniques of L.L. Thurstone or R.A. Likert. Only those deriving from samples in excess of one thousand respondents are discussed here, and for details of lesser research readers are referred to the series of thesis abstracts prepared by John Daines [B.92] and to a valuable bibliographical article by Leslie Francis [B.113].

4.1.1.2 An early barometer of the interest shown by boys and girls in spiritual matters is provided by a survey undertaken by R. Rallison [B.316] at 141 schools throughout Newcastle-upon-Tyne and Northumberland at the beginning of the 1940s. Given a week in which to compile a list of everything they would most like to know, 3,514 pupils in the eleven plus to thirteen plus range eventually submitted a total of 17,264 individual non-scientific questions which were sorted into seventeen groupings of which religion was one.

4.1.1.3 A further attempt to quantify childhood preoccupation with religious issues and the prevalence of doubt was made by James Bradbury [B.34] in twenty-two modern, central, technical and grammar schools across Cheshire, Lancashire, Leicestershire, Westmorland and Yorkshire between July 1944 and November 1945. The subjects comprised 696 boys and 842 girls, mainly in the eleven to fifteen year band.

4.1.1.4 An investigation of the leisure activities of some five thousand secondary pupils at Ilford in 1946-47, carried out by Mary Stewart [B.375] [B.376] and students from a London University tutorial class, included details of the membership of churches and chapels, Sunday schools and other ecclesiastical organisations. The enquiry was replicated with the aid of a Workers Educational Association group in 1958, the number of respondents on this occasion exceeding seven thousand which was equivalent to 88% of the relevant age range in the borough [B.377].

4.1.1.5 John Daines presented 'A psychological Study of the Attitude of Adolescents to Religion and Religious Instruction' as a doctoral thesis in 1949 [B.91]. His sample consisted of 1,090 children drawn from grammar schools in both urban and rural areas of Greater London and the Midlands.

4.1.1.6 The results of a three year project established at the University of Sheffield Institute of Education in December 1956 are described in [B.527]. Tests were completed by 1,233 fourteen to fifteen year olds, 607 males and 626 females, from four grammar, three technical and eight modern schools in various parts of the Institute region, the twenty questions being chiefly designed to assess Bible knowledge on the one hand and religious practices and opinions on the other.

4.1.1.7 Research carried out by Kenneth Hyde at the University of Birmingham from 1958 to 1961 centred on a series of six separate papers given to 1,977 pupils, 1,035 boys and 942 girls, in forms one to six of four state schools, two grammar and two modern, situated in the West Midlands conurbation. These covered religious behaviour and attitudes, images of God, definitions of key spiritual concepts, awareness of scripture stories, Christian festivals, and the life of Jesus. The earliest phase of the work is discussed in [B.204], whilst final figures appear in [B.203].

4.1.1.8 Frank Garrity surveyed 4,040 eleven to fifteen year old children, 2,088 males and 1,952 females, from eight secondary modern schools in the County Borough of Stockport. Use was made both of a questionnaire to ascertain regularity of church or Sunday school attendance and home Bible reading and of a twenty-two statement scale to measure opinions about religious education. The full results are contained in an unpublished thesis of 1960 [B.126] which has been summarised in [B.127].

4.1.1.9 A parallel study was conducted by Winston Johnson [B.215] amongst first and fourth year pupils at twelve modern schools, ten mixed and two single sex, in Manchester and Stockport during the early 1960s. An initial sample of 1,440 children were asked a number of basic questions about their background and religious practices, and from these were selected, on the basis of quota controls for sex, age, church attendance and stream, a sub-group of 640 to complete a two part spiritual attitude scale.

4.1.1.10 Colin Alves [B.5] reported the findings of a multi-stage enquiry launched by the BCC in 1964. The first phase was conducted amongst 637 county secondary schools in England and Wales, 293 of them chosen for their success in religious instruction and the remainder according to random principles, of which 520 (185 grammar and 335 modern) eventually co-operated in setting a spiritual knowledge, attitude and behaviour test to the highest ability stream of their fourth formers, the resulting fifteen thousand pupil schedules being scored and analysed on a school basis. The second stage involved the completion of a questionnaire by the headmasters and religious education staff of 80 of the 98 highest and 62 of the 102 lowest scoring schools. During the third phase, 60 of the surviving high scoring institutions administered a further written examination, this time to their eldest children, fifteen to sixteen year olds in modern and seventeen to eighteen year olds in grammar schools, which produced some 1,360 individual responses.

4.1.2 *Recent research*

4.1.2.1 Philip May, currently Reader in Education at the University of Durham, was responsible for a nationwide survey of children's attitudes to prayer, church-going, the Bible, life after death, loving God, and human goodness during 1973-76. A random selection of 160 maintained primary and secondary schools throughout England took part, and information was gathered from some 4,943 pupils of whom 49% were boys, 51% girls, 25% were ten to eleven year olds, 42% were aged fourteen to fifteen, and 33% were in the sixth form. Some of the data have appeared in periodical articles [B.261] [B.262].

4.1.2.2 Brian Gates [B.128] has examined the level of religious understanding amongst boys and girls from six to fifteen years. Written tests involving the comprehension of two stories, sentence completion exercises and an attempt at picturing God were administered to approximately one thousand pupils from eight schools. Oral interviews embracing a very broad spectrum of spiritual ideas and concepts extending, at one extreme, to superstitions, belief in Father Christmas, and the like were also held with samples of eighty-two Anglican, thirty-eight Nonconformist, forty Roman Catholic, forty-one Jewish, thirty-nine Sikh, seventeen Muslim and eighty-one denominationally unattached children from a total of fifteen schools.

4.1.2.3 Leslie Francis devised a twenty-four item Likert-type attitude scale concerning the Church, church-going, prayer, the Bible, God, Jesus, religious instruction and assembly [B.112] for use in two surveys conducted in Essex, Suffolk and Cambridgeshire during 1974. The first was designed to monitor changes in religious outlook between the initial year of the junior and the fifth year of the secondary school; some nine hundred pupils from four local education authority establishments were involved, and results are presented in a doctoral thesis [B.115] and in a Farmington Institute Occasional Paper [B.114]. The second sought to isolate the effects of differing kinds of agreed syllabus and institutional foundation (LEA, Anglican or Catholic) on the views of 2,272 third and fourth year pupils in mixed primary schools; findings are recorded in an unpublished dissertation [B.118] and in two periodical articles [B.117] [B.119]. With assistance from John Rust and Boyd Wesley at the University of London Institute of Education, both investigations were replicated in 1978, the new project being described in ESRC Research Report HR 5580 which is available through the BLLD.

4.1.2.4 Three independent and four state schools contributed to a survey carried out by Mary Spain [B.567] in 1977 during which pupils were asked to write a free essay on 'What I believe' as part of their English language instruction. Some 1,973 manuscripts were received, rather inequitably distributed between boys (56.6%) and girls (43.4%) as well as between children aged eight to ten (6.2%), eleven to fifteen (79.0%) and sixteen to eighteen (14.7%), the content being subjected to fairly arbitrary statistical analysis by Susan Major.

4.1.2.5 Timothy Mark undertook 'A Study of cognitive and affective Elements in the religious Development of Adolescents' [B.254] in two comprehensive schools on the outskirts of Sheffield in January-March 1978. His questionnaire, which dealt with attitudes to faith and to other people, religious and compassionate behaviour, and the knowledge and understanding of spiritual concepts, was completed by 1,997 pupils from eleven to sixteen, 991 of them boys and 1,006 girls. The research has been summarised in [B.255].

4.1.2.6 One of the samples included in the *National Survey on religious Attitudes of young People, 1978* [B.507], jointly sponsored by the BS, Scripture Union, the Evangelical Alliance (EA) and *Buzz* magazine, consisted of 810 fourth and 151 lower sixth formers from seven English and Scottish secondary schools. The schedule covered self-assessed spirituality, beliefs about God, Jesus and the Bible, church attendance, religious education, moral opinions, paranormal behaviour, and leisure activities. Useful digests of the fourth form data are provided in [QRL.73], 28 September 1978 and [QRL.48], 15 March 1979.

4.1.2.7 The following year, in April and May 1979, John Greer [B.148] [B.151] of the University of Ulster investigated some 2,149 mainly average ability children aged eight to sixteen attending a random selection of Protestant and Roman Catholic schools in Belfast. His research instrument consisted of Peatling's 'Thinking about the Bible' test, designed to assess the capacity for concrete/abstract thought, Francis's Likert scale [B.112], and items about belief in God, the importance of religion to the respondent, and church-going. Similar ground was also covered in a further study by Greer, undertaken in April and May 1981, which involved the administration of a lengthy battery of questions, including Turner's measure of religious attitudes as well as Francis's, to 2,133 first to fifth formers from nineteen secondary schools across the whole of Northern Ireland [B.147].

4.1.2.8 The latest expert in the field is William Kay [B.226] [B.227] [B.228] [B.229] who has examined, mainly by means of multiple regression techniques, the beliefs, practices and opinions of 3,116 pupils, 48.2% of them boys and 51.8% girls, drawn from the first four years of thirty-three state and denominational secondary schools situated in predominantly semi-urban areas of England (1,687 children from seventeen institutions), Ulster (784 from eight), and the Irish Republic (645 from eight). The massive three hundred and forty item questionnaire comprised, in addition to numerous measures of Kay's own construction, the verbal component of Thorndike and Hagen's cognitive abilities test, Francis's religious attitude [B.112] and behaviour scales, Peatling's 'Thinking about the Bible', literalism and exposure indicators, and the Junior Eysenck Personality Inventory.

4.2 Young Adults

4.2.1 *General surveys*
4.2.1.1 The earliest statistics, reproduced in Bryan Reed's book [B.320], relate to attendance at church-based activities amongst 1,004 fourteen to twenty year olds (49.8% male, 50.2% female, 22.2% at school, 35.6% in industrial employment, 36.3% in other occupations, 6.0% in the armed forces) resident in the city of Birmingham during the late 1940s.

4.2.1.2 The next set of data derive from a review of the religious and historical knowledge of over a thousand fifteen to twenty year olds, two thirds of them female, which was undertaken by the Reverend J.W. Packer [QRL.124], 2 January 1953, [B.526] in 1950-51. The sample appears to have been recruited from schools, training colleges and youth clubs in and around Leeds.

4.2.1.3 The third major study was conducted in January and February 1957 by the Roman Catholic Young Christian Workers movement with technical assistance from the NDS. Interviews were held with 8,196 persons aged fifteen to twenty-four living in randomly selected streets of twenty-eight London boroughs and thirty English provincial towns and cities with a population in excess of forty thousand. The full questionnaire, which was given to all non-Anglican respondents and to thirty per cent of the five thousand Church of England adherents, covered socio-demographic characteristics, belief in God, Christ, heaven and hell, attendance at Sunday school or catechism, public worship and Holy Communion, and confirmation. Proper weighting (to correct for the overrepresentation of Catholics and fifteen to nineteen year olds) and analysis of the data was never completed on account of shortages both of time and money, and the only significant publication to have arisen from the project was a special double issue of *New Life* [B.578] which was summarised in [QRL.119], 12-19 April 1958.

4.2.1.4 Two years later, in January 1959, the Gallup Poll entered the field with an enquiry amongst adults aged fifteen to twenty-nine throughout Great Britain carried out on behalf of the *News Chronicle* [QRL.51] 26 March 1959; [QRL.64], January 1963; [QRL.74], 16-18 March 1959. Various spiritual topics were dealt with including denominational affiliation, the importance of faith, willingness to approach a clergyman or priest in the event of a serious personal problem, admiration for religious people, and the influence of the Churches over the country's future.

4.2.1.5 Encouraged by the success of this experiment, Gallup progressed to a longitudinal study of the opinions of youth. The original panel, created in September and October 1960, comprised a national, random sample of one thousand eight hundred individuals aged sixteen to eighteen who were asked about their church-going, their preference for ecclesiastical or civil marriage ceremonies, and the role of religion in their own lives and, relative to politics, in the world generally. Informants were reinterviewed in 1961, 1962 and 1963 when they were additionally questioned about their confessional allegiance and their attitudes towards Jews and Catholics. Data for 1960, 1961 and 1963 are held by the ESRC DA, those for 1962 by the Roper Center at the University of Connecticut.

4.2.1.6 At much the same time, in 1962-64, David Bleakley [B.25] was mounting 'an inquiry into the attitudes to religion of young Ulster people in the 15-20 age group, with special reference to Church membership, participation, Sunday observance and to the way in which Christian teaching is viewed'. The sample comprised several hundred students and workers of both sexes and from each side of the sectarian divide.

4.2.1.7 A survey by NOP Market Research, carried out during 1967, of more than a thousand adolescent Britons between twelve and twenty is reported in [QRL.55], 27-30 November 1967. Several relevant topics were covered including belief in God and in Christianity as the one true faith.

4.2.1.8 The Youth Bureau of the Office of the Prime Minister of Japan has commissioned two world-wide polls of young people aged eighteen to twenty-four, British fieldwork being undertaken by Gallup in October-November 1972 (n = 2,031) and December 1977 - January 1978 (n = 1,994). There were questions about spiritual goals in life, denominational affiliation, church attendance, and, in the second study only, the willingness to discuss worries with a clergyman and religion as a source of family disputes and national pride. Results have been published in [QRL.13], 1978 [B.350] [B.580] [B.581].

4.2.1.9 ORC interviewed 494 adults aged sixteen to twenty throughout Scotland during the first week of April 1976. Respondents were asked about the importance of their faith in everyday life, belief in God, church membership, religious practices over the previous seven days, prejudices against Protestants or Catholics, integrated schooling, and the spiritual upbringing of children. The investigation was sponsored by *The Scotsman* [QRL.104], and figures appear in the issue of that paper for 29 April 1976.

4.2.1.10 Young persons aged twelve to thirteen, seventeen to eighteen and twenty-two to twenty-three were the subject of a study conducted in France, West Germany and Great Britain (n = 904) during the summer of 1977 under the auspices of the Jugendwerk der Deutschen Shell, Hamburg. Information was gathered about assurance in religious belief, denominational profession, the ability to name one of the Old Testament prophets, and the readiness to seek the advice of a minister over a private problem. The data set is deposited at the ESRC DA, University of Essex (SN 1225).

4.2.1.11 NOP questioned 1,847 British adults aged fifteen to twenty-one for BBC Radio's Jimmy Young programme during August 1978. Statistics relative to self-assessed religiosity, sectarian affiliation and frequency of church attendance have been printed in [B.577] or may be extracted from the original data set which is held by the ESRC DA as SN 1636.

4.2.1.12 Leslie Francis's *Youth in Transit* [B.121] was the product of research, undertaken between January 1979 and February 1980, into 'the attitudes and values of the sixteen to twenty-five year old young people working and living in the city...who become members of London Central YMCA'. The 1,085 respondents (56.8% male and 43.2% female, 64.2% born in the United Kingdom and 35.8% abroad, 30.7% students and 69.3% in employment, 81.6% with some full time education after the age of sixteen and just 18.4% without) completed a twenty-six point questionnaire and a one hundred and forty statement opinion scale which together included items on the nature and strength of religious identification, habits of public worship, prayer and Bible reading, belief in God, Jesus Christ, life after death, reincarnation, luck, horoscopes and the existence of intelligent beings on other planets, willingness to approach a clergyman for counselling needs, the provision of spiritual instruction in schools, and on the relevance of scripture and the Church to modern society. Results were disaggregated by sex, age, academic qualifications, occupational experience, social class, country of birth, type of accommodation, and denomination. A parallel enquiry amongst 2,074 persons aged twenty-six to thirty-nine is reported in [B.116].

4.2.1.13 At much the same time, in August 1979, Market and Opinion Research International (MORI) investigated the attitudes and life style of an interlocking quota sample of 891 Britons from fifteen to twenty-four on behalf of *Now!* magazine [QRL.79] 14 September 1979; [QRL.80] October 1979; [B.579]. They were asked, amongst other things, to state whether they believed in God or not and to identify, from a list which included going to church, the activities which they enjoyed most.

4.2.1.14 Within a month of this last poll, Survey Research Associates had examined the opinions of a representative group of Scottish fifteen to twenty year olds. The interview schedule covered the strength of religious conviction, belief in God, confessional allegiance, attendance at services, preference for an ecclesiastical or civil wedding ceremony, and the denominational segregation of day schools. Findings are reproduced in [QRL.80], December 1979 and [B.111].

4.2.1.15 MORI reviewed the experiences of a quota sample of 580 unemployed Britons aged sixteen to twenty-one at the request of Granada Television in August 1981. Besides the standard enquiries about belief in a deity, religious profession and church-going, respondents were invited to say whether they thought increased emphasis should be placed on the spiritual and less on the material side of life. Basic results were published in [QRL.88], May-October 1981, and the full data set has now been deposited at the ESRC DA (SN 1618).

4.2.1.16 Virtually simultaneously, in August and September 1981, MORI also questioned 585 persons aged fifteen to twenty-four and resident in Croydon or Newcastle-upon-Tyne about their belief in God, denomination and attendance at worship. Summary figures appear in [QRL.88], May-October 1981 and [QRL.123], 9 October 1981, whilst the actual data set is available at the ESRC DA (SN 1620).

4.2.1.17 The most recent commercial poll was conducted by NOP (JN 7172) amongst a quota sample of 1,326 fifteen to twenty-one year old Britons in January 1982. The thirty page research instrument contained four items of specifically religious interest: preference for an ecclesiastical or civil marriage, belief in a God, frequency of church-going, and attitudes to children attending services at school. Data for these topics were omitted from the overall account of the survey printed in [QRL.55], 24-28 January 1983 but are readily available from NOP upon request.

4.2.1.18 The foregoing profiles of the general young adult population have been supplemented by several in-depth analyses of the activist Christian minority. Notable examples include the appraisal of Methodism's work amongst eighteen to thirty year olds in 1978 [B.421], the 791 schedules returned by readers of *Buzz* magazine as a contribution to the *National Survey on religious Attitudes of young People, 1978* [B.507], and the report on the ecclesiastical involvement, faith and secular opinions of some one thousand three hundred persons aged thirteen to twenty who frequented ninety different places of worship (forty-two Anglican, twenty-two Catholic and twenty-six Free Church) in the Clitheroe, Lancaster, Morecambe, Preston and Skelmersdale areas during November 1979 - April 1980 [B.576].

4.2.2 *Sixth formers*
4.2.2.1 Really detailed research in this field originated with a study, sponsored by the Christian Education Movement, of 2,276 second year sixth formers, 49.6% male and 50.4% female, drawn from a random sample of ninety-six maintained grammar schools throughout England in October 1963, the self-completion schedule dealing with belief in God, Jesus and an afterlife, the Bible, church-going, private prayer, religious instruction, moral judgments, and related matters. Results are discussed in a series of publications by Derek Wright and Edwin Cox [B.85] [B.430] [B.431] who were also responsible for a replication of the survey at sixty-six of the original schools in February and March 1970, the respondents on this occasion numbering 1,574 of whom 48.1% were male and 51.9% female [B.428] [B.429].

4.2.2.2 Nearly four thousand students from some twenty-five institutions took part in an investigation conducted by *Sixth Form Opinion* magazine in 1965 and summarised in an article by Michael Spencer [B.370]. The data, which relate to belief in God, denominational affiliation, church attendance, attitudes to compulsory assemblies and to the rights of atheists to teach, are of only limited value on account of the lack of disaggregation by sex of informant or by type and location of establishment.

4.2.2.3 Questionnaires completed by 1.631 second year sixth formers from forty-two Protestant grammar and secondary intermediate schools across Northern Ireland in January-February 1968 form the basis of both a book [B.150] and papers [B.146] [B.152] [B.153] by John Greer. Topics covered comprised frequency of worship, prayer and Bible reading, belief in God, Christ, heaven, hell, life after death and reincarnation, opinions of the Church, of religious education and on ethical matters. All but seven of the same schools contributed to a replication of the enquiry in 1978 when the sample totalled 1,870 [B.149].

4.2.2.4 Philip May's work apart (4.1.2.1), the final investigation of note was undertaken by Oxford University's Bloxham Project Research Unit in 1971. Scales measuring involvement in youth culture, radicalism/conservatism, idealism/realism, alienation/satisfaction, religious beliefs and practices were administered to 2,842 sixth formers, 74,4% male and 25.6% female, 39.2% day and 60.8% boarding pupils, from thirty-two independent and seven maintained schools throughout Britain. Results are presented in *Images of Life* by Robin Richardson and John Chapman [B.328].

4.2.3 *Higher education students*
4.2.3.1 Basic material on denominational affiliation and/or church attendance is contained in numerous general surveys of undergraduate attitudes and life styles during the 1950s and 1960s. Significant examples include those conducted at Birmingham University (in 1951-52), Oxford (1956 and 1961), Cambridge (1958 and 1959), Belfast (1959), Edinburgh (1960), Liverpool (1960), London (1961), Nottingham (1962), Cardiff (1962), Essex (1964, 1965 and 1966), Sussex (1966), and Warwick (1968). Detailed findings were initially reported in student or other fairly recondite publications, but key facts have also been summarised in the articles by Paul Black [B.23] and Joan Brothers [B.42]. Data sets for some of these investigations are held by the ESRC DA (SN 65008, 65009, 66004, 68006, 1622, 1623).

4.2.3.2 More in-depth analysis has been pioneered by Geoffrey Pilkington and associates who have devised a scale to measure the religious faith and practice of undergraduates at the University of Sheffield. Complete cross-sections [B.311] [B.308] were taken in 1961 (n=463) and 1972 (n=761), specialised samples of third year [B.307] and unmarried female students [B.315] in 1962 (n=106) and the mid-1970s (n=238) respectively.

4.2.3.3 Cedric Sandford and S.Griffin [B.343] investigated the religious belief and church attendance of over four hundred first degree students at the Bristol College of Science and Technology, subsequently elevated to university status at Bath, in 1963. The majority were pursuing sandwich courses in architecture, biology, chemistry and engineering, and only one in eight was a woman.

4.2.3.4 Reginald Rees's *Background and belief* [B.322] was based upon a postal survey of a random selection of 433 third year undergraduates at Oxford, Cambridge and Bangor Universities in February-March 1966. The thirty-one questions covered personal characteristics, frequency of church-going and private prayer, self-assessed spiritual commitment, immortality, reactions to the Bishop of Woolwich's *Honest to God*, Bible truths, and opinions of religious teaching received in the sixth form.

4.2.3.5 Judith Brown's recent book [B.47] contains the results of an enquiry amongst honours students in the Department of History, University of Manchester in 1978. A total of 263 were approached of whom 106 or 40% eventually replied. Topics discussed comprised denominational affiliation, attendance at worship, prayer, Bible reading and ownership, belief in God, the influence of religion in the respondent's life and in British society as a whole, religious instruction and toleration.

4.2.3.6 Investigations of the religious attitudes and values of students at Colleges of Education have been completed by John Daines [B.90] in 1962 (n=368), M.Gray [B.143] in 1963 (n=571), E.C. Prichard [B.314] in 1965 (n=193), Trafford Walker [B.399] in 1966 (n=420), D.B. Evans [B.105] in 1968 (n=approximately 250), and by John McLeish [B.248] in 1970 (n=1,671, 130 men and 1,541 women).

4.3 Other Groups

4.3.1 *Women*

4.3.1.1 Although there have been no full-length studies of female religiosity, small amounts of relevant data have been gathered as part of broader surveys of women's social attitudes. One of the earliest known instances of this was a MO poll of two hundred and fifty middle class housewives carried out on behalf of *Good Housekeeping* magazine in 1950 in which information was collected about attendance at worship and the influence of the Church [B.461].

4.3.1.2 Four years later, Eustace Chesser [B.72] examined female sexual, marital and family relationships on the basis of questionnaires distributed to women nominated by general practitioners all over England from lists of their adult patients. A less than random selection process and a low response rate (only 33%) resulted in a sample of some two thousand individuals biased towards single persons, the younger age groups, and the upper end of the social scale. Answers were tabulated according to strength of religious background, denomination, and church-going habits of the informant, her parents, spouse and children.

4.3.1.3 The British Market Research Bureau (BMRB) interviewed 669 married women aged eighteen to twenty-seven in London, Birmingham and Leeds during January 1957. The investigation, commissioned by the United Kingdom Alliance, was designed to isolate circumstances surrounding home and family formation with particular reference to 'mode of living, expenditures, deficiencies and savings'. The findings, which include a detailed breakdown by frequency of public worship, appear in [B.442] and [B.547].

4.3.1.4 Polls conducted on behalf of the Population Investigation Committee in 1966 (n=3,000) and 1967-68 (n=2,262) probed the factors determining family size amongst samples of married women across Great Britain. Confessional affiliation was used as one variable, and its influence is considered in the articles by Ru-Chi Chou and Susannah Brown [B.74] and by David Glass [B.134] as well as in a book by Christopher Langford [B.237].

4.3.1.5 T.Kidd surveyed some two thousand young female recruits to the Royal Air Force in preparation for a Nottingham M.Phil. thesis [B.231]. A battery of tests measuring attitudes to moral issues was administered, and the results were analysed in terms of declared religious practices.

4.3.1.6 *Honey* magazine appointed the Schlackman Research Organisation to undertake a study of 'Sex and the single Girl' [B.548] in December 1976, the subjects comprising two hundred and ninety unmarried women aged eighteen to twenty-six throughout Great Britain. There were questions on denominational allegiance, church attendance, religious reasons for failure to have intercourse or to use contraceptives, and willingness to contemplate involvement with a man of a different faith.

4.3.1.7 Christine Player's *A national Portrait* [B.309] was based upon interviews, conducted in the spring and summer of 1978, with 2,385 women resident in thirty-three Anglican dioceses who had children under twelve years but did not belong to any Mothers' Union or Young Family Groups. The sample was not constructed according to recognised random or quota principles and was especially biased towards the owner occupied housing sector. Respondents were questioned, *inter alia*, about their degree of contact with and interest in the Church.

4.3.1.8 *19* magazine asked its readers, in October 1981, 'What do you really think about sex today?' and received more than six thousand replies which were tabulated in the issues for April, May and June 1982 [B.285]. Informants tended to be well-educated, unmarried females in the sixteen to twenty-four age range who were either still studying or had white collar occupations. The research instrument included items on religious affiliation and church-going with a view to assessing the impact of faith on sexual behaviour and attitudes.

4.3.1.9 Eight months later, in May 1982, the evangelical publication *Family* canvassed the opinions of its readership on the role which women did and should play in the organisational, pastoral and liturgical life of the Christian Church. There were 466 replies, preponderantly from females (61.2%), married people (86.1%), twenty-five to forty-four year olds (70.8%), and Anglicans or Baptists (63.2%). Results, processed manually and disaggregated only by sex, are given in Anne Townsend's article [B.389].

4.3.2 *Old people*
4.3.2.1 One of the first attempts to examine religion in old age was made at Birmingham in 1948, a random sample of 2,230 persons over seventy years and living in private households being asked about their outside interests including the Church. Findings are reported by Barbara Shenfield [B.349].

4.3.2.2 Peter Townsend [B.391] investigated the family life of a representative group of 203 pensioners, 64 men and 139 women, from Bethnal Green, London between October 1954 and November 1955. His schedule contained enquiries about denominational allegiance and frequency of public worship.

4.3.2.3 Pauline Callard's study of 'The Church and older People' [B.60] was based upon information supplied by ecclesiastical agencies in Torquay, a town with an abnormally large population of retired persons, in 1956. Figures, which related to average winter conditions and to permanent residents only, were obtained regarding membership, attendance at Sunday services and weekday meetings, and office-holding by those over sixty years of age.

4.3.2.4 Howard Bracey [B.33] interviewed 155 pensioners, 63 male and 92 female, from a random sample of one hundred households in the parish of Filton, Gloucestershire in 1961. Respondents were questioned about their current level of involvement with a church or chapel and the likelihood of their worshipping more regularly if specifically invited to come and/or if transport was provided.

4.3.2.5 Peter Townsend and Sylvia Tunstall [B.392] summarise the results of an enquiry undertaken by the Government Social Survey (GSS) amongst 2,591 individuals aged sixty-five and over living in a probability sample of private households throughout Great Britain in May-July 1962. Data were obtained about religious 'membership' as indicated by at least occasional attendance at services.

4.3.2.6 A review of 'Communication and isolation among the elderly' was carried out by Market Advertising and Product Studies Limited at the request of the Post Office in November 1968, a random group of 583 Britons aged sixty-five years and above being asked, *inter alia*, whether they had frequented a place of worship during the past year and, if so, what its denomination was. The data set is deposited at the ESRC DA, University of Essex (SN 68011).

4.3.2.7 Valerie Karn's *Retiring to the Seaside* [B.225] derived from interviews, conducted by ORC from November 1968 to January 1969, with 990 persons of fifty-five and over who had moved to Clacton or Bexhill either after or in anticipation of retirement. Attendance at church and religious societies and the willingness to turn to a clergyman in times of need were amongst the topics covered.

4.3.2.8 *The Attitudes of the Retired and the Elderly* [B.443] were explored by Social Policy Research on behalf of Age Concern between February and June 1974. The sample consisted of 2,702 adults of pensionable age (men of sixty-five and above, women of sixty and over) living in private households across Great Britain south of the Caledonian Canal, whilst the actual questions dealt with attendance at public worship and religious clubs, extent of interest in the Church, and the receipt of visits from representatives of local congregations. The data set is held at the ESRC DA (SN 441).

4.3.2.9 Scott Reid was awarded a doctorate for his thesis, submitted in 1975 [B.326], on the spiritual life of 184 old people in Edinburgh, 66 of them residing in institutions and 118 in their own homes. Information was gathered on a wide range of issues including church membership and attendance, prayer, Bible reading, religious broadcasting, death and the afterlife.

4.3.2.10 Audrey Hunt's *The Elderly at Home* [B.202] was the final report of an investigation conducted by the GSS in January and February 1976 at the request of the DHSS. The sample comprised 2,622 persons aged sixty-five and over randomly selected from private dwellings across England in such a way as to secure an overrepresentation of individuals of seventy-five years and above. Respondents were asked whether they had received a visit from a minister during the six months prior to interview and whether they were members of any church-based organisations. The data set is available at the ESRC DA (SN 702).

4.3.2.11 In March-May 1977, some three years after its first enquiry (4.3.2.8), Age Concern commissioned a poll from Research Services Limited (RSL) of 1,646 adults aged sixty-five and above living in Hove, Merton, Northampton, and the Moss Side district of Manchester. They were questioned about their membership of, date of joining, and actual attendance at religious groups and about their activities, including presence at public worship, on the previous Sunday. Results are tabulated in two reports by Mark Abrams [B.3] [B.4].

4.3.2.12 The experiences of 155 old people in residential care across London and the Home Counties north of the River Thames were examined by NOP in February and March 1978. Data were collected about denominational affiliation, church-going and self-assessed religiosity, and these, together with other findings, are discussed in the monograph by Sheila Peace, John Hall and Graham Hamblin [B.296].

4.3.2.13 The most recent statistics, which relate only to attendance at services, are contained in a report on *The Elderly in the Community* [B.470] prepared by North Tyneside's Social Services Department. These derived from a survey, undertaken between October 1978 and July 1979, of a random sample of 1,047 persons aged sixty-five and over who held concessionary bus passes and lived in the borough.

4.3.3 *Coloured people*
4.3.3.1 Various investigations have been conducted which throw light on the involvement of the coloured population with organised Christianity in Britain. One of the earliest was a Gallup Poll of West Indians from Birmingham and the Brixton, Paddington and Stepney districts of London in 1955 which included a question on attendance at church or chapel. Figures are cited by Sheila Patterson [B.292].

4.3.3.2 Robert Davison carried out a longitudinal study amongst a random sample of 272 Jamaican men and women who came to England in 1961. His book [B.95] provides statistics, disaggregated by sex, of the proportion of church members and attenders at the end of the first and second years of residence.

4.3.3.3 Clifford Hill [B.175] circulated all the Anglican (n = 854), Baptist (n = 246), Congregational (n = 164), Methodist (n = 279), Presbyterian (n = 90), and Roman Catholic (n = 155) churches in London, Middlesex and the metropolitan parts of Essex, Kent, and Surrey in March 1963 with a view to determining the amount of immigrant support which they commanded. Separate returns, grossed by denomination within county, were made of the number of West Indian adherents, worshippers, communicants, attendants at ordinary meetings, office-holders, choristers, Sunday scholars, members of uniformed organisations and youth clubs, infant baptisms, and weddings.

4.3.3.4 Robin Ward [B.404] surveyed the religious life of an immigrant area of Manchester in 1966-67 on the basis of participant observation at services, discussions with local clergy, and structured interviews with a representative group of 765 adults.

Special attention was paid to the religious behaviour and attitudes of the 275 West Indian respondents, almost all of whom lived in Moss Side.

4.3.3.5 Peter Evans [B.106] reported the results of a poll of coloured men in the sixteen to twenty-four age range conducted by Marplan for *The Times* in November and December 1970. The four hundred and fifty informants, equally divided between West Indians from Handsworth, Indians from Southall and Pakistanis from Bradford, were asked about their religious affiliations and attendance at a place of worship.

4.3.3.6 NOP [QRL.77], May 1971 questioned 534 West Indian, Indian and Pakistani adults from Brent and Bradford on the subject of racial integration and discrimination in April 1971. In particular, they were invited to register their membership of religious clubs or organisations, to assess the importance of spiritual differences as a barrier to ethnic harmony, and to state which of five factors (class, colour, creed, education or type of job) they regarded as the prime social division in Britain. Their replies were contrasted with those of a control group of 568 white people from Brent and Pudsey.

4.3.3.7 A rather different perspective was adopted by Peter Jarvis and A.G. Fielding [B.213] in their study of a West Midlands borough with a large migrant population during the summer of 1971. They approached the clerical and lay leadership of seventy-eight individual churches in order to ascertain the number of immigrants in the congregations, worshippers' attitudes towards coloured persons, and the level of ecclesiastical involvement in community relations.

4.3.3.8 David Pearson [B.298] [B.299] has examined the religiosity of one hundred and eight West Indians in 'Easton', a city with two hundred and eighty thousand inhabitants somewhere in the Midlands, during the years 1971-73. Especially interesting comparisons were made between patterns of denominational affiliation and church-going in the pre-migration (Caribbean) and post-migration ('Easton') phases.

4.3.3.9 Jean Morton-Williams and Richard Stowell's profile of the residents of *Small Heath, Birmingham* [B.274] included a brief but significant analysis of religion and worship frequency by nationality. The data set (ESRC DA, SN 717) comprised 1,578 adults of all ethnic origins, white British as well as New Commonwealth, from 854 households, fieldwork being conducted by Social and Community Planning Research (SCPR) between February and May 1974.

4.3.3.10 Political and Economic Planning's report on *The Facts of racial Disadvantage* [B.358] derived from interviews with samples of 1,189 West Indians and 2,102 Asians aged sixteen and over throughout England and Wales in June-December 1974. Enquiries were made concerning religious profession and regularity of attendance at church, mosque or temple. The data set, deposited at the ESRC DA as SN 427/428, must be subjected to complex weighting procedures before it can be used for secondary analysis.

4.3.3.11 The next year, 1975, SCPR undertook a 'Housing Choice Survey' amongst 1,674 coloured people from Bradford, Leicester, Lambeth, and Haringey on behalf of the Community Relations Commission. Respondents were asked about their denominational allegiance and their presence at public worship. The data set is archived at the ESRC DA (SN 791).

4.3.3.12 The findings of a poll carried out by NOP for Professor John Rex in May and June 1976 are discussed in Peter Ratcliffe's book [B.318]. Interviews were held with 395 West Indian, 305 Asian and 400 white British heads of households in the Handsworth area of Birmingham, the topics covered including religious affiliation, attendance at services, the enrolment of informants' children at Sunday school or its equivalent, and the willingness to contact a minister or priest over a local problem. The data set is preserved at the ESRC DA (SN 1395).

4.3.3.13 A study of the *Elders of the minority ethnic Groups* [B.19] was undertaken by MAFS (Market Research) Limited on behalf of AFFOR (All Faiths for One Race) in the Deritend, Handsworth, Soho and Sparkhill districts of Birmingham from September to November 1979. The four hundred respondents, a random selection of men aged sixty-five or over and women of sixty years or above, comprised 179 Afro-Caribbeans, 169 Asians, and 52 Europeans. They were asked about their regularity of public worship, their actual and desired contact with local religious workers, and their preparedness to avail themselves of any day time recreational facilities that churches or equivalent centres might provide.

4.3.3.14 The most recent survey, commissioned by the ESRC Centre for Research in Ethnic Relations, was conducted by SCPR within five electoral wards of three Midland cities (Deritend, Perry Barr and Selly Oak in Birmingham, Foleshill in Coventry, Graisely in Wolverhampton) between February and May 1981. The sample consisted of 366 Afro-Caribbean, 878 Asian, and 917 white heads of households or their spouses, whilst the questionnaire contained items on confessional identification, frequency of worship, and membership of clubs or societies connected with churches, mosques or temples.

CHAPTER 5

PERSONAL RELIGION: BELIEFS

5.1 Overall Religiosity

5.1.1 *General indicators*

5.1.1.1 Six principal indicators have been employed in polls of the adult population conducted both nationally and locally since the early 1940s. First, informants have been asked to state whether they regarded life as either having or needing some kind of spiritual meaning and purpose; this approach was followed in investigations carried out across Britain in August-September 1967 (n = 1.001 fifteen to forty year olds, ESRC DA, SN 67025), February 1968 [QRL.94], January 1973 [QRL.91], August 1974 [QRL.108], July 1979 [QRL.79], 21 December 1979 and September-October 1979 [QRL.92], Northern Ireland in March-August 1968 [QRL.26] and December 1968 - January 1969 [QRL.94] [QRL.95], and Greater London in February - March 1978 (2.2.2.16).

5.1.1.2 Secondly, interviewees have been invited to say whether they considered themselves to be religious or not. This line of enquiry was pursued throughout the United Kingdom in March 1981 [QRL.70], 1982-83 and March-April 1982 (ESRC DA, SN 1792), Britain in March 1963 [QRL.12], August 1966 [QRL.12], February 1968 [QRL.94], January 1973 [QRL.91], October 1973 - February 1974 (ESRC DA, SN 672), August 1974 [QRL.108] [QRL.123], 14 October 1974 and February 1980 (by BMRB), Northern Ireland in March-August 1968 [QRL.26], December 1968 - January 1969 [QRL.94] [QRL.95], August 1973 - July 1974 (n = 2,416 males aged eighteen to sixty-four) [B.243] and June - November 1978 [QRL.24], in seven major conurbations (n = 593) in October - November 1971 (ESRC DA, SN 248), at Machynlleth and Newtown, Montgomeryshire in September 1974 (2.3.2.4), Greater London in February - March 1978 (2.2.2.16), and at Coventry a few weeks later (2.2.2.17).

5.1.1.3 Thirdly, respondents have been required to estimate the importance which they attached to their beliefs and/or their willingness to make sacrifices for the sake of them. This information was gathered across the United Kingdom in October 1975 (ESRC DA, SN 789), May -June 1976 (ESRC DA, SN 933), November 1976 (ESRC DA, SN 934), April - May 1977 (ESRC DA, SN 936), October - November 1977 (ESRC DA, SN 1029), April 1979 (ESRC DA, SN 1396), October 1979 (ESRC DA, SN 1397), March 1981 [QRL.70], 1982-83 and March - April 1982 [QRL.59], June 1982, Britain in June 1970 [QRL.101], January 1972 [QRL.77], July 1972, November 1974 - January 1975 [QRL.13], 1979; [QRL.14], [QRL.28], [QRL.69], [QRL.87], March-May 1979, August 1976 [QRL.21], September- October 1979 [QRL.70],

1980-81 and March 1982 [QRL.90]; [QRL.123], 12 May 1982, Northern Ireland (males only) in August 1973 - July 1974 [B.243], and in the Associated Rediffusion Television Area in 1960 (2.2.2.7).

5.1.1.4 Fourthly, subjects have been asked to assess the extent to which religion affected them in their daily actions. This question was included in ORC surveys undertaken throughout Britain in February 1968 [QRL.94], September 1972 (JN 7238) and January 1973 [QRL.91], Northern Ireland in December 1968 - January 1969 [QRL.94] [QRL.95], and Greater London in February - March 1978 (2.2.2.16).

5.1.1.5 Fifthly, attempts to measure the degree to which people claim to derive comfort and strength from their faith were made in polls carried out within Britain in January 1941 [QRL.9] [QRL.12], seven major conurbations (n = 593) in October - November 1971 (ESRC DA, SN 248), and the United Kingdom in March 1981 [QRL.70], 1982-83.

5.1.1.6 Lastly, the frequency with which religion formed a topic of everyday conversation was investigated across Britain in April - May 1972 [QRL.83], March 1976 [QRL.84], June 1980 [QRL.85] and September 1982 [QRL.80], February 1983 as well as at Machynlleth and Newtown, Montgomeryshire in September 1974 (2.3.2.4).

5.1.1.7 The chief limitation of all these data is that 'religion' and its related concepts were never defined or qualified in any way at all, and there are strong grounds for supposing that many interviewees will have interpreted them in ethical rather than in strictly spiritual terms. Thus, in ORC's British survey of February 1968 [QRL.94], 39% of the sample asserted that the most important aspect of religion was 'what you do to others', and 77% stated that its main function was 'to provide a set of rules to live by'.

5.1.2 *Religious experience*
5.1.2.1 Recent work in this area originated with the Religious Experience Research Unit (RERU) which Professor Sir Alister Hardy, the eminent zoologist, established at Manchester College, Oxford in 1969. As a result of appeals for volunteers appearing in the secular press, over four thousand detailed accounts of awareness of or influence by a presence or power, whether referred to as God or not, different from the everyday self have now been received. An elementary quantitative analysis of the first three thousand records is given in *The spiritual Nature of Man* [QRL.17], and a follow-up study amongst a sub-group of 362 individuals claiming experiences which occurred during childhood is discussed by Edward Robinson [B.330].

5.1.2.2 RERU correspondents, being an entirely self-selecting body, were far from typical of the overall population; in particular, they were disproportionately recruited from the ranks of women and older people. More representative and reliable data have been collected during the course of three enquiries mounted by the Religious Experience Research Project, School of Education, University of Nottingham and described in a series of publications by its Director, David Hay [QRL.20], [QRL.21], [QRL.119], 23 July 1977; [B.169]. Subjects comprised one hundred postgraduate students contacted during the 1972-73 academic session, 1,865 adults aged sixteen and over interviewed across Great Britain in August 1976, and 172 electors from the city of Nottingham and immediately adjacent districts.

5.1.2.3 One highly specific form of religious experience, conversion, was examined by an EA Commission early in 1968. The sample consisted of some four thousand members of evangelical churches throughout England, apparently chosen in a fairly arbitrary fashion, who supplied information as to their age, sex, occupation, region of residence, and home circumstances as well as about the date, method, and context of their decision for the Lord. Statistics are reproduced in [B.444] and [B.511].

5.2 Specific Beliefs

5.2.1 *God*
5.2.1.1 Variants on the simple 'Do you believe in God?' question have been employed in surveys of the general adult population of the United Kingdom in March 1981 [QRL.70], 1982-1983, of Britain in April-May 1964 (ESRC DA, SN 64009), February 1968 [QRL.94], May 1968 [QRL.62] [QRL.64], August 1968, June 1970 [QRL.101], September 1972 [QRL.113], 22 April 1973, January 1973 (by ORC, JN 7/1337), April-May 1973 [QRL.64], May 1973; [QRL.112], 13 May 1973, November 1974 - January 1975 [QRL.13], 1979; [QRL.28] [QRL.69], [QRL.87], March-May 1979, May-June 1975 [QRL.12] [QRL.64] June 1975, March 1977 [QRL.99], March 1979 [QRL.25] [QRL.64] May 1979 [QRL.112] 15 April 1979, July 1979 [QRL.79], 21 December 1979; [QRL.93], September-October 1979 [QRL.70], 1980-81, June 1980 [QRL.80], August 1980 and April 1981 [QRL.31], 1981 [QRL.64], April 1981 [QRL.103], [QRL.112] 19 April 1981, of Scotland in August 1976 [QRL.66] 11 October 1976; [QRL.103], of Northern Ireland in December 1968 - January 1969 [QRL.94] [QRL.95], of Hammersmith in 1944-45 (2.2.2.3), of the Associated Rediffusion Television Area in 1960 (2.2.2.7), of Dawley during the summer of 1969 (2.2.2.14), of Altrincham in September 1977 (2.2.2.15), of Greater London in February-March 1978 (2.2.2.16), of Coventry in the spring of 1978 (2.2.2.17), and of Hertford in September 1982 [QRL.44], 4 November 1982. A similar enquiry has also been put to readers of the *Sun* (n = 12,000) in 1967 [QRL.111], 27 June 1967 and of *New Society* (n = 3,180) in 1982 [QRL.73], 25 November 1982.

5.2.1.2 The distinction between belief in a personal God on the one hand and in some sort of spirit or life force on the other was first drawn in the *Daily News* and *Nation and Athenaeum* readership profiles of 1926 (2.2.1.2); it has been repeated in polls conducted throughout the United Kingdom in March 1981 [QRL.70], 1982-83, Britain in December 1947 [QRL.12] [QRL.74] 13 January 1948, February 1957 [QRL.12] [QRL.74] 15-17 April 1957, March-April 1963 [QRL.12] [QRL.23] [QRL.64] April 1963, February 1968 [QRL.94], April 1970 [QRL.53] 13 May 1970 [QRL.100], June 1970 [QRL.101], August 1974 [QRL.108], [QRL.113], 13 October 1974; [QRL.123], 14 October 1974. March 1979 [QRL.25] [QRL.64] May 1979

[QRL.112] 15 April 1979 and April 1981 [QRL.31] 1981; [QRL.64], April 1981; [QRL.112] 19 April 1981, England in December 1963 - January 1964 [QRL.120] [QRL.121], and Northern Ireland in December 1968 - January 1969 [QRL.94] [QRL.95]. More specialised research into concepts of the Deity has been undertaken by R.S.Dawes [B.96], Frederick Hilliard [B.179] and D.J.C. Walker [B.398] amongst secondary school children, and by Glanville Rees [B.321] with one hundred and twenty Anglican, Catholic, Nonconformist, Quaker, Jewish, and agnostic adults.

5.2.1.3 Other relevant data derive from investigations carried out by ORC across Britain in February 1968 [QRL.94] and January 1973 (JN 7/1337), Northern Ireland in December 1968 - January 1969 [QRL.94] [QRL.95] and Greater London in February - March 1978 (2.2.2.16), and by Gallup within the United Kingdom in March 1981 [QRL.70], 1982-83 and Britain in March 1982 [QRL.42] [QRL.64] April 1982, April-May 1982 [QRL.4], June 1982 [QRL.36] and November 1982 (JN CQ.845). ORC's respondents were asked to comment on the statements that 'God watches what each person does and thinks' and that 'without belief in God life is meaningless' as well as to identify the kind of circumstances which tended to bring Him to their minds; Gallup's were invited to estimate, by means of a ten point scale, the importance of God in their lives.

5.2.2 *Jesus Christ*
5.2.2.1 Public attitudes towards the divinity of Jesus were first explored by the *Daily News* and *Nation and Athenaeum* as long ago as 1926 (2.2.1.2). Amongst more recent enquiries may be mentioned those conducted within Britain in February 1957 [QRL.12] [QRL.74] 15 April 1957, March-April 1963 [QRL.12] [QRL.23] [QRL.64] April 1963, February 1968 [QRL.94], June 1970 [QRL.101], March 1979 [QRL.25] [QRL.64] May 1979 [QRL.112], 15 April 1979, April 1981 [QRL.31] 1981; [QRL.64], April 1981; [QRL.112], 19 April 1981 and December 1981 [QRL.56], 24 December 1981; [QRL.88], October-December 1981, England in December 1963 - January 1964 [QRL.120] [QRL.121], Scotland in November 1981 [QRL.88] October - December 1981; [QRL.104], 21 December 1981, Northern Ireland in December 1968 - January 1969 [QRL.94] [QRL.95], Hammersmith in 1944-45 (2.2.2.3), Dawley in the summer of 1969 (2.2.2.14), and Altrincham in September 1977 (2.2.2.15).

5.2.2.2 Other aspects of Christ's life and teachings have been less often studied. Popular allegiance to His nativity in a Bethlehem stable and subsequent visitation by the three wise men and the shepherds was tested across Scotland in November 1981 [QRL.88] October - December 1981; [QRL.104] 21 December 1981 and Britain in December 1981 [QRL.56], 24 December 1981; [QRL.88] October-December 1981, whilst attachment to the doctrine of the Virgin Birth was measured at Hammersmith in 1944-45 (2.2.2.3) as well as nationally in June 1970 [QRL.101]. Acceptance of the Resurrection was monitored in one part of Coventry during the spring of 1978 (2.2.2.17), and reactions to the statement that 'people who believe in Jesus as the Son of God can expect salvation' were examined throughout the United Kingdom between February 1968 and January 1969 [QRL.94] [QRL.95].

5.2.3 *The Devil*
5.2.3.1 The prevalence of belief in the Devil has been quantified in surveys of the adult population of the United Kingdom in March 1981 [QRL.44], 17 December 1981; [QRL.70], 1982-83; [QRL.119], 26 February 1983; [QRL.125], 11 December 1981, Britain in February 1957 [QRL.12] [QRL.30], [QRL.74], 15 April 1957, March-April 1963 [QRL.12] [QRL.23] [QRL.64], April 1963, May 1968 [QRL.12] [QRL.28] [QRL.62] [QRL.64], August 1968, June 1970 [QRL.101], April-May 1973 [QRL.12] [QRL.64] May 1973; [QRL.112], 13 May 1973, May-June 1975 [QRL.12] [QRL.64], June 1975, March 1979 [QRL.25] [QRL.64], May 1979; [QRL.112], 15 April 1979, June 1980 [QRL.80], August 1980 and April 1981 [QRL.31], 1981; [QRL.64], April 1981; [QRL.112], 19 April 1981, England in December 1963-January 1964 [QRL.120] [QRL.121], and Dawley during the summer of 1969 (2.2.2.14).

5.2.3.2 Additional data have been gathered by Geoffrey Gorer on the basis of two more specialised samples. The first comprised some five thousand English readers of the *People* who completed multi-purpose questionnaires in January 1951 (2.2.1.3). The second consisted of 359 persons who had been bereaved of a primary relative during the five years previous to their interview by RSL in April-May 1963; results, disaggregated by sex and region, appear in *Death, Grief and Mourning in contemporary Britain* [B.140].

5.2.4 *The Afterlife*
5.2.4.1 The extent of the general public's belief in a life after death has been assessed in enquiries carried out across the United Kingdom in March 1981 [QRL.70], 1982-83, Britain in March 1939 [QRL.74], 27 April 1939, December 1947 [QRL.12] [QRL.74], 13 January 1948, February 1957 [QRL.12] [QRL.30] [QRL.74], 15 April 1957, March 1960 [QRL.1], March-April 1963 [QRL.12] [QRL.23] [QRL.64], April 1963, April-May 1963 (5.2.3.2, n = 359 bereaved individuals), May 1968 [QRL.12]; [QRL.28]; [QRL.64], August 1968, April 1970 [QRL.53], 13 May 1970; [QRL.100], June 1970 [QRL.101], April-May 1973 [QRL.12], [QRL.64], May 1973; [QRL.112], 13 May 1973, September-October 1973 [QRL.64], October 1973, October 1973 [QRL.12] [QRL.64], October 1973, August 1974 [QRL.108] [QRL.123], 14 October 1974, November 1974-January 1975 [QRL.13], 1979; [QRL.14] [QRL.69] [QRL.87], March-May 1979, May-June 1975 [QRL.12], [QRL.64], June 1975, February 1978 [QRL.13], 1978; [QRL.64], March 1978, July 1979 [QRL.79], 21 December 1979; [QRL.93], September-October 1979 [QRL.70], 1980-81, June 1980 [QRL.80], August 1980, November 1981 [QRL.31], 1981; [QRL.64], December 1981; [QRL.112], 27 December 1981 and October 1982 (n = 3,180 *New Society* readers) [QRL.73], 25 November 1982, England in January 1951 (2.2.1.3) and December 1963-January 1964 [QRL.120] [QRL.121], Scotland in August 1976 [QRL.66], 11 October 1976; [QRL.103], at Hammersmith in 1944-45 (2.2.2.3), Dawley during the summer of 1969 (2.2.2.14), Altrincham in September 1977 (2.2.2.15), and Coventry in the Spring of 1978 (2.2.2.17). On none of these occasions did the actual form of question used contain any kind of definition or qualification of the term 'life after death', and on only four (December 1947, April-May 1963, June 1970, and July 1979) were

respondents themselves subsequently given the opportunity to describe their own interpretations of it.

5.2.4.2 More concretely, Gallup has probed adults' commitment to the notions of heaven, hell and reincarnation in May 1968 [QRL.12]; [QRL.62]; [QRL.64], August 1968; [QRL.112], 21 July 1968, April-May 1973 [QRL.12]; [QRL.64], May 1973; [QRL.112], 13 May 1973, May-June 1975 [QRL.12]; [QRL.64], June 1975, March 1979 [QRL.25]; [QRL.64], May 1979; [QRL.112], 15 April 1979, March 1981 [QRL.44], 17 December 1981; [QRL.70], 1982-83; [QRL.125], 11 December 1981, and April 1981 [QRL.31], 1981; [QRL.64], April 1981; [QRL.112], 19 April 1981. Information about hell has also been collected in the *People* social study of January 1951 (2.2.1.3) and by NOP in June 1970 [QRL.101], whilst Hertford residents were quizzed in September 1982 about their certainty of admission to heaven in the event of their sudden death [B.502].

5.2.5 *Other beliefs*
5.2.5.1 Beyond the limits of orthodox faith lie a variety of superstitious, paranormal and other marginal belief systems which, although they may lack a specifically Christian foundation and content, constitute a vital element within British folk religion and thus lay claim to a brief consideration in this review. Nationally, there are two main sources of quantitative data on the subject. First, eighteen opinion polls have been undertaken since March 1940, the most important of them by ORC early in 1968 [QRL.113], 5 May 1968, by NOP in June 1970 [QRL.101], by Gallup in October 1973 [QRL.12]; [QRL.64], October 1973, May-June 1975 [QRL.12] [QRL.64], June 1975, February 1978 [QRL.13], 1978; [QRL.64], March 1978 and November 1981 [QRL.31], 1981; [QRL.64], December 1981; [QRL.112], 27 December 1981, and by Marplan in December 1979 [QRL.37]; [QRL.79], 29 February 1980; full details of all of these are given in the QRL. Secondly, and less representatively, surveys have been conducted amongst self-selecting samples of the readerships of the *People* (n=4,983) in January 1951 (2.2.1.3), *New Scientist* (n=1,416, 63% of whom were graduates) in November 1972 [B.104], *The Times* (n=1,314) in October 1980 [QRL.123], 20 December 1980, and *New Society* (n=3,180) in October 1982 [QRL.73], 25 November 1982.

5.2.5.2 More localised research has been carried out by Nicholas Abercrombie, John Baker, Sebastian Brett and Jane Foster [B.1] at Islington during the spring and summer of 1968 (n=181), by Geoffrey Nelson and Rosemary Clews at Dawley in the summer of 1969 (2.2.2.14), by Peter Jarvis (of the Department of Adult Education, University of Surrey) within a Midlands industrial town during the spring of 1974 (n=172), and by Max Hammerton and A.C.Downing [B.159] amongst 105 undergraduate students at the University of Newcastle-upon-Tyne in the late 1970s.

CHAPTER 6

PERSONAL RELIGION: PRACTICES

6.1 Private Practices

6.1.1 *Prayer*

6.1.1.1 Data concerning the incidence and frequency of private prayer have been collected from samples of the adult population of the United Kingdom in March 1981 [QRL.70], 1982-83, Britain in January 1950 [QRL.3]; [QRL.12]; [QRL.74], 9 February 1950, April-May 1963 (5.2.3.2, bereaved persons only), June 1970 [QRL.101] and September 1972 [QRL.113], 22 April 1973, England in January 1951 (2.2.1.3) and December 1963- January 1964 [QRL.120]; [QRL.121], Hammersmith in 1944-45 (2.2.2.3), two South Norfolk communities in 1962 (2.2.2.9), Balsall Heath, Birmingham in September-October 1965 (2.2.2.11), the Clun Valley of Shropshire in 1968 (2.2.2.11), Dawley in the summer of 1969 (2.2.2.14), and Coventry during the spring of 1978 (2.2.2.17).

6.1.1.2 Other lines of enquiry have been less often pursued. Details of the actual content of prayers were recorded at Hammersmith in 1944-45 (2.2.2.3), and ideas about potentially suitable subjects were gathered by ORC throughout Great Britain in February 1968 [QRL.94] and Northern Ireland in December 1968- January 1969 [QRL.94]; [QRL.95]. Belief in the power and efficacy of prayer was monitored nationally in January 1950 [QRL.3]; [QRL.12]; [QRL.74], 9 February 1950 and December 1954 [QRL.97], whilst parental teaching of prayers to children has been examined in the *People* social survey of January 1951 (2.2.1.3), by Gallup in February 1957 [QRL.12]; [QRL.74], 15 April 1957, and by NOP in June 1970 [QRL.101]. Finally, the prevalence of formal family prayers and/or grace at mealtimes has been measured across the entire country in July 1948 [QRL.54], 10 August 1948, at Dawley during the summer of 1969 (2.2.2.14), and at Machynlleth and Newtown, Montgomeryshire in September 1974 (2.3.2.4).

6.1.2 *The Bible*

6.1.2.1 The overall level of Bible ownership amongst adults has been studied in polls conducted throughout Britain in July 1948 [QRL.54], 10 August 1948, February 1954 [QRL.12] [QRL.74], 8 March 1954, April 1973 [QRL.45], April 1976 [QRL.72], 30 September 1976, and April-May 1982 [QRL.4] as well as at Derby in February-April 1953 (2.2.2.4). The actual process of Bible purchase and acquisition both by individuals and institutions has recently been scrutinised by the BS (of Stonehill Green, Westlea, Swindon, SN5 7DG); samples comprised four representative groups of the British public interviewed in February 1979 [QRL.44],

11 October 1979; [QRL.51], 12 October 1979 and April-May 1982 [QRL.4], 760 Protestant Christians contacted by post during 1979, and one thousand eight hundred English churches, schools, and prison, hospital or armed forces chaplains circularised in May 1979 [QRL.44], 28 February 1980; [QRL.51], 29 February 1980.

6.1.2.2 Surveys of Bible readership have been undertaken amongst elements of the general population of Great Britain in July 1948 [QRL.54], 10 August 1948, February 1954 [QRL.12]; [QRL.74], 8 March 1954, December 1954 [QRL.97], June 1970 [QRL.101], September 1972 [QRL.113], 22 April 1973, April 1973 [QRL.45], April 1976 [QRL.72], 30 September 1976 and April-May 1982 [QRL.4], England in December 1963-January 1964 [QRL.120]; [QRL.121], Derby in February-April 1953 (2.2.2.4), two south Norfolk communities in 1962 (2.2.2.9), Machynlleth and Newtown, Montgomeryshire in September 1974 (2.3.2.4), Altrincham in September 1977 (2.2.2.15), and Coventry in the spring of 1978 (2.2.2.17). Broader aspects of the usage of scripture in both private and public devotion have been examined by the BS on the basis of questionnaires mailed to 1,290 clergy or laity in September 1979 and of diaries kept by 257 church-goers over a six week period in 1980, and by Pearl Sjolander [B.355] [B.356] with two hundred ministers from various Protestant denominations between November 1979 and January 1980.

6.1.2.3 The earliest investigation of attitudes towards the inerrancy of the Old and/or New Testaments took place amongst readers of the *Daily News* and *Nation and Athenaeum* in 1926 (2.2.1.2); more recently, the topic has featured in polls of British adults held in December 1954 [QRL.97], February 1957 [QRL.12]; [QRL.74], 15 April 1957, January 1960 [QRL.64], May 1979, June 1970 [QRL.101], January 1973 [QRL.12] [QRL.64], February 1973, March 1979 [QRL.25]; [QRL.64], May 1979; [QRL.112], 15 April 1979, and April 1981 [QRL.31], 1981; [QRL.64], April 1981; [QRL.112], 19 April 1981. Belief in the historical genuineness of the miracles recorded in the Bible was measured across Great Britain in February 1968 [QRL.94], Northern Ireland in March-August 1968 [QRL.26], December 1968-January 1969 [QRL.94] [QRL.95] and August 1973-July 1974 (n = 2,416 males aged eighteen to sixty-four) [B.243], and at Dawley in the summer of 1969 (2.2.2.14).

6.1.2.4 Three further indicators may be more briefly mentioned. The popularity of the Bible in relation to other works of literature was assessed in February 1938 [QRL.9] [QRL.12], May 1948 [QRL.12], and February 1954 [QRL.12] [QRL.74], 8 March 1954. The public's ability to name any of the four gospels was tested in October 1949 [QRL.12] [QRL.74], 3 January 1950, whilst their knowledge of modern translations of scripture was checked in April 1973 [QRL.45] and April 1976 [QRL.72], 30 September 1976.

6.1.3 *Religious broadcasting*
6.1.3.1 Although listening and viewing figures for individual programmes have been gathered on a serial basis since the early 1940s, initially by the BBC and IBA but latterly by the Broadcasters' Audience Research Board, the illumination of public attitudes towards the theory, practice and achievements of religious broadcasting has

mainly been tackled through non-recurrent survey methods. The QRL gives details of fourteen national opinion polls conducted in this field between February 1938 and October 1982, seven of which are of sufficient importance to warrant a fuller description here.

6.1.3.2 The first study of note was undertaken by *News Review* [QRL.75], 6 November 1947 during the middle of 1947 using a sample composed of 'several thousand' adults of eighteen years and above drawn from one hundred and ten locations across England, Wales and Scotland. Respondents were asked how often they listened to religious worship on the radio, whether they did so intentionally or simply because the set happened to be turned on, if they ever deliberately switched off to avoid hearing a broadcast, and whether they regarded wireless services as a substitute for attending church.

6.1.3.3 Seven years later, in December 1954, Gallup interviewed a representative group of 1,859 Britons aged sixteen and over on behalf of the BBC. Informants spoke about their frequency of listening to religious programmes, their reasons for doing so, their preferences for talks, discussions and plays revolving around spiritual themes, and the extent to which they felt they had been helped by any radio preacher. Results, broken down by eight variables, appeared in [QRL.97].

6.1.3.4 A further Gallup enquiry, carried out in December 1963 and January 1964, covered 2,211 persons living in the London, Midlands and Northern Independent Television Areas of England. Twenty-one of the seventy-two questions dealt either with matters affecting religious broadcasting as a whole or with the audience for and reactions to ABC TV's 'Sunday Break' series. Findings have been published in [QRL.120] and [QRL.121], whilst the original data set is preserved at the ESRC DA, University of Essex.

6.1.3.5 The next two significant investigations were conducted by ORC amongst random samples of the adult population of Great Britain in February 1968 (n = 1,071) and Northern Ireland in December 1968-January 1969 (n = 694). Informants on each occasion were asked to state whether they would purposely switch on their television to watch a religious item, to say how much attention they paid to such a feature if transmission began when the set was already on, and to express their ideas about the content and objectives of religious broadcasting. Statistics are reproduced in [QRL.94] and [QRL.95].

6.1.3.6 Another ORC poll, undertaken in January 1973, was 'designed to discover the characteristics by which religious programmes are recognised' [QRL.91]. The 647 respondents, 317 of them from England and Wales and 330 from Scotland, were each given a thirty dimension semantic scale with which to rate six programmes drawn from a master list of eleven religious and nineteen secular titles. Scores were disaggregated according to a four point index of personal spirituality which derived, in its turn, from nine variables.

6.1.3.7 The most recent major national survey was carried out by BMRB during the first week of February 1980 amongst a quota sample of 1,126 adults aged fifteen and over resident in Great Britain south of the Caledonian Canal. They were invited to say whether they liked three particular types of religious broadcast (hymns and music, documentaries and news, general items about Christianity) or not, and whether they considered 'there is too little, too much or just the right amount of religious programming on television'. The research was commissioned by London Weekend Television to whom any requests for figures should be addressed.

6.1.3.8 More localised data have been compiled for Derby in February-April 1953 (2.2.2.4), two south Norfolk communities in 1962 (2.2.2.9), Dawley during the summer of 1969 (2.2.2.14), and, most importantly of all, Greater London in February-March 1978 (2.2.2.16). This last investigation, which aimed to measure the pastoral success of the media in alleviating the problems of loneliness, contained several items relative to the identification, consumption, and impact of religious broadcasts.

6.1.4 *Observance of Christian festivals*
6.1.4.1 The festival which has been most consistently examined in the national opinion polls is that of Christmas. Various questions have been asked of which only two are of immediate relevance. The first concerns the extent to which respondents regarded Christmas as a religious, family or other kind of occasion; this enquiry was put in surveys conducted throughout Great Britain in December 1964 [QRL.12] [QRL.64], January 1965; [QRL.112], 27 December 1964, 10-15 December 1969 [QRL.77], December 1969, 11-14 December 1969 [QRL.12]; [QRL.57], 23 December 1969; [QRL.64], December 1969, December 1970 [QRL.12] [QRL.64], January 1971, November-December 1972 (ESRC DA, SN 069), December 1972 [QRL.113], 24 December 1972, December 1974 [QRL.12]; [QRL.64], January 1975, November 1975 [QRL.12]; [QRL.64], December 1975, and November 1976 [QRL.64], December 1976. The second invited people to say whether they considered Christmas was becoming more or less of a spiritual event than it had been during their childhood; this information was sought in December 1964 [QRL.12]; [QRL.64], January 1965; [QRL.112], 27 December 1964, December 1969 [QRL.12] [QRL.57], 23 December 1969; [QRL.64], December 1969, and December 1970 [QRL.12]; [QRL.64], January 1971.

6.1.4.2 The principal local study of attitudes towards Christmas was carried out in Oxford on St.Nicholas's Day, 1980 by a group calling themselves Christians in Communications. The sample comprised a somewhat arbitrary selection of 175 city centre shoppers who were asked particularly about the importance which they attached and/or would like to see given to the religious dimension of the occasion. Results are briefly reported in [QRL.44], 18 December 1980; [QRL.47], 19 December 1980; [QRL.51], 19 December 1980.

6.1.4.3 Other festivals in the Christian calendar have attracted little attention. Gallup explored the extent of and motives for self-denial during Lent in February 1939

[QRL.9]; [QRL.12]; [QRL.74], 8 March 1939, and NOP covered part of the same ground in June 1970 [QRL.101]. The degree to which Easter was popularly viewed as a spiritual event was investigated in April 1968 [QRL.112], 14 April 1968.

6.2 Public Practices

6.2.1 *Rites of passage*
6.2.1.1 Overall figures relative to the incidence of baptism are only available at the community level. Direct comparisons of the number of births and of christenings have been made by William Pickering for Rawmarsh and Scunthorpe in 1951 (2.2.2.5) and by Peter Kaim-Caudle for Billingham in 1957 and 1964-65 (2.2.2.6). Information as to the percentage of the adult population claiming to have been baptised is given in surveys undertaken in Hodge Hill and Balsall Heath, Birmingham in 1965 (2.2.2.11) and in Dawley in 1969 (2.2.2.14).

6.2.1.2 Attitudes to infant baptism have been explored nationally by Gallup in February 1957 [QRL.12]; [QRL.74], 15 April 1957 and locally by Richard Kingsbury within the Anglican Diocese of Oxford in 1980. The latter study, which was based upon replies to questionnaires received from 112 of 230 parents in two parishes and from 110 of 300 priests, is described in an unpublished report available from the Mid-Service Clergy Course at St. George's House, Windsor Castle and, more briefly, in [QRL.51], 19 September 1980.

6.2.1.3 Statistics of the form of marriage solemnisation, ecclesiastical or civil, have been obtained from representative groups of adults in Great Britain in mid-1947 [QRL.75], 30 October 1947, April 1952 [QRL.12], February 1957 [QRL.12] and March 1977 [QRL.99], Swansea in May-June 1960 (2.3.2.2), Hodge Hill and Balsall Heath during the summer and autumn of 1965 (2.2.2.11), and Machynlleth and Newtown, Montgomeryshire in September 1974 (2.3.2.4). The extent of public agreement/disagreement with the proposition that 'It is better to get married in church than in a registry office' was measured by MORI in May 1981 [QRL.88], May-October 1981.

6.2.1.4 Details of the proportion of funerals conducted with religious rites were gathered by William Pickering for Rawmarsh and Scunthorpe in the mid-1950s (2.2.2.5), by Peter Kaim-Caudle for Billingham in 1957 (2.2.2.6), and by Geoffrey Gorer [B.140] from a national sample of 359 bereaved persons in April-May 1963. Popular preferences for an ecclesiastical burial as opposed to baptism or marriage in church were expressed in a NOP survey of June 1970 [QRL.101].

6.2.2 *Denominational affiliation*
6.2.2.1 Since, for politico-historical causes best explained by Michael Drake [B.101], no comprehensive enumeration of confessional allegiance has been carried out in Great Britain subsequent to the censuses of 1603 (2.1.1), 1676 (2.1.2) and 1755 (2.4.1.1), reliance must again be placed upon commercial opinion polls as the

principal source of national data. Details of relevant studies are given in the QRL, and it is not proposed to repeat them here but merely to direct attention to a number of general factors which will condition their interpretation and use. First, it is quite certain that the list as it stands is seriously incomplete in that many more polls have been conducted over the years than the ones for which it has proved possible to obtain precise information; Joan Brothers [B.43], for example, quotes aggregate statistics of denominational profession drawn from twenty separate Gallup investigations in 1963 of which only half can now be traced in Gallup's own archives or elsewhere. Secondly, religious persuasion has mostly been examined less for its own sake than as an added background variable against which to analyse replies to other questions; this is the reason why so many entries lack publication references of any kind and why still fewer can boast documentation which includes some degree of breakdown of the results. Thirdly, the standard 'What is your religious denomination?' form of enquiry is highly tendentious in that it implies and assumes that respondents either do or should have a confessional label to report; it thus triggers the 'prestige' effect (2.1.4.6) and leads, in particular, to exaggerated claims of commitment to the established Churches of England and Scotland on the part of nominal Christians. Fourthly, the range of sectarian categories adopted for coding purposes is frequently far too narrow to be of much practical benefit; even with surveys specifically designed for cumulation to provide extra large data bases, such as those undertaken in February-April 1978 [QRL.96] and April-May 1979 [QRL.13], 1979; [QRL.64], May 1979, Gallup has often refused to advance beyond its traditional 'Church of England, Church of Scotland, Nonconformist, Roman Catholic, other, none' classification scheme.

6.2.2.2 Local figures, which are subject to much the same sort of qualifications and limitations, first appeared during the latter half of the eighteenth century with, for instance, investigations at Stockport in 1754 (Bodleian Library, Ms.Top. Cheshire b.1, fo.129), Armagh City in 1770 (Armagh Public Library, Ms. 9/5/20), and Woodbridge, Suffolk in 1770 and 1777 [B.435]. They became plentiful during the 1830s and 1840s (2.2.2.1) and again towards the end of the Victorian era when Abraham Hume [B.199] organised a census of religious profession within the Anglican Diocese of Liverpool in 1881 and the Free Churches canvassed the population of several major towns and cities during the 1890s (2.2.2.2). Interest then waned a little, only to revive in the period since the Second World War when many relevant sample surveys have been conducted; notable examples, deriving from a base of at least one thousand adults, comprise studies of Banbury in July 1950 [B.371] and April-May 1967 (ESRC DA, SN 67016) [B.372], Derby in February-April 1953 (2.2.2.4), Newcastle-under-Lyme in November 1959-March 1960 [B.10], the Associated Rediffusion Television Area in 1960 (2.2.2.7), Swansea in May-June 1960 (2.3.2.2), Stockton-on-Tees and Morpeth in the early 1960s [B.294], Bishop's Stortford in the autumn of 1966 [B.367], Preston in April-June 1968 (3.1.1.3), thirty-seven parishes of the Diocese of Bangor *circa* 1970 (3.1.2.1), Runcorn in April-July 1972 (ESRC DA, SN 1668) [B.18], Belfast between August 1972 and January 1974 (ESRC DA, SN 921), and the Hillhead division of Glasgow in March 1982 (by MORI, JN 7806, JN 7924).

6.2.3 *Church membership*

6.2.3.1 Subjective data are neither especially numerous nor, since they are mostly incapable of independent verification and tend to derive from questions employing an ill-defined concept of membership, of outstanding quality. Claims to active membership of a Christian Church were registered by readers of the *Daily News* and *Nation and Athenaeum* in 1926 (2.2.1.2) and by representative samples of electors across Great Britain in October 1974-January 1975 (ESRC DA, SN 666), Scotland in October 1974-January 1975 (ESRC DA, SN 681) and May-October 1979 (ESRC DA, SN 1604), and Wales in May-September 1979 (ESRC DA, SN 1591). Ordinary membership was reported by adults throughout Britain in November 1937 [QRL.9]; [QRL.12], February 1968 [QRL.94] and September 1972 (fieldwork by ORC, JN 7238), Northern Ireland in December 1968-January 1969 [QRL.94]; [QRL.95], two south Norfolk communities in 1962 (2.2.2.9), Dawley during the summer of 1969 (2.2.2.14), Falkirk in February- March 1970 (2.4.2.2), and Machynlleth and Newtown, Montgomeryshire in September 1974 (2.3.2.4).

6.2.3.2
Inter-denominational censuses would be an extremely valuable and objective source of information were it not for the fact that lack of standardisation in the actual criteria of membership makes meaningful aggregations and comparisons difficult. Significant national investigations include those undertaken in England by the Congregational Union in 1834 (2.2.1.1) and by the NIE in 1979 (2.2.1.5 - 2.2.1.9), in Wales by a Royal Commission in 1906-10 (2.3.1.2 - 2.3.1.3) and by the BS in conjunction with WfC in 1982 (2.3.1.6), and in Scotland by a Government board of enquiry in 1835-39 (2.4.1.3). Amongst fairly recent local studies may be mentioned those of 'Squirebridge', an English country town with a population of about fifteen thousand, in April-August 1950 [B.30], Glasgow in the mid-1950s (2.4.2.1), south Norfolk in 1962 (2.2.2.9), and Leeds during the late 1970s (2.2.2.18).

6.2.3.3 Data collected internally by individual religious bodies present the fewest problems, and most of these are available on a serial basis. Relevant non-recurrent statistics which have already been noted throughout chapter 3 will not be discussed again here, but attention may perhaps be drawn to two pieces of research into the mechanics of membership growth and decline which have been conducted within the Methodist Church. First, a series of surveys of lapsed members were carried out in the Manchester (n = 357), Sheffield (n = 225), London South-West (n = 34), and Nottingham and Derby (n = 82) Districts during the early 1960s; summary figures have been reproduced by Bernard Jones [B.218], whilst a full account of the last of these four investigations is given by J.R. Butler [B.58]. Secondly, a postal questionnaire sent to a one in ten sample of circuit ministers in June 1977 elicited an 88% response and yielded information relative to the sex, age, marital status, education, occupation, and other characteristics of some three thousand new and former members gained or lost during the period 1 September 1976 to 31 May 1977; the work was co-ordinated by Peter Jarvis of the Department of Adult Education, University of Surrey and is described in a pamphlet which he co-authored with Jeffrey Harris [B.164].

6.2.4 *Religious organisations*

6.2.4 1 The extent of the general public's membership of one or more religious organisations has been examined in polls undertaken throughout the United Kingdom in March 1981 [QRL.70], 1982-83, Great Britain in July-August 1947 (n = 3,000 gainfully employed adults) [B.472], June-July 1959 (ESRC DA, SN 370), August-September 1967 (n = 1,001 persons aged fifteen to forty, ESRC DA, SN 67025) [B.488] and June-August 1970 (ESRC DA, SN 173), England and Wales in September 1965-March 1966 (urban areas only, n = 2,682) [B.351] and April-October 1972 (n = 10,309 males from twenty to sixty-four years, ESRC DA, SN 1097), England in December 1963-January 1964 [QRL.120] [QRL.121] and April-July 1967 [QRL.52], Scotland in May 1974-September 1975 (n = 4,887 men aged twenty to sixty- four, ESRC DA, SN 981), and Northern Ireland in March-August 1968 [QRL.26]. More localised research on the same theme has been carried out at Hammersmith in 1944-45 (2.2.2.3), Aston (n = 200) in 1946 [B.472], 'Squirebridge' in April- August 1950 [B.30], Derby in February-April 1953 (2.2.2.4), Swansea in May-June 1960 (2.3.2.2), two south Norfolk communities in 1962 (2.2.2.9), inner London (n = 1,321) and eight new towns (n = 1,732) in September 1965-March 1966 [B.351], Banbury (n = 1,449) in April-May 1967 (ESRC DA, SN 67016) [B.372], Sheffield (n = 584) in November 1967 [B.160], the Clun Valley of Shropshire in 1968 (2.2.2.11), Cublington, Foulness, Nuthampstead, Thurleigh and immediately adjacent districts (n = 932) in August 1969 (ESRC DA, SN69017), Falkirk in February-March 1970 (2.4.2.2), and Salford (n = 604) in March-April 1970 (ESRC DA, SN 70003).

6.2.4.2 Actual attendance at meetings of religious clubs and groups has been less often studied. Seebohm Rowntree [B.337] seems to have been first in the field with a census of weekday church activities in York conducted during the fortnight 27 October-10 November 1935. His example has since been followed by Peter Varney in south Norfolk in 1962 (2.2.2.9) and by Martin Reardon at Sheffield in 1965-67 (2.2.2.13).

CHAPTER 7

PERSONAL RELIGION: CHURCH ATTENDANCE

7.1 Censuses of Attendance

7.1.1 *1851 religious census*

7.1.1.1 Partial returns of church attendance in England in 1834 (2.2.1.1), Scotland in 1835-39 (2.4.1.3), and Wales in 1847 (2.3.1.1) paved the way for a full official ecclesiastical census of Great Britain in 1851. General methodological aspects of this enquiry have already been considered elsewhere (2.1.3, 2.4.1.4), and the present discussion will concentrate upon the three factors which have the most critical bearing on the interpretation and use of the statistics relating to public worship. These are the reliability of the data as a record of attendance on 30 March 1851, the extent to which turn-out on that day can be regarded as typical of other Sundays throughout the year, and the adjustments which are necessary to convert gross figures to an estimate of the total worshipping community.

7.1.1.2 The intrinsic accuracy of the returns for 30 March is dependent upon both their completeness of coverage and the care with which they were compiled. With regard to the first point, it is certain that a measure of underregistration will have occurred owing to the fact that some churches were overlooked by the enumerators and others failed to reply to the questions which were asked of them (2.1.3.4, 2.1.3.5, 2.4.1.4). So far as the second is concerned, comments on the original schedules as well as widespread rounding of statistics to the nearest ten or hundred clearly indicate that only in a minority of cases, more so in smaller than in larger meetings and in Anglican than in Nonconformist ones, was an exact count of worshippers made. Many informants seem merely to have estimated the size of their congregations on the basis of the apparent rate of occupancy of the available sittings, a procedure which is notoriously liable to lead to some exaggeration; as the minister of Ebenezer Street Chapel in Swansea remarked: 'Most people would suppose we had 800... last evening by viewing the assembly, but when numbered they were found short of 500' [B.522].

7.1.1.3 Allegations that attendances on 30 March fell below the norm were commonplace. Ignoring purely local circumstances, we may identify three major causes which were thought to have kept people from public worship. First, the census was taken on Mid-Lent or Mothering Sunday which was traditionally marked in many parts of England, not least in Cheshire, Lancashire, Yorkshire and several Midland counties, by family reunions, visits to friends, and Simnel feasts or fairs. Secondly, the enumeration was held at an especially busy point in the agricultural calendar when farmers and labourers were hard at work seven days a week tending cattle and, since it was the lambing season, sheep. Thirdly, weather conditions on 30 March were reported as being exceptionally bad, a contention which it has been possible to substantiate from records at the National Meteorological Library, Bracknell which reveal high winds, rain, hail, and thunderstorms to have been prevalent throughout the country on that day; individual congregations were said to have suffered reductions of anything between ten and fifty per cent as a result, those in rural districts being the worst affected on account of the poor state of the roads there and the relatively greater distances from home to church. Many respondents noted that their largest attendances were registered during the summer months.

7.1.1.4 Against these arguments must be weighed others, no less widespread, which suggested that deliberate and successful attempts were made, principally by the Dissenters of England and Wales and by the Free Church in Scotland, to maximise support on census day by means of advance exhortation or 'whipping' of their adherents, the multiplication of services, the deployment of special preachers, and even by the wholesale movement of congregations and Sunday schools from one chapel to another in order to ensure they were counted twice over. Whilst such charges may not have been entirely without foundation, they were probably grossly exaggerated, and it is certainly interesting that when the Bishop of Oxford, who had voiced them so eloquently during the course of debates in the House of Lords, canvassed the views of his own clergy in 1854, no more than 33 of 595 of them were prepared to accuse their Nonconformist neighbours of distorting the returns which they had made in 1851.

7.1.1.5 The net effect of these and other conflicting claims can be assessed, if only tentatively, in one of two ways. First, attendances on 30 March may be contrasted with the approximate twelve month averages which were supplied by one half to three quarters of all churches. Such a comparison suggests that turn-out at the census did indeed tend to fall below the norm but not universally so nor always by a serious amount; in London Methodism, for example, the net discrepancy between the two sets of data was just 7% [B.110]. Secondly, the figures can be matched with results from independent local enumerations which were conducted at about the same time and along methodologically similar lines (7.1.3.1); although no consistent picture emerges from this type of correlation, it is perhaps significant that in three towns at least (Canterbury, Carlisle, and Lincoln) morning congregations actually encompassed some four per cent *more* of the population in 1851 than they did three years earlier.

7.1.1.6 However accurate or representative the statistics may or may not be, there can be absolutely no doubt that they require careful adjustment before any assessment of the size of the total worshipping community can be reached. An initial complication is that a good many people will have frequented two or more services on the census day, not necessarily in the same building nor even with the same denomination, and that, as a consequence, the number of separate attenders will have been less than the sum of all attendances. Some analysts have sought to evade the problem by constructing a minimum participation index on the basis of the largest single congregation at each individual church; this procedure, which was adopted in Table N of the official report for England and Wales [B.450] with disaggregations to registration county level and for four broad ecclesiastical groupings, is obviously unsatisfactory in that it omits from the reckoning those persons who solely worshipped at the least popular times. Other commentators have tried to devise formulae whereby, for any given geographical unit in the published tabulations, the whole attendance at one service is counted together with a varying proportion of that recorded at other meetings; all such devices, quite apart from being entirely without empirical foundation, have perpetrated three fundamental methodological errors. First, they have assumed that each place of worship and/or sect registered its peak turn-out on the same part of the day. This was most definitely not the case; Horace Mann's classic equation (morning + one half afternoon + one third evening), for example, was grossly unfair to Nonconformists whose principal gatherings were at night. Secondly, they have ignored the fact that a substantial number of churches (29.6% throughout Great Britain, 28.8% in England and Wales, 39.7% in Scotland, 13.9% in towns, 34.1% in rural districts, 33.7% with the Anglicans, 25.4% with other English and Welsh religious bodies) only ever held one service anyway. Thirdly, they have disregarded the considerable inter-denominational differences in twicing which are revealed in the local sources. Scottish Presbyterians appear to have been the most devout (at Aberdeen, for instance, it has been calculated [B.247] that their 31,155 attendances were made by just 19,316 individuals); then came, in descending order, Protestant Dissenters, Anglicans, and, finally, Roman Catholics amongst whom double duty was least common.

7.1.1.7 If some people were zealous enough to frequent divine service twice in one day, then it is equally certain that others were too lethargic or too busy to attend church regularly week by week. Direct evidence on this point is limited, but such as there is tends to support Horace Mann's assumption, expressed in a paper read before the Statistical Society of London in December 1854 [B.252], that about half of the total Anglican and Catholic constituency and three fifths of the Nonconformist and sectarian one would have been present on any particular Sunday.

7.1.2 *1979 and 1982 Bible Society censuses*
7.1.2.1 One hundred and eight years were to elapse before the next co-ordinated national survey, a sample census of public worship in Scotland in 1959 (2.4.1.6), and a further twenty were to pass before any more full-scale enumerations were undertaken, this time not by the Government but by the BS Research Department acting on behalf of the NIE and WfC, two ecumenical home missionary organisations. The data, which are not methodologically perfect, covered the number, sex and ages of attenders at Christian churches on a 'normal Sunday' throughout both England in November 1979 (2.2.1.5-2.2.1.9) and Wales in May 1982 (2.3.1.6).

7.1.2.2 As in 1851, reductions are necessary to take account of those who frequented two services on census day. According to a study of thirteen to twenty year olds in five areas of Lancashire in 1979-80 (4.2.1.18), such persons comprised 28% of

Nonconformist, 18% of Anglican, and 3% of Catholic church-goers. The proportion amongst older people is undoubtedly rather higher; indeed, results from a miscellaneous sample of 483 evangelical Christians published in *Today* magazine in April 1982 [B.455] suggest that double duty was twice as common in the over-40 age group as in the under-40 range.

7.1.2.3 Opinion polls give an approximate indication of the allowances which require to be made for irregular worshippers. An unpublished cumulation of six Gallup surveys conducted during April and May 1982, for example, revealed that, of the 56.4% of adult Britons who claimed ever to come to church other than for baptisms, weddings or funerals, 14.9% went once a week or more, 9.2% once a month, 19.8% at least annually, and 12.5% less frequently. Denominationally, reported attendance within the previous year varied from 37.0% of professing Anglicans to 69.8% of Catholics.

7.1.2.4 Detailed examination of local ecclesiastical records and censuses clearly demonstrates that such irregularity is not an entirely random phenomenon but that, for all the major Christian bodies with the possible exception of the Catholics, it follows a fairly predetermined cyclical pattern. Congregations in January and February tend to be appreciably below the norm, mainly because of adverse climatic conditions and illness which especially affect the elderly on whom the Churches increasingly depend for their support. Attendances in March, April and May show a big improvement on account of finer weather and the appeal of Easter Day services with the Anglicans (who, during the 1950s and 1960s at least, were present in twice their usual number for the occasion) and of chapel or Sunday school anniversaries with the Nonconformists. A new trough develops in June, July and August which is associated with summer recreations and the holiday period. Then, towards the end of the year, comes a further, if uneven, recovery which is assisted, markedly so in rural Anglican parishes, by the harvest festival season and culminates in a relatively high level of observance at Christmastide.

7.1.3 *Local censuses*
7.1.3.1 The earliest local surveys were undertaken during the two decades preceding the 1851 religious census. Returns of average attendances were made at Nottingham by Richard Hopper in 1833 [B.71], Hull by Thomas Stratten in 1834 [B.378], York by James Riddal Wood in 1837 (Manchester Central Library, Ms.f310.6, M5, vol.IV, no.139), Penzance and Madron by Richard Edmonds in 1838 [B.102], Hetton by the British Association for the Advancement of Science in 1838 [B.217], Trevethin and Blaenavon by G.S. Kenrick *circa* 1840 [B.230], Bristol by the city's Statistical Society in 1841 [B.456], Malton by William Charles Copperthwaite in 1841 [B.497], Oldham in 1845 [B.287], and Ipswich by John Glyde in 1850 [B.135]. Actual enumerations were held at Preston on 9 January 1834 [B.414], Spitalfields in 1843 [B.440], Greenwich in October 1846 [B.485], Carlisle on 7 May 1848 (as described in the *Carlisle Journal* of 19 May 1848), Canterbury and Lincoln on 14 May 1848 (as reported in Edward Horsman's speech before the House of Commons on 16 May of

that year), Hammersmith in June 1848 [B.463], Chiswick on 16 July 1848 [B.454], and Cripplegate in January 1849 [B.462].

7.1.3.2 The first major investigation to be conducted after 1851 was at Liverpool in 1855 [B.495]; it was organised by Nathaniel Caine over a period of some six months, great care being taken to survey each place of worship on a day when attendances were likely to have been at their maximum (many Anglican congregations, for instance, were counted on Easter Sunday). Little of substance was accomplished during the 1860s, but on 14 October 1871 the *Stratford Express* published the results of its census of morning and evening services in West Ham, and on 31 January 1873 the *Lincoln, Rutland and Stamford Mercury* printed data from a similar enquiry in the city of Lincoln [B.176]. Up in Scotland, as can be seen from Robert Howie's volume [B.196], the *North British Daily Mail* examined church-going amongst the Protestants of Glasgow and forty-seven other towns in the west of the country during the spring of 1876, and the *Northern Daily News* carried the findings of an enumeration at Aberdeen in 1878.

7.1.3.3 On 2 October 1881 the *Newcastle Daily Chronicle* decided to mark the Church Congress then meeting in the city by arranging for a census of attendance in the Tyneside boroughs. Its example was quickly taken up by the *Liverpool Daily Post* on 16 October and thereafter by, mainly Liberal, provincial newspapers throughout the Kingdom until, by mid-February 1882, no fewer than 142 separate places and districts had been surveyed, six of them (Bradford, Cheltenham, Gosport, Ipswich, Nottingham, and Portsmouth) on more than one occasion or by more than one journal. Of these 142, listed in full in Appendix 2, 87 were in England, 4 in Wales, and 51 in Scotland; 13 were cities with populations in excess of one hundred thousand, 13 were large towns with fifty to one hundred thousand inhabitants, 48 were medium sized towns with ten to fifty thousand residents, 55 were small towns with between two and ten thousand people, and 13 were very small towns (with less than two thousand persons) or groups of villages. General overviews of the results, together with details of fieldwork dates and names of the newspapers concerned, were prepared by Andrew Mearns [B.267] and by *The Nonconformist and Independent* [B.510], 2, 23 February, 9 March 1882, whilst complete returns may be found in the columns of the local press or, exceptionally [B.452] [B.489], in book form.

7.1.3.4 Valuable although the 1881-82 data undoubtedly are, it is important to recognise that they are difficult to use for comparative purposes because of the greatly differing methodologies involved; in particular, attention is drawn to four basic points. First, the counting was sometimes undertaken by neutral observers but in other cases by officials connected with each church. Secondly, Sunday scholars were included in a bare majority of instances but omitted from the rest. Thirdly, there was no standardisation in the range of services which were covered; at one extreme, many of the Scottish censuses and a few of the English and Welsh ones (for example, Gateshead, Llanelly, Newcastle-upon-Tyne, and Stockport) were confined to a single session of worship only, yet at the other, especially in the smaller towns and villages, morning, afternoon, and evening gatherings were all enumerated. Fourthly, the weather conditions in which the surveys were made varied from bright and spring-like to the most appalling wintry ones. Some indication of the effect of this factor can be gained from the enquiry at Cheltenham which was held both on 29 January (an exceedingly wet day) and 5 February 1882 (a reasonably fine one); total attendances on the former occasion were equivalent to 47.7% of the population, on the latter to 61.4%.

7.1.3.5 The main census movement ground to a halt at Darwen in February 1882, but sporadic local initiatives continued with enumerations at Southport and Birkdale on 17 September 1882 and 2 March 1884 [B.24], Swansea by the *South Wales Daily News* (26 March 1884) in 1884, Cardiff by the *Cardiff Times* (22 November 1884) in 1884, Kidderminster on the evening of 9 November 1886 as reported in the *Kidderminster Shuttle* of 13 November 1886, Bacup, Cloughfold, Crawshawbooth, Lumb, Newchurch, Rawtenstall, Stacksteads, and Waterfoot by the *Bacup Times and Rossendale Advertiser* (29 January, 5 February 1887) on 23 and 30 January 1887, Birmingham by the *Birmingham Daily Times* (31 May 1887) on the morning of 22 May 1887, and Gainsborough by the *Retford, Worksop, Isle of Axholme and Gainsborough News* in 1887 and on Whit Sunday 1888 [B.14].

7.1.3.6 By far the biggest single achievement of the late 1880s, however, was a study of attendances in the twenty-nine registration districts of inner London (population 4,100,000) organised by the *British Weekly* in two stages on 24 October 1886 (permanent churches and chapels) and 28 November 1887 (mission halls). Sunday scholars were included when they formed part of the general congregation, but no account was taken of special children's meetings, of any adult gatherings, whether Anglican early communions or Roman Catholic masses, preceding the 11 a.m. service, nor, except for the missions, of afternoon worship. Figures originally appeared in [QRL.46], 5 November-17 December 1886, 13-20 January 1888 but were subsequently revised and reprinted as a book [B.523].

7.1.3.7 Of the eight surveys carried out during the course of the 1890s, the most important were at Liverpool on the morning of 18 October and the evening of 15 November 1891 and at Birmingham on 30 November 1892. The Liverpool data, reported in the *Liverpool Daily Post* for 22, 24 October and 19, 24 November 1891, may be supplemented by a fuller record of mass-goers in the city given in the *Catholic Times* of 30 October 1891; those for Birmingham, which covered Sunday school as well as church attendance, were initially published in the *Birmingham News* on 3, 10 December 1892 but have recently been reanalysed by Roy Peacock [B.297]. Four of the other six communities were in Scotland (Broughty Ferry, Dundee, and Newport examined by the *Dundee Advertiser* on 5 April 1891, Aberdeen by the *Northern Daily News* also in 1891), and two in England - Wednesbury towards the close of 1894 [B.154] and Bolton on the evening of 22 December 1895 (as documented in the *Bolton Journal & Guardian* for 25 January 1896).

7.1.3.8 During the opening years of the twentieth century enumerations of public worship were made at Dewsbury on the evening of 10 February 1901 [B.77], York by Seebohm Rowntree [B.336] on 17 and 24 March 1901, Aberdeen on a wet and stormy day in 1901 and by the *Aberdeen Daily Journal* on a finer one in April 1911,

Dundee by the *Dundee Advertiser* in 1901, Liverpool by the *Liverpool Daily Post* (11 November 1902, 13 December 1912) on 2 November 1902 and 8 December 1912, thirty-nine towns (including Cockermouth, Keswick, Whitehaven, Wigton, and Workington) and rural districts within the circulation area of the *West Cumberland Times* (20 December 1902) on 14 December 1902, Lincoln on a brilliant Sunday in March 1903 as reported by the *Lincoln Leader and County Advertiser* for 14 March 1903 and subsequently by Francis Hill [B.176], Chester and Hoole by the *Cheshire Observer* on 25 October 1903, Newport (Isle of Wight) by the local Free Church Council in 1903 [B.568], Middlesbrough by the town's Temperance Society on 1, 8, 15 and 22 May 1904 as documented in the *North-Eastern Daily Gazette* of May-July 1904 and in a thesis by Peter Stubley [B.379], Carnarvon by the *Carnarvon and Denbigh Herald and North and South Wales Independent* (31 January, 7 February, 10 July 1908) first on a bitterly cold day in January and then on a warm sunny one in July 1908, and Tredegar by the community's Free Church Council in December 1909 [B.528]. A novel feature of the enquiries in Dewsbury, York, West Cumberland, Lincoln, Chester, and Middlesbrough was that the adult returns were disaggregated by sex; the York survey also attempted a crude distinction between upper and working class worshippers.

7.1.3.9 Pride of place amongst all the various censuses of the Edwardian era must undoubtedly go to an enumeration, by paid agents of the *Daily News*, of attendances of men, women and children at the principal morning and evening services held at 4,026 churches in the eighty-one boroughs and districts of inner and outer London (total non-institutionalised population 6,240,000); fieldwork was spread over thirty-six separate Sundays (nineteen of them fine, two dull, three unsettled, one damp, three showery, six wet, two very wet) between 30 November 1902 and 8 November 1903. The main count was supplemented by, first, a special study in sixty-nine 'representative' congregations which revealed that 17.0% of non-Roman Catholic worshippers were 'twicers' (17.3% in the inner ring, 16.3% in the outer zone, 18.5% in fine weather, 15.5% in wet, 11.7% of Anglicans, 18.9% of Nonconformists), and, secondly, a review of all gatherings in Chelsea on 17 May 1903 and of fifty-one adult schools, two hundred and twenty-eight early communion, fifty-nine afternoon, ten open air, thirty-three week evening, and two week morning services elsewhere in the capital. Full details of methodology and results may be found in Richard Mudie-Smith's book [B.529]. Plans for a replication of the entire census in 1911 were frustrated by opposition from certain ecclesiastical quarters [B.163].

7.1.3.10 During the inter-war years investigations were conducted at Ipswich by the Ipswich Local Committee of the Conference on Christian Politics, Economics and Citizenship on three successive Sundays in October and November 1923 [B.491], in one working class and one suburban area of London by Arthur Black in 1927 [QRL.46], 23 February, 1 March 1928; [B.22], at Wallsend and South Shields on behalf of the Bureau of Social Research for Tyneside on 26 February and 13 May 1928 respectively [B.271], Liverpool by *The Social Survey of Merseyside* [B.550] amongst a sample of fifty-six churches in May 1930 and May 1931, Hertford by E.R. Roper Power on 2 June 1935 [B.313], and York by Seebohm Rowntree on 27 October and 3 November 1935 [B.337]. Adult attendances were divided by sex at

Wallsend, South Shields and Hertford, by sex, age and social status at Liverpool and York.

7.1.3.11 The only significant wartime enumeration was carried out, somewhat haphazardly, by MO in the Paddington district of London on four separate dates in 1941: 23 March (a National Day of Prayer), 13 April (Easter), 11 May (in the wake of a blitz), and 8 June ('a normal Sunday'). Documentation survives amongst the 'Topic Collections: Religion' and the 'File Reports' at the Tom Harrisson MO Archive, University of Sussex.

7.1.3.12 Since the Second World War, censuses have been undertaken, with varying degrees of completeness, by Seebohm Rowntree and George Lavers [B.338] at High Wycombe in October 1947 and York in October 1948, at Redfield, Bristol by the Redfield United Front on 22 March 1953 [B.520], by William Pickering [B.303] at Scunthorpe on 4, 11, 18 April 1954 and at Rawmarsh on 27 March, 3, 10 April 1955, at Glasgow by John Highet [B.171] on 25 April, 2, 9 May 1954, 1, 8, 15 May 1955 and 29 April, 6, 13 May 1956, at Billingham by Peter Kaim-Caudle on 29 March, 12 April 1959 [B.224] and 10, 24 April 1966 [B.223], in south Norfolk by Peter Varney [B.396] in 1962, the Birmingham suburb of 'Brookton' by Kofi Busia [B.57] over a thirty-four week period in 1963-64, the Abercromby, Childwall, South Scotland and Speke wards of Liverpool by William Shannon [B.348] mostly on 9 August 1964, Banbury by Colin Bell [QRL.73], 30 May 1968 on 31 March 1968, Congleton by the local History Society and Council of Churches also on 31 March 1968 [B.373], Hemel Hempstead by Peter Bridges [B.39] in June 1968, Falkirk by Peter Sissons [B.354] in eleven congregations in September 1969, and at Newtown and Machynlleth, Montgomeryshire by Graham Day in October 1974 (2.3.2.4). Worshippers were classified according to sex and age at High Wycombe, York, Billingham, 'Brookton', Banbury and Hemel Hempstead, sex, age and occupation at Scunthorpe and Rawmarsh, sex, age, marital status, earnings and education at Redfield, sex, age, marital status, occupation and length of residence at Falkirk, Newtown and Machynlleth.

7.1.4 *Denominational censuses*
7.1.4.1 Although the Church of England did not begin to collect attendance figures on a national basis until 1968, returns of average congregations were being made during the course of episcopal visitations from as early as the 1820s in dioceses such as Chester, Llandaff, Oxford and Winchester. Actual censuses have been conducted in the see of Liverpool by Abraham Hume [B.198] on 4 June 1882, and, more recently, at Rotherham, with disaggregations by sex, age, marital status, occupation and residence, by the Sheffield Industrial Mission in March 1963 [QRL.73], 29 April 1965; [B.100] and at Preston in April-June 1968 (3.1.1.3).

7.1.4.2 The most important general Nonconformist enumeration was carried out at Liverpool on 14 June 1908 [B.335]. For the Methodists, besides materials already noted in Section 3.2.4 above, we may mention connexional investigations by the Primitives on 7 April 1861 [B.479] and by the Free Methodists on 10 April 1881

[B.26] and 24 March 1901 [B.83] as well as local ones by the Wesleyans in Melton Mowbray and vicinity on 6 October 1907 [B.132] and the Windsor and Maidenhead circuit on 26 March and 2 April 1911 [B.161]. Quaker worshippers were counted throughout Britain on 9, 16, 23, 30 October 1904 [B.575], Congregationalist ones in Greater Manchester on five separate Sundays in 1966 and 1967 [B.353].

7.1.4.3 For the Roman Catholics of England and Wales, *ad hoc* censuses of mass attendance, such as those which were undertaken in the dioceses of Salford in 1875 and Liverpool in 1881 and 1891, have long since been superseded by centrally gathered serial data. The Scottish Church has been far less fortunate in this respect, and returns secured by the Pastoral Research Centre in 1967 (3.3.2.2) remain a principal source of national statistics in this field.

7.2 Opinion Polls

7.2.1 *Basic attendance*
7.2.1.1 Subjective data, relating to claimed rather than observed attendance at church, are available from opinion polls conducted amongst the general adult public. Nationally, over one hundred relevant surveys are known to have been undertaken since November 1937, full details of which may be found in the QRL; particular attention is drawn to the Gallup *Religion Study* [QRL.96] of February-April 1978 in which 11,061 people were interviewed. Locally, major enquiries, those deriving from samples in excess of five hundred persons, have been carried out on twenty-five occasions during the period 1944-81 as recorded in Appendix 3.

7.2.1.2 At the risk of some slight over-simplification, we may identify four principal types of question, none of them entirely free from methodological difficulties, which have been used in these polls over the years. First, and least satisfactorily, there is the vague 'Do you ever go to a place of worship?' form of enquiry which facilitates and encourages quite misleading claims of religious activity; in MO's survey of Hammersmith in 1944-45, for example, it was discovered that one avowed 'church-goer' had not actually been since parade services during the 1914-18 war [B.518]. Secondly, and most commonly, respondents have been asked to define the regularity of their attendance in terms of a time scale extending from once or twice a week at one end to never at the other; this procedure too results in some exaggeration, especially, as Graham Day and Martin Fitton have shown at Machynlleth [B.97], amongst the allegedly once a month or more category. Thirdly, informants have been required to state when they last went to church, an approach whose outcome is dependent upon both the accuracy of recall and, because of seasonal fluctuations in participation levels (7.1.2.4), the date at which the investigation was made. Fourthly, contacts have been invited to record, generally with only a minimal degree of prompting and without any specific mention of the church or chapel option, their activities on the Sunday immediately prior to their interview; this device, whilst it has the undoubted merit of neutralising the 'prestige' factor (2.1.4.6), has sometimes been found, for instance in the 'Youth and Religion' study of January-February 1957 (4.2.1.3), to lead to a marked underregistration of committed worshippers.

7.2.2 *Other matters*

7.2.2.1 Contrasts between respondents' past and present church-going habits were attempted in surveys undertaken throughout Great Britain in January 1941 [QRL.9] [QRL.12], mid-1947 [QRL.75], 30 October 1947, December 1954 [QRL.97] and February 1957 [QRL.12]; [QRL.74], 16-17 April 1957, England in December 1963-January 1964 [QRL.120] [QRL.121], and at Machynlleth and Newtown, Montgomeryshire in September 1974 (2.3.2.4). Comparisons with the religious behaviour of other members of the informant's family were made across Britain in mid-1947 [QRL.75], 30 October 1947, England in December 1963-January 1964 [QRL.120] [QRL.121], and at Machynlleth and Newtown in September 1974 (2.3.2.4).

7.2.2.2 The reasons for non-attendance at worship were explored throughout Britain in mid-1947 [QRL.75], 30 October 1947, December 1954 [QRL.97], February 1957 (by Gallup, JN CS.1717) and August 1974 [QRL.108] [QRL.123], 14 October 1974, England in December 1963-January 1964 [QRL.120] [QRL.121], and at Dawley during the summer of 1969 (2.2.2.14). Factors considered likely to improve participation in the future were discussed in national polls of mid-1947 [QRL.75], 30 October 1947 and April 1970 [QRL.100].

7.2.2.3 Belief in the possibility of being a Christian or leading a useful life without going to church was measured in Great Britain in February 1957 [QRL.12] [QRL.74], 15 April 1957, England in December 1963-January 1964 [QRL.120] [QRL.121], and at Machynlleth and Newtown in September 1974 (2.3.2.4).

CHAPTER 8

PERSONAL RELIGION: ATTITUDES

8.1 Religious Attitudes

8.1.1 *Religious influences on national life*
8.1.1.1 As can be seen from the QRL, attempts to measure the extent and nature of the impact of religion in general on society have been made in twenty-five separate investigations extending from February 1947 to November 1982. Eighteen different types of question have been used over the years, one of them ('At the present time, do you think religion as a whole is increasing its influence on British life or losing its influence?') by Gallup on no fewer than eight occasions in February 1957 [QRL.12], December 1963-January 1964 [QRL.120] [QRL.121], May 1965 [QRL.23], May 1967 [QRL.12] [QRL.23] [QRL.64], May 1967, April-May 1973 [QRL.12] [QRL.64], May 1973; [QRL.112], 13 May 1973, May-June 1975 [QRL.12] [QRL.64], June 1975, March 1982 [QRL.42] [QRL.64], April 1982, and November 1982 (JN CQ.845).

8.1.1.2 The role played by the institutional Church in the nation's affairs has formed the subject of twenty polls conducted amongst the adult population of constituent parts of the United Kingdom between June 1942 and April 1983; as the QRL indicates, thirteen distinct approaches have been adopted of which the commonest, employed by Gallup in January 1963 [QRL.12] [QRL.64] January 1963, June 1968 [QRL.12] [QRL.64], June 1968, December 1968 [QRL.12] [QRL.64], January 1969, June 1969 [QRL.12] [QRL.64], October 1969, February 1973 [QRL.12] [QRL.64] February 1973, January 1976 [QRL.64], February 1976 and November 1982 [QRL.64], December 1982, examined the relative contribution of the Churches and of eleven other major groups or organisations to the country's future. More elitist viewpoints were registered in a postal study of 2,548 persons listed in *Who's Who* which was undertaken by RSL on behalf of *The Times* in June-July 1971 [QRL.123], 1 October 1971.

8.1.2 *Ecumenism*
8.1.2.1 Attitudes of the public towards inter-Church relationships have been canvassed in eighteen surveys carried out over the period February 1938-June 1982, sixteen of them in Great Britain and two in Northern Ireland; these enquiries have included a total of thirty-two questions, many with similar or identical wordings, of which nine have dealt with Anglican-Nonconformist reunion, nine with Protestant-Catholic unity, and fourteen with wider ecumenical matters. The usefulness of all the data is limited by the high proportion of respondents, often in

the region of a quarter to a third, falling into the 'don't know' or 'don't mind' categories. Full methodological and bibliographical details are provided in the QRL.

8.1.2.2 Studies of more religiously committed samples are only available from the beginning of the 1960s. Amongst general investigations may be mentioned those by Nicholas Kokosalakis [B.235] of 148 adults drawn from five places of worship in the socially mixed inner residential district of Liverpool in 1965-67, by Martin Reardon of *Christian Unity in Sheffield* (2.2.2.13), by Kenneth Sansbury, Robert Latham and Pauline Webb [B.344] of the denominational and geographical distribution of participants in the 'People Next Door Programme' which flourished across the British Isles during 1967, and by R.M.C. Jeffery of *Areas of ecumenical Experiment* [B.214] as they existed in 1968. Within Anglican circles, surveys of opinions about intercommunion were completed by the *Church of England Newspaper* [QRL.50], 8-15 December 1961 amongst 4,244 or 40.9% of incumbents in the Provinces of Canterbury and York towards the close of 1961 and by a Commission of the Scottish Episcopal Church amongst 243 or 87.1% of the ministers and 1,689 local office-bearers of that body in 1969 [B.490] [B.558], whilst Alan Bryman, Robin Hinings and Stewart Ranson [B.49] [B.50] have examined the views on ecumenical co-operation and organic union expressed by 213 of 257 clergymen and 228 of 310 lay representatives to deanery synods approached in the Diocese of Birmingham during the early 1970s. The ill-fated Anglican-Methodist Conversations of 1956-72 gave rise to two major pieces of research, one by David Clark [B.76] into the social background and ideas about worship, ministry, polity, unity and moral issues of members of Anglican Church Councils (n = 248) and Methodist Leaders' Meetings (n = 244) in Rugby, Trowbridge, Ellesmere Port and Bromley during the spring of 1962 and the summer of 1964, the other by Michael Hill and Peter Wakeford [B.178] into the religious practices and convictions of 328 Methodists from the congregations at Byfleet, Crawley, Forest Hill and Upper Norwood in September 1967 whose pivotal feature was an AID (Algorithm for Interaction Detection) presentation of factors affecting attitudes towards the Established Church. Finally, Roman Catholic perspectives on ecumenism have been documented in various readership profiles (3.3.3) and Gallup Polls (3.3.4) as well as by David Hay [B.168] amongst 638 mass-goers at Nottingham Cathedral one Sunday in July 1978.

8.1.3 *Religious prejudices*

8.1.3.1 Evidence relating to the incidence and nature of religious bigotry may be derived from the thirty-four national surveys, the earliest conducted in August 1939 and the latest in November 1982, which are described in the QRL; twenty-nine of these were carried out in mainland Britain, two in Scotland, one in the United Kingdom, one in England, and, reflecting the fact that polls illustrative of the troubles in Ulster have been excluded from the review's terms of reference (1.1.1.6), just one in Northern Ireland. Several of the questions posed are so vague as to be of little real value, but the majority have been directed towards the measurement of overt or latent bias against specific target groups and thus command serious attention; most commonly studied victims of prejudice have been Roman Catholics (examined on twenty-two occasions), Jews (on thirteen), Protestants (on five), church-goers, adherents of fringe sects, and atheists (three each).

8.1.3.2 Of the twenty-two investigations covering attitudes towards the Church of Rome, half have been of a miscellaneous character in which respondents have been asked, for example, whether they were prepared to vote for a Catholic as a parliamentary candidate or to have one as a neighbour. The other eleven, all undertaken by Gallup between March and November 1982 [QRL.35] [QRL.36] [QRL.38] [QRL.39] [QRL.40] [QRL.42] [QRL.43] [QRL.64], April, June 1982; [QRL.112], 16 May 1982; [QRL.125], 26 March, 23 April, 7-14 May, 30 July 1982, monitored the adult population's interest in, approval of, and, in most instances, anticipated or actual attendance at events connected with Pope John Paul II's historic pastoral visit to Great Britain which took place from 28 May to 2 June in that year. Interpretation of the resulting data, which were disaggregated by denominational affiliation and frequency of worship as well as by standard demographic variables, is rendered difficult by the operation of the so-called 'Falklands factor', the devastating three month armed conflict in the South Atlantic for the repossession of the Falkland Islands, seized by Argentinian troops on 2 April, which quite dominated the public mood throughout this period and at one stage, because of the Holy See's desire to denounce the use of force on both sides and to remain diplomatically and ecclesiastically neutral in the affair, even threatened to lead to the complete cancellation of the visit.

8.1.3.3 The prevalence of anti-semitism in society as a whole was assessed in five Gallup surveys extending from August 1939 to January 1960 [QRL.9] [QRL.12], the question being 'Among the people you know, is anti-Jewish feeling increasing, decreasing or about the same?'. An impression of interviewees' own prejudices in this area was gathered in eight further country-wide polls commencing in November 1958 and terminating in June 1970 as well as in two localised pieces of research conducted by MO in July-August 1946 (n = 180) and April 1951 (n = 200) which are documented in File Report 2411 at the Tom Harrisson MO Archive, University of Sussex.

8.2 Moral Attitudes

8.2.1 *General surveys*
8.2.1.1 The overall interdependence of faith and ethics has been investigated in twelve national and two community-based studies undertaken between 1944 and 1981. Four main approaches have been adopted. First, respondents have been asked to estimate the value of religion in providing a set of standards to support the moral fabric of society; this line of enquiry has been pursued across Britain in February 1968 [QRL.94], June 1970 [QRL.101], January 1973 (by ORC, JN 7/1337) and July 1979 [QRL.93], Northern Ireland in December 1968- January 1969 [QRL.94], and Greater London in February-March 1978 (2.2.2.16). Secondly, informants have been invited to suggest reasons, including spiritual ones, why they should be honest, truthful and kind; this question was posed throughout Britain in December 1954 [QRL.97] and February 1957 [QRL.12], and in England in December 1963-January

1964 [QRL.120] [QRL.121]. Thirdly, views concerning the Ten Commandments have been canvassed at Hammersmith in 1944-45 (2.2.2.3), in Great Britain in June 1970 [QRL.101], and across the whole of the United Kingdom in March 1981 [QRL.31], 1981; [QRL.70], 1982-83. Fourthly, readers of *New Society* [QRL.73] 9-23 May 1963, 30 November, 7 December 1972 have been called upon to assess the vitality of 'traditional Christian morality' and its relevance to the country's past and future greatness both in March 1963 (n = 7,344) and October 1972 (n = 2,859).

8.2.1.2 Although space does not permit a comprehensive listing of polls of the adult population in which attitudes to a general range of moral issues have been broken down according to religious characteristics, reference should certainly be made to two important recent examples of the genre which have been carried out in Britain by MORI (JN 5285) on behalf of *The Sunday Times* in January 1980 and in the United Kingdom by Gallup (JN S.2131) at the request of the EVSSG in March 1981. Amongst similarly wide-ranging surveys conducted with samples of committed Christians may be mentioned those by Cyril Rodd of 473 church members at Hall Green, Birmingham in 1966 (2.2.2.12), by Kevin Mayhew [QRL.47], 19 January 1968 of over 1,350 teenage readers of the *Catholic Herald* towards the close of 1967, by Christopher Murray [B.280] of 1,284 Catholic adolescents with a modal age of fourteen years during the mid-1970s, by Roy Wallis and Richard Bland [B.400] of 1,106 participants at a rally held by the Nationwide Festival of Light in Trafalgar Square on 25 September 1976 (ESRC DA, SN 957), of one thousand three hundred young people attending ninety different places of worship in five parts of Lancashire in November 1979-April 1980 (4.2.1.18), and of 483 evangelicals of whom 35% had been present at the Keswick Convention in July 1981, 37% had frequented the Greenbelt Arts Festival in August 1981, and 28% were distribution agents for *Crusade* (since renamed *Today*) magazine [B.455].

8.2.2 Sexual questions

8.2.2.1 Various attempts have been made since the Second World War to determine the extent to which denominational affiliation and/or church attendance condition the public's thinking and behaviour with regard to a broad spectrum of sexual matters. One of the earliest surveys, modelled on Kinsey's American work, was undertaken by MO amongst a cross-section of 2,051 British adults in 1949 (Tom Harrisson MO Archive, University of Sussex, File Report 3110). Subsequent investigations have included those by Eustace Chesser of some two thousand English women in 1954 (4.3.1.2), by Michael Schofield [B.345] of 1,873 teenagers resident in seven areas in 1962-63, by ORC of 1,987 sixteen to forty-five year olds throughout England in April-May 1969 as described in a series of articles [QRL.113], 15-29 March 1970 and a book [B.141] by Geoffrey Gorer, by the Institute for Social Studies in Medical Care [B.108] of 1,556 youngsters aged sixteen to nineteen living in twelve English and Welsh districts in 1974-75 (ESRC DA, SN 1317), by the Schlackman Organisation of 290 single girls in the eighteen to twenty-six year band in December 1976 (4.3.1.6), by Glenn Wilson [B.419] of 4,767 individuals (1,862 men and 2,905 women with mean ages of 30.84 and 27.72 respectively) who replied to a questionnaire appearing in the *Sun* newspaper during 1980, and by *19* magazine amongst more than six thousand of its female readers in October 1981 (4.3.1.8).

8.2.2.2 Of particular sex-related issues, contraception, abortion, and homosexuality have attracted most attention in recent decades. The connection between religious allegiance on the one hand and attitudes to and the practice of birth control on the other has been explored by MO [B.447] amongst 787 married women aged twenty to forty-five from London and Gloucester during the early 1940s, by the Royal College of Obstetricians and Gynaecologists [B.107] with 3,281 married female patients drawn from non-maternity wards of hospitals in ten regions of Britain in August 1946-June 1947, by the Population Investigation Committee on the basis of national samples of three thousand adults from sixteen to fifty-nine years in December 1959-March 1960 [B.339] and of 2,262 married women below the age of sixty in June 1967-March 1968 [B.134] [B.237] [B.238], by Ann Cartwright [B.68] [B.67] amongst two distinct groups of 1,495 and 1,473 newly delivered mothers across England and Wales in October 1967-May 1968 (ESRC DA, SN 400) and March-August 1973 (ESRC DA, SN 396), and by Gallup [QRL.89] in a poll of one thousand Britons carried out for the Family Planning Association in October 1968. Public reactions to the Church of Rome's teaching on birth control were examined in February-March 1965 [QRL.12] [QRL.57], 11 March 1965, [QRL.64], March 1965 and, in the aftermath of the papal encyclical *Humanae Vitae*, on 1-4 August 1968 [QRL.12] [QRL.64] August 1968; [QRL.112], 11 August 1968 and 14-19 August 1968 [QRL.77] August 1968, whilst the views of rank and file Catholics themselves have been canvassed throughout Great Britain in March 1967 (3.3.4.1), July-August 1968 [QRL.113], 4 August 1968, June 1970 [QRL.101] and February 1977 (3.3.4.2), England and Wales in February-March 1978 (3.3.4.4), and Scotland in December 1977-February 1978 (3.3.4.3); those of the Catholic intelligentsia may be gauged from surveys of the memberships of the Guild of St.Luke, St. Cosmas and St Damian (a doctors' body) and of the Newman Association (an organisation for graduates and professional people) which were undertaken during 1965 [QRL.67], 10 September, 6 October 1965.

8.2.2.3 There have been so many investigations of attitudes to abortion in which the results are broken down by religious denomination that it is only possible to include a small selection here. Omnibus polls amongst the adult population of Britain have been conducted in March 1965 [QRL.29] [QRL.32] [QRL.77] May 1965, February 1966 [QRL.23], January 1967 [QRL.23], February 1967 [QRL.117], September 1967 (ESRC DA, SN 67027), October-November 1969 [QRL.57], 18 November 1969; [QRL.65] [QRL.123], 18 November 1969, January 1970 [QRL.118], July 1971 (by Louis Harris Research - LHR, JN 119), March 1972 [QRL.58] [QRL.76] [QRL.77] May 1972, November 1973 [QRL.34], November 1979 [QRL.33] [QRL.127], 9 February 1980, January 1980 [QRL.86] [QRL.113], 3 February 1980, and February-March 1982 [QRL.73], 10 June 1982. Medical comment has been obtained from national samples of general practitioners in January-February 1970 (n = 1,248) [B.557], November 1970-March 1971 (n = 601, ESRC DA, SN 402) [B.69], March 1972 (n = 1,448) [QRL.77], June 1972; [B.436] [B.480] and September 1973 (n = 1,221) [B.484], of consultant or senior registrar obstetricians and gynaecologists in 1970 (n = 402, ESRC DA, SN 912) [B.397] and early 1977 (n = 602) [B.506], of 374 consultant psychiatrists in 1970 (ESRC DA, SN 911), and of 682 nurses working in non-specialist hospitals in April-June 1972 [B.498].

8.2.2.4 The people's desire for the continuance of homosexuality as a criminal offence was monitored throughout England in December 1963-January 1964 [QRL.120] [QRL.121] and Great Britain in October 1965 [QRL.77], November 1965; findings on each occasion were disaggregated by confessional allegiance. Confidence in the ability of homosexuals to be good members of the Christian, Jewish or other faiths and approval of their recruitment as ministers of religion have been tested by Gallup in August 1977 [QRL.64], August 1977, July 1979 [QRL.64], July 1979, and October-November 1981 [QRL.64], November 1981.

8.2.3 *Marriage and divorce*
8.2.3.1 The prevalence of denominational intermarriage within the population has been documented locally at, amongst other places, Swansea (n = 1,962) in May-June 1960 (2.3.2.2), Bishop's Stortford (n = 1,892) in the autumn of 1966 [B.367], Banbury (n = 1,449) in April-May 1967 [B.372], Machynlleth and Newtown (n = 535) in September 1974 (2.3.2.4), whilst public commendation of such unions has been measured across Britain in May 1968 [QRL.12] [QRL.28] [QRL.62] [QRL.64], August 1968, January-March 1969 [QRL.115], June 1970 [QRL.101], April 1971 (ESRC DA, SN 71001), August 1973 [QRL.12] [QRL.64], September 1973 and November 1977 [QRL.13], 1978; [QRL.64], January 1978 as well as in Northern Ireland in June-November 1978 [QRL.24]. The importance attached to shared religious beliefs in making for a happy and successful conjugal relationship has been surveyed nationally by Gallup in January 1950 [QRL.74], 7 February 1950, April 1952 (JN S.302A), March 1981 [QRL.70], 1982-83, and April 1982 [QRL.64], May 1982. Finally, the five hundred replies received to a questionnaire appearing in the October 1980 issue of *Family*, a monthly magazine with a readership largely composed of evangelical Anglicans, offer a revealing picture of the practical outworking of Christian marriage with special reference to sources of stress, prayer life and Church commitments [B.390] [B.474].

8.2.3.2 Reviews of people's attitudes towards divorce which include a breakdown of the results by sectarian affiliation and/or frequency of attendance at worship have been regularly conducted throughout Great Britain between March 1948 [QRL.74] 15 April 1948 and May 1981 (ESRC DA, SN 1617). Opinions of the Church's rules on the remarriage of divorcees have been gathered from samples of the general population in May 1947 [QRL.12], November 1955 [QRL.12], February 1957 [QRL.12] [QRL.74] 16 April 1957 and July 1978 [QRL.53] 20 July 1978, from Anglican clergymen in the Diocese of Southwark (n = 200) in 1976 [QRL.46], 29 October 1976 and across England (n = 405) in 1977 [QRL.50], 15 July 1977; [QRL.51] 15 July 1977, from several thousand members of parochial councils in the Bishopric of Chester in 1979 [QRL.51], 13 July 1979, and from Roman Catholics in Scotland in December 1977-February 1978 (3.3.4.3) and England and Wales in February-March 1978 (3.3.4.4). The religious differences between two separate groups of divorcees (n = 184 men and 336 women) and continuing married persons (n = 199 and 371) drawn at random from an area of the West Midlands were investigated by Barbara Thornes and Jean Collard [B.387] in September 1972-January 1973.

8.3 Political Attitudes

8.3.1 *General surveys*

8.3.1.1 The interaction of religion and politics at the institutional level has been examined in twenty-one national or local surveys carried out during the last forty years. Four main lines of enquiry have been pursued. First, respondents have been asked to identify the extent to which the Church should become involved in public life and/or the issues on which it ought to speak out; this approach was adopted throughout Great Britain in June 1942 [QRL.9] [QRL.74] 4 July 1942, May 1956 [QRL.12], February 1957 [QRL.12] [QRL.74], 16 April 1957, August 1968 [QRL.12] [QRL.64], August 1968, June 1969 [QRL.12] [QRL.64] October 1969 and July 1979 [QRL.79], 21 December 1979 [QRL.93], England in December 1963-January 1964 [QRL.120] [QRL.121], Hodge Hill and Balsall Heath, Birmingham during the summer and autumn of 1965 (2.2.2.11), the Clun Valley of Shropshire around Eastertide 1968 (2.2.2.11), Machynlleth and Newtown, Montgomeryshire in September 1974 (2.3.2.4). Secondly, views concerning the preservation of the official link between Anglicanism and the state have been sought in February 1957 [QRL.12], April 1970 [QRL.53], 13 May 1970 [QRL.100], and June 1970 [QRL.101]. Thirdly, comments on the relations between the Vatican and the Kremlin and their effect upon the international situation were gathered in October 1961 [QRL.12] [QRL.47], 12 January 1962; [QRL.64], November 1961, April 1963 [QRL.12] [QRL.64], July 1963, and June-July 1963 [QRL.12] [QRL.64], July 1963; [QRL.112], 14 July 1963. Fourthly, the importance attached to religious liberty relative to the other major freedoms was measured in September 1963 [QRL.12] [QRL.81], Spring 1965, June 1969 [QRL.12] [QRL.64] October 1969, and, on behalf of the United States Information Communication Agency, in 1977 [QRL.70], 1978-79.

8.3.1.2 The association between denominational allegiance, church attendance or self-assessed religiosity on the one hand and personal voting behaviour or political attitudes on the other is best illuminated through secondary analysis of key national data sets held at the ESRC DA, University of Essex; especially useful in this regard are nine academic psephological surveys undertaken in May-August 1963 (SN 1090), October-December 1964 (SN 1091), April-June 1966 (SN 1092), June-July 1969 (SN 1093), October 1974 - January 1975 (SN 666 for Britain, SN 681 for Scotland) and May-October 1979 (SN 1533 for Britain, SN 1591 for Wales, SN 1604 for Scotland), eighteen pre-election polls commissioned by the *Daily Telegraph* and *Sunday Telegraph* in May-June 1970 (SN 1353), February 1974 (SN 658), September-October 1974 (SN 659) and April-May 1979 (SN 1352), and thirteen enquiries funded by the European Economic Community in September-October 1973 (SN 864), October 1975 (SN 789), May-June 1976 (SN 933), November 1976 (SN 934), April-May 1977 (SN 936), October-November 1977 (SN 1029), May 1978 (SN 1224), October-November

1978 (SN 1284), April 1979 (SN 1396), October 1979 (SN 1397), April 1980 (SN 1615), October 1981 (SN 1759) and March-April 1982 (SN 1792). Amongst comparable local investigations may be mentioned those at Greenwich (n=914) in December 1949- February 1950 [B.16], Droylsden (n=545) in October 1951 [B.61], Glossop (n=657) in 1953-54 [B.20], Bristol North-East (n=528) in May 1955 [B.273], Acton, Blackley, Coventry South, Halifax, Ilford South and Paddington (n=604 working class adults) in June-July 1958 [B.246], Newcastle-under-Lyme (n=1,516) in November 1959-March 1960 [B.10], Brentford and Chiswick (n=147) in February- July 1962 (ESRC DA, SN 62001), Cathcart (n=191) in May 1964 (ESRC DA, SN 64001) [B.52], Craigton (n=186) in March-April 1965 (ESRC DA, SN 65004) [B.52], Sheffield (n=584) in November 1967 [B.160], Dundee (n=584) in May 1968 [B.27], Peterhead (n=194) in the autumn of 1969 [B.9], Salford (n=604) in March-April 1970 (ESRC DA, SN 70003), Cardiganshire (n=713) in May-June 1971 (ESRC DA, SN 71006) [B.251], Crosby (n=739, n=937, n=1,006) in November 1981 by NOP [QRL.80] December 1981 and MORI (JN 7524, JN 7525), and Glasgow, Hillhead (n=994, n= 978) in March 1982 (by MORI, JN 7806, JN 7924). An interesting feature of the Salford and the first of the three Crosby studies was that respondents were asked outright whether religion had any influence on their political views.

8.3.2 Sunday observance

8.3.2.1 Nowhere is the continuing political impact of the Christian Church in this country more keenly felt than in the laws governing the observance of Sunday and the provision of religious education and worship in state schools. Sabbatarianism in particular has an exceedingly long legislative history (even the statutes in force date back to 1780) which has been only slowly dismantled during recent decades. Inevitably, the advocates of reform, both inside Parliament and without, have sought to mobilise public opinion on their side, and no fewer than twenty-nine relevant national attitude surveys have been carried out since the eve of the Second World War; five of these, conducted throughout Great Britain in May 1958 [QRL.12] [QRL.98] [QRL.104] 15 May 1958, February 1965 [QRL.12] [QRL.57], 22 February 1965; [QRL.64], February 1965, October 1971 (by LHR, JN 140) and January 1973 [QRL.12] [QRL.64], February 1973 and in Scotland in September-October 1980 [QRL.66] 27 October 1980; [QRL.102], have included questions of a general and miscellaneous nature, but the majority have been designed to elicit judgements on more specific aspects of the topic.

8.3.2.2 Liberalisation of the regulations covering the Sunday opening of cinemas and theatres, effected by the acts 1972 c.19 and c.26, was preceded by a series of polls undertaken across Britain in April 1941 [QRL.12] [QRL.74], 15 May 1941, January 1943 [QRL.12] [QRL.74], 20 March 1943, January 1944 [QRL.9] [QRL.12] [QRL.74], 7 February 1944, January 1953 [QRL.12] [QRL.74], 31 January 1953, February 1957 [QRL.12] [QRL.74], 16 April 1957, May 1958 [QRL.12] [QRL.98] [QRL.104], 15 May 1958, February 1965 [QRL.12] [QRL.57], 22 February 1965; [QRL.64], February 1965, March 1966 [QRL.57], 29 April 1966 [QRL.122], January 1968 [QRL.12] [QRL.57], 31 January 1968; [QRL.64], January 1968, and March 1969

[QRL.12] [QRL.64], March 1969. Cinema hours were also the subject of numerous local plebiscites held in the towns of South Wales during the early 1950s, the most important being at Swansea in 1950 [B.552] and Cardiff in 1952 [QRL.126], 27 September 1952, whilst 1,244 members of Equity, the actors' trade union, were successfully balloted about Sunday theatrical performances in February 1963 [QRL.98].

8.3.2.3 Views concerning the staging of professional sport as a whole and of football, cricket, and horse racing in particular on the Lord's Day have been obtained from random or quota samples of the adult population of Great Britain in January 1953 [QRL.12] [QRL.74],31 January 1953, February 1957 [QRL.12]; [QRL.74], 16 April 1957, May 1958 [QRL.12] [QRL.98] [QRL.104], 15 May 1958, February 1965 [QRL.12] [QRL.57], 22 February 1965; [QRL.64], February 1965, March 1966 [QRL.57], 29 April 1966; [QRL.122], January 1968 [QRL.12]; [QRL.57], 31 January 1968; [QRL.64], January 1968, late 1968 [QRL.55], 28 February 1969, March 1969 [QRL.12] [QRL.64], March 1969, October 1971 (by LHR, JN 140), January 1974 [QRL.77], January 1974, January-February 1977 [QRL.55], 18 February 1977; [QRL.109] and November 1980 [QRL.55], 19 December 1980; [QRL.80] February 1981, [QRL.110], England in December 1966 [QRL.55], 10 February 1967, and Scotland in September-October 1980 [QRL.66], 27 October 1980; [QRL.102]. Additional, though less reliable, statistics derive from a self-selection of one thousand one hundred *Daily Mail* readers at the beginning of 1977 [QRL.55], 12 January 1977.

8.3.2.4 Attitudes towards the revision of Sunday licensing laws have been expressed by representative groups of Britons in May 1958 [QRL.12] [QRL.104], 15 May 1958, July 1959 [QRL.12], February 1965 [QRL.12] [QRL.57], 22 February 1965; [QRL.64], February 1965, March 1969 [QRL.12] [QRL.64], March 1969, October-November 1970 [QRL.5], and October 1971 (fieldwork by LHR, JN 140) as well as by 3,992 persons, 243 of them publicans, who responded to an advertisement placed by Whitbread & Co. Ltd. in a variety of leading newspapers in the autumn of 1976 [B.492]. In Wales, a blanket closure of licensed premises on the Sabbath was enforced from 1881 until the first local option referendum in November 1961 [QRL.123], 10 November 1961 which split the principality into 'wet' and 'dry' areas; further plebiscites have been taken, wherever requested by a quorum of electors, on 6 November 1968 [QRL.123], 8 November 1968; [B.66], 5 November 1975 [QRL.123], 7 November 1975; [B.65] and 3 November 1982 [QRL.57], 5 November 1982, whilst sample polls have also been conducted nationally in the autumn of 1968 [QRL.126], 24 October 1968 and May-September 1979 (ESRC DA, SN 1591), in Swansea (n = 1,962) in May-June 1960 (2.3.2.2), Cardiganshire (n = 713) in May-June 1971 (ESRC DA, SN 71006) [B.251], and Machynlleth and Newtown, Montgomeryshire (n = 535) in September 1974 (2.3.2.4). The regular Sunday opening of public houses in Scotland was not legally permitted until October 1977, and Scottish reactions to this change were monitored in the third phase of a panel study (n = 1,143) carried out by the OPCS Social Survey Division in the four major cities and central belt of the country in October-November 1978 [B.234]. The situation in the Channel Islands is complicated by the requirements of the tourist industry as was demonstrated in a recent canvass of Guernsey residents [QRL.123], 13 November 1982.

8.3.2.5 Opinions about Sunday shopping restrictions have been gathered in enquiries undertaken amongst adults across Great Britain in April 1962 [QRL.64] February 1965, February 1965 [QRL.12] [QRL.57], 22 February 1965; [QRL.64], February 1965, October-November 1970 [QRL.6], October 1971 (by LHR, JN 140), September 1978 [QRL.106] [QRL.114], November-December 1981 [QRL.70], 1981-82; [QRL.88], January 1982, September 1982 [QRL.70], 1982-83; [QRL.88], October 1982; [QRL.105], and March 1983 [QRL.80], April 1983. Supplementary data derive from surveys of 1,338 members of the Federation of Consumer Groups in 1963 [QRL.98], of three thousand readers of *Woman* magazine, younger, better-off and more likely to live in the South-East of England than average, in September 1978 [B.570], of over forty thousand correspondents and customers of Dickie Dirts, the London retail chain specialising in jeans and casual clothing which habitually traded from 9 a.m. until 11 p.m. seven days a week in open defiance of the law,in 1980-81 [QRL.123], 27 November 1980, 22 January, 19 February, 4 June, 15 September 1981, and of approximately two hundred readers of *Living*, a monthly publication sold in supermarkets, in July 1982 [B.563].

8.3.2.6 Attitudes towards Sunday observance may be usefully contrasted with evidence about the ways in which people actually spend the Sabbath. National figures are available from interviews carried out by Gallup in September-October 1948 [QRL.12] [QRL.74], 1 November 1948, May 1952 [QRL.116], February 1957 [QRL.12], May 1958 [QRL.12] [QRL.74], 22 May 1958; [QRL.98], December 1963-January 1964 [QRL.120] [QRL.121], March 1966 [QRL.122] and April 1968 [QRL.112], 14 April 1968, by IPC Surveys Division in January and August 1968 [QRL.68], by LHR (JN 140) in October 1971, and from one week time budget diaries kept, at the request of the British Broadcasting Corporation [B.514], by 3,545 persons aged five and upwards from 1,383 households in August-September 1974 and February-March 1975 (ESRC DA, SN 1425). Amongst more localised studies may be mentioned those of 328 church-goers at Horwich, Oldham and Witham in April-May 1955 [B.184] and of children from Priestlands Comprehensive School, Lymington in 1980 [QRL.67], 8 July 1980.

8.3.3 *Religious education*
8.3.3.1 Christian influence over the country's educational system is perpetuated not only by the existence of separate Church schools but also by the requirements of United Kingdom law (dating from 1944 in England and Wales, 1945 in Scotland, and 1947 in Northern Ireland) that, unless exempted by parental request, all pupils in the maintained sector should receive religious instruction according to an agreed, undenominational syllabus and participate in a daily, unsectarian, collective act of worship. Succeeding paragraphs will consider research into the implicit or explicit views of children, adults/parents, and teachers on the desirability of these arrangements and into the institutional resources for, and extent of, their actual implementation.

8.3.3.2 General investigations of pupils' opinions on the topic have been completed by L.D.Rixon [B.329] in 1959 (n = 555), J.A. Jones [B.220] in 1962 (n = 280), H.

Marchant [B.253] in 1970 (n = 265), Charles Povall [B.312] in 1971 (n = 800), and Anthony Russell [B.340] in 1978 (n = 266] as well as by several other authors whose works have already been discussed in Sections 4.1.1, 4.1.2 and 4.2.2 above. The popularity of religious education relative to fourteen or more other subjects has been tested by E.O. Lewis [B.240] in London and South Wales on the eve of the First World War (n = 8,000), J.J. Shakespeare [B.347] in Worcestershire during the 1930s (n = 9,127), N.L. Houslop and E.J.Weeks [B.194] amongst the evacuated boys of Battersea Grammar in 1942 (n = 215), 1943 (n = 222) and 1944 (n = 204), the GSS [B.416] with a national sample of thirteen to sixteen year olds in 1966 (n = 4,618), and by M.B. Ormerod [B.288] at nineteen schools across England in the early 1970s (n = 1,204). Attitudes towards corporate worship have been studied by Edith Smith [B.359] in the 1940s (n = 1,200 eleven to fourteen year olds) and by Clifford Jones [B.219], Peter McPhail [B.250] and James Brimer [B.40] [B.41] during the late 1960s (n = 1,459 secondary children from Yorkshire, 2,207 secondary pupils from the area served by the Oxford University Institute of Education, and 293 fourth form juniors from Birmingham respectively).

8.3.3.3 The views of samples of the entire adult population about the importance and/or content of religious instruction in schools have been canvassed throughout Great Britain in February 1944 [QRL.9] [QRL.12], November 1951 [QRL.12], December 1954 [QRL.97], February 1957 [QRL.12], January-February 1963 [QRL.82], March 1965 [QRL.73], 27 May 1965 and March 1969 [QRL.78], England in December 1963-January 1964 [QRL.120] [QRL.121], and Hammersmith in 1944-45 (2.2.2.3). Parental opinions alone have been examined by Philip May and Raymond Johnston [B.264] [B.266] in an enquiry conducted in Northumberland and Durham in 1965 (n = 1,730, comprising 303 fathers, 394 mothers, and 1,033 married couples) whose methodology has been severely criticised by the secularist Maurice Hill [B.177], by the GSS [B.416] across England and Wales in February-May 1966 (n = 4,546, mostly females), by John Greer [B.146] [B.150] in Northern Ireland in January-February 1968 (n = 832), by *Woman's Own* magazine [QRL.127], 30 July 1977 amongst its readership in 1977 (n = 3,000), and by NOP [QRL.80], February 1980 in January 1980 (n = 400).

8.3.3.4 Denominationally segregated schooling is a fairly uncontroversial issue throughout most of Great Britain, and adults' attitudes towards it have only been investigated nationally in January and December 1943 (by Gallup, JN S.95 and S.104), November 1951 [QRL.12] and May 1959 [QRL.12] [QRL.74], 12 June 1959, and in the Anglican Diocese of Hereford (n = 202) in 1977-78 [B.471]. In Scotland, however, it has proved to be more contentious, and opinions have been taken from samples of the whole population in October 1974-January 1975 [QRL.104], 15 October 1975, August 1976 [QRL.66], 12 October 1976; [QRL.103] and May-October 1979 (ESRC DA, SN 1604), fifteen/sixteen to twenty year olds in April 1976 (4.2.1.9) and September 1979 (4.2.1.14), and Roman Catholics in December 1977-February 1978 (3.3.4.3). Interesting data about the educational and occupational effects of the sectarian system are also available from the Scottish Mobility Study of May 1974 -September 1975 (ESRC DA, SN 981) which involved interviews with 4,887 men aged twenty to sixty-four [B.295].

8.3.3.5 The attitudes of fully qualified teachers towards the principle and practice of religious instruction and worship in schools have been surveyed nationally by MO (Tom Harrisson MO Archive, University of Sussex, File Reports 2014, 2016, 2017) [QRL.124], 11 March 1944 in January 1944 (n = 312 elementary and secondary), R.B. Dierenfield [B.98] in the mid-1960s (n = 216 secondary), Philip May [B.260] [B.263] [B.265] in 1967 (n = 2,615 primary and secondary), the Schools Council [B.525] in 1970 (n = 538 primary), the Order of Christian Unity [B.566] in March 1973 (n = 2,302 state secondary headmasters and mistresses), and NOP in March-June 1977 [QRL.124], 2 September 1977 (n = 847 primary, secondary, and independent), January 1980 [QRL.80], February 1980 (n = 200 secondary) and May 1983 [QRL.124], 27 May 1983 (n = 559 primary and secondary); more localised enquiries have been carried out, all during the 1960s or 1970s, by Richard Acland [QRL.124], 20 October 1961 in Devon (n = 124 secondary), T.H. Marriott [B.257] (n = 99 secondary), the Belfast branch of the Christian Education Movement [B.477], S.H.Nicholls [B.286] in a northern town (n = 238 primary), Charles Povall [B.312] in the North-West (n = 188 secondary), Peter McPhail [B.250] within the catchment area of the Oxford University Institute of Education (n = 383 secondary), a Government committee [B.505] in two mixed urban-rural districts of Scotland (n = 330 primary and secondary), Peter Jarvis [B.207] [B.210] [B.211] [B.212] in Warley (n = 238 junior), J. Marvell [B.259] in a southern community (n = 102 secondary), Bernard George Burgess [B.53] [B.54] amongst primary staff in Essex (n = 259 in 1968, n = 712 in 1977) and Walsall (n = 289), and J.P. Bysh [B.59] in some Cheshire comprehensives. Studies of the opinions of trainee teachers at Colleges of Education have been produced by John Daines [B.90] in 1962 (n = 368), M.Gray [B.143] in 1963 (n = 571), E.C.Prichard [B.314] in 1965 (n = 193), Trafford Walker [B.399] in 1966 (n = 420), D.B.Evans [B.105] in 1968 (n = 250), S.H. Nicholls [B.286] in 1969 (n = 194), and Robert Crawford [B.88] in 1979 (n = 280).

8.3.3.6 Statistics relative to the extent and/or nature of the religious instruction and worship provided within the maintained sector have been gathered from schools across England with or without Wales during the early 1950s (n = 908 grammar) [B.526], the late 1950s (n = 216 grammar) [B.73], 1963 (n = 116 secondary) [B.551], 1970 (n = 213 primary) [B.525], October-November 1975 (n = over 1,100 secondary) [QRL.124] 3 June, 16 December 1977; [B.524], 1975-78 (n = 384 secondary) [B.441] and the autumn of 1977 (n = 505 secondary) [B.545], Scotland (n = 363 primary and secondary) around 1970 [B.505], five Midland counties (n = 869 primary, secondary, and all-age) in 1948-49 [B.31] [B.526], Norfolk and Norwich (n = 380) in 1949-50 [B.526], Lancashire (n = 245 secondary) in 1973 [B.15], North Yorkshire (n = 25 secondary) in 1977 [B.346], Lincolnshire (n = 71 secondary) in 1977 [B.7], Salford (n = 164 primary and secondary) during the summer of 1978 (further information available from the city's Chief Education Officer), and Hampshire (n = 227 primary and secondary) in 1981 [QRL.124], 10 September 1982, [B.362]. Evidence concerning the number and qualifications of religious studies teachers was collected by the Government for Scotland in 1970 [B.546] and England and Wales in 1977 [B.545], whilst reviews of their recruitment and training were prepared by the BCC in 1971 [B.519] and by the Religious Education Council in 1978 [B.464] and 1979 [B.256].

CHAPTER 9

THE INSTITUTIONAL CHURCH

9.1 Resources

9.1.1 *Plant*

9.1.1.1 The 1851 ecclesiastical census of Great Britain [B.449] [B.450] is the principal source of national data for the nineteenth century, information being returned as to, first, the number of places of worship belonging to each denomination (somewhat underestimated as we have seen in paragraphs 2.1.3.5 and 2.4.1.4 above), distinguishing buildings that were separate from those which were not and, except in 13.3% of cases, dates of erection and/or adaptation for religious use, and, secondly, the amount of sitting accommodation available in 92.5% of enumerated congregations, differentiating, save for 12.1% of the total, between free and appropriated. More localised statistics, also covering both churches and seating capacity, were collected for Hull in 1834 [B.378], Glasgow in 1836 [B.82], London in 1838 [B.504], 1865 [B.509], 15 November 1865 and 1885 [B.521], English and Welsh towns with more than ten thousand inhabitants in 1872-73 [B.509], 23 October, 6 November, 4 December 1872, 8 January, 17 December 1873, Derbyshire in 1876 [B.241], Nottinghamshire in 1879 [B.242], Bolton, Liverpool, Manchester, Oldham, Rochdale, St. Helens, Salford and Warrington in 1880 [B.530] as well as in connection with many of the counts of attendance which were carried out during the Victorian era and especially in 1881-82 (7.1.3.3 and Appendix 2).

9.1.1.2 Twentieth century data have mostly been of a serial nature, and, the Royal Commission examining the religious state of Wales and Monmouthshire in 1906-10 apart (2.3.1.2-2.3.1.3), it is only within the last ten to twenty years that there are any general non-recurrent surveys which are at all worthy of note. Figures for places of worship throughout the entire United Kingdom, derived from a combination of primary research and synthesis of existing materials, have recently been published in [B.561] and [B.572], whilst English and Welsh ones, disaggregated to county level, were gathered by the BS in 1979 (2.2.1.5-2.2.1.9) and 1982 (2.3.1.6) respectively. Locally, basic statistics of churches and accommodation have been assembled for Sheffield in 1965-67 (2.2.2.13) and elsewhere, and attitudes to the use of ecclesiastical property for secular and community purposes have been investigated amongst samples of the adult population of Hodge Hill and Balsall Heath, Birmingham in 1965 (2.2.2.11) and within 133 congregations at Bradford, Derby and Lambeth in 1972 [B.186].

9.1.2 *Clergy: general surveys*

9.1.2.1 Interdenominational studies of ministerial characteristics, career patterns and opinions on a range of professional, theological, social or political issues have been conducted by Stephen Mayor (now of Westminster College, Cambridge) in Cheshire, Derbyshire, Leicestershire, Lincolnshire and Nottinghamshire in 1968 (n = 957 Anglican, Baptist, Congregational, Methodist, and Presbyterian clergy), Stewart Ranson, Alan Bryman and Robin Hinings [B.317] within nine English dioceses or districts during 1970-73 (n = 1,227, 564 Anglican, 251 Methodist, and 412 Roman Catholic), D.J.D. Roche, W.D. Birrell and John Greer [B.331] across Northern Ireland in 1972-73 (n = 192), Peter Jarvis [B.208] [B.209] throughout the United Kingdom in 1974 (n = 999 Anglican, Baptist, Methodist and URC, 524 in parochial and 475 in other situations), Professor Anthony Coxon (of the Department of Sociology, University College, Cardiff) within South Wales in 1978 (n = 630, 333 Anglican, 112 Baptist, 70 Independent, 45 Methodist, and 70 Roman Catholic) as described in unpublished ESRC Research Report HR 4712 which is available from the BLLD, and Marplan [QRL.79], 21 December 1979; [B.457] across Great Britain in 1979 (ESRC DA, SN 1366, n = 230, 124 Anglican and 106 Catholic). Amongst more thematic surveys of the nation's clergy may be mentioned those of attitudes to foreign missionary work undertaken by BMRB [B.503] in August-September 1969 (n = 200 Anglican, Baptist, Congregational, and Methodist), of higher education chaplaincy by Monroe Wright [B.432] in February-December 1974 (ESRC DA, SN 445, n = 367 Anglican, Baptist, Methodist, URC, Church of Scotland and Catholic), of job satisfaction by *Money Which?* [QRL.51], 9 September 1977; [B.487] in December 1976, of ministerial mail by the BS [QRL.44], 28 August 1980; [QRL.47], 8 August 1980; [QRL.51], 8 August 1980; [QRL.72], 7 August 1980 in November 1979 (n = 143, 62 Anglican and 81 others), and of scripture use by Pearl Sjolander [B.355] [B.356] in November 1979-January 1980 (n = 200, 63 Anglican, 29 Baptist, 69 Methodist, 31 Seventh-Day Adventist, and 8 miscellaneous).

9.1.2.2 Lay perceptions of the Christian ministry have been examined on at least forty-one occasions since the end of the Second World War. The extent of public contact with parsons and/or willingness to approach them for advice or help with a personal problem has been investigated amongst samples of the adult population of Great Britain in September 1948 [QRL.12], April 1952 [QRL.12] [QRL.74], 1 May 1952, the first week of February 1968 [QRL.94], June 1970 [QRL.101], September 1972 [QRL.113], 22 April 1973, August 1974 [QRL.108], 23-29 July 1979 [QRL.93] and April 1981 [QRL.64], May 1981; [QRL.73], 7 May 1981, England in December 1963-January 1964 [QRL.120] [QRL.121], and Northern Ireland in December 1968-January 1969 [QRL.94] [QRL.95] as well as with young folk (4.2.1.4, 4.2.1.8, 4.2.1.10, 4.2.1.12), the elderly (4.3.2.7, 4.3.2.10), and coloured people (4.3.3.12). The ranking of clergymen and of four to twenty-nine other occupational groups in terms of their relative usefulness and influence for good within the community has been recorded nationally in August 1950 [QRL.12], the summer of 1960 [QRL.19], December 1963-January 1964 [QRL.120] [QRL.121], the beginning of June 1964 [QRL.12] [QRL.112], 14 June 1964, 23-30 June 1964 [QRL.64], August 1964, 7-13 February 1968 [QRL.77], February 1968, January-March 1969 [QRL.115], October 1973-February 1974 [QRL.22], May 1974 [QRL.12] [QRL.64], May 1974, May 1979

[QRL.73], 2 August 1979, April 1981 [QRL.64], May 1981; [QRL.73], 7 May 1981 and May 1981 [QRL.88], May-October 1981, and locally by Noel Richards [B.327] during the early 1960s, Bryan Turner and David Smith [B.395] at Aberdeen in the late 1960s (n = 600 eleven to twelve year old schoolchildren), Frank Bealey and John Sewel [B.9] at Peterhead in the autumn of 1969 (n = 194 electors), and Graham Day at Machynlleth and Newtown, Montgomeryshire in September 1974 (2.3.2.4). Other aspects of ministerial functions and behaviour upon which adults have been asked to comment include stipends in December 1963-January 1964 [QRL.120] [QRL.121] and June 1970 [QRL.101], the performance of parochial duties in December 1963-January 1964 [QRL.120] [QRL.121], June 1970 [QRL.101] and 23-29 July 1979 [QRL.93], political involvement in March-August 1968 [QRL.26] and 23-29 July 1979 [QRL.79], 21 December 1979; [QRL.93], hospital chaplaincy (n = 127 ward sisters/charge nurses and 521 patients from a Midlands conurbation) towards the end of the 1960s [B.420], marriage in March 1970 [QRL.77], November 1970, female ordination in June 1970 [QRL.101], March 1976 [QRL.64], April 1976, July 1978 [QRL.48], 7 September 1978; [QRL.49], 23-29 July 1979 [QRL.79], 21 December 1979 and September 1981 [QRL.80], February 1982, the recruitment of working class parsons in January 1972 [QRL.77], July 1972 and of homosexual ones in August 1977, 4-9 July 1979 and October-November 1981 (8.2.2.4).

9.1.3 *Clergy: denominational surveys*
9.1.3.1 Besides the surveys already noted in paragraph 9.1.2.1 above, attitudinal research amongst the Anglican clergy has been undertaken by the *Church of England Newspaper* [QRL.50], 8-15 December 1961 in 1961 on the subject of intercommunion (n = 4,244 incumbents from the Provinces of Canterbury and York), by Leslie Paul [B.294] into ministerial work-loads in July-December 1962 (n = 905) and incomes in December 1962 (n = 204), by Michael Daniel [B.94] throughout Greater London in 1967 (n = 96 men ordained from 1955 to 1965), by Leslie Paul again [B.293] with 295 parsons who had attended courses at St George's House, Windsor Castle between October 1966 and July 1968, by the Advisory Council for the Church's Ministry [B.438] in 1975 on reactions to theological education (n = 175 individuals who had completed their training during 1969-73), by W.H. Saumarez Smith [B.361] into the non-stipendiary priesthood in March 1976 (n = 131 honorary ministers), by the radical 'Parish and People' movement [QRL.50], 15 July 1977; [QRL.51], 15 July 1977 in 1977 on the question of the remarriage of divorcees (n = 405 clerics from deaneries in the South, Midlands, and North of the country), by various *ad hoc* groups in the Dioceses of Chester [QRL.123], 26 September 1977, Liverpool (n = 158) [QRL.51], 19 May 1978, Newcastle (n = 194) [QRL.48], 7 September 1978, Guildford (n = approximately 150) [QRL.51], 29 September 1978 and Manchester (n = 279) [QRL.48], 2 November 1978 during 1977-78 on the topic of female ordination, by Richard Kingsbury (6.2.1.2) into infant baptism in 1980 (n = 110 incumbents from Berkshire, Buckinghamshire, and Oxfordshire), by Michael Walker [QRL.51], 26 June 1981 in 1981 on the theme of the pastoral care of clergymen and their families (n = 100 participants at a conference held in Swanwick), and by ORC [QRL.44], 21 October 1982; [QRL.51], 22 October 1982; [QRL.57], 18 October 1982; [QRL.67], 18 October 1982 in September 1982 on the

relationship between the Church and political life (n= 500 men randomly selected from *Crockford's Clerical Directory*). Analyses of the backgrounds and opinions of ordinands have been carried out by Anthony Coxon [B.86] [B.87] [B.388] with a national sample of 494 students in November 1962 and by Anthony Russell [B.341] in the early 1970s. Finally, the views of active and nominal lay Anglicans regarding their vicars were explored in some detail in a NOP poll conducted on behalf of the *Daily Mail* [QRL.55], 6 April 1960 in March 1960, and those of the general British public concerning the issue of women priests in the Church of England were canvassed, also by NOP, in July 1978 [QRL.48], 7 September 1978; [QRL.49] and September 1981 [QRL.80], February 1982.

9.1.3.2 Relatively few studies of the Nonconformist ministry have been undertaken additional to those listed in paragraph 9.1.2.1. The attitudes of Methodist clergy towards total abstinence have been examined connexionally by the Christian Economic and Social Research Foundation in May 1962 (n=2,138) [QRL.72], 1 November 1962; [B.500], May 1972 (n=2,471) [QRL.72], 16 November 1972; [B.539] and June 1982 (n=886) [QRL.72], 21 October 1982, whilst their morale, experience of stress, and financial circumstances were investigated by the Reverend Peter Nock (currently of 11 Kingsley Road, Kingsbridge, Devon, TQ7 1EY) within the Oxford and Leicester District (n=80) during the spring of 1978 [QRL.72], 2 August 1979. Stephen Mayor (now of Westminster College, Cambridge) charted the socio-political beliefs of some 125 Congregational ministers around 1960, and a report on alcohol use amongst both Congregational and Presbyterian Church of England ones was published in 1962 [B.501]. For the Baptists, Eric Carlton [B.62] has looked at the situation of probationer clergy in the early 1960s, and Raymond Burnish [QRL.44], 6 August 1981 has monitored the ways in which 330 pastors prepared candidates for baptism and membership in 1981.

9.1.3.3 With regard to the Church of Rome, the two major profiles of clerical opinion, one researched by Stewart Ranson, Alan Bryman and Robin Hinings in 1970-73 and the other by Marplan in 1979 (9.1.2.1), have been complemented by various surveys of lay Catholics' images of the priesthood. Nationally, support for a relaxation in the Vatican's rules on ministerial celibacy has been assessed in March 1967 (3.3.4.1), 1972 [QRL.123], 4 October 1972, January 1977 (3.3.3.1) and February 1977 (3.3.4.2), whilst satisfaction with priestly performance, solutions to the vocations crisis, and sympathy for those who had renounced holy orders so that they might marry were discussed throughout Scotland in December 1977- February 1978 (3.3.4.3) and England and Wales in February-March 1978 (3.3.4.4). Locally, Conor Ward [B.402] and R.E.S. Tanner [B.381] have canvassed parishioners' views on clerical duties and activities within two separate districts of Liverpool in 1957 (n=96) and October 1969 (n=219) respectively.

9.1.4 *Lay agency*
9.1.4.1 Overall statistics of the full-time lay employees of the various British denominations were last published in the 1968 edition of the *World Christian Handbook* [B.573]. A basic enumeration of voluntary workers was undertaken by

Peter Varney [B.396] across South Norfolk in 1962, whilst more detailed comparative studies of their socio-economic backgrounds, ecclesiastical opinions or wider community involvements have been conducted by Thomas Brennan, E.W. Cooney and Harold Pollins [B.37] in the Swansea area in 1951 (n = 2,281 officials and leading members from 212 Church in Wales, Baptist, Congregational, Methodist, and Welsh Presbyterian places of worship), David Clark [B.76] at Rugby, Trowbridge, Ellesmere Port and Bromley in 1962-64 (n = 248 Anglicans and 244 Methodists), Peter Sissons [B.354] at Falkirk in 1969 (n = 130 Church of Scotland elders, 28 minor Protestants, and 11 Catholics), and by Frank Bealey and John Sewel [B.9] at Peterhead during the early 1970s (n = 118 Kirk elders and 84 others).

9.1.4.2 A sample survey (n = 482) of accredited and salaried lay ministry in the Established Church was concluded in 1975 [B.195], and a sociological portrait of 237 representatives to the parochial councils of the Battersea Deanery in 1970 is appended to [B.476]. Within Methodism, reports on the recruitment and qualifications of local preachers were produced by the Wesleyans [B.64] in 1919 (after research in 261 of the connexion's 755 circuits) and by the United Methodists [B.536] in 1921 (on the basis of replies received from 255 of 362 circuits), whilst attempts to measure their utilisation and deployment have recently been made by Roger Thorne [B.386] in the Plymouth and Exeter District in 1970 and by Richard Smith [B.360] across England and Wales in 1978. For the Roman Catholics, Gallup has investigated the labours of 98 members of the Association of Parish Sisters by means of questionnaires and one week diaries completed in February 1978 (JN S.477).

9.2 Modernisation

9.2.1 *Structural change*
9.2.1.1 Many denominations have tried to recast and democratize the basis of their ecclesiastical polity in the period since the Second World War, but few have made such rapid strides in this direction as the Anglicans and Catholics. The major administrative development within the Church of England, the introduction of a system of full synodical government in 1969-70, has given rise to several relevant pieces of statistical research. At the national level, socio-demographic profiles of the membership of the quinquennial General Synods have been prepared by Kathleen Jones [B.221] [B.222] in 1970 (n = 235 or 94% of lay delegates) and 1975 (n = all 52 bishops, 232 or 93% of the clergy, and 233 or 95% of the laity), and by George Moyser [B.275] in 1980 (n = 69% of proctors and laity); Moyser and Kenneth Medhurst [B.268] [B.276] [B.278] [B.279] have also examined the religious and political opinions of 682 or 80% of the 855 candidates who offered themselves for election to the General Synod, whether successfully or not, in September 1975 (ESRC DA, SN 1777), whilst BBC Television's 'Newsnight' programme of 8 February 1983 broadcast the results of a special poll (n = 300, equivalent to a 55% response) of members' attitudes towards disarmament in anticipation of the debate on 'The Church and the Bomb' which took place later that same week. Locally, Alan Bryman and Robin Hinings [B.48] [B.49] have surveyed the views on 'Participation,

reform and ecumenism' expressed by 228 lay members of twelve Deanery Synods in the Diocese of Birmingham in November 1971, and Leslie Francis [B.120] has monitored the degree of interest in synodical structures shown by their clerical and lay counterparts from a more rural see.

9.2.1.2 Organisational renewal within the Roman Church has largely stemmed from the work of the Second Vatican Council of 1962-65. Reactions of the faithful to the changes implemented as a result of the Council and especially to the increased amount of lay involvement in ecclesiastical affairs which it helped to promote have been tested across Great Britain in March 1967 (3.3.4.1) and February 1977 (3.3.4.2), England and Wales in February-March 1978 (3.3.4.4), and Scotland in December 1977-February 1978 (3.3.4.3) as well as with samples of the readership of the *Catholic Herald* in 1968 and 1977 (3.3.3.1) and of priests in 1970-73 [B.317]. One practical step towards the achievement of greater democracy was the establishment by the Bishops' Conference of a series of consultative commissions, 141 of whose lay members were interviewed or contacted by mail during the early 1970s [B.191]. Another was the convening of a National Pastoral Congress at Liverpool in May 1980, the delegates to which have been studied from a demographic standpoint by George Moyser [B.277] for the Salford Diocese and from an attitudinal perspective by Michael Hornsby-Smith (of the Department of Sociology, University of Surrey) throughout the entire country; the latter's seven page, thirty-three item postal questionnaire, completed retrospectively in November and December 1981 and scheduled for published analysis during the summer of 1983, seems to have elicited a fairly healthy response even without the use of reminder letters and despite strong criticisms of its theological content aired by some clerical participants [QRL.47], 4-25 December 1981, 15 January 1982.

9.2.2 *Liturgical change*
9.2.2.1 The process of liturgical revision within the Church of England which commenced with the passage through Parliament of the Prayer Book (Alternate and Other Services) Measures in 1965 and culminated in the publication of the *Alternative Service Book* in 1980 has prompted a variety of quantitative surveys. First, attempts to record the forms of worship used in the parishes have been made throughout the Provinces of Canterbury and York (on a 10% sample basis) in 1980 [B.103], the Dioceses of Chester in 1978 [QRL.51], 5 May 1978, Carlisle in 1978 [QRL.48], 7 September 1978 and Rochester in 1978 [QRL.51], 14 April 1978 and 1981 [QRL.51], 19 June 1981, and the Archdeaconries of Sheffield in 1968 [B.401], Colchester in 1980 [QRL.123], 20 April 1981 and Berkshire in 1982 [QRL.51], 1 October 1982. Secondly, the association between service types and trends in electoral roll membership was explored by Roger Homan [B.187] [B.188] in an enquiry conducted within the Archdeaconry of Chichester during the spring of 1980 whose impartiality has been vigorously disputed in some quarters [QRL.51], 10-31 October, 7 November 1980. Thirdly, the preferences of a nationally representative body of 1,178 professed Anglicans concerning traditional and modern styles of the Lord's Prayer and the wedding rite and of a sub-group of 490 active ones (attending worship at least once or twice a year) regarding the use of the Book of Common

Prayer or the Series 3 liturgies and of the Authorized or an updated version of the Bible for public lessons were investigated by Gallup on behalf of Professor David Martin in April-May 1980 [QRL.31], 1980; [QRL.50], 13 June 1980; [QRL.51], 13 June 1980; [QRL.57], 12 June 1980; [QRL.64], June 1980; [QRL.67], 12 June 1980; [QRL.123], 12 June 1980.

9.2.2.2 Liturgical controversy within Methodism during the past decade has centred less around the reformulation of any ecclesiastical offices than the preparation of a new hymn book for eventual publication in December 1983. This circumstance reflects the overriding importance which Methodists have always attached to hymn-singing relative to all other aspects of worship, a paramountcy which was strikingly demonstrated in research undertaken by David Clark [B.76] at Rugby, Trowbridge, Ellesmere Port and Bromley in 1962-64 (n = 244 leaders) and by Michael Hill and Peter Wakeford [B.178] at Byfleet, Crawley, Forest Hill, and Upper Norwood in 1967 (n = 328 members). The principal statistical contributions to the latest debate comprise, first, a census of utilisation of hymns from the existing 1933 book and its supplement of 1969 carried out by Bryan Spinney [QRL.72], 13 April 1978 at 139 churches throughout the connexion in 1977, and, secondly, a study, directed by the Reverend Malcolm Braddy (of 7 Mayfield Road, Timperley, Cheshire, WA15 7TB), of the responses of 68 congregations in the Manchester and Stockport District to the appearance, in October 1980, of the initial draft of the proposed replacement volume.

9.2.2.3 The major liturgical development in Roman Catholicism during recent years, and yet another direct consequence of Vatican II, has been the substitution of mass in the vernacular for the traditional Latin rite. Reactions of the Catholic laity to this change have been tested across Great Britain in March 1967 (3.3.4.1), June 1970 [QRL.101], September 1976 [QRL.47], 8 October 1976; [QRL.64], September 1976; [QRL.67], 8 October 1976 and February 1977 (3.3.4.2), England and Wales in February-March 1978 (3.3.4.4), Scotland in December 1977- February 1978 (3.3.4.3), and at St. Timothy's Church, West Derby, Liverpool (n = 219) in October 1969 [B.380]; less scientifically, the *Catholic Herald* has canvassed the views of its readership in 1968 and 1977 (3.3.3.1), and *The Universe* [QRL.125], 31 October, 7 November 1980 ran a ballot in 1980 whose 14,614 voters are known to have included vast numbers of members of the Latin Mass Society, of Archbishop Lefebvre's Society of St. Pius X, and of other groups renowned for their opposition to the new liturgy. Priestly attitudes seem only to have been recorded on one occasion, in the Diocese of Portsmouth as far back as 1961 [QRL.57], 3 April 1961.

9.3 Outreach

9.3.1 *Sunday schools*
9.3.1.1 Non-recurrent institutional data sources for this topic are relatively few and far between. Nationally, returns of the number of Sunday schools and of total pupil enrolments were compiled, with varying degrees of accuracy, by Government agencies throughout Great Britain in 1818 [B.481] [B.482] [B.483] and 1851 [B.448]

[B.449] and England and Wales in 1833 [B.469] and 1858-59 [B.534], whilst censuses of scholars' attendances on a particular day have been undertaken across Britain in 1851 [B.448] [B.449] and by the BS within England in 1979 (2.2.1.5-2.2.1.9) and Wales in 1982 (2.3.1.6). Denominationally, detailed reports on the nature and effectiveness of Sunday school work have been prepared for the Free Churches as a whole (n= approximately 500 schools) in 1956 [B.555], the Scottish Kirk (n=60% of ministers) in 1960 [B.142], Methodism (n= 10 societies in the Leeds District) in 1973 [QRL.72], 8 November 1973; [B.323] [B.325], and the Church of England (n=714 parishes) in 1981 [QRL.51], 27 November 1981; [B.103].

9.3.1.2 Additional evidence is available from opinion polls. Samples of the adult population have been asked, first, about their own involvement with Sunday school when younger across Great Britain in mid-1947 [QRL.75], 6 November 1947, July 1948 [QRL.54], 10 August 1948, December 1954 [QRL.97] and February 1957 [QRL.12], Hodge Hill and Balsall Heath during the summer and autumn of 1965 (2.2.2.11), the Rhondda Valley early in 1966 (2.3.2.3), Machynlleth and Newtown, Montgomeryshire in September 1974 (2.3.2.4), and, secondly, about past or present attendances by their children throughout Britain in mid-1947 [QRL.75], 6 November 1947, December 1954 [QRL.97], February 1957 [QRL.12], March 1966 [QRL.122] and June 1970 [QRL.101], England in January 1951 (2.2.1.3) and December 1963-January 1964 [QRL.120] [QRL.121], Derby in February-April 1953 (2.2.2.4), Machynlleth and Newtown in September 1974 (2.3.2.4), and Handsworth in May-June 1976 (4.3.3.12). Adolescents have been questioned about their attitudes to and/or contact with Sunday schools in several of the surveys discussed in Section 4.1 above, whilst Ivan Reid [B.324] [B.325] has contrasted the religious beliefs, knowledge and practices of eighty-two members of the Young People's Departments of three Yorkshire Nonconformist places of worship with those of two hundred fourth and fifth year comprehensive pupils from the same county.

9.3.2 *Evangelism*

9.3.2.1 There are three principal types of non-recurrent data relating to home missionary activity. First, statistics of hearers and enquirers at major post-war crusades are either given in the *World Christian Encyclopedia* [B.572] or may be obtained from the various individuals and organisations listed in [B.466]. Secondly, studies of the longer term success of aggressive evangelism in promoting church membership and/or attendance have been made by S.Herron [QRL.46], 10 February 1955 for the Harringay outreach of 1954, John Highet [B.171] [B.173] for the 'Tell Scotland' movement of 1955, the EA [B.511] for the Greater London campaigns of 1966 and 1967, and David Wasdell for Church Army missions held at All Saints', Bury St. Edmunds in 1963 and 1977 [B.408] and at St.Oswald's, Preesall in 1977-78 [B.409]. Thirdly, public attitudes towards Billy Graham have been measured in polls conducted amongst Britons in March 1954 [QRL.12], May-June 1954 [QRL.12], and June 1966 [QRL.12] [QRL.64], July 1966 and listeners to BBC Radio's 'Sunday' programme early in 1979 [QRL.44], 8 March 1979.

9.3.2.2 Records of the country's total human and material investment in foreign missionary work have been assembled in a number of sources extending from the *World Missionary Atlas* of 1925 [B.574] to the six editions of the *UK Christian Handbook* which have been published between June 1964 and November 1982 [B.561]. Images of, and personal support for, overseas evangelism were investigated amongst samples of both clergy (n = 200) and regular church-goers (n = 1,030) from the Anglican, Baptist, Congregational and Methodist denominations who were interviewed throughout England and Wales by BMRB in August-October 1969 [B.503].

CHAPTER 10

FUTURE NEEDS AND PROSPECTS

10.1 Content

10.1.1 *Survey populations*

10.1.1.1 Geographically (chapter 2), it is Northern Ireland (2.5), of all four countries within the United Kingdom, which is least well served with non-recurrent sources, a circumstance which may perhaps be attributed, first, to the existence of an official, decennial census of confessional allegiance in the province, secondly, to the diversion of scholarly interest away from religious questions as such and towards Ulster's politico-sectarian troubles, and, thirdly, to the fact that the leading commercial opinion polling agencies have normally confined their sphere of operations to mainland Britain. Scotland (2.4), too, has received less attention than it deserves, especially since John Highet (2.4.1.6, 2.4.2.1) ceased his labours in the early 1960s, and it is heartening to learn that the National Bible Society of Scotland and MARC Europe are now planning some sort of enumeration of membership and attendance here similar to those which were carried out by the BS in England in 1979 (2.2.1.5 - 2.2.1.9) and Wales in 1982 (2.3.1.6). At the community level (2.2.2, 2.3.2, 2.4.2, 2.5.2), there have been many valuable studies of towns and cities but only two serious quantitative investigations of rural conditions, one by Peter Varney of South Norfolk in 1962 (2.2.2.9) and the other by Robin Hinings of the Clun Valley in 1968 (2.2.2.11); David Clark's recently published account of religious life in the North Yorkshire fishing village of Staithes in 1975-76 [B.75] is essentially a qualitative enquiry in the anthropological mould.

10.1.1.2 Denominationally (chapter 3), the Roman Catholics (3.3) have been most extensively surveyed, although, as Michael Hornsby-Smith [B.189] makes clear, the research potential cannot yet be said to be wholly exhausted. For the Established (3.1) and Free Churches (3.2), the really pressing requirement is for comprehensive examinations of the beliefs and opinions of the man in the pew comparable to those which have already been undertaken for the clergy (9.1.2.1, 9.1.3.1, 9.1.3.2); the only full-length national poll of the Anglican laity, for example, was conducted as far back as March 1960 (3.1.1.2). As for the sects, many of them are vehemently opposed, generally on fundamentalist grounds (1.1.1.8), to the collection of detailed ecclesiastical statistics, and it seems unlikely that much improvement can be hoped for in this direction.

10.1.1.3 Demographically (chapter 4), there has been no shortage of work amongst children (4.1) and young adults (4.2) unless, perhaps, in the case of sixth-formers for whom a replication of enquiries made by Derek Wright and Edwin Cox in October

1963 and February-March 1970 (4.2.2.1) would be desirable. With just one partial exception [B.116], the years of parenthood and middle age, by contrast, have suffered neglect, and there is special scope here for some investigation of men's attitudes towards religion, particularly into how they may vary from one occupational group to another. Studies of older people (4.3.2) have tended to concentrate on links with the institutional Church, and more evidence is needed regarding their personal faith and private practices.

10.1.2 *Survey topics*
10.1.2.1 Data relating to popular beliefs (chapter 5) are lacking less in terms of actual quantity than in their quality, many deriving from questions which are either ambiguous, biased, superficial or unduly restrictive of the respondent's choices (2.1.4.7, 5.1.1.7, 5.2.4.1). Serious consideration should be given to the improvement of standards of survey design in this area, notably through the provision of more precise yet simply worded definitions of key concepts such as 'religion', 'God' or 'life after death', and by the introduction of a wider range of preformulated reply codes or the greater use of open-ended interviewing techniques.

10.1.2.2 In the realm of general practices (chapter 6), there is room for more research into the frequency and nature of private prayer (6.1.1), the observance of Church festivals other than Christmas (6.1.4), the persistence of rites of passage (6.2.1), and participation in religious organisations (6.2.4). With regard to attendance at Sunday services (chapter 7), the main requirements are for local enumerations to be carried out in towns and cities such as Aberdeen, Billingham, Bolton, Dundee, Glasgow, Ipswich, Lincoln, Liverpool, London, Newtown (Montgomeryshire), Whitehaven, and York where a series of counts have already been made over time (7.1.3), for weekly congregational records to be kept in a representative sample of places of worship so that the pattern of seasonal fluctuation (7.1.2.4) may be more exactly determined, and for the quality of poll figures (7.2) to be raised by the employment of sophisticated filtering methods such as those described by Malcolm Macourt [B.249] for the North-East Area Study of April-May 1974.

10.1.2.3 Two very obvious needs in the field of religious attitudes (chapter 8) are for reviews of public and committed Christian opinion concerning, first, future ecumenical options (8.1.2) in the wake of the Anglican General Synod's rejection of the 'Towards Visible Unity' proposals and the subsequent dissolution of the Churches' Council for Covenanting during July 1982, and, secondly, Sabbath observance (8.3.2) in the light of the repeated clamours for legislative change which are now being heard in this area. Less essential, but still desirable, improvements would include investigations of the extent and character of anti-semitism (8.1.3.3), of the interaction of religion and ethics which go beyond simple cross-tabulations of specific moral beliefs by denominational allegiance (8.2), and of the support for disestablishment (8.3.1.1).

10.1.2.4 At the institutional level (chapter 9), some form of total or sample census of voluntary lay agency (9.1.4) and of Sunday school work (9.3.1.1) would be beneficial, whilst the continuing debates about the *Alternative Service Book* in the Church of England (9.2.2.1), hymnological revision with the Methodists (9.2.2.2), and the demise of the Latin mass in Roman Catholicism (9.2.2.3) will require periodic testing of grass roots feeling for several years to come. On the evangelistic front (9.3.2), 'Mission England', the major interdenominational initiative with an anticipated £1.5 million budget which was launched in November 1982 and is destined to culminate in a crusade led by Billy Graham in May-July 1984, would repay close sociological and statistical inspection at each phase of its development and aftermath; consideration might also be given to a thorough evaluation of practical support for, and perceptions of, foreign missionary enterprise in the post-imperial age.

10.2 Methodology

10.2.1 *Data collection*

10.2.1.1 Probably the greatest single deficiency in the non-recurrent sources is the almost total lack of Government involvement in their collection. Nationally, in view of the historical experience outlined by Michael Drake [B.101] and of the doubts expressed by the BCC Executive at its meeting in November 1978, it is probably too much to ask that a religious enquiry should ever again form part of the decennial census of Great Britain, but it is to be hoped that official departments might be persuaded to help in other ways. Perhaps the most obvious means of doing so would be by the insertion of a handful of basic items in the OPCS General Household Survey which is capable of generating an annual data base of approximately twenty thousand individual cases; there is, in fact, just a very slight precedent for this, since in 1977 church-going was included as one of the codes in a question about leisure activities, although the resultant figures, briefly noted in [QRL.107], no.9, were apparently deemed to be so methodologically imperfect that they were omitted from the final report as published by HMSO. Locally, a proportion of authorities now conduct their own voluntary censuses of population as an aid to the planning of services, and it might be feasible to gather evidence on, say, confessional allegiance through this medium where such information could be shown to be strategically relevant, for example to the determination of the number of places required in Roman Catholic schools.

10.2.1.2 There seems to be little prospect of any meaningful, long term co-ordination of the statistical efforts of the various Christian denominations. Two recent attempts to further this goal, one made by the BCC in 1972-73 and the other by an *ad hoc* Inter-Church Research Group in 1978-79, never advanced beyond the talking stage, whilst the NIE, which did score a notable success in the field (2.2.1.5-2.2.1.9), was wound up in July 1983 after less than five years' existence.

10.2.1.3 The problem with commercial polling organisations arises less from the level of their commitment, which, as we have seen throughout this review, is really quite substantial, as from its nature. Specifically, key topics such as religious profession and attendance need to be explored on the basis of samples far in excess of the customary one or two thousand respondents if an exhaustive analysis by ecclesiastical and demographic variables is ever to be undertaken, and other matters would be better concentrated into fewer and more purpose-designed surveys, where a degree of methodological refinement can be obtained, rather than fragmented amongst investigations of the omnibus type which are often hurried and superficial. Such reforms could be relatively cost-effective provided that potential clients were prepared to pool their research funds, as happened, for instance, with the Gallup-EVSSG 'Values' enquiry of 1981 [QRL.16] [QRL.31], 1981; [QRL.70], 1982-83 which attracted sponsorship from an international range of business, charitable, Church, educational, and governmental sources.

10.2.2 *Data retrieval*
10.2.2.1 The retrieval of data could be facilitated in any or all of five ways. First, some sort of regular current awareness service might be devised, perhaps by an ecumenical agency such as the BS or by an academic one like the British Sociological Association's Sociology of Religion Study Group, in order to advertise the existence and availability of new material. At the very least, this would have to take the form of an update to the bibliographies which appeared in David Martin's *A Sociology of English Religion* [B.258] and in the 1970-75 editions of *A sociological Yearbook of Religion in Britain* [B.78] [B.79] [B.80] [B.81] [B.206] [B.270].

10.2.2.2 Secondly, publication of actual statistics could be extended either through the use of established outlets such as *Social Trends* [QRL.107] or by the creation of some kind of printed or, for cheapness, microform digest which would complement the work done by Robert Currie, Alan Gilbert and Lee Horsley [B.89] in abstracting the time series evidence.

10.2.2.3 Thirdly, whenever in machine-readable format, either as a deck of punched cards or on magnetic tape, major data sets should be deposited at the ESRC DA, University of Essex where they can be fully processed and cleaned, securely stored, and, for a handling charge, made available for secondary analysis to any interested enquirer. As yet, the DA holds data for only about one hundred and twenty-five of the surveys which have been referred to throughout this review.

10.2.2.4 Fourthly, efforts ought to be made to ensure that all unpublished reports, schedules, and other documents which are no longer required by the original researcher are preserved at an appropriate library or record office. The wanton destruction or mysterious disappearance of many potentially valuable sources has been a constant cause of frustration and hindrance in the preparation of the present text; some of the material collected by Kofi Busia for his 'Brookton' study of 1963-64 (2.2.2.10), for instance, ended up as the scrap paper supply for staff at one Midlands college!

10.2.2.5 Finally, steps might be taken to improve access to data which have been retained by private individuals or organisations. Opinion poll companies are an obvious case in point, for whilst some, like Gallup, MORI and NOP, treat academic investigators with a kindness and a liberality for which no praise can be too high, others make consultation of their files either difficult or impossible; perhaps this is an issue which could be considered by the Market Research Society, the industry's watchdog, to see whether any guidelines on future policy can be established.

NOTES TO THE QUICK REFERENCE LIST

Scope

For reasons explained in paragraph 1.2.2.1, the QRL has been restricted to surveys involving personal interviews with quota or random samples of the adult population (aged fifteen/sixteen/eighteen/twenty-one and over) of the United Kingdom, Great Britain, England, Wales, Scotland or Northern Ireland. It contains more than six hundred and eighty separate entries deriving from approximately three hundred and thirty polls conducted by twenty-two research agencies between 1937 and 1983.

Type of data

Topic descriptions, which ordinarily represent a paraphrase of the actual question(s) asked, are grouped by twenty-eight subject headings which broadly correspond to the divisions used throughout chapters 5-9 of the text.

Breakdown

This column simply relates to the level of breakdown offered in the relevant primary publication source(s); obviously, whenever an original data set is extant, the potential for detailed disaggregation of the results is almost limitless.

Date

Within each category, surveys are listed in strict chronological order of fieldwork. Interviewing dates are given as precisely as possible in one of the following, contracted, forms: 3/1963 March 1963 3-4/1968 March-April 1968 20-25/8/1974 20-25 August 1974 30/6-5/7/1982 30 June-5 July 1982

QRL Publication

References are given by QRL number only in the case of non-recurrent publications and by QRL number and contracted date for those issued on a daily, weekly, monthly, quarterly or annual basis; a key to QRL numbers follows the QRL itself. Where no printed source is mentioned, requests for data should be directed to the appropriate polling agency or sponsoring body. *Text Reference and remarks*

Sample size: Unweighted totals are given as far as possible. A modal base of plus or minus one thousand to plus or minus two thousand respondents may be assumed for the 27% of entries where no exact figure has been ascertained.

Fieldwork: the names of polling agencies have been abbreviated as follows: BMRB British Market Research Bureau DEP Daily Express Poll of Public

Opinion GP Social Surveys (Gallup Poll) Limited, formerly the British Institute of Public Opinion IMS Irish Marketing Surveys IPC IPC Surveys Division IS Interscan LHR Louis Harris Research MAFS Mary Agar Fieldwork Services MAR Marplan MO Mass-Observation MORI Market & Opinion Research International NOP NOP Market Research, formerly National Opinion Polls OPCSSSD Office of Population Censuses and Surveys, Social Survey Division ORC Opinion Research Centre RSGB Research Surveys of Great Britain RSL Research Services Limited RSNR Research Section, News Review RSOP Research Section, Odhams Press SCPR Social and Community Planning Research SPR Social Policy Research STS System Three Scotland UOS Ulster Opinion Surveys Job numbers are given in parentheses where known.

Sponsor: The following abbreviations are used: AA Advertising Association ALRA Abortion Law Reform Association BBC British Broadcasting Corporation BES British Election Study, University of Essex BHA British Humanist Association BS Bible Society CEC Commission of the European Communities CFKF Charles F. Kettering Foundation DE *Daily Express* DG *Daily Graphic* DM *Daily Mail* DS *Daily Star* DT *Daily Telegraph* EERT European Educational Research Trust EM European Movement EVSSG European Value Systems Study Group GH *Glasgow Herald* IBA Independent Broadcasting Authority ITA Independent Television Authority LDC Leisure Development Center, Tokyo LWT London Weekend Television NC *News Chronicle* NCC National Consumer Council NR *News Review* NS *New Society* QUB Department of Political Science, Queen's University of Belfast RCC Royal Commission on the Constitution RCLG Royal Commission on Local Government in England RDA Reader's Digest Association RERP Religious Experience Research Project, University of Nottingham RPA Rationalist Press Association SC *The Scotsman* SES Scottish Election Study, University of Strathclyde SPUC Society for the Protection of the Unborn Child ST *Sunday Times* STE *Sunday Telegraph* SU *Sunday* U *The Universe* UTV Ulster Television VES Voluntary Euthanasia Society WES Welsh Election Study, University College of Wales, Aberystwyth WM *Western Mail* WO *Woman's Own*

Data set: This tag signifies that the data set for the survey is located at the ESRC Data Archive, University of Essex. Where a precise study number (SN) has been allocated to such a set, this information too is recorded.

Multinational: This word serves to identify polls in which the same questions were put simultaneously to samples in several different countries.

QUICK REFERENCE LIST - TABLE OF CONTENTS

QUICK REFERENCE LIST

PERSONAL RELIGION: BELIEFS

General indicators of religiosity

Type of data	Breakdown	Area	Date	QRL Publication	Text Reference and remarks
Religion as a source of comfort and strength		GB	1/1941	[QRL.9] [QRL.12]	5.1.1.5. Fieldwork: GP
Past/present interest in religion	age, sex, social class	GB	1947	[QRL.75], 23/10/1947	Fieldwork: RSNR. Sponsor: NR
Religion v. politics as the greater influence on respondent's life		GB	6/1948	[QRL.12]	Fieldwork: GP
Whether politics, religion, hobbies or work meant most to respondent		GB	4/1955		Fieldwork: GP (S.431B)
Self-assessed religiosity		GB	3/1963	[QRL.12]	5.1.1.2. Fieldwork: GP
Self-assessed religiosity		GB	8/1966	[QRL.12]	5.1.1.2. Fieldwork: GP
Self-assessed religiosity - extent to which life has a spiritual purpose - necessity for religious belief to lead a good life - effect of beliefs on respondent's everyday life	age, sex, social class, denominational affiliation, other religious variable	GB	2/1968	[QRL.94]	5.1.1.1, 5.1.1.2, 5.1.1.4, Sample size: 1,071. Fieldwork: ORC. Sponsor: ITA
Certainty of belief that religion provides the best guide to life - religiosity of respondent compared with father/mother at same age	denominational affiliation	Northern Ireland	3-8/1968	[QRL.26]	5.1.1.1 - 5.1.1.2. Sample size: 1,291. Fieldwork: UOS. Sponsor: R.Rose. Data set: SN 1040

Subject	Variables	Location	Date	Reference	Details
Self-assessed religiosity - extent to which life has a spiritual purpose - necessity for religious belief to lead a good life - effect of beliefs on respondent's everyday life	denominational affiliation, other religious variable	Northern Ireland	2/12/1968 -10/1/1969	[QRL.94] [QRL.95]	5.1.1.1, 5.1.1.2, 5.1.1.4. Sample size: 694. Fieldwork: ORC. Sponsor: ITA, UTV and the Churches
Strength of religious beliefs	age, sex, marital status, social class, education, region	GB	8-15/6/1970	[QRL.101]	5.1.1.3. Sample size: 1,395. Fieldwork: NOP (4233). Sponsor: DM
Importance of religious beliefs to respondent	social class , frequency of church attendance	GB	20-22/1/1972	[QRL.77], 7/1972	5.1.1.3. Sample size:1,000. Fieldwork: NOP. Sponsor: DM
Subjects (including religion) talked about most/about which strongest opinions held	sex, education	GB	4-5/1972	[QRL.83]	5.1.1.6. Sample size: 1,260. Fieldwork: BMRB. Sponsor: AA
Effect of religious beliefs on respondent's everyday life		GB	20-24/9/1972		5.1.1.4. Sample size: 1,026. Fieldwork: ORC (7238). Sponsor: ST. Data set
Self-assessed religiosity - necessity for religious belief to lead a good life - effect of religious beliefs on respondent's everyday life		GB	15-20/1/1973	[QRL.91]	5.1.1.1, 5.1.1.2, 5.1.1.4. Sample size: 647. Fieldwork: ORC (7/1337). Sponsor: IBA

Type of data	Breakdown	Area	Date	QRL Publication	Text Reference and remarks
Self-assessed religiosity		GB	1/10/1973 -7/2/1974		5.1.1.2. Sample size: 1,802. Fieldwork: MAFS. Sponsor: M.Abrams and A.Marsh. Data set: SN 672
Extent to which life has a spiritual purpose - self-assessed religiosity - sense of an increasing dissatisfaction with material objects and an increasing awareness of spiritual things	age, sex, social class, region	GB	20-25/8/1974	[QRL.108] [QRL.123], 14/10/1974	5.1.1.1 - 5.1.1.2. Sample size: 1,093. Fieldwork: ORC (34333). Sponsor: BBC
Importance of religious beliefs to respondent		GB	11/1974-1/1975	[QRL.13], 1979 [QRL.14] [QRL.28] [QRL.69] [QRL.87], 3-5/1979	5.1.1.3. Sample size: 307. Fieldwork: GP. Sponsor: CFKF. Multinational
Importance of religion to respondent		UK	13-25/10/1975		5.1.1.3. Sample size: 1,438. Fieldwork: GP. Sponsor CEC. Data set: SN 789. Multinational
Subjects (including religion) talked about most/about which strongest opinions held	age, sex, social class	GB	3/1976	[QRL.84]	5.1.1.6. Sample size: 1,067. Fieldwork: BMRB. Sponsor: AA

Subject	Country	Date	Ref	Details
Importance of religion to respondent	UK	7/5-7/6/1976		5.1.1.3. Sample size: 1,340. Fieldwork: GP. Sponsor: CEC. Data set: SN 933. Multinational
Importance of spiritual side of life to respondent	GB	8/1976	[QRL.21]	5.1.1.3. Sample size: 1,865. Fieldwork: NOP. Sponsor: RERP
Importance of religion in respondent's life	UK	2-21/11/1976		5.1.1.3. Sample size: 1,351. Fieldwork: GP. Sponsor: CEC. Data set: SN 934. Multinational
Importance of religion in respondent's life	UK	23/4-12/5/1977		5.1.1.3. Sample size: 1,417. Fieldwork: GP (S.309/7). Sponsor: CEC. Data set: SN 936. Multinational
Importance of religion in respondent's life	UK	24/10 -7/11/1977		5.1.1.3. Sample size: 1,350. Fieldwork: GP (S.309/8). Sponsor: CEC. Data set: SN 1029. Multinational

Type of data	Breakdown	Area	Date	QRL Publication	Text Reference and remarks
Self-assessed religiosity	denominational affiliation	Northern Ireland	6-11/1978	[QRL.24]	5.1.1.2. Sample size: 1,277. Fieldwork: IMS (5234). Sponsor: QUB. Data set: SN 1347
Importance of religion in respondent's life		UK	9-21/4/1979		5.1.1.3. Sample size: 1,317. Fieldwork: GP (S.4009/11). Sponsor: CEC. Data set: SN 1396. Multinational
Whether it is more important to help people than to believe - belief that nothing matters except what happens on earth	age, sex, denominational affiliation	GB	23-29/7/1979	[QRL.79], 21/12/1979 [QRL.93]	5.1.1.1. Sample size: 988. Fieldwork: MAR (51809/1). Sponsor: *Now!*. Data set: SN 1366
Personal goal to lead a Christian life - importance of religion in respondent's life	age, sex, social class, education	GB	9-10/1979	[QRL.70], 1980-81 [QRL.92]	5.1.1.1, 5.1.1.3. Sample size: 987. Fieldwork: GP (S.5077). Sponsor: LDC. Multinational

Subject	Breakdown	Area	Date	Reference	Details
Importance of religion in respondent's life		UK	11-26/10/1979		5.1.1.3. Sample size: 1,403. Fieldwork: GP (S.4009/12). Sponsor: CEC. Data set: SN 1397. Multinational
Self-assessed religiosity		GB	2/1980		5.1.1.2. Sample size: 1,126. Fieldwork: BMRB. Sponsor: LWT
Subjects (including religion) talked about most/about which strongest opinions held	age, sex, social class, party political preference	GB	6/1980	[QRL.85]	5.1.1.6. Sample size: 1,116. Fieldwork: BMRB. Sponsor: AA
Willingness to sacrifice everything for religious beliefs - self-assessed religiosity - religion as a source of comfort and strength		UK	3/1981	[QRL.70], 1982-83 [QRL.113], 13/3/1983	5.1.1.2, 5.1.1.3, 5.1.1.5. Sample size: 1,543. Fieldwork: GP (S.2131). Sponsor: EVSSG. Multinational
Importance of religion in respondent's life		GB	1-8/3/1982	[QRL.90], [QRL.123], 12/5/1982	5.1.1.3. Sample size: 1,076. Fieldwork: GP (S.2202). Sponsor: Birds Eye Wall's Ltd.

Type of data	Breakdown	Area	Date	QRL Publication	Text Reference and remarks
Ideas and causes (including religious faith) considered sufficiently worthwhile to do something about even if this might involve risk or giving up other things - self-assessed religiosity		UK	31/3-29/4/1982	[QRL.59], 6/1982 [QRL.70], 1982-83	5.1.1.2 , 5.1.1.3. Sample size: 1,419. Fieldwork: GP (S.4009/17). Sponsor: CEC. Data set: SN 1792. Multinational
Subjects (including religion) talked about most/about which strongest opinions held		GB	24-28/9/1982	[QRL.80], 2/1983	5.1.1.6. Sample size: 1,076. Fieldwork: NOP (8510). Sponsor: The Mail on Sunday

Religious experience

Type of data	Breakdown	Area	Date	QRL Publication	Text Reference and remarks
Sense of awareness of, or of being influenced by, a presence or power, whether referred to as God or not, which different from the everyday self - feeling of being close to a powerful spiritual force that seemed to lift respondent out of himself	age, sex, social class, education, region, denominational affiliation, frequency of church attendance, other religious variable	GB	8/1976	[QRL.17] [QRL.20] [QRL.21] [QRL.119], 23/7/1977	5.1.2.2. Sample size: 1,865. Fieldwork: NOP. Sponsor: RERP
Feeling of being close to a powerful spiritual life force that seemed to lift respondent out of himself - extent to which this experience had altered his outlook on life		UK	3/1981	[QRL.70], 1982-83	Sample size: 1,543. Fieldwork: GP (S.2131). Sponsor: EVSSG. Multinational

God

Belief in a personal God/Spirit or vital force	age, sex, social class, denominational affiliation	GB	12/1947	[QRL.12] [QRL.74], 13/1/1948	5.2.1.2. Fieldwork: GP (S.159). Sponsor: NC. Multinational
Belief in a personal God/spirit or life force	age	GB	2-12/2/1957	[QRL.12] [QRL.74], 15-17/4/1957	5.2.1.2. Sample size: 2,261. Fieldwork : GP (CS.1717). Sponsor: NC
Belief in a personal God/spirit or life force	age, sex, social class, denominational affiliation	GB	29/3-4/4/1963	[QRL.12] [QRL.23] [QRL.64], 4/1963	5.2.1.2. Fieldwork: GP
Belief in a personal God/spirit or vital force	age, sex, social class, region, denominational affiliation, frequency of church attendance, other religious variable	England	16/12/1963-20/1/1964	[QRL.57], 20/9/1965 [QRL.113], 19/9/1965 [QRL.120] [QRL.121]	5.2.1.2. Sample size: 2,211. Fieldwork: GP (CS.5480). Sponsor: ABC TV. Data set
Belief in God - knowledge of any organisation representing the views of humanists, agnostics and atheists		GB	29/4-3/5/1964		5.2.1.1. Sample size: 2,431. Fieldwork: NOP (868). Sponsor: BHA. Data set: SN 64009
Certainty of belief/disbelief in God - conception of God - belief that God watches what each person does and thinks - kind of situation in which most likely to think of God - words and concepts associated with God - likelihood to think of God when worried or happy - belief that God can forgive sins - belief that God created the universe - support for the statement that 'without belief in God life is meaningless'	age, sex, social class, denominational affiliation, other religious variable	GB	2/1968	[QRL.94]	5.2.1.1 , 5.2.1.2 , 5.2.1.3. Sample size: 1,071. Fieldwork: ORC. Sponsor: ITA

Type of data	Breakdown	Area	Date	QRL Publication	Text Reference and remarks
Belief in God	denominational affiliation	GB	23-26/5/1968	[QRL.12] [QRL.28] [QRL.62] [QRL.64], 8/1968 [QRL.112], 21/7/1968	5.2.1.1. Fieldwork: GP. Sponsor: STE. Multinational
Certainty of belief/disbelief in God - conception of God - belief that God watches what each person does and thinks - kind of situation in which most likely to think of God - words and concepts associated with God - likelihood to think of God when worried or happy - belief that God can forgive sins - belief that God created the universe - support for the statement that 'without belief in God life is meaningless'	denominational affiliation, other religious variable	Northern Ireland	2/12/1968-10/1/1969	[QRL.94] [QRL.95]	5.2.1.1, 5.2.1.2, 5.2.1.3. Sample size: 694. Fieldwork: ORC. Sponsor: ITA, UTV and the Churches
Belief in a personal God who can respond to individual human beings	age, sex	GB	13-19/4/1970	[QRL.53], 13/5/1970 [QRL.100]	5.2.1.2. Sample size: 2,472. Fieldwork: LHR (032). Sponsor: DE. Data set
Belief in God - conception of God as a personal/impersonal being	age, sex, marital status, social class, education, region	GB	8-15/6/1970	[QRL.55], 5/1/1971 [QRL.101]	5.2.1.1, 5.2.1.2. Sample size: 1,395. Fieldwork: NOP (4233). Sponsor: DM
Certainty of belief/disbelief in God	age, sex	GB	20-24/9/1972	[QRL.113], 22/4/1973	5.2.1.1. Sample size: 1,026. Fieldwork:ORC (7238). Sponsor: ST. Data set

Support for the statement that 'without belief in God life is meaningless'- certainty of belief/disbelief in God - belief that God watches what each person does and thinks - likelihood to think of God when worried or happy		GB	15-20/1/1973		5.2.1.1, 5.2.1.3. Sample size: 647. Fieldwork: ORC (7/1337). Sponsor: IBA
Belief in God	age, sex, denominational affiliation, other religious variable	GB	27/4-1/5/1973	[QRL.12] [QRL.57], 14/5/1973 [QRL.64], 5/1973 [QRL.112], 13/5/1973	5.2.1.1. Sample size: 892. Fieldwork: GP (CQ.848). Sponsor: STE
Belief in a personal God/some sort of spirit or life force	age, sex, social class, region	GB	20-25/8/1974	[QRL.108] [QRL.113], 13/10/1974 [QRL.123], 14/10/1974	5.2.1.2. Sample size: 1,093. Fieldwork: ORC (34333). Sponsor: BBC
Belief in God or universal spirit - belief that this God or spirit observes actions and rewards/punishes them		GB	11/1974-1/1975	[QRL.13], 1979 [QRL.28] [QRL.69] [QRL.87], 3-5/1979	5.2.1.1. Sample size: 307. Fieldwork: GP. Sponsor: CFKF. Multinational
Belief in God		GB	29/5-2/6/1975	[QRL.12] [QRL.64], 6/1975	5.2.1.1. Fieldwork: GP (CQ.962)
Belief in God	age, sex, social class, denominational affiliation	Scotland	23-30/8/1976	[QRL.66], 11/10/1976 [QRL.103]	5.2.1.1. Sample size: 1,044. Fieldwork: STS (SOS.876). Sponsor: GH
Belief in God	age, sex, marital status, social class, region	GB	23-28/3/1977	[QRL.99]	5.2.1.1. Sample size: 1,050. Fieldwork: ORC (17704). Sponsor: BBC

Type of data	Breakdown	Area	Date	QRL Publication	Text Reference and remarks
Belief in God - belief in a personal God/some sort of spirit or life force	age, sex, social class, frequency of church attendance	GB	21-26/3/1979	[QRL.25] [QRL.57], 16/4/1979 [QRL.64], 5/1979 [QRL.70], 1978-79 [QRL.112], 15/4/1979	5.2.1.1, 5.2.1.2. Sample size: 918. Fieldwork: GP (CQ.662). Sponsor: STE
Belief in God - desire to believe in God	age, sex, denominational affiliation	GB	23-29/7/1979	[QRL.79], 21/12/1979 [QRL.93]	5.2.1.1. Sample size: 988. Fieldwork: MAR (51809/1). Sponsor: Now! Data set: SN 1366
Belief that there is only one true God/many different Gods - belief that God can save only individual souls/society as a whole	age, sex, social class, education	GB	9-10/1979	[QRL.92] [QRL.70], 1980-81	5.2.1.1. Sample size: 987. Fieldwork: GP (S.5077). Sponsor: LDC. Multinational
Belief in God/a supreme being	age, sex, social class	GB	19-24/6/1980	[QRL.80], 8/1980	5.2.1.1. Sample size: 2,067. Fieldwork: NOP (5803)

Subject	Breakdown	Country	Date	QRL references	Details
Belief in God - belief in a personal God/some sort of spirit or life force- importance of God in respondent's life		UK	3/1981	[QRL.44], 17/12/1981 [QRL.51], 11/12/1981 [QRL.70], 1982-83 [QRL.119], 26/2/1983 [QRL.125], 11/12/1981	5.2.1.1, 5.2.1.2, 5.2.1.3. Sample size: 1,543. Fieldwork: GP (S.2131). Sponsor: EVSSG. Multinational
Belief in God - belief in a personal God/some sort of spirit or life force	age, sex, frequency of church attendance	GB	8-13/4/1981	[QRL.31], 1981 [QRL.57], 20/4/1981 [QRL.64], 4/1981 [QRL.70], 1980-81 [QRL.112], 19/4/1981	5.2.1.1, 5.2.1.2. Sample size: 994. Fieldwork: GP (CQ.763). Sponsor: STE
Importance of God in respondent's life	age, sex, social class , region, denominational affiliation, frequency of church attendance, other religious variable	GB	11-15/3/1982	[QRL.42] [QRL.64], 4/1982 [QRL.70], 1982-83	5.2.1.3. Sample size: 1,032. Fieldwork: GP (CQ.808). Sponsor: U
Importance of God in respondent's life		GB	28/4-4/5/1982	[QRL.4]	5.2.1.3. Sample size: 947. Fieldwork: GP (CQ.815A). Sponsor: U
Importance of God in respondent's life	age, sex, social class , region, party political preference, denominational affiliation, frequency of church attendance, other religious variable	GB	9-15/6/1982	[QRL.36]	5.2.1.3. Sample size: 1,000. Fieldwork: GP (CQ.821B).

R-L

Type of data	Breakdown	Area	Date	QRL Publication	Text Reference and remarks
Importance to respondent of following God's will	age, sex	GB	30/6-5/7/1982	[QRL.64], 7/1982 [QRL.70], 1982-83 [QRL.112], 11/7/1982	Sample size: 885. Fieldwork: GP (CQ.824). Sponsor: STE
Importance of God in respondent's life		GB	11/1982		5.2.1.3. Sample size: 991. Fieldwork: GP (CQ.845)
Jesus Christ					
Belief that Christ was the Son of God/just a man	age, social class	GB	2-12/2/1957	[QRL.12] [QRL.30] [QRL.74], 15/4/1957	5.2.2.1. Sample size: 2,261. Fieldwork: GP (CS.1717). Sponsor: NC
Belief that Christ was the Son of God/just a man	age, sex, social class, denominational affiliation	GB	29/3-4/4/1963	[QRL.12] [QRL.23] [QRL.64], 4/1963	5.2.2.1. Fieldwork: GP
Belief that Christ was the Son of God/just a man	age, sex, social class, region, denominational affiliation, frequency of church attendance, other religious variable	England	16/12/1963-20/1/1964	[QRL.57], 20/9/1965 [QRL.113], 19/9/1965 [QRL.120] [QRL.121]	5.2.2.1. Sample size: 2,211. Fieldwork: GP (CS.5480). Sponsor: ABC TV. Data set
Belief that Christ is the Son of God - agreement with the proposition that 'people who believe in Jesus as the Son of God can expect salvation'	age, sex, social class, other religious variable	GB	2/1968	[QRL.94]	5.2.2.1, 5.2.2.2. Sample size: 1,071. Fieldwork: ORC. Sponsor: ITA

Belief	Attributes	Area	Date	References	Details
Belief that Christ is the Son of God - agreement with the proposition that 'people who believe in Jesus as the Son of God can expect salvation'		Northern Ireland	2/12/1968-10/1/1969	[QRL.94] [QRL.95]	5.2.2.1, 5.2.2.2. Sample size: 694. Fieldwork: ORC. Sponsor: ITA, UTV and the Churches
Belief that Christ is the Son of God - belief that Mary is the virgin mother of Jesus	age, sex, marital status, social class, education, region	GB	8-15/6/1970	[QRL.101]	5.2.2.1, 5.2.2.2. Sample size: 1,395. Fieldwork: NOP (4233). Sponsor: DM
Belief that Christ was the Son of God/just a man	age, sex, social class, frequency of church attendance	GB	21-26/3/1979	[QRL.25] [QRL.64], 5/1979 [QRL.70], 1978-79 [QRL.112], 15/4/1979	5.2.2.1. Sample size: 918. Fieldwork: GP (CQ.662). Sponsor:STE
Belief that Christ was the Son of God/just a man		GB	8-13/4/1981	[QRL.31], 1981 [QRL.64], 4/1981 [QRL.112], 19/4/1981 [QRL.57], 20/4/1981 [QRL.70], 1980-81	5.2.2.1. Sample size: 994. Fieldwork: GP (CQ.763). Sponsor: STE
Belief that someone called Jesus was born about 2,000 years ago, that he was born in a stable in Bethlehem, that he was visited in the stable by three wise men and shepherds soon after birth, that he was the Son of God	age, sex, denominational affiliation	Scotland	25-29/11/1981	[QRL.70], 1981-82 [QRL.88], 10-12/1981 [QRL.104], 21/12/1981	5.2.2.1, 5.2.2.2. Sample size: 1,079. Fieldwork: MORI (7477). Sponsor: SC

Type of data	Breakdown	Area	Date	QRL Publication	Text Reference and remarks
Belief that someone called Jesus was born about 2,000 years ago, that he was born in Bethlehem, that he was visited in the stable by three wise men and shepherds soon after birth, that he was the son of God	age, sex, denominational affiliation	GB	10-14/12/1981	[QRL.56], 24/12/1981 [QRL.70], 1981-82 [QRL.88], 10-12/1981	5.2.2.1, 5.2.2.2. Sample size: 1,523. Fieldwork: MORI (7550). Sponsor: DS
The Devil					
Belief in a Devil	age, social class	GB	2-12/2/1957	[QRL.12] [QRL.30] [QRL.74], 15/4/1957	5.2.3.1. Sample size: 2,261. Fieldwork: GP (CS.1717). Sponsor: NC
Belief in a Devil	age, sex, social class, denominational affiliation	GB	29/3-4/4/1963	[QRL.12] [QRL.23] [QRL.64], 4/1963	5.2.3.1. Fieldwork: GP
Belief in a Devil	age, sex, social class, region, denominational affiliation, frequency of church attendance, other religious variable	England	16/12/1963-20/1/1964	[QRL.120] [QRL.121]	5.2.3.1. Sample size: 2,211. Fieldwork: GP (CS.5480). Sponsor: ABC TV. Data set
Belief in the Devil		GB	23-26/5/1968	[QRL.12] [QRL.28] [QRL.62] [QRL.64], 8/1968	5.2.3.1. Fieldwork: GP. Sponsor: STE. Multinational
Belief in the Devil	age, sex, marital status, social class, education, region	GB	8-15/6/1970	[QRL.55], 5/1/1971 [QRL.101]	5.2.3.1. Sample size: 1,395. Fieldwork: NOP (4233). Sponsor: DM

Belief in the Devil	age, sex, denominational affiliation, other religious variable	GB	27/4-1/5/1973	[QRL.12] [QRL.57], 14/5/1973 [QRL.64], 5/1973 [QRL.112], 13/5/1973	5.2.3.1. Sample size: 892. Fieldwork: GP (CQ.848). Sponsor: STE
Belief in the Devil		GB	29/5-2/6/1975	[QRL.12] [QRL.64], 6/1975	5.2.3.1. Fieldwork: GP (CQ.962)
Belief in the Devil	age, sex, social class	GB	21-26/3/1979	[QRL.25] [QRL.64], 5/1979 [QRL.70], 1978-79 [QRL.112], 15/4/1979	5.2.3.1. Sample size: 918. Fieldwork: GP (CQ.662). Sponsor: STE
Belief in the Devil or an identifiable force of evil in this world	age, sex, social class	GB	19-24/6/1980	[QRL.80], 8/1980	5.2.3.1. Sample size: 2,067. Fieldwork: NOP (5803)
Belief in the Devil		UK	3/1981	[QRL.16] [QRL.51], 11/12/1981 [QRL.44], 17/12/1981 [QRL.119], 26/2/1983 [QRL.125], 11/12/1981 [QRL.70], 1982-83	5.2.3.1. Sample size: 1,543. Fieldwork: GP (S.2131). Sponsor: EVSSG. Multinational

Type of data	Breakdown	Area	Date	QRL Publication	Text Reference and remarks
Belief in the Devil	age, sex	GB	8-13/4/1981	[QRL.31], 1981 [QRL.64], 4/1981 [QRL.112], 19/4/1981 [QRL.57], 20/4/1981 [QRL.70], 1980-81	5.2.3.1. Sample size: 994. Fieldwork: GP (CQ.763). Sponsor: STE
The Afterlife					
Belief in life after death	age, sex, social class	GB	3/1939	[QRL.64], 10/1973 [QRL.74], 27/4/1939	5.2.4.1. Sample size: 1,761. Fieldwork: GP (S.56). Sponsor: NC. Data set: SN 2037-2045
Belief in life after death - form of life after death	age, sex, social class, denominational affiliation	GB	12/1947	[QRL.1] [QRL.10] [QRL.12] [QRL.74], 13/1/1948	5.2.4.1. Fieldwork: GP (S.159). Sponsor: NC. Multinational
Belief that present behaviour affects our destiny after death	frequency of church attendance, other religious variable	GB	1-15/12/1954	[QRL.97]	Sample size: 1,859. Fieldwork: GP. Sponsor: BBC
Belief in life after death	age, social class, party political preference	GB	2-12/2/1957	[QRL.12] [QRL.30] [QRL.74], 15/4/1957	5.2.4.1. Sample size: 2,261. Fieldwork: GP (CS.1717). Sponsor: NC

Topic	Variables	Country	Date	References	Notes
Belief in life after death	sex	GB	3/1960	[QRL.1]	5.2.4.1. Fieldwork: GP. Multinational
Belief in life after death	age, sex, social class, denominational affiliation	GB	29/3-4/4/1963	[QRL.12], [QRL.23], [QRL.64], 4/1963	5.2.4.1. Fieldwork: GP
Belief in life after death	age, sex, social class, region, denominational affliation, frequency of church attendance, other religious variable	England	16/12/1963-20/1/1964	[QRL.57], 20/9/1965 [QRL.113], 19/9/1965 [QRL.120] [QRL.121]	5.2.4.1. Sample size: 2,211. Fieldwork: GP (CS.5480), Sponsor: ABC TV. Data set
Belief in life after death - belief in heaven - belief in hell - belief in reincarnation	denominational affiliation	GB	23-26/5/1968	[QRL.12] [QRL.28] [QRL.62] [QRL.64], 8/1968 [QRL.112], 21/7/1968	5.2.4.1, 5.2.4.2. Fieldwork: GP. Sponsor: STE. Multinational
Belief in life after death	age, sex	GB	13-19/4/1970	[QRL.53], 13/5/1970 [QRL.100]	5.2.4.1. Sample size: 2,472. Fieldwork: LHR (032). Sponsor: DE. Data set
Belief in hell - description of hell - belief that death is absolutely the end - nature of life after death	age, sex, marital status, social class, education, region	GB	8-15/6/1970	[QRL.55], 5/1/1971 [QRL.101]	5.2.4.1, 5.2.4.2. Sample size: 1,395. Fieldwork: NOP (4233). Sponsor: DM

Type of data	Breakdown	Area	Date	QRL Publication	Text Reference and remarks
Belief in life after death - belief in hell - belief in heaven - belief in reincarnation	age, sex, denominational affiliation, other religious variable	GB	27/4-1/5/1973	[QRL.12], [QRL.57], 14/5/1973 [QRL.64], 5/1973 [QRL.112], 13/5/1973	5.2.4.1, 5.2.4.2. Sample size: 892. Fieldwork: GP (CQ.848). Sponsor: STE
Belief in life after death		GB	26/9-1/10/1973	[QRL.64], 10/1973	5.2.4.1. Fieldwork: GP
Belief in life after death		GB	9-15/10/1973	[QRL.12] [QRL.64], 10/1973	5.2.4.1. Fieldwork: GP
Belief in life after death	age, sex, social class, region	GB	20-25/8/1974	[QRL.108] [QRL.113], 13/10/1974 [QRL.123], 14/10/1974	5.2.4.1. Sample size: 1,093. Fieldwork: ORC (34333). Sponsor: BBC
Belief in life after death		GB	11/1974-1/1975	[QRL.13], 1979 [QRL.14] [QRL.28] [QRL.69] [QRL.87], 3-5/1979	5.2.4.1. Sample size: 307. Fieldwork: GP. Sponsor: CFKF. Multinational
Belief in life after death - belief in hell - belief in heaven - belief in reincarnation		GB	29/5-2/6/1975	[QRL.12] [QRL.64], 6/1975	5.2.4.1, 5.2.4.2. Fieldwork: GP (CQ.962)
Belief in life after death	age, sex, social class, denominational affiliation	Scotland	23-30/8/1976	[QRL.66], 11/10/1976 [QRL.103]	5.2.4.1. Sample size: 1,044. Fieldwork: STS (SOS.876). Sponsor: GH

Subject	Breakdown	Region	Date	QRL references	Details
Belief in life after death		GB	22-27/2/1978	[QRL.13], 1978 [QRL.64], 3/1978	5.2.4.1. Fieldwork: GP
Belief in hell - belief in heaven - belief in reincarnation	age, sex, social class, frequency of church attendance	GB	21-26/3/1979	[QRL.25] [QRL.64], 5/1979 [QRL.70], 1978-79 [QRL.112], 15/4/1979	5.2.4.2. Sample size: 918. Fieldwork: GP (CQ.662). Sponsor: STE
Belief in life after death - nature of life after death	age, sex, denominational affiliation	GB	23-29/7/1979	[QRL.79], 21/12/1979 [QRL.93]	5.2.4.1. Sample size: 988. Fieldwork: MAR (51809/1). Sponsor: Now! Data set: SN 1366
Belief in life after death	age, sex, social class, education	GB	9-10/1979	[QRL.92] [QRL.70], 1980-81	5.2.4.1. Sample size: 987. Fieldwork: GP (S.5077). Sponsor: LDC. Multinational
Belief in life after death	age, sex, social class	GB	19-24/6/1980	[QRL.80], 8/1980	5.2.4.1. Sample size: 2,067. Fieldwork: NOP (5803)

R-L*

Type of data	Breakdown	Area	Date	QRL Publication	Text Reference and remarks
Belief in life after death - belief in hell - belief in heaven - belief in reincarnation		UK	3/1981	[QRL.16] [QRL.44], 17/12/1981 [QRL.51], 11/12/1981 [QRL.70], 1982-83 [QRL.119], 26/2/1983 [QRL.125], 11/12/1981	5.2.4.1, 5.2.4.2. Sample size: 1,543. Fieldwork: GP (S.2131). Sponsor: EVSSG. Multinational
Belief in hell - belief in heaven - belief in reincarnation	age, sex, frequency of church attendance	GB	8-13/4/1981	[QRL.31], 1981 [QRL.64], 4/1981 [QRL.112], 19/4/1981 [QRL.57], 20/4/1981 [QRL.70], 1980-81	5.2.4.2. Sample size: 994. Fieldwork: GP (CQ. 763). Sponsor: STE
Belief in life after death	age, sex	GB	25-30/11/1981	[QRL.31], 1981 [QRL.64], 12/1981 [QRL.70], 1981-82 [QRL.112], 27/12/1981	5.2.4.1. Sample size: 968. Fieldwork: GP (CQ.796). Sponsor: STE

Other beliefs

Topic	Breakdown	Location	Date	Reference	Notes
Belief in the possibility of exchanging messages with the dead		GB	3/1940	[QRL.9] [QRL.12]	Sample size: 1,796. Fieldwork: GP (S.68). Data set: SN 2037-2045
Superstitions in which respondent believed - extent to which respondent threw salt over his shoulder, touched wood and walked under ladders	age, sex, social class	GB	5/1946	[QRL.9] [QRL.12]	Sample size: 1,830. Fieldwork: GP (SS.133). Data set: SN 2037-2045
Belief in telepathy	age, sex, social class	GB	9/1949	[QRL.12] [QRL.74], 26/10/1949	Fieldwork: GP (S.190)
Belief in ghosts - sighting of a ghost	age, sex, social class, region, education	GB	3/1950	[QRL.12] [QRL.74], 12/6/1950	Fieldwork: GP (S.210)
Use of lucky mascots - whether respondent had a specially lucky/unlucky day - visits to a fortune-teller - experience of fortune-telling coming true - extent of horoscope reading - notice taken of advice in horoscopes - credence given to horoscopes	age, sex, marital status, social class, region	England	1/1951	[QRL.15]	Sample size: 1,760. Fieldwork: RSOP. Sponsor: *People*
Belief in foretelling the future	sex	GB	3/1951	[QRL.12] [QRL.74], 11/8/1951	Fieldwork: GP (S.232)
Belief in the possibility of exchanging messages with the dead		GB	2-12/2/1957	[QRL.12]	Sample size: 2,261. Fieldwork: GP (CS.1717). Sponsor:NC
Extent to which respondent threw salt over his shoulder, avoided walking under ladders, regarded a black cat as lucky/unlucky, considered bad luck attached to a particular colour	sex	GB	1968	[QRL.61], 27/2/1968	Fieldwork: ORC

Type of data	Breakdown	Area	Date	QRL Publication	Text Reference and remarks
Extent of horoscope reading - credence given to horoscopes - belief in the ability of faith-healers to cure - visits to a faith-healer - belief in telepathy - incidence of telepathic experience - belief in fortune-telling - visits to a fortune-teller - belief in the possibility of communicating with a dead person - belief in water-divining	age, sex, social class	GB	1968	[QRL.113], 5/5/1968	5.2.5.1. Fieldwork: ORC. Sponsor: ST
Belief in ghosts - belief in the possibility/desirability of speaking with the dead - attempts at speaking with the dead - belief in witchcraft - attendance at magic rites - extent to which respondent superstitious - particulars of superstitions held by respondent - use of lucky charm/mascot - knowledge of birth sign - frequency of horoscope reading - notice taken of horoscopes - visits to a fortune-teller - premonitions of future events - sense of having lived through a situation before	age, sex, marital status, social class, education, region	GB	8-15/6/1970	[QRL.55], 5/1/1971 [QRL.101]	5.2.5.1. Sample size: 1,395. Fieldwork: NOP (4233). Sponsor: DM
Reading of horoscopes - accuracy of horoscopes - importance attached to horoscopes by respondent - knowledge of birth sign	sex	GB	20-24/9/1972	[QRL.113], 22/4/1973	Sample size: 1,026. Fieldwork: ORC (7238). Sponsor: ST. Data set
Belief in horoscopes		GB	4-8/1/1973	[QRL.12] [QRL.64], 2/1973	Fieldwork: GP

Variables	Breakdown	Country	Date	Source	Notes
Sense of having lived through a situation before - sighting of a ghost - incidence of paying to have fortune told - belief in hypnotism, black magic, horoscopes, thought transference, ghosts, flying saucers, faith-healing, the ability to forecast something before it happens, lucky charms/mascots, and exchanging messages with the dead		GB	9-15/10/1973	[QRL.12] [QRL.64], 10/1973	5.2.5.1. Fieldwork: GP
Belief in hypnotism, black magic, horoscopes, thought transference, ghosts, flying saucers, faith-healing, the ability to forecast something before it happens, lucky charms/mascots, and exchanging messages with the dead - sense of having lived through a situation before -sighting of a ghost - incidence of paying to have fortune told		GB	29/5-2/6/1975	[QRL.12] [QRL.64], 6/1975	5.2.5.1. Fieldwork: GP (CQ.962)
Belief in hypnotism, black magic, horoscopes, thought transference, ghosts, flying saucers, faith-healing, the ability to forecast something before it happens, lucky charms/mascots, and exchanging messages with the dead - sense of having lived through a situation before - sighting of a ghost - incidence of paying to have fortune told		GB	22-27/2/1978	[QRL.13], 1978 [QRL.64], 3/1978	5.2.5.1. Fieldwork: GP
Frequency of horoscope reading - attention paid to horoscopes in planning daily life - visits to astrologer/fortune-teller in past twelve months - accuracy of fortune-teller's predictions - extent and nature of fortune-teller's influence - degree to which respondent superstitious - practice of particular superstitions - role of fate/luck in life	age, sex	GB	18-19/12/1979	[QRL.37] [QRL.79], 29/2/1980	5.2.5.1. Sample size: 961. Fieldwork: MAR (51896). Sponsor: Now! Telephone poll

Type of data	Breakdown	Area	Date	QRL Publication	Text Reference and remarks
Experience of feeling in touch with someone who was far away, of seeing events that occurred at a great distance as they were happening, and of feeling in touch with someone who had died		UK	3/1981	[QRL.70], 1982-83	Sample size: 1,543. Fieldwork: GP (S.2131). Sponsor: EVSSG. Multinational
Belief in hypnotism, black magic, horoscopes, thought transference, ghosts, flying saucers, faith-healing, the ability to forecast something before it happens, lucky charms/mascots, and exchanging messages with the dead - sense of having lived through a situation before - sighting of a ghost - incidence of paying to have fortune told	age, sex	GB	25-30/11/1981	[QRL.31], 1981 [QRL.64], 12/1981 [QRL.70], 1981-82 [QRL.112], 27/12/1981	5.2.5.1. Sample size: 968. Fieldwork: GP (CQ.796). Sponsor: STE

PERSONAL RELIGION: PRACTICES

Prayer

Type of data	Breakdown	Area	Date	QRL Publication	Text Reference and remarks
Prevalence of formal family prayers/grace	age	GB	7/1948	[QRL.54], 10/8/1948	6.1.1.2. Sample size: 2,055. Fieldwork: MO (09/1). Sponsor: DG
Belief in prayer - incidence of regular prayer by any adult member of respondent's household	age, sex, social class, denominational affiliation	GB	1/1950	[QRL.3] [QRL.12] [QRL.74], 9/2/1950	6.1.1.1, 6.1.1.2. Fieldwork: GP. Sponsor: NC
Belief that God answers prayer	frequency of church attendance, other religious variable	GB	1-15/12/1954	[QRL.97]	6.1.1.2. Sample size: 1,859. Fieldwork: GP. Sponsor: BBC

Belief in teaching children to say prayers		GB	2-12/2/1957	[QRL.12] [QRL.74], 15/4/1957	6.1.1.2. Sample size: 2,261. Fieldwork: GP (CS.1717). Sponsor: NC
Incidence of regular prayer	age, sex, social class, region, denominational affiliation, frequency of church attendance, other religious variable	England	16/12/1963-20/1/1964	[QRL.120] [QRL.121] [QRL.57], 20/9/1965	6.1.1.1. Sample size: 2,211. Fieldwork: GP (CS.5480). Sponsor: ABC TV. Data set.
Belief that it is a good/bad thing to pray to God for peace/the life of a sick friend or relative/help for other people/a happier family life/victory in war/success in one's job/relief from money problems	other religious variable	GB	2/1968	[QRL.94]	6.1.1.2. Sample size: 1,071. Fieldwork: ORC. Sponsor: ITA
Belief that it is a good/bad thing to pray to God for peace/the life of a sick friend or relative/help for other people/a happier family life/victory in war/success in one's job/relief from money problems		Northern Ireland	2/12/1968-10/1/1969	[QRL.94] [QRL.95]	6.1.1.2. Sample size: 694. Fieldwork: ORC. Sponsor: ITA, UTV and the Churches
Frequency of prayer - habit of praying regularly/only in moments of crisis - whether respondent did/would teach his children to pray - kind of prayers taught to children	age, sex, marital status, social class, education, region	GB	8-15/6/1970	[QRL.55], 5/1/1971 [QRL.101]	6.1.1.1, 6.1.1.2. Sample size: 1,395. Fieldwork: NOP (4233). Sponsor: DM
Whether respondent had said a prayer on the previous day	age, sex	GB	20-24/9/1972	[QRL.113], 22/4/1973	6.1.1.1. Sample size: 1,026. Fieldwork: ORC (7238). Sponsor: ST. Data set

Type of data	Breakdown	Area	Date	QRL Publication	Text Reference and remarks
Prevalence of prayer, meditation or contemplation		UK	3/1981	[QRL.70], 1982-83	6.1.1.1. Sample size: 1,543. Fieldwork: GP (S.2131). Sponsor: EVSSG. Multinational.
The Bible					
The Bible as the book which had impressed respondent most	sex	GB	2/1938	[QRL.9] [QRL.12]	6.1.2.4. Fieldwork: GP
The Bible as the best book which respondent had ever read		GB	5/1948	[QRL.12]	6.1.2.4. Fieldwork: GP
Availability of a Bible in respondent's house - precise whereabouts of Bible - sort of occasions on which Bible used		GB	7/1948	[QRL.54], 10/8/1948	6.1.2.1, 6.1.2.2. Sample size: 2,055. Fieldwork: MO (09/1). Sponsor: DG
Ability to name any of the four Gospels	age, sex, social class, denominational affiliation	GB	10/1949	[QRL.12] [QRL.74], 3/1/1950	6.1.2.4. Fieldwork: GP
Choice of the Bible as one of three books with which to be banished to a desert island - availability of a Bible in respondent's home - recall of having read anything in the Bible since leaving school - views about modern translations of the Bible		GB	18-29/2/1954	[QRL.12] [QRL.74], 8/3/1954	6.1.2.1, 6.1.2.2, 6.1.2.4. Fieldwork: GP (S.390)
Length of time since last looking at the Bible - belief in the literal truth and contemporary relevance of the Old Testament - belief that a man can be a Christian even if he does not consider every word of the Bible to be true	frequency of church attendance, other religious variable	GB	1-15/12/1954	[QRL.97]	6.1.2.2, 6.1.2.3. Sample size: 1,859. Fieldwork: GP. Sponsor: BBC

Belief/Topic	Variables	Country	Date	Reference	Details
Belief that a person can be a Christian even if he does not consider every word of the New Testament to be true	age	GB	2-12/2/1957	[QRL.12] [QRL.74], 15/4/1957	6.1.2.3. Sample size: 2,261. Fieldwork: GP (CS.1717). Sponsor: NC
Belief in the divine authority of the Old/New Testament - extent to which idea of the divine authority of the Bible is essential to the Christian Church		GB	1/1960	[QRL.64], 5/1979	6.1.2.3. Fieldwork: GP
Prevalence of regular Bible-reading	age, sex, social class, denominational affiliation, region, frequency of church attendance, other religious variable	England	16/12/1963-20/1/1964	[QRL.57], 20/9/1965 [QRL.120] [QRL.121]	6.1.2.2. Sample size: 2,211. Fieldwork: GP (CS.5480), Sponsor: ABC TV. Data set.
Belief that the miracles of the Bible really happened	age, sex, social class, other religious variable	GB	2/1968	[QRL.94]	6.1.2.3. Sample size: 1,071. Fieldwork: ORC. Sponsor : ITA
Belief that the miracles in the Bible happened as described there	denominational affiliation	Northern Ireland	3-8/1968	[QRL.26]	6.1.2.3. Sample size: 1,291. Fieldwork: UOS. Sponsor: R.Rose. Data set: SN 1040
Belief that the miracles of the Bible really happened	other religious variable	Northern Ireland	2/12/1968-10/1/1969	[QRL.94] [QRL.95]	6.1.2.3. Sample size: 694. Fieldwork: ORC. Sponsor: ITA, UTV and the Churches

Type of data	Breakdown	Area	Date	QRL Publication	Text Reference and remarks
Belief that the Bible should be taken literally - length of time since last reading the Bible	age, sex, marital status, social class, education, region	GB	8-15/6/1970	[QRL.55], 5/1/1971 [QRL.101]	6.1.2.2, 6.1.2.3. Sample size: 1,395. Fieldwork: NOP (4233). Sponsor: DM
Whether respondent had read the Bible/other religious books on the previous day	age, sex	GB	20-24/9/1972	[QRL.113], 22/4/1973	6.1.2.2. Sample size: 1,026. Fieldwork: ORC (7238). Sponsor: ST. Data set.
Belief in Bible truth		GB	4-8/1/1973	[QRL.12] [QRL.64], 2/1973	6.1.2.3. Fieldwork: GP
Personal ownership of a Bible - version of the Bible owned - method by which the Bible was obtained - ownership of a Bible by other members of household - length of time since last reading the Bible - particular part of the Bible which was read on that occasion - ability to name any modern translations of the Bible	age, sex, social class, region	GB	10-15/4/1973	[QRL.45] [QRL.107], no.10	6.1.2.1, 6.1.2.2, 6.1.2.4. Sample size: 2,033. Fieldwork: NOP (6746). Sponsor: BS
Personal ownership of a Bible - version of the Bible owned - method by which the Bible was obtained - ownership of a Bible by other members of household- length of time since last reading the Bible - particular part of the Bible which was read on that occasion - ability to name any modern translations of the Bible	age, social class, region	GB	4/1976	[QRL.72] 30/9/1976 [QRL.107], no.10	6.1.2.1, 6.1.2.2, 6.1.2.4. Sample size: 2,055. Fieldwork: NOP. Sponsor: BS

Subject	Breakdown variables	Area	Date of fieldwork	QRL references	Reference / Sample / Fieldwork / Sponsor
Acquisition of a Bible by purchase or gift within the last year - source of acquisition - version of the Bible obtained		GB	15-21/2/1979		6.1.2.1. Sample size: 993. Fieldwork: BMRB. Sponsor: BS
Personal purchase of a Bible within the past year either to keep or to give to someone else - source of purchase - version of the Bible bought		GB	21-26/2/1979	[QRL.44] 11/10/1979 [QRL.51], 12/10/1979	6.1.2.1. Sample size: 2,024. Fieldwork: RSGB (6907). Sponsor: BS
Belief in the divine authority of the Old/New Testament - extent to which idea of the divine authority of the Bible is essential to the Christian Church	sex, social class, frequency of church attendance	GB	21-26/3/1979	[QRL.25] [QRL.64], 5/1979 [QRL.70], 1978-79 [QRL.112], 15/4/1979	6.1.2.3. Sample size: 918. Fieldwork: GP (CQ.662). Sponsor: STE
Belief in the divine authority of the Old/New Testament - extent to which idea of the divine authority of the Bible is essential to the Christian Church		GB	8-13/4/1981	[QRL.31], 1981 [QRL.57], 20/4/1981 [QRL.64], 4/1981 [QRL.70], 1980-81 [QRL.112], 19/4/1981	6.1.2.3. Sample size: 994. Fieldwork: GP (CQ.763). Sponsor: STE
Personal ownership of a Bible - ownership of a Bible by other members of household - version of Bibles owned - occasion on which the Bible was last read - part of the Bible which was read on that occasion - situation in which the Bible-reading occurred - personal purchase of a Bible within the past year - source of purchase - person for whom the Bible was bought - version of the Bible bought	age, sex, social class, region, denominational affiliation, frequency of church attendance, other religious variable	GB	28/4-4/5/1982	[QRL.4] [QRL.107], no.14	6.1.2.1, 6.1.2.2. Sample size: 947. Fieldwork: GP (CQ.815A). Sponsor: BS.

Type of data	Breakdown	Area	Date	QRL Publication	Text Reference and remarks
Personal purchase of a Bible within the past year - source of purchase - person for whom the Bible was bought - version of the Bible bought	age, sex, social class, frequency of church attendance	GB	19-24/5/1982	[QRL.4]	6.1.2.1. Sample size: 963. Fieldwork: GP (CQ.818). Sponsor: BS
Religious broadcasting					
Use of radio services as a reason for staying away from church		GB	2/1938	[QRL.9] [QRL.12]	Fieldwork: GP
Tendency to regard BBC religious services as a substitute for attending church - frequency of listening to BBC religious services - whether the reason for listening to such services was deliberate/because the wireless happened to be on - incidence of switching off the radio if a religious service came on	age, sex, region, denominational affiliation, frequency of church attendance, other religious variable	GB	1947	[QRL.75], 6/11/1947	6.1.3.2. Fieldwork: RSNR. Sponsor: NR
Prevalence of listening to BBC religious broadcasts - normal/previous Sunday's radio audience for 'The Morning Service'/ 'The people's service'/ 'Sunday Half Hour'/The Evening Service' - appreciation of talks, discussions and plays about religious subjects - help received in the past from any preacher on the radio - reasons for listening to religious broadcasts	age, sex, marital status, social class, region, denominational affiliation, frequency of church attendance, other religious variable	GB	1-15/12/1954	[QRL.7] [QRL.97]	6.1.3.3. Sample size: 1,859. Fieldwork: GP. Sponsor: BBC
Frequency of listening to/watching religious services on wireless/television		GB	2-12/2/1957	[QRL.12]	Sample size: 2,261. Fieldwork: GP (CS.1717). Sponsor: NC

Extent of listening to/watching religious services on TV - opinion of the usefulness of such services - extent to which TV services were a substitute for church-going amongst people who could go - whether BBC/ITV provided religious programmes out of choice/necessity - recognition of religious TV programmes - attitude to religious programmes being shown on week-evenings - which of five religious TV programmes ('Meeting Point', 'Songs of Praise', 'Sunday Break', 'About Religion', 'Living your Life') seen on previous Sunday - whether respondent made a point of watching the programme(s)/ another member of the family insisted on viewing/the TV happened to be on at the time - occasion on which 'Meeting Point'/'Songs of Praise'/'Sunday Break'/'About Religion' last seen - rating of the content and presentation of 'Sunday Break'	age, sex, social class, region, denominational affiliation, frequency of church attendance, other religious variable	England	16/12/1963-20/1/1964	[QRL.120] [QRL.121]	6.1.3.4. Sample size: 2,211. Fieldwork: GP (CS.5480). Sponsor: ABC TV. Data set

Type of data	Breakdown	Area	Date	QRL Publication	Text Reference and remarks
Viewing of individual religious TV programmes - recognition of religious TV programmes - action taken when a religious programme came on TV (switch off the set/leave the set on but not really listen/pay attention) - incidence of switching on the TV set in order to listen to religious programmes - kinds of people thought likely to watch religious TV programmes - appropriateness of the content of present religious TV programmes - whether religious TV programmes should be mainly for people who go/do not often go to church - whether TV should concern itself with giving religious instruction to children - perceptions of the main purpose of religious TV - extent of agreement with reasons sometimes given for not watching religious TV - TV programmes (including religious ones) considered likely to help people with their problems	age, sex, other religious variable	GB	2/1968	[QRL.94]	6.1.3 5. Sample size: 1,071. Fieldwork: ORC. Sponsor: ITA
Incidence of watching/listening to religious TV/radio programmes last Sunday - intention of doing so on Easter Sunday		GB	4/1968	[QRL.112], 14/4/1968	Fieldwork: GP. Sponsor: STE

Description		Region	Date	QRL	Reference
Action taken when a religious programme came on TV (switch off the set/leave the set on but not really listen/pay attention) - incidence of switching on the TV set in order to listen to religious programmes - kinds of people thought likely to watch religious TV programmes - appropriateness of the content of present religious TV programmes - whether religious TV programmes should be mainly for people who go/do not often go to church - whether TV should concern itself with giving religious instruction to children - perceptions of the main purpose of religious TV - extent of agreement with reasons sometimes given for not watching religious TV - TV programmes (including religious ones) considered likely to help people with their problems		Northern Ireland	2/12/1968-10/1/1969	[QRL.94] [QRL.95]	6.1.3.5. Sample size: 694. Fieldwork: ORC. Sponsor: ITA, UTV and the Churches
Desire for more/same/less time to be given to religious TV programmes		GB	19-25/9/1971		Fieldwork: LHR (135). Data set
Belief that there were too many religious TV programmes on Sundays		GB	18-24/10/1971		Fieldwork: LHR (140). Data set
Recognition of the religious nature of designated religious TV programmes - other attributes of such programmes	region, other religious variable	GB	15-20/1/1973	[QRL.91]	6.1.3.6. Sample size: 647. Fieldwork: ORC (7/1337). Sponsor: IBA
Appreciation of hymns and religious music programmes/ documentaries and news programmes about religious questions/general programmes about Christianity presented from a Christian point of view - belief that there was too little/ too much/the right amount of religious programming on TV		GB	2/1980		6.1.3.7. Sample size: 1,126. Fieldwork: BMRB. Sponsor: LWT

Type of data	Breakdown	Area	Date	QRL Publication	Text Reference and remarks
Belief that there was too much/too little/the right amount of religious programming on TV - whether BBC or ITV had the best religious programmes	sex	GB	9-12/5/1980	[QRL.70], 1980-81 [QRL.88], 1980 [QRL.113], 8/6/1980	Sample size: 1,140. Fieldwork: MORI (5726). Sponsor: ST
Belief that there was too much/too little/the right amount of religious programming on TV - whether BBC or ITV had the best religious programmes		GB	16-18/10/1982	[QRL.70], 1982-83 [QRL.88], 10/1982 [QRL.113], 7/11/1982	Sample size: 1,107. Fieldwork: MORI (2097). Sponsor: ST
Christian festivals					
Extent of, and reasons for, self-denial during Lent	age, sex, social class	GB	2/1939	[QRL.9] [QRL.12] [QRL.74], 8/3/1939	6.1.4.3. Sample size: 1,523. Fieldwork: GP (S.55). Sponsor: NC. Data set: SN 2037-2045
Extent to which Christmas was regarded mainly as a religious festival/ holiday/ opportunity to meet family and friends/ occasion for eating and drinking - whether Christmas was becoming more/less religious than it had been during respondent's childhood	sex	GB	16-21/12/1964	[QRL.12] [QRL.64], 1/1965 [QRL.112], 27/12/1964	6.1.4.1. Fieldwork: GP. Sponsor: STE
Extent to which Easter was regarded mainly as a religious festival/holiday	age, sex, social class, region, denominational affiliation	GB	4/1968	[QRL.57], 15/4/1968 [QRL.112], 14/4/1968	6.1.4.3. Fieldwork: GP. Sponsor: STE

Subject	Variables	Area	Date	Reference	Details
Extent to which Christmas was regarded mainly as a family/religious occasion	age	GB	10-15/12/1969	[QRL.77], 12/1969	6.1.4.1. Sample size: 1,744. Fieldwork: NOP (4000). Data set: SN 69038
Extent to which Christmas was regarded mainly as a religious festival/ holiday/ opportunity to meet family and friends/ occasion for eating and drinking - whether Christmas was becoming more/less religious than it had been during respondent's childhood	sex	GB	11-14/12/1969	[QRL.12] [QRL.57], 23/12/1969 [QRL.64], 12/1969	6.1.4.1. Fieldwork: GP. Sponsor: DT
Incidence of meat-eating on Friday - Incidence of self-denial during Lent	age, sex, marital status, social class, education, region	GB	8-15/6/1970	[QRL.101]	6.1.4.3. Sample size: 1,395. Fieldwork: NOP (4233). Sponsor: DM
Extent to which Christmas was regarded mainly as a religious festival/opportunity to meet family and friends/holiday/occasion for eating and drinking - whether Christmas was becoming more/less religious than it had been during respondent's childhood		GB	17-20/12/1970	[QRL.12] [QRL.64], 1/1971	6.1.4.1. Fieldwork: GP
Extent to which Christmas was regarded as a family/religious occasion		GB	28/11-3/12/1972		6.1.4.1. Fieldwork: NOP (6401). Data set: SN 069
Extent to which Christmas was regarded mainly as a family/religious occasion		GB	12/1972	[QRL.113], 24/12/1972	6.1.4.1. Sample size: 912. Fieldwork: ORC. Sponsor: ST
Extent to which Christmas was regarded mainly as a religious festival/holiday/opportunity to meet family and friends/occasion for eating and drinking		GB	16-23/12/1974	[QRL.12] [QRL.64], 1/1975	6.1.4.1. Fieldwork: GP

Type of data	Breakdown	Area	Date	QRL Publication	Text Reference and remarks
Extent to which Christmas was regarded mainly as a religious festival/holiday/opportunity to meet family and friends/occasion for eating and drinking		GB	21-28/11/1975	[QRL.12], [QRL.64], 12/1975	6.1.4.1. Sample size: 937. Fieldwork: GP. Sponsor: STE
Extent to which Christmas was regarded mainly as a religious festival/holiday/opportunity to meet family and friends/occasion for eating and drinking		GB	24-29/11/1976	[QRL.64], 12/1976	6.1.4.1. Fieldwork: GP
Extent to which people were more/less religious at Christmas than during the rest of the year		Scotland	25-29/11/1981	[QRL.88], 10-12/1981	Sample size: 1,079. Fieldwork: MORI (7477). Sponsor: SC
Rites of passage Incidence of church marriage	frequency of church attendance	GB	1947	[QRL.75], 30/10/1947	6.2.1.3. Fieldwork: RSNR. Sponsor: NR
Incidence of church/registry office marriage		GB	5-16/4/1952	[QRL.12]	6.2.1.3. Fieldwork: GP (S.302A)
Attitude towards infant baptism - incidence of church/registry office marriage		GB	2-12/2/1957	[QRL.12], [QRL.74], 15/4/1957	6.2.1.2, 6.2.1.3. Sample size: 2,261. Fieldwork: GP (CS.1717). Sponsor: NC
Preference for a church baptism/church marriage/church burial if forced to choose only one of the three - reasons for making this choice	age, sex, marital status, social class, education, region	GB	8-15/6/1970	[QRL.101]	6.2.1.4. Sample size: 1,395. Fieldwork: NOP (4233). Sponsor: DM

Incidence of/preference for church marriage	age, sex, marital status, social class, region	GB	23-28/3/1977	[QRL.99]	6.2.1.3. Sample size: 1,050. Fieldwork: ORC (17704). Sponsor: BBC
Extent of agreement with the proposition that 'it is better to get married in church than in a registry office'	region	GB	29-30/5/1981	[QRL.88], 5-10/1981	6.2.1.3. Sample size: 1,886. Fieldwork: MORI (6756). Sponsor: ST. Data set: SN 1617

Denominational affiliation

Religious denomination		GB	8/1943		Sample size: 1,937. Fieldwork: GP (S.101). Data set: SN 2037-2045
Religious denomination		GB	12/1943		Sample size: 1,773. Fieldwork: GP (S.104). Data set: SN 2037-2045
Religious denomination		GB	5/1947		Fieldwork: GP (S.150)
Religious denomination		GB	1947	[QRL.75], 6/11/1947	Fieldwork: RSNR. Sponsor: NR
Religious denomination		GB	9/1947	[QRL.15]	Sample size: 3,019. Fieldwork: RSOP

Type of data	Breakdown	Area	Date	QRL Publication	Text Reference and remarks
Religious denomination		GB	12/1947		Fieldwork: GP (S.159). Sponsor: NC Multinational
Religious denomination		GB	3/1948		Fieldwork: GP (S.164)
Religious denomination		GB	4-5/1948		Sample size: 6.114. Fieldwork: MO (48C). Sponsor: DT
Religious denomination		GB	1948		Fieldwork: GP (S.166)
Religious denomination		GB	1948		Fieldwork: GP (S.168)
Religious denomination		GB	1948	[QRL.53], 20/9/1948	Fieldwork: DEP. Sponsor: DE
Religious denomination		GB	9/1948		Fieldwork: GP (S.171)
Religious denomination		GB	10/1948		Fieldwork: GP (S.172)
Religious denomination		GB	1/1949		Fieldwork: GP (S.175A)
Religious denomination		GB	1949		Sample size: 2,051. Fieldwork: MO
Religious denomination		GB	8/1949		Fieldwork: GP
Religious denomination		GB	10/1949		Fieldwork: GP
Religious denomination	social class	GB	1/1950	[QRL.3] [QRL.15]	Fieldwork: GP
Religious denomination		GB	5-16/4/1952		Fieldwork: GP (S.302A)

Religious denomination		England & Wales	6-21/5/1952	[QRL.116]	Sample size: 4,948. Fieldwork: GP. Sponsor: NC
Religious denomination		GB	1/1953		Fieldwork: GP (S.340)
Religious denomination	frequency of church attendance, other religious variable	GB	1-15/12/1954	[QRL.7] [QRL.97]	Sample size: 1,859. Fieldwork: GP Sponsor: BBC
Religious denomination- former religious denomination- whether other members of family/parents belonged to the same denomination as respondent		GB	2-12/2/1957	[QRL.12] [QRL.74], 16/4/1957	Sample size: 2,261. Fieldwork: GP (CS.1717). Sponsor: NC
Religious denomination		GB	7-12/3/1958		Fieldwork: GP (CQ.63)
Religious denomination		GB	3-7/5/1958		Fieldwork: GP (CQ.70B).
Religious denomination Church to which respondent belonged		GB GB	11/1958 6-7/1959		Sponsor: NC Fieldwork: GP Sample size: 963. Fieldwork: RSL. Sponsor: G.A. Almond and S. Verba. Data set: SN 370. Multinational
Religious denomination		GB	11/1959		Fieldwork: GP
Religious denomination		GB	3/1960		Fieldwork: GP. Multinational
Religious denomination	other religious variable	GB	3-7/11/1960	[QRL.64], 11/1960	Sample size: 1,150. Fieldwork: GP
Religious denomination		GB	19-24/10/1961		Fieldwork: GP

Type of data	Breakdown	Area	Date	QRL Publication	Text Reference and remarks
Religious denomination		England and Wales	3/1962		Sample size: 1,415. Fieldwork: RSL. Sponsor: W.G.Runciman. Data set: SN 028
Religious denomination		GB	6/1962		Sample size: 1,000. Fieldwork: GP (CQ.275)
Religious denomination		GB	29/9-6/10/1962		Fieldwork: GP
Religious denomination		GB	11/1962		Fieldwork: GP
Religious denomination		GB	12/1962		Fieldwork: GP
Religious denomination		GB	29/3-4/4/1963		Fieldwork: GP
Religious denomination		GB	12-20/4/1963		Sample size: 1,088. Fieldwork: GP (CQ.313)
Religious denomination		GB	26/4-3/5/1963		Sample size: 1,091. Fieldwork: GP (CQ.315)
Religion - parents' religion when respondent was young		GB	24/5-13/8/1963		Sample size: 2,009. Fieldwork: BMRB. Sponsor: D.Butler and D.Stokes. Data set: SN 1090
Religious denomination		GB	28/6-2/7/1963		Fieldwork: GP. Sponsor: STE

Subject	Variables	Area	Date	References	Details
Religious denomination		GB	12-17/7/1963		Fieldwork: GP Sample size: 1,057.
Religious denomination		GB	25-30/7/1963		Fieldwork: GP (CQ.328) Sample size: 1,048.
Religious denomination		GB	1-6/8/1963		Fieldwork: GP (CQ.329) Sample size: 1,081.
Religious denomination		GB	8-13/8/1963		Fieldwork: GP (CQ.330) Sponsor: STE Sample size: 1,068.
Religious denomination		GB	17-24/9/1963		Fieldwork: GP (CQ.336) Sample size: 2,211.
Religious denomination	age, sex, social class, region, frequency of church attendance, other religious variable	England	16/12/1963-20/1/1964	[QRL.113], 19/9/1965 [QRL.120] [QRL.121]	Fieldwork: GP (CS.5480). Sponsor: ABC TV. Data set
Religious denomination	party political preference	GB	17/9 -13/10/1964	[QRL.63]	Sample size: 11,270. Fieldwork: GP. Sponsor: DT. Six separate surveys. Data set: SN 2051
Religious denomination		GB	10/1964		Sample size: 1,005. Fieldwork: MO. Sponsor: L.M.Harris

Type of data	Breakdown	Area	Date	QRL Publication	Text Reference and remarks
Religion - parents' religion when respondent was young		GB	16/10 -5/12/1964		Sample size: 1,769. Fieldwork: BMRB. Sponsor: D.Butler and D.Stokes. Data set: SN 1091
Religious denomination		GB	15-20/1/1965		Fieldwork: GP. Sponsor: DT
Religious denomination		GB	26/2-2/3/1965		Sample size: 1,000. Fieldwork: GP. Sponsor: DT
Religion	age, sex, social class	GB	3/1965	[QRL.73], 27/5/1965	Sample size: 2,160. Fieldwork: NOP. Sponsor: NS
Religion		GB	25-29/3/1965	[QRL.32]	Sample size: 1,997. Fieldwork: NOP (1284). Sponsor: ALRA
Religious denomination		GB	6-11/5/1965		Fieldwork: GP
Religious denomination		GB	10-15/9/1965		Sample size: 1,000. Fieldwork: GP
Religious denomination		GB	7-12/10/1965		Fieldwork: GP

Topic	Area	Date	Reference	Details
Religion	GB	19-25/10/1965		Sample size: 1,042. Fieldwork: NOP. Sponsor: DM
Religious denomination	GB	4-9/11/1965		Fieldwork: GP
Religious denomination	GB	31/12/1965 - 4/1/1966		Fieldwork: GP
Religious denomination	GB	11-15/2/1966		Fieldwork: GP
Religion - parents' religion when respondent was young	GB	1/4-14/6/1966		Sample size: 1,874. Fieldwork: BMRB. Sponsor: D.Butler and D.Stokes. Data set: SN 1092
Religious denomination	GB	23-29/1/1967	[QRL.117]	Fieldwork: GP
Religion	GB	15-20/2/1967		Sample size: 1,899. Fieldwork: NOP (2171). Sponsor: ALRA
Religious denomination	GB	2-7/5/1967		Fieldwork: GP. Sponsor: STE
Religion	GB	13-18/9/1967		Sample size: 1,810. Fieldwork: NOP (2449). Sponsor: ALRA. Data set: SN 67027
Religion	Wales	3-4/1968	[QRL.27]	Sample size: 1,381. Fieldwork: ORC. Sponsor: R.Rose

Type of data	Breakdown	Area	Date	QRL Publication	Text Reference and remarks
Religion	social class	Northern Ireland	3-8/1968	[QRL.26]	Sample size: 1,291. Fieldwork: UOS. Sponsor: R.Rose. Data set: SN 1040
Religious denomination		GB	4/1968		Fieldwork: GP. Sponsor: STE
Religious denomination		GB	23-26/5/1968		Fieldwork: GP. Sponsor: STE. Multinational
Religious denomination		GB	1-4/8/1968		Fieldwork: GP
Religion		GB	14-19/8/1968		Sample size: 1,218. Fieldwork: NOP (3099). Data set: SN 68019
Religion		Wales	31/8-9/9/1968		Sample size: 760. Fieldwork: ORC. Sponsor: WM
Religious denomination		GB	10/1968	[QRL.89]	Sample size: 1,000. Fieldwork: GP. Sponsor: Family Planning Association

Topic	Variables		Date	Refs	Notes
Church in which respondent was brought up		GB	1-3/1969	[QRL.115]	Sample size: 1,490. Fieldwork: IS. Sponsor: RDA. Data set: SN 987. Multinational
Religion		GB	26-31/3/1969	[QRL.78]	Sample size: 1,905. Fieldwork: NOP (3490). Sponsor: BHA
Religion - parents' religion when respondent was young		GB	9/6-31/7/1969		Sample size: 1,114. Fieldwork: BMRB (49440). Sponsor: D.Butler and D.Stokes. Data set: SN 1093
Religious denomination		GB	30/10 -4/11/1969	[QRL.65] [QRL.123], 18/11/1969	Sample size: 1,001. Fieldwork: GP. Sponsor: SPUC
Religion	age, sex, social class, region	GB	7-12/1/1970	[QRL.77], 2/1970 [QRL.118]	Sample size: 1,705. Fieldwork: NOP (4051). Sponsor: ALRA
Religion		GB	19-23/1/1970		Sample size: 984. Fieldwork: NOP (4010). Sponsor: DM

Type of data	Breakdown	Area	Date	QRL Publication	Text Reference and remarks
Religion		GB	2-3/1970		Sample size: 1,975. Fieldwork: LHR. Sponsor: University of Michigan. Data set: SN 375
Religion		GB	3/1970		Sample size: 1,978. Fieldwork: NOP
Religion		GB	13-19/4/1970	[QRL.100]	Sample size: 2,472. Fieldwork: LHR (032). Sponsor: DE. Data set
Religious denomination		GB	23/5-16/6/1970		Sample size: 9,634. Fieldwork: GP. Sponsor: DT and STE. Data set: SN 1353. Four separate surveys
Religious group - parents' religion during respondent's childhood - religion in which respondent was brought up	age, sex, marital status, social class, education, region	GB	8-15/6/1970	[QRL.101]	Sample size: 1,395. Fieldwork: NOP (4233). Sponsor: DM

Religion	GB		6-8/1970		Sample size: 4,892. Fieldwork: SCPR (P.153). Sponsor: RCC. Data set: SN 173
Religion	GB		2-3/1971		Sample size: 2,030. Fieldwork: SCPR. Sponsor: EM. Data set: SN 084
Religion	GB		15-21/3/1971		Fieldwork: LHR (095). Data set
Religion	GB		21-28/6/1971		Fieldwork: LHR (110). Data set
Religion	GB		19-25/7/1971		Fieldwork: LHR (119). Data set
Religion - connection with any other religion in the past	GB		19-25/9/1971		Fieldwork: LHR (135). Data set
Religion - connection with any other religion in the past	GB		18-24/10/1971		Fieldwork: LHR (140). Data set
Religion - connection with any other religion in the past	GB		22-29/11/1971		Fieldwork: LHR (146). Data set
Religion	GB		14-20/3/1972		Sample size: 2,344. Fieldwork: NOP. Sponsor: RPA
Religious group	GB	age, sex, social class, region	10-15/4/1973	[QRL.45]	Sample size: 2,033. Fieldwork: NOP (6746). Sponsor: BS

Type of data	Breakdown	Area	Date	QRL Publication	Text Reference and remarks
Religious denomination		GB	27/4-1/5/1973		Sample size: 892. Fieldwork: GP (CQ.848). Sponsor: STE
Religion		GB	6-9/1973		Sample size: 1,319. Fieldwork: SCPR. Sponsor: EERT. Data set: SN 117
Religious denomination		GB	9-10/1973		Sample size: 1,933. Fieldwork: GP. Sponsor: CEC. Data set: SN 864. Multinational
Religious denomination		GB	1/10/1973-7/2/1974		Sample size: 1,802. Fieldwork: MAFS. Sponsor: M.Abrams and A. Marsh. Data set: SN 672
Religious denomination		GB	7-12/11/1973	[QRL.34]	Sample size: 1,085. Fieldwork: GP (CQ.876). Sponsor: SPUC

Religious denomination	party political preference	GB	8-27/2/1974	[QRL.12] [QRL.64], 2/1974	Sample size: 9,540. Fieldwork: GP. Sponsor: DT and STE. Data set: SN 658. Five separate surveys
Religious denomination	party political preference	GB	19/9-3/10/1974	[QRL.12] [QRL.64], 10/1974	Sample size: 8,428. Fieldwork: GP. Sponsor: DT and STE. Data set: SN 659. Four separate surveys
Religious denomination		GB	15/10/1974 - 20/1/1975		Sample size: 2,365. Fieldwork: SCPR. Sponsor: BES. Data set: SN 666
Religious denomination	party political preference	Scotland	15/10/1974 - 20/1/1975	[QRL.104], 15/10/1975	Sample size: 1,178. Fieldwork: SCPR. Sponsor: BES. Data set: SN 681
Religious denomination		GB	29/5-2/6/1975		Fieldwork: GP (CQ.962)
Religious denomination	age	GB	18-23/6/1975	[QRL.11]	Sample size: 944. Fieldwork: GP (CQ.965)

Type of data	Breakdown	Area	Date	QRL Publication	Text Reference and remarks
Religious faith		GB	6-7/1975		Sample size: 1,450. Fieldwork: SPR (5024). Sponsor: SSRC Survey Unit. Data set: SN 680
Religion		UK	13-25/10/1975		Sample size: 1,438. Fieldwork: GP. Sponsor: CEC. Data set SN 789. Multinational
Religious group		GB	4/1976		Sample size: 2,055. Fieldwork: NOP. Sponsor: BS
Religion		UK	7/5-7/6/1976		Sample size: 1,340. Fieldwork: GP. Sponsor: CEC. Data set SN 933. Multinational
Religious group	other religious variable	GB	8/1976	[QRL.21]	Sample size: 1,865. Fieldwork: NOP. Sponsor: RERP

Religion	age, sex, social class	Scotland	23-30/8/1976	[QRL.66], 12/10/1976 [QRL.103]	Sample size: 1,044. Fieldwork: STS (SOS.876). Sponsor: GH
Religion		GB	14-19/9/1976	[QRL.60]	Sample size: 2,121. Fieldwork: NOP (9698). Sponsor: VES
Religion		UK	2-21/11/1976		Sample size: 1,351. Fieldwork: GP. Sponsor: CEC. Data set: SN 934. Multinational
Religion		UK	23/4-12/5/1977		Sample size: 1,417. Fieldwork: GP (S.309/7). Sponsor: CEC. Data set: SN 936. Multinational
Religion		UK	24/10 -7/11/1977		Sample size: 1,350. Fieldwork: GP (S.309/8). Sponsor: CEC. Data set: SN 1029. Multinational

Type of data	Breakdown	Area	Date	QRL Publication	Text Reference and remarks
Religious denomination	age, sex, marital status, social class, education, region, party political preference	GB	22/2-17/4/1978	[QRL.96]	Sample size: 11,061. Fieldwork: GP (CQ.608-615A). Eleven separate surveys
Religion		UK	5-25/5/1978		Sample size: 1,420. Fieldwork: GP (S.4009/9). Sponsor: CEC. Data set: SN 1224. Multinational
Church to which respondent belonged - parents' religion		Northern Ireland	6-11/1978		Sample size: 1,277. Fieldwork: IMS (5234). Sponsor: QUB. Data set: SN 1347
Religious group	age, sex, social class, region, frequency of church attendance, other religious variable	GB	13-19/7/1978	[QRL.44], 31/8/1978 [QRL.48], 7/9/1978 [QRL.49] [QRL.123], 25/8/1978	Sample size: 1.989. Fieldwork: NOP (3594)
Religious group		GB	3-9/8/1978		Sample size: 1,856. Fieldwork: NOP

Religion		UK	26/10 -4/11/1978		Sample size: 1,339. Fieldwork: GP (S.4009/10B). Sponsor: CEC. Data set: SN 1284. Multinational
Religion		GB	16-22/11/1978		Sample size: 1,952. Fieldwork: NOP (4008). Sponsor: VES
Religious denomination	sex, social class	GB	21-26/3/1979	[QRL.25]	Sample size: 918. Fieldwork: GP (CQ.662). Sponsor: STE
Religious denomination	party political preference	GB	6/4-1/5/1979	[QRL.13], 1979 [QRL.64], 5/1979	Sample size: 11,097. Fieldwork: GP. Sponsor: DT and STE. Data set: SN 1352. Five separate surveys
Church/religious group		GB	5-7/1979		Sample size: 1,893. Fieldwork: RSL. Sponsor: BES. Data set: SN 1533
Religion		Wales	15/5-9/9/1979		Sample size: 858. Fieldwork: GP (S.5061). Sponsor: WES. Data set: SN 1591

Type of data	Breakdown	Area	Date	QRL Publication	Text Reference and remarks
Church/religious denomination		Scotland	5-10/1979		Sample size: 729. Fieldwork: RSL (J.1279). Sponsor: SES. Data set: SN 1604
Religion	age, sex, region	GB	23-29/7/1979	[QRL.93]	Sample size: 988. Fieldwork: MAR (51809/1). Sponsor: *Now!*. Data set: SN 1366
Religion		GB	9-10/1979		Sample size: 987. Fieldwork: GP (S.5077). Sponsor: LDC. Multinational
Religious denomination		GB	21-26/11/1979	[QRL.33]	Sample size: 1,004. Fieldwork: GP (CQ.698). Sponsor: WO
Religion		GB	18-19/1/1980		Sample size: 1,090. Fieldwork: MORI (5312). Sponsor: ST
Religion		GB	24-28/1/1980		Sample size: 1,930. Fieldwork: MORI (5285). Sponsor: ST

Religion	UK	11-25/4/1980			Sample size: 1,454. Fieldwork: GP (S.4009/13). Sponsor: CEC. Data set: SN 1615. Multinational
Religious denomination	GB	30/4-6/5/1980	[QRL.31], 1980 [QRL.64], 6/1980		Sample size: 2,117. Fieldwork: GP (CQ.717/717A). Sponsor: D.Martin
Religious denomination	Scotland	27/9-7/10/1980	[QRL.102]	age, sex, social class, frequency of church attendance, other religious variable	Sample size: 1,014. Fieldwork: STS (SOS.980). Sponsor: GH
Religion	GB	18-19/12/1980	[QRL.88], 12/1980 -1/1981		Sample size: 1,071. Fieldwork: MORI (6423). Sponsor: ST
Religious denomination	UK	3/1981			Sample size: 1,543. Fieldwork: GP (S.2131). Sponsor: EVSSG. Multinational
Religious denomination	GB	8-13/4/1981			Sample size: 994. Fieldwork: GP (CQ.763). Sponsor: STE

Type of data	Breakdown	Area	Date	QRL Publication	Text Reference and remarks
Religion		GB	9-11/5/1981	[QRL.88], 7/1981	Sample size: 1,077. Fieldwork: MORI (6878). Sponsor: DS
Religion	region	GB	29-30/5/1981	[QRL.88], 5-10/1981	Sample size: 1,886. Fieldwork: MORI (6756). Sponsor: ST. Data set: SN 1617
Religious group	age, sex, social class, region, frequency of church attendance	GB	3-8/9/1981	[QRL.80], 2/1982	Sample size: 1,991. Fieldwork: NOP (7191)
Religion		GB	14-18/9/1981	[QRL.88], 10-12/1981	Sample size: 1,996. Fieldwork: MORI (7250). Sponsor: BBC
Religion		UK	15-26/10/1981		Sample size: 1,395. Fieldwork: GP (S.4009/16). Sponsor: CEC. Data set: SN 1759. Multinational

Topic	Variables	Country	Date	QRL ref	Details
Religion		Scotland	25-29/11/1981	[QRL.88], 10-12/1981	Sample size: 1,079. Fieldwork: MORI (7477). Sponsor: SC
Religion		GB	10-14/12/1981	[QRL.88], 10-12/1981	Sample size: 1,523. Fieldwork: MORI (7550). Sponsor: DS
Religious denomination		GB	24/2-1/3/1982		Sample size: 1,042. Fieldwork: GP (CQ.806). Sponsor: ALRA and Doctors for a Woman's Choice on Abortion
Religious denomination	age, sex, social class, region, frequency of church attendance, other religious variable	GB	11-15/3/1982	[QRL.42] [QRL.64], 4/1982	Sample size: 1,032. Fieldwork: GP (CQ.808). Sponsor: U
Religious denomination		UK	31/3-29/4/1982		Sample size: 1,419. Fieldwork: GP (S.4009/17). Sponsor: CEC. Data set: SN 1792. Multinational
Religious denomination		GB	7-12/4/1982	[QRL.40]	Sample size: 944. Fieldwork: GP (CQ.812). Sponsor:U

Type of data	Breakdown	Area	Date	QRL Publication	Text Reference and remarks
Religious denomination		GB	13-20/4/1982		Sample size: 1,882. Fieldwork: GP (CQ.813/813B). Sponsor: STE
Religious denomination		GB	21-26/4/1982		Sample size: 968. Fieldwork: GP (CQ.814). Sponsor: U
Religious denomination		GB	28/4-4/5/1982	[QRL.4]	Sample size: 947. Fieldwork: GP (CQ.815A). Sponsor: U
Religious denomination		GB	5-10/5/1982		Sample size: 958. Fieldwork: GP (CQ.816)
Religious denomination		GB	12-17/5/1982		Sample size: 934. Fieldwork: GP (CQ.817A)
Religious denomination		GB	14-15/5/1982		Sample size: 1,038. Fieldwork: GP (S.4023). Sponsor: STE
Religious denomination		GB	19-24/5/1982	[QRL.4]	Sample size: 963. Fieldwork: GP (CQ.818)
Religious denomination	age, sex, social class, region, party political preference, frequency of church attendance, other religious variable	GB	9-15/6/1982	[QRL.36]	Sample size: 1,000. Fieldwork: GP (CQ.821B)

Church membership

Religious denomination	GB	30/6-5/7/1982		Sample size: 936. Fieldwork: GP (CQ.824)
Religious denomination	GB	11/1982		Sample size: 991. Fieldwork: GP (CQ.845)
Church membership	GB	11/1937	[QRL.9] [QRL.12]	6.2.3.1. Fieldwork: GP
Church membership	GB	2/1968	[QRL.94]	6.2.3.1. Sample size: 1,071. Fieldwork: ORC. Sponsor: ITA
Church membership	Northern Ireland	2/12/1968-10/1/1969	[QRL.94] [QRL.95]	6.2.3.1. Sample size: 694. Fieldwork: ORC. Sponsor: ITA, UTV and the Churches
Church membership	GB	20-24/9/1972		6.2.3.1. Sample size: 1,026. Fieldwork: ORC (7238). Sponsor: ST. Data set
Practising membership	GB	15/10/1974-20/1/1975		6.2.3.1. Sample size: 2,365. Fieldwork: SCPR. Sponsor: BES. Data set: SN 666
Practising membership	Scotland	15/10/1974-20/1/1975		6.2.3.1. Sample size: 1,178. Fieldwork: SCPR. Sponsor: BES. Data set: SN 681

Type of data	Breakdown	Area	Date	QRL Publication	Text Reference and remarks
Practising membership		Wales	15/5-9/9/1979		6.2.3.1. Sample size: 858. Fieldwork: GP (S.5061). Sponsor WES. Data set: SN 1591
Practising membership		Scotland	5-10/1979		6.2.3.1. Sample size: 729. Fieldwork: RSL (J.1279). Sponsor: SES. Data set SN 1604
Religious organisation membership					
Membership of religious organisations		GB	6-7/1959		6.2.4.1. Sample size: 963. Fieldwork: RSL. Sponsor: G.A. Almond and S.Verba. Data set: SN 370. Multinational
Membership of local church groups by respondent or any of his family	age, sex, social class, region, denominational affiliation, frequency of church attendance, other religious variable	England	16/12/1963-20/1/1964	[QRL.120] [QRL.121]	6.2.4.1. Sample size: 2,211. Fieldwork: GP (CS.5480). Sponsor: ABC TV. Data set

Subject	Attributes	Location	Date	Reference	Details
Membership of church clubs/groups		England	24/4-13/7/1967	[QRL.52]	6.2.4.1. Sample size: 2.199. Fieldwork: RSL. Sponsor: RCLG. Data set: SN 030
Membership of, and experience of holding office in, any kind of church organisation	denominational affiliation	Northern Ireland	3-8/1968	[QRL.26]	6.2.4.1. Sample size: 1,291. Fieldwork: UOS. Sponsor: R.Rose. Data set: SN 1040
Membership of church clubs/groups		GB	6-8/1970		6.2.4.1. Sample size: 4,892. Fieldwork: SCPR (P.153). Sponsor: RCC. Data set: SN 173
Membership of, and unpaid voluntary work for, churches/religious organisations		UK	3/1981	[QRL.70], 1982-83	6.2.4.1. Sample size: 1,543. Fieldwork: GP (S.2131). Sponsor: EVSSG. Multinational
Church attendance					
Regular church attendance		GB	11/1937	[QRL.9] [QRL.12]	Fieldwork: GP
Frequency of church attendance	age, sex, social class	GB	1/1939	[QRL.9] [QRL.12] [QRL.74], 7/2/1939	Sample size: 1,608. Fieldwork: GP (S.54). Sponsor: NC. Data set: SN 2037-2045

Type of data	Breakdown	Area	Date	QRL Publication	Text Reference and remarks
Current and pre-war church attendance compared		GB	1/1941	[QRL.9] [QRL.12]	7.2.2.1. Sample size: 2,175. Fieldwork: GP (S.74). Data set: SN 2037- 2045
Frequency of church attendance - last occasion on which current non-attenders went to church - current and pre-war church attendance compared - reasons for not attending as frequently as in the past - action which the Church could take to secure/improve attendance - likely effect on church attendance if the main services were to be held on weekday evenings instead of on Sundays - church attendance by other members of household - impact of experiences in the forces upon attitudes towards church-going	age, sex, social class, region, denominational affiliation	GB	1947	[QRL.75], 30/10 -6/11/1947	7.2.2.1, 7.2.2.2. Fieldwork: RSNR. Sponsor: NR
Frequency of church attendance	sex, social class, denominational affiliation	GB	9/1947	[QRL.3] [QRL.15]	Sample size: 3,019. Fieldwork: RSOP
Church attendance on either of the two previous Sundays		GB	12/1947	[QRL.12]	Fieldwork: GP (S.159). Sponsor: NC
Church attendance		GB	4-5/1948		Sample size: 6,114. Fieldwork: MO. Sponsor: DT

Subject	Variables	Region	Date	QRL	Notes
Church attendance - length of time since last attendance	age, sex, region, denominational affiliation	GB	7/1948	[QRL.54], 10-11/8/1948	Sample size: 2,055. Fieldwork: MO (09/1). Sponsor: DG
Frequency of church attendance	sex, region, denominational affiliation	GB	1948	[QRL.53], 20/9/1948	Fieldwork: DEP. Sponsor: DE
Church attendance on the previous Sunday	sex, region, denominational affiliation	GB	9-10/1948	[QRL.12], [QRL.74], 1/11/1948	Fieldwork: GP (S.171/172). Two separate surveys
Frequency of church attendance		GB	1949		Sample size: 2,051. Fieldwork: MO
Church attendance on the previous Sunday	age, social class	England and Wales	6-21/5/1952	[QRL.116]	Sample size: 4,948. Fieldwork: GP. Sponsor: NC
Frequency of church attendance - current and past church attendance compared - reasons for not going to church	age, sex, marital status, social class, region, denominational affiliation, other religious variable	GB	1-15/12/1954	[QRL.97]	7.2.2.1, 7.2.2.2. Sample size: 1,859. Fieldwork: GP. Sponsor: BBC
Frequency of church attendance	sex	GB	3/1955	[QRL.53], 19/3/1955	Fieldwork: DEP. Sponsor: DE
Church attendance		GB	4-7/11/1955		Sample size: 896. Fieldwork: GP (S.452A)
Church attendance on the previous Sunday-frequency of church attendance - age at which church-going ceased - reasons for not going to church - current and past church attendance compared - reasons for attending more/less frequently than in the past - belief that a person can be a Christian if he does not go to church	age, sex, social class, party political preference, denominational affiliation	GB	2-12/2/1957	[QRL.12], [QRL.30], [QRL.74], 16-17/4/1957	7.2.2.1, 7.2.2.2, 7.2.2.3. Sample size: 2,261. Fieldwork: GP (CS.1717). Sponsor: NC

Type of data	Breakdown	Area	Date	QRL Publication	Text Reference and remarks
Church attendance on the previous Sunday	sex	GB	3-7/5/1958	[QRL.12] [QRL.98] [QRL.74], 22/5/1958	Fieldwork: GP (CQ.70B). Sponsor: NC
Frequency of church attendance		GB	6-7/1959		Sample size: 963. Fieldwork: RSL. Sponsor: G.A.Almond and S. Verba. Data set: SN 370. Multinational
Frequency of church attendance		GB	3/1960	[QRL.1]	Fieldwork: GP. Multinational
Most recent church attendance		England & Wales	3/1962		Sample size: 1,415. Fieldwork: RSL. Sponsor: W.G. Runciman. Data set: SN 028
Frequency of church attendance	sex, denominational affiliation	GB	24/5-13/8/1963	[QRL.8]	Sample size: 2,009. Fieldwork: BMRB. Sponsor: D.Butler and D. Stokes. Data set: SN 1090

Topic	Variables	Area	Date	Reference	Details
Church attendance on the previous Sunday - belief that a person can lead a good life if he does not go to church - main reasons why people go to church - frequency of church attendance - age at which church-going ceased - reasons for not going to church - current and past church attendance compared - church attendance by other members of family	age, sex, social class, region, denominational affiliation, frequency of church attendance, other religious variable	England	16/12/1963-20/1/1964	[QRL.113], 19/9/1965 [QRL.120] [QRL.121]	7.2.2.1, 7.2.2.2, 7.2.2.3. Sample size: 2,211. Fieldwork: GP (CS.5480). Sponsor: ABC TV. Data set
Frequency of church attendance		GB	10/1964		Sample size: 1,005. Fieldwork: MO. Sponsor: L.M.Harris
Frequency of church attendance		GB	16/10 -5/12/1964		Sample size: 1,769. Fieldwork: BMRB. Sponsor: D.Butler and D. Stokes. Data set: SN 1091
Church attendance on Christmas Day		GB	16-21/12/1964	[QRL.12] [QRL.64], 1/1965	Fieldwork: GP. Sponsor: STE
Most recent church attendance	age, sex, social class, region, denominational affiliation	GB	3/1965	[QRL.73], 27/5/1965	Sample size: 2,160. Fieldwork: NOP. Sponsor: NS
Frequency of church attendance	sex	GB	3/1966	[QRL.57], 29/4/1966 [QRL.122]	Sample size: 1,501. Fieldwork: GP. Sponsor: SU

Type of data	Breakdown	Area	Date	QRL Publication	Text Reference and remarks
Frequency of church attendance		GB	1/4-14/6/1966		Sample size: 1,874. Fieldwork: BMRB. Sponsor: D.Butler and D.Stokes. Data set: SN 1092
Church attendance	age, sex, social class, education, region	England	24/4-13/7/1967	[QRL.52]	Sample size: 2,199. Fieldwork: RSL. Sponsor: RCLG. Data set: SN 030
Church attendance on the previous Sunday	age, sex, social class, region	GB	15-17/1/1968	[QRL.68]	Sample size: 968. Fieldwork: IPC
Frequency of church attendance	age, denominational affiliation	Northern Ireland	3-8/1968	[QRL.26]	Sample size: 1,291. Fieldwork: UOS. Sponsor: R.Rose. Data set: SN 1040
Frequency of church attendance - church attendance on the previous Sunday - intention to go to church on Easter Sunday	age, sex, social class, region, denominational affiliation	GB	4/1968	[QRL.112], 14/4/1968	Fieldwork: GP. Sponsor: STE
Frequency of church attendance		GB	23-26/5/1968	[QRL.62] [QRL.64], 8/1968	Fieldwork: GP. Sponsor: STE. Multinational
Church attendance on the previous Sunday	age, sex, social class, region	GB	19-21/8/1968	[QRL.68]	Sample size: 955. Fieldwork: IPC
Church attendance on the previous Sunday - intention to go to church over Christmas	age, sex	GB	12/1968	[QRL.113], 22/12/1968	Fieldwork: ORC. Sponsor: ST

Topic	Variables	Area	Date	Reference	Details
Attendance at a religious service during the past year/on the previous Sunday		Northern Ireland	2/12/1968-10/1/1969		Sample size: 694. Fieldwork: ORC. Sponsor: ITA, UTV and the Churches
Church attendance over the previous Christmas	age, social class, education, denominational affiliation	GB	1-3/1969	[QRL.115]	Sample size: 1,490. Fieldwork: IS. Sponsor: RDA. Data set: SN 987. Multinational
Frequency of church attendance		GB	9/6-31/7/1969		Sample size: 1,114. Fieldwork: BMRB (49440). Sponsor: D.Butler and D.Stokes. Data set: SN 1093
Church attendance over Christmas	age, sex, social class	GB	10-15/12/1969	[QRL.77], 12/1969	Sample size: 1,744. Fieldwork: NOP (4000). Data set: SN 69038
Church attendance on Christmas Day	age	GB	11-14/12/1969	[QRL.12] [QRL.57], 23/12/1969 [QRL.64], 12/1969	Fieldwork: GP. Sponsor: DT
Church attendance		GB	19-23/1/1970		Sample size: 984. Fieldwork: NOP (4010). Sponsor: DM

Type of data	Breakdown	Area	Date	QRL Publication	Text Reference and remarks
Frequency of church attendance		GB	2-3/1970		Sample size: 1,975. Fieldwork: LHR. Sponsor: University of Michigan. Data set: SN 375
Frequency of church attendance - changes in religious services which might induce more frequent attendance - reasons for the decline in church attendance during the previous twenty years	age, sex, denominational affiliation	GB	13-19/4/1970	[QRL.53], 13/5/1970 [QRL.100]	7.2.2.2. Sample size: 2,472. Fieldwork: LHR (032). Sponsor: DE. Data set
Frequency of church attendance - reasons for attending religious services - attendance at special Easter/Christmas services	age, sex, marital status, social class, education, region	GB	8-15/6/1970	[QRL.55], 5/1/1971 [QRL.101]	Sample size: 1,395. Fieldwork: NOP (4233). Sponsor: DM
Church attendance on Christmas Day		GB	17-20/12/1970	[QRL.12] [QRL.64], 1/1971	Fieldwork: GP
Frequency of church attendance		GB	2-3/1971		Sample size: 2,030. Fieldwork: SCPR. Sponsor: EM. Data set: SN 084
Church attendance during the previous four weeks		GB	18-24/10/1971		Fieldwork: LHR (140). Data set
Frequency of church attendance	sex, social class	GB	20-22/1/1972	[QRL.77], 7/1972	Sample size: 1,000. Fieldwork: NOP. Sponsor: DM

Whether respondent visited a church/took part in a religious service on the previous day	age, sex	GB	20-24/9/1972	[QRL.113], 22/4/1973	Sample size: 1,026. Fieldwork: ORC (7238). Sponsor: ST. Data set
Church attendance over Christmas		GB	28/11 -3/12/1972		Fieldwork: NOP (6401). Data set: SN 069
Intention to go to church on Christmas Day	age	GB	12/1972	[QRL.113], 24/12/1972	Sample size: 912. Fieldwork: ORC. Sponsor: ST
Frequency of church attendance		GB	6-9/1973		Sample size: 1,319. Fieldwork: SCPR. Sponsor: EERT. Data set: SN 117
Frequency of church attendance		GB	9-10/1973		Sample size: 1,933. Fieldwork: GP. Sponsor: CEC. Data set: SN 864. Multinational
Church attendance		GB	1/10/1973 -7/2/1974		Sample size: 1,802. Fieldwork: MAFS. Sponsor: M.Abrams and A.Marsh. Data set: SN 672
Frequency of church attendance - reasons for not attending religious services	age, sex, social class, region	GB	20-25/8/1974	[QRL.108] [QRL.113], 13/10/1974 [QRL.123], 14/10/1974	7.2.2.2. Sample size: 1,093. Fieldwork: ORC (34333). Sponsor: BBC

Type of data	Breakdown	Area	Date	QRL Publication	Text Reference and remarks
Most recent church attendance	denominational affiliation	GB	18-23/6/1975	[QRL.11]	Sample size: 944. Fieldwork: GP (CQ.965)
Frequency of church attendance		UK	13-25/10/1975		Sample size: 1,438. Fieldwork: GP. Sponsor: CEC. Data set: SN 789. Multinational
Frequency of church attendance		UK	7/5-7/6/1976		Sample size: 1,340. Fieldwork: GP. Sponsor: CEC. Data set: SN 933. Multinational
Frequency of church attendance	other religious variable	GB	8/1976	[QRL.20] [QRL.21]	Sample size: 1,865. Fieldwork: NOP. Sponsor: RERP
Frequency of church attendance	age, sex, social class, denominational affiliation	Scotland	23-30/8/1976	[QRL.66], 11/10/1976 [QRL.103]	Sample size: 1,044. Fieldwork: STS (SOS.876). Sponsor:GH

Frequency of church attendance	UK	2-21/11/1976		Sample size: 1,351. Fieldwork: GP. Sponsor: CEC. Data set: SN 934. Multinational
Frequency of church attendance	UK	23/4-12/5/1977		Sample size: 1,417. Fieldwork: GP (S.309/7). Sponsor: CEC. Data set: SN 936. Multinational
Frequency of church attendance	UK	24/10 -7/11/1977		Sample size: 1,350. Fieldwork: GP (S.309/8). Sponsor: CEC. Data set: SN 1029. Multinational
Frequency of church attendance	GB	22/2-17/4/1978 [QRL.96]	age, sex, social class, education, region, party political preference, denominational affiliation	Sample size: 11,061. Fieldwork: GP (CQ.608-615A). Eleven separate surveys.
Frequency of church attendance	UK	5-25/5/1978		Sample size: 1,420. Fieldwork: GP (S.4009/9). Sponsor: CEC. Data set: SN 1224. Multinational

Type of data	Breakdown	Area	Date	QRL Publication	Text Reference and remarks
Frequency of church attendance	age, region, denominational affiliation	Northern Ireland	6-11/1978	[QRL.24]	Sample size: 1,277. Fieldwork: IMS (5234). Sponsor: QUB. Data set: SN 1347
Frequency of church attendance	age, sex, social class, region, denominational affiliation, other religious variable	GB	13-19/7/1978	[QRL.48], 7/9/1978 [QRL.49]	Sample size: 1,989. Fieldwork:NOP (3594)
Frequency of church attendance		GB	3-9/8/1978		Sample size: 1,856. Fieldwork: NOP
Frequency of church attendance		UK	26/10 -4/11/1978		Sample size: 1,339. Fieldwork: GP (S.4009/10B). Sponsor: CEC. Data set: SN 1284. Multinational
Frequency of church attendance	sex, social class	GB	21-26/3/1979	[QRL.25]	Sample size: 918. Fieldwork: GP (CQ.662). Sponsor: STE
Frequency of church attendance		GB	5-7/1979		Sample size: 1,893. Fieldwork: RSL. Sponsor: BES. Data set: SN 1533

Frequency of church attendance	15/5-9/9/1979	Wales			Sample size: 858. Fieldwork: GP (S.5061). Sponsor: WES. Data set: SN 1591
Frequency of church attendance	5-10/1979	Scotland			Sample size: 729. Fieldwork: RSL (J.1279). Sponsor: SES. Data set: SN 1604
Most recent church attendance other than for a wedding/funeral/christening - frequency of church attendance	23-29/7/1979	GB	age, sex, region	[QRL.79], 21/12/1979 [QRL.93]	Sample size: 988. Fieldwork: MAR (51809/1). Sponsor: *Now!*. Data set: SN 1366
Frequency of church attendance	21-26/11/1979	GB		[QRL.33]	Sample size: 1,004. Fieldwork: GP (CQ.698). Sponsor: WO.
Frequency of church attendance	11-25/4/1980	UK			Sample size: 1,454. Fieldwork: GP (S.4009/13). Sponsor: CEC. Data set: SN 1615. Multinational
Frequency of church attendance	27/9-7/10/1980	Scotland	age, sex, social class, denominational affiliation	[QRL.66], 27/10/1980 [QRL.102]	Sample size: 1,014. Fieldwork: STS (SOS.980). Sponsor: GH

Type of data	Breakdown	Area	Date	QRL Publication	Text Reference and remarks
Frequency of church attendance other than for weddings/funerals/baptisms		UK	3/1981	[QRL.70], 1982-83	Sample size: 1,543. Fieldwork: GP (S.2131). Sponsor: EVSSG. Multinational
Frequency of church attendance		GB	8-13/4/1981		Sample size: 994. Fieldwork: GP (CQ.763). Sponsor: STE
Frequency of church attendance	region	GB	29-30/5/1981	[QRL.70], 1981-82 [QRL.88], 5-10/1981	Sample size: 1,886. Fieldwork: MORI (6756). Sponsor: ST. Data set: SN 1617
Frequency of church attendance	age, sex, social class, region, denominational affiliation	GB	3-8/9/1981	[QRL.80], 2/1982	Sample size: 1,991. Fieldwork: NOP (7191)
Frequency of church attendance		UK	15-26/10/1981	[QRL.31], 1981	Sample size: 1,395. Fieldwork: GP (S.4009/16). Sponsor: CEC. Data set: SN 1759. Multinational

Topic	Breakdown		Date	QRL references	Details
Intention to go to church/carol service over Christmas	age, sex, social class	GB	10-14/12/1981	[QRL.56], 24/12/1981 [QRL.70], 1981-82 [QRL.88], 10-12/1981	Sample size: 1,523. Fieldwork: MORI (7550). Sponsor: DS
Church-going as a favourite leisure activity	age, sex, social class	GB	21-25/1/1982	[QRL.53], 6/2/1982 [QRL.70], 1981-82 [QRL.88], 2/1982	Sample size: 1,812. Fieldwork: MORI (7677). Sponsor: DE
Frequency of church attendance other than for weddings/funerals/baptisms	age, sex, social class, region, denominational affiliation, other religious variable	GB	11-15/3/1982	[QRL.42], [QRL.64], 4/1982 [QRL.70], 1982-83 [QRL.119], 3/4/1982	Sample size: 1,032. Fieldwork: GP (CQ.808). Sponsor: U
Frequency of church attendance other than for weddings/funerals/baptisms		GB	7-12/4/1982		Sample size: 944. Fieldwork: GP (CQ.812). Sponsor: U
Frequency of church attendance other than for weddings/funerals/baptisms		GB	21-26/4/1982		Sample size: 968. Fieldwork: GP (CQ.814). Sponsor: U
Frequency of church attendance other than for weddings/funerals/baptisms		GB	28/4-4/5/1982	[QRL.4]	Sample size: 947. Fieldwork: GP (CQ.815A). Sponsor: U
Frequency of church attendance other than for weddings/funerals/baptisms		GB	5-10/5/1982		Sample size: 958. Fieldwork: GP (CQ.816)
Frequency of church attendance other than for weddings/funerals/baptisms		GB	12-17/5/1982		Sample size: 934. Fieldwork: GP (CQ.817A)

R-N

Type of data	Breakdown	Area	Date	QRL Publication	Text Reference and remarks
Frequency of church attendance other than for weddings/funerals/baptisms		GB	19-24/5/1982	[QRL.4]	Sample size: 963. Fieldwork: GP (CQ.818)
Frequency of church attendance other than for weddings/funerals/baptisms	age, sex, social class, region, party political preference, denominational affiliation, other religious variable	GB	9-15/6/1982	[QRL.36]	Sample size: 1,000. Fieldwork: GP (CQ.821B)
Frequency of church attendance other than for weddings/funerals/baptisms		GB	30/6-5/7/1982		Sample size: 936. Fieldwork: GP (CQ.824)
Frequency of church attendance other than for weddings/funerals/baptisms		GB	11/1982		Sample size: 991. Fieldwork: GP (CQ.845)
Church attendance at least once every two to three months - whether, when going to church, respondent would normally meet people he knew well/be on his own		GB	25-29/11/1982	[QRL.113], 11/12/1983	Sample size: 1,801. Fieldwork: MORI (2106). Sponsor: ST

PERSONAL RELIGION: ATTITUDES

Religious influences on national life

Type of data	Breakdown	Area	Date	QRL Publication	Text Reference and remarks
Opinion of the role which the Churches were playing in the life of the country		GB	6/1942	[QRL.9] [QRL.74], 4/7/1942	Sample size: 1,981. Fieldwork: GP (S.88). Data set: SN 2037-2045
Belief that religion had a mission to fulfil in modern Britain/was fulfilling this mission	age, sex, social class, denominational affiliation	GB	2/1947	[QRL.10] [QRL.12] [QRL.74], 3/4/1947*	Fieldwork: GP

Extent to which the Churches were carrying out their job - main job which the Churches should have been doing	age, sex, social class, region, denominational affiliation	GB	1947	[QRL.75], 23/10 -6/11/1947	Fieldwork: RSNR. Sponsor: NR
Extent to which the Churches were doing their job	social class	GB	9/1947	[QRL.3]	Sample size: 3,019. Fieldwork: RSOP
Religion versus politics as the greater influence in people's lives		GB	6/1948	[QRL.12]	Fieldwork: GP
Extent to which the Churches were succeeding in their work	denominational affiliation, frequency of church attendance	GB	7/1948	[QRL.54], 11/8/1948	Sample size: 2,055. Fieldwork: MO (09/1). Sponsor: DG
Religion versus politics as the greater influence on people's lives and circumstances - confidence in the ability of religion to provide answers to all or most contemporary problems - influence of religion on British life - economic security versus religion as the world's greater need	age	GB	2-12/2/1957	[QRL.12] [QRL.74], 15/4/1957	8.1.1.1. Sample size: 2,261. Fieldwork: GP (CS.1717). Sponsor:NC
Spiritual virtues/religion as objects of national pride		GB	6-7/1959		Sample size: 963. Fieldwork: RSL. Sponsor: G.A.Almond and S.Verba. Data set: SN 370. Multinational
Influence of the Churches on the country's future		GB	4-11/1/1963	[QRL.12] [QRL.64], 1/1963	8.1.1.2. Fieldwork: GP

Type of data	Breakdown	Area	Date	QRL Publication	Text Reference and remarks
Religion versus the opinions of friends/workmates as the greater influence on the way people behave - confidence in the ability of religion to provide answers to all or most contemporary problems - actual/desired influence of religion on British life - class interests which the Anglican/Roman Catholic/Nonconformist Churches served best - problems for which people could get help and comfort from the Church	age, sex, social class, region, denominational affiliation, frequency of church attendance, other religious variable	England	16/12/1963-20/1/1964	[QRL.113], 19/9/1965 [QRL.120] [QRL.121]	8.1.1.1. Sample size: 2,211. Fieldwork: GP (CS.5480). Sponsor: ABC TV. Data set
Religion versus politics as the greater influence on people's lives and circumstances		GB	17-23/6/1964	[QRL.12] [QRL.64], 7/1964	Fieldwork: GP
Extent to which Britain was a Christian country	age, region, denominational affiliation	GB	3/1965	[QRL.73], 27/5/1965	Sample size: 2,160. Fieldwork: NOP. Sponsor: NS
Influence of religion on British life	sex, denominational affiliation	GB	6-11/5/1965	[QRL.23]	8.1.1.1. Fieldwork: GP
Influence of religion on British life	age, sex, social class, denominational affiliation	GB	2-7/5/1967	[QRL.12] [QRL.23] [QRL.64], 5/1967 [QRL.112], 14/5/1967	8.1.1.1. Fieldwork: GP. Sponsor: STE
Importance attached to this being a Christian country	other religious variable	GB	2/1968	[QRL.94]	Sample size: 1,071. Fieldwork: ORC. Sponsor: ITA

Description	Other variable	Country	Date	References	Details
Influence of the Church on the country's future		GB	7-9/6/1968	[QRL.12] [QRL.64], 6/1968	8.1.1.2. Fieldwork: GP
Importance attached to this being a Christian country	other religious variable	Northern Ireland	2/12/1968 -10/1/1969	[QRL.94] [QRL.95]	Sample size: 694. Fieldwork: ORC. Sponsor: ITA, UTV and the Churches
Influence of the Churches on the country's future		GB	12-29/12/1968	[QRL.12] [QRL.64], 1/1969	8.1.1.2. Fieldwork: GP
Attitude of the British people towards religion		GB	3/1969	[QRL.12]	Fieldwork: GP. Sponsor: STE
Influence of the Church on the country's future - desirability of the Church attempting to increase its influence over the life of the nation		GB	6/1969	[QRL.12] [QRL.64], 10/1969	8.1.1.2. Fieldwork: GP
Desire to see the Church concentrate upon adherence to its traditional forms/adaptation to the ways of the modern world	age, sex, denominational affiliation	GB	13-19/4/1970	[QRL.100]	Sample size: 2,472. Fieldwork: LHR (032). Sponsor: DE. Data set
Importance of the part which the Church played/should play in the world	age, sex, marital status, social class, education, region	GB	8-15/6/1970	[QRL.55], 5/1/1971 [QRL.101]	Sample size: 1,395. Fieldwork: NOP (4233). Sponsor: DM
Extent to which religion needed immediate attention and change	sex, social class, education, party political preference	GB	4-5/1972	[QRL.83]	Sample size: 1,260. Fieldwork: BMRB. Sponsor: AA
Influence of the Church on the country's future		GB	1-5/2/1973	[QRL.12] [QRL.64], 2/1973	8.1.1.2. Fieldwork: GP
Degree of confidence in the leaders of religion		GB	4/1973	[QRL.123], 30/4/1974	Fieldwork: ORC

Type of data	Breakdown	Area	Date	QRL Publication	Text Reference and remarks
Influence of religion on British life	age, sex, social class, region, denominational affiliation	GB	27/4-1/5/1973	[QRL.12] [QRL.57], 14/5/1973 [QRL.64], 5/1973 [QRL.112], 13/5/1973	8.1.1.1. Sample size: 892. Fieldwork: GP (CQ.848). Sponsor: STE
Degree of confidence in the leaders of religion		GB	13-19/4/1974	[QRL.123], 30/4/1974	Sample size: 1,100. Fieldwork: ORC. Sponsor:*The Times*
Influence of religion in British life		GB	29/5-2/6/1975	[QRL.12] [QRL.64], 6/1975	8.1.1.1. Fieldwork: GP (CQ.962)
Influence of the Church on the country's future		GB	21-26/1/1976	[QRL.64], 2/1976	8.1.1.2. Fieldwork: GP
Extent to which religion needed immediate attention and change	age, sex, social class	GB	3/1976	[QRL.84]	Sample size: 1,067. Fieldwork: BMRB. Sponsor: AA
Influence of the Churches on everyday life in Scotland - desire to see the Churches doing more to keep up to date with life in Scotland	age, sex, social class, denominational affiliation	Scotland	23-30/8/1976	[QRL.66], 12/10/1976 [QRL.103]	Sample size: 1,044. Fieldwork: STS (SOS.876). Sponsor: GH

Importance of religion in the lives of the people of Northern Ireland	age, region, denominational affiliation	Northern Ireland	6-11/1978	[QRL.24]	Sample size: 1,277. Fieldwork: IMS (5234). Sponsor: QUB. Data set: SN 1347
Extent to which the Church was complacent, old-fashioned and out of touch - conviction that many of the problems in Britain stemmed from a lack of religious belief	denominational affiliation	GB	23-29/7/1979	[QRL.79], 21/12/1979	Sample size: 988. Fieldwork: MAR (51809/1). Sponsor: *Now!*. Data set: SN 1366
Actual/desired influence of the Church over the lives of the people in Britain		GB	19-24/6/1980	[QRL.80], 8/1980	Sample size: 2,067. Fieldwork: NOP (5803)
Extent to which religion needed immediate attention and change	age, sex, social class, party political preference	GB	6/1980	[QRL.85]	Sample size: 1,116. Fieldwork: BMRB. Sponsor: AA
Extent to which the Church was giving adequate answers to the moral problems and needs of the individual/the problems of family life/man's spiritual needs - future importance of religion for people in this country - degree of confidence in the Church		UK	3/1981	[QRL.44], 17/12/1981 [QRL.51], 11/12/1981 [QRL.70], 1982-3	Sample size: 1,543. Fieldwork: GP (S.2131). Sponsor: EVSSG. Multinational
Extent to which the Church was giving adequate answers to the problems of family life/man's spiritual need/the problems of society - consciousness/approval of the Christian/multi-faith nature of British society		GB	1-7/9/1981	[QRL.31], 1981 [QRL.64], 9/1981 [QRL.70], 1981-82	Sample size: 1,031. Fieldwork: GP (CQ.784). Sponsor: BBC

Type of data	Breakdown	Area	Date	QRL Publication	Text Reference and remarks
Influence of religion on British life	age, sex, social class, region, denominational affiliation, frequency of church attendance, other religious variable	GB	11-15/3/1982	[QRL.42] [QRL.64], 4/1982 [QRL.70], 1982-83 [QRL.119], 3/4/1982	8.1.1.1. Sample size: 1,032. Fieldwork: GP (CQ.808). Sponsor: U
Influence of religion on British life		GB	11/1982		8.1.1.1. Sample size: 991. Fieldwork: GP (CQ.845)
Influence of the Church on the country's future		GB	24-30/11/1982	[QRL.64], 12/1982 [QRL.70], 1982-83	8.1.1.2. Fieldwork: GP
Degree of confidence in the Church		GB	20-26/4/1983	[QRL.64], 5/1983 [QRL.70], 1982-83	Sample size: 1,016. Fieldwork: GP (CQ.863A)
Ecumenism					
Approval of the unification of all Protestant Churches		GB	2/1938	[QRL.9]	Fieldwork: GP
Approval of the creation of a single Christian Church in this country	sex, denominational affiliation, frequency of church attendance	GB	7/1948	[QRL.54], 11/8/1948	Sample size: 2,055. Fieldwork: MO (09/1). Sponsor: DG
Approval of unity negotiations between the Anglican and Nonconformist Churches/between the Roman Catholic and all other Churches in this country		GB	11/1949	[QRL.12]	Fieldwork: GP (S.195X/Y).

Subject	Breakdown	Country	Date	References	Notes
Approval of unity negotiations between the Anglican and Nonconformist Churches		GB	2-12/2/1957	[QRL.12]	Sample size: 2,261. Fieldwork: GP (CS.1717). Sponsor: NC
Interest in/approval of the Archbishop of Canterbury's visit to the Pope	denominational affiliation	GB	3-7/11/1960	[QRL.12] [QRL.64], 11/1960 [QRL.74], 14/11/1960	Sample size: 1,150. Fieldwork: GP
Approval of unity negotiations between the Anglican and Nonconformist Churches/between the Roman Catholic and all other Churches in this country	denominational affiliation	GB	19-24/10/1961	[QRL.12] [QRL.47], 12/1/1962 [QRL.64], 11/1961	Fieldwork: GP
Approval/likely success of unity negotiations between the Roman Catholic, Greek Orthodox, Anglican and all the other Churches in the world	sex, denominational affiliation	GB	29/9-6/10/1962	[QRL.23]	Fieldwork: GP
Approval of unity negotiations between the Anglican and Nonconformist Churches/between the Roman Catholic and all other Churches in this country	denominational affiliation	GB	28/6-2/7/1963	[QRL.12] [QRL.64], 7/1963 [QRL.112], 14/7/1963	Fieldwork: GP. Sponsor: STE
Approval of unity negotiations between the Anglican and Nonconformist Churches/between the Roman Catholic and all other Churches in this country	age, sex, social class, denominational affiliation	GB	23-29/1/1967	[QRL.12] [QRL.23] [QRL.64], 2/1967	Fieldwork: GP
Desirability/feasibility of the unification of the Protestant and Roman Catholic Churches	age, denominational affiliation	Northern Ireland	3-8/1968	[QRL.26]	Sample size: 1,291. Fieldwork: UOS. Sponsor: R.Rose. Data set: SN 1040
Approval of unity negotiations between the Roman Catholic and all other Churches in this country		GB	9-11/8/1968	[QRL.12] [QRL.64], 8/1968	Fieldwork: GP

Type of data	Breakdown	Area	Date	QRL Publication	Text Reference and remarks
State of relations between the Churches in Northern Ireland - approval, within the Northern Irish context, of regular meetings between the main Churches to discuss their problems/a closer relationship between the Roman Catholic and Protestant Churches/movement towards the unity of all major Christian Churches - obstacles to the improvement of relations between the different Churches in Northern Ireland - role of television as a help/hindrance to relations between the different Churches in Northern Ireland	denominational affiliation	Northern Ireland	2/12/1968 -10/1/1969	[QRL.94] [QRL.95]	Sample size: 694. Fieldwork: ORC. Sponsor: ITA, UTV and the Churches
Approval of the Churches joining together - approval of Anglican-Methodist reunion	age, sex, marital status, social class, education, region	GB	8-15/6/1970	[QRL.101]	Sample size: 1,395. Fieldwork: NOP (4233). Sponsor: DM
Belief that the Church was too divided within itself	denominational affiliation	GB	23-29/7/1979	[QRL.79], 21/12/1979	Sample size: 988. Fieldwork: MAR (51809/1). Sponsor: *Now!*. Data set: SN 1366
Desirability of having friendly relations with people of different religions		GB	9-10/1979	[QRL.92]	Sample size: 987. Fieldwork: GP (S.5077). Sponsor: LDC. Multinational

	Variables		Date	Reference	Details
Approval of unity negotiations between the Church of England/Scotland and the Roman Catholic Church - approval of unity negotiations between the Church of England/Scotland and the Free Churches - prospects for unity between the Anglican and Catholic Churches/unity between the Anglican and Free Churches/unity between the Anglican, Catholic and Nonconformist Churches/ the Churches remaining the way they were/the Churches moving further apart Approval of the Pope becoming universal primate of the Anglican and Roman Catholic Churches	age, sex, social class, region, denominational affiliation, frequency of church attendance, other religious variable	GB	11-15/3/1982	[QRL.42] [QRL.47], 2/4/1982 [QRL.64], 4/1982 [QRL.70], 1982-83 [QRL.119], 3/4/1982 [QRL.125], 26/3/1982	Sample size: 1,032. Fieldwork: GP (CQ.808). Sponsor: U
	denominational affiliation, frequency of church attendance	GB	7-12/4/1982	[QRL.40], [QRL.51], 30/4/1982	Sample size: 944. Fieldwork: GP (CQ.812). Sponsor: U
Approval of unity negotiations between the Anglican and Roman Catholic Churches/between the Anglican and Free Churches - prospects for unity between the Anglican and Catholic Churches/unity between the Anglican and Free Churches/unity between the Anglican, Catholic and Nonconformist Churches/the Churches remaining the way they were/the Churches moving further apart	age, sex, social class, region, party political preference, denominational affiliation, frequency of church attendance, other religious variable	GB	9-15/6/1982	[QRL.35] [QRL.36] [QRL.125], 30/7/1982	Sample size: 1,000. Fieldwork: GP (CQ.821B)

Religious prejudices

			Date	Reference	Details
Increase/decrease in anti-Jewish sentiment amongst people known to respondent		GB	8/1939	[QRL.9]	8.1.3.3. Sample size: 1,811. Fieldwork: GP (S.61). Data set: SN 2037-2045
Increase/decrease in anti-Jewish sentiment amongst people known to respondent		GB	11/1940	[QRL.9]	8.1.3.3. Sample size: 2,285. Fieldwork: GP (S.73). Data set: SN 2037-2045

Type of data	Breakdown	Area	Date	QRL Publication	Text Reference and remarks
Increase/decrease in anti-Jewish sentiment amongst people known to respondent		GB	1/1942	[QRL.9]	8.1.3.3. Sample size: 2,002. Fieldwork: GP (S.83). Data set: SN 2037-2045
Increase/decrease in anti-Jewish sentiment amongst people known to respondent		GB	1/1943	[QRL.9]	8.1.3.3. Sample size: 1,996. Fieldwork: GP (S.95). Data set: SN 2037-2045
Friendliness, good citizenship and trustworthiness of church-goers relative to other people	frequency of church attendance, other religious variable	GB	1-15/12/1954	[QRL.97]	Sample size: 1,859. Fieldwork: GP. Sponsor: BBC
Dislike of any particular denomination or creed		GB	2-12/2/1957	[QRL.12]	Sample size: 2,261. Fieldwork: GP (CS.1717). Sponsor: NC
Willingness to vote for a well-qualified parliamentary candidate who was a Roman Catholic/Jew/atheist	social class , party political preference, denominational affiliation	GB	11/1958	[QRL.12] [QRL.74], 6/2/1959 [QRL.104], 6/2/1959	Fieldwork: GP
Degree of power exercised by Jews/Catholics in this country		GB	8/1959	[QRL.12]	Fieldwork: GP
Increase/decrease in anti-Jewish sentiment amongst people known to respondent		GB	9-14/1/1960	[QRL.12]	8.1.3.3. Fieldwork: GP (CQ.147B)
Attitude towards Roman Catholics/Jews		GB	21/12/1961 -1/1/1962	[QRL.12] [QRL.64], 1/1962	Fieldwork: GP

Description	Variables	Area	Date	References	Details
Attitude towards parents having the power to refuse, on religious grounds, to let their children have blood transfusions		GB	1963	[QRL.77], 7/1963	Fieldwork: NOP
Attitude towards having an atheist/practising Jew/practising Roman Catholic/practising Anglican/practising Nonconformist/someone who seldom gave religion a thought as a neighbour - estimation of the age/receptiveness to new ideas/sincerity of belief/quality of life of regular church-goers	age, sex, social class, region, denominational affiliation, frequency of church attendance, other religious variable	England	16/12/1963-20/1/1964	[QRL.113], 19/9/1965 [QRL.120] [QRL.121]	Sample size: 2,211. Fieldwork: GP (CS.5480). Sponsor: ABC TV. Data set
Willingness to vote for a well-qualified parliamentary candidate who was a Roman Catholic/Jew/atheist	age, sex, social class, denominational affiliation	GB	10-15/9/1965	[QRL.12] [QRL.23]	Sample size: 1,000. Fieldwork: GP
Attitude towards Jews/Roman Catholics		GB	2-10/12/1967	[QRL.12] [QRL.64], 12/1967	Sample size: 1,000. Fieldwork: GP
Belief that no one Church or faith could claim to be the only true religion	age, sex, social class	GB	2/1968	[QRL.94]	Sample size: 1,071. Fieldwork: ORC. Sponsor: ITA
Likes/dislikes about the Protestant/Roman Catholic Churches in Northern Ireland - denial of freedom to preach to men whose religious doctrines were false	denominational affiliation	Northern Ireland	3-8/1968	[QRL.26]	Sample size: 1,291. Fieldwork: UOS. Sponsor: R.Rose. Data set: SN 1040
Degree of power exercised by Jews/Catholics in this country		GB	6/1969	[QRL.12] [QRL.64], 10/1969	Fieldwork: GP
Familiarity with/estimation of the truth of individual religions and sects	age, sex, marital status, social class, education, region	GB	8-15/6/1970	[QRL.101]	Sample size: 1,395. Fieldwork: NOP (4233). Sponsor: DM

Type of data	Breakdown	Area	Date	QRL Publication	Text Reference and remarks
Extent to which religious differences were a serious problem in Scotland	age, sex, social class, denominational affiliation	Scotland	23-30/8/1976	[QRL.66], 11/10/1976 [QRL.103]	Sample size: 1,044. Fieldwork: STS (SOS.876). Sponsor: GH
Seriousness of conflict between Protestants and Catholics - extent of agreement with Protestants/Catholics		Scotland	5-10/1979		Sample size: 729. Fieldwork: RSL (J.1279). Sponsor: SES. Data set: SN 1604
Belief that religious people are usually kinder, more honest and more generous than non-believers, that just as many good people do not go to church as do, that most people go to church to keep up appearances	denominational affiliation	GB	23-29/7/1979	[QRL.79], 21/12/1979	Sample size: 988. Fieldwork: MAR (51809/1). Sponsor: Now!. Data set: SN 1366
Attitude towards having members of minority religious sects or cults as neighbours - belief that there are basic truths to be found in all the great religions of the world/there is only one true religion/none of the great religions has any truths to offer		UK	3/1981	[QRL.31], 1981 [QRL.70], 1982-83 [QRL.125], 11/12/1981	Sample size: 1,543. Fieldwork: GP (S.2131). Sponsor: EVSSG. Multinational

Topic	Variables	Country	Date	References	Sample
Interest in/approval of the papal visit to Britain - reasons for approval/disapproval of the visit	age, sex, social class, region, denominational affiliation, frequency of church attendance, other religious variable	GB	11-15/3/1982	[QRL.42], [QRL.47], 2/4/1982 [QRL.64], 4/1982 [QRL.67], 25/3/1982 [QRL.70], 1982-3 [QRL.119], 3/4/1982 [QRL.123], 25/3/1982 [QRL.125], 26/3/1982	8.1.3.2. Sample size: 1,032. Fieldwork: GP (CQ.808). Sponsor: U
Interest in/approval of the papal visit to Britain - intention to attend any of the papal functions or ceremonies/see the Pope pass through the streets/watch televised coverage of the events - places where it was intended to see the Pope - approval of protests or demonstrations against the Pope during his visit	age, sex, social class, region, denominational affiliation, frequency of church attendance, other religious variable	GB	7-12/4/1982	[QRL.40], [QRL.51], 30/4/1982 [QRL.64], 6/1982 [QRL.125], 23/4/1982, 14/5/1982	8.1.3.2. Sample size: 944. Fieldwork: GP (CQ.812). Sponsor: U
Attitude towards having members of minority religious sects or cults as neighbours		GB	13-20/4/1982	[QRL.64], 5/1982 [QRL.70], 1982-83	Sample size: 1,882. Fieldwork: GP (CQ.813/813B). Sponsor: STE
Interest in/approval of the papal visit to Britain - intention to attend any of the papal functions or ceremonies/see the Pope pass through the streets/watch televised coverage of the events - places where it was intended to see the Pope	age, sex, social class, region, denominational affiliation, frequency of church attendance	GB	21-26/4/1982	[QRL.38], [QRL.64], 6/1982 [QRL.125], 7-14/5/1982	8.1.3.2. Sample size: 968. Fieldwork: GP (CQ.814). Sponsor: U

Type of data	Breakdown	Area	Date	QRL Publication	Text Reference and remarks
Interest in/approval of the papal visit to Britain - intention to attend any of the papal functions or ceremonies/see the Pope pass through the streets/watch televised coverage of the events - places where it was intended to see the Pope	region, denominational affiliation, frequency of church attendance	GB	28/4-4/5/1982	[QRL.39] [QRL.125], 14/5/1982	8.1.3.2. Sample size: 947. Fieldwork: GP (CQ.815A). Sponsor: U
Interest in/approval of the papal visit to Britain - intention to attend any of the papal functions or ceremonies/see the Pope pass through the streets/watch televised coverage of the events - places where it was intended to see the Pope	age, sex, social class, region, denominational affiliation, frequency of church attendance	GB	5-10/5/1982	[QRL.43] [QRL.64], 6/1982 [QRL.112], 16/5/1982	8.1.3.2. Sample size: 958. Fieldwork: GP (CQ.816)
Interest in/approval of the papal visit to Britain - intention to attend any of the papal functions or ceremonies/see the Pope pass through the streets/watch televised coverage of the events - places where it was intended to see the Pope	region, denominational affiliation, frequency of church attendance	GB	12-17/5/1982	[QRL.35] [QRL.64], 6/1982	8.1.3.2. Sample size: 934. Fieldwork: GP (CQ.817A)
Approval of the papal visit to Britain - support for cancellation of the visit in the light of the Falklands crisis	denominational affiliation	GB	14-15/5/1982	[QRL.112], 16/5/1982	8.1.3.2. Sample size: 1,038. Fieldwork: GP (S.4023). Sponsor: STE
Interest in/approval of the papal visit to Britain - intention to attend any of the papal functions or ceremonies/see the Pope pass through the streets/watch televised coverage of the events - places where it was intended to see the Pope	region, denominational affiliation, frequency of church attendance	GB	19-24/5/1982	[QRL.35] [QRL.64], 6/1982 [QRL.70], 1982-83	8.1.3.2. Sample size: 963. Fieldwork: GP (CQ.818)

Question	Breakdown	Area	Date	Reference	Sample details
Interest in/approval of the papal visit to Britain - incidence of attendance at any of the papal functions or ceremonies/seeing the Pope pass through the streets/watching televised coverage of the events	age, sex, social class, region, party political preference, denominational affiliation, frequency of church attendance, other religious variable	GB	9-15/6/1982	[QRL.35] [QRL.36] [QRL.125], 30/7/1982	8.1.3.2. Sample size: 1,000. Fieldwork: GP (CQ.821B)
Interest in/approval of the papal visit to Britain - incidence of attendance at any of the papal functions or ceremonies/seeing the Pope pass through the streets/watching televised coverage of the events	region, denominational affiliation, frequency of church attendance	GB	30/6-5/7/1982	[QRL.35]	8.1.3.2. Sample size: 936. Fieldwork: GP (CQ.824)
Approval of the papal visit to Britain		GB	11/1982		8.1.3.2. Sample size: 991. Fieldwork: GP (CQ.845)

Religion and morals

Question	Breakdown	Area	Date	Reference	Sample details
Reasons (including religious ones) for being honest, truthful and kind	frequency of church attendance, other religious variable	GB	1-15/12/1954	[QRL.97]	8.2.1.1. Sample size: 1,859. Fieldwork: GP. Sponsor: BBC
Reasons (including religious ones) for being honest, truthful and kind		GB	2-12/2/1957	[QRL.12]	8.2.1.1. Sample size: 2,261. Fieldwork: GP (CS.1717). Sponsor: NC
Reasons (including religious ones) for being honest, truthful and kind - extent to which the Church was too strict/not strict enough in its standards of behaviour	age, sex, social class, region, denominational affiliation, frequency of church attendance, other religious variable	England	16/12/1963-20/1/1964	[QRL.120] [QRL.121]	8.2.1.1. Sample size: 2,211. Fieldwork: GP (CS.5480). Sponsor: ABC TV. Data set
Belief that religion helped to maintain the standards and morals of society, that the main purpose of religion was to provide a set of rules to live by	age, sex, social class, other religious variable	GB	2/1968	[QRL.94]	8.2.1.1. Sample size: 1,071. Fieldwork: ORC. Sponsor: ITA

Type of data	Breakdown	Area	Date	QRL Publication	Text Reference and remarks
Belief that religion helped to maintain the standards and morals of society, that the main purpose of religion was to provide a set of rules to live by	other religious variable	Northern Ireland	2/12/1968 -10/1/1969	[QRL.94]	8.2.1.1. Sample size: 694. Fieldwork: ORC. Sponsor: ITA, UTV and the Churches.
Extent to which people could be moral without believing in God - belief that the Ten Commandments should be the basis of modern life	age, sex, marital status, social class, education, region	GB	8-15/6/1970	[QRL.55], 5/1/1971 [QRL.101]	8.2.1.1. Sample size: 1,395. Fieldwork: NOP (4233). Sponsor: DM
Belief that religion helped to maintain the standards and morals of society		GB	15-20/1/1973		8.2.1.1. Sample size: 647. Fieldwork: ORC (7/1337). Sponsor: IBA
Extent to which the main value of having a religious faith was to provide a moral standard to live by	age, sex, denominational affiliation	GB	23-29/7/1979	[QRL.93]	8.2.1.1. Sample size: 988. Fieldwork: MAR (51809/1). Sponsor: *Now!*. Data set: SN 1366
Necessity for people's daily lives to be governed by religious commandments		GB	9-10/1979	[QRL.92]	Sample size: 987. Fieldwork: GP (S.5077). Sponsor: LDC. Multinational

Question/Topic	Breakdown	Area	Date	References	Details
Continuing applicability of each of the Ten Commandments both for respondent and for people as a whole		UK	3/1981	[QRL.31], 1981 [QRL.70], 1982-83 [QRL.87], 4-5/1982 [QRL.125], 11/12/1981	8.2.1.1. Sample size: 1,543. Fieldwork: GP (S.2131). Sponsor: EVSSG. Multinational
Religion and sexual questions					
Desire to see the Roman Catholic Church accept the use of birth control - likely effect of such acceptance upon attitudes towards the Catholic Church	denominational affiliation	GB	26/2-2/3/1965	[QRL.12], [QRL.57], 11/3/1965 [QRL.64], 3/1965	8.2.2.2. Sample size: 1,000. Fieldwork: GP. Sponsor: DT
Extent to which Roman Catholics should/would follow the Pope's ban on the use of contraceptive methods - likely effect of the Pope's decision upon respect for the Catholic Church	denominational affiliation	GB	1-4/8/1968	[QRL.12], [QRL.64], 8/1968 [QRL.112], 11/8/1968	8.2.2.2. Fieldwork: GP
Legitimacy of the Church concerning itself with the use of contraceptive methods by married couples		GB	9-11/8/1968	[QRL.12], [QRL.64], 8/1968	Fieldwork: GP
Approval of the Pope's decision to ban the use of artificial methods of birth control by Catholics - likely effect of the Pope's statement upon the chances for Christian unity	denominational affiliation	GB	14-19/8/1968	[QRL.77], 8/1968	8.2.2.2. Sample size: 1,218. Fieldwork: NOP (3099). Data set: SN 68019
Attitude towards the recruitment of homosexuals for the clergy - possibility of a homosexual being a good Christian/Jew		GB	3-8/8/1977	[QRL.64], 8/1977	8.2.2.4, 9.1.2.2. Fieldwork: GP
Attitude towards the recruitment of homosexuals for the clergy - possibility of a homosexual being a good Christian/Jew		GB	4-9/7/1979	[QRL.13], 1979 [QRL.64], 7/1979 [QRL.70], 1979-80	8.2.2.4, 9.1.2.2. Sample size: 905. Fieldwork: GP

Type of data	Breakdown	Area	Date	QRL Publication	Text Reference and remarks
Attitude towards the recruitment of homosexuals for the clergy - possibility of a homosexual being a good Christian/Jew		GB	28/10 -2/11/1981	[QRL.31], 1981 [QRL.64], 11/1981 [QRL.70], 1981-82	8.2.2.4, 9.1.2.2. Sample size: 998. Fieldwork: GP (CQ.792)
Religious aspects of marriage and divorce					
Agreement with the rules which made it practically impossible for a divorced person to be remarried by a minister of religion		GB	5/1947	[QRL.12]	8.2.3.2. Fieldwork: GP (S.150)
Common religion as a factor contributing to a happy marriage	denominational affiliation	GB	1/1950	[QRL.74], 7/2/1950	8.2.3.1. Fieldwork: GP
Strong religious beliefs as a factor making for a successful marriage		GB	5-16/4/1952		8.2.3.1. Fieldwork: GP (S.302A). Sponsor: NC
Agreement with the Archbishop of Canterbury's ruling that the Church of England should not remarry a divorced person so long as the other party was still alive - whether an innocent party should come under this ban or not - desire to see the clergy having discretion to remarry divorced people after acquainting themselves with the circumstances of the case	frequency of church attendance	GB	4-7/11/1955	[QRL.12]	8.2.3.2. Sample size: 896. Fieldwork: GP (S.452A)

Description	Variables	Country	Date	QRL	Notes
Agreement with the Archbishop of Canterbury's ruling that the Church of England should not remarry any divorced person so long as the other party was still alive - whether an innocent party should be included under this ban or not - desire to see the clergy having discretion to remarry divorced people after acquainting themselves with the circumstances of the case		GB	2-12/2/1957	[QRL.12] [QRL.74], 16/4/1957	8.2.3.2. Sample size: 2,261. Fieldwork: GP (CS.1717). Sponsor: NC
Approval of marriage between Catholics and Protestants/between Jews and non-Jews		GB	23-26/5/1968	[QRL.12] [QRL.28] [QRL.62] [QRL.64], 8/1968	8.2.3.1. Fieldwork: GP. Sponsor: STE. Multinational
Attitude towards people who married outside of their own religion	age, sex, education	GB	1-3/1969	[QRL.115]	8.2.3.1. Sample size: 1,490. Fieldwork: IS. Sponsor: RDA. Data set: SN 987. Multinational
Advice to friends whose daughter wanted to marry a man of a different religion	age, sex, marital status, social class, education, region	GB	8-15/6/1970	[QRL.101]	8.2.3.1. Sample size: 1,395. Fieldwork: NOP (4233). Sponsor: DM
Advice to friends whose daughter wanted to marry a man of a different religion		GB	4/1971		8.2.3.1. Sample size: 2,266. Fieldwork: NOP (4975). Data set: SN 71001
Approval of marriage between Catholics and Protestants/between Jews and non-Jews		GB	22-28/8/1973	[QRL.12] [QRL.64], 9/1973	8.2.3.1. Fieldwork: GP

Type of data	Breakdown	Area	Date	QRL Publication	Text Reference and remarks
Belief that marriage was just a legal arrangement in which religion played no part/a marriage without religion was no marriage at all	age, sex, marital status, social class, region	GB	23-28/3/1977	[QRL.99]	Sample size: 1,050. Fieldwork: ORC (17704). Sponsor: BBC
Attitude towards people who married outside of their own religion		GB	8-28/11/1977	[QRL.13], 1978 [QRL.64], 1/1978 [QRL.70], 1978-79	8.2.3.1. Sample size: 1,267. Fieldwork: GP. Sponsor: RDA
Attitude towards a son/daughter marrying someone of the opposite religion	denominational affiliation	Northern Ireland	6-11/1978	[QRL.24]	8.2.3.1. Sample size: 1,277. Fieldwork: IMS (5234). Sponsor: QUB. Data set: SN 1347
Approval of Prince Charles' speech criticising the Roman Catholic Church's doctrine on marriage - desire to see divorced people being allowed to remarry in church		GB	11/7/1978	[QRL.53], 20/7/1978	8.2.3.2. Sample size: 1,080. Fieldwork: MORI. Sponsor: DE
Attitude towards Prince Charles marrying, and still becoming king if he did marry, a Roman Catholic	age	GB	11-12/2/1980	[QRL.111], 15/2/1980	Sample size: 793. Fieldwork: MAR. Sponsor: *Sun.* Telephone poll

Extent to which marriage partners shared the same attitudes towards religion - importance of shared religious beliefs in making for a successful marriage		UK	3/1981	[QRL.70], 1982-83	8.2.3.1. Sample size: 1,543. Fieldwork: GP (S.2131). Sponsor: EVSSG. Multinational
Importance of shared religious beliefs in making for a successful marriage		GB	13-20/4/1982	[QRL.64], 5/1982 [QRL.70], 1982-83	8.2.3.1. Sample size: 1,882. Fieldwork: GP (CQ.813/813B). Sponsor: STE.

Religion and politics

Extent to which the Churches should interest themselves in questions of social reform		GB	6/1942	[QRL.9], [QRL.74], 4/7/1942	8.3.1.1. Sample size: 1,981. Fieldwork: GP (S.88). Data set: SN 2037-2045
Extent to which Church leaders such as the Archbishop of Canterbury should be involved in politics		GB	19-27/5/1956	[QRL.12]	8.3.1.1. Fieldwork: GP (S.464)
Extent to which the Church should express its views on day to day social and political questions - support for the disestablishment of the Church of England		GB	2-12/2/1957	[QRL.12], [QRL.74], 16/4/1957	8.3.1.1. Sample size: 2,261. Fieldwork: GP (CS.1717). Sponsor: NC
Approval of a formal diplomatic agreement between the Vatican and the Kremlin	denominational affiliation	GB	19-24/10/1961	[QRL.12] [QRL.47], 12/1/1962 [QRL.64], 11/1961	8.3.1.1. Fieldwork: GP

Type of data	Breakdown	Area	Date	QRL Publication	Text Reference and remarks
Approval of a formal diplomatic agreement between the Vatican and the Kremlin - implications of such an agreement for world peace - approval of the Pope's appeal for universal disarmament and greater understanding amongst nations - likely effect of this appeal upon the international situation		GB	4/1963	[QRL.12] [QRL.64], 7/1963	8.3.1.1. Fieldwork: GP
Approval of a formal diplomatic agreement between the Vatican and the Kremlin - approval of Pope Paul's stated intention to press for greater East-West understanding - likely effect of such pressure upon the international situation	denominational affiliation	GB	28/6-2/7/1963	[QRL.12] [QRL.64], 7/1963 [QRL.112], 14/7/1963	8.3.1.1. Fieldwork: GP. Sponsor: STE
Importance attached to freedom of religion relative to the other major freedoms		GB	17-24/9/1963	[QRL.12] [QRL.81], Spr. 1965	8.3.1.1. Sample size:1,068. Fieldwork: GP (CQ.336)
Extent to which the Churches should express their views on day to day social questions - extent to which the Churches should be concerned with housing/the unemployed/disarmament and nuclear weapons/the colour bar/the hungry people of the world/marriage counselling/education/automation/ racially mixed marriages	age, sex, social class, region, denominational affiliation, frequency of church attendance, other religious variable	England	16/12/1963-20/1/1964	[QRL.120] [QRL.121]	8.3.1.1. Sample size: 2,211. Fieldwork: GP (CS. 5480). Sponsor: ABC TV. Data set.
Extent to which a monarchy/republic was better for the religious life of any country	age, sex, social class	GB	10/1964	[QRL.18]	Sample size: 1,005. Fieldwork: MO. Sponsor: L.M.Harris

Compatibility of political activism with Christian discipleship	denominational affiliation	Northern Ireland	3-8/1968	[QRL.26]	Sample size: 1,291. Fieldwork: UOS. Sponsor: R.Rose. Data set: SN 1040
Extent to which the Church should express its views on day to day social and political questions		GB	9-11/8/1968	[QRL.12] [QRL.64], 8/1968	8.3.1.1. Fieldwork: GP
Importance of freedom of religion relative to the other major freedoms - extent to which the Church should express its views on day to day social and political questions		GB	6/1969	[QRL.12] [QRL.64], 10/1969	8.3.1.1. Fieldwork: GP
Support for the disestablishment of the Church of England	denominational affiliation	GB	13-19/4/1970	[QRL.53], 13/5/1970 [QRL.100]	8.3.1.1. Sample size: 2,472. Fieldwork: LHR (032). Sponsor: DE. Data set
Agreement with the presence of the senior Anglican bishops in the House of Lords	age, sex, marital status, social class, education, region	GB	8-15/6/1970	[QRL.101]	8.3.1.1. Sample size: 1,395. Fieldwork: NOP (4233). Sponsor: DM
Extent to which freedom to practise one's own religion was a basic human right/a privilege granted by the state		GB	1977	[QRL.70], 1978-79	8.3.1.1. Sample size: 2,000. Sponsor: United States Information Communication Agency. Multinational

Type of data	Breakdown	Area	Date	QRL Publication	Text Reference and remarks
Extent to which the Church should be involved in politics - extent to which the Church should raise money for charities that helped people in Britain/charities that helped people overseas/political movements in Britain/peaceful political movements overseas/political movements overseas which resorted to violence/refugees like the 'boat people'/victims of natural disasters/anti-apartheid movements - extent to which members of the clergy were/should be allowed to join political parties - eligibility of members of the clergy to stand for Parliament	age, sex, denominational affiliation	GB	23-29/7/1979	[QRL.79], 21/12/1979 [QRL.93]	8.3.1.1. Sample size: 988. Fieldwork: MAR (51809/1). Sponsor: *Now!*. Data set: SN 1366
Likelihood of political parties based on religious beliefs gaining popular support	age, sex, social class, education	GB	9-10/1979	[QRL.70], 1980-81 [QRL.92]	Sample size: 987. Fieldwork: GP (S.5077). Sponsor: LDC. Multinational
Sunday observance					
Desire to see the BBC include a regular dance-band broadcast in its Sunday programmes	age, social class	GB	12/1938	[QRL.9] [QRL.12] [QRL.74], 31/12/1938	Sample size: 1,868. Fieldwork: GP (S.53). Sponsor: NC. Data set: SN 2037-2045
Approval of the wartime Sunday opening of theatres/cinemas	age, sex, social class	GB	4/1941	[QRL.12] [QRL.74], 15/5/1941	8.3.2.2. Sample size: 2,192. Fieldwork: GP (S.77). Data set: SN 2037-2045

Approval of the Sunday opening of theatres	GB		1/1943	[QRL.12] [QRL.74], 20/3/1943	8.3.2.2. Sample size: 1,996. Fieldwork: GP (S.95). Data set: SN 2037-2045
Approval of the wartime Sunday opening of cinemas/theatres - support for a change in the law to allow the Sunday opening of cinemas and theatres	GB	age, social class, region	1/1944	[QRL.9] [QRL.12] [QRL.74], 7/2/1944	8.3.2.2. Sample size: 1,451. Fieldwork: GP (S.105). Data set: SN 2037-2045
Approval of/participation in Sunday games	GB	age, sex, region	13/9-6/10/1948	[QRL.71] [QRL.54], 20/10/1948	Sample size: 2,078. Fieldwork: MO. Sponsor: DG
Approval of the opening of theatres/professional sport/horse-racing on Sundays	GB	party political preference, denominational affiliation	1/1953	[QRL.12] [QRL.74], 31/1/1953	8.3.2.2, 8.3.2.3. Fieldwork: GP (S.340)
Approval of the opening of theatres/professional sport/horse-racing on Sundays	GB	age	2-12/2/1957	[QRL.12] [QRL.74], 16/4/1957	8.3.2.2, 8.3.2.3. Sample size: 2,261. Fieldwork: GP (CS. 1717). Sponsor: NC

Type of data	Breakdown	Area	Date	QRL Publication	Text Reference and remarks
Support for the appointment of a Royal Commission to investigate the laws affecting Sunday observance - support for a change in the law to allow public houses to open the same hours on Sundays as on weekdays/places of entertainment such as theatres and cinemas to open on Sundays as on weekdays/professional sport such as cricket and football to be played on Sundays - agreement with special legal restrictions on what people could do on Sundays - knowledge/approval of the action of the Lord's Day Observance Society in opposing a Sunday ballet performance sponsored by the Bishop of Coventry	sex, region, denominational affiliation, frequency of church attendance	GB	3-7/5/1958	[QRL.12] [QRL.64], 2/1965 [QRL.98] [QRL.104], 15/5/1958	8.3.2.1, 8.3.2.2, 8.3.2.3, 8.3.2.4. Fieldwork: GP (CQ.70B). Sponsor: NC
Approval of the Sunday opening of public houses and other licensed premises		GB	23-27/7/1959	[QRL.12]	8.3.2.4. Fieldwork: GP (CQ.123)
Current and past attitudes towards Sunday shopping		GB	4/1962	[QRL.64], 2/1965	8.3.2.5. Fieldwork: GP
Agreement with special legal restrictions on what people could do on Sundays - support for a change in the law to allow public houses to open the same hours on Sundays as on weekdays/places of entertainment such as theatres and cinemas to open on Sundays as on weekdays/professional cricket, football and other sports to be played on Sundays - current and past attitudes towards Sunday shopping		GB	4-9/2/1965	[QRL.12] [QRL.57], 22/2/1965, [QRL.64], 2/1965	8.3.2.1, 8.3.2.2, 8.3.2.3, 8.3.2.4, 8.3.2.5. Sample size: 1,000. Fieldwork: GP. Sponsor: DT

Subject	Classification	Area	Date	Source	Details
Likelihood of attending theatres/professional sporting events on Sundays	sex, frequency of church attendance	GB	3/1966	[QRL.57], 29/4/1966 [QRL.122]	8.3.2.2, 8.3.2.3. Sample size: 1,501. Fieldwork: GP. Sponsor: SU
Approval of professional sport being played on Sundays - likelihood of attending league football matches on Sundays	age	England	5-13/12/1966	[QRL.55], 10/2/1967	8.3.2.3. Sample size: 1,556. Fieldwork: NOP. Sponsor: DM
Approval of amateur sport/professional sport/theatres, cinemas and other entertainments being allowed to charge for admission after 2 o'clock on Sundays	age, sex, region	GB	13-21/1/1968	[QRL.12] [QRL.57], 31/1/1968 [QRL.64], 1/1968	8.3.2.2, 8.3.2.3. Sample size: 1,000. Fieldwork: GP. Sponsor: DT
Attitude towards the Sunday opening of public houses - intention to vote in the forthcoming referendum on the Sunday opening of public houses - approval of clubs/hotels and restaurants being allowed to serve alcoholic drinks on Sundays - support for a change in the law to allow sports and public dancing to take place on Sundays	age, party political preference, denominational affiliation	Wales	1968	[QRL.126], 24/10/1968	8.3.2.4. Fieldwork: ORC. Sponsor: WM
Approval of professional sport being played on Sundays - likelihood of attending league football matches on Sundays		GB	1968	[QRL.55], 28/2/1969	8.3.2.3. Fieldwork: NOP. Sponsor: DM
Support for a change in the law to allow public houses to open the same hours on Sundays as on weekdays/places of entertainment such as theatres and cinemas to open on Sundays as on weekdays/professional cricket, football and other sports to be played on Sundays		GB	14-16/3/1969	[QRL.12] [QRL.64], 3/1969	8.3.2.2, 8.3.2.3, 8.3.2.4. Fieldwork: GP

Type of data	Breakdown	Area	Date	QRL Publication	Text Reference and remarks
Incidence of Sunday shopping - knowledge of, and support for a change in, existing Sunday trading regulations - attitude towards the Sunday opening of public houses	age, sex, social class, education, region	GB	5/10 -30/11/1970	[QRL.5] [QRL.6]	8.3.2.4, 8.3.2.5. Sample size: 2,747. Fieldwork: OPCSSSD (SS.443). Sponsor: Home Office and Scottish Home and Health Dept.
Desire to see more shops open on Sundays/more professional sport on Sundays/Sunday being kept as a day of quiet/extended Sunday opening hours for public houses/more attention being paid to religion on Sundays		GB	18-24/10/1971		8.3.2.1, 8.3.2.3, 8.3.2.4, 8.3.2.5. Fieldwork: LHR (140). Data set
Approval of Sunday observance		GB	4-8/1/1973	[QRL.12] [QRL.64], 2/1973	8.3.2.1. Fieldwork: GP
Approval of professional football being played on Sundays during/after the power crisis - preferred kick-off time if professional football matches were to be played on Sundays	age, sex	GB	8-13/1/1974	[QRL.77], 1/1974	8.3.2.3. Sample size: 2,104. Fieldwork: NOP
Approval of all sports (including horse-racing and league football)/the opening of betting shops being allowed on Sundays	age, sex, social class, region	GB	27/1-2/2/1977	[QRL.55], 18/2/1977 [QRL.109]	8.3.2.3. Sample size: 1,955. Fieldwork: NOP (2073). Sponsor: DM

Subject	Breakdown	Area	Fieldwork dates	References	Details
Demand for/likely utilisation of extended Sunday shopping facilities	age, sex, marital status, social class, region	GB	21-27/9/1978	[QRL.106] [QRL.114]	8.3.2.5. Sample size: 1,946. Fieldwork: NOP (3826). Sponsor: NCC
Attitude towards the Sunday opening of public houses in Wales		Wales	15/5-9/9/1979		8.3.2.4. Sample size: 858. Fieldwork: GP (S.5061). Sponsor: WES. Data set: SN 1591
Desire to see continental-style Sundays in Scotland - approval of professional football being played on Sundays - opinion of the Church's influence over what was/was not allowed on Sundays - respect for the views of people who wished to see society as a whole strictly observe the Sabbath	age, sex, social class, denominational affiliation, frequency of church attendance	Scotland	27/9-7/10/1980	[QRL.66], 27/10/1980 [QRL.102]	8.3.2.1, 8.3.2.3. Sample size: 1,014. Fieldwork: STS (SOS.980). Sponsor: GH
Approval of league football/test cricket/horse-racing/the opening of betting shops being allowed on Sundays	age, sex, social class, region	GB	20-25/11/1980	[QRL.55], 19/12/1980 [QRL.80], 2/1981 [QRL.110]	8.3.2.3. Sample size: 1,911. Fieldwork: NOP (6341). Sponsor: DM
Support for a change in the law to allow shops besides those selling newspapers and certain types of food to open on Sundays	age, sex, social class, region	GB	27/11-1/12/1981	[QRL.88], 1/1982 [QRL.70], 1981-82	8.3.2.5. Sample size: 2,005. Fieldwork: MORI (7534). Sponsor: Dickie Dirts.
Support for a change in the law to allow shops besides those selling newspapers and certain types of food to open on Sundays	age, sex, social class, region, party political preference	GB	23-27/9/1982	[QRL.70], 1982-83 [QRL.88], 10/1982 [QRL.105]	8.3.2.5. Sample size: 2,016. Fieldwork: MORI. Sponsor: NCC

Type of data	Breakdown	Area	Date	QRL Publication	Text Reference and remarks
Importance of allowing all shops to open on Sundays	party political preference	GB	22-23/3/1983	[QRL.80], 4/1983	8.3.2.5. Sample size: 2,135. Fieldwork: NOP (9056). Sponsor: General Election Co-ordinating Committee on Animal Protection.
Religious education Support for/personal experience of church elementary schools		GB	1/1943		8.3.3.4. Sample size: 1,996. Fieldwork: GP (S.95). Data set: SN 2037-2045
Support for/personal experience of church elementary schools		GB	12/1943		8.3.3.4. Sample size: 1,773. Fieldwork: GP (S.104). Data set: SN 2037-2045
Desire to see religious education being given a more defined place in the life and work of the schools		GB	2/1944	[QRL.9] [QRL.12]	8.3.3.3. Fieldwork: GP (S.106)
Importance attached to the provision of religious instruction in schools - approval of the use of state funds to build and repair denominational schools		GB	1-13/11/1951	[QRL.12]	8.3.3.3, 8.3.3.4. Fieldwork: GP (S.274A)
Attitude towards the provision of religious instruction in day schools	frequency of church attendance, other religious variable	GB	1-15/12/1954	[QRL.97]	8.3.3.3. Sample size: 1,859. Fieldwork: GP. Sponsor: BBC

Topic	Breakdown variables	Country	Date	Reference	Details
Extent to which religion and scripture should be taught in schools		GB	2-12/2/1957	[QRL.12]	8.3.3.3. Sample size: 2,261. Fieldwork: GP (CS. 1717). Sponsor: NC
Support for an increase in the grants paid to denominational schools	party political preference	GB	16-20/5/1959	[QRL.12] [QRL.74], 12/6/1959	8.3.3.4. Fieldwork: GP (CQ.114). Sponsor: NC
Importance attached to a religious background in children's education	age, sex, social class, education, region	GB	1-2/1963	[QRL.82]	8.3.3.3. Sample size: 2,000. Fieldwork: BMRB. Sponsor: RDA. Data set: SN 1511
Extent to which religion and scripture should be taught in schools	age, sex, social class, region, denominational affiliation, frequency of church attendance, other religious variable	England	16/12/1963-20/1/1964	[QRL.113], 19/9/1965 [QRL.120] [QRL.121]	8.3.3.3. Sample size: 2,211. Fieldwork: GP (CS.5480). Sponsor: ABC TV. Data set
Support for the continuance of the arrangement whereby all schoolchildren had to participate in religious instruction and daily worship unless excused by parental request - preference for a comparative/Christian approach to religious instruction in schools - preference for the abolition of religious instruction in state primary/secondary schools - receipt of religious instruction by respondent's own school age children	age, sex, region	GB	3/1965	[QRL.73], 27/5/1965	8.3.3.3. Sample size: 2,160. Fieldwork: NOP. Sponsor: NS

R-O

Type of data	Breakdown	Area	Date	QRL Publication	Text Reference and remarks
Importance of providing information about Christianity and other world religions/help in becoming a convinced Christian to schoolboys/girls over the age of twelve years - knowledge of the law relating to the provision of religious instruction/a daily act of worship in state schools	age, sex, social class, region, party political preference, denominational affiliation	GB	26-31/3/1969	[QRL.78]	8.3.3.3. Sample size: 1,905. Fieldwork: NOP (3490). Sponsor: BHA.
Attitude towards the maintenance of separate schools for Roman Catholics	party political preference	Scotland	15/10/1974-20/1/1975	[QRL.104], 15/10/1975	8.3.3.4. Sample size: 1,178. Fieldwork: SCPR. Sponsor: BES. Data set: SN 681
Attitude towards the existence of denominational schools	age, sex, social class, denominational affiliation	Scotland	23-30/8/1976	[QRL.66], 12/10/1976 [QRL.103]	8.3.3.4. Sample size: 1,044. Fieldwork: STS (SOS.876). Sponsor: GH
Attitude towards the maintenance of separate schools for Roman Catholics		Scotland	5-10/1979		8.3.3.4. Sample size: 729. Fieldwork: RSL (J.1279). Sponsor: SES. Data set: SN 1604

THE INSTITUTIONAL CHURCH
Clergy

Type of data	Breakdown	Area	Date	QRL Publication	Text Reference and remarks
Willingness to contact a minister of religion over family troubles		GB	9/1948	[QRL.12]	9.1.2.2. Fieldwork: GP (S.171)
Extent to which the ordained ministry was regarded as a suitable profession for a young man to follow		GB	8/1950	[QRL.12]	9.1.2.2. Fieldwork: GP (S.214)

Willingness to seek a priest's advice in the event of marital difficulties		GB	5-16/4/1952	[QRL.12] [QRL.74], 1/5/1952	9.1.2.2. Fieldwork: GP (S.302A). Sponsor: NC
Usefulness of the clergy		GB	1960	[QRL.19]	9.1.2.2. Fieldwork: MO
Clergymen's influence for good within the community - extent to which clergymen's motives were altruistic/personal - extent to which the clergy were receptive to new ideas/sincere in their beliefs/useful workers in their parishes/overworked/underpaid - contact with the local clergy	age, sex, social class, region, denominational affiliation, frequency of church attendance, other religious variable	England	16/12/1963-20/1/1964	[QRL.57], 20/9/1965 [QRL.113], 19/9/1965 [QRL.120] [QRL.121]	9.1.2.2. Sample size: 2,211. Fieldwork: GP (CS.5480). Sponsor: ABC TV. Data set
Admiration for the clergy		GB	6/1964	[QRL.12], [QRL.57], 15/6/1964 [QRL.112], 14/6/1964	9.1.2.2. Fieldwork: GP. Sponsor: STE
Admiration for the clergy		GB	23-30/6/1964	[QRL.64], 8/1964	9.1.2.2. Fieldwork: GP
Willingness to turn to a clergyman for comfort and help	other religious variable	GB	2/1968	[QRL.94]	9.1.2.2. Sample size: 1,071. Fieldwork: ORC. Sponsor: ITA
Usefulness of the clergy within the community	age, social class	GB	7-13/2/1968	[QRL.77], 2/1968 [QRL.81], 1967-68	9.1.2.2. Sample size: 1,834. Fieldwork: NOP (2682). Data set: SN 68013
Importance of church members obeying their minister or priest - extent to which respondent's minister or priest should/did speak his views on public matters	denominational affiliation	Northern Ireland	3-8/1968	[QRL.26]	9.1.2.2. Sample size: 1,291. Fieldwork: UOS. Sponsor: R.Rose. Data set: SN 1040

Type of data	Breakdown	Area	Date	QRL Publication	Text Reference and remarks
Willingness to turn to a clergyman for comfort and help	other religious variable	Northern Ireland	2/12/1968 -10/1/1969	[QRL.94] [QRL.95]	9.1.2.2. Sample size: 694. Fieldwork: ORC. Sponsor: ITA, UTV and the Churches
Admiration for the clergy		GB	1-3/1969	[QRL.115]	9.1.2.2. Sample size: 1,490. Fieldwork: IS. Sponsor: RDA. Data set: SN 987. Multinational
Approval of clerical marriage	denominational affiliation	GB	3/1970	[QRL.77], 11/1970	9.1.2.2. Sample size: 1,978. Fieldwork: NOP
Approval of the ordination of women - willingness to turn to a clergyman in the event of a personal problem - knowledge of any of the local clergy by name - extent to which the clergy did a good/bad job, were well/badly paid	age, sex, marital status, social class, education, region	GB	8-15/6/1970	[QRL.101]	9.1.2.2. Sample size: 1,395. Fieldwork: NOP (4233). Sponsor: DM
Relative chances of a working class person and a middle class person of becoming a Church of England vicar/a Methodist minister	sex, social class	GB	20-22/1/1972	[QRL.77], 7/1972	9.1.2.2. Sample size: 1,000. Fieldwork: NOP. Sponsor: DM
Whether respondent had sought the advice of a vicar or priest on the previous day	age, sex	GB	20-24/9/1972	[QRL.113], 22/4/1973	9.1.2.2. Sample size: 1,026. Fieldwork: ORC (7238). Sponsor: ST. Data set

Topic	Breakdown	Area	Date	Source	Notes
Sympathy for the clergy		GB	1/10/1973 -7/2/1974	[QRL.22]	9.1.2.2. Sample size: 1,802. Fieldwork: MAFS. Sponsor: M.Abrams and A.Marsh. Data set: SN 672
Clergymen's influence for good within the community - extent to which clergymen's motives were altruistic/personal		GB	8-13/5/1974	[QRL.12] [QRL.64], 5/1974	9.1.2.2. Fieldwork: GP
Willingness to turn to religious leaders for answers to personal problems	age, sex, social class, region	GB	20-25/8/1974	[QRL.108]	9.1.2.2. Sample size: 1,093. Fieldwork: ORC (34333). Sponsor: BBC
Approval of the ordination of women		GB	17-22/3/1976	[QRL.64], 4/1976	9.1.2.2. Fieldwork: GP
Awareness of discussions about, and attitude towards, the admission of women to the priesthood of the Church of England - reasons for opposing their admission	age, sex, social class, region, denominational affiliation, frequency of church attendance	GB	13-19/7/1978	[QRL.44], 31/8/1978 [QRL.47], 1/9/1978 [QRL.48], 7/9/1978 [QRL.49] [QRL.51], 1/9/1978 [QRL.123], 25/8/1978	9.1.2.2, 9.1.3.1. Sample size: 1,989. Fieldwork: NOP (3594)
Usefulness of the clergy - expertise of the clergy in dealing with social problems such as baby-battering and loneliness in old age		GB	5/1979	[QRL.73], 2/8/1979	9.1.2.2. Sample size: 1,018. Fieldwork: BMRB. Sponsor: LWT

Type of data	Breakdown	Area	Date	QRL Publication	Text Reference and remarks
Willingness to consult a vicar or priest over family/job/health/religious/ sexual/marital problems - frequency of, and reasons for, contact with the local vicar or priest - most important function which the local clergy had to perform - belief that most local clergymen did a good job for their parishioners - extent to which members of the clergy were/should be allowed to join trade unions - approval of the ordination of women	age, sex, denominational affiliation	GB	23-29/7/1979	[QRL.79], 21/12/1979 [QRL.93]	9.1.2.2. Sample size: 988. Fieldwork: MAR (51809/1). Sponsor: *Now!*. Data set: SN 1366
Clergymen's value to the community - experience of consulting a clergyman over a personal problem		GB	8-13/4/1981	[QRL.64], 5/1981 [QRL.70], 1980-81 [QRL.73], 7/5/1981	9.1.2.2. Sample size: 994. Fieldwork: GP (CQ.763). Sponsor: NS and the National Institute for Social Work
Effectiveness of the clergy in looking after people	region	GB	29-30/5/1981	[QRL.88], 5-10/1981 [QRL.70], 1981-82	9.1.2.2. Sample size: 1,886. Fieldwork: MORI (6756). Sponsor: ST. Data set: SN 1617
Awareness of discussions about, and attitude towards, the admission of women to the priesthood of the Church of England - reasons for opposing their admission	denominational affiliation, frequency of church attendance	GB	3-8/9/1981	[QRL.80], 2/1982 [QRL.123], 13/11/1981	9.1.2.2, 9.1.3.1. Sample size: 1,991. Fieldwork: NOP (7191)

Sunday schools

Description	Variables	Country	Date	Reference	Notes
Sunday school attendance by respondent's children - reasons for sending children to Sunday school - Sunday school attendance by respondent when a child	frequency of church attendance	GB	1947	[QRL.75], 6/11/1947	9.3.1.2. Fieldwork: RSNR. Sponsor: NR
Sunday school attendance by respondent when a child - willingness to send own children to Sunday school - reasons for sending/not sending children to Sunday school	frequency of church attendance	GB	7/1948	[QRL.54], 10/8/1948	9.3.1.2. Sample size: 2,055. Fieldwork: MO (09/1). Sponsor: DG
Sunday school or Bible class attendance by respondent when a child - desirability of childen attending Sunday school - Sunday school attendance by respondent's children	age, frequency of church attendance, other religious variable	GB	1-15/12/1954	[QRL.7] [QRL.97]	9.3.1.2. Sample size: 1,859. Fieldwork: GP. Sponsor: BBC
Sunday school attendance by respondent when a child - desirability of children attending Sunday school - Sunday school attendance by respondent's children		GB	2-12/2/1957	[QRL.12] [QRL.74], 15/4/1957	9.3.1.2. Sample size: 2,261. Fieldwork: GP (CS.1717). Sponsor: NC
Voluntary/involuntary Sunday school attendance by respondent's children	age, sex, social class, region, denominational affiliation, frequency of church attendance, other religious variable	England	16/12/1963-20/1/1964	[QRL.120] [QRL.121]	9.3.1.2. Sample size: 2,211. Fieldwork: GP (CS.5480). Sponsor: ABC TV. Data set
Sunday school attendance by respondent's children		GB	3/1966	[QRL.122]	9.3.1.2. Sample size: 1,501. Fieldwork: GP. Sponsor: SU
Actual/intended encouragement of own children to attend Sunday school	age, sex, marital status, social class, education, region	GB	8-15/6/1970	[QRL.101]	9.3.1.2. Sample size: 1,395. Fieldwork: NOP (4233). Sponsor: DM

Evangelism

Description	Variables	Country	Date	Reference	Notes
Knowledge of/attitude towards Billy Graham		GB	20-31/3/1954	[QRL.12]	9.3.2.1. Fieldwork: GP (S.399)

Type of data	Breakdown	Area	Date	QRL Publication	Text Reference and remarks
Knowledge of/attitude towards Billy Graham		GB	19/5-2/6/1954	[QRL.12]	9.3.2.1. Fieldwork: GP (S.406)
Knowledge of/attitude towards Billy Graham		GB	10-15/6/1966	[QRL.12] [QRL.64], 7/1966	9.3.2.1. Sample size: 1,000. Fieldwork: GP

QUICK REFERENCE LIST KEY TO PUBLICATIONS

Reference	Author or Organisation	Title	Publisher	Frequency or Date	Remarks
[QRL.1]	Alan, P.	'The statistics of belief', *The Humanist*, Vol.76, pp.169-71		1961	
[QRL.2]	Alford, Robert Ross	*Party and Society: the Anglo-American Democracies*	John Murray, London	1964	
[QRL.3]	Argyle, Michael	*Religious Behaviour*	Routledge & Kegan Paul, London	1958	
[QRL.4]	Barley, Lynda	*Individual Bible Purchasing and Ownership: Results of 1982 Omnibus Study carried out by Gallup Polls Ltd.*	Bible Society, London	1982	
[QRL.5]	Bradley, Michael & Fenwick, David	*Public Attitudes to Liquor Licensing Laws in Great Britain: an Enquiry carried out in October-November 1970 by OPCS Social Survey Division on behalf of the Home Office and the Scottish Home and Health Department*	HMSO, London	1974	
[QRL.6]	Bradley, Michael & Fenwick, David	*Shopping Habits and Attitudes to Shop Hours in Great Britain: an Enquiry carried out in October-November 1970 by OPCS Social Survey Division on behalf of the Home Office and the Scottish Home and Health Department*	HMSO, London	1975	
[QRL.7]	Briggs, Asa	*The History of Broadcasting in the United Kingdom, Volume IV: Sound and Vision*	Oxford University Press, Oxford	1979	
[QRL.8]	Butler, David Henry Edgeworth & Stokes, Donald Elkinton	*Political Change in Britain: the Evolution of electoral Choice*	Macmillan, London	1974	Second Edition
[QRL.9]	Cantril, Albert Hadley	*Public Opinion, 1935-1946*	Princeton University Press, Princeton, New Jersey	1951	

[QRL.10]	Eysenck, Hans Jurgen	The Psychology of Politics	Routledge & Kegan Paul, London	1954	
[QRL.11]	Gaine, John J.	Young Adults today and the Future of the Faith	(Liverpool Institute of Socio-Religious Studies, Liverpool)	(1976)	
[QRL.12]	Gallup, George Horace	The Gallup international public Opinion Polls: Great Britain, 1937-1975	Random House, New York	1976	2 volumes
[QRL.13]	Gallup, George Horace	The international Gallup Polls: public Opinion	Scholarly Resources, Wilmington, Delaware	1980-81	2 volumes only published, containing data for 1978-79
[QRL.14]	Gallup, George Horace	'What mankind thinks about itself', Reader's Digest, vol.109, no.654, pp.51-6		October 1976	
[QRL.15]	Gorer, Geoffrey Edgar Solomon	Exploring English Character	Cresset Press, London	1955	
[QRL.16]	Gorton, Ted	'Belief in Britain', The Listener		17/24 December 1981	
[QRL.17]	Hardy, Alister	The spiritual Nature of Man: a Study of contemporary religious Experience	Clarendon Press, Oxford	1979	
[QRL.18]	Harris, Leonard Mortimer	Long to reign over us? The Status of the royal Family in the Sixties	William Kimber, London	(1966)	
[QRL.19]	Harrisson, Tom	Britain revisited	Victor Gollancz, London	1961	
[QRL.20]	Hay, David	Exploring inner Space: Scientists and religious Experience	Penguin Books, Harmondsworth	1982	
[QRL.21]	Hay, David & Morisy, Ann	'Reports of ecstatic, paranormal or religious experience in Great Britain and the United States: a comparison of trends' Journal for the Scientific Study of Religion, vol.17, pp.255-68		1978	
[QRL.22]	Marsh, Alan	Protest and Political Consciousness	Sage Publications, Beverly Hills	1977	

Reference	Author or Organisation	Title	Publisher	Frequency or Date	Remarks
[QRL.23]	Martin, Bernice	'Comments on some Gallup Poll statistics', *A Sociological Yearbook of Religion in Britain*, ed. David Martin, pp.146-97	SCM Press, London	1968	
[QRL.24]	Moxon-Browne, Edward	'Attitudes towards religion in Northern Ireland: some comparisons between Catholics and Protestants', *PACE*, vol.12, no.2, pp.21-3		Summer/ Autumn 1980	
[QRL.25]	Reid, Ivan	*Social Class Differences in Britain*	Grant McIntyre, London	1981	Second edition
[QRL.26]	Rose, Richard	*Governing without Consensus: an Irish Perspective*	Faber and Faber, London	1971	
[QRL.27]	Rose, Richard & McAllister, Ian	*United Kingdom Facts*	Macmillan, London	1982	
[QRL.28]	Sigelman, Lee	'Multi-nation surveys of religious beliefs', *Journal for the Scientific Study of Religion*, vol.16, pp.289-94		1977	
[QRL.29]	Simms, Madeleine	'Abortion and public opinion', *Family Planning*, vol.14, pp.51-2		1965-66	
[QRL.30]	Stark, Rodney	'Class, radicalism and religious involvement in Great Britain', *American Sociological Review*, vol.29, pp.698-706		1964	
[QRL.31]	Webb, Norman L.& Wybrow, Robert J.	*The Gallup Report*	Sphere Books, London	1981-82	2 volumes only published, containing data for 1980-81
[QRL.32]	National Opinion Polls Ltd.	*Abortion Law: a Survey carried out by National Opinion Polls Limited*	National Opinion Polls, London	1965	
[QRL.33]	Social Surveys (Gallup Poll) Ltd.	*Abortion Study, 28 November- 3 December 1979: conducted on behalf of 'Woman's Own'*	Social Surveys (Gallup Poll) Ltd., London	1979	

[QRL.34]	Social Surveys (Gallup Poll) Ltd.	*Abortions Study, November 1973*	Gallup, London	1973	
[QRL.35]	Social Surveys (Gallup Poll) Ltd.	*Assessing the Impact of the Papal Visit*	Social Surveys (Gallup Poll) Ltd., London	1982	
[QRL.36]	Social Surveys (Gallup Poll) Ltd	*Assessment of Papal Visit, 9-15 June 1982*	Social Surveys (Gallup Poll) Ltd., London	1982	
[QRL.37]	Marplan Ltd.	*Astrology, Superstition and Fortune-Telling: prepared for 'Now!' Magazine*	Marplan Ltd., London	1980	
[QRL.38]	Social Surveys (Gallup Poll) Ltd.	*Attitudes towards the Papal Visit and an Assessment of Attendance at Functions, 21-26 April 1982*	Social Surveys (Gallup Poll) Ltd., London	1982	
[QRL.39]	Social Surveys (Gallup Poll) Ltd.	*Attitudes towards the Papal Visit and an Assessment of Attendance at Functions, 28 April-4 May 1982*	Social Surveys (Gallup Poll) Ltd., London	1982	
[QRL.40]	Social Surveys (Gallup Poll) Ltd.	*Attitudes towards the Papal Visit and an initial Assessment of Attendance at Functions, April 1982*	Social Surveys (Gallup Poll) Ltd., London	1982	
[QRL.41]	Social Surveys (Gallup Poll) Ltd.	*Attitudes towards the Papal Visit and Church Unity (cumulative Sample)*	Social Surveys (Gallup Poll) Ltd., London	1982	
[QRL.42]	Social Surveys (Gallup Poll) Ltd.	*Attitudes towards the Papal Visit and Church Unity, March 1982*	Social Surveys (Gallup Poll) Ltd., London	1982	2 volumes
[QRL.43]	Social Surveys (Gallup Poll) Ltd.	*Attitudes towards the Papal Visit, 5 May-10 May 1982*	Social Surveys (Gallup Poll) Ltd., London	1982	
[QRL.44]	Baptist Times Ltd.	*Baptist Times*	Baptist Times Ltd., London	weekly	
[QRL.45]	NOP Market Research Ltd.	*Bibles: a Report on a Survey carried out by NOP Market Research Limited for Word in Action*	NOP Market Research Ltd., London	1973	
[QRL.46]	Christian Weekly Newspapers	*British Weekly*	Christian Weekly Newspapers, London	weekly	

Reference	Author or Organisation	Title	Publisher	Frequency or Date	Remarks
[QRL.47]	Catholic Herald Ltd.	*Catholic Herald*	Catholic Herald Ltd., London	weekly	
[QRL.48]	Christian World Newspapers Ltd.	*Christian World*	Christian World Newspapers Ltd., Oxford	weekly	ceased publication, 1979
[QRL.49]	NOP Market Research Ltd.	*Church Going: a Report on a Survey carried out by NOP Market Research Limited*	NOP Market Research Ltd., London	1978	
[QRL.50]	Christian Weekly Newspapers	*Church of England Newspaper*	Christian Weekly Newspapers, London	weekly	
[QRL.51]	G.J. Palmer & Sons Ltd.	*Church Times*	G.J. Palmer & Sons Ltd., London	weekly	
[QRL.52]	Research Services Ltd.	*Community Attitudes Survey, England: prepared for the Government Social Survey by Research Services Limited*	HMSO, London	1969	Royal Comm. on Local Gov. in England, Research Studies, 9
[QRL.53]	Express Newspapers Ltd.	*Daily Express*	Express Newspapers Ltd., London	daily	
[QRL.54]	Daily Graphic and Daily Sketch	*Daily Graphic and Daily Sketch*	Daily Graphic and Daily Sketch, London	daily	Renamed *The Daily Sketch*, 1954 and merged with *Daily Mail*, 1971
[QRL.55]	Associated Newspapers Group Ltd.	*Daily Mail*	Associated Newspapers Group Ltd., London	daily	

Ref	Organization	Title	Publisher	Frequency/Date	Notes
[QRL.56]	Express Newspapers Ltd.	*Daily Star*	Express Newspapers Ltd., Manchester	daily	
[QRL.57]	Daily Telegraph Ltd.	*Daily Telegraph*	Daily Telegraph Ltd., London	daily	
[QRL.58]	National Opinion Polls Ltd.	*Electors' Opinions on Abortion and the Abortion Act, 1967: a Report prepared by National Opinion Polls Limited on behalf of the Rationalist Press Association*	National Opinion Polls Ltd., London	1972	
[QRL.59]	Commission of the European Communities	*Eurobarometer*	Commission of the European Communities, Brussels	Biannual	
[QRL.60]	NOP Market Research Ltd.	*Euthanasia: a Report on a Survey carried out by NOP Market Research Limited for Voluntary Euthanasia Society*	NOP Market Research Ltd, London	1976	
[QRL.61]	Evening Standard	*Evening Standard*	Evening Standard, London	daily	Absorbed *Evening News* and renamed *The Standard*, 1980
[QRL.62]	Institut NIPO & Institut EMNID	'Foi, religion, morale et vie familiale dans dix pays d'Europe', *Social Compass*, vol.XVIII, pp.279-84		1971	
[QRL.63]	Social Surveys (Gallup Poll) Ltd.	*The Gallup Election Handbook, March 1966*	Social Surveys (Gallup Poll) Ltd., London	1966	
[QRL.64]	Social Surveys (Gallup Poll) Ltd.	*Gallup Political Index*	Social Surveys (Gallup Poll) Ltd., London	monthly	
[QRL.65]	Social Surveys (Gallup Poll) Ltd.	*Gallup Poll on Abortion Act*	Gallup Poll, London	1969	
[QRL.66]	George Outram & Co. Ltd.	*Glasgow Herald*	George Outram & Co. Ltd. Glasgow	daily	

Reference	Author or Organisation	Title	Publisher	Frequency or Date	Remarks
[QRL.67]	Guardian Newspapers Ltd.	*The Guardian*	Guardian Newspapers Ltd., London	daily	
[QRL.68]	IPC Surveys Division	*How People spend their Sundays*	IPC Surveys Division, London	1968	
[QRL.69]	Gallup International Research Institutes	*Human Needs and Satisfactions: a global Survey conducted for the Charles F. Kettering Foundation by Gallup International Research Institutes*	Gallup International Research Institutes, (no place)	1977	14 volumes
[QRL.70]	Survey Research Consultants International	*Index to international public Opinion*	Macmillan, London	annual	
[QRL.71]	Mass-Observation	*Meet yourself on Sunday*	Naldrett Press, London	1949	
[QRL.72]	Methodist Newspaper Co.	*Methodist Recorder*	Methodist Newspaper Co., London	weekly	
[QRL.73]	IPC Magazines Ltd.	*New Society*	IPC Magazines Ltd., London	weekly	
[QRL.74]	News Chronicle	*News Chronicle*	News Chronicle, London	daily	Renamed *News Chronicle and Daily Dispatch*, 1955 and merged with *Daily Mail*, 1960
[QRL.75]	News Review	*News Review*	News Review, London	weekly	incorporated with *Illustrated*, 1950
[QRL.76]	National Opinion Polls Ltd.	'NOP Abortion Survey', *New Humanist*, vol. LXXXVIII, pp.30-3		1972-73	

	Author/Organisation	Title	Publisher	Frequency/Year	Notes
[QRL.77]	National Opinion Polls Ltd.	*NOP Political Bulletin*	National Opinion Polls Ltd., London	monthly	continued as *Political, Social, Economic Review* [QRL.80]
[QRL.78]	National Opinion Polls Ltd.	*NOP Survey, moral & religious Education: what the People want*	British Humanist Association, London	1969	
[QRL.79]	Cavenham Communications Ltd.	*Now!*	Cavenham Communications Ltd., London	weekly	ceased publication, 1981
[QRL.80]	NOP Market Research Ltd.	*Political, Social, Economic Review*	NOP Market Research Ltd., London	bimonthly	continuation of *NOP Political Bulletin* [QRL.77] ceased publication, 1968
[QRL.81]	Keesing's Systems	*Polls*	Keesing's Systems, Amsterdam	quarterly	
[QRL.82]	Reader's Digest Association	*Products and People: the Reader's Digest European Surveys*	Reader's Digest Association, London	1963	
[QRL.83]	Advertising Association	*Public Attitudes to Advertising: a Survey, April 1972*	Advertising Association, London	1972	
[QRL.84]	Advertising Association	*Public Attitudes to Advertising, 1976: a Survey commissioned by the Advertising Association*	Advertising Association, London	1976	
[QRL.85]	Advertising Association	*Public Attitudes to Advertising, 1980/1981: a Survey commissioned by the Advertising Association*	Advertising Association, London	1981	
[QRL.86]	Market & Opinion Research International	*Public Attitudes towards Abortion, January 1980: Research Study conducted for 'The Sunday Times'*	Market & Opinion Research International, London	1980	

Reference	Author or Organisation	Title	Publisher	Frequency or Date	Remarks
[QRL.87]	American Enterprise Institute for Public Policy Research	*Public Opinion*	American Enterprise Institute for Public Policy Research, Washington, D.C.	bimonthly	
[QRL.88]	Market & Opinion Research International	*Public Opinion in Great Britain*	Market & Opinion Research International, London	monthly	Renamed *British Public Opinion* from 1983
[QRL.89]	Family Planning	'Public opinion poll on family planning', *Family Planning*,vol.17, pp.87-8		1968-69	
[QRL.90]	Birds Eye Wall's Ltd.	*The Quest for Values: Birds Eye Report, 1982*	Birds Eye Wall's Ltd., Walton -on -Thames	1982	
[QRL.91]	Opinion Research Centre	*Reactions to religious Programmes: carried out for Independent Broadcasting Authority*	Opinion Research Centre, London	1973	
[QRL.92]	International Conference on Human Values	*Reference Materials for the 1980 International Conference on Human Values*	International Conference on Human Values Secretariat Office, Tokyo	1980	
[QRL.93]	Marplan Ltd.	*Religion and the Public in Britain today: prepared for Cavenham Communications Ltd.*	Marplan Ltd., London	1979	
[QRL.94]	Independent Television Authority	*Religion in Britain and Northern Ireland: a Survey of popular Attitudes*	Independent Television Authority, London	1970	
[QRL.95]	Opinion Research Centre	*Religion in Northern Ireland*	(Ulster Television, Belfast)	(1969)	

				Notes
[QRL.96]	Social Surveys (Gallup Poll) Ltd.	*Religion Study, 22 February -17 April 1978*	Social Surveys (Gallup Poll) Ltd., London	1978	
[QRL.97]	British Broadcasting Corporation Audience Research Department	*Religious Broadcasts and the Public: a social Survey of the Differences between Non-listeners and listeners to religious Broadcasts*	British Broadcasting Corporation Audience Research Department, London	1955	
[QRL.98]	Home Office	*Report of the Departmental Committee on the Law on Sunday Observance*	HMSO, London	1964	Parl. Papers, House of Commons, 1964-65, vol.XXIII
[QRL.99]	Opinion Research Centre	*Report on a Poll on Religion and Marriage: conducted for BBC TV Religious Department*	Opinion Research Centre, London	1977	
[QRL.100]	Louis Harris Research	*Report on a Survey carried out from 13-19 April on the religious Beliefs of the British People*	Louis Harris Research, London	1970	
[QRL.101]	National Opinion Polls Ltd.	*Report on Attitudes to and Practice of Religion and Superstition: prepared for the 'Daily Mail' by National Opinion Polls Ltd.*	National Opinion Polls Ltd., London	1970	2 volumes
[QRL.102]	System Three Scotland Ltd.	*Research on Attitudes to Sunday Activities and the Status of Women*	System Three Scotland Ltd., Edinburgh	1980	
[QRL.103]	System Three Scotland Ltd.	*Scots' Attitudes to the Church and Religion*	System Three Scotland Ltd., Dundee	1976	
[QRL.104]	The Scotsman Publications Ltd.	*The Scotsman*	The Scotsman Publications Ltd., Edinburgh	daily	

Reference	Author or Organisation	Title	Publisher	Frequency or Date	Remarks
[QRL.105]	Market & Opinion Research International	Shop Opening Hours, September 1982: Research Study conducted for National Consumer Council	Market & Opinion Research International, London	1982	
[QRL.106]	NOP Market Research Ltd.	Shopping Hours: a Report on a Survey carried out by NOP Market Research Limited for National Consumer Council	NOP Market Research Ltd., London	1978	
[QRL.107] [QRL.108]	Central Statistical Office Louis Harris International	Social Trends Spiritual Attitudes: conducted for BBC TV by Louis Harris International	HMSO, London Louis Harris International, London	annual 1974	
[QRL.109]	NOP Market Research Ltd.	Sports: a Report on a Survey carried out by NOP Market Research Limited for 'Daily Mail'	NOP Market Research Ltd., London	1977	
[QRL.110]	NOP Market Research Ltd.	Sports: a Report on a Survey carried out by NOP Market Research Limited for the 'Daily Mail'	NOP Market Research Ltd., London	1980	
[QRL.111]	News Group Newspapers Ltd.	Sun	News Group Newspapers Ltd., London	daily	
[QRL.112]	Sunday Telegraph	Sunday Telegraph	Sunday Telegraph, London	weekly	
[QRL.113]	Times Newspapers Ltd.	Sunday Times	Times Newspapers Ltd., London	weekly	
[QRL.114]	National Consumer Council	Sunday Trading: the Consumers' View	National Consumer Council, London	1979	
[QRL.115]	Reader's Digest Association	A Survey of Europe today: The Peoples and Markets of sixteen European Countries	Reader's Digest Association, London	1970	
[QRL.116]	Gallup Poll	Survey of Readership of Newspapers: England and Wales	Gallup Poll, London	1952	

[QRL.117]	National Opinion Polls Ltd.	*Survey on Abortion: Report on a Survey carried out by National Opinion Polls Limited for the Abortion Law Reform Association*	National Opinion Polls Ltd., London	1967
[QRL.118]	National Opinion Polls Ltd.	*Survey on Abortion: Report on a Survey carried out by National Opinion Polls Limited for the Abortion Law Reform Association*	National Opinion Polls Ltd., London	1970
[QRL.119]	Tablet Publishing Co.Ltd.	*The Tablet*	Tablet Publishing Co. Ltd., London	weekly
[QRL.120]	Social Surveys (Gallup Poll) Ltd.	*Television and Religion: full statistical Tables of a Survey Research from ABC TV*	ABC Television, London	1964
[QRL.121]	Social Surveys (Gallup Poll) Ltd.	*Television and Religion: prepared by Social Surveys (Gallup Poll) Ltd. on behalf of ABC Television Ltd.*	University of London Press, London	1965
[QRL.122]	Social Surveys (Gallup Poll) Ltd.	'This is your Sunday', *Sunday*, vol.1, no.1, pp.4-6		May 1966
[QRL.123]	Times Newspapers Ltd.	*The Times*	Times Newspapers Ltd., London	daily
[QRL.124]	Times Newspapers Ltd.	*The Times Educational Supplement*	Times Newspapers Ltd., London	weekly
[QRL.125]	Associated Catholic Newspapers (1912) Ltd.	*The Universe*	Associated Catholic Newspapers (1912) Ltd., London	weekly
[QRL.126]	Western Mail and Echo Ltd.	*Western Mail*	Western Mail and Echo Ltd., Cardiff	daily
[QRL.127]	IPC Magazines Ltd.	*Woman's Own*	IPC Magazines Ltd., London	weekly

BIBLIOGRAPHY

[B.1] Abercrombie, Nicholas, Baker, John, Brett, Sebastian & Foster, Jane, 'Superstition and religion: The God of the gaps', *A Sociological Yearbook of Religion in Britain, 3*, ed. David Martin & Michael Hill, SCM Press, London, 1970, pp.93-129.

[B.2] Abrams, Mark, 'Aspects of life satisfaction', *Profiles of the Elderly, Volume 1*, Age Concern, Mitcham, 1977, pp.31-48.

[B.3] Abrams, Mark, *Beyond three-score and ten: a first Report on a Survey of the Elderly*, Age Concern, Mitcham, 1978.

[B.4] Abrams, Mark, *Beyond three-score and ten: a Second Report on a Survey of the Elderly*, Age Concern, Mitcham, 1980.

[B.5] Alves, Colin, *Religion and the secondary School: a Report undertaken on behalf of the Education Department of the British Council of Churches*, SCM Press, London, 1968.

[B.6] Attfield, David George, *East Hull Church of England social Survey (1981)*, (The author, Hull, 1982).

[B.7] Bailey, John R., 'Religious education in Lincolnshire secondary Schools', *British Journal of Religious Education*, vol.1, 1978-79, pp.89-94.

[B.8] Barker, Eileen, 'Who'd be a Moonie? A comparative study of those who join the Unification Church in Britain', *The social Impact of new religious Movements*, ed. Bryan Wilson, Rose of Sharon Press, New York, 1981, pp.59-96.

[B.9] Bealey, Frank & Sewel, John, *The Politics of Independence: a study of a Scottish Town*, Aberdeen University Press, Aberdeen, 1981.

[B.10] Bealey, Frank, Blondel, Jean & McCann, William Phillip, *Constituency Politics: a Study of Newcastle-under-Lyme*, Faber & Faber, London, 1965.

[B.11] Beasley-Murray, Paul & Wilkinson, Alan, *Turning the Tide: an Assessment of Baptist Church Growth in England*, Bible Society, London, 1981.

[B.12] Beaumont, Luke, 'Our churches to-day', *Congregational Quarterly*, vol. X, 1932, pp.345-50.

[B.13] Beckford, James Arthur, *The Trumpet of Prophecy: a sociological Study of Jehovah's Witnesses*, Basil Blackwell, Oxford, 1975.

[B.14] Beckwith, Ian S., 'Religion in a working men's parish, 1843-1893', *Lincolnshire History and Archaeology*, vol.V, 1970, pp.29-38.

[B.15] Benfield, Gordon, 'Religious education in secondary Schools: a close look at one Area', *Learning for Living*, vol.14, 1974-75, pp.173-8.

[B.16] Benney, Mark, Gray, A.P.& Pear, Richard Hatherley, *How People vote: a Study of electoral Behaviour in Greenwich*, Routledge & Kegan Paul, London, 1956.

[B.17] Bentley, James, *Cry God for England: the Survival and Mission of the British Churches*, Bowerdean Press, London, 1978.

[B.18] Berthoud, Richard & Jowell, Roger, *Creating a Community: a Study of Runcorn Residents, 1972*, Social and Community Planning Research, London, 1973.

[B.19] Bhalla, Anil & Blakemore, Ken, *Elders of the Minority ethnic Groups*, All Faiths for One Race, Birmingham, 1981.

[B.20] Birch, Anthony Harold, *Small-Town Politics: a Study of political Life in Glossop*, Oxford University Press, London, 1959.

[B.21] Bird, Arthur H., 'Rhondda Valley survey', *Free Church Chronicle*, vol. XXI, no.4, April 1966, pp.8-11.

[B.22] Black, Arthur, *London Church and Mission Attendances*, Botolph Printing Works, London, 1928.

[B.23] Black, Paul, 'The religious scene: belief and practice in the universities', *Dublin Review*, vol.234, 1960-61, pp.105-25.

[B.24] Bland, E., *Annals of Southport and District: a chronological History of North Meols, A.D.1086 to 1886*, A.Heywood, Manchester, (1888).

[B.25] Bleakley, David, *Young Ulster and Religion in the Sixties*, Christian Youth Committee, Belfast, 1964.

[B.26] Boaden, Edward, 'Statistics of chapels, schools &c, 1881', *Minutes of Proceedings of the twenty-fifth annual Assembly of Representatives of the United Methodist Free Churches, held in London, July and August 1881*, T. Newton, London, 1881, pp.110-2.

[B.27] Bochel, John Main & Denver, D.T., 'Religion and voting: a critical review and a new analysis', *Political Studies*, vol. XVIII, 1970, pp.205-19.

[B.28] Booth, Charles, *Life and Labour of the People in London, Third Series: religious influences*, 7 vol., Macmillan, London, 1902.

[B.29] Bossy, John, *The English Catholic Community, 1570-1850*, Darton, Longman & Todd, London, 1975.

[B.30] Bottomore, Thomas, 'Social stratification in voluntary organizations', *Social Mobility in Britain*, ed. David Victor Glass, Routledge & Kegan Paul, London, 1954, pp.349-82.

[B.31] Bowden, Jean S., 'Religious education: some results of a preliminary inquiry in schools in the area administered by sixteen Local Education Authorities of the West Midlands', *Educational Review*, vol.3, 1950-51, pp.129-38.

[B.32] Boyle, Joseph F., 'Educational attainment, occupational achievement and religion in Northern Ireland', *Economic and Social Review*, vol.8, 1976-77, pp.79-100.

[B.33] Bracey, Howard Edwin, *In Retirement: Pensioners in Great Britain and the United States*, Routledge and Kegan Paul, London, 1966.

[B.34] Bradbury, James Bernard, 'The religious Development of the Adolescent', University of Manchester M.Ed. thesis, 1947.

[B.35] Bradley, James Edwin, 'Whigs and Nonconformists: Presbyterians, Congregationalists and Baptists in English Politics, 1715-1790', University of Southern California Ph.D. thesis, 2 vol., 1978.

[B.36] Braithwaite, Richard Bevan, *The State of religious Belief: an inquiry based on 'The Nation and Athenaeum' Questionnaire*, Hogarth Press, London, 1927.

[B.37] Brennan, Thomas, Cooney, E.W. & Pollins, Harold, *Social Change in South-West Wales*, Watts & Co., London, 1954.

[B.38] Bressan, Vanni, *La structure sociale d'une paroisse urbaine: The Holy Ghost and St. Stephen, Shepherd's Bush, London, W12*, Louvain, 1961.

[B.39] Bridges, Peter, 'Congregational cluster patterns in Hemel Hempstead New Town', *University of Birmingham Institute for the Study of Worship and Religious Architecture Research Bulletin*, 1971, pp.20-37.

[B.40] Brimer, James W., 'School worship with juniors', *Learning for Living*, vol.11, no.5, May 1972, pp.6-12.

[B.41] Brimer, James W., 'Worship in the junior School', University of Birmingham M.Ed. thesis, 1971.

[B.42] Brothers, Joan B., 'Religion in the British universities: the findings of some recent surveys', *Archives de Sociologie des Religions*, no.18, July-December 1964, pp.71-82.

[B.43] Brothers, Joan B., *Religious Institutions*, Longman, London, 1971.

[B.44] Brown, Graham D., 'Decline and fall?', *The Harvester*, vol.LX, no.9, September 1981, pp.5-7.

[B.45] Brown, Graham D., 'How can we improve our evangelism? Deductions from a survey of assemblies', *Journal of the Christian Brethren Research Fellowship*, no. 21, May 1971, pp.44-57.

[B.46] Brown, Graham D. & Mills, Brian, *The Brethren today: a factual Survey*, Paternoster Press, Exeter, 1980.

[B.47] Brown, Judith Margaret, *Men and Gods in a changing World: some Themes in the religious Experience of Twentieth-Century Hindus and Christians.* SCM Press, London, 1980.

[B.48] Bryman, Alan & Hinings, Christopher Robin, 'Lay perceptions of Church issues', *University of Birmingham Institute for the Study of Worship and Religious Architecture Research Bulletin,* 1973, pp.81-6.

[B.49] Bryman, Alan & Hinings, Christopher Robin, 'Participation, reform and ecumenism: the views of laity and clergy', *A Sociological Yearbook of Religion in Britain, 7,* ed. Michael Hill, SCM Press, London, 1974, pp. 13-25.

[B.50] Bryman, Alan, Ranson, Stewart & Hinings, Christopher Robin, 'Churchmanship and ecumenism', *Journal of Ecumenical Studies,* vol.11, 1974, pp.467-75.

[B.51] Buckle, Robert, 'Mormons in Britain: a survey', *A Sociological Yearbook of Religion in Britain, 4,* ed. Michael Hill, SCM Press, London, 1971, pp.160-79.

[B.52] Budge, Ian & Urwin, Derek William, *Scottish political Behaviour: a Case Study in British Homogeneity,* Longmans, London, 1966.

[B.53] Burgess, Bernard George, 'A further Study of Opinions of Essex primary Teachers about religious Education and School Assembly in the Context of contemporary Controversy', University of London Ph.D. thesis, 2 vol. 1980.

[B.54] Burgess, Bernard George, 'A Study of the Attitudes of primary Teachers in Essex and Walsall to religious Education and collective Worship', University of London M.Phil. thesis, 1975.

[B.55] Burton, Lewis, 'Social class in the local church: a study of two Methodist churches in the Midlands', *A Sociological Yearbook of Religion in Britain, 8,* ed. Michael Hill, SCM Press, London, 1975, pp. 15-29.

[B.56] Burton, Lewis, 'The social Stratification of two Methodist Churches in the Midlands in respect of Leadership, Membership and Adherence: a Study of the social Structure of the local Church', University of London Ph.D. thesis, 1972.

[B.57] Busia, Kofi Abrefa, *Urban Churches in Britain: a Question of Relevance,* Lutterworth Press, London, 1966.

[B.58] Butler, J.R., 'A sociological study of lapsed membership', *London Quarterly and Holborn Review,* 6th. Series, vol.XXXV, 1966, pp.236-44.

[B.59] Bysh, J.P., 'Teachers' Attitudes towards School Assembly in some Cheshire comprehensive Schools', University of Wales (Bangor) M.Ed. thesis, 1979.

[B.60] Callard, Pauline, 'The Church and older people', *Social Service Quarterly,* vol.XXXIII, 1959-60, pp.115-8.

[B.61] Campbell, Peter, Donnison, David & Potter, Allen, 'Voting behaviour in Droylsden in October 1951', *Manchester School of Economic and Social Studies,* vol.XX, 1952, pp.57-65.

[B.62] Carlton, Eric J., 'The Probationer Minister: a Study among English Baptists', University of London M.Sc. thesis, 1965.

[B.63] Carlton, Eric J., 'The Unitarian Movement in England', University of London M.Phil. thesis, 1972.

[B.64] Carter, G. Wallace, 'Local preachers' Commission', *Wesleyan Methodist Conference Agenda: Representative Session,* 1919, pp.313-33.

[B.65] Carter, Harold, 'Y Fro Gymraeg and the 1975 referendum on Sunday closing of public houses in Wales', *Cambria,* vol.3, 1976, pp.89-101.

[B.66] Carter, Harold & Thomas, J.G., 'The referendum on the Sunday opening of licensed premises in Wales as a criterion of a culture region', *Regional Studies,* vol.3, 1969, pp.61-71.

[B.67] Cartwright, Ann, *How many Children?,* Routledge & Kegan Paul, London, 1976.

[B.68] Cartwright, Ann, *Parents and Family Planning Services,* Routledge & Kegan Paul, London, 1970.

[B.69] Cartwright, Ann & Waite, Marjorie, 'General practitioners and abortion: evidence to the Committee on the Working of the Abortion Act', *Journal of the Royal College of General Practitioners,* vol.22, Supplement no. 1, 1972.

[B.70] Cauter, Theodore & Downham, John Stanley, *The Communication of Ideas: a Study of contemporary Influences on urban Life*, Chatto and Windus, London, 1954.

[B.71] Chapman, Stanley David, 'The Evangelical Revival and education in Nottingham', *Transactions of the Thoroton Society of Nottinghamshire*, vol.LXVI, 1962, pp.35-66.

[B.72] Chesser, Eustace, Maizels, Joan, Jones, Leonard & Emmett, Brian, *The sexual, marital and family Relationships of the English Woman*, Hutchinson's Medical Publications, (London), 1956.

[B.73] Chetwood, N., 'Religious Teaching in grammar Schools, with special Reference to the Period after 1944', University of Nottingham M.Ed. thesis, 1958.

[B.74] Chou, Ru-Chi & Brown, Susannah, 'A comparison of the size of families of Roman Catholics and non-Catholics in Great Britain', *Population Studies*, vol.XXII, 1968, pp.51-60.

[B.75] Clark, David, *Between Pulpit and Pew: folk Religion in a North Yorkshire fishing Village*, Cambridge University Press, Cambridge,1982.

[B.76] Clark, David B., *Survey of Anglicans and Methodists in four towns*, Epworth Press, (London), 1965.

[B.77] Coates, George, 'Temperance notes', *Methodist New Connexion Magazine*, vol.CIV, 1901, p.81.

[B.78] Coles, Robert W., 'Bibliography of work in the sociology of British religion, July 1969', *A Sociological Yearbook of religion in Britain, 3*, ed. David Martin & Michael Hill, SCM Press, London, 1970, pp. 162-75.

[B.79] Coles, Robert W., 'Bibliography of work in the sociology of British religion, 1970 supplement', *A Sociological Yearbook of Religion in Britain, 4*, ed. Michael Hill, SCM Press, London, 1971, pp.180-4.

[B.80] Coles, Robert W.& Graham, Hilary, 'Bibliography of work in the sociology of British religion, 1971 supplement', *A Sociological Yearbook of Religion in Britain, 5*, ed. Michael Hill, SCM Press, London, 1972, pp.192-6.

[B.81] Coles, Robert W. & Iphofen, Ronald, 'Bibliography of work in the sociology of British religion, 1972 supplement', *A Sociological Yearbook of Religion in Britain, 6*, ed. Michael Hill, SCM Press, London, 1973, pp.235-9.

[B.82] Collins, William, *Statistics of the Church Accommodation of Glasgow, Barony and Gorbals, presented to the Royal Commissioners appointed to inquire into the Means of religious Instruction and pastoral Superintendance afforded to the People of Scotland*, W. Collins, Glasgow, 1836.

[B.83] Cornish, Ebenezer Darrel, 'Statistics of chapels, schools, &c., 1901', *Minutes of Proceedings of the Forty-Fifth Annual Assembly of Representatives of the United Methodist Free Churches held in Fore Street chapel, Redruth, July 1901*, Andrew Crombie, London, 1901, pp. 124-7.

[B.84] Coverdale, Philip F., 'The number of Essex papists in 1706', *Essex Recusant*, vol.2, 1960, pp.16-29.

[B.85] Cox, Edwin, *Sixth Form Religion: a Study of the Beliefs and of the Attitudes to Religion, religious Instruction and Morals of a Sample of grammar School sixth Form Pupils, based on an Investigation sponsored by the Christian Education Movement*, SCM Press, London,1967.

[B.86] Coxon, Anthony Peter Macmillan, 'Patterns of occupational recruitment: the Anglican ministry', *Sociology*, vol.1, 1967, pp.73-9.

[B.87] Coxon, Anthony Peter Macmillan, 'A sociological Study of the social Recruitment, Selection and professional Socialization of Anglican ordinands', University of Leeds Ph.D. thesis, 1965.

[B.88] Crawford, Robert G., *Student Attitudes and Beliefs concerning religious Education*, Association for Religious Education Occasional Paper no.17, Association for Religious Education, Birmingham, 1979.

[B.89] Currie, Robert, Gilbert, Alan David & Horsley, Lee, *Churches and Churchgoers: Patterns of Church Growth in the British Isles since 1700*, Clarendon Press, Oxford, 1977.

[B.90] Daines, John Wilfred, *An Enquiry into the Methods and Effects of religious Education in sixth Forms*, University of Nottingham Institute of Education, Nottingham, 1962.

[B.91] Daines, John Wilfred, 'A psychological Study of the Attitude of Adolescents to Religion and religious Instruction', University of London Ph.D. thesis, 1949.

[B.92] Daines, John Wilfred, *Religious Education: a Series of Abstracts of unpublished Theses in religious Education*, 4 pt., University of Nottingham Institute of Education, Nottingham, 1963-72.

[B.93] Dallas, Alexander Robert Charles, *Pastoral Superintendence: its Motive, its Detail and its Support*, James Nisbet & Co., London, 1841.

[B.94] Daniel, Michael G., 'London Clergymen: the Ways in which their Attitudes to themselves and their Work have changed in the first ten Years of their Ministry', University of London M.Phil. thesis, 1967.

[B.95] Davison, Robert Barry, *Black British: Immigrants to England*, Oxford University Press, London, 1966.

[B.96] Dawes, R.S., 'The Concepts of God among secondary School Children (10-14)', University of London M.A. thesis, 1954.

[B.97] Day, Graham A.S. & Fitton, Martin, 'Religious organization and community in mid-Wales', *Social and cultural Change in contemporary Wales*, ed. Glyn Williams, Routledge & Kegan Paul, London, 1978, pp. 242-52.

[B.98] Dierenfield, R.B., 'The Cinderella subject: religion for the county secondary schools of England', *Religious Education*, vol.LXII, 1967, pp.38-45.

[B.99] Dobson, Mary J., 'Original Compton Census returns: the Shoreham Deanery', *Archaeologia Cantiana*, vol.XCIV, 1978, pp.61-73.

[B.100] Dodd, Peter, *Census of Attendance in Anglican Churches in the County Borough of Rotherham, 1963*, Steel, Peech and Tozer, (No place), 1964.

[B.101] Drake, Michael, 'The census, 1801-1891', *Nineteenth-Century Society: Essays in the Use of quantitative Methods for the Study of social Data*, ed. Edward Anthony Wrigley, Cambridge University Press, Cambridge, 1972, pp.7-46.

[B.102] Edmonds, Richard, 'A statistical account of the parish of Madron, containing the borough of Penzance, in Cornwall', *Journal of the Statistical Society of London*, vol.II, 1839-40, pp. 198-233.

[B.103] Egan, Pamela, *Voluntary religious Education national Survey*, Church of England Board of Education, (London), 1981.

[B.104] Evans, Christopher, 'Parapsychology: what the questionnaire revealed', *New Scientist*, 25 January 1973.

[B.105] Evans, D.B., 'Religious Concepts and their Development in Students at Colleges of Education during the training Course', University of Nottingham M.Ed. thesis, 1968.

[B.106] Evans, Peter, *The Attitudes of young Immigrants*, Runnymede Trust, London, 1971.

[B.107] Faning, Ernest Lewis, *Report on an Enquiry into Family Limitation and its Influence on human Fertility during the past fifty Years*, Papers of the Royal Commission on Population vol.1, HMSO, London, 1949.

[B.108] Farrell, Christine & Kellaher, Leonie, *My Mother said ··· : the Way young People learned about Sex and Birth Control*, Routledge & Kegan Paul, London, 1978.

[B.109] Field, Clive Douglas, 'The 1851 religious census: a select bibliography of materials relating to England and Wales', *Proceedings of the Wesley Historical Society*, vol.XLI, 1977-78, pp.175-82.

[B.110] Field, Clive Douglas, 'Methodism in metropolitan London, 1850-1920: a social and sociological Study', University of Oxford D.Phil. thesis, 1974.

[B.111] Finlayson,John, 'Just like Mum and Dad', *Sunday Mail*, 7 October 1979.

[B.112] Francis, Leslie John, 'Attitude and Longitude: a study in measurement', *Character Potential*, vol.8, 1976-78, pp.119-30.

[B.113] Francis, Leslie John, 'The child's attitude towards religion: a review of research', *Educational Research*, vol.21, 1978-79, pp.103-8.

[B.114] Francis, Leslie John, *Christianity and the Child today: a Research Perspective on the Situation in England*, Farmington Institute for Christian Studies Occasional Paper no.6, Farmington Institute for Christian Studies, Oxford, (1980).

[B.115] Francis, Leslie John, 'An Enquiry into the Concept "Readiness for Religion"', University of Cambridge Ph.D. thesis, 1976.

[B.116] Francis, Leslie John, *Experience of Adulthood: a Profile of 26-39 Year Olds*, Gower, Aldershot, 1982.

[B.117] Francis, Leslie John, 'Paths of holiness? Attitudes towards religion among 9-11 year old children in England', *Character Potential*, vol. 9, 1979-81, pp. 129-38.

[B.118] Francis, Leslie John, 'School Influence and Pupil Attitude in religious Education', University of London M.Sc. thesis, 1977.

[B.119] Francis, Leslie John, 'School influence and pupil attitude towards religion', *British Journal of Educational Psychology*, vol,49, 1979, pp.107-23.

[B.120] Francis, Leslie John, 'The secular evaluation of sacred institutions: synods and the social sciences', *Modern Churchman*, New Series, vol. XXII, 1978-79, pp.12-7.

[B.121] Francis, Leslie John, *Youth in Transit: a Profile of 16-25 Year Olds*, Gower, Aldershot, 1982.

[B.122] Francis, Leslie John & Carter, Marian, 'Church aided secondary schools, religious education as an examination subject and pupil attitude towards religion', *British Journal of Educational Psychology*, vol.50, 1980, pp.297-300.

[B.123] Francis, Leslie John, Pearson, Paul R., Carter, Marian & Kay, William K., 'Are introverts more religious?', *British Journal of Social Psychology*, vol.20, 1981, pp.101-4.

[B.124] Francis, Leslie John, Pearson, Paul R., Carter, Marian & Kay, William K., 'The relationship between neuroticism and religiosity among English 15- and 16-year-olds', *Journal of Social Psychology*, vol.114, 1981, pp.99-102.

[B.125] Galway,R., 'The Perception and Manipulation of the religious Identities in a Northern Irish Community', Queen's University of Belfast M.A. thesis, 1978.

[B.126] Garrity, Frank Deane, 'A Study of the Attitude of some secondary modern School Pupils towards religious Education', University of Manchester M.Ed. thesis, 1960.

[B.127] Garrity, Frank Deane, 'A study of the attitude of some secondary modern school pupils towards religious education', *Religious Education*, vol. LVI, 1961, pp.141-3.

[B.128] Gates, Brian E., 'Religion in the developing World of Children and young People', University of Lancaster Ph.D. thesis, 1976.

[B.129] Gay, John Dennis, *The Geography of Religion in England*, Duckworth, London, 1971.

[B.130] Gerard, David, *Roman Catholic Opinion*, Catholic Truth Society, London, 1980.

[B.131] Gilbert, Alan David, *The Making of post-Christian Britain: a History of the Secularization of modern Society*, Longman, London, 1980.

[B.132] Gill, Josiah, *The History of Wesleyan Methodism in Melton Mowbray and the vicinity, 1769-1909*, J.W.Warner, Melton Mowbray, 1909.

[B.133] Gill, Robin, 'Who goes to church in Scotland? A further sociological perspective', *Liturgical Review*, vol.VI, no.1, 1976, pp.48-53.

[B.134] Glass, David Victor, 'Contraception in marriage', *Family Planning*, vol.17, 1968-69, pp.55-6.

[B.135] Glyde, John, *The moral, social and religious Condition of Ipswich in the middle of the nineteenth Century, with a Sketch of its History, Rise and Progress*, J.M.Burton and Co., Ipswich, 1850.

[B.136] Glyn, Edward Carr, *A Charge delivered to the Clergy and Churchwardens of the Diocese of Peterborough... at his primary Visitation, June 1901*, Harrison & Sons, London, 1901.

[B.137] Glyn, Edward Carr, *A Charge delivered to the Clergy and Churchwardens of the Diocese of Peterborough... at his secondary visitation, May-June 1905*, London, 1905.

[B.138] Goldstein, Reine, 'La minorite catholique d'une petite ville industrielle anglaise', *Archives de Sociologie des Religions*, no.9, January-June 1960, pp.113-27.

[B.139] Goldstein, Reine, 'Types de comportement religieux et cadres sociaux dans deux paroisses catholiques anglaises', *Revue Francaise de Sociologie*, vol.VI, 1965, pp.58-67.

[B.140] Gorer, Geoffrey Edgar Solomon, *Death, Grief and Mourning in contemporary Britain*, Cresset Press, London, 1965.

[B.141] Gorer, Geoffrey Edgar Solomon, *Sex & Marriage in England today: a study of the Views and Experience of the Under-45s*, Nelson, London, 1971.

[B.142] Gray, John & Sutherland, John, *A Survey of Sunday Schools and Bible Classes in the Church of Scotland*, Church of Scotland Youth Committee, Edinburgh, 1960.

[B.143] Gray, M., 'Religious Beliefs and Attitudes in Training College Students', University of Nottingham M.Ed. thesis, 2 vol., 1963.

[B.144] Greenslade, Michael Washington, 'The 1767 return of Staffordshire papists', *Staffordshire Catholic History*, no.17, 1977, pp.1-59.

[B.145] Greenslade, Michael Washington, 'Staffordshire papists in 1705 and 1706', *Staffordshire Catholic History*, no.13, 1973, pp.1-55.

[B.146] Greer, John Edmund, 'The attitudes of parents and pupils to religion in school', *Irish Journal of Education*, vol.4, 1970.pp.39-46.

[B.147] Greer, John Edmund, 'A comparison of two attitude to religion scales', *Educational Research*, vol.24, 1981-82, pp.226-7.

[B.148] Greer, John Edmund, 'Growing up in Belfast: a study of religious development', *CORE*, vol.6, no.1, March 1982, microfiche no.1, frames A.14-F.7.

[B.149] Greer, John Edmund, 'The persistence of religion: a study of adolescents in Northern Ireland', *Character Potential*, vol.9, 1979-81, pp.139-49.

[B.150] Greer, John Edmund, *A questioning Generation: a Report on sixth Form Religion in Northern Ireland prepared for the Northern Ireland Committee of the Church of Ireland Board of Education*, Northern Ireland Committee of the Church of Ireland Board of Education, Belfast, 1972.

[B.151] Greer, John Edmund, 'Religious attitudes and thinking in Belfast pupils', *Educational Research*, vol.23, 1980-81, pp.177-89.

[B.152] Greer, John Edmund, 'Religious belief and church attendance of sixth form pupils and their parents', *Irish Journal of Education*, vol.5, 1971, pp.98-106.

[B.153] Greer, John Edmund, 'Sixth form religion in Northern Ireland: religious belief, religious practice and moral judgment in a sample of Protestant boys and girls', *Social Studies*, vol.1, no.3, 1972, pp.325-40.

[B.154] Hackwood, Frederick William, *Religious Wednesbury: its Creeds, Churches & Chapels*, Herald Press, Dudley, 1900.

[B.155] Haigh, William Buckley, *Synopsis of Wesleyan Methodism in Yorkshire, and Companion to the County Plan of Circuits*, printed for the author, Leeds, 1830.

[B.156] Haldane, Ian R., 'Who and what is religious broadcasting for?', *Independent Broadcasting*, no.18, November 1978, pp.13-6.

[B.157] Hall, John & Perry, Norman, *Aspects of Leisure in two industrial Cities: first Results from the Life Satisfaction Surveys carried out in Sunderland and Stoke-on-Trent, November 1973 to February 1974, compared with Data from a national urban Sample*, Occasional Papers in Survey Research 5, Social Science Research Council Survey Unit, London, 1974.

[B.158] Hall, John, Lord, David, Marsh, Cathie & Ring, James, *Quality of Life Survey (urban Britain, 1973), volume 1: Distribution of Responses and Questionnaire*, Social Science Research Council, London, 1976.

[B.159] Hammerton, Max & Downing, A.C., 'Fringe beliefs amongst undergraduates', *Theology*, vol.LXXXII, 1979, pp.433-6.

[B.160] Hampton, William A., *Democracy and Community: a Study of Politics in Sheffield*, Oxford University Press, London, 1970.

[B.161] Hardiment, Peter, *Methodism in Maidenhead, 1829-1979*, Barracuda Books, Buckingham, 1979.

[B.162] Harris, Christopher Charles, *Facing the Future together: the Report of the Bangor Diocesan Survey*, Diocesan Office, Bangor, (1973).

[B.163] Harris, Henry Wilson, *Life so far*, Jonathan Cape, London, 1954.

[B.164] Harris, Jeffrey W. & Jarvis, Peter, *Counting to some Purpose*, Methodist Church Home Mission Division, London, (1979).

[B.165] Harris, Rosemary, *Prejudice and Tolerance in Ulster: a study of Neighbours and "Strangers" in a Border Community*, Manchester University Press, Manchester, 1972.

[B.166] Hassall, W.O., 'Papists in early eighteenth-century Oxfordshire', *Oxoniensia*, vol.XIII, 1948, pp.76-82.

[B.167] Hawksley, R.E., 'A sociological Study of a suburban Church', University of Liverpool M.A. thesis, 1963.

[B.168] Hay, David, 'Attitudes towards the ecumenical movement in an English parish', *Clergy Review*, vol.LXIV, 1979, pp.393-402.

[B.169] Hay, David, 'Religious experience amongst a group of post-graduate students: a qualitative study', *Journal for the Scientific Study of Religion*, vol.18, 1979, pp.164-82.

[B.170] Hickey, John, 'Religion, values and daily life: a case study in Northern Ireland', *Actes 16eme, Conference Internationale de Sociologie des Religions, Lausanne 1981*, Conference Internationale de Sociologie des Religions, Paris, 1981, pp.301-16.

[B.171] Highet, John, 'The Churches', *The Third Statistical Account of Scotland: Glasgow*, ed. James Cunnison & John Brodie Smith Gilfillan, Collins, Glasgow, 1958, pp.713-50.

[B.172] Highet, John, *The Churches in Scotland to-day: a Survey of their Principles, Strength, Work and Statements*, Jackson Son & Co., Glasgow, 1950.

[B.173] Highet, John, *The Scottish Churches: a Review of their State 400 Years after the Reformation*, Skeffington, London, 1960.

[B.174] Highet, John, 'Scottish religious adherence', *British Journal of Sociology*, vol.4, 1953, pp.142-59.

[B.175] Hill, Clifford Stanley Horace, *West Indian Migrants and the London Churches*, Oxford University Press, London, 1963.

[B.176] Hill, James William Francis, *Victorian Lincoln*, Cambridge University Press, London, 1974.

[B.177] Hill, Maurice, *RI and Surveys: Opinion Polls on religious Education in State Schools*, National Secular Society, London, 1968.

[B.178] Hill, Michael & Wakeford, Peter, 'Disembodied ecumenicalism: a survey of the members of four Methodist churches in or near London', *A Sociological Yearbook of Religion in Britain, 2*, ed.David Martin, SCM Press, London, 1969, pp.19-46.

[B.179] Hilliard, Frederick Hadaway, 'Ideas of God among secondary school children', *Religion in Education*, vol.XXVII, 1959-60, pp.14-9.

[B.180] Hine, Margaret Clare, '1706 recusant returns for the City of London', *London Recusant*, vol.5, 1975, pp.88-90.

[B.181] Hinings, Christopher Robin, 'The Balsall Heath survey: a report', *University of Birmingham Institute for the Study of Worship and Religious Architecture Research Bulletin*, 1967, pp.56-72.

[B.182] Hinings, Christopher Robin, 'Church and community: the Hodge Hill survey', *University of Birmingham Institute for the Study of Worship and Religious Architecture Research Bulletin*, 1968, pp.21-37.

[B.183] Hinings, Christopher Robin, 'Religiosity and attitudes towards the Church in a rural setting: the Clun Valley', *Religion in the Birmingham Area: Essays in the Sociology of Religion*, ed. Alan Bryman, University of Birmingham Institute for the Study of Worship and Religious Architecture, Birmingham, 1975, pp.112-22.

[B.184] Hodgkins, William, *Sunday: Christian and social Significance*, Independent Press, London, 1960.

[B.185] Hollingsworth, Thomas Henry, *Historical Demography*, Sources of History Ltd., London, 1969.

[B.186] Holmes, Ann, *Church, Property and People: a Study of the Attitudes of Churches to their Property in three multi-racial, multi-faith Areas- Bradford, Derby and Lambeth*, British Council of Churches, London, 1973.

[B.187] Homan, Roger, 'Church membership and the liturgy: report of a survey in the Archdeaconry of Chichester', *Faith and Worship*, no.9, Winter 1980-81, pp.19-24.

[B.188] Homan, Roger, 'Sociology and the questionable truth', *No Alternative: the Prayer Book Controversy*, ed. David Martin & Peter Mullen, Basil Blackwell, Oxford, 1981, pp. 183-90.

[B.189] Hornsby-Smith, Michael Peter, 'The statistics of the Church', *The Church now: an Inquiry into the present State of the Catholic Church in Britain & Ireland*, ed. John Cumming & Paul Burns, Gill and Macmillan, Dublin, 1980, pp.55-65.

[B.190] Hornsby-Smith, Michael Peter & Lee, Raymond M., *Roman Catholic Opinion: a Study of Roman Catholics in England and Wales in the 1970s- final Report*, University of Surrey, (Guildford), 1979.

[B.191] Hornsby-Smith, Michael Peter & Mansfield, Penny, 'Overview of the Church Commissions', *The Month*, Second New Series, vol.8, 1975, pp. 84-9.

[B.192] Hornsby-Smith, Michael Peter & Turcan, Kathryn A., 'Are northern Catholics different?', *Clergy Review*, vol.LXVI, 1981, pp.231-41.

[B.193] Hornsby-Smith, Michael Peter, Lee, Raymond M. & Turcan, Kathryn A., 'A typology of English Catholics', *Sociological Review*, New Series, vol.30, 1982, pp.433-59.

[B.194] Houslop, N.L. & Weeks, E.J., 'The interests of schoolchildren - I', *School Science Review*, vol. XXIX, 1947-48, pp.281-94.

[B.195] Howard, Christian, *Survey of accredited lay Ministry*, Advisory Council for the Church's Ministry Occasional Paper no.2, Advisory Council for the Church's Ministry, London, 1975.

[B.196] Howie, Robert, *The Churches and the Churchless in Scotland: Facts and Figures*, David Bryce and Son, Glasgow, 1893.

[B.197] Hudson, Kenneth, *An awkward Size for a Town: a Study of Swindon at the 100,000 Mark*, David & Charles, Newton Abbot, 1967.

[B.198] Hume, Abraham, 'Census of religious worship for the Diocese of Liverpool', *Liverpool Diocesan Calendar*, 1883, pp.67-84.

[B.199] Hume, Abraham, *Ecclesiastical Census of the City and Suburbs of Liverpool*, J.A.Thompson, Liverpool, 1882.

[B.200] Hume, Abraham, *Missions at Home; or, A Clergyman's Account of a Portion of the Town of Liverpool*, Rivington, London, 1850.

[B.201] Hume, Abraham, *Remarks on the Census of religious Worship for England and Wales, with Suggestions for an improved Census in 1861, and a Map illustrating the religious Condition of the Country*, Longman, Green, Longman & Roberts, London, 1860.

[B.202] Hunt, Audrey, *The Elderly at Home: a Survey carried out on behalf of the Department of Health and Social Security*, HMSO, London, 1978.

[B.203] Hyde, Kenneth Edwin, *Religious Learning in Adolescence*, University of Birmingham Institute of Education, Educational Monographs no.7, Oliver and Boyd, Edinburgh, 1965.

[B.204] Hyde, Kenneth Edwin, 'A Study of some Factors influencing the Communication of religious Ideas and attitudes among secondary School Children', University of Birmingham Ph.D. thesis, 2 vol., 1959.

[B.205] Inglis, Kenneth Stanley, 'Patterns of religious Worship in 1851', *Journal of Ecclesiastical History*, vol. 11, 1960, pp.74-86.

[B.206] Iphofen, Ronald & Edmiston, James, 'Bibliography of Work in the sociology of British religion, 1973 supplement', *A Sociological Yearbook of Religion in Britain, 7*, ed. Michael Hill, SCM Press, London, 1974, pp.154-8.

[B.207] Jarvis, Peter, 'The class teacher and religious education in the junior school', *Learning for Living*, vol.14, 1974-75, pp.26-31.

[B.208] Jarvis, Peter, 'Job satisfaction and the Protestant and Reformed ministry', *University of Birmingham Institute for the Study of Worship and Religious Architecture Research Bulletin*, 1978, pp.36-55.

[B.209] Jarvis, Peter, 'A Profession in Process: the Relationship between occupational Ideology, occupational Position and the Role Strain, Satisfaction and Commitment of Protestant and Reformed Ministers of Religion', University of Aston Ph.D.thesis, 1977.

[B.210] Jarvis, Peter, 'Religious education as a vehicle for moral education?', *Journal of Moral Education*, vol.2, 1972-73, pp. 69-73.

[B.211] Jarvis, Peter, 'Religious socialization in the junior school', *Educational Research*, vol.16, 1973-74, pp.100-6.

[B.212] Jarvis, Peter, 'Teachers report their aims', *Learning for Living*, vol.11, no.5, May 1972, pp.12-5.

[B.213] Jarvis, Peter & Fielding, A.G., 'The Church, clergy and community relations', *Religion in the Birmingham Area: Essays in the Sociology of Religion*, ed.Alan Bryman, University of Birmingham Institute for the Study of Worship and Religious Architecture, Birmingham, 1975, pp.85-98.

[B.214] Jeffery, Robert Martin Colquhoun, *Areas of ecumenical Experiment: a Survey and Report to the British Council of Churches*, British Council of Churches, London, (1968).

[B.215] Johnson, Winston Peter Leacock, 'The religious Attitude of secondary modern County School Pupils', University of Manchester M.Ed. thesis, 1966.

[B.216] Johnston, James, *The ecclesiastical and religious Statistics of Scotland, showing 1st. the Number of Adherents in each Denomination, 2d. that there are more than half a Million of the Population unconnected with any Church*, D.Bryce & Son, Glasgow, 1874.

[B.217] Johnston, James F.W., 'First report of a Committee of the British Association for the Advancement of Science, appointed at Newcastle, to inquire into the statistics of the collieries upon the Tyne and Wear', *Journal of the Statistical Society of London*, vol.II, 1839-40, pp. 345-56.

[B.218] Jones, Bernard Ewart, *Family Count: a Study-Pamphlet about Methodism today*, Home Mission Occasional Papers no.11, Methodist Church Home Mission Department, London, 1970.

[B.219] Jones, Clifford Merton, *Worship in the secondary School: an Investigation and Discussion*, Religious Education Press, Oxford, 1969.

[B.220] Jones, J.A. 'An Investigation into the Response of Boys and Girls respectively to Scripture as a School Subject in certain co-educational grammar Schools in industrial South Wales', University of Wales (Swansea) M.A.thesis, 1962.

[B.221] Jones, Kathleen, 'The General Synod: 1975 version', *Crucible*, 1976, pp.152-8.

[B.222] Jones, Kathleen, 'The House of Laity in the General Synod: a membership analysis', *Crucible*, 1971, pp.104-8.

[B.223] Kaim-Caudle, Peter Robert, 'Church & social change: a study of religion in Billingham, 1959-66', *New Christian*, 9 March 1967.

[B.224] Kaim-Caudle, Peter Robert, *Religion in Billingham, 1957-59*, Billingham Community Association, Billingham-on-Tees, 1962.

[B.225] Karn, Valerie Ann, *Retiring to the Seaside*, Routledge & Kegan Paul, London, 1977.

[B.226] Kay, William K., 'Conversions among 11-15 year olds', *Spectrum*, vol. 13, no.2, Spring 1981, pp.26-31.

[B.227] Kay, William K., 'Religious Thinking, Attitudes and Personality amongst secondary Pupils in England and Ireland: a Study with particular Reference to religious Education', University of Reading Ph.D. thesis, 1981.

[B.228] Kay, William K., 'Subject preference and attitude to religion in secondary school', *Educational Review*, vol.33, 1981, pp.47-51.

[B.229] Kay, William K., 'Syllabuses and attitudes to Christianity', *Irish Catechist*, vol.5, no.2, 1981.

[B.230] Kenrick, G.S., 'Statistics of the population in the parish of Trevethin (Pontypool) and at the neighbouring works of Blaenavon in Monmouthshire, chiefly employed in the iron trade, and inhabiting part of the district recently disturbed', *Journal of the Statistical Society of London*, vol.III, 1840-41, pp.366-75.

[B.231] Kidd, T., 'An Investigation into the Attitudes of a Sample of young Women joining H.M. Forces towards some moral issues and the Relationship between these and their declared religious Practice', University of Nottingham M.Phil. thesis, 2 vol., 1971.

[B.232] King, G.M., Mercer, Alan & Smith, D.K., 'Towards diocesan planning', *Journal of the Operational Research Society*, vol.29, 1978, pp.859-66.

[B.233] Kirk, John Fraser, 'A comparative statistical Analysis of the Churches of the Presbytery of Edinburgh from 1960 to 1974', University of Aberdeen Ph.D. thesis, 2 vol., 1978.

[B.234] Knight, Ian & Wilson, Paul, *Scottish Licensing Laws: a Survey carried out on behalf of the Scottish Home and Health Department*, HMSO, London, 1980.

[B.235] Kokosalakis, Nicholas, 'The Impact of Ecumenism on Denominationalism: a sociological Study of five Christian Congregations in Liverpool', University of Liverpool Ph.D. thesis, 1969.

[B.236] Langdale, Eugene, 'Survey of Eastcote parish', *New Life*, vol.11, 1955, pp.109-14.

[B.237] Langford, Christopher M., *Birth Control Practice and marital Fertility in Great Britain: a Report on a Survey carried out in 1967-68*, Population Investigation Committee, London School of Economics, London, 1976.

[B.238] Langford, Christopher M., 'Birth control practice in Britain', *Family Planning*, vol.17, 1968-69, pp.89-92.

[B.239] Lesourd, Jean-Alain, *Sociologie du catholicisme anglais, 1767-1851*, Publications Universite Nancy II, Nancy, 1981.

[B.240] Lewis, E.O., 'Popular and unpopular school-subjects', *Journal of Experimental Pedagogy and Training College Record*, vol.II, 1913-14, pp.89-98.

[B.241] Mabbs, Goodeve, *The Churches in Derbyshire; or, Provision for public Worship in the Country Districts: an Analysis of the Accommodation provided by all religious Bodies in the Divisions, Districts and Parishes of the County*, Bemrose & Sons, London, 1876.

[B.242] Mabbs, Goodeve, *The Churches in Nottinghamshire; or, Provision for public Worship in the Midland Districts: a full Analysis of the Accommodation provided by all religious Bodies*, Bemrose & Sons, London, 1879.

[B.243] McAllister, Ian, 'The Devil, miracles and the Afterlife: the political sociology of religion in Northern Ireland', *British Journal of Sociology*, vol.XXXIII, 1982, pp.330-47.

[B.244] MacGrath, Kevin M., *Catholicism in Devon and Cornwall, 1767*, (Abbey of St Mary, Buckfastleigh), 1960.

[B.245] MacGrath, Kevin M., 'Devon and Cornwall Catholics in 1705', *Buckfast Chronicle*, vol.XXXII, 1962, pp.1-36.

[B.246] McKenzie, Robert & Silver, Allan, *Angels in Marble: working Class Conservatives in urban England*, Heinemann, London, 1968.

[B.247] MacLaren, Archibald Allan, *Religion and social Class: the Disruption Years in Aberdeen*, Routledge & Kegan Paul, London, 1974.

[B.248] McLeish, John, *Students' Attitudes and College Environments*, Cambridge Institute of Education, Cambridge, 1970.

[B.249] Macourt, Malcolm P.A., *Church Attenders: their Identification and their Characteristics*, North-East Area Study Working Paper 27, North-East Area Study, University of Durham, Durham, 1976.

[B.250] McPhail, Peter, Ungoed-Thomas, Jasper Rhodri & Chapman, Hilary, *Moral Education in the secondary School*, Longman, London, 1972.

[B.251] Madgwick, Peter James, Griffiths, Non & Walker, Valerie, *The Politics of rural Wales: a Study of Cardiganshire*, Hutchinson, London, 1973.

[B.252] Mann, Horace, 'On the statistical position of religious bodies in England and Wales', *Journal of the Statistical Society of London*, vol.XVIII, 1855, pp.141-59.

[B.253] Marchant, H.G., 'An Investigation into the Attitudes of young people to religious and moral Education, with special reference to five Schools and Colleges of Further Education in mid-Wales', University of Wales (Aberystwyth) M.A.thesis, 1970.

[B.254] Mark, Timothy John, 'A Study of cognitive and affective Elements in the religious Development of Adolescents', University of Leeds Ph.D. thesis, 1979.

[B.255] Mark, Timothy John, 'A study of religious attitudes, religious behaviour and religious cognition', *Educational Studies*, vol.8, 1982,pp. 209-16.

[B.256] Marratt, Howard, *Religious Education and the Training of primary Teachers: Report of a Survey*, Religious Education Council of England and Wales, Rowledge, 1979.

[B.257] Marriott, T.H., 'The role of religious Instruction: a comparative Study of the Conceptions held by secondary School Teachers of the Role of religious Instruction', University of Birmingham M.Ed.thesis, 1967.

[B.258] Martin, David Alfred, *A Sociology of English Religion*, Heinemann, London, 1967.

[B.259] Marvell, J., 'Religious beliefs and moral values: the influence of the School', *Educational Research*, vol.16, 1973-74, pp.94-9.

[B.260] May, Philip Radford, *Moral Education in School*, Methuen, London, 1971.
[B.261] May, Philip Radford, 'Pupil attitudes to the Bible', *Spectrum*, vol.10, no.2, January 1978, pp.31-3.
[B.262] May, Philip Radford, 'Religious judgments in children and adolescents: a research report', *Learning for Living*, vol.16, 1976-77, pp.115-22.
[B.263] May, Philip Radford, 'Teachers' attitudes to religious education', *Educational Research*, vol.11, 1968-69, pp.66-70.
[B.264] May, Philip Radford, 'Why parents want religion in School', *Learning for Living*, vol.6, no.4, March 1967, pp.14-8.
[B.265] May, Philip Radford, 'Why teachers want religion in school', *Learning for Living*, vol.8, no.1, September 1968, pp.13-7.
[B.266] May, Philip Radford & Johnston, Olaf Raymond, 'Parental attitudes to religious education in state schools', *Durham Research Review*, vol.5, 1965-68, pp.127-38.
[B.267] Mearns, Andrew, *The Statistics of Attendance at public Worship, as published in England, Wales and Scotland by the local press between October 1881 and February 1882*, Hodder & Stoughton, London, 1882.
[B.268] Medhurst, Kenneth & Moyser, George, 'The Open Synod Group', *Living the Faith: a Call to the Church*, ed. Kathleen Jones, Oxford University Press, Oxford, 1980, pp.132-49.
[B.269] Mercer, Alan, O'Neil, Jennifer S.& Shepherd, Alan J., 'The churching of urban England', *OR 69: Proceedings of the fifth International Conference on Operational Research, Venice, 1969*, ed.J.Lawrence, Tavistock, London, 1970, pp.725-39.
[B.270] Meredith, Philip J., 'Bibliography of work in the sociology of British religion, 1974 supplement', *A Sociological Yearbook of Religion in Britain, 8*, ed. Michael Hill, SCM Press, London, 1975, pp.181-4.
[B.271] Mess, Henry Adolphus, *Industrial Tyneside: a social Survey made for the Bureau of Social Research for Tyneside*, Ernest Benn, London, 1928.
[B.272] Miller, John, *Popery and Politics in England, 1660-1688*, Cambridge University Press, Cambridge, 1973.
[B.273] Milne, Robert Stephen & MacKenzie, Hugh Cormack Henderson, *Marginal Seat, 1955: a Study of Voting Behaviour in the Constituency of Bristol North East at the General Election of 1955*, Hansard Society for Parliamentary Government, London, 1958.
[B.274] Morton-Williams, Jean & Stowell, Richard, *Small Heath, Birmingham: a social Study*, Department of the Environment, London, 1975.
[B.275] Moyser, George, 'The 1980 General Synod: patterns and trends', *Crucible*, 1982, pp.75-86.
[B.276] Moyser, George, 'Patterns of representation in the elections to the General Synod in 1975', *Crucible*, 1979, pp.73-9.
[B.277] Moyser, George, 'Patterns of social representation in the National Pastoral Congress: a preliminary report', *The Month*, Second New Series, vol.13, 1980, pp.95-101.
[B.278] Moyser, George, 'The political organisation of the middle class: the case of the Church of England', *The middle Class in Politics*, ed. John Garrard, David Jary, Michael Goldsmith & Adrian Oldfield, Saxon House, Farnborough, (1978), pp.262-93.
[B.279] Moyser, George & Medhurst, Kenneth, 'Political participation and attitudes in the Church of England', *Government and Opposition*, vol. 13, 1978, pp.81-95.
[B.280] Murray, Christopher, 'The moral and religious beliefs of Catholic adolescents: scale development and structure'. *Journal for the Scientific Study of Religion*, vol.17, 1978, pp.439-47.
[B.281] Mutton, N., 'Shropshire recusants in 1706, 1767 and 1780', *Worcestershire Recusant*, no.24, December 1974, pp.18-31.
[B.282] Mutton, N., 'Shropshire recusants in 1767 and 1780', *Worcestershire Recusant*, no.25, June 1975, pp.28-42, no.26, December 1975, pp.21-5.
[B.283] Nelson, Geoffrey Kenneth & Clews, Rosemary A., 'Geographical mobility and religious behaviour', *Sociological Review*, New Series, vol.21, 1973, pp.127-35.

[B.284] Nelson, Geoffrey Kenneth & Clews, Rosemary A., *Mobility and religious Commitment*, University of Birmingham Institute for the Study of Worship and Religious Architecture, Birmingham, 1971.

[B.285] Newman, Linda, 'Sex', *19*, April 1982, pp. 31-7, May 1982, pp. 37-41, June 1982, pp.65-7.

[B.286] Nicholls, S.H., 'The Opinions on religious Education in primary Schools of the County primary Teachers of a northern Town and final Year Students of a neighbouring College of Education', University of Newcastle upon Tyne M.Ed. thesis, 1969.

[B.287] Oats, Henry C., 'On the social statistics of certain boroughs and townships in Lancashire and Cheshire during the last twenty years', *Transactions of the Manchester Statistical Society*, 1866-67, pp.33-63.

[B.288] Ormerod, M.B., 'Subject preference and choice in co-educational and single-sex secondary schools', *British Journal of Educational Psychology*, vol.45, 1975, pp.257-67.

[B.289] Owen, Trefor M., 'Chapel and community in Glan-Llyn, Merioneth', *Welsh rural Communities*, ed. Elwyn Davies & Alwyn D.Rees, University of Wales Press, Cardiff, 1960, pp.185-248.

[B.290] Pagden, Frank, 'An analysis of the effectiveness of Methodist churches of varying sizes and types in the Liverpool District', *A Sociological Yearbook of Religion in Britain*, ed. David Martin, SCM Press, London, 1968, pp.124-34.

[B.291] Patterson, George, 'The Religious Census: a test of its accuracy in South Shields', *Durham County Local History Society Bulletin*, no.21, April 1978, pp.14-7.

[B.292] Patterson, Sheila, *Dark Strangers: a sociological Study of the Absorption of a recent West Indian migrant Group in Brixton, South London*, Tavistock Publications, London, 1963.

[B.293] Paul, Leslie Allen, *A Church by Daylight: a Reappraisement of the Church of England and its Future*, Geoffrey Chapman, London, 1973.

[B.294] Paul, Leslie Allen, *The Deployment and Payment of the Clergy: A Report*, Church Information Office, London, 1964.

[B.295] Payne, Geoff & Ford, Graeme, 'Religion, class and educational policy: some evidence on the educational record of Scotland's religiously segregated secondary Schools', *Scottish Educational Studies*, vol.9, 1977, pp.83-99.

[B.296] Peace, Sheila M., Hall, John F. & Hamblin, Graham, *The Quality of Life of the Elderly in residential Care: a Feasibility Study of the Development of Survey Methods*, Survey Research Unit, Polytechnic of North London, London, 1979.

[B.297] Peacock, Roy, 'The 1892 Birmingham religious census',*Religion in the Birmingham Area: Essays in the Sociology of Religion*, ed. Alan Bryman, University of Birmingham Institute for the Study of Worship and Religious Architecture, Birmingham, 1975, pp.12-28.

[B.298] Pearson, David G., *Race, Class and political Activism: a Study of West Indians in Britain*, Gower, Farnborough, 1981.

[B.299] Pearson, David G., 'Race, religiosity and political activism: some observations on West Indian participation in Britain', *British Journal of Sociology*, vol.XXIX, 1978, pp.340-57.

[B.300] Perman, David, *Change and the Churches: an Anatomy of Religion in Britain*, Bodley Head, London, 1977.

[B.301] Pickering, William Stuart Frederick, 'Children pose the problems', *Christian News-Letter*, vol.5, no.4, October 1957, pp.24-8.

[B.302] Pickering, William Stuart Frederick, 'The 1851 Religious Census- a useless experiment?', *British Journal of Sociology*, vol.XVIII, 1967, pp.382-407.

[B.303] Pickering, William Stuart Frederick, 'The Place of Religion in the social Structure of two English industrial Towns (Rawmarsh, Yorkshire and Scunthorpe, Lincolnshire)', University of London Ph.D. thesis, 1958.

[B.304] Pickering, William Stuart Frederick, 'Quelques resultats d'interviews religieuses', *Vocation de la sociologie religieuse, sociologie des vocations: Conference Internationale de Sociologie Religieuse, Louvain, 1956*, Casterman, Tournai, 1958, pp.54-76.

[B.305] Pickering, William Stuart Frederick, '"Religious movements" of church members in two working-class towns in England', *Archives de Sociologie des Religions*, no.11, January-June 1961, pp.129-40.

[B.306] Piggott, Charles Antony, 'A Geography of Religion in Scotland', University of Edinburgh Ph.D. thesis, 1978.

[B.307] Pilkington, Geoffrey W., Poppleton, Pamela K. & Robertshaw, Gillian, 'Changes in religious attitude and practices among students during university degree courses', *British Journal of Educational Psychology*, vol.XXXV, 1965, pp.150-7.

[B.308] Pilkington, Geoffrey W., Poppleton, Pamela K., Gould, Judith B. & McCourt, Margaret M., 'Changes in religious beliefs, practices and attitudes among university students over an eleven-year period in relation to sex differences, denominational differences and differences between Faculties and years of study', *British Journal of Social and Clinical Psychology*, vol.15, 1976, pp.1-9.

[B.309] Player, Christine M., *A national Portrait: young Families in Britain*, Young Families Department of the Mothers' Union, (London), 1979.

[B.310] Poole, Michael A., 'Religious residential segregation in urban Northern Ireland', *Integration and Division: geographical Perspectives on the Northern Ireland Problem*, ed. Frederick W.Boal & J.Neville H. Douglas, Academic Press, London, 1982, pp.281-308.

[B.311] Poppleton, Pamela K. & Pilkington, Geoffrey W., 'The measurement of religious attitudes in a university population', *British Journal of Social and Clinical Psychology*, vol.2, 1963, pp.20-36.

[B.312] Povall, Charles Herbert, 'Some Factors affecting Pupils' Attitudes to religious Education', University of Manchester M.Ed. thesis, 1971.

[B.313] Power, E.R.Roper, 'The social Structure of an English County Town', University of London Ph.D. thesis, 1937.

[B.314] Prichard, E.C., 'An Enquiry into the Extent and Content of religious Instruction in some Welsh secondary Schools in the light of Sections 25-28 of the 1944 Act', University of Wales (Cardiff) M.A.thesis, 1965.

[B.315] Priestnall, Robin, Pilkington, Geoffrey W. & Moffat, Gillian, 'Personality and the use of oral contraceptives in British university students', *Social Science & Medicine*, vol.12A, 1978, pp.403-7.

[B.316] Rallison, R., 'The interests of senior school children in non-scientific subjects', *British Journal of Educational Psychology*, vol.XIII, 1943, pp.39-47.

[B.317] Ranson, Stewart, Bryman, Alan & Hinings, Christopher Robin, *Clergy, Ministers and Priests*, Routledge & Kegan Paul, London, 1977.

[B.318] Ratcliffe, Peter, *Racism and Reaction: a Profile of Handsworth*, Routledge & Kegan Paul, London, 1981.

[B.319] Reardon, Martin, *Christian Unity in Sheffield*, Sheffield Council of Churches, Sheffield, 1967.

[B.320] Reed, Bryan Holwell, *Eighty Thousand Adolescents: a Study of young people in the City of Birmingham by the Staff and Students of Westhill Training College*, George Allen & Unwin, London, 1950.

[B.321] Rees, D. Glanville, 'A psychological Investigation into denominational Concepts of God', University of Liverpool M.A. thesis, 1967.

[B.322] Rees, Reginald Jackson, *Background and Belief: a Study of Religion and religious Education as seen by third-year Students at Oxford, Cambridge and Bangor*, SCM Press, London, 1967.

[B.323] Reid, Ivan, 'Some views of Sunday school teachers', *Learning for Living*, vol.17, 1977-78, pp.79-81.

[B.324] Reid, Ivan, 'Sunday school attendance and adolescents' religious and moral attitudes, knowledge and practice', *Learning for Living*, vol. 17, 1977-78, pp.3-8.

[B.325] Reid, Ivan, 'Sunday schools as socialisation agencies', *Understanding Socialisation*, ed. Graham White & Rashid Mufti, Studies in Education Ltd., Nafferton, 1979, pp.41-58.

[B.326] Reid, W. Scott, 'The Role of the Church in the Life of the Elderly: Studies of the religious Attitudes of the Elderly in Institutions and those domiciled privately', University of Edinburgh Ph.D. thesis, 1975.

[B.327] Richards, Noel D., 'An empirical Study of the Prestige of selected Occupations', University of Nottingham M.A. thesis, 1962.

[B.328] Richardson, Robin & Chapman, John, *Images of Life: Problems of religious Belief and human Relations in Schools*, SCM Press, London, 1973.

[B.329] Rixon, L.D., 'An experimental and critical Study of the Teaching of Scripture in secondary Schools', University of London Ph.D. thesis, 1959.

[B.330] Robinson, Edward, *The original Vision: a Study of the religious Experience of Childhood*, Religious Experience Research Unit, Manchester College, Oxford, 1977.

[B.331] Roche, D.J.D., Birrell, W.D. & Greer, John Edmund, 'A socio-political opinion profile of clergymen in Northern Ireland', *Social Studies*, vol.4, 1975-76, pp.143-51.

[B.332] Rodd, Cyril S., 'Church affiliation and denominational values', *Sociology*, vol.2, 1968, pp.79-90.

[B.333] Rodd, Cyril S., 'Religiosity and its correlates: Hall Green, Birmingham', *Religion in the Birmingham Area: Essays in the Sociology of Religion*, ed. Alan Bryman, University of Birmingham Institute for the Study of Worship and Religious Architecture, Birmingham, 1975, pp. 99-111.

[B.334] Rosser, Colin & Harris, Christopher Charles, *The Family and Social Change: a Study of family and Kinship in a South Wales Town*, Routledge & Kegan Paul, London, 1965.

[B.335] Rowland, Wilfrid James, *The Free Churches and the People: a Report of the Work of the Free Churches in Liverpool by the Special Commissioner*, London, 1908.

[B.336] Rowntree, Benjamin Seebohm, *Poverty: a Study of Town Life*, Second Edition, Macmillan, London, 1902.

[B.337] Rowntree, Benjamin Seebohm, *Poverty and Progress: a second social Survey of York*, Longmans, Green and Co., London, 1941.

[B.338] Rowntree, Benjamin Seebohm & Lavers, George Russell, *English Life and Leisure: a social Study*, Longmans, Green and Co., London, 1951.

[B.339] Rowntree, Griselda & Pierce, Rachel M., 'Birth control in Britain', *Population Studies*, vol.XV, 1961-62, pp.3-31, 121-60.

[B.340] Russell, Anthony, 'The Attitude of primary School Children to religious Education', University of Nottingham M.Phil. thesis, 1978.

[B.341] Russell, Anthony John, *Two Surveys of Ordinands in the Church of England: a comparative Analysis*, Advisory Council for the Church's Ministry Occasional Paper no.4, Advisory Council for the Church's Ministry, London, 1976.

[B.342] Saint Moulin, Leon de, 'Social class and religious behaviour in England', *Clergy Review*, vol.LIII, 1968, pp.20-35.

[B.343] Sandford, Cedric Thomas & Griffin, S., 'Religious belief and church attendance of students at a College of Science and Technology', *Church Quarterly Review*, vol.CLXVI, 1965, pp.337-43.

[B.344] Sansbury, Kenneth, Latham, Robert & Webb, Pauline, *Agenda for the Churches: a Report on the People Next Door Programme*, SCM Press, (London), 1968.

[B.345] Schofield, Michael, *The sexual Behaviour of young People*, Longmans, London, 1965.

[B.346] Sellick, David, 'R.E. in North Yorkshire', *British Journal of Religious Education*, vol.1, 1978-79, pp.95-101.

[B.347] Shakespeare, J.J., 'An enquiry into the relative popularity of school subjects in elementary schools', *British Journal of Educational Psychology*, vol.VI, 1936, pp.147-64.

[B.348] Shannon, William D., 'A Geography of organised Religion in Liverpool', University of Liverpool B.A. dissertation, 1965.

[B.349] Shenfield, Barbara Estelle, *Social Policies for old Age: a Review of social Provision for old Age in Great Britain*, Routledge and Kegan Paul, London, 1957.

[B.350] Shirakashi, Sanshiro, 'Religious attitudes and ways of life of the world's youth: the 1972 International Youth Survey of the Office of the Prime Minister of Japan', *Journal of Church and State*, vol.18, 1976, pp.523-36.

[B.351] Sillitoe, K.K., *Planning for Leisure: an Enquiry into the present Pattern of Participation in outdoor and physical Recreation and the Frequency and Manner of Use of public open spaces among People living in the urban Areas of England and Wales*, HMSO, London, 1969.

[B.352] Sinclair, John, *The statistical Account of Scotland; drawn up from the Communications of the Ministers of the different Parishes*, 21 vol., W.Creech, Edinburgh, 1791-99.

[B.353] Sissons, Peter Lawson, 'Ethical, social and theological Diversity in contemporary Manchester Congregationalism', University of Manchester M.A. thesis, 1967.

[B.354] Sissons, Peter Lawson, *The social Significance of Church Membership in the Burgh of Falkirk: a Report to the Hope Trust and the Church and Ministry Department of the General Assembly of the Church of Scotland*, Church of Scotland, Edinburgh, 1973.

[B.355] Sjolander, Pearl M., 'A Survey on the use of Bible versions', *Worship & Preaching*, vol.10, no.3, June 1980,pp.37-8.

[B.356] Sjolander, Pearl M., 'Versions of the Bible used by British clergy today: a Report of a questionnaire survey, November 1979', *Bible Distributor*, no.15, June 1980, pp.18-25.

[B.357] Slack, Kathleen Mary, *Constancy and Change in the Society of Friends*, Friends Home Service Committee, London, 1967.

[B.358] Smith, David John, *The Facts of racial Disadvantage: a national survey*, PEP Broadsheet no.560, Political and Economic Planning, London, 1976.

[B.359] Smith, Edith M., 'Corporate religious Worship as practised in a Group of secondary modern Schools, and its Value to Adolescents', University of Birmingham M.A. thesis, 1946.

[B.360] Smith, Richard, 'Methodist preaching power in England and Wales', *Worship & Preaching*, vol.8, no.1, February 1978, pp.38-40.

[B.361] Smith, W.H. Saumarez, *An Honorary Ministry: a Review of non-stipendiary Ministry in the Church of England consequent upon the Bishops' Regulations of 1970*, Advisory Council for the Church's Ministry Occasional Paper no.8, Advisory Council for the Church's Ministry, London, 1977.

[B.362] Souper, Patrick C. & Kay, William K., *The School Assembly in Hampshire: Report of a Pilot Study*, School Assembly Project Working Paper Two, University of Southampton Department of Education, Southampton, 1982.

[B.363] Spencer, Anthony E.C.W., 'The demography and sociography of the Roman Catholic community of England and Wales',*The committed Church*, ed. Laurence Bright & Simon Clements, Darton, Longman & Todd, London, 1966, pp.60-85.

[B.364] Spencer, Anthony E.C.W., 'How effective are Catholic schools?', *Slant*, vol.1, no.4, Spring 1965, pp.9-13.

[B.365] Spencer, Anthony E.C.W., 'The Newman Demographic Survey, 1953-62: nine years of progress', *Wiseman Review*, vol.236, no.492, Summer 1962, pp. 139-54.

[B.366] Spencer, Anthony E.C.W., 'The Newman Demographic Survey, 1953-64: reflections on the birth, life and death of a Catholic institute of socio-religious research', *Social Compass*, vol.XI, no.3-4, 1964, pp. 31-7.

[B.367] Spencer, Anthony E.C.W., 'Religious census of Bishop's Stortford', *A Sociological Yearbook of Religion in Britain*, ed.David Martin, SCM Press, London, 1968, pp.135-45.

[B.368] Spencer, Anthony E.C.W., *Report on the Parish Register, religious Practice & Population Statistics of the Catholic Church in Scotland, 1967*, Pastoral Research Centre, Harrow, 1969.

[B.369] Spencer, Anthony E.C.W., *Report on the Parish Register Statistics of the Catholic Church in Scotland, 1966*, Pastoral Research Centre, Harrow, 1967.

[B.370] Spencer, Michael, 'Religion and sixth formers', *Sixth Form Opinion*, no.13, Summer 1965, pp.14-5.

[B.371] Stacey, Margaret, *Tradition and Change: a Study of Banbury*, Oxford University Press, London, 1960.

[B.372] Stacey, Margaret, Batstone, Eric, Bell, Colin & Murcott, Anne, *Power, Persistence and Change: a second study of Banbury*, Routledge & Kegan Paul, London, 1975.

[B.373] Stephens, William Brewer, Dunning, Robert W., Alcock, Joan P. & Greenslade, Michael Washington, 'Religion in Congleton', *History of Congleton: published to celebrate the 700th. Anniversary of the Granting of the Charter to the Town*, ed. William Brewer Stephens, Manchester University Press, Manchester, 1970, pp.201-71.

[B.374] Stewart, D.A., 'The Geography of the Church of Scotland in Edinburgh', University of Edinburgh M.A. dissertation, 1975.

[B.375] Stewart, Mary, 'The leisure activities of grammar school children', *British Journal of Educational Psychology*, vol.XX, 1950, pp.11-34.

[B.376] Stewart, Mary, *The Leisure Activities of School Children*, Workers Educational Association, London, 1948.

[B.377] Stewart, Mary, *The Leisure Activities of School Children: a Report of an Investigation by Mary Stewart and the Students of a Holborn Advanced Tutorial Class*, Workers Educational Association London District, London, 1960.

[B.378] Stratten, Thomas, *Review of the Hull Ecclesiastical Controversy*, Hull, 1834.

[B.379] Stubley, Peter, 'The Churches and the Iron and Steel Industry in Middlesbrough, 1890-1914', University of Durham M.A. thesis, 1979.

[B.380] Tanner, R.E.S., *Reactions to liturgical Change: a Study of some Parishioners' Responses in a Liverpool Parish*, English Province of the Society of Jesus Social Survey Memorandum 6, Heythrop College, (London), 1970.

[B.381] Tanner, R.E.S., *Reactions to pastoral Change: a Study of some Parishioners' Responses in a Liverpool Parish*, English Province of the Society of Jesus Social Survey Memorandum 7, Heythrop College, (London), 1970.

[B.382] Theobald, Robin C., 'The Seventh-Day Adventist Movement: a sociological Study with particular reference to Great Britain', University of London Ph.D. thesis, 1979.

[B.383] Thompson, David Michael, 'The 1851 Religious Census: problems and possibilities', *Victorian Studies*, vol.11, 1967-68, pp.87-97.

[B.384] Thompson, David Michael, 'The Religious Census of 1851', *The Census and social Structure: an interpretative Guide to Nineteenth Century Censuses for England and Wales*, ed.Richard Lawton, Frank Cass, London, 1978, pp.241-86.

[B.385] Thompson, Richard Huberht Thurlow, *The Church's Understanding of itself: a Study of four Birmingham Parishes*, SCM Press, London, 1957.

[B.386] Thorne, Roger, 'An analysis of services on three Sundays in 1970', *Cirplan*, vol.5, 1972-75, pp.19-23.

[B.387] Thornes, Barbara & Collard, Jean, *Who divorces?*, Routledge & Kegan Paul, London, 1979.

[B.388] Towler, Robert & Coxon, Anthony Peter Macmillan, *The Fate of the Anglican Clergy: a sociological Study*, Macmillan, London, 1979.

[B.389] Townsend, Anne, 'A woman's place ···', *Family*, November 1982, pp.23-4.

[B.390] Townsend, Anne, 'Your marriage', *Family*, March 1981, pp.12-3.

[B.391] Townsend, Peter, *The Family Life of old People: an Inquiry in East London*, Routledge & Kegan Paul, London, 1957.

[B.392] Townsend, Peter & Tunstall, Sylvia, 'Isolation, desolation and loneliness', *Old People in three industrial Societies*, by Ethel Shanas, Peter Townsend, Dorothy Wedderburn, Henning Friis, Paul Milhoj & Jan Stehauwer, Routledge & Kegan Paul, London, 1968, pp.258-87.

[B.393] Turner, Bryan Stanley, 'Belief, ritual and experience: the case of Methodism', *Social Compass*, vol.XVIII, 1971, pp.187-201.

[B.394] Turner, Bryan Stanley, 'The Decline of Methodism: an Analysis of religious Commitment and Organisation', University of Leeds Ph.D.thesis, 1970.

[B.395] Turner, Bryan Stanley & Smith, David, 'The Child's view of the minister of religion', *Crucible*, 1970, pp.110-4.

[B.396] Varney, Peter D., 'Religion in rural Norfolk', *A Sociological Yearbook of Religion in Britain, 3*, ed. David Martin & Michael Hill, SCM Press, London, 1970, pp.65-77.

[B.397] Waite, Marjorie, *Consultant Gynaecologists and Birth Control*, Birth Control Trust, London, 1974.

[B.398] Walker, D.J.C., 'A Study of Children's Conceptions of God', University of Glasgow Ed.B. dissertation, 1950.

[B.399] Walker, L.Trafford, 'A Study of Attitudes of Training College Students towards religious Education and Religion', University of London Ph.D. thesis, 1966.

[B.400] Wallis, Roy, *Salvation and Protest: Studies of social and religious Movements*, Frances Pinter, London, 1979.

[B.401] Walton, Mary, *A History of the Diocese of Sheffield, 1914-1979*, Sheffield Diocesan Board of Finance, Sheffield, 1981.

[B.402] Ward, Conor Kieran, *Priests and People: a Study in the Sociology of Religion*, Liverpool University Press, Liverpool, 1961.

[B.403] Ward, Conor Kieran, 'Some aspects of the social structure of a Roman Catholic parish', *Sociological Review*, New Series, vol.6, 1958, pp.75-93.

[B.404] Ward, Robin Harwood, 'Some aspects of religious life in an immigrant area in Manchester', *A Sociological Yearbook of Religion in Britain, 3*, ed. David Martin & Michael Hill, SCM Press, London, 1970, pp.12-29.

[B.405] Wasdell, David, *Case Study no.1, unit I: basic Parameters*, Urban Church Project, London, (1979).

[B.406] Wasdell, David, *Case Study no.1, unit II: Congregation Survey (first Part)*, Urban Church Project, London, (1979).

[B.407] Wasdell, David, *Facing the Future: a Report submitted to Billericay Methodist Church*, Urban Church Project, London, 1980.

[B.408] Wasdell, David, *Mission Appraisal no.1: a Study of the Development of a City Parish in East Anglia including Coverage of two Church Army Missions and Assessment of their Effects*, Urban Church Project, London, (1981).

[B.409] Wasdell, David, *Mission Appraisal no.2: a Study of the Impact and Effects of a Church Army Mission and its Follow-Through in a Lancashire Parish*, Urban Church Project, London, (1981).

[B.410] Wasdell, David, *1781-1981, 200 Years of Methodism: a Study of Barking Methodist Church*, Urban Church Project, London, (1981).

[B.411] Watson, Gillian I., 'To examine the Perception of the Church of Scotland as seen by its Members', University of Edinburgh M.A. dissertation, 1975.

[B.412] Watts, Michael Robert, *The Dissenters: from the Reformation to the French Revolution*, Clarendon Press, Oxford, 1978.

[B.413] Whiteman, Anne, 'The census that never was: a problem in authorship and dating', *Statesmen, Scholars and Merchants: Essays in Eighteenth-Century History presented to Dame Lucy Sutherland*, ed, Anne Whiteman, J.S. Bromley & P.G.M. Dickson, Clarendon Press, Oxford, 1973, pp.1-16.

[B.414] Whittle, Peter, *The History of the Borough of Preston in the County Palatine of Lancaster*, 2 vol., P. & H. Whittle, Preston, 1837.

[B.415] Whyte, John Henry, 'The Vicars Apostolics' returns of 1773', *Recusant History*, vol.9, 1967-68, pp.205-14.

[B.416] Williams, Roma Morton & Finch, Stewart, *Young School Leavers: Report of a Survey among young People, Parents and Teachers*, Schools Council Enquiry 1, HMSO, London, 1968.

[B.417] Willmott, Peter, *The Evolution of a Community: a Study of Dagenham after forty Years*, Routledge & Kegan Paul, London, 1963.

[B.418] Willmott, Peter & Young, Michael, *Family and Class in a London Suburb*, Routledge & Kegan Paul, London, 1960.

[B.419] Wilson, Glenn Daniel, 'Cross-generational stability of gender differences in sexuality', *Personality and Individual Differences*, vol.2, 1981, pp.254-7.

[B.420] Wilson, Michael, *The Hospital - a Place of Truth: A Study of the Role of the Hospital Chaplain*, University of Birmingham Institute for the Study of Worship and Religious Architecture, Birmingham, 1971.

[B.421] Winwood, David J., *Before it's too late*, Methodist Division of Education and Youth, London, 1980.

[B.422] Withrington, Donald J., 'The 1851 Census of Religious Worship and Education: with a note on church accommodation in mid-19th.-Century Scotland', *Records of the Scottish Church History Society*, vol.XVIII, 1972-74, pp.133-48.

[B.423] Wolfe, James Nathaniel & Pickford, Michael, *The Church of Scotland: an economic Survey*, Geoffrey Chapman, London, 1980.

[B.424] Wollaston, Barbara K., *Saint Andrew's Presbyterian Church of England, Woolwich: Membership Study, Winter 1966*, St.Mary's Parish Office, London, (1966).

[B.425] Wollaston, Barbara K., *Saint Mary's Parish Church, Woolwich: Membership Study, Spring 1965*, St. Mary's Parish Office, London, (1965).

[B.426] Worrall, E.S., 'The Catholic recusant minority in Middlesex in 1706', *London Recusant*, vol.III, 1973, pp.47-53.

[B.427] Worrall, E.S., 'The recusant minority in Hertfordshire, 1705-1706', *Essex Recusant*, vol.XI, 1969, pp.32-8.

[B.428] Wright, Derek & Cox, Edwin, 'Changes in attitudes towards religious education and the Bible among sixth-form boys and girls', *British Journal of Educational Psychology*, vol. 41, 1971, pp.328-31.

[B.429] Wright, Derek & Cox, Edwin, 'Changes in moral belief among sixth-form boys and girls over a seven-year period in relation to religious belief, age and sex difference', *British Journal of Social and Clinical Psychology*, vol.10, 1971, pp.332-41.

[B.430] Wright, Derek & Cox, Edwin, 'Religious belief and co-education in a sample of sixth-form boys and girls', *British Journal of Social and Clinical Psychology*, vol.6, 1967, pp.23-31.

[B.431] Wright, Derek & Cox, Edwin, 'A Study of the relationship between moral judgment and religious belief in a sample of English adolescents', *Journal of Social Psychology*, vol.72, 1967, pp.135-44.

[B.432] Wright, M.Monroe, *Occupational Career Patterns of British Chaplains to Higher Education*, Sociological Research Unit, University College, Cardiff, 1977.

[B.433] Wrigley, Edward Anthony & Schofield, Roger S., *The Population History of England, 1541-1871: a Reconstruction*, Edward Arnold, London, 1981.

[B.434] Wykes, David, 'A reappraisal of the reliability of the 1676 "Compton Census" with respect to Leicester', *Leicestershire Archaeological and Historical Society Transactions*, vol.LV, 1979-80, pp.72-7.

[B.435] Young, Arthur, *General View of the Agriculture of the County of Suffolk; drawn up for the consideration of the Board of Agriculture and Internal Improvement*, Third Edition, Richard Phillips, London, 1804.

[B.436] 'Abortion: defining GPs' attitudes', *New Humanist*, vol.LXXXVIII, 1972-73, pp.74-6.

[B.437] *Agency and Progress of Wesleyan-Methodism as exemplified by statistical details, and considered with reference to its Facilities for promoting and sustaining a general Revival of Religion throughout the Country*, Simpkin, Marshall and Co., London, 1845.

[B.438] *Alternative Patterns of Training: a Report prepared by a Working Party for the Advisory Council for the Church's Ministry*, General Synod GS.265, Church Information Office, London, 1975.

[B.439] *The annual Monitor for 1849: or, Obituary of the Members of the Society of Friends in Great Britain and Ireland for the year 1848*, Executors of the late William Alexander, York, 1848.

[B.440] 'An appeal for the London City Mission', *London City Mission Magazine*, vol.XI, 1846, pp.1-14.

[B.441] Department of Education and Science, *Aspects of secondary Education in England: a Survey by HMI Inspectors of Schools*, HMSO, London, 1979.

[B.442] Christian Economic and Social Research Foundation, *Aspects of the Problem facing the Churches: an Analysis of certain Findings of the Survey of Factors affecting Setting up a Home, made in Birmingham, Leeds and London in January 1957*, Christian Economic and Social Research Foundation, London, 1960.

[B.443] Age Concern, *The Attitudes of the Retired and the Elderly*, Age Concern, Mitcham, 1974.

[B.444] *Background to the Task: Supplement to 'On the other Side', the Report of the Evangelical Alliance Commission on Evangelism*, Scripture Union, London, 1968.

[B.445] 'The Baptist interest under George I', *Transactions of the Baptist Historical Society*, vol.II, 1910-11, pp.95-109.

[B.446] Census Office, *Bedfordshire Ecclesiastical Census, 1851*, ed.D.W. Bushby, Publications of the Bedfordshire Historical Record Society, vol.54, the Society, Luton, 1975.

[B.447] *Britain and her Birth-Rate: a Report prepared by Mass-Observation for the Advertising Service Guild*, John Murray, London, 1945.

[B.448] Census Office, *Census of Great Britain, 1851: Education, England and Wales, Report and Tables*, Parliamentary Papers, House of Commons, 1852-53, vol.XC.

[B.449] Census Office, *Census of Great Britain, 1851: Religious Worship and Education, Scotland, Report and Tables*, Parliamentary Papers, House of Commons, 1854, vol.LIX.

[B.450] Census Office, *Census of Great Britain, 1851: Religious Worship, England and Wales, Report and Tables*, Parliamentary Papers, House of Commons, 1852-53, vol.LXXXIX.

[B.451] *Census of Great Britain, 1851: Religious Worship in England and Wales, abridged from the official Report made by Horace Mann, Esq. to George Graham, Esq., Registrar-General*, George Routledge and Co., London, 1854.

[B.452] *Census of public Worship in Bradford: being Statistics of the Attendance at religious Services in the Borough on Dec.11 and Dec.18, 1881, with Press and Pulpit Comments, revised and reprinted from 'The Bradford Observer'*, Bradford Observer, Bradford, 1882.

[B.453] Foy Society Survey Group, *A Census of Unitarian Congregations in Britain*, General Assembly of Unitarian & Free Christian Churches, London, 1967.

[B.454] 'Chiswick', *London City Mission Magazine*, vol.XIII, 1848, pp.273-82.

[B.455] 'Christian behaviour: exclusive survey', *Today*, April 1982, pp.32-5.

[B.456] 'Church accommodation', *Bristol Statistical Society Annual Report*, 1841, pp.13-6.

[B.457] Marplan Ltd., *The Clergy of Britain: prepared for Cavenham Communications Ltd.*, Marplan Ltd., London, 1979.

[B.458] 'Comparative statistics of religion in Wales', *The Congregational Calendar for 1848*, Jackson and Walford, London, 1848, pp.71-6.

[B.459] 'A comparative view of the hearers, communicants and scholars belonging to Churchmen, Dissenters & Wesleyan Methodists in two hundred and three towns and villages of England, compiled from local returns', *Congregational Magazine*, New Series, vol.X, 1834, Supplement.

[B.460] *Country Pattern: the first Report of the Church in Rural Life Committee*, Home Mission Occasional Papers no.14, Methodist Church Home Mission Department, London, 1970.

[B.461] Mass-Observation, 'Current problems', *Mass-Observation Reprint*, vol. 1, no.22, April 1951, pp.1-4.

[B.462] 'Descriptive report of Cripplegate Without', *London City Mission Magazine*, vol.XIV, 1849, pp.67-86.

[B.463] 'Descriptive report of Hammersmith', *London City Mission Magazine*, vol XIII, 1848, pp.223-35.

[B.464] Religious Education Council of England and Wales, *The Development of religious Education: a Report on the Recruitment and Training of RE Teachers*, Religious Education Council of England and Wales, Rowledge, 1978.

[B.465] Community Resources Centre, *A Directory of Christian Communities and Groups*, Community Resources Centre, Westhill College, Birmingham, 1980.

[B.466] *Directory of Evangelists and evangelistic Organisations*, ed.John M. Parr, Church Growth Centre, Cheltenham, 1980.

[B.467] *The Distribution & Statistics of the Scottish Churches*, MacNiven & Wallace, Edinburgh, 1886.

[B.468] 'District report', *The Methodist Church (Leeds District): Agenda of May Synod*, 1970, pp.17-9.

[B.469] *Education Enquiry: Abstract of the Answers and Returns made pursuant to an Address of the House of Commons, dated 24th. May 1833*, Parliamentary Papers, House of Commons, 1835, vol.XLI, XLII, XLIII.

[B.470] Metropolitan Borough of North Tyneside Social Services Department, *The Elderly in the Community: a Study of People aged sixty five and over living in North Tyneside in 1979*, Metropolitan Borough of North Tyneside Social Services Department, (Newcastle upon Tyne, 1981).

[B.471] Hereford Diocesan Council of Education, *An Enquiry into the Role of Village Church Schools: a Summary*, Hereford Diocesan Council of Education, Hereford, (1978).

[B.472] *The Evidence for voluntary Action, being Memoranda by Organisations and Individuals and other Material relevant to voluntary Action*, ed. William Henry Beveridge & Alan Frank Wells, George Allen and Unwin, London, 1949.

[B.473] Statistical Unit of the Central Board of Finance of the Church of England, *Facts and Figures about the Church of England*, 3 vol., Church Information Office, London, 1959-65.

[B.474] *'Family' Marriage Survey: Analysis of the first 500 Replies to a questionnaire in 'Family' Magazine, October 1980*, Family, London, (1981).

[B.475] *The final Report of the Priorities and Resources Group with Resolutions of the General Assembly, 1980*, United Reformed Church, London, 1980.

[B.476] Church of England Battersea Deanery Organisation Committee, *First Report, Jan.1971*, Battersea Deanery Organisation Committee, London, 1971.

[B.477] *The fourth R: the Report of the Commission on Religious Education in Schools appointed in 1967 under the Chairmanship of the Bishop of Durham*, National Society, London, 1970.

[B.478] *Gallup Poll with Roman Catholics*, Social Surveys (Gallup Poll) Ltd., London, 1967.

[B.479] *General Minutes made at the forty-second annual Conference of the Primitive Methodist Connexion held at Derby, June 5-14, 1861*, Richard Davies, London, 1861.

[B.480] *General Practitioners' Attitudes to the Operation of the Abortion Act, 1967: a Report prepared for the Rationalist Press Association by NOP Market Research Limited*, NOP Market Research Ltd., London, 1972.

[B.481] *A general Table showing the State of Education in England*, Parliamentary Papers, House of Commons, 1820, vol.XII.

[B.482] *A general Table showing the State of Education in Scotland*, Parliamentary Papers, House of Commons, 1820, vol.XII.

[B.483] *A general Table showing the State of Education in Wales*, Parliamentary Papers, House of Commons, 1820, vol.XII.

[B.484] 'GPs' attitudes to the Abortion Act', *New Humanist*, vol.LXXXIX, 1973-74, pp.225-7.

[B.485] 'Greenwich', *London City Mission Magazine*, vol.XI, 1846, pp.273-96.

[B.486] *House-to-house Visitation of Bradford, 1892: being an Account of the Movement*, Thomas Brear & Co., Bradford, (1892).

[B.487] 'How you rate your jobs', *Money Which?*, September 1977, pp.489-93.

[B.488] *Images of the World in the Year 2000: a comparative ten nation Study*, ed. H. Ornauer, H. Wiberg, A. Sicinski & J. Galtung, Publications of the European Coordination Centre for Research and Documentation in Social Sciences 7, Mouton, the Hague, 1976.

[B.489] *The Independent's religious Census of Sheffield, Rotherham, Chesterfield, Barnsley, Worksop and Retford taken on Sunday, Nov.20, 1881, reprinted, with corrections and additions, from the 'Sheffield and Rotherham Independent'*, Leader & Sons, Sheffield, 1881.

[B.490] *Intercommunion: a Scottish Episcopalian Approach, being a Report of the Commission on Intercommunion to the Provincial Synod of the Scottish Episcopal Church together with a Postscript recording the Decisions of the Provincial Synod at its Meeting in Perth on 4th.-5th. November 1969*, Representative Church Council, Scottish Episcopal Church, Edinburgh, 1969.

[B.491] Conference on Christian Politics, Economics and Citizenship Ipswich Local Committee, *Ipswich: a Survey of the Town*, (East Anglian Daily Times, Ipswich, 1924).

[B.492] Whitbread & Co. Ltd., *Is there anything to be said for our Licensing Hours? How did you vote?*, Whitbread & Co. Ltd., London, (1977).

[B.493] *Lambeth Conference, 1968: preparatory Information*, SPCK, London, 1968.

[B.494] Census Office, *Lincolnshire Returns of the Census of Religious Worship, 1851*, ed. R.W. Ambler, Publications of the Lincoln Record Society, vol.72, the Society, (Lincoln), 1979.

[B.495] *Liverpool Mercury*, Liverpool, 28 September 1855.

[B.496] Independent Broadcasting Authority Audience Research Department, *Lonely people and the Media: Report on a Study, March 1978*, Independent Broadcasting Authority Audience Research Department, London, 1978.

[B.497] *Malton in the early nineteenth Century*, ed. D.J. Salmon, North Yorkshire County Record Office Publications no.26, North Yorkshire County Council, Northallerton, 1981.

[B.498] Social Surveys (Gallup Poll) Ltd., *Medical Survey: Opinions of nursing Staff of the Working of the Abortion Act*, Gallup, London, 1972.

[B.499] Anglican Consultative Council, *Membership, Manpower and Money in the Anglican Communion: a survey of 27 Churches and 360 Dioceses*, Anglican Consultative Council, London, 1973.

[B.500] Christian Economic and Social Research Foundation, *Methodist Ministers and total Abstinence: Report on an Inquiry made with the Goodwill of the Christian Citizenship Department of the Methodist Church* , Christian Economic and Social Research Foundation, London, 1962.

[B.501] Christian Economic and Social Research Foundation, *Ministers of the Congregational Church and Presbyterian Church of England and total Abstinence: Report*, Christian Economic and Social Research Foundation, London, 1962.

[B.502] 'Mission '82', *Hertford Baptist Church News Letter*, October 1982.

[B.503] *Missionary Societies: Report on a Research Programme prepared for the Home Council of the Conference of Missionary Societies by the British Market Research Bureau Limited*, 2 vol., British Market Research Bureau, London, 1969.

[B.504] 'Moral and ecclesiastical statistics of London', *Congregational Magazine*, New Series, vol.II, 1838, pp.325-34, 465-71, 557-65, 827-48.

[B.505] Scottish Education Department, *Moral and religious Education in Scottish Schools: Report of a Committee appointed by the Secretary of State for Scotland*, HMSO, Edinburgh, 1972.

[B.506] Social Surveys (Gallup Poll) Ltd., *National Survey of Attitudes towards Abortion amongst Obstetricians and Gynaecologists*, 2 vol., Social Surveys (Gallup Poll) Ltd., London, 1977.

[B.507] *National Survey on religious Attitudes of young People, 1978*, ed. Janet Harrison, Bible Society, (London), 1978.

[B.508] *The new statistical Account of Scotland; by the Ministers of the respective Parishes under the Superintendence of a Committee of the Society for the Benefit of the Sons and Daughters of the Clergy*, 15 vol., W. Blackwood & Sons, Edinburgh, 1845.

[B.509] *The Nonconformist*, London, 1841-79.

[B.510] *The Nonconformist and Independent*, London, 1880-90.

[B.511] *On the other Side: the Report of the Evangelical Alliance's Commission on Evangelism*, Scripture Union, London, 1968.

[B.512] *Original Records of early Nonconformity under Persecution and Indulgence*, ed. George Lyon Turner, 3 vol., T. Fisher Unwin, London, 1911-14.

[B.513] Parochus, 'A parish survey', *Clergy Review*, vol.XLII, 1957, pp. 449-56.

[B.514] British Broadcasting Corporation Audience Research Department, *The People's Activities and Use of Time: a Reference Book based on two Surveys in Great Britain, 1974-5*, British Broadcasting Corporation, (London), 1978.

[B.515] *Primitive Methodism as represented in metropolitan London*, (Primitive Methodist Church, London, 1906).

[B.516] *Primitive Methodist Church: Statistics supplied by Circuits in the Metropolitan Area, March 1918*, (Primitive Methodist Church, London, 1918).

[B.517] *Prospects for the Eighties: from a Census of the Churches in 1979 undertaken by the Nationwide Initiative in Evangelism*, Bible Society, London, 1980.

[B.518] Mass-Observation, *Puzzled People:a Study in popular Attitudes to Religion, Ethics, Progress and Politics in a London Borough*, Victor Gollancz, London, 1947.

[B.519] *The Recruitment, Employment and Training of Teachers concerned with religious Education in Schools in England and Wales: the Report of a Working Party set up by the Education Department of the British Council of Churches with the Support of the Department of Education and Science*, British Council of Churches, London, 1971.

[B.520] 'The Redfield United Front Survey', *Redfield Review*, May 1953, pp.3-5.

[B.521] 'Religious accommodation in London', *Primitive Methodist Magazine*, New Series, vol.VIII, 1885, pp. 252-3.

[B.522] Census Office, *The Religious Census of 1851: a Calendar of the Returns relating to Wales*, ed. Ieuan Gwynedd Jones & David Williams, Board of Celtic Studies History and Law Series no.30-31, 2 vol., University of Wales Press, Cardiff, 1976-81.

[B.523] *The religious Census of London: reprinted from 'The British Weekly'*, Hodder & Stoughton, London, 1888.

[B.524] Assistant Masters Association, *Religious Education*, (Assistant Masters Association, no place, 1977).

[B.525] Schools Council, *Religious Education in primary Schools*, Schools Council Working Paper 44, Evans Brothers, London, 1972.

[B.526] *Religious Education in Schools: the Report of an Inquiry made by the Research Committee of the Institute of Christian Education into the Working of the 1944 Education Act*, National Society, London, 1954.

[B.527] University of Sheffield Institute of Education, *Religious Education in secondary Schools: a Survey and a Syllabus*, Thomas Nelson and Sons, London, 1961.

[B.528] 'Religious investigation work', *Free Church Year Book*, 1910, pp.155-7.

[B.529] *The religious Life of London*, ed. Richard Mudie-Smith, Hodder and Stoughton, London, 1904.

[B.530] *Religious Statistics of eight Towns in South Lancashire: collected at the Request of the Committee of the Congregational Union of England & Wales*, Thos. Dornan, Oldham, 1880.

[B.531] *Report from the Clergy of a District in the Diocese of Lincoln, convened for the Purpose of considering the State of Religion in the several parishes in the said District, as well as the best Mode of promoting the belief and Practice of it; and of guarding, as much as possible, against the Dangers arising to the Church and Government of this Kingdom from the alarming Increase of Profaneness and Irreligion on the one Hand and from the false Doctrines and evil Designs of fanatic and seditious Teachers on the other*, Second Edition, F. & C. Rivington, London, 1800.

[B.532] *Report from the Select Committee on Church Rates; together with the Proceedings of the Committee, Minutes of Evidence, Appendix and Index*, Parliamentary Papers, House of Commons, 1851, vol.IX.

[B.533] 'Report of our work in towns and Villages', *Minutes made at the seventy-seventh annual Conference of the Primitive Methodist Connexion held at Burnley, June 10-19, 1896*, Thomas Mitchell, London, 1896, pp.137-40.

[B.534] *Report of the Commissioners appointed to inquire into the State of popular Education in England, vol.I*, Parliamentary Papers, House of Commons, 1861, vol.XXI, part I.

[B.535] *Report of the Commissioners of religious Instruction, Scotland*, Parliamentary Papers, House of Commons, 1837, vol.XXI, 1837-38, vol. XXXII, XXXIII, 1839, vol.XXIII, XXIV, XXV, XXVI.

[B.536] 'Report of the Local Preachers' Commission of the United Methodist Church', *Minutes of the annual Conference of the United Methodist Church held in Salem Church, Newcastle-on-Tyne from July 13th. to July 19th. 1921*, United Methodist Publishing House, London, 1921, pp.173-87.

[B.537] *Report of the Royal Commission on the Church of England in Wales and other religious Bodies in Wales and Monmouthshire*, Parliamentary Papers, House of Commons, 1910, vol.XIV, XV, XVI, XVII, XVIII, XIX.

[B.538] *Report on a Survey of Churches in the Liverpool Methodist District undertaken by a Sub-Committee of the District General Purposes Committee, October 1976*, Liverpool Methodist District General Purposes Committee, Liverpool, 1976.

[B.539] Christian Economic and Social Research Foundation, *Report on Methodist Ministers and total Abstinence: the Change in Attitudes, 1962 to 1972*, Christian Economic and Social Research Foundation, (London, 1972).

[B.540] Council for Wales and Monmouthshire, *Report on the Welsh Language today*, Parliamentary Papers, House of Commons, 1963-64, vol.XX.

[B.541] *Return of the Number of Parish Churches and Chapels and Chapels of Ease of the Church of England, and of the Number of Places of Worship not of the Church of England; so far as regards the County of Lancaster*, Parliamentary Papers, House of Commons, 1830, vol.XIX.

[B.542] *Returns of Papists, 1767: Diocese of Chester*, transcribed under the direction of E.S. Worrall, Catholic Record Society Occasional Publication no.1, the Society, (London), 1980.

[B.543] Methodist Church Commission on Rural Methodism, *Rural Methodism: Commission's Report to 1958 Conference, with a Summary of Evidence*, Epworth Press, London, 1958.

[B.544] *Scottish Population Statistics, including Webster's Analysis of Population, 1755*, ed. James Gray Kyd, Publications of the Scottish History Society, Third Series, vol.XLIV, the Society, Edinburgh, 1952.

[B.545] 'The Secondary School Staffing Survey', *Department of Education & Science Statistical Bulletin*, 6/80, July 1980, 5/82, March 1982.

[B.546] Scottish Education Department, *Secondary Schools Staffing Survey, 1970*, 3 vol., HMSO, Edinburgh, 1972.

[B.547] Christian Economic and Social Research Foundation, *Setting up a Home: Results of an Enquiry into the Mode of Living, Expenditures, Deficiencies and Savings of 669 Housewives aged between 18 and 27 among the working Populations of London, Leeds and Birmingham around about January 1957 - Preliminary Report*, Christian Economic and Social Research Foundation, London, 1957.

[B.548] 'Sex and the single British girl', *Honey*, May 1977, pp.40-3.

[B.549] Baptist Union Denominational Enquiry Group, *Signs of Hope: an Examination of the numerical and spiritual State of Churches in membership with the Baptist Union of Great Britain and Ireland*, Baptist Union of Great Britain and Ireland, London, 1979.

[B.550] *The social Survey of Merseyside*, ed. David Caradog Jones, 3 vol., University Press of Liverpool, Liverpool, 1934.

[B.551] *Some aspects of religious Education in secondary Schools: an Inquiry by the British Council of Churches and the National Union of Teachers*, (National Union of Teachers, London, 1965).

[B.552] *South Wales Evening Post*, Swansea, 10 November 1950.

[B.553] 'Spiritual advance', *Minutes of several Conversations at the one hundred and seventy-fifth yearly Conference of the People called Methodists in the Connexion established by the late Rev. John Wesley, A.M., begun in Manchester on Tuesday, July 16, 1918*, Wesleyan Conference Office, London, 1918, pp.22-33.

[B.554] 'Summary of District survey of 1972', *The Methodist Church (Leeds District): Agenda of May Synod*, 1972, pp.17-20.

[B.555] *Sunday Schools today: an Investigation of some Aspects of Christian Education in English Free Churches*, Free Church Federal Council, London, (1956).

[B.556] Social Surveys (Gallup Poll) Ltd., *A Survey of English Catholics*, 3 vol., Social Surveys (Gallup Poll) Ltd., London, (1978).

[B.557] *Survey of General Practitioners: Report on a Survey conducted by National Opinion Polls Limited for Abortion Law Reform Association*, National Opinion Polls Ltd., London, 1970.

[B.558] Scottish Episcopal Church Commission on Intercommunion, *A Survey of Practices in and Attitudes to Matters relevant to the Work of the Commission*, (Representative Church Council, Scottish Episcopal Church, Edinburgh), 1969.

[B.559] *The Testing of the Churches, 1932-1982: a Symposium*, ed. Rupert Davies, Epworth Press, London, 1982.

[B.560] '25 p.c. of men uninterested in religion', *The Observer*, 16 April 1961.

[B.561] *UK Christian Handbook, 1983 Edition*, ed. Peter Brierley, Evangelical Alliance/Bible Society/MARC Europe, London, 1982.

[B.562] 'Unitarian statistics', *Unitarian Chronicle*, 1832, pp.145-7, 197-9, 234-5, 243-4.

[B.563] 'Verdict: "Shops should be allowed to open on Sundays"', *Living*, December 1982, p.131.

[B.564] 'A view of English Nonconformity in 1773', *Transactions of the Congregational Historical Society*, vol.V, 1911-12, pp.205-22, 261-77, 372-85.

[B.565] *Village Life in Hampshire: a Report by Mass-Observation Ltd. and Hampshire County Planning Department*, Hampshire County Council, Winchester, 1966.

[B.566] Order of Christian Unity Education Committee, *Ways whereby Christian Education in State Schools should be saved: a Submission to the Secretary of State for Education and Science, including a Survey of Head Teachers' Views, an Appeal to Local Education Authorities*, Revised Edition, Order of Christian Unity, London, 1976.

[B.567] *What do I Believe? Answers from the Young*, ed. Mary Spain, Shepheard- Walwyn, London, 1978.

[B.568] 'What the Councils are doing', *Free Church Chronicle*, vol.V, 1903, pp. 252-3.

[B.569] 'Where now? Gallup Poll examines the Church', *Flourish*, 29 April 1979.

[B.570] 'Who wants longer shopping hours ···', *Woman*, 18 August 1979.

[B.571] *The Work of the Churches: the Report of a Commission appointed by the General Assembly of Unitarian and Free Christian Churches*, General Assembly of Unitarian and Free Christian Churches, London, 1946.

[B.572] *World Christian Encyclopedia: a comparative Study of Churches and Religions in the modern World, A.D. 1900-2000*, ed. David B. Barrett, Oxford University Press, Nairobi, 1982.

[B.573] *World Christian Handbook, 1968*, ed. H. Wakelin Coxill & Kenneth Grubb, Lutterworth Press, London, 1967.

[B.574] *World missionary Atlas: containing a directory of missionary Societies, classified summaries of Statistics, Maps showing the Location of Mission Stations throughout the World, a descriptive Account of the principal Mission Lands and comprehensive Indices*, ed. Harlan Page Beach & Charles Harvey Fahs, Edinburgh House Press, London, 1925.

[B.575] Society of Friends, *Yearly Meeting Proceedings*, 1905, pp.95-126.

[B.576] *Young People and the Church: the Report of a Working Party set up by the British Council of Churches Youth Unit*, British Council of Churches, London, 1981.

[B.577] NOP Market Research Ltd., *The Young Report: a Survey of the Attitudes of Young People undertaken for the Jimmy Young Programme*, 2 vol., NOP Market Research Ltd., London, 1978.

[B.578] 'Youth and religion: a scientific inquiry into the religious attitudes, beliefs and practice of urban youth', *New Life*, vol.14, 1958, pp.1-59.

[B.579] Market & Opinion Research International, *Youth in Britain: Attitudes and Life Style*, Market & Opinion Research International, London, 1979.

[B.580] Youth Bureau, Prime Minister's Office of Japan, *The Youth of the World and Japan: the Findings of the Second World Youth Survey*, Youth Bureau, Prime Minister's Office of Japan, Tokyo, 1978.

[B.581] Youth Bureau, Prime Minister's Office of Japan, *The Youth of the World: from the World Youth Survey Report*, Printing Bureau, Ministry of Finance, Tokyo, (1973).

APPENDIX 1 - SPECIMEN FORMS

Introductory notes.

As explained in paragraph 1.2.2.2, documentation in this appendix is limited to the three most important national ecclesiastical censuses conducted across Great Britain in 1851 (2.1.3, 2.4.1.4, 7.1.1, 9.1.1.1), England in 1979 (2.2.1.5-2.2.1.9, 7.1.2), and Wales in 1982 (2.3.1.6). Data were gathered on each occasion by means of a self-completion questionnaire delivered to the minister or lay leader of, supposedly, every congregation within the survey area.

The first three forms with accompanying instructions derive from the 1851 enquiry and relate to places of worship of, respectively, the Church of England, all other English and Welsh religious bodies, and the Scottish Kirk. A fourth schedule, issued to non-established meetings throughout Scotland, was virtually indistinguishable from the second and has not been reproduced; however, it does appear in both [B.384] and [B.449].

Six separate forms and covering letters were used in connection with the 1979 study, but the Anglican version alone is reprinted here. The remaining five questionnaires differed from this with regard to terminology rather than substance:

Denomination	Question 1	Question 2	Question 4
Roman Catholic	Parish Priest	Assistant clergy	Estimated Catholic population (aged 17 and over)
Methodist	Minister in pastoral charge	Circuit superintendent	Membership roll
Baptist	Church secretary	Minister	Membership roll
United Reformed	Church secretary	Minister	Membership roll
Other	Minister/church leader	Other minister	Adult membership

The 1982 census schedule was also available in a variety of denominational formats as well as in English and Welsh language editions. The English text of the Presbyterian Church of Wales return has been selected to indicate the range of the investigation.

Form A.

CENSUS OF GREAT BRITAIN, 1851.
(13 & 14 Victoriæ, Cap. 53.)

A RETURN of the several Particulars to be inquired into respecting the under-mentioned Church or Chapel in England, belonging to the United Church of England and Ireland.

A similar Return (*mutatis mutandis*) will be obtained with respect to Churches belonging to the Established Church in Scotland, and the Episcopal Church there, and also from Roman Catholic Priests, and from the Ministers of every other Religious Denomination throughout Great Britain, with respect to their Places of Worship.]

I.	**NAME AND DESCRIPTION OF CHURCH OR CHAPEL.**

II.	**WHERE SITUATED.**	Parish, Ecclesiastical Division or District, Township, or Place.	Superintendent Registrar's District.	County and Diocese.

III.	**WHEN CONSECRATED OR LICENSED.**	**UNDER WHAT CIRCUMSTANCES CONSECRATED OR LICENSED.**

IV.	**IN THE CASE OF A CHURCH OR CHAPEL CONSECRATED OR LICENSED SINCE THE 1st JANUARY 1800 ; STATE**	
	HOW OR BY WHOM ERECTED.	**COST, HOW DEFRAYED.**
		By Parliamentary Grant - - - Parochial Rate - - - Private Benefaction or Subscription, or from other Sources - } Total Cost - - £

V.	VI.
HOW ENDOWED.	**SPACE AVAILABLE FOR PUBLIC WORSHIP.**
£ ... £	£
Land - - - Pew Rents - - - Tithe - - - Fees - - - - Glebe - - - Dues - - - Other Permanent Endowment - } Easter Offerings - - Other Sources - -	Free Sittings - - - Other Sittings - - - Total Sittings -

VII.	**ESTIMATED NUMBER OF PERSONS ATTENDING DIVINE SERVICE ON SUNDAY, MARCH 30, 1851.**				**AVERAGE NUMBER OF ATTENDANTS during Months next preceding March 30, 1851. (See Instruction VII.)**				
		Morning.	Afternoon.	Evening.		Morning.	Afternoon.	Evening.	
	General Congregation - } Sunday Scholars -				General Congregation - } Sunday Scholars -				
	Total -				Total -				

VIII.	**REMARKS.**

I certify the foregoing to be a true and correct Return to the best of my belief.
Witness my hand this _____ day of _____1851.

   IX. (*Signature*) _____

     (*Official Character*) _____ of the above-named.

    (*Address by Post*) _____

CENSUS OF GREAT BRITAIN, 1851.

INSTRUCTIONS FOR FILLING UP THE SCHEDULE ON THE ADJOINING PAGE.

(Prepared under the direction of one of Her Majesty's Principal Secretaries of State.)

I.—*Name and Description of Church or Chapel.*—In the column thus headed insert—1st. The Name given to the Church on its Consecration, or the Name by which it is commonly known, if only licensed for Public Worship by the Bishop of the Diocese:—2ndly. Its Description,—(that is to say) Whether it be an ancient Parish Church, or the Church of an ancient Chapelry, the Church of a distinct and separate Parish, District Parish, District Chapelry or Consolidated District, or of a new Parish under the provisions of 6 & 7 Vict. c. 37. (Sir R. Peel's Act,) or of a District under the provisions of 1 & 2 W. 4. c. 38. (the Private Patronage Act), or a Chapel of Ease, or a Church or Chapel built under the authority of a local or private Act of Parliament; and if such information can be given, state the year, reign, and chapter of such Act.

II.—*Where situated.*—Describe accurately in the proper columns,—
The Parish, Ecclesiastical Division or District, Township, or Place, in which the Church is situated; and if it be in a Town, the Name of the Street or other locality.
The Superintendent Registrar's District or Poor Law Union.
The County and Diocese.

III.—*When consecrated or licensed.*—State in this Column whether the Church was consecrated, or only licensed by the Bishop of the Diocese. This will be sufficiently done by writing the word "Consecrated," or "Licensed," as the case may require. And if the Consecration or License was *before the 1st January* 1800, write after "Consecrated" or "Licensed" as follows,—"Before 1800." But if it took place *on or after the 1st January* 1800, insert, as nearly as can be, the *precise date* of such Consecration or License.
Under what circumstances Consecrated or Licensed.—If the Consecration or License was *before* the 1st January 1800, this column *may be left blank*; but, if it was on or after that date, state under this heading whether the Church, if consecrated, was consecrated as an additional Church, or in lieu of an old or previously existing one.

IV.—*How or by whom erected.*—If the Church was consecrated *before* the year 1800, the column thus headed, and also the column headed "Cost, how defrayed," *are to be left blank.* If the Church was consecrated or licensed *since* the 1st January 1800, and as an additional Church, *but not else,*—insert under this heading the words "By Parliamentary Grant,"—"By Parochial Rate,"—"By Private Benefaction or Subscription,"—or the Name of the individual at whose expense the Church was built, or such other words as will briefly express the facts of the case.
Cost.—And, in the same circumstances, *but not else,*—state in the column headed "Cost, how defrayed," as nearly as may be known, the total cost of the Building. And if it was erected partly by Parliamentary Grant and partly by Private Subscription, or from other sources, state also the respective proportions contributed.

V.—*How endowed.*—Insert under this heading in what manner it is endowed,—whether by land, tithe, glebe, or other permanent endowment; by pew rents, fees, dues, Easter-offerings, or now otherwise, and the aggregate annual amount of such endowment.

VII.—*Estimated Number of Attendants on March* 30, 1851.—
If—as is sometimes the case in Wales and elsewhere—two or more Congregations successively assemble in the Building during the same part of the day,—and also in all cases where two or more distinct services are performed in the morning, afternoon, or evening, either by the same Minister, or by different Ministers,—denote the fact by drawing a line immediately *under* the gross number of attendants during that part of the day, thus | 750 | —in order to show that it expresses the aggregate of persons attending at *all* such distinct services. Make a × under each portion of the day—if there be any—during which *no* service is performed.

Average Number.—
If from any cause the figures in the first three columns of Division VII. should not truly represent the numbers *usually* in attendance, the person making the Return is at liberty to add in the fourth, fifth, and sixth columns of the same Division, the estimated *average* number of attendants on Sunday during the 12 calendar months next preceding March 30, 1851, or during such portion of that period as the Building has been open for Public Worship, stating in the heading over the numbers so inserted the exact number of months for which the additional Return is made.
And if, in consequence of repairs, or from any other temporary cause, the Building should not be open for Public Worship on March 30, 1851, write across the first three columns the words "No Service," and insert in the remaining columns the average number who are supposed to have attended at each Sunday during twelve months next preceding the Sunday on which Divine Service was last performed.

VIII.—*Remarks.*—Any observations in explanation of the Return may be inserted in this column; or—if the space provided for the purpose be insufficient—they may be written on a separate paper and appended to the Return.

IX.—*Signature, &c.*—The Return is to be made and signed by the Minister, or by a Church or Chapel Warden, or other recognized and competent officer; and the person signing will have the goodness to state in what capacity he signs, by writing immediately below his name the word "Minister," "Churchwarden," &c., as the case may be. He will also add his *Address by the Post*, in order that, if necessary, he may be communicated with direct from the Census Office in London, on the subject of the return.

Approved,   GEORGE GRAHAM,
                                                  Registrar General.

Whitehall, } G. GREY.
28th Jan. 1851. }

N.B.—The Return must not relate to more than ONE *Church or Chapel. Clergymen having the charge of two or more Churches will be furnished with a separate Form for each. And any Minister, Warden, or other person requiring an additional supply of Forms, may obtain them, free of postage or other charge, on application by letter (the postage of which may be left unpaid), addressed to "Horace Mann, Esq., Census Office, Craig's Court, London."*

FORM B.

CENSUS OF GREAT BRITAIN, 1851.

(13 & 14 Victoriæ, Cap. 53.)

A RETURN of the several Particulars to be inquired into respecting the under-mentioned Place of Public Religious Worship.

[N.B.—A similar Return will be obtained from the Clergy of the Church of England, and also from the Ministers of every other Religious Denomination throughout Great Britain.]

I.	II.			III.	IV.	V.	VI.	VII.				VIII.				IX.
Name or Title of Place of Worship.	Where situate; specifying the			Religious Denomination.	When erected.	Whether a separate and entire Building.	Whether used exclusively as a Place of Worship (except for a Sunday School).	Space available for Public Worship.				Estimated Number of Persons attending Divine Service on Sunday March 30, 1851.				REMARKS.
	Parish or Place.	District.	County.					Number of Sittings already provided.								
								Free Sittings.	Other Sittings.				Morning.	Afternoon.	Evening.	
	(1)	(2)	(3)					(4)	(5)			General Congregation				
												Sunday Scholars				
												TOTAL -				
								Free Space or *Standing Room* for				Average Number of Attendants during Months. (See Instruction VIII.)				
												General Congregation				
												Sunday Scholars				
												TOTAL -				

I certify the foregoing to be a true and correct Return to the best of my belief. Witness my hand this _____ day of _____ 1851.

X. (*Signature*) _____

(*Official Character*) _____ of the above-named Place of Worship.

(*Address by Post*) _____

The *Particulars to be inserted in Divisions I. to VI. inclusive, and in IX., may be written either along or across the Columns, as may be more convenient.*

CENSUS OF GREAT BRITAIN, 1851.

INSTRUCTIONS FOR FILLING UP THE SCHEDULE ON THE ADJOINING PAGE.
(Prepared under the direction of one of Her Majesty's Principal Secretaries of State.)

I.—*Name or Title of Place of Worship.*—In the column thus headed insert the distinguishing Name, Title, or other Appellation by which the Place of Worship is commonly known. But if by reason of its being only a *part* of some Dwelling House or other Building, or from any other cause it have *no* distinguishing Name write in this column the word " None."

II.—*Where situate.*—Describe accurately,
(1.) The Parish, Township, or Place in which the Building is situated; and if it be in a Town, the Name of the Street or other locality.
(2.) The Superintendent Registrar's District or Poor Law Union.
(3.) The County.

III.—*Religious Denomination.*—Insert here the name of the Religious Denomination or Society now occupying the Building.

IV.—*When erected.*—If the Building was erected *before* the year 1800—or, if it has been erected since 1800 on the site or in lieu of one which existed before that year,—in either of those cases write "Before 1800." If it was erected *in* the year 1800, or has been erected *since* and *not* on the site or in lieu of a previously existing Building, insert, as nearly as can be ascertained, the precise year in which it was built, thus—"*In the year* 1800," or—"*About the year* 1801," according to the fact of the case.

V.—*Whether a separate and entire Building*—as contra-distinguished from a mere *Room* or *Part of a Building.*—Insert in this column " Yes " or " No," as the case may be.
Bear in mind that, for the purposes of this Return, a building must not be deemed the less a "separate" Building by reason of its adjoining, or having an internal communication with, a Dwelling House or other Building, as frequently happens in the case of Roman Catholic Chapels and those of some other Religious Denominations; the term "separate" being employed simply to denote a Building which is *separated or set apart* for religious uses.
In this Division (V.) should also be included *Private or Domestic* Chapels, if commonly used as places of *Public Religious* Worship, but not else.

VI.—*Whether exclusively a Place of Worship* (except as it may be also used as a Sunday School).—Write also in this column " Yes " or " No," according to the fact.

VII.—*Space available for Public Worship.*—
(4.) The term " Free Sittings " is used to denote sittings which are not appropriated for the use of particular individuals, and to which, therefore, *any* person is entitled to have free access.
(5.) " Other Sittings " are those which are either let, or have become private property, or which for any other reason do not answer strictly the description of *free* sittings.
" Free Space or Standing Room."—If, as is the case in some *Roman Catholic* Churches and Chapels there is, besides or instead of *free sittings*, an open space allotted as *standing room*, for the accommodation of the poor, state immediately below this heading the number of persons that such space will accommodate.

VIII.—*Number of Attendants.*—
If—as is sometimes the case in Wales and elsewhere—two or more Congregations successively assemble in the Building during the same part of the day, and also in all cases where two or more distinct services are performed in the morning, afternoon, or evening, either by the same Minister or by different Ministers, denote the fact by drawing a line immediately *under* the gross number of attendants during that part of the day, thus [750]—in order to show that it expresses the aggregate of persons attending at *all* such distinct services. Make a × under each portion of the day—if there be any—during which *no* service is held.

Average Number.—
If from any cause the figures in the *upper* section of Division VIII. should not truly represent the numbers *usually* in attendance, the person making the Return is at liberty to add in the *lower* columns of the same Division, the estimated *average* number of attendants on Sunday during the 12 calendar months next preceding March 30, 1851, or during such portion of that period as the Building has been open for Public Worship, stating in the heading over the numbers so inserted the exact number of months for which the additional Return is made.
And if, in consequence of repairs, or from any other temporary cause, the Building should not be open for Public Worship on March 30, 1851, write across the *upper* columns the words "No Service," and insert in the *lower* columns the average number who are supposed to have attended on Sundays during twelve months next preceding the Sunday on which Divine Service was last performed.

IX.—*Remarks.*—Any observations which it may be deemed requisite to make in explanation of the Return may be written along this column; or—if the space provided for the purpose should be insufficient—may be written on a separate paper and appended to the Return.

X.—*Signature, &c.*—The Return is to be made and signed by the Minister, or by some person acting under his authority; if there be no Minister, by an Elder, Deacon, Manager, Steward, or other recognized and competent officer : and the person signing will have the goodness to state in what capacity he signs, by writing immediately below his name the word " Minister," " Elder," " Deacon," " Manager," " Steward," &c., as the case may be. He will also add his *Address by the Post*, in order that, if necessary, he may be communicated with direct from the Census Office, in London, on the subject of the Return.

Approved.
                                        GEORGE GRAHAM,
Whitehall,   } G. GREY.   *Registrar-General.*
28th Jan. 1851.}

N.B.—*The Return must relate to only* ONE *Place of Worship. Ministers having the charge of two or more such Places will be furnished with a separate Form for each. And any person requiring an additional supply of Forms, may obtain them free of postage or other charge, on application by letter (the postage of which may be left unpaid) addressed to "Horace Mann, Esq., Census Office, Craig's Court, London."*

CENSUS OF GREAT BRITAIN, 1851.
(13 & 14 Victoriæ, Cap. 53.)

A RETURN of the several Particulars to be inquired into respecting the under-mentioned Church or Chapel in SCOTLAND, belonging to the Established Church of Scotland.

[A similar Return (*mutatis mutandis*) will be obtained with respect to Churches belonging to the Established Church in England, and also from Roman Catholic Priests, and from the Ministers of every other Religious Denomination throughout Great Britain, with respect to their Places of Worship.]

I.	**NAME AND DESCRIPTION OF CHURCH OR CHAPEL.**		

		Parish, *Quoad Sacra* Parish, or Burgh.	County.
II.	**WHERE SITUATED.**		

	WHEN OPENED FOR WORSHIP.	**UNDER WHAT CIRCUMSTANCES OPENED FOR WORSHIP.**
III.		

IN THE CASE OF A CHURCH OR CHAPEL OPENED FOR WORSHIP SINCE THE 1st JANUARY 1800; STATE

	HOW OR BY WHOM ERECTED.	COST, HOW DEFRAYED.
IV.		By Parliamentary Grant - - - Church Extension Fund - - Contribution of Heritors - Private Benefaction or Subscription, or from other Sources - } Total Cost - - £

V.	**VI.**
STIPEND OF MINISTER.	SPACE AVAILABLE FOR PUBLIC WORSHIP
£ £ Grain Stipend - - Salary - - - Money Stipend - - Land Mortified, &c. - Glebe - - - Other Permanent En- } Manse - - - dowment - -}	Free Sittings - - - Other Sittings - - - Total Sittings -

	ESTIMATED NUMBER OF PERSONS ATTENDING DIVINE SERVICE ON SUNDAY, MARCH 30, 1851.				**AVERAGE NUMBER OF ATTENDANTS during Months next preceding March 30, 1851. (See Instruction VII.)**			
VII.		Morning.	Afternoon.	Evening.		Morning.	Afternoon.	Evening.
	General Congregation - -} Sunday Scholars -				General Congregation - -} Sunday Scholars -			
	Total -				Total -			

VIII.	**REMARKS.**

I certify the foregoing to be a true and correct Return to the best of my belief.

Witness my hand this_____ day of_____1851.

IX. (*Signature*) _____

    (*Official Character*) _____ *of the above-named.*

    (*Address by Post*) _____

CENSUS OF GREAT BRITAIN, 1851.

Instructions for filling up the Schedule on the adjoining Page.

(Prepared under the direction of one of Her Majesty's Principal Secretaries of State.)

.*. *It is requested that all the Particulars in this Return, except those under Heading VII., may be filled in as soon as possible after the Schedule is delivered; those under Heading VII. early on the morning of the 31st March.*

I.—*Name and Description of Church or Chapel.*—In the column thus headed insert—1st. The Name by which it is commonly known:—2dly. Its Description,—(that is to say) Whether it be an ancient Parish Church, *Quoad Sacra* Church, Chapel of Ease, Preaching Station, &c., as the case may be.

II.—*Where situated.*—Describe accurately in the proper columns,—
The Parish, *Quoad Sacra* Parish, or Burgh, in which the Church is situated; and if it be in a Town, the Name of the Street or other locality.
The County.

III.—*When opened for Worship.*—State in this Column when the Church was opened under the authority of the Presbytery, or otherwise. If *before the 1st January* 1800, write,—"Before 1800." But if it took place *on or after the 1st January* 1800, insert, as nearly as can be, the *precise date.*
Under what circumstances opened for Worship.—If *before* the 1st January 1800, this column *may be left blank;* but, if it was on or after that date, state under this heading whether the Church was opened as an additional Church, or in lieu of an old or previously existing one.

IV.—*How or by whom erected.*—If the Church was opened *before* the year 1800, the column thus headed, and also the column headed "Cost, how defrayed," *are to be left blank.* If opened *since* the 1st January 1800, and as an additional Place of Worship *but not else,*—insert under this heading the words "By Parliamentary Grant,"—"By Contributions of Heritors,"—"By Private Benefaction or Subscription,"—or the Name of the individual at whose expense the Church was built, or such other words as will briefly express the facts of the case.
Cost.—And, in the same circumstances, *but not else,*—state in the column headed "Cost, how defrayed," as nearly as may be known, the total cost of the Building, with the proportions thereof, derived from each of the sources specified.

V.—*Stipend of Minister.*—Insert under this heading the provision for the Officiating Minister under each of the heads specified; giving the annual value in money. Where the amount is fixed, state it; where otherwise, state the average annual receipt for the last seven years, or for such shorter period as the present Minister has held the charge.

VI.—Under "Free Sittings" insert only such sittings as are permanently set apart as *free,* and cannot be let as pews, or otherwise appropriated. Where the Church, having been built *since* 1800 in lieu of a former Church, is larger than such old Church, state the number of *additional* sittings it contains over and above those in the old Church.

VII.—*Estimated Number of Attendants on March 30, 1851.*—
Insert the number at each diet of worship; leaving a blank at any part of the day when there was no service.
Average Number.—
If from any cause the figures in the first three columns of Division VII. should not truly represent the numbers *usually* in attendance, the person making the Return is at liberty to add in the fourth, fifth, and sixth columns of the same Division, the estimated *average* number of attendants on Sunday during the 12 calendar months next preceding March 30, 1851, or during such portion of that period as the Building has been open for Public Worship, stating in the heading over the numbers so inserted the exact number of months for which the additional Return is made.
And if, in consequence of repairs, or from any other temporary cause, the Building should not be open for Public Worship on March 30, 1851, write across the first three columns the words "No Service," and insert in the remaining columns the average number who are supposed to have attended at each Sunday during twelve months next preceding the Sunday on which Divine Service was last performed.

VIII.—*Remarks.*—Any observations in explanation of the Return may be inserted in this column; or—if the space provided for the purpose be insufficient—they may be written on a separate paper and appended to the Return. State particularly whether the charge is Sole or Collegiate; and if there be an ordained Assistant and Successor, specify that fact.

IX.—*Signature, &c.*—The Return is to be made and signed by the Minister, or by an Elder, the Session Clerk, or other recognized and competent officer; and the person signing will have the goodness to state in what capacity he signs, by writing immediately below his name the word "Minister," &c., as the case may be. He will also add his *Address by the Post,* in order that, if necessary, he may be communicated with direct from the Census Office in London, on the subject of the Return.

GEORGE GRAHAM,
Registrar General.

Approved.
Whitehall,
19th Feb. 1851.} G. GREY.

N.B.—*The Return must not relate to more than* ONE *Church or Chapel. Clergymen having the charge of two or more Churches will be furnished with a separate Form for each. And any Minister or other person requiring an additional supply of Forms, may obtain them, free of postage or other charge, on application by letter (the postage of which may be left unpaid), addressed to "Horace Mann, Esq., Census Office, Craig's Court, London."*

H 2

Nationwide Initiative in Evangelism

146 Queen Victoria Street
London EC4V 4BX
Telephone: 01-248 4616
(if unobtainable: 01-248 4751)

Dear Incumbent,

The General Synod of the Church of England commended the Nationwide
Initiative in Evangelism to the dioceses in November 1977. In
particular it encouraged "dioceses, and through them, the deaneries
and parishes to consider participation in the proposed National
Assembly".

At that Assembly, which is to be held at Nottingham University in
September next year, it is planned to present a picture of the present
state of the church in England. Among other things, this inevitably
involves the collection of a small number of statistics from as large
a proportion of the existing churches as possible. We would be very
grateful therefore if you could spend a few minutes completing the
enclosed form and return it in the envelope provided not later than
28th November 1979. The information on individual churches will be
treated as strictly confidential, and will not be released at all.
We regret that it is not possible to secure this information in any
other way.

The study is designed to cover life in all churches in the country;
if you know, therefore, of any independent churches or worshipping
communities in your locality whose addresses are unlikely to be
readily available to us, we would be grateful if you would kindly
list these on the reverse side of the form.

This is only one part of the wide programme of research which the NIE
is launching. There are plans for careful studies of particular areas
of our society and of particular groups of people which will attempt
to understand their needs more fully and to indicate the ways in which
the Gospel may be presented sensitively and effectively. The Board
for Mission and Unity's paper "Evangelism in England Today" (GS.411,
50p plus postage from Church House Bookshop, Great Smith Street,
London SW1) is a contribution to that process.

These different strands which make up the whole picture will be the
base on which the National Assembly does its work of considering
strategies for evangelism at local level. The fuller the response
to the questionaire by Church of England parishes, the more realistic
that process will be.

With Christian greetings,

Yours sincerely,

David Brown
Bishop of Guildford
Chairman of the Board for Mission and Unity

Donald English
Chairman
Initiative Committee

Chairman: The Rev. Donald English, M.A.   Executive Secretary: Mr. David Taylor, M.A.

CHURCH LIFE IN ENGLAND TODAY   26286.

Ihe purpose of this study is to help to describe a total picture of life in all the churches in England today.   Would you, therefore, be kind enough to spare a few minutes to answer the questions below.

PLEASE USE BLOCK CAPITALS

1   Incumbent   2   Assistant Clergyman (if any)

Name: ----------------------------------   Name: ----------------------------------

Address: -------------------------------   Address: -------------------------------

        -------------------------------   -------------------------------

        -------------------------------   -------------------------------

Post Code: -----------------------------   Post Code: -----------------------------

3   Church

Name: ----------------------------------   Village/District: ----------------------

Post Town: -----------------------------   Postal County: -------------------------

Post Code: -----------------------------   Administrative County: -----------------
                                                  (if different)

4   Church Membership   1979   1975

    Number of names on the Electoral Roll, as presented
    at the Parochial Church Meeting   ____   ____

5   Church Attendance

a) Total adult attendance (15 and over) at all morning
    services, on a normal Sunday in November.   ____   ____

b) Total adult attendance (15 and over) at evening
    service on a normal Sunday in November.   ____   ____

c) Children (under 15) attending Church or Sunday School
    on a normal Sunday in November   ____   ____

d) Estimated 1979 attendance composition   APPROXIMATE PERCENTAGES

                                                 MALE   FEMALE

                    15-19 years   ___ %   ___ %

                    20-29 years   ___ %   ___ %

                    30-44 years   ___ %   ___ %

                    45-64 years   ___ %   ___ %

                    65 years and over   ___ %   ___ %

6   Shared Clergy

a) Does your church share its clergy with any other church(es)?   YES / NO

b) If "YES", which? _____

7   Midweek Meetings

a) Does your church have a midweek Bible Study/Fellowship/House Group/Prayer/Worship Meeting?   YES/NO

b) If "YES", which? _____

Name of respondent _____   Date _____

Please return this form by 28th November 1979 in the reply paid envelope provided to:
Nationwide Initiative in Evangelism, 146 Queen Victoria Street, London EC4B 4BL

Bible Society

146 Queen Victoria Street,
London, EC4V 4BX

Telephone: 01-248 4751

Telegrams: Testaments London EC4.

April 1982

Dear Friend,

We all know how much easier it is to understand something, when we can see a picture of it. We are writing to ask if you will be good enough to spare a short time from your busy schedule to help "Wales for Christ" to draw a picture of church life in Wales today.

"Wales for Christ", as you may know, is supported by most of the churches in Wales. It tries to help churches to reach out to non-church going people, as well as to strengthen the faith and commitment of those who are already part of the churches' life.

Wales for Christ has asked the Bible Society to assist it by carrying out a national study of the churches in Wales. The questions on the enclosed form represent the first stage of this undertaking and we write to ask you if you would please be kind enough to answer them and return the form to the above address in the envelope provided, not later than 25th May 1982. The Welsh and English versions of the form are of course identical; please feel free to complete whichever side of the form you wish. There is no need to fill in both sides.

The results of this study we hope will be published in the first half of 1983, and information about this will be sent to you in due season. The study is designed to cover life in all churches in the country; if you should know therefore of any Christian Fellowships or worshipping communities in your locality whose addresses we might not have, we would be very grateful if you could kindly give such information as you can on a separate piece of paper.

To give the most complete picture possible of church life in Wales today, it is very important that the enclosed sheet relating to your church(es) be completed and returned to us. If you have any query, please phone either Rev Byron Evans, ex-Secretary of Wales for Christ, working as Head of Local Support for the Bible Society, (Swansea (0792) 892687), or Peter Brierley, our Programme Director, who is co-ordinating the study in London (01-248 4751 ext 249 or 253). Please be assured that the information given on individual churches will be treated as strictly confidential and will not be released in any way; only aggregated figures will be published.

We look forward to hearing from you.

                With warmest Christian greetings,

                                Yours sincerely,

D H Owen
General Secretary, Mission Board

L. D. Richards
Clerk of General Assembly.

Tom Houston
Executive Director

CHURCH ATTENDANCE IN WALES

The purpose of this study is to provide information which can help to stimulate more effective action in all the churches in Wales, both locally and nationally.   Would you please be kind enough to give the time necessary to answer the questions below?   Please fill in one form for each church, and return to Mr P W Brierley, Bible Society, 146 Queen Victoria Street, London EC4V 4BX by 25th May 1982, in the stamped addressed envelope provided.

PLEASE USE BLOCK CAPITALS

1   Minister   2   Church Secretary

    Name: _____   Name: _____

    Address: _____   Address _____

             _____   _____

             _____   _____

    Post Code: _____   Post Code: _____

3   Church

    Name: _____   Village/District: _____

    Town: _____   Postal County: _____

    Post Code: _____

4a Is the Minister named in (1) above responsible for churches other than that named in (3) above? YES/NO*

4b If 'YES', please give the names and town/village in which those churches are located

        _____   _____

        _____   _____

5   Church Membership   1982   1978

    Number of Church Members for church named in (3) above   ____   ____

6   Church Attendance for church named in (3) above for a normal Sunday in May (excluding Whitsun)

a) Total adult attendance (15 and over) at morning service(s)   ____   ____

b) Total adult attendance (15 and over) at afternoon and evening service(s)   ____   ____

c) Estimated number of individual adults attending both morning and evening
    services on a normal Sunday   ____   ____

d) Children (under 15) attending Sunday School   ____   ____

e) Estimated composition of attendance (including Sunday School) in 1982   APPROXIMATE NUMBERS

                                                                    MALE   FEMALE

                                    Under 15 years   ____   ____
                                    15-19 years   ____   ____
                                    20-29 years   ____   ____
                                    30-44 years   ____   ____
                                    45-64 years   ____   ____
                                    65 and over   ____   ____

7   Midweek Meetings/Services

    Does your church hold any midweek meetings? YES/NO*   If 'YES', please state what those are

        _____   _____

        _____   _____

8   What is the normal language of worship in your church?   Welsh/English/Bilingual*

9   Name of Respondent: _____   Date: _____

    Thank you for your help

                            * Please delete as appropriate

APPENDIX 2 - LOCAL CENSUSES OF CHURCH ATTENDANCE, OCTOBER 1881-FEBRUARY 1882

Community type	England	Wales	Scotland
Cities	Bolton		Dundee
	Bradford		Edinburgh
	Bristol		Glasgow
	Hull		
	Leicester		
	Liverpool		
	Newcastle- upon- Tyne		
	Nottingham		
	Portsmouth		
	Sheffield		
Large towns	Bath		Greenock
	Burnley		Leith
	Derby		Paisley
	Gateshead		
	Hanley		
	Ipswich		
	Northampton		
	Southampton		
	Stockport		
	Wolverhampton		
Medium-sized towns	Accrington	Llanelly	Abbotshall, Kirkcaldy, Dysart and Kinghorn
	Barnsley	Wrexham	Arbroath
	Barrow-in-Furness		Ayr
	Bournemouth		Berwickshire
	Burslem		Bute
	Cheltenham		Dalry
	Chesterfield		Forfar
	Colne		Galashiels
	Coventry		Hawick and Wilton
	Darlington		Inverness

492

Darwen
Douglas
Frome
Gloucester
Gosport
Hastings and
St.Leonards
Kettering
Longton
Margate
Newcastle- under-
Lyme
Newton and
Earlestown
Peterborough
Rotherham
Runcorn
Scarborough
Stockton-on-Tees
Stoke
Trowbridge
Warrington
Wellingborough
Whitehaven
Widnes
Worksop

Kilmarnock
Montrose
Perth

Small towns

Basingstoke

Bradford-on-Avon
Charlton Kings

Chippenham
Christchurch
Corsham
Daventry
Diss
Egremont
Halstead
Holbeach
Latchford
Leckhampton
Long Buckby

Long Sutton
Lymm

Melksham

Newtown

Ardrossan and
Saltcoats
Bannockburn
Blairgowrie and
Rattray
Brechin
Broughty Ferry
Burntisland
Ceres
Colinton
Cupar Angus
Cupar Fife
Dreghorn
Gourock
Helensburgh
Irvine and
Fullarton
Kilbirnie
Kilmaurs, Fenwick
and Hurlford
Kilwinning

Community type	England	Wales	Scotland
	Mexborough		Kirriemuir
	Midsomer Norton		Largo
	Nantwich		Melrose
	Padiham		Row and Rosneath
	Pinchbeck		St.Andrews
	Retford		St.Ninians
	Shepton Mallet		Scoonie
	Spalding		Selkirk
	Towcester		Stewarton
			Troon
			Wemyss
Very small towns and villages	Blisworth	Conway	Aberdour
	Donington		Carnbee
	Needham Market		Newport
	Prestbury		Torryburn
	Surfleet		
	Swindon		
	Villages around Bath		
	Villages around Warrington		

APPENDIX 3 - LOCAL SAMPLE SURVEYS OF CHURCH ATTENDANCE, 1944-81

Fieldwork date	Location	Sample size	Text reference or source
1944-45	Hammersmith	500	2.2.2.3
July 1950	Banbury	3,387	[B.371]
February-April 1953	Derby	1,205	2.2.2.4
1953-54	Glossop	657	[B.20]
1958	Dagenham	877	[B.417]
Spring 1959	Wanstead and Woodford	939	[B.418]
November 1959-March 1960	Newcastle-under-Lyme	1,516	[B.10]
1960	Associated Rediffusion Television Area	7,205	2.2.2.7
May-June 1960	Swansea	1,962	2.3.2.2
September-October 1965	Hampshire villages and hamlets	1,694	[B.565]; ESRC DA, SN 65006
November 1967	Sheffield	584	[B.160]
August 1969	Cublington, Foulness, Nuthampstead, Thurleigh and immediately adjacent districts	932	ESRC DA, SN 69017
circa 1970	Diocese of Bangor	2,500	3.1.2.1
March-April 1970	Salford	604	ESRC DA, SN 70003
May-June 1971	Cardiganshire	713	[B.251]; ESRC DA, SN 71006
August 1972-January 1974	Belfast	2,203	ESRC DA, SN 921
March-May 1973	Glasgow and Bishopbriggs	963	ESRC DA, SN 031
November 1973-February 1974	Stoke-on-Trent	764	[B.157]; ESRC DA, SN 250
November 1973-February 1974	Sunderland	788	[B.157]; ESRC DA, SN 251
April 1974	Edinburgh	818	[B.133]

Fieldwork date	Location	Sample size	Text reference or source
April-May 1974	Newton Aycliffe, Peterlee and Washington	679	[B.249]; ESRC DA, SN 522
September 1974	Machynlleth and Newtown	535	2.3.2.4
September 1977	Altrincham, Bowdon Vale, Broadheath, Hale, Timperley and Wellgreen	2,300	2.2.2.15
Spring 1978	Coventry	972	2.2.2.17
August 1981	Greater London	2,734	[QRL.61], 24 September 1981

SUBJECT INDEX

35: JUDAISM

Dr BARRY A. KOSMIN

Research Unit

Board of Deputies of British Jews

REFERENCE DATE OF SOURCES REVIEWED

All sources are post 1930 except where publications include time series data prior to this date. Terminating date is January 1983.

ADDENDUM ON RECENT CHANGES

The most important recent developments have been in the demographic field. They were linked to the completion of a new population estimate for British Jewry for the period 1975-9 which was referred to in section 4.3. The preferred estimate of 336,000 was published in S. Haberman, B.A. Kosmin anc C. Levy, 'Mortality Patterns of British Jews 1975-79: Insights and applications for the Size and Structure of British Jewry', *The Journal of the Royal Statistical Society*, Series A. (General) Volume 146, Part 3, 1983, pp 294-310.

On the basis of this study an attempt was made to produce a tentative age and sex structure. This was published as 'Estimated Population of British Jewry by Age and Sex in 1977', *On Board*, No. 24, April 1983. (Obtainable from Research Unit, Board of Deputies of British Jews).

The study of mortality patterns also indicated much greater migration effects on the Jewish population than imagined heretofore. This finding was confirmed using official census data of countries with a religious or ethnic census question. It was discovered that British-born Jews resident abroad totalled 12 per cent of the estimated total of British Jewry in 1971. The data was published as: B.A. Kosmin & C. Levy, 'Jewish Emigration from the United Kingdom', *On Board*, No. 45, June 1985. (Obtainable from the Research Unit, Board of Deputies of British Jews).

Renewed attempts to investigate the Jewish birth-rate based upon the collection of data on ritual circumcisions (section 3.2.2.) were made and proved largely successful. These were published as: B.A. Kosmin & C. Levy, 'Jewish circumcisions and the demography of British Jewry, 1965-82, *The Jewish Journal of Sociology*, XXVII,I, (June 1985). 5-11.

Finally, the collection and analysis of time-series data on synagogue membership (section 3.1.3) was extended to 1983 by the study: B.A. Kosmin and C. Levy, *Synagogue Membership in the United Kingdom, 1983*, London, Research Unit of Board of Deputies of British Jews, 1983.

CONTENTS OF REVIEW 35

CHAPTER 1

INTRODUCTION

1.1

Since the resettlement of Jews in Britain in 1656 there has been no official attempt to organise a census of its Jewish population. The only official statistics relating to Jews, as such, are the Registrar General's returns from marriage secretaries and for the number of buildings licensed as synagogues. The only real attempt at a religious count was the Census of Worship made at the time of the 1851 Census, when the numbers who attended religious services at the weekend nearest to the census day, were collected.

1.2

Lacking the necessity, or authority to collect statistics for communal taxation purposes, and in keeping with the *laisser-faire* attitude of the State authorities on this matter, the Jewish community has never made any attempt to maintain communal registers on a consistent and coherent basis. Thus membership of the Jewish community in Britain has been, and is, a purely voluntary and informal act which necessitates a positive act of affiliation by the individual.

1.3

The impetus to collect information on the Jewish population by established Jewish organisations has largely arisen from particular political concerns. In the period of the struggle for Jewish political emancipation of the 1840s and 50s the first comprehensive attempts were launched. In 1845 Chief Rabbi Nathan Adler issued an elaborate questionnaire asking all the congregations in Britain under his control for detailed information about synagogal, charitable and educational activities. These *Statistical Accounts of All The Congregations in the British Empire* were published, only in part, in the *Jewish Chronicle* of 23rd July, 1847.

1.4

In these years the London Committee of Deputies of the British Jews, founded in 1760 and commonly known as the Board of Deputies of British Jews, decided to take on a more influential and representative role. One of its self-appointed tasks was the collection of basic demographic data from its menber synagogues. These comprised annual returns of births, marriages, interments and seatholders in each congregation. Unfortunately, this was a purely voluntary system and the coverage was only adequate for the years 1852 and 1856-9. It was revived from time to time with varying rates of success and coverage.

1.5

Mass Immigration of Jews after 1881 led to another political struggle known as "the aliens question". This immigration debate which lasted until the Alien's Act of 1905, created the need for statistical data to support the political arguments of the day. Thus, at the end of the last century some note-worthy contributions were made by Joseph Jacobs in his *Studies in Jewish Statistics* (1891); and while Jacobs was editor of the *Jewish Year Book*, original contributions appeared year by year in its statistical section. When Jacobs left London for New York to help edit the *Jewish Encyclopedia*, the work in the *Year Book* was continued under the editorship of I. Harris. As a result of their efforts, the issues of that annual preceding the 1914 war remain of considerable interest to the statistician of today, both on grounds of method, and as providing valuable source material for historical series. In the same period there was formed in London a Society for Jewish Statistics at which members read prepared papers; S. Rosenbaum (later Rowson), whose paper in the *Journal of the Royal Statistical Society* (1905) is well-known, was secretary of the society.

1.6

After the First World War, interest in statistics lapsed (the *Year Book's* statistical section did not even appear every year). The rise of political antisemitism in Europe and its resulting creation of a "new Jewish refugee" issue in Britain, led to another spurt in statistical enquiry on the Jews. Thus, in the 1930s, we find a Jewish Health 0rganisation newly established with a Statistical Committee engaged in research. The papers by Trachtenberg [QRL.23] and Kantorowitsch [QRL.24] were prepared for that Committee. These published contributions, however, all remark on the general sparseness of information and indicate that the hopeful start made by Jacobs was not pursued by the community.

1.7

In the post-war period Dr. Neustatter [QRL.10] made a brave attempt to survey the available material on the contemporary community. She highlighted the lack of comprehensive information on births, deaths and marriages that were centrally collected by the community. at the turn of the century.

1.8

The establishment of the State of Israel and the Holocaust created a new political climate and conflicting pressures as regards the collection of statistical material on Jews. The concern of Jews, and particularly Israelis , to know the size and details of Jewish populations was undoubtedly partly an outcome of the 1939-45 European Holocaust. The slaughter of up to one-third of the Jewish people and the destruction of some of the oldest and most populous national communities not only completely changed the demographic balance of the Jewish world, but made the survivors particularly conscious of the value, both quantitatively and qualitatively, of each Jewish life.

1.9

However, the experience of the Holocaust also produced a contradictory trend for Jewish population studies. This is a marked reluctance by both the leaders and the mass to let outsiders, and even insiders, know details concerning the Jewish communities. Considering that the Jews were treated literally as mere numbers and that the census and other statistical information was often an instrument of destruction, this attitude is understandable, if rather frustrating for those scholars working in the field.

1.10

In response to an Israeli initiative, directed at all surveying Western Jewish communities , in 1962 the Board of Deputies in association with the Institute of Contemporary Jewry of the Hebrew University, Jerusalem, convened a conference on "Jewish Life in Modern Britain". The gap in factual information for communal policy and planning which was revealed at this gathering led directly to the establishment in 1965 of the Statistical and Demographic Research Unit of the Board of Deputies of British Jews. The Unit was directed expressly to compile statistical data on various aspects of the community and prepare interpretive studies of social and demographic trends among the Jewish population. It was also hoped that the Research Unit would act as a catalyst for further work in the field and so remedy the paucity of statistics on the Jewish population. Thus the period since 1967 has seen a spate of publications concerned with statistical information on British Jewry and the revival of a central institution empowered to collect it from synagogue groups.

CHAPTER 2

PROBLEMS OF DEFINITION AND MEASUREMENT

2.1

The problem of definition is a fundamental issue in the collection of statistics relating to Jews and the practice of Judaism. This basic problem of definition which is often raised as an obstacle to work in this field concerns who or who is not to be counted as a Jew. According to Jewish religious law, *halacha*, a Jew is a person who is born of a Jewish mother or a person who has been converted according to traditional Jewish practice as recognised by a Rabbinical court, known as a *Beth Din*. This Orthodox definition has been supplemented over the last century and a half by the "progressive" movement, whose legitimacy is not recognised by the Orthodox majority for the purposes of conversions. The Reform congregations accept the definition of a Jew as coming through the maternal line, but the Liberal Wing of the "progressive" movement also regard a person as Jewish if they have only a Jewish father and are brought up in a " Jewish home. "

2.2

In Jewish thinking and law a person born a Jew never ceases to be a Jew even though the person may disown this identity and convert to another religion. The really crucial dilemma for definitional purposes is the lack of differentiation among Jews between their religious and ethnic identities. A person converting to Judaism automatically joins the Jewish people.

2.3

The spread of Jews across the world over several millennia into different societies has meant they have had variable personal or group status as a religious minority, a national minority or an ethnic group. To comprehend the contemporary situation in the United Kingdom, it must be remembered that Britain has been a country of Jewish immigration for more than three centuries during which time there have been no barriers to assimilation and very little overt persecution which would tend to encapsulate the Jewish population. In practice the Jewish population is self-defined, as is the case where there is a census question on religion among the small Jewish population in Northern Ireland. The mass of British Jewry which is an unenumerated population in terms of the national census , is increasingly a sociologically identified rather than biological population. Historical, social and family pressures are the defining agents. A definition of Jew according to *halacha* is often unacceptable to the person involved and to out-groups. Yet we must recognise that if we do not have a means of self-identification through a religious or ethnic question in the census and if there is no external authority (such as the Nuremberg laws) to define the term Jew, we inevitably operate in a rather imprecise or grey area on the boundary or extremity of this population.

2.4

Nevertheless, one must define the term Jew and consistently operate it across the whole society. In Britain as a result of historical circumstances, particularly the emancipation process, the Jewish population is more likely to define itself in terms of a religious identity than do Jews in many other Western countries. British Jewry is a synagogue-centred community. In 1977 it had over 400 congregations and 100,000 households with paid-up membership. No other form of organisational affiliation can compete with this coverage. Many social studies have moved beyond this core population and approached persons whom people consider as probably Jews. Such work thus relies on a social network of knowledgeable local informants. There is also the Distinctive Jewish Name Method to identify potential households. It is up to these persons when approached to accept or reject the Jewish label offered to them. However, in the light of the tradition described above, most studies only include as Jews those who are born of a Jewish mother or have been formally converted by an Orthodox or progressive (Reform or Liberal) *Beth Din*.

2.5

What then is one to make of this predicament? All the totals and indices are inevitably estimates and subject to varying degrees of error. People who regard themselves as Jewish today may in the light of future social and political developments negate that identity. On the other hand, others outside the community may, like some of the descendants of the Spanish *Marannos*, return to the fold in changed circumstances. One solution is merely to accept the given data with the proviso that they are more open to interpretation and subjective bias in collection and presentation than even most other social statistics. Another alternative is to argue that there are a number of Jewish populations, depending on the social context. These can be presented in the form of overlapping concentric rings, depending on the type of identification or affiliation whether religious, social, national, political or cultural. It is doubtful however, if this model is acceptable to some Jews on intellectual or political grounds, as well as religious grounds. Definitional issues of this kind are familiar grist to the applied statistician.

2.6

In the context of the definitional issue it is relevant that a division can be made between the type of data collected at the national and local levels. The national data normally arise from an administrative process and relate to the religiously affiliated population. On the other hand, local studies relating to Jewish topics encompass a wider Jewish population which may be termed the "ethnic" Jewish population i.e. self-defined Jews. In recent years the impetus has been towards studies and the collection of data on Jews at the local level using sample surveys. This cannot be explained only in terms of a religious versus ethnic debate, but reflects structural and organisational changes. The lack of a widely accepted and clearly defined religious hierarchy has led increasingly to pluralism. The organisational structure of British Jewry reflects this pluralism and most of the power, finance and decision-making process in communal affairs lies at the local level. As a result national and even regional bodies are usually merely confederations with representative rather than executive functions. They are therefore rarely empowered or able to organise the collection of statistics. The Research Unit of the Board of Deputies of British Jews is an exception. However, while their annual collection of deaths and marriages is on the national level [QRL.1] their in-depth studies have mirrored the trend towards localism and pluralism in the community They have concentrated on a number of local community investigations as have the few academic studies which have yielded statistical data.

2.7

It must be understood that Judaism is a way of life, and its practice permeates and structures every aspect of daily life, e.g. what people eat and when, how they dress and their sexual mores. It imposes a hierarchy of commandments, laws (written and oral) rabbinical interpretations and traditions which can vary according to gender, stage in the life cycle, familial condition, and geographical location. In such a situation it is very difficult to measure their behaviour against a set standard without detailed knowledge of the individuals or aggregate groups under investigation.

2.8

When compared to other religious denominations in the U.K. Judaism itself creates certain problems of definition. The evolution of rabbinical Judaism can be seen as a reaction to the hierarchical and hereditary structures of the Biblical priesthood *(Cohanim)*. Since the destruction of the second Temple in Jerusalem by the Romans, Judaism as we know it today has rejected the need for an intermediary between Jews and God. Therefore, rabbis and ministers do not have exclusive sacred or priestly duties. For example, not every authorised marriage officer in the community is a rabbi. The title "rabbi" is an indication of a qualification in Jewish learning. Thus not every rabbi has a congregation and, since every Jewish male over the age of 13 (and females over the age of 12 in "progressive" congregations) can lead a religious service, not every congregation has a rabbi. Some large congregations employ cantors in addition to a rabbi. Statistics on the number of rabbi's or rabbinical students would therefore merely be an indicator of the level of Jewish education rather than of religious manpower. However, there is no system of collection of such data. Any attempts to collect statistics on the clergy and trainees would be faced by definitional problems as well as "international traffic" of students both in and out of the U.K. The limited statistics on training that are available can be found under "Education" in the category of students in *Yeshivot*.

2.9

Similarly Jewish people do not need a consecrated place in which to pray or even be married. Therefore, although the Registrar General published the number of buildings registered for worship by religious denomination, this does not provide comprehensive coverage of places of worship or the synagogue population. Many of the small congregations (*Minyanim*) are not officially registered. In addition those synagogues in existence before 1850 are also excluded from the registration requirement.

CHAPTER 3

AVAILABLE SOURCES

3.1 Membership

3.1.1

Membership of a synagogue is the most widely held point of identity for British Jews. All contemporary studies in this country have shown that synagogue membership covers around two-thirds of identifying Jews. The formation of a synagogue or congregation does not necessitate a building or even a minister. Membership is a voluntary act and requires payment of membership dues.

3.1.2

Lack of a clearly defined religious hierarchy in the U.K. means that outside of the London based United Synagogue, congregations are independent entities. Some have joined together for mutual aid and benefit based on their standing in the theological spectrum, e.g. Federation of Synagogues (Orthodox); Reform Synagogues of Great Britain. Synagogues do not generally publish statistical reports, except for private circulation. In recent years it has become practice to classify synagogues into two main streams; Orthodox and "progressive". Within the Orthodox majority there are three sub-groups: the *Sephardim* who hold to the rites of the Spanish and Portuguese tradition; the *Ashkenazim* (German-Polish Jewish rites) are divided between the Central Orthodox (mainstream modern Orthodoxy) and the Right Wing Orthodox (traditional and Hassidic sects). The "progressives" are divided between Reform congregations and the even less traditional, Liberal and Progressive Congregations.

3.1.3

For representative purposes it is necessary for member synagogues to provide the Board of Deputies of British Jews triannually with a return indicating the number of members or seatholders. Although the Registrar General's certification of buildings does not provide comprehensive coverage, a complete coverage of all Jewish congregations in the country i.e. including those unrepresented in the Board of Deputies, has only taken place twice in this century, in 1970 and 1977 [QRL.61], [QRL.59].

3.1.4

Even these sources must be approached with some reservation since there is a small amount of over-enumeration because of the possibility of dual membership by individuals. In some of the London boroughs affiliation is unrealistic with regard to residence. Notably, in Tower Hamlets there is a generational lag as many former residents of the borough retain membership for sentimental reasons, and in Westminster social prestige rather than convenient access is often the motivation for membership of the many large, fashionable synagogues. The lack of synagogues in an area reflects the small number of Jews living there not their total absence. In areas of sparse Jewish population a synagogue in a particular town often draws its membership from a wide area and there can be overlapping "catchments" between synagogues.

3.1.5

The distribution of membership among the various religious groupings shows a greater preponderance of the Central Orthodox outside London. The capital offers a variety of types of synagogue to its large Jewish population. Only Greater Manchester shares this heterogeneity. Comparative figures of the proportional breakdown over time are only available for Greater London and these show a relatively static position.

3.1.6

Certain adjustments have to be made in respect of female membership because of the different policies towards women. In Orthodox synagogues married women are not counted as members unless they themselves join and pay an individual subscription, whereas in progressive synagogues (Reform and Liberal) women and men have equal membership and total membership therefore includes two adults per household.

3.1.7

There is a dearth of information concerning the membership of secular organisations e. g. Zionist groups , Association of Jewish Ex-Servicemen. The exception to the general lack of data from official sources is that on professing Jews in the Armed Forces [QRL.6]

3.2 Demography and rites of passage

3.2.1 *Population Estimates and Mortality*

In the absence of direct facts one has to rely on various indirect methods of estimating the size of the Jewish community. These have been based on counts of deaths since such figures can often be obtained more easily because, for example, of some existing registration procedure. This number is then inflated by the reciprocal of the corresponding proportion in the general population. Particular emphasis has been placed upon mortality based studies since the main motivation for synagogue membership has been found to be access to religious burial. Certainly this is the most widely practised Jewish rite and covers people who have had only minimal contact with Jewish communal activities during their lifetime. Since 1967 all Jewish interments under religious auspices (including cremations for progressive Jews) have been collected by the Research Unit of the Board of Deputies, and the figures published annually, [QRL.1].

A population estimate based on death statistics is somewhat easier to apply, in view of the relative accessibility of the basic data. As far as the reliability of the method is concerned, it is often objected that the Jewish death-rate is not necessarily the same as that of the general population, partly because of the different age and sex structure resulting from migrations , and partly because of differing economic or other conditions of life. The former need not prove an obstacle if the statistics are classified by sex and age-group, and death-rates specific to each group are applied; whether an adjustment is advisable on grounds of social class is an open question. A problem mainly exists for the younger age-groups , say 0-15, where Jewish mortality appears to be lower; but some adjustment of the estimates for these age-groups may be made on the basis of other information.

3.2.2 Births
In Britain births are not registered by religion, so no information exists from official sources. For some years in the 1960s and 1970s a system of collection of birth data from male circumcisions was operated but administrative problems developed, and this ceased. The principal difficulty with statistics based on the return of *Mohalim* (circumcisers) was one of definition; there are undoubtedly many cases attended by doctors not registered with the Initiation Society (and hence not authorised to officiate by the *Beth Din*). Such births would on this approach not be classified as Jewish though, for other purposes , the families concerned may regard themselves as Jewish. In addition the coverage of circumcision among the different elements of the Jewish population was never established. Nevertheless, a single year's collection has been used as the basis for fertility data on Jewish sub-groups, [QRL.27].

3.2.3 Marriage
Data are only available on the endogamous synagogue affiliated population, i.e. the religious section of British Jewry which accounts for around 70% of the total. Annual statistics of synagogue marriages in Britain are collected by the Research Unit of the Board of Deputies of British Jews, the community's representative body. These figures are analysed by synagogue grouping and geographical area and published in an annual press release, [QRL.1]. In addition in-depth studies of the characteristics of marriage cohorts have been undertaken. This communal data supplements official data collected by the Registrar General through authorised local marriage officers [QRL.26]. In England and Wales, where 96% of British Jewry reside, the Registrar General's figures have covered 89% of all synagogue marriages during the 1970s. The remainder which are only collected by the Board

of Deputies, consist of those marriages which are not combined civil and religious ceremonies but merely of a religious nature only, a civil marriage having been performed previously. The official coverage is much better for Orthodox than progressive (Reform and Liberal) ceremonies , since the communally collected figures show that the latter has an undercount of around 20%. Comparative data on the characteristics of Jewish marriages alongside other religious groups, have been published for the years 1974, 1975 and 1978 [QRL.26].

The synagogue marriages which do not fall into the official net have specific characteristics in addition to the theological bias already mentioned. They often follow conversions, or what is more relevant here, are second marriages for one or both partners. These national figures have been bolstered by local area studies which all provide useful supplementary material on marital status and marriage cohort patterns.

3.2.4 *Divorce*

The various *Batei Din* are understandably much more reluctant to allow close inspection and analysis of application for religious divorce because of the personal nature of such information. The only usable data gathered have been the annual total of *gittin* (religious divorces) written in London by the London Beth Din, i.e. for the London Ashkenazi Orthodox community for the period 1955 to 1980, and by the Beth Din of the Reform Synagogues of Great Britain, i. e. the Reform community nationally, but only for the years 1976-80 [QRL.11]. The Union of Liberal and Progressive Synagogues, which accounts for 8-9% of synagogue marriages does not have religious divorce and accepts the civil procedure.

Official divorce statistics on Jews are also much less adequate than on synagogue marriages. In fact, the only direct information available is a proportionate total of marriages dissolved by manner of solemnization for 1966. No figures are available on divorce decrees by the original marriage ceremony. This is a real problem since it is impossible to determine what proportion of civil divorces among Jews, who originally married in a synagogue, are regularised by a *get*. Both Orthodox and Reform rabbis encourage their congregants to obtain *gittin* and so regularise their religious matrimonial status but it is generally accepted that only those who contemplate quick remarriage within the Jewish community will go through the formality of a *get* at the time of their civil proceedings. Thus, not only will some divorcees never obtain the *get* but they may obtain it years after their civil divorce which can further complicate statistics.

In order to fill these lacunae on the subject and obtain a measure of the cumulative experience of divorce rather than merely the usual picture of present marital status, specific questions on marriage termination have been included in local surveys. In addition during 1977 a questionnaire was administered to a sample of the rabbinate as to their knowledge of divorce within their congregations. This survey covered 30 rabbis, 20 in London and 10 in the provinces and again two-thirds Orthodox and one-third progressive [QRL.11].

3.3 Practice and rituals

Judaism being a way of life, there are a large number of rituals associated with the Sabbath, the festivals and different facets of daily life. No comprehensive or representative sample data on such issues exist. What data do exist, relate to specific local or sample populations. It is difficult to use this material for comparative analysis or to combine it for a more general picture of religious practice, since the wording in the questions and the response categories vary widely. Moreover, it should be noted that given the theological spectrum and pluralism which exists in British Jewry, inappropriate questions and anomalies are a hazard when considering some populations.

3.4 Beliefs and attitudes

Under this heading is included social and political beliefs as well as religious ones. The boundaries between these are not always clearly demarcated. For example, attitudes towards Israel have a religious as well as a political aspect. Again the samples are small and largely unrepresentative of a national Jewish population and comparative analysis is fraught with difficulties. A recent local study on Jewish identity has collated the results from studies over the last two decades [QRL.36].

3.5 Education

This is a topic for which universal coverage has been attempted, largely because of international interest for the purposes of comparison with communities abroad. The existence of state-aided and recognised Jewish day schools for which returns to the Department of Education are mandatory, provided a useful base from which to build. The coverage is largely limited to numbers of students and pupils on the rolls of Jewish educational institutions. The division given usually reflects full-time and part-time or supplementary classes, and the type of school by synagogue grouping or allegiance. There is no information on the potential market for this education since there are no reliable figures on the numbers of Jews by age cohort. This means that the proportionate take-up of religious education at any point in time or by generations is unavailable. This has not however prevented "guesstimates" from being made. Nevertheless education is the topic on which time series data is most readily available.

3.6 Welfare and Health

The collection of statistical data from the many Jewish welfare and philanthropic organisations is largely non-existent. Most have excluded a quantitative analysis of their work from their reports which are mainly irregularly produced for private circulation, amongst their donors and supporters. The London Jewish Board of Guardians, now known as the Jewish Welfare Board, is the exception to this

[QRL.4] As regards health, there have been a small number of medically related studies in the U.K. which make passing reference to Jews in their samples. Although individual hospital admission procedures , including those at the Jewish hospitals in London and Manchester, have required the patient to give religion as part of their personal details, there is no known attempt to collate this material. This source is as yet untapped, but usage and access will depend on the practice of each hospital records officer.

3.7 Socio-economic data

The socio-economic data relates to aggregates of individual Jews and not to Jews as a corporate body. No income or direct expenditure statistics are available. The Jewish Chronicle Readership Survey series [QRL.30], [QRL.31] has attempted to identify consumer patterns, but the representative nature of their samples is unknown. The local surveys have concentrated on the classification of their Jewish populations in terms of the official system i.e. by employment, occupation, industry and social class. The only national data relate to the social class structure distribution for 1961 and are based on an analysis of a sample of death certificates [QRL.51].

CHAPTER 4

IMPROVEMENTS AND FUTURE DEVELOPMENTS

4.1

The unsatisfactory nature of the material available on the Jewish population is clearly evident. Essential demographic details , such as national age distribution and population size, are unavailable or else synagogue-based. Overall counts cannot be obtained with precision from the existing documentary material without resorting to a full census-type survey. This option is currently beyond the resources of the interested parties in the organised Jewish community. Moreover, it is realised that national global totals are of no practical value for planning or provision of communal services. The urgent social concerns and problems in our hetergeneous communities are in the fields of education, housing for the elderly, youth facilities, welfare etc., i.e. local needs. Even concerns such as religiosity, assimilation and identity cannot be usefully analysed and the information utilised at a national level.

4.2

The question of using the official administrative system e.g. in hospitals, for Jewish social statistics is worthy of serious consideration. Data gathered in this way would have the advantage of being standardised in terms of the category "Jew" and directly comparable with national data. In realistic terms though it is only by a combination of a wide range of methods, i.e. censuses, area sample surveys, collection of vital statistics and indirectly gathered official data that we shall be able to assemble a worthwhile body of knowledge on Jewish social statistics.

4.3

A realistic aim at this stage would be to replicate a number of surveys and studies in order to create time-series data. This is already being attempted with regard to a mortality based national population estimate for the quinquennum 1975-1979. It is essential that there is consistent use of standardised questions and categories in any further study for this purpose.

526

4.4

The motivation for the collection of statistics on Jews is not primarily academic or theoretical, but for problem solving and applied purposes. Therefore, realistic improvements and future developments will have to rely on the short-term practical gains they offer to decision makers in influential and leadership positions in Jewish community organisations. As heretofore discussed the actual Jewish populations studied will vary between the religiously affiliated and the socially or ethnically defined populations depending on the context. These definitional and ideological issues which have existed for centuries, will remain in all future statistical accounts of British Jewry.

QUICK REFERENCE LIST - TABLE OF CONTENTS

QUICK REFERENCE LIST

Type of data	Breakdown	Area	Frequency	QRL Publication	Text Reference
Membership					
Seatholders					
Membership of *Jewish Chronicle* readers	Member/non-member of a synagogue; synagogue affiliation, (United, Federation, Reform, Liberal Synagogue, none).	UK	1974 1976 1980	[QRL.31]	
Synagogue membership in the UK	Male and female members and affiliated households by English County/ Scotland /Wales /Northern Ireland /Jersey; male & female membership by synagogue.	UK	1977 (to be repeated for 1983)	[QRL.59] [QRL.61]	Synagogues are identified by name, religious group (Federation, Reform, Liberal & Progressive, Orthodox Hebrew congregations, United, non-affiliated Orthodox & Reform) and town.
Buildings certified as synagogues	Standard regions, metropolitan counties, non-metropolitan counties	England and Wales	Annual	[QRL.43]	Inadequate coverage of actual congregations. (See discussion in section 2.9).

Membership of the United Synagogue	Male seat holders by synagogue	London	Every 10 years from 1870 to 1970	[QRL.63]	Also includes date of admission of each synagogue to the United synagogue
Synagogue membership	Male membership in main centres	London, Manchester, Leeds, Glasgow, Liverpool, Brighton & Hove, Birmingham, Southend & Westcliff; other provincial centres.	1970	[QRL.67]	
Prisons & Forces					
Jews in the three forces	Number of Jews by age, rank and location in all three forces	GB	6 monthly	[QRL.6]	
Demography and Rites of Passage					
Demographic characteristics					
Demographic characteristics	Age and sex distribution; marital condition; nationality at birth and at present	UK	1952	[QRL.10]	1667 forms returned covering 5225 people in selected towns in the UK

Type of data	Breakdown	Area	Frequency	QRL Publication	Text Reference
Demographic characteristics	Households by household size; age distribution; sex ratio by age group; marital status by sex; age at first marriage of heads of household & their wives; mean number of children born to women aged under 5 year by marriage duration.	Edgware	1963	[QRL.12]	Based on a sample of 382 households (1,29 people) using a multiphase probability technique.
	Age and sex distribution, fertility and population projections	London Borough of Hackney	1971	[QRL.41]	Sample size of 2700 people from Census S.A.S. (Small Area Statistics) 1971 via voters roll using name and other supplementary techniques. pp. 13-18.
	Age and sex distribution; household size and composition; marital status, reproductive and death rates; population projection.	Sheffield	1975	[QRL.56]	Based on a census of the Sheffield Jewish households. pp.12-16.
	Age and sex distribution; household size and composition, marital status and patterns; place of birth; birth and death rates; fertility, residential characteristics; population projections.	London Borough of Redbridge.	1978	[QRL.52]	Based on a survey of 500 households (1,552 people) using a stratified random sample.
Demographic characteristics

Death statistics | 10 year cohort age breakdown | Chapeltown, Leeds | 1979 | [QRL.19] | Based on a survey of 48 households |

Deaths	By synagogue group, by geographical distribution (London and the provinces)	Britain	Annual (from 1965)	[QRL.1]	Based on return from all Jewish burial societies (& cremation where appropriate) in Britain
Marriage statistics					
Marriage statistics	Number of marriages by synagogue group and by geographical distribution	England (from 1965)		[QRL.1]	Based on returns from synagogues
Marriage statistics in Great Britain	Synagogue marriages by type of ceremony (Orthodox, Reform etc.) marital status, age at marriage, place of birth of partners, place of marriage	Great Britain	1901-1965	[QRL.54]	Synagogue marriage by type of ceremony based on records of 50 synagogues in the country; other information based on sample of 200 marriages for selected years
	Synagogue marriage by type of ceremony	Great Britain	1966-1968	[QRL.60]	Analysis based on [QRL.18]
Marriage statistics in a London suburb	Marital status; marriage patterns; how marriages end; single parent families	London borough of Redbridge	1978	[QRL.52]	Based on a survey of 500 households OPCS
Marriage statistics	Number of Jewish marriages	England & Wales		[QRL.26]	Based on official statistics (available every 5 th year till 1934)
Marriage statistics	Number of marriages solemnized by religious rites		1934	[QRL.53]	
Marriage trends		UK		[QRL.62]	Based on figures from the OPCS

Type of data	Breakdown	Area	Frequency	QRL Publication	Text Reference
Marriage statistics	Religious marriages by type of church e.g., church of England, Roman Catholic, Methodist, Baptist, *Jewish* and other	England & Wales	Annually till 1973	[QRL.47]	Trends since 1844 shown
Divorce					
Divorce statistics	Age at divorce	England	1950s & 60s	[QRL.17]	Based on Beth Din report; limited interpretation
	Divorce rate	England & Wales	1966	[QRL.55]	Part of Statistical Review, Registrar General, Pt III, p.32
	Divorce rate; rate of religious divorce, causes of divorce	UK	1970-1980	[QRL.11]	Based on a survey of internal community sources; supported by OPCS material
Exogamy					
Exogamy			1947	[QRL.45]	Based on a survey of 50 Jewish soldiers who were patients in a neurosis ward of a hospital - 231 marriages among patients & their relatives analysed

Fertility

Fertility data	Fertility Ratio: fertility of marriage cohorts; fecundity, family size, fertility trends	London Borough of Redbridge	1978	[QRL.52]	Based on a survey of 500 households; pp.17-21
	Family size, distribution of births according to number of years married; average number of years elapsed since marriage till birth of children of given parity; fertility by religious sub-group	Britain	1970-71	[QRL.27]	Based on 694 birth returns from 20 Mohelim
Fertility & influence of family limitation	By religion - contraception, inter-marriage, social class	UK	1949	[QRL.25]	Sample included 113 Jewish women

Population Size, Structure and Distribution

Population size		United Kingdom	1901	[QRL.8]	Estimate based on Jewish deaths and marriages
	Total male and female population for New London Survey Area, for Greater London and Administrative County of London	London	1929	[QRL.23]	Estimates base on burial returns to Jewish Health Organisation and age-specific death rates. (revision of Rosenbaum method)
Population size and structure	Total, male and female population for New London Survey Area, Greater London, and Administrative County of London; age-sex distribution for each of the three geographic units	London	1929-33 (age-sex figures for 1931-33 only)	[QRL.24]	Estimates are based on Trachtenberg's methods with revised assumptions on age-specific death rates

Type of data	Breakdown	Area	Frequency	QRL Publication	Text Reference
Population size and structure	Total population by main towns; estimated total for London and the Provinces; population by synagogue affiliation	Britain	1960-65	[QRL.50]	Estimates based on Trachtenberg's method and Kantorowitsch's London estimates
Population size and geographic distribution.	Population by London Borough	London	1970	[QRL.61]	Estimates based on synagogue membership and general knowledge of the community
Population size and distribution	Population in urban and rural districts by religion for county level; men and women shown separately	Northern Ireland	1971 and at 10 yearly intervals prior to this	[QRL.9]	
Population size and distribution	Population by town	Gt.Britain & Northern Ireland	Annual	[QRL.46]	Figures are based on a 1968 study by Prais [QRL.33] and no attempt is made to update them from year to year
Population size and Geographical distribution	Population distribution by town	England, Wales & Scotland	1974	[QRL.28]	Estimates based on indirect indicators (telephone directories, synagogue statistics, etc.)

Practice and Rituals

Practice of selected rituals	Percentage practising selected rituals	UK	1947-48	[QRL.58]	Based on an unrepresentative and self-selected sample of 3365 Jewish adults and 2523 Jewish children
	percentage practising selected rituals	Edgware, London	1962-63	[QRL.13]	Based on a sample of 382 households (1,290 people) using a multiphase probability technique
	percentage practising selected rituals	UK	1970	[QRL.48]	Quota sample of religious groups with age, sex and class quota controls; 1395 adults were interviewed (214 Jews)
	percentage practising selected rituals	Newton Mearns, Scotland	1973-74	[QRL.16]	Based on interviews with 280 Jewish heads of households (part of a larger study of inter-group relations in which 221 non-Jewish heads of households were also interviewed)

Type of data	Breakdown	Area	Frequency	QRL Publication	Text Reference
	Percentage practising selected rituals by household size, synagogue grouping, age and gender	London Borough of Redbridge	1978	[QRL.36]	
Practice among university students	percentage practising selected rituals	Oxford	1954-55	[QRL.22]	Based on a postal questionnaire
			1969-70	[QRL.35]	Based on an analysis of 133 questionnaires (51% response rate from all Jewish known students at Oxford)
Synagogue attendance	Attendance of *Jewish Chronicle* readers regularly, less often, festivals only, never	UK	1974, 1976, 1980	[QRL.31]	
	Synagogue attendance by household size, synagogue grouping, age and gender	London Borough of Redbridge	1978	[QRL.36]	
Beliefs and Attitudes					
Beliefs and attitudes of Jewish university students	percentage for and against a wide range of Jewish issues, and local and international situations with Jewish links	Oxford	1969-70	[QRL.35]	Based on an analysis of 133 questionnaires (51% response rate from all known Jewish students in Oxford).

	Description	Location	Date	Reference	Notes
	Nos. for and against intermarriage by parents' affiliation; affiliation by parents' affiliation; observance by university; beliefs about Jews and Jewish community	Cambridge, Manchester, Essex, London	1966-1967	[QRL.18]	Based on a survey of 155 students at universities of Cambridge, Manchester, Essex & Imperial College, University College, & L.S.E. London
Comparison of attitudes of different religious groups	Comparison of Jewish attitudes to a number of issues with other religious group (Protestants, Roman Catholics, Atheist or Agnostics); Jewish attitudes to selected Jewish related issues	UK	1970	[QRL.48]	Quota sample of religious groups with age, sex & class quota controls; 1395 adults were interviewed (214 Jews)
Political attitudes among Jews	Voting patterns in 1970; intended voting patterns in 1974; reasons for changing party reference	Mill Hill, Hale and Edgware, London	February 1974	[QRL.44]	150 Jews interviewed; random selection
	Voting patterns 1974	Hendon North London	October 1974	[QRL.39]	178 Jews interviewed, random selection as a basis for comparison with [QRL.50]
	Voting patterns in 1974 and intended voting pattern in 1978 by-election and 1977 general election	Ilford North	March 1978	[QRL.39]	Based on a survey of 143 Jewish voters selected at random from annotated electoral registers

Type of data	Breakdown	Area	Frequency	QRL Publication	Text Reference
Jewish interests	Attitudes to a wide range of Jewish issues	UK	1947-48	[QRL.58]	Based on an unrepresentative and self-selected sample of 3365 Jewish adults and 2523 Jewish children
Beliefs	By household size, age, sex, synagogue affiliation	London Borough of Redbridge	1978	[QRL.36]	
Attitudes to Israel	By adults, teenagers	London Borough of Redbridge	1978	[QRL.36]	A sample of 425 adults and 104 teenagers
Attitudes to Exogamy	Parents' attitudes	London Borough of Redbridge	1978	[QRL.36]	A sample of 206 parents
Attitudes to Jewish Day School	By parents, children, synagogue affiliation, reasons for and against Jewish education, attitude to Jewish Festivals and Shabbat	London Borough of Redbridge	1978	[QRL.36]	This sample varies with each table; basic table based on 209 parents and 105 teenagers
Education Children and teachers involved in Jewish Religious Education	Numbers of children on roll; average attendance; list of teachers at each institution.	London	Annually 1895-1935	[QRL.2]	Separate sections in a short annual report
Children in Jewish Religious Education	Numbers of children by institution (for synagogue and withdrawal classes); average attendance (Sundays & weekdays); age and sex of children	London	Annually- 1948	[QRL.3]	Separate sections in a short annual report
Children in Jewish Religious Education	Numbers of children by institution	Provinces, UK	Annually - 1953	[QRL.20]	Section called "Register of Classes"

Topic	Description	Location	Year	QRL ref	Notes
Children in Jewish Religious Education	Numbers of children by type of class (synagogue, Talmud Torah, withdrawal) children in Jewish Day Schools in London; number of pupils in Provincial community; percentage of Jewish, children receiving Jewish education, f.t. & p.t. students in the main Yeshivot	Greater London & the Provinces	1950 1957 1958 1961 (most figures 1958 only)	[QRL.33]	Secondary analysis based on [QRL.2] [QRL.4]
Jewish children, types of schools, and distribution of religious instruction	Average number of Jewish children per school; estimate of number of Jewish school children; percentage in Jewish/non-Jewish schools, religious instruction by primary/secondary school attended; religious instruction by age	London	1972/73	[QRL.49]	Based on a stratified sample of London schools with a secondary sample stage to select 200 Jewish children to complete a questionnaire. (86% response rate)
Types of Jewish Educational Experience	By age, sex and synagogue affiliation	London Borough of Redbridge	1978	[QRL.36]	
Attitudes to Jewish Day School	By parents, children, synagogue affiliation, reasons for and against Jewish education, attitudes to Jewish Festivals and Shabbat	London Borough of Redbridge	1978	[QRL.36]	The sample varies with each table; basic table based on 209 parents and 105 teenagers
Development of Jewish Day School enrollment	Numbers of children and numbers of schools; numbers of children by primary/secondary and grammar schools	London and the Provinces	1952-1957	[QRL.32]	Based on figures obtained from Jewish Day Schools
Enrollment in Jewish Schools	Numbers of children in nursery, primary and secondary schools; numbers of children by name of nursery, secondary and primary school	London and the Provinces. (breakdown by town)	1952, 1954, 1958, 1959, & bi-annually till 1971	[QRL.42]	

Type of data	Breakdown	Area	Frequency	QRL Publication	Text Reference
	Number of children by name of school	UK & Ireland (by town)	1973, 1975, plus bi-annual summary of totals 1959 to 1975	[QRL.57]	
	Numbers of students enrolled; number of Jewish children, distribution of students by type of Jewish education	UK London, Provinces (including separate figures for Manchester, Leeds, Liverpool, Glasgow, Birmingham)	Non-recurrent, but summary of figures for 1967, 1971/73, 1975, 1977/78	[QRL.15]	Table 2, Section 7, pp.76-77
Jewish children in schools in Glasgow	Number and geographical distribution of Jewish school-children	Greater Glasgow	1964	[QRL.29]	
Education data of *Jewish Chronicle* readers	Last educational institute attended; age f.t. education finished	UK	1967, 1974, 1976, 1980	[QRL.30] [QRL.31]	
State Aided and Independent Jewish schools	Type of school by enrollment by primary/secondary schools	London, Manchester, other centres	1977	[QRL.32]	Based on figures obtained from Jewish Day schools
Jewish students in universities	Nos. of Jewish students in universities	Gt. Britain (excluding London) and Ireland	1936, 1939	[QRL.38]	Based on two surveys

Welfare & Health

Jewish Homes for the Aged	Bed capacity by institution	UK	1980 non-recurrent	[QRL.34]	Pages 54 to 97; includes additional information on accessibility of inst.; criteria for admission; fees; services offered etc.
The Jewish Board of Guardians	Main operations by cases dealt with, nationality of applicants; type of relief granted; destination of emigrants dealt with and length of residence in UK	G.London	1861-1945	[QRL.7]	Based on annual reports of the Board
Jewish Welfare Board	Cases at Board's Homes by age	G.London	1951-1957		
	Numbers in Board's Homes	London & S.E.	1959	[QRL.4]	
Jewish Mentally Handicapped at Home	Numbers of families interviewed by borough; numbers of siblings & family size by Borough; social class of primary earner; diagnosis; additional handicaps; numbers using selected services by Borough; numbers in contact with selected Jewish organisations; numbers in contact with non-Jewish voluntary groups; type of services needed (percentage support); analysis of parents' comments on provision of services; those requiring transport by Borough; numbers approving of mixed sex facilities by Borough; distribution of synagogue affiliation; attitudes surveys; degree of handicap.	North London	1982	[QRL.37]	Based on a survey of 110 families identified through contact Jewish organisations and local authorities
Addiction, heroin and cocaine	Proportion of male and female Jews in sample who are addicts	London	1964	[QRL.46]	Analysis is based on 100 addicts attending the medical practice of the authors

Type of data	Breakdown	Area	Frequency	QRL Publication	Text Reference
Infant health and care	Proportion of Jewish infants; birth weights recorded; frequency of weighing infants; incidence of breast feeding; type and incidence of illness	Tower Hamlets, Hackney and City of London	1979-80	[QRL.5]	Based on 3,712 babies born in areas listed (89% of all babies born in these areas) information collected by Health Visitors of the districts when babies were about 4 weeks old
Socio-Economic Data Socio-economic data on *Jewish Chronicle* (J.C.) Readers	Social Grade; J.C. reading; car & T.V. ownership; hh. appliances; leisure activities; holidays; smoking	UK	1958 1959	[QRL.30]	
	Readership selection; age; sex; hh. status; attitudes to J.C. reporting; occupation	UK	1967	[QRL.30]	
	Age; sex; residential area; work status (F.t.,p.t., unempl.); industrial occupation + status of head of hh; number, destination & transport for/of holidays; T.V. viewing; ownership of hh goods, cars, financial items; petrol buying; home ownership & length of tenure; frequency of eating out in a restaurant; leisure activities; readership attitudes	UK	1974, 1976 1980	[QRL.31]	The 1980 survey also had additional survey material on T.V. ownership; entertaining at home; type of drink currently in home; home improvement undertaken in the last 12 months

Social-class structure of Anglo-Jewry	Social-class distribution of Jews (%); social-class distribution of synagogue members & non-members (%); social-class distribution of Jews aged 15 to 44 years and 45 to 75 years (%)	England & Wales	1961	[QRL.51]	Based on 1,216 Jewish deaths registered in England and Wales in 1961, identified in the records of the Registrar General by Jewish names from registers of Jewish burial societies; estimate of social-class distribution of live population also made
Economic activity occupation and social class of suburban Jewry	Occupation distribution (scale D); economically active population; industrial distribution; occupation distribution (scale D) by respondents' children aged 15 and over; Social class of respondents by social class of father; comparisons with general population in Edgware and UK	Edgware	1963	[QRL.14]	Based on a sample of 382 Jewish households (1,290 people) using a multiphase probability sampling technique
	Economically active pattern; SEG by industrial classification; self-employment by industry for Jewish & general Hackney population	London borough of Hackney	1971	[QRL.41]	Sample size of 2,700 people selected from 1971 Census S.A.S. using name and other supplementary techniques

Type of data	Breakdown	Area	Frequency	QRL Publication	Text Reference
	Economically active population; comparison of Jewish SEG distribution with that for Ecclesall ward, Sheffield City & Hackney Jewry; SEG by gender	Sheffield	1975	[QRL.56]	Based on a census of the 483 Sheffield Jewish households
Economic activity, occupation and social class of suburban Jewry	Age distribution of economically active population; age specific activity rates; dependent occupation; employment status (f.t; p.t.) by sex; economically active retired; percentage unemployed; distribution by employment category; employment by industry; occupation of head of household; SEG by industry; social class distribution; percentage of earner in household size; industry & employment status by place of work; percentage distribution of voluntary work workers by age & sex; time in voluntary work by employment status	London Borough of Redbridge	1978	[QRL.52]	Based on a survey of 500 households (1552 people) using a stratified random sample.
Occupations	Occupation by kind of employment (own account; employed; managerial; technician; professional; clerical and manual) by selected demographic characteristics	UK	1952	[QRL.10]	1667 forms returned covering 5225 people in selected towms in UK

QUICK REFERENCE LIST KEY TO PUBLICATIONS

Reference	Author or Organisation	Title	Publisher	Frequency or Date	Remarks
[QRL.1]	Research Unit, Board of Deputies of British Jews	*Annual Marriage and Death Statistics*	London, Board of Deputies of British Jews (mimeographed)	Annual	Research Unit Board of Deputies of British Jews
[QRL.2]	Jewish Religious Education Board	*Annual Report*	London, Jewish Religious Education Board	Annual (1895-1935)	Jews' College Library, Board itself
[QRL.3]	London Board of Jewish Religious Education	*Annual Report*	London, London Board of Jewish Religious Education	Annual (1948 to present)	Jews' College Library London Board itself
[QRL.4]	Jewish Welfare Board	*Annual Reports*	London, Jewish Welfare Board	Annual	Jewish Welfare Board
[QRL.5]	Cullinan, T.R. and Treuherz, J.	*Born in East London 1979-1980*	London, St. Bartholomews Hospital	1981	
[QRL.6]	Senior Jewish Chaplain to HM Forces	*Census of Religion of service personnel*		6 monthly	Senior Jewish Chaplain to HM Forces, Woburn House, Upper Woburn Place, London, WC1H OEP

[QRL.7]	V.D. Lipman	*A Century of Social Service 1859-1959, The Jewish Board of Guardians*	London, Routledge and Kegan Paul	1959	
[QRL.8]	S. Rosenbaum	*A Contribution to the Study of the Vital and other Statistics of the Jews in the United Kingdom in Journal of the Royal Statistical Society Vol.68, 526*		1905	
[QRL.9]	Census of Northern Ireland	*County Reports*	HMSO, Belfast	1971 and 10 yearly intervals prior to this	HMSO, 80 Chichester Street, Belfast B21 4JY
[QRL.10]	H. Neustatter	*Demographic and other statistical aspects of Anglo-Jewry in M.Freedman (Ed) A Minority in Britain.*	London, Vallentine, Mitchell and Co. Ltd	1955	
[QRL.11]	B.Kosmin	*Divorce in Anglo-Jewry 1970-1980: An Investigation*	London, West Central Counselling and Community Research	1982	West Central; Research Unit, Board of Deputies of British Jews
[QRL.12]	E. Krausz	*The Edgware Survey: Demographic Results in The Jewish Journal of Sociology Vol.X, No. 1 June 1968*	London	1968	
[QRL.13]	Krausz, E.	*The Edgware Survey: Factors in Jewish identification in The Jewish Journal of Sociology, Vol.XI, No.2, Dec.1969*	London	1969	
[QRL.14]	E.Krausz	*The Edgware Survey; Occupation & Social Class in The Jewish Journal of Sociology, Vol.XI, No.1, June 1969*	London	1969	

Reference	Author or Organisation	Title	Publisher	Frequency or Date	Remarks
[QRL.15]	Harold S. Himmelfarb & Segio Dellapergola	*Enrollment in Jewish Schools in the Diaspora Late 1970s*	Jerusalem, Institute of Contemporary Jewry, Hebrew University of Jerusalem	1982	
[QRL.16]	Benski T.	"Identification, Group Survival and Inter-Group Relations: the case of a middle-class Jewish community in Scotland" in *Ethnic and Racial Studies*, Vol.4, No.3, July 1981		1981	
[QRL.17]	M. Benjamin	*The incidence of divorce among the Jews of England* in J. Fried (Ed) *Jews & Divorce*	Ktav Publishing House, New York Inc., 1968 (pp 187-190)	1968	
[QRL.18]	V. West	*The Influence of Parental Background on Jewish University Students* in *The Jewish Journal of Sociology* Vol.X, No.2, Dec.1968	London	1968	
[QRL.19]	N. Grizzard, P. Raisman	*Inner City Jews in Leeds*	London, Research Unit Board of Deputies of British Jews (reprinted from the *Jewish Journal of Sociology*, Vol.XXII, No.1, June 1980)	1980	Part of Reprint Series, Research Unit, Board of Deputies of British Jews

[QRL.20]	Central Council for Jewish Religious Education	*Inspectors' Report*	London, Central Council for Jewish Religious Education	Annual	Jews' College Library Central Council itself
[QRL.21]	G. Cromer	*Intermarriage and Communal Survival in a London Suburb in The Jewish Journal of Sociology, XVI (pp 155-169), 1974*	London	1974	
[QRL.22]	Baron, R.V.	*I.U.J.F. Survey of Jewish University Students 1954/55 in Jewish Academy Winter 1955-6*	London	1955-6	
[QRL.23]	H.L. Trachtenberg	*Estimate of the Jewish Population of London, 1929 in Journal of the Royal Statistical Society Vol.96, 87, 1933*	London	Non-recurrent (but subsequent estimates using the same method have been made for 1929-33, 1960-65 & 1980-82)	
[QRL.24]	M.Kantorowitsch	*Estimate of the Jewish population of London, 1929-33 in Journal of the Royal Statistical Society Vol.99, 372, 1936*	London	1936 (see [QRL.23])	
[QRL.25]	E.Lewis-Fanning	*Family limitation and its influence on human fertility in the past fifty years*	London, HMSO (Papers on the Royal Commission on Population, vol.i)	1949	HMSO
[QRL.26]	OPCS	*Family Monitor: Marriage and Divorce*	London, OPCS (FM 2, No.1, 1977 & FM 2, No.2, 1978)	Non-recurrent with respect to marriages	

Reference	Author or Organisation	Title	Publisher	Frequency or Date	Remarks
[QRL.27]	S.J.Prais, M.Schmool	*The Fertility of Jewish Families in Britain 1971*	London, Board of Deputies of British Jews (reprinted from the *Jewish Journal of Sociology*, Vol.XV, No.2, Dec.1973)	1973	Part of Reprint Series, Research Unit, Board of Deputies of British Jews
[QRL.28]	B.Kosmin , N.Grizzard	*Geographical Distribution; Estimates of Ethnically Jewish Population in the United Kingdom, 1974*	London, Board of Deputies of British Jews (mimeographed)	1974	Research Unit, Board of Deputies pf British Jews
[QRL.29]	P.Vincent	*Glasgow Jewish schoolchildren* in *The Jewish Journal of Sociology*, Vol.Vi, No.2, Dec:1964, pp.220-231	London	1964	
[QRL.30]	Research Services Ltd. (Research Division of the London Press Exchange Organisation)	*Jewish Chronicle Readership Survey*	London,*Jewish Chronicle*	1958 1959 1967	
[QRL.31]	Gordon Simmons Research Ltd	*Jewish Chronicle Readership Survey*	London, Survey Chronicle	1974 1976 1980	*Jewish Chronicle*
[QRL.32]	Dr.J.Braude	*Jewish Education in Britain Today* in S.L. & V.D.Lipman, *Jewish Life in Britain 1962-1977*	New York, K.G. Sauer	1981	
[QRL.33]	I.Fishman, H.Levy	*Jewish Education in Great Britain* in G.Gould & S.Esh *Jewish Life in Modern Britain*	London, Routledge and Kegan Paul	1964	
[QRL.34]	European Council of Jewish Community Services	*Jewish Homes for the Aged in Europe*	Paris, European Council of Jewish Community Services	1980	*Jewish Chronicle* Library

[QRL.35]	B.Wasserstein	Jewish Identification among Students at Oxford in The Journal of Sociology, Vol.XIII, No.2. Dec.1971	London		
[QRL.36]	B.Kosmin , C. Levy	Jewish Identity in an Anglo-Jewish Community	London, Research Unit Board of Deputies of British Jews	1983	
[QRL.37]	Michael Jimack	The Jewish Mentally Handicapped at Home	London, Central Council for Jewish Social Services	1982	Contact Council for Jewish Social Services, 221 Golders Green Road, London, N.W.11.
[QRL.38]	G.D.M. Black	Jewish students at Universities of Gt. Britain & Ireland, excluding London, 1936-9 in Sociological Review		1942	
[QRL.39]	G. Alderman	The Jewish Vote in Great Britain since 1945 in Studies in Political Policy No.72	Centre for the Study of Public Policy, University of Strathclyde, Glasgow	1980	
[QRL.40]	Michael Wallach (Editor)	The Jewish Year Book	London,Jewish Chronicle Publications	Annual	Jewish Chronicle Pub, 25 Furnival Street, London, EC4A 1JT
[QRL.41]	B.Kosmin, N.Grizzard	Jews in an Inner London Borough	London, Research Unit Board of Deputies of British Jews	1975	Research Unit, Board Deputies of British Jews

Reference	Author or Organisation	Title	Publisher	Frequency or Date	Remarks
[QRL.42]	M.Davies (Editor)	*Let my People know*	London, Office of the Chief Rabbi	1971	Office of the Chief Rabbi
[QRL.43]	OPCS	*Marriage and Divorce Statistics*	HMSO	Annual	
[QRL.44]	G. Alderman	*Not Quite British. The Political Attitudes of Anglo-Jewry* in I. Crewe (Ed) *British Political Sociology Year Book*, Vol.II,	London	1975 (Alderman carried out further surveys - see [QRL.39]	
[QRL.45]	E.Slater	*A note on Jewish-Christian Intermarriage* in *Eugenics Reviews*; Vol.39, 17.1947			
[QRL.46]	Hewetson, J. and Ollendorff, R.	*Preliminary Survey of One Hundred London Heroin and Cocaine Addicts* in *The British Journal of Addiction*, Vol.60, No.1 August 1964		1964	
[QRL.47]	Registrar General	*Registrar General's Review of England & Wales, Part II*	HMSO, London	Annually till 1975	HMSO
[QRL.48]	NOP Market Research Ltd	*Report on Attitudes to and Practices of Religion and Superstition*	London, NOP Market Research Ltd	1970	
[QRL.49]	S.J. Prais	*A Sample Survey on Jewish Education in London 1972-73*	London, Board of Deputies of British Jews (reprinted from *The Jewish Journal of Sociology*, Vol.XVI, No.2.Dec.1974	1974	Part of Reprint Series Research Unit, Board of Deputies of British Jews

[QRL.50]	S.J.Prais and M.Schmool	*The Size and Structure of the Anglo-Jewish Population 1960-65*	London, Board of Deputies of British Jews (reprinted from *The Jewish Journal of Sociology*, Vol.X, 1, June 1968)	1968 (see [QRL.23]	Part of Reprint Series Research Unit, Board Deputies of British Jews
[QRL.51]	S.J.Prais, M Schmool	*The Social Class Structure of Anglo-Jewry 1961*	London, Board of Deputies of British Jews (reprinted from *The Jewish Journal of Sociology* Vol.XVI, June 1975	1975	Part of Reprint Series Research Unit, Board of Deputies of British Jews
[QRL.52]	B.Kosmin, C.Levy, P.Wigodsky	*The Social Demography of Redbridge Jewry*	London, Research Unit Board of Deputies of British Jews	1979	Research Unit, Board of Deputies of British Jews
[QRL.53]	M. Kantorowitsch	*On the Statistics of Jewish marriages in England and Wales in Population Vol. 2, 74, 1936*		1936	
[QRL.54]	S.J. Prais, M.Schmool	*Statistics of Jewish Marriages in Great Britain:1901-1965*	London, Board of Deputies of british Jews (reprinted from the *Jewish Journal of Sociology*, vol.IX, No.2, Dec.1967)	1967	Part of Reprint Series, Research Unit, Board of Deputies of British Jews

Reference	Author or Organisation	Title	Publisher	Frequency or Date	Remarks
[QRL.55]	Registrar General	*Statistical Review of England and Wales for 1967, Part III*	London, HMSO	Last Published in 1967; information on divorce in 1967 publication only.	HMSO
[QRL.56]	B. Kosmin, M. Bauer, N. Grizzard	*Steel City Jews*	London, Research Unit Board of Deputies of British Jews	1976	Research Unit, Board of Deputies of British Jews
[QRL.57]	Dr.J.Braude	*Survey of Jewish Day Schools in the United Kingdom*	London, Institute of Jewish Affairs	1975	I.J.A.
[QRL.58]	R.L.Henriques (editor)	*Survey of Jewish Interests*	London, Jewish Research Unit	1949	
[QRL.59]	B. Kosmin, D. de Lange	*Synagogue Affiliation in the United Kingdom 1977*	London, Research Unit, Board of Deputies of British Jews	To be repeated for 1982	Research Unit, Board of Deputies of British Jews
[QRL.60]	S.J.Prais, M. Schmool	*Synagogue Marriages in Great Britain 1966-8* in *The Jewish Journal of Sociology*, Vol.XII, Number 1, June 1970	London	1970	Off-prints available from Research Unit, Board of Deputies of British Jews

[QRL.61]	S.J. Prais	*Synagogue Statistics and the Jewish Population of Great Britain 1900-70*	London; Board of Deputies of British Jews (reprinted from *The Jewish Journal of Sociology*, Vol.XIV, 2 December, 1972)	Updated in 1977 [QRL.59] and repeated 1983	Off-prints available from Research Unit, Board of Deputies of British Jews
[QRL.62]	J. Haskey	*Trends in Marriages: Church, Chapel and Civil ceremonies in Population Trends* (Pop. Trends 18, Winter 1980)		1980	
[QRL.63]	A. Newman	*The United Synagogue 1870-1970*	London, Henley & Boston, Routledge & Kegan Paul	1977	

BIBLIOGRAPHY

[B.1] Adler, H. 'Jewish Life and Labour in East London' in *The New Survey of London Life and Labour*, VI, London, King, 1934

[B.2] de Lange, Deborah, J. and Kosmin, Barry A. *Community Resources for a Community Survey*. London, Research Unit, Board of Deputies of British Jews, 1979.

[B.3] Freedman, Maurice, 'The Jewish Population in Great Britain', *The Jewish Journal of Sociology*, Vol.IV, No.1. June 1962. p.92-100.

[B.4] Kosmin, B.A., 'The Structure and demography of British Jewry in 1976', *Gesher*, XXXIII (1977), 87-97 (Hebrew). English translation, London World Zionist Organisation, n.d.

[B.5] Kosmin, B.A. 'Demography and sampling problems', in D. Bensimon, *Communautees Juives (1880-1978) Sources et Methodes de Recherche*, Clichy, Centre de Documentation D'Etudes et de Recherche Habraiques et Juives Modernes et Contemporaines, 1979.

[B.6] Kosmin, B.A. 'The case for the local perspective in the Study of Contemporary British Jewry' in S.L. and V.D. Lipman, eds., *Jewish Life in Britain 1962-1977*, New York, K.G. Sauer, 1981, pp. 83-94.

[B.7] Kosmin, B.A. 'Nuptiality and fertility patterns of British Jewry 1850-1980: an immigrant transition?" in D. Coleman, ed., *The Demography of Immigrants and Minority Groups in the United Kingdom*, London, Academic Press, 1982, pp.245-261.

[B.8] Krausz, Ernest, 'A demographic report on Jews in Great Britain', in U.O. Schmelz, S.Della Pergola, and P. Glikson, eds. *Papers in Jewish Demography 1973*, Jerusalem, The Hebrew University of Jerusalem, pp.289-295.

[B.9] Lipman, V.D. *Social History of the Jews in England 1850-1950*, London, Watts & Co, 1954.

[B.10] Prais, S.J. 'Statistical research: needs and prospects' in Gould, Julius and Shaul Esq (eds.) *Jewish Life in Modern Britain*, London, Routledge & Kegan Paul, 1964, pp.111-126.

[B.11] Prais, S.J. 'Polarization or decline' in S.L. and V.D. Lipman, eds, *Jewish Life in Britain 1962-1977*, New York, K.G. Sauer, 1981, pp.3-16.

[B.12] Schmool, Marlene and Prais, S.J. 'Methodes de recherches demographiques sur le Judaisme Britannique-Rapport sur les travaux du groupe de recherche statistique du Board of Deputies', in *Deuxieme colloque sur la vie juive dans l'Europe contemporaine*. Bruxelles, Centre National des Hautes Etudes Juives and Institute of Contemporary Jewry of the Hebrew University, 1967.

SUBJECT INDEX

Act 1905, Aliens, 1.5
Adler Chief Rabbi, 1.3
Aliens Act 1905, 1.5
Antisemitism, 1.6
Armed forces, 3.1.7
Armed Forces, Jews in, 3.1.7
Ashkenazi Orthodox Jews, London, 3.2.4
Association of Jewish Ex-servicemen, 3.1.7

Beliefs, Personal, 3.4
Beth din, 2.1; 2.4; 3.2.4
Births, 1.4; 1.7; 3.2.2
Board of Deputies of British Jews, 1.4; 1.10; 2.6; 3.1.3; 3.2.1
Burial data, 3.2.1

Census 1851, Religious, 1.1
Census, Northern Ireland, 2.3
Central Orthodox Jews, 3.1.5
Circumcision, 3.2.2
Comparative marriage data, 3.2.3
Comparisons, International, 3.5
Coversions, 2.1; 2.4; 3.2.3
Cremations, 3.2.1

Deaths, 1.7; 3.2.1; 3.7
Definition of a Jew, 2.1; 2.2; 2.3
Demographic data, 1.4; 1.10; 3.2; 4.1
Department of Education, 3.5
Distinctive Jewish Name Method, 2.4
Divorce, 3.2.4

Education, 3.5
Education, Department of, 3.5
Ethnic Jews, 2.2; 2.6

Federation of Synagogues, 3.1.2
Fertility data, 3.2.2
Festivals, 3.3

Get, 3.2.4
Gittin, 3.2.4

Halacha, 2.1; 2.3
Health, 3.6

Health Organisation, Jewish, 1.6
Hebrew University Jerusalem, 1.10
Holocaust, 1.8; 1.9
Hospitals, 3.6

Immigration, 1.5
Initiation Society, 3.2.2
Interments, 1.4; 3.2.1
International comparisons, 3.5
Isreal, 1.8; 3.4

Jacobs Joseph, 1.5
Jerusalem, Hebrew University, 1.10
Jewish Chronicle Readership Survey, 3.7
Jewish Ex-servicemen, Association of, 3.1.7
Jewish Health Organisation, 1.6
Jewish life style, 2.7
Jewish sub-groups, 3.1.2
Jewish Welfare Board, 3.6
Jews in Armed Forces, 3.1.7

Liberal and Progressive Synagogues, Union of, 3.2.4
Life style, Jewish, 2.7
Local needs, 4.1
London, 3.1.4; 3.1.5; 3.6
London Ashkenazi Orthodox Jews, 3.2.4
London, Tower Hamlets, 3.1.4
London, United Synagogue, 3.1.2
London, Westminster, 3.1.4

Manchester, 3.1.5; 3.6
Manpower, 2.8
Marriage data, Comparative, 3.2.3
Marriages, 1.1; 1.4; 1.7; 2.8; 3.2.3
Members, Women, 3.1.6
Membership, 3.1
Membership payment, 3.1.1
Membership, Synagogue, 2.4; 2.6; 3.1.1
Minyanim, 2.9
Mohalion, 3.2.2
Mortality studies, 3.2.1; 4.3

Name Method, Distinctive Jewish, 2.4
Northern Ireland Census, 2.3

36: OTHER RELIGIONS

Dr JORGEN S. NIELSEN

Selly Oak Colleges

Birmingham

REFERENCE DATE OF SOURCES REVIEWED

Generally, material published before January 1983 has been included, although a few later items have also been noted. In addition, reference is also made to survey data accessible to the researcher at that time although not yet published.

ACKNOWLEDGEMENTS

A number of libraries have been helpful in tracing material for this survey, among them the Birmingham Public Library and the University of Birmingham. Particularly useful has been the assistance of the library staffs at the ESRC Centre for Research in Ethnic Relations, University of Warwick, at the Commission for Racial Equality and at the Runnymede Trust.

I am grateful to those individuals and organizations who responded to requests for information, and to the Commission for Racial Equality for circulating the local Community Relations Councils, even though the response was negligible.

Coming into this project at a late stage, I am especially indebted to my colleagues for their advice and assistance in locating material and in determining structure and frame of reference.

ABBREVIATIONS USED IN TEXT

AFFOR   All Faiths for One Race
CARAF   Campaign Against Racism and Fascism
CRC   Community Relations Commission (now Commission for Racial Equality)
GLC   Greater London Council
NCW   New Commonwealth
NCWP   New Commonwealth and Pakistan
OPCS   Office of Population Censuses and Surveys
PEP   Political and Economic Planning (now Policy Studies Institute)
RUER   Research Unit on Ethnic Relations (now Centre for Research in Ethnic Relations)
SCPR   Social and Community Planning Research
SSRC   Social Sciences Research Council (now Economic and Social Research Council)

CONTENTS OF REVIEW 36

CHAPTER 1

INTRODUCTION

1.1

The identification of sources for statistical information on religions other than Christianity and Judaism in the United Kingdom presents the researcher with a complex of problems. Immediate among them is the glaring lack of material. The organisations representing these religions are not, on the whole, statistics conscious. In some instances this may be a matter of principle, a concern for quality and the transcendental rather quantity and the material. Since the major religions in question are closely identified with communities whose origins are to be found in South Asia during the last half century, the reason is often cultural, manifesting itself in an interest in orders of magnitude rather than accuracy of detail. For the same reason, there is a deep-seated reluctance to divulge membership and finance statistics which, it is feared, may be used to adverse effect by opponents or government departments.

1.2

A deeper problem is the institutional expression of the various religions. The structures being developed in the United Kingdom among, for example, Muslims and Sikhs are often radically different from the traditional structures of these religions. So, one is dealing with new institutions which are searching for new ways of performing traditional functions or, indeed, are becoming aware that new functions are necessary if they are to serve their communities constructively in a new context. To expect institutions to produce reliable and regular statistical information at such a stage in their existence would be unreasonable. The total absence of structure precludes any treatment of some religious groups, for example the Rastafarians.

1.3

A further problem is the identification, at least among Muslims, Hindus and Sikhs, of religion, culture and ethnicity. Certainly for the present and probably for a long time to come it is not possible to distinguish between strictly "religious" and the wider cultural and social data, in the way this has been done with sources on Protestantism and Catholicism in Northern Ireland elsewhere in this volume. Similarly, it follows that data on membership will, unless otherwise stated, refer to the whole population with no age group excluded.

1.4

A large part of the source material potentially under consideration reflects the approach of the social anthropologist rather than the sociologist, in consequence of which sources, including statistical, material are further limited in number. Additionally, most of the material included was not written with the purpose of providing statistical source material on religion. The authors' emphases and concerns are usually in other areas. This partly peripheral nature of any religious data means that it often has to be treated with the greatest of care. Several surveys have recently used religious identity more conspicuously. This is the case when the sample base is the electoral register where family name is an indication of the religion of individuals of South Asian origin. However, while religious identity is central to sampling method, it often remains peripheral to the use and analysis of the data thus gained. The varieties of emphasis and method should warn the user against too facile a comparative utilization of the data. (See also Section 3.2.3 below).

1.5

As a general rule, only sources which include an analysis explicitly by religion have been considered. Apart from a few governmental sources (Section 2.3), the material therefore comprises mainly unique studies and surveys. While this is definitely not a consideration of statistical sources on ethnic minorities, brief note has been taken of the census (Section 2.1) and to sources on intercensal changes (Section 2.2), since these are frequently used as a basis on which to calculate the size and distribution of the minority religious communities. Material which merely repeats figures from elsewhere without further treatment has, on the whole, been excluded.

1.6

Although the subject is statistical data on religion, it was decided not to arrange the material strictly by religion. Because this has not been the main concern of the vast majority of sources listed, it would be misleading to impose such a framework on the material. Section 3 contains sources whose basic frame of reference is geographical or ethnic. Material with a single religion as the frame of reference is to be found in section 4, while in section 5 the reference is that of limited social or other issues. In other words, the placing of an item has been determined by the emphasis of the author, and the researcher who wishes to investigate one particular religion will have to refer to each of sections 2 to 5 or to the Quick Reference List.

1.7

No attempt has been made to achieve a consistency of terminology with material which is characterized by the lack of such consistency. Thus terms such as black, coloured, immigrant and British will all appear, as will ethnic minority, Asian, white,

European and New Commonwealth. The terms used are those used in the source
material itself.

CHAPTER 2

RECURRENT DATA

2.1 The Census

2.1.1

In connection with the 1851 census an effort was made to collect also information on religious adherence. Returns included some estimates also for religions other than Christianity. This census is discussed in more detail elsewhere in this volume.

In subsequent censuses, information on place of birth has occasionally and unsatisfactorily been used as a basis on which to estimate the size and distribution of minority religious groups. The 1961 census [QRL.28] was the first to show substantial numbers of residents of England and Wales born in countries where religions other than Christianity predominate. The 1966 10% sample census [QRL.29] repeated the question. In 1971 an attempt was made to get as much information as possible without asking a direct question on ethnicity or religion [QRL.66]. The schedule included a question on parents' place of birth and, in addition to the usual county reports, two volumes of Country of Birth Supplementary Tables based on a 10% sample appeared [QRL.67]. In these, place of birth was correlated with household composition, occupation and time of migration. The 1971 county reports have been reissued with the data reorganized to take account of the new local government boundaries which came into effect in 1974.

2.1.2

As pointed out, these data are sometimes used to estimate membership of a particular religious community. The nature of the census data makes such an attempt unreliable for a number of reasons. The country of birth data relating to Commonwealth countries has included a substantial, although over time decreasing, proportion of people of white British parentage. In his appendix III,3 Rose [QRL.88] offers detailed calculations aimed at determining the exact extent to which the figures in the 1951, 1961 and 1966 censuses should be adjusted to take this factor into account. Knott and Toon have attempted a similar exercise on the 1971 census [QRL.57]. A related problem is definition of country of birth, particularly with regard to the Indian subcontinent. As Anwar [B.1] and Knott [B.13], among many others, have pointed out, many people arriving from Pakistan and Bangladesh have put India as their birth place if they were born before the 1947 partition, or if they moved to these countries later. Some people, arrived from India, have put Pakistan as their birthplace if their place of birth became part of Pakistan in 1947. The third problem is underenumeration of the ethnic minorities in the census, a problem partly related to country of birth. Peach and Winchester [B.19] in a paper which also considers the previous points, suggest that for a complex of reasons underenumeration of the Pakistan-born population in the 1971 census may be as high as 29%.

2.1.3

These considerations mean, in effect, that any attempts to estimate especially the number of Muslims in Britain, which rely on census data relating to people born in Pakistan, are likely to be unreliable. A possible way out of this problem has been to consider the population born in India, Pakistan and Bangladesh as one population, subtract the estimated number of white British origin, and then seek gross percentages of the relative sizes of the three main religious communities represented in Great Britain: Muslims, Hindus and Sikhs. The first such remotely reliable percentages to become available are those of the 1974 PEP survey (cf.sect.3.1.3). The conclusions reached in that survey have, however, been criticized and somewhat amended by Knott and Toon [QRL.57] in a way which particularly affects estimates of the Muslim and Sikh populations in Britain. The disadvantage of this approach is, of course, that it does not include groups from other parts of the world where particularly Islam is prevalent.

2.1.4

Given the only partially satisfactory outcome of the 1971 census with regard to data on ethnic origin, the Office of Population Censuses and Surveys (OPCS) was asked to test the feasibility of including a question on "racial and ethnic origin" in the 1981 census. Aspects of the debate provoked by this experiment have been discussed by Bulmer [B.5], and the problems involved in the experiment itself are discussed by one of the researchers involved, Ken Sillitoe, in an OPCS publication [B.17]. The main concern was to devise a question which, both in its formulation and presentation, would produce reliable results. During the early stages, religious adherence was considered as a possible supplementary question. However, this question was asked only of those whose place of birth was entered as being India, Pakistan, Bangladesh or Sri Lanka, not of other categories such as Arab, Turk or African, which appeared in various versions of the experimental census form. The results of the experiments have been published by the OPCS [B.23], but as the purpose was to test reliability, the religious data is of no value. In the event, a combination of the public controversy surrounding the field trials in Haringey in April 1979 and an increasingly cost-conscious government led to this and several other questions being omitted. To compensate, the OPCS has analysed the 1981 census data by the country of birth of heads of household. These data are published in the separate volume of tables on country of birth [QRL.68].

2.1.5

The decennial census of Scotland has, for the purposes of this study, been conducted on lines similar to those for England and Wales. For the 1971 census [QRL.77], a separate volume of usual residence and birthplace tables [QRL.78] brought together figures on place of birth and parents' place of birth. For the 1981 census, the data on place of birth have been incorporated in the volume for Great Britain [QRL.68].

2.1.6

The decennial censuses of Northern Ireland differ from the others, in that they do include information on religious affiliation. Such affiliation is analysed by county for any denomination, including non-Christian religions, with more than ten adherents. Small numbers of minority religions became identifiable in 1971 [QRL.64].

2.2 Intercensal changes

2.2.1

Since the census is taken only at ten-year intervals, other data are needed to trace the movements in the intervening periods. Like the other statistical sources discussed throughout this section, they can only assist in reaching approximate conclusions regarding the sizes of ethnic minority groups rather than specifically religious minority groups. A recent study by the Runnymede Trust and the Radical Statistics Race Group [B.21] and the older work by Rose [QRL.88] are useful guides to the problems inherent in using such data and also provide detailed biblographies.

2.2.2

The OPCS publishes annual figures on immigration and emigration based on the International Passenger Survey (see [B.21], pp.24f). Until 1973, these tables were part of The *Registrar General's Statistical Review of England and Wales* [QRL.72], which also included statistics of live births analysed by the country of birth of the mother and the father. Since 1974, the two sections have been published separately [QRL.65] [QRL.69]. A more detailed discussion is to be found in volume 8, Tourism , of the present series.

2.2.3

More detailed figures on international arrivals, covering the whole of the United Kingdom, have been published annually by the Home Office. One series [QRL.39] covers citizens of Commonwealth origin, the other covers foreign citizens [QRL.43]. The two have been published together since 1973 [QRL.40] [QRL.41]. Both series analyse by type of entry and by nationality. The Home Office's annual tables on persons acquiring UK citizenship [QRL.44] [QRL.45] also analyse by previous nationality.

2.2.4

Another set of serial data providing information on the regional, age and sex distribution as well as the employment and socio-economic situation of ethnic minorities is the *Labour Force Survey* conducted in alternate years starting in 1973

[QRL.70]. The first three surveys classified only by country of birth, while the 1979 and 1981 surveys have also included analyses by self-assessed ethnicity.

2.2.5

Overseas students are a small but significant group in terms of ideological and structural impact, especially among Muslims in Britain. Annual figures analysed by country of nationality are published by the Department of Education and Science [QRL.24]. These tables include only students in public sector institutions in England and Wales. The British Council's annual statistics include figures of students in private institutions and cover the whole of the United Kingdom [QRL.15]. Again, these figures can only be used as a rough guide to religious adherence, and then only as regards Muslims.

2.3 Sources on religion - governmental

2.3.1

Despite the controversy surrounding the trials for the 1981 census (section 2.1.4 above), a few sets of official statistics are published including direct reference to minority religions. There is clearly no general policy regarding the extent to which the collection of such data is useful or legitimate, merely the practice of analysing separately figures for these religions when they have become of a significant magnitude in already existing religious data. The *Sources of Statistics on Religion* [B.8] is, perhaps, overconfident in the ability of some government departments to produce data of much value.

2.3.2

An early attempt on the part of government departments to give overall estimates of religious adherence has been a haphazard and ultimately unsuccessful section in the annual *Britain: An Official Handbook* [QRL.20]. The Muslim, Sikh, Hindu and Buddhist presence in Britain is acknowledged. The 1960 edition, for the first time, ventured to estimate the number of Muslims. Over the next few years, the figure slowly grew, until in 1969 it suddenly increased six-fold to 1.5 million. In the following year, the Central Office of Information must have realized that its informant was unreliable, and it gave a much vaguer "several hundred thousand". Similar vague estimates were given over the next several editions, except in 1974 and 1975 when no figures were presented at all. No estimates of the sizes of other religious communities have been given, and since the 1979 edition the attempt to do so for Muslims has also been abandoned. On the other hand, the Central Statistical Office has included, for the first time, data on non-Christian religions, specifically Muslims and Sikhs, in the 1983 edition of *Social Trends* [B.7]. The source for these data is the 1983 edition of the *UK Christian Handbook* (see sect.3.1.7 below).

2.3.3

The major official source to present data of relevance in England and Wales is the OPCS's *Marriage and Divorce Statistics* [QRL.71], one of the successors to the *Registrar-General's Statistical Review* (see sect. 2.2.2 above). This includes the category "other" in its analysis of the manner of solemnization in registered buildings by denomination. On request, the OPCS (St.Catherine's House, 10 Kingsway, London WC2B 6JP) will provide an analysis of this category by Sikh, Muslim and "other" going as far back as 1969. The same data is further analysed by the prior marital status of the parties. A further two tables list the number of buildings registered for the purposes of public worship and the number of such buildings authorized for solemnization of marriage. These tables include columns for Muslim, Sikh and a remaining unanalysed "other". Part III of the Registrar-General's *Official List* [B.16] is a register of all the buildings summarized in both these tables and can thus be used to analyse further the category "other", which includes Hindu, Buddhist and Bahai buildings. The data presented in these sources is to be treated with caution. It is correct but only within the strict definitions stated. The data has to be interpreted in the light of the traditions of the communities concerned. Among groups originating in South Asia it is by no means common to solemnize marriage in a place of worship. That it is more common among Sikhs than among Muslims is clearly reflected in the OPCS annual statistics. The figures for mosques in Birmingham, given by Hodgins [QRL.38], also suggest that many mosques, as opposed to Sikh gurdwaras (see sect.4.3.2 below), may not be registered as such, even if they have obtained the relevant planning permission.

2.3.4

For Scotland, the *Registrar-General's Annual Report* [QRL.76] has, since the 1978 edition, included entries for the number of marriages solemnized in Muslim and Sikh buildings. The figures are broken down by religion only in 1978, but in the 1979 edition, figures are listed against named buildings.

2.3.5

The Home Office Prison Department has, since 1970, included in its annual census of the religion of inmates figures on Muslims, Hindus, Sikhs and Buddhists. The census is normally published in the *Report on the Work of the Prison Department* [QRL.42], although it was omitted from 1980 edition for administrative reasons. The Home Office has not yet recognized Rastafarianism as a religion for the purposes of this census. In view of the beliefs of Rastafarians (cf. [B.6]) and the experience of the Prison Department itself, it is probably justified to suggest that most, if not all, of those registered as Ethiopian Orthodox are, in fact, Rastafarian, although it is unlikely that this category reflects the true extent of adherence to Rastafarianism among prison inmates. Another uncertainty concerning the Prison Department's census is the extent to which inmates declare adherence to a religion with a view to gaining related privileges, a practice which has individual inmates declaring different religious adherence at successive admissions.

2.3.6

The Ministry of Defence does not publish statistics on the religious adherence of servicemen, but the figures are available on request from Stats (M)1, Ministry of Defence, Northumberland House, Northumberland Avenue, London WC2N 5BP. The religious census is carried out by the chaplaincies of the three services, and there is no common policy regarding the analysis of non-Christian serving personnel. The Royal Navy/ Royal Marines quinquennial census included this analysis for the first time in 1971, while the Army until the present does not. The census of Royal Air Force personnel has included figures on Muslims, Hindus, Sikhs and Buddhists since the first census in 1963. According to information from the Ministry of Defence, the Army and RAF data cover only personnel whose units are head-quartered in the UK. However, the Royal Navy/Royal Marines figures include personnel recruited locally in the Far East, especially Hong Kong. In comparison with other figures, those for Buddhist/Confucian are therefore likely to reflect a preponderance of personnel recruited in Hong Kong.

2.4 Sources on religion - non-governmental

2.4.1

Outside the government publications mentioned above, very little statistical information is published in any recurrent form. An uneven and haphazard source of information on particular localities in Great Britain are the annual reports of the approximately 150 Community Relations Councils (addresses available from the Commission for Racial Equality, 10/12 Allington Street, London SW1E 5EH). Occasionally such reports will include estimates of the sizes of particular religious communities in a given area. More regularly, however, they include a list of members of the council. Among such members are usually religious organizations, and the lists can thus be a useful initial source of local data. They cannot, however, be used alone, as many religious organizations are either not members of such councils or are represented through umbrella organizations.

2.4.2

Compared with Christian and Jewish organizations, the religions under consideration here produce very little regular statistical information. The researcher will normally have to hope that correspondence or personal visits to the officers of relevant organizations may yield some kind of fruit. In the following are listed the main national organizations with their addresses and, where necessary, details of their functions and regular publications.

2.4.2.1 *Muslim organizations* The Islamic Cultural Centre, Regent's Lodge, 146 Park Rd, London NW8 7RG, is linked to the London Central Mosque. It does occasionally produce reports on its activities but not an annual report.

The Islamic Foundation , 223 London Rd, Leicester LE2 1LD, is engaged in research and publishing. Its annual report has occasionally been published but includes no regular statistics.

The Muslim Educational Trust , 130 Stroud Green Rd, London N4 3RZ, is concerned with Islamic instruction of children. Although it does not publish an annual report, it does make available information on the number of peripatetic teachers employed, of children taught as well as details of the schools admitting its teachers.

The Muslim Institute , 6 Endsleigh St, London WC1H ODS, is another body engaged in research and publication. It does not produce an annual report.

Union of Muslim Organizations of the UK and Eire, 109 Campden Hill Rd. London W8, brings together a number of smaller Muslim associations and mosques in the UK. The programme of its annual conference [QRL.100] includes a list of member bodies.

UK Islamic Mission , 202 North Gower St, London NW1 2LY, maintains a number of mosques, Islamic centres, mosque schools and bookshops. Its regular annual report [QRL.99] includes detailed figures on correspondence, distribution of literature, collective and individual membership, aspects of finances, numbers of staff and pupils and library holdings in its local branches.

The Ahmadiyyat Movement in Islam, the London Mosque, 16 Gressenhall Rd, London SW18 5QL, is the UK representation of the Rabwah section of a movement which the majority of the Islamic world has declared not to be Islamic. Its monthly journal *The Muslim Herald* includes reports of the movements' activities and regularly lists its regional branches.

The Ahmadiyya Anjuman Isha'at Islam , 15 Stanley Avenue, Wembley, HAO 4JQ, represents the smaller section, the Lahore branch, of the Ahmadi movement. In addition to religious and educational functions, the organization publishes the journals *Al-Ahmadiyya* and *The Islamic Guardian*.

2.4.2.2 *Hindu organizations* Brahma Kumaris World Spiritual University (Raja Yoga Centre), 98 Tennyson Rd, London NW6, is involved in education and information. It compiles an annual report [QRL.12] for the headquarters in India. This report, which is available on request, includes figures on the number of centres in the UK, teachers, class size and frequency, as well as data on the type and frequency of other activities and the size of attendance.

The Hindu Centre , 39 Grafton Terrace, London NW5 4JA, is a broad-based religious centre involving many different Hindu tendencies; it also organizes educational activity.

The International Society for Krishna Consciousness, Chaitanya College, Groome Court, Severn Stoke, Worcester WR4 9DW, is the centre of the so-called Hare Krisna movement and has an extensive educational and publications programme. It publishes *Mahabarata Times*.

Ramakrishna Vedanta Centre, Bourne End, Bucks. SL8 5LG, runs educational and spiritual programmes. Its annual report [QRL.74] is mainly an account of activities, but it also includes figures on membership and on distribution of its magazine.

World Government and the Age of Enlightenment , Mentmore Towers, Mentmore, Leighton Buzzard, Bucks. LU7 OQH, was founded by the Maharishi Mahesh Yogi and teaches transcendental meditation.

2.4.2.3 *Sikh organizations*

The Sikh Cultural Society of Great Britain , 88 Mollison Way, Edgware, Middlesex, HA8 5QW, seeks to cater to the educational needs of the Sikh community and provides general information on Sikhism. It publishes a journal, *The Sikh Courier*.

The Sikh Educational and Cultural Association , Satnam Cottage, Compton Gardens, Kinver, West Midlands, DY7 6DS, produces information pamphlets on aspects of Sikhism.

Supreme Council of Sikhs in the UK , 162 Great West Rd, Hounslow, Middlesex, is an umbrella organization and will provide information regarding the Sikh communities in the UK.

2.4.2.4 *Other organizations*

The Beshara School of Esoteric Education , Stable Block, Sherborne House, Sherborne, Cheltenham, Glos. GL 54 3DZ, runs courses in contemplation, meditation and study based on the writings of the 12th century Spanish Muslim mystic Ibn 'Arabi.

The Buddhist Society , 58 Eccleston Way, London SW1V 1PH, is engaged in education and information work. The annual report of the president is published in the Society's magazine *The Middle Way*. Although some figures are given, none recur regularly [QRL.17].

The Meditation Society , 158 Holland Park Ave, London W11 4UH, is the parent body of the School of Meditation, established to teach methods of meditation. The Society keeps a register of adult members, and its annual accounts are available for inspection, as are the annual reports of the Principal of the School.

National Spiritual Assembly of the Baha'is of the UK, 27 Rutland Gate, London, SW7 1PD, coordinates and supports the more than 150 local assemblies in the UK. The annual *Supplementary Report* includes data on the number of local Spiritual Assemblies and the number of districts with at least one resident Baha'i.

The Sufi Order in the West , Barton Farm, Pund Lane, Bradford-on-Avon, Wilts, BA15 1LF, is the English branch of an international group with headquarters in Paris. Its background is in the Chisti Sufi order of South Asia. It publishes a quarterly magazine *The Flute*.

CHAPTER 3

AREA AND ETHNIC STUDIES

3.1 National and multi-local

3.1.1

One of the earliest relevant systematic surveys to be carried out was commissioned by the Economist Intelligence Unit and conducted in 1961 by Mass Observation Ltd [QRL.26]. Using a sample of 3000 from eleven different areas of immigrant concentration in England and Scotland, the survey was intended to provide a profile of immigrants from the Commonwealth. The basic category used was nationality, and religious adherence was used only as a supplementary category for Cypriots, Indians and Pakistanis. Among the former, a very small proportion of Muslims are identifiable, while among the latter only Muslims and Hindus are identified.

3.1.2

Social and Community Planning Research (SCPR) have on a number of occasions been commissioned to conduct studies in the field of ethnic minority research. During 1975, a survey into ethnic residential choice was carried out in Bradford, Leicester, Lambeth and Haringey with oral interviews of a sample of 1,674 [QRL.94]. The schedule included questions on religious affiliation and attendance at worship. Although a methodological report has been published [B.22], the results of the survey have not. However, the data are accessible on magnetic tape at the SSRC Data Archive, study no.791.

3.1.3

A PEP survey published in 1976 by David Smith [QRL.93] under the title *The Facts of Racial Disadvantage* was also carried out by SCPR. Its estimate of the relative proportions of Muslims, Hindus and Sikhs among people originating in South Asia (including those from East Africa) has come to be regarded in many circles as authoritative (but see section 3.1.5 below). In addition to this overall estimate, however, the published data also contribute to a statistical description of the social situation of adherents of the three religions in England and Wales. Tables are included analysing aspects of housing conditions, household size and structure, and job levels by Muslim, Hindu and Sikh. Most of the remaining data dealing with immigration, settlement, family, language ability, education, employment, housing and discrimination are analysed in such a way as to distinguish Pakistani (including Bangladeshi) from Indian and African Asian. Since the survey shows 95% of Pakistanis to be Muslims, these data can be used for a more detailed description of at least part of the Muslim community in England and Wales. In addition to the published material, the raw data are also accessible at the SSRC Data Archive, study no.427/428.

3.1.4

A much more recent survey was conducted by SCPR during January-April 1981 for a study on urban institutions being conducted by the SSRC's Research Unit on Ethnic Relations, University of Aston in Birmingham [QRL.79]. The survey covers a sample of 2161 persons of all ethnic backgrounds selected from inner and outer parts of Birmingham, and from Coventry and Wolverhampton. The schedule included a question on religious identity covering Christian denominations and Judaism as well as Islam, Hinduism and Sikhism. Another question sought information on attendance at religious worship. No results of this survey have as yet been published, but one aspect of the project is specifically the religious perspective. When completed the data will be accessible in the SSRC Data Archive.

3.1.5

An attempt to develop more accurate estimates of the relative strengths of Islam, Hinduism and Sikhism among South Asians in Britain has been carried out by the SSRC-sponsored Community Religions Project based at the University of Leeds. In a first exercise, unpublished, Knott and Toon [B.14] had amended 1971 census figures (see sect.2.1.2 above), brought them up to 1977 by using statistics on births, deaths and migration. The results were distributed among the three religions according to Smith's percentages (sect.3.1.3 above). These figures were subsequently refined [B.13] by taking into account data on parents' place of birth and Smith's tables on areas of residence prior to migration to Britain. In consequence, the authors are able both significantly to adjust Smith's proportions of the three religions and to analyse them by several regional ethnic subdivisions. The two stages have been brought together in published form [QRL.57].

3.1.6

Other published material suggesting national totals for membership of the three religions under discussion is not uncommon, but as the major part merely reproduces estimates unsystematically based on census data or repeats figures given by representatives of the communities themselves, they will be ignored here. Even such comparatively sound works as Gay's *The geography of religion in England* [B.9] or the more recent *World Christian Encyclopaedia* [QRL.7], although apparently more accurate than most similar sources, can only give rough estimates in this area.

3.1.7

The *UK Christian Handbook* 1983 Edition [QRL.13], a new combined edition of previously separately published volumes, includes in its statistical section estimates of the numbers of members, ministers and buildings for 1975 and 1980 of the main religions under discussion. The figures are analysed by individual country in the UK, and a supplementary table indicating annual rates of change (presumably between 1975 and 1980), and worship attendance rates are included. Most of the figures are estimates obtained by contacting community representatives. The Buddhist figures, however, are the result of a postal inquiry conducted by the Bible Society in cooperation with the Buddhist Society and the Central Statistical Office.

3.2 Single localities and ethnic groups

3.2.1

Statistical data and published material, in which the primary perspective is that of a particular ethnic group or locality in the United Kingdom, may occasionally yield some useful information relevant to the researcher whose starting point is religious identification. It is, however, to be hoped that not too many readers will repeat the approach of Richmond [B.20], who amalgamates West Indians and Asians into a single unanalysable group and then proceeds to ask, "Are you a member of a religious group?" without further differentiating among the various religions. At the other extreme is the survey by Bristow, Adams and Pereira [QRL.14] of one definable migrant group, namely the Ugandan Asians, which is analysed by age, religion, education and family origin. In fact, the vast majority of such studies have selected a locality as the primary focus.

3.2.2

The Community Relations Councils can be a source of information on the distribution of religions within their areas (see sect.2.4.1 above). In some cases, they have produced reports which provide such data, although the figures given vary in their reliability, since it is often not clear whether they are extrapolated from 1971 census figures, statements by community representatives, or the results of independent assessments. The experience of Knott with regard to Leeds ([QRL.56], see sect.3.2.4 below) is salutary. Thus, it would appear, for example, that Jabbal's estimates for 1979 of Hindus, Sikhs and Bengalis and Pakistanis in Nottingham [QRL.47], have been drawn from an estimate based on the 1971 census. On the other hand, the Tayside CRC has produced locally researched estimates of the number of families of Indian subcontinent background [QRL.97]. It has been assumed that Pakistanis and Bangladeshis are Muslim, but the Indians have been distinguished by Hindu and Sikh. The Hawkins study of Pakistanis in Bradford [QRL.35] accounts for Muslims, Hindus and Sikhs, but it is unlikely that figures relating to non-Pakistanis are much more than a compromise between 1971 extrapolations and the statements of community representatives.

3.2.3

A small number of local studies do exist which have a sound statistical base or provide numerical data regarding the minority religious groups. Muhammad Anwar's study of Rochdale Pakistani society [QRL.5] includes information regarding the level of attendance and staffing at six centres of Muslim teaching during 1975. For the same year, Hahlo has researched the Gujarati community of Bolton [QRL.33]. On a sample of 258, he has examined the correlation between religion (Muslim or Hindu) and length of residence, age structure, and occupation. A much larger base has been utilized by Robinson in studying the residential patterns in Blackburn [QRL.86]. A selection of 1,693 households was chosen from the electoral registers and identified as Muslim, Hindu or Sikh by reference to their names. This was supplemented by in-depth interviewing of a sample of 364 households. Conclusions are drawn as regards patterns of residence and degrees of separation among the various groups. A recent study by Sims [QRL.90] has compared these conclusions with those suggested by performing a similar exercise with data from Manchester and Birmingham. He concludes that spatial separation is as much a function of the relative sizes of communities and of immigration patterns as of religion. What may be the pattern in Blackburn does not necessarily apply in Manchester or Birmingham. The problems associated with identifying religion or ethnicity by names in electoral or rates registers are discussed by Smith in a Linguistic Minorities Project Working Paper [B.24].

3.2.4

In 1971 the Yorkshire Committee for Community Relations published a report covering the whole county [QRL.101]. The information was provided by the local Community Relations Officers and is very uneven, making internal comparisons difficult. Estimates of the number of Gujarati Muslims are included for Batley and Dewsbury. The Community Religions Project has surveyed the electoral register of Leeds for 1979 and produced a significantly different assessment of the numbers of Hindus and Sikhs from that offered by the local Council for Community Relations [QRL.56]. Saifullah Khan's study of Mirpuris in Bradford [QRL.89] includes 1972-73 estimates of the overall number of Pakistanis, as well as the Mirpuri component, in the city. A survey of the Muslim Asians in Batley was conducted in 1973 by McGrath [QRL.60]. However, out of the initial sample of 850 households, only 54 were Asian immigrants. This search was supplemented by a survey of one in seven immigrant households carried out with the help of the local Muslim Welfare Society. The results include data on age structure, educational background and the nature and conditions of employment.

3.2.5

Communities in the Midlands are among the best researched from the point of view also of religion. Some of the published material is like Jenkins'study of Leamington Spa [QRL.51], which reproduces locally estimated totals of the Sikh community relative to all South Asians in the city in 1970. The main emphasis of the study is on employment, housing, social conditions and education. Incidental information of secondary value covering parts of Birmingham is provided in a collection of short articles edited by Tiptaft [B.25], which includes some population estimates and notes on the construction of religious buildings. In a historical study of religion in Handsworth, Nelson [QRL.62] lists the number of religious organizations based in the area in 1974-5, including Hindu, Sikh, and Muslim.

3.2.6

Several surveys of primary value have also been carried out in Birmingham. The earliest major survey is that of Rex and Moore [QRL.80] relating to Sparkbrook in 1964. Out of a sample of 800, 39 were Pakistani Muslims, regarding whom data is presented on attendance at prayer and festivals. An overall figure for the Sikh population is also given. This 1964 sample of Muslims is, of course, too small to give much more than an indication of the situation during an early stage in the appearance of a Muslim community in Birmingham. Ten years later, it was possible for a survey of Small Heath, conducted by SCPR, to find a more useful data base [QRL.61]. Over 1500 New Commonwealth adults are analysed by nationality and religion, including Muslims, Hindus and Sikhs. In the published form, however, data is presented in an almost useless form. One table presents religion by nationality, but nationality (in fact, place of birth) is only analysed by West Indian and Asian. In a further table, worship attendance is analysed by the same nationalities but not by religion. Under the auspices of RUER, Rex returned to Birmingham in 1976 with a detailed quota sample of 900 heads of household, consisting of equal members of whites, Asians and West Indians selected from 128 enumeration districts in Handsworth, supplemented by 200 Newtown council tenants equally divided between black and white. Rex and Tomlinson [QRL.81] were primarily concerned with housing, social and economic conditions and published only an analysis of religious affiliation by West India, Asian and white British. Utilizing the same data, Ratcliffe [QRL.75] includes a chapter on "Religion, culture and spatial patterns" in which religion figures prominently. The chapter includes analyses by religion of country of origin, frequency of worship attendance both by religion and ethnic group, and the spatial distribution of Asians by ward and by religion. Using electoral registers and 1971 census data, Phillips has produced estimates of the ethnic composition of the Asian population of Leicester for 1978 [QRL.73]. The data has been converted into maps showing the distribution of Muslim, Sikh and Hindu households preparatory to a consideration of patterns and ratios of segregation and dispersal. The debate between Sims and Robinson regarding the conclusions to be drawn from such material (Sect.3.2.3 above) should be kept in mind here.

3.2.7

For the south west, one study is of secondary interest, namely that by Jeffery on Pakistanis in Bristol [QRL.50]. Her overall figures are based on the 1961 and 1966 censuses, which she realizes are unreliable by the time her research was conducted in 1971-72. She offers estimates, based on conversations with informants, on the numbers of Muslim and Christian Pakistanis in Bristol.

3.2.8

There is only little material covering the south east. Alavi's estimate of the percentage of Pakistani Muslims observing Ramadan in the early 1960's [QRL.3] is not based on detailed research. Israel's study of Slough in 1962 [QRL.46] includes survey results in which Hindus, Sikh, and Muslims as well as Christians are tabulated. Since most of the questions are analysed by country of origin, and the sample is a mere 165, the results are of only limited use. For 1969, Brown [QRL.16] provides estimates of the sizes of religious communities in Bedford, including Sikhs and Muslims. Ladbury's work [QRL.58] on the traditionally Muslim Turkish Cypriots in London includes population figures and historical immigration statistics. Bhatti's later article [QRL.9] is to a great extent based on the former, but he includes also more recent information from Turkish Cypriot representatives on the total population, the numbers of professional people, mosque attendance and Islamic classes for children. The 1981 CARAF report of the black community in Southall [QRL.19] includes historical and present estimates of the Sikh population.

CHAPTER 4

SINGLE RELIGIONS

4.1 Muslims

4.1.1

Reliable estimates of the total Muslim population of the United Kingdom are difficult to come by. Statements by officials of Muslim organizations often suggest 1.5 million and occasionally even two million. Reasoned estimates suggest a much lower total. Ahmad's figure of one million for 1975 [QRL.2] claims to be based on Smith's percentages of relative community size among South Asians and on a questionnaire circulated to Muslim organizations by the Islamic Foundation, Leicester. Nielsen's attempt to produce up-to-date estimates of the size of European Muslim communities [QRL.63] suffers from being based mainly on extrapolations from 1971 census. Ally's study of Muslims in Britain [QRL.4] well illustrates the problem with his reference to a number of wildly varying figures given by different sources, one of which is as low as 499 000 for 1975. This same study, however, discusses not only the total size of the community but also gives numbers of mosques and centres of religious instruction. The reliability of these figures is, however, open to some question since, for example, his 1978 estimate of the numbers of mosques registered for the solemnization of marriage bears no relationship to that given by the OPCS (sect.2.3.3 above). His information on the construction history and costs, as well as the funding sources, of some of Britain's main mosques is much more reliable.

4.1.2

During 1972-73, Ritchie conducted surveys of the Muslim communities in Glasgow, South Shields, Bradford, and Birmingham [QRL.82], [QRL.83], [QRL.84] and [QRL.85]. These reports are impressionistic and based on information gathered during a 4-6 day visit in each city. Consequently, there is hardly any useful statistical data, and what there is is secondary in nature. Thus estimates for the total populations are given for Glasgow and Birmingham, and estimates of attendance at single mosques are given for South Shields and Bradford. The report on South Shields also includes information on the costs of the Azheri mosque.

4.1.3

Two more detailed studies of particular Muslim communities are useful, since they include reasonably reliable figures on aspects of religious activity. Harrison and Shepherd's handbook on Islam in Preston [QRL.34] has 1975 and 1979 estimates of the total Muslim population and their countries of origin, which are not solely dependent on the 1971 census. The handbook includes also details of the Preston mosques, costs of purchase or construction and maintenance, and average attendance. Where there are mosque schools, information is given regarding the tuition fees and also the income from almsgiving (zakat). The other study is by Gibson on Birmingham [QRL.31]. A more individual study based on personal interviews and visits, the author quotes local figures for the city estimated from the 1971 census and compared to the 1974 figures given by the Pakistani, Bangladeshi and Yemeni diplomatic representative. She includes material on attendance at Friday noon prayers at Birmingham University and the Central Mosque, as well as attendance at several mosque schools. Her details on the cost of constructing the Central Mosque bring up to date earlier estimates given by the mosque itself [QRL.10].

4.2 Hindus

4.2.1

There is only limited relevant source material on Hindus in the United Kingdom. In a study such as that on Gujaratis by Tambs-Lyche [QRL.95] the emphasis is totally that of the social anthropologist, and the fact that the Gujarati Patidars can be identified as Hindu is of no immediate significance. His 1970 figures for the sizes of the Patidar communities of Coventry and Rugby are estimates based on local informants. Hawkin's description of Hinduism in Bradford [B.10], while it does include a good deal of general information, does not give any figures at all.

4.2.2

The Community Religions Project at Leeds University has led to two useful sources on Hinduism. Bowen has edited a collection of information seeking to cover most of England [QRL.11]. Besides a general introduction on Hinduism, the book includes information about the worship and educational attendance at named Hindu centres in Bradford, Huddersfield and Coventry. Building cost estimates are given for a temple in Bradford and in Coventry. For the latter there is also statistical information on the numbers of families belonging to each of the main castes. In another paper, Knott [QRL.56] provides sound statistical data regarding the Hindu population of Leeds based on the October 1979 draft electoral register. She provides figures enabling an analysis by regional origin, by caste and by organized structures.

4.3 Sikhs

4.3.1

Source material on Sikhs in the United Kingdom is more readily available, but it is usually of a general nature with only the odd cases of statistical information. Desai's book on Indian immigrants in Britain [QRL.25] includes a few late 1950's estimates of Indian immigrants by area of origin. In discussing associations Desai does, however, include some early (1957) figures on purchase cost, membership fees and worship attendance at the Guru Nanak Gurdwara, Smethwick. Discussing Sikh children, James [QRL.48] includes 1964 and 1969 estimates of the Sikh population of Huddersfield. Unfortunately, two recent thorough studies on Sikhism in Britain do not include much statistical data. Helweg [QRL.36] has some detailed information on the Gravesend gurdwara and gives figures on the number of Indians living outside India, without clarifying how many might be Sikhs. Cole and Sambhi [QRL.22] give only estimates of the total Sikh population and of the number of gurdwaras with their distribution between England, Wales and Scotland.

4.3.2
Two recent studies on Sikhs include useful statistical data. Ramindar Singh's study of Sikhs in Bradford [QRL.91] is based on a search through the 1977-78 electoral register. With this raw material an overall total is reached and analysed by ward relative to the overall Asian population. The subsequently gathered survey data are also analysed by domestic circumstances, length of stay, employment, education, and linguistic ability. The study includes information on the purchase or construction costs of Bradford gurdwaras as well as worship and educational attendance levels. The other study is that by Ghuman on the Bhattra Sikhs of Cardiff [QRL.30]. Besides giving the 1979 total Sikh population, he presents the results of interviews with one third of the Bhattra Sikh households. The study seeks to quantify language proficiency and the levels of acculturation and cultural affinity. One weakness of this study is that the collection and interviewing has been carried out in cooperation with the leaders of the community.

4.3.3
In addition to other sources, the book by Janjua [QRL.49] is useful. Each gurdwara in Britain is listed with a description of its history, construction or purchase costs and of its activities. Each entry also lists the names of the management committee. OPCS figures [QRL.71], *The Official List* [B.16] and Janjua's collection generally corroborate each other.

4.4 Buddhists

The Buddhist Society (see sect.2.4.2.4 above) has published two works which provide some useful data. *Sixty Years of Buddhism in England* [B.4] is primarily a history and includes estimates of historical figures. *The Buddhist Directory* [B.3] lists individuals and local and regional organizations.

4.5 Zoroastrians

Most of this community are Parsis from India but in recent years have come to include also people from Iran and East Africa. A study by Hinnells [QRL.37] surveys the history of particularly Parsi settlement in Britain and of its main organizing body, the Zoroastrian Association. The main part of the paper is a summary of a 1976 survey carried out by the author for that Association and the Open University. The data describe the community under four headings: 1) a profile of the Association's membership in terms of regional distribution, sex and age distribution and educational standards; 2) extent of community solidarity; 3) the religious practices, especially with reference to frequency of worship and the language used in prayer; and 4) religious beliefs. The questionnaire for the survey was initially sent to names on the mailing list of the Zoroastrian Association, and the final response represented between 8% and 16% of the community in the UK, depending on estimates of its total size. The author is confident from the nature of the response that the method of sampling has not introduced an excessive bias into the results. A fuller study of the survey is promised. Mehta [B.15] has published the results of interviews conducted in 1979 and 1980 and compared them with Hinnell's survey, although there are no new statistical data.

CHAPTER 5

SINGLE ISSUES

5.1 Marriage

5.1.1
Only a few studies of ethnic minority marriage patterns include data analysed by religious affiliation. Jones and Shah [QRL.53] have conducted a useful study of cases in which one party has entered the UK from the Indian subcontinent to marry a UK resident. The study is based on a random sample encompassing 25% of all landing cards completed by citizens of India, Pakistan and Bangladesh entering for marriage during the period October 1978-January 1979 - 404 entrants in all. Religion is identified by reference to name, father's name, nationality and script. The data is utilized to provide an analysis by religion, area of origin and destination, sex and age. Origin and destination in the UK of the arriving fiance(e) are analysed by religion, and this is also correlated with the religion of the UK resident fiance(e).

5.1.2
In a study conducted in the mid-1960's, Kannan has investigated interracial marriages in London [QRL.55]. The author traced 100 couples through personal contacts. The resulting data are analysed by the religion of the parties. In addition, tables analyse the woman's response to the man's proposal of marriage and the response of both parties' parents by religion. A further table analyses the religion of the parties by the form of solemnization of the marriage. Kannan's book is primarily of historical interest, since the nature of the sample and the topic itself preclude valid generalizations.

5.1.3
A team of students has studied family planning in Haringey over a period of eight years [QRL.21]. The 1,297 cards included information on the ethnic origin and religion of the women referred. Only a very small group are not Christian, and the analysis by ethnic and religion includes a few Muslims and Hindus. Most of the further discussion concentrates on indigenous Roman Catholics, but one set of tables also analyses the 22 Muslim Turkish Cypriots by social class and conditions and by resort to sterilization. The figures are too small to be more than interesting, especially since they are not compared to the ethnic and religious composition of the total potential population.

5.2 School and youth

5.2.1

Research on issues connected with education is usually based on broad definitions of ethnic identity. However, an early Youth Development Trust survey of the November 1965 coloured population in Manchester's schools [QRL.102] does divide Indians into Sikhs and others. Townsend's study of the response of education authorities to the presence of immigrant pupils [QRL.98] includes figures on the number of local education authorities which have been approached by Muslim or Sikh bodies on questions of school uniform and physical education, or which have been requested to allow provision of Muslim or Sikh religious instruction in schools.

5.2.2

An unusual and very detailed survey of the leisure needs of 8-14 year old Asian boys in Slough has been carried out by Livingstone for The Scout Association [QRL.59]. The survey sample of 423 consists of Asian boys in picked classes at selected schools in Slough. They were asked to complete a wide-ranging questionnaire to discover what they currently did with their spare time, what they would like to do, their reasons for being satisfied or dissatisfied with existing facilities, and their image of scouting. One chapter of the report analyses the responses to all questions by religion.

5.2.3

Several surveys have investigated the attitudes of young people to the culture and society of their country of origin and to their own situation in Britain. An early survey by Taylor [QRL.96] questioned 67 Asians who had left school in Newcastle-upon-Tyne during 1962-67. The resulting report includes an analysis by religion of levels of and reasons for religious adherence, frequency of worship attendance and adherence to dietary rules, as well as the frequency of interreligious friendships.

5.2.4

The Community Relations Commission in 1976 published the results of a major survey of cultural attitudes among young Asians [QRL.23]. Commissioned from the Opinion Research Centre, the survey questioned 1117 Asian youth and 944 Asian parents in nine different locations in England and Scotland. An analysis by religion is given of children's and parents' perceptions of the effects of attendance at British schools. Specific reference is made to Christian assemblies, girls' preference for western dress and to single-sex education. Preference in social mixing and marriage patterns, as well as attitudes to Asian women in employment are analysed in the same manner. Most answers are also analysed by parent/youth. Muhammad Anwar, who was responsible for the survey, has since extracted the Muslim data and published it separately with additional comments [B.2].

R-T

5.2.5

A small sample of 176, including 28 of mixed race marriage, is the base for Kannan's study of the cultural adaptation of Asian immigrants [QRL.54]. The chapter on religion seeks to assess the extent of involvement in or deviation from traditional forms of religious practice with particular attention being paid to the children of mixed race marriage. The sample is claimed to be random, but the high proportion of children of mixed race marriages suggests a link to the author's earlier study on such marriages (see sect.5.1.2 above), where personal contacts had determined the sample.

5.3 The elderly

A unique study has been conducted by the Birmingham-based All Faiths for One Race (AFFOR) on the conditions and attitudes of the elderly among the ethnic minorities [QRL.1]. Four hundred elderly from among the Asian, Afro-Caribbean and European population in four inner wards of Birmingham were interviewed. The lower age limits used were 65 years from men and 60 for women. No direct question on religious adherence was asked, and the data as presented is analysed by the three main ethnic groupings mentioned. The data include information on attendance at places of worship and attitudes to religious officials and institutions providing social services. Since the question on worship attendance codes church, mosque, temple and gurdwara separately, this would be a basis on which to attempt an analysis of the raw data by religion. The completed questionnaires are accessible at AFFOR, 173 Lozells Rd. Lozells, Birmingham B19 1 RN.

5.4 Language

5.4.1

Hardly any linguistic research includes an analysis by religion. The Linguistic Minorities Project, based at the University of London Institute of Education, has not as yet published the results of its work. The Project is currently working on four distinct surveys, of which three include questions on religion. The Adult Language Use Survey includes questions on religious adherence, perceived personal importance of religion and participation in the activities of religious groups. The Secondary Pupils Survey, using a questionnaire which is designed as a useful teaching aid, seeks information on whether language classes include religious content, are given in religious centres, as well as the basic question on religious adherence. *The Mother Tongue Teaching Directory* will include information on languages taught for religious purposes. The Project is concerned with all linguistic and ethnic minorities and so includes Judaism and Christian denominations as well as Islam, Hinduism, Sikhism and Buddhism.

5.4.2

A recent study of 67 5-17 year-old children in Oxford by Johnstone [QRL.52] concentrates on language use. The data includes information on the numbers of children in the process of learning to read the Qur'an, as well as whether they are learning at home or at a mosque school.

5.5 Planning permission

Two studies of the problems of acquiring planning permission for religious buildings in Birmingham have been carried out. A short one by Hodgins [QRL.38] includes information on the number of mosques in the city. A more detailed study by Grudzinska [QRL.32] analyses the number of mosques and Sikh and Hindu temples in Birmingham by the nature of the building and its legal status under the Town and Country Planning Act 1971. She also includes a detailed tabulation of the planning history of all Muslim, Sikh and Hindu places of worship which have had contacts with the planning authorities.

5.6 Employment

A team of researchers at the University of Glasgow has investigated the employment prospects of male school leavers [QRL.27]. The sample of 54 Asian boys and 56 white boys was interviewed on leaving school in 1972 and again in mid-July 1973. The published report provides an analysing of the group by religion, but the remaining data is not thus analysed. However, the material is accessible in the SSRC Data Archive, study no.663.

5.7 Retailing

5.7.1

A study of ethnic minority shopping patterns in Bradford has been undertaken by the National Consumer Council in early 1982 [QRL.92]. The South Asian part of the sample is analysed by Pakistani, Indian Punjabi, Gujarati and Bangladeshi with no reference to religion. However, the responses given for preferring ethnic shops include the availability of Halal meat. This can be used as a guide to the Muslim element in the sample and also, if correlated with the sample base of Pakistanis and Bangladeshis, as an indication of the level of Muslim insistence on Halal meat. But the tables can not be more than a guide in this respect, as the Bangladeshi sample of thirty is, by the author's own admission, low enough to warrant caution.

5.7.2

A survey of Asian retailers in the Foleshill area of Coventry was conducted in the autumn of 1980 by Robinson and Flintoff [QRL.87]. The sample of forty businesses interviewed represents less than 50% of those in the area covered, and when analysed by religion gives a very low base, especially with only six Muslims. Despite this hesitation, the authors conclude from observations made generally during field work that the statistical data are valid. The study includes information on the retailers' occupation prior to migration, the type and number of shops owned, opening hours, identity of staff and customers as well as language most commonly used.

5.8 Broadcasting

Among the studies carried out by the Commission for Racial Equality in recent years is one by Anwar [QRL.6] on the listening and viewing habits and desires of Asians. The survey was carried out in Leicester in the summer of 1977 with a sample of 1192 Asians. Questions were limited to the programmes of the BBC. As in so many other surveys, a question on religious adherence was included, but the results are nowhere in the published version analysed by religion.

5.9 Interfaith attitudes

There are two studies on the mutual attitudes of minority religions and Christianity, both, as it happens, relating to Muslims. In 1966 Butterworth [QRL.18] surveyed the attitudes of Christian clergy and lay people in Bradford towards the Muslims living in their vicinity. A much more recent survey by Bhai [QRL.8] suffers from serious weaknesses in sampling. The result of interviewing one hundred mainly educated Muslims in the Birmingham area, selected by personal contacts, it does all the same remain of interest. The sample has been analysed by age, sex, duration of residence, occupation and the religious identity of neighbours. These factors have been correlated with attitudes to and knowledge of Christian belief, worship and life style, as well as with images held of Christians' motivation for social involvement and cooperation with Muslims. Perceptions of common ground between Islam and Christianity are also analysed.

CHAPTER 6

POSTSCRIPT

6.1

Two factors combine to explain the scarcity of useful statistical material relating to religions other than Judaism and Christianity in the UK. One is the general reluctance on the part of government departments to take account of religious affiliation, which is reflected particularly in the census, but also, for example, in the lack of religious statistics from the Health Service. The other factor is the very novelty of the presence of these religions. British society and institutions have not yet seriously taken account of their existence, nor have these religious communities yet defined their place and function. Only when that has been achieved is there likely to develop a felt need for statistical information.

6.2

The point at which public debate has most conspicuously considered these religions in statistics has been in the experiment prior to the 1981 census (sect.2.1.4 above). The frame of reference was clearly a desire to get more direct data on ethnic minorities, and the question on religious affiliation was included merely to refine the large South Asian category. The concern with ethnic minorities opened the question to accusations of racism, and this ultimately contributed to its omission. The context of the supplementary question on religion would, in any case, have made the results most unsatisfactory, if not almost useless, to those concerned with statistics on religion. The main deficiency would have been the failure to distinguish between Muslim and Christian among the Arab and African categories. The conclusion must be that the only satisfactory way of dealing with religion in the census is to include a question on religious affiliation. The fact that it has been a regular feature of the Northern Ireland census suggests that it is quite feasible, especially if it is done on the basis of self-description. Whether such a question is desirable is a different debate, in which the assumption must be that since the churches are, on the whole, able to cater for their own needs in this regard, and the government does not seem interested in a religious census for its own sake, it should be these minority religious communities themselves which should decide.

6.3

The social survey type of material, which accounts for most of this review, is associated with a different set of problems but also with as yet unexplored opportunities. In only a few instances, such as the CRC study of young Asians' cultural attitudes [QRL.23], is religious affiliation a primary frame of reference. In most instances, it is merely part of the general description of a sample population. In virtually all these instances, however, religion has been included as a question, and it is only in the published reports that the bulk of the data collected has not been analysed by religion. The data in several of these surveys remains accessible, either in the SSRC Data Archive at the University of Essex or with the authors. There are possible advantages in utilizing such data in an analysis by religion. The relationship between religion and behaviour has not been a primary concern, and one might therefore expect responses free of a desire to conform to perceived religious ideals, which might not be the case with a survey explicitly aimed at relating religion to behaviour and attitudes. A further advantage might be that such an analysis of existing data could take us a step nearer to determining the extent to which such a relationship exists.

6.4

It is unfortunate that most of the relevant religious organizations do not publish statistical data with any degree of regularity. It is, however, understandable. Generally speaking, the institutional structures of the religious communities in question are still very fluid. Many are based only partly in the communities they seek to serve and retain strong links with structures in the countries of origin. Many Muslim organizations additionally cultivate various types of connections with actual or potential sponsors in the Middle East. It is not to be expected that religious organizations in such circumstances will divulge reliable information regarding membership or finances, either to their own communities or to the public at large. On the other hand, it is to be expected that once they have established themselves securely and have defined their functions in ways perceived to be relevant and related to their communities in this country, such organzations will begin to gather and publish useful statistical information. They will need to do so, both so as to enable them to perform their chosen functions satisfactorily and in response to the need to be accountable to their constituencies.

QUICK REFERENCE LIST - TABLE OF CONTENTS

QUICK REFERENCE LIST

Type of data	Breakdown	Area	Frequency	QRL Publication	Text Reference and Remarks
General Topics					
Census Data					
Country of birth	Population totals	England and Wales by district	Decennial; 1966	[QRL.28] [QRL.29] [QRL.66] [QRL.68]	2.1.1
Country of birth of parents	Population totals	England and Wales by district	1971	[QRL.66]	2.1.1
Household composition	Country of birth of head of household, economic supporter, wife, and parents; occupation; date of immigration	England and Wales	1971	[QRL.67]	2.1.1
Country of birth	Population totals	Scotland by district	Decennial till 1971	[QRL.77]	2.1.5
Usual residence	Country of birth, of parents' birth	Scotland	1971	[QRL.78]	2.1.5
Country of birth	Population totals by sex, age, marital status, and birthplace of head of household	GB, standard regions, metropolitan counties, GLC	1981	[QRL.68]	2.1.4
Country of birth	Ethnic origin	GB	1951, 1961, 1966	[QRL.88]	2.1.2
Population movements					
Commonwealth arrivals	Nationality; type of entry	UK	Annual 1963-72	[QRL.39]	2.2.3
Foreign arrivals and departures	Nationality; type of entry	UK	Annual 1967-72	[QRL.43]	2.2.3
All arrivals	Nationality; type of entry	UK	Annual 1973 onwards	[QRL.40] [QRL.41]	2.2.3
Immigration and emigration	Last, future country of residence; country of birth by sex; citizenship	England and Wales	Annual	[QRL.72] [QRL.69]	2.2.2

Persons acquiring UK citizenship	Previous nationality; method of acquisition		Annual	[QRL.44] [QRL.45]	2.2.3
Overseas students in public and private higher education	Country of origin	UK	Annual from 1956	[QRL.15]	2.2.5
Overseas students in public sector higher education	Country of origin	England and Wales till 1977, England 1978-	Annual	[QRL.24]	2.2.5
Social profiles					
Live births	NCWP birth place of mother; NCWP origin of parents; usual residence of mother	England and Wales by metropolitan counties, GLC, and other districts with more than 10% foreign live births	Annual	[QRL.72] [QRL.65]	2.2.2
Economically active persons aged 16+	Country of birth	GB	Biennial from 1973	[QRL.70]	2.2.4 regionally weighted sample of 105000 extrapolated to total population
Unemployment rates	Country of birth	GB	Biennial from 1973	[QRL.70]	2.2.4 (cf.previous remark)
Economic activity of persons aged 16+	Sex; ethnic origin	GB	1979, 1981, 1983	[QRL.70]	2.2.4 (cf.previous remark)
Country of birth and ethnic origin	Sex; residence	GB by standard region	1979, 1981, 1983	[QRL.70]	2.2.4 (cf.previous remark)
Population aged under 15	Ethnic origin, country of birth of head of household	GB	1979, 1981, 1983	[QRL.70]	2.2.4 (cf.previous remark)
Local data					
NCW communities	Country of origin	Yorks. urban districts	June 1971	[QRL.101]	3.2.4
Pakistani community	District of origin	Bradford	1972-3	[QRL.89]	3.2.4

R-T*

Type of data	Breakdown	Area	Frequency	QRL Publication	Text Reference and Remarks
Ethnic minority elderly worship attendance and attitudes to social welfare	Asian, Afro-Caribbean, European	Inner Birmingham	Sept-Nov. 1979	[QRL.1]	5.3
Several Religions Specified					
Population estimates					
Numbers, growth and projections of population	Bahai, Buddhist Hindu, Muslim, Sikh	UK	1980	[QRL.7]	3.1.6
Membership, ministers and buildings	Ahmadi, Buddhist, Hindu, Jew, Krishna, Muslim, School of Meditation, Sikh	UK by country	1975, 1980	[QRL.13]	3.1.7
South Asian population	Country of birth; ethnicity; religion by Hindu, Muslim, Sikh	GB	1971, 1977	[QRL.57]	3.1.5
NCWP immigrants	Christian, Hindu, Muslim, Sikh	England and Wales	July-Oct. 1974	[QRL.93]	3.1.3
Religious adherence	Sex; incl. Bahai, Buddhist, Hindu, Muslim, Sikh	Northern Ireland	Decennial	[QRL.64]	2.1.6
Community membership	Hindu, Sikh, Pakistani/Bangladeshi	Nottingham	n.a.	[QRL.47]	3.2.2
Community membership	Hindu, Muslim, Sikh	Bradford	n.a.	[QRL.35]	3.2.2
Numbers of families	Hindu, Muslim, Sikh	Tayside	n.a.	[QRL.97]	3.2.2
Community membership	Muslim, Sikh	Bedford	1969	[QRL.16]	3.2.8
Commonwealth immigrants	Nationality; Cypriots by Christian, Muslim; Indians, Pakistanis by Hindu, Muslim	England and Scotland	1961	[QRL.26]	3.1.1
Community membership	Incl. Hindu, Muslim, Sikh	Slough	1962	[QRL.46]	3.2.8
Religious adherence and practice					
Degree of adherence to traditional practice	Buddhist, Christian, Hindu, Muslim, Sikh	London	n.a.	[QRL.54]	5.2.5
Worship attendance	West Indian, Asian by Christian, Hindu, Muslim, Sikh	Small Heath, Birmingham	Feb-May 1974	[QRL.61]	3.2.6

Worship attendance	Country of origin; Asians by Hindu, Muslim, Sikh	Handsworth, Newtown (Birmingham) by ward, enumeration district	1976	[QRL.75]	3.2.6
Religious affiliation	West Indian, Asian, white by Christian, Hindu, Muslim, Sikh	ditto	1976	[QRL.81]	3.2.6
Worship attendance	Incl. Hindu, Muslim, Sikh	West Midlands	Jan-April 1981	[QRL.79]	3.1.4
Residential distribution					
Distribution of Asian households	Hindu, Muslim, Sikh	Leicester by ward, enumeration district	1978	[QRL.73]	3.2.6
Distribution of Asian households	Hindu, Muslim, Sikh	Blackburn by ward, enumeration district	1977	[QRL.86]	3.2.3
Distribution of Asian households	Hindu, Muslim, Sikh	Manchester, Birmingham	1971-76	[QRL.90]	3.2.3
Residential distribution by worship attendance	Hindu, Muslim, Sikh	Bradford, Haringey, Lambeth, Leicester	1975	[QRL.94]	3.1.2
Organizations and buildings					
Buildings registered for worship	Muslim, Sikh, other	England and Wales by standard region and metropolitan county	Annual from 1975	[QRL.71]	2.3.3

Type of data	Breakdown	Area	Frequency	QRL Publication	Text Reference and Remarks
Buildings authorized for marriage	Muslim, Sikh, other	England and Wales by standard region and metropolitan county	Annual from 1975	[QRL.71]	2.3.3
Organizations listed Planning permission	Christian, Hindu, Muslim, Sikh Hindu, Muslim, Sikh	Handsworth Birmingham	1974-5 1981	[QRL.62] [QRL.32]	3.2.5 5.5
Government institutions					
Education authorities approached regarding concessions for religious groups	Muslim, Sikh	England	Until 1970	[QRL.98]	5.2.1
Royal Navy and Royal Marines personnel	Buddhist, Hindu, Muslim, Sikh	UK and Far East	Quinquennial from 1971	Ministry of Defence	2.3.6
Army personnel	'Other'	UK	Annual since 1975	ditto	2.3.6
Royal Air Force personnel	Buddhist, Hindu, Muslim, Sikh	UK	1963, 1969, 1971, 1974, annual from 1977	ditto	2.3.6
Inmates of Prison Dept. establishments	Incl. Buddhist, Hindu, Muslim, Sikh	England and Wales	Annual from 1970	[QRL.42]	2.3.5
Economic and social surveys					
Asian household size and structure	Hindu, Muslim, Sikh	England and Wales	July-Oct. 1974	[QRL.93]	3.1.3
Asian households: types of occupancy	Hindu, Muslim, Sikh	England and Wales	July-Oct.1974	[QRL.93]	3.1.3
Asian employment patterns	Hindu, Muslim, Sikh	England and Wales	July-Oct. 1974	[QRL.93]	3.1.3

Description	Details	Location	Date	Reference	Section
Asian women in trades unions	Hindu, Muslim, Sikh	England and Wales	July-Oct. 1974	[QRL.93]	3.1.3
Gujaratis' length of residence, age, and occupation	Hindu, Muslim	Bolton	1975-76	[QRL.33]	3.2.3
Ugandan Asians' origin, age, education and occupation	Hindu, Ismaili Muslim, other Muslim, Sikh, Goan	GB, Canada, India	1973	[QRL.14]	3.2.1
Female clients of family planning service	Incl. Hindu, Muslim	Haringey	1968-76	[QRL.21]	5.1.3
Asian retailers'family and ethnic background, type of shop and ownership, staff and customers' language	Hindu, Muslim, Sikh	Coventry Foleshill	Aug-Sept.1980	[QRL.87]	5.7.2
Asians'viewing and listening habits	Hindu, Muslim, Sikh	Leicester	May-July 1977	[QRL.6]	5.8
Marriage					
Manner of solemnization	Incl. Muslim, Sikh	Scotland	Annual since 1978	[QRL.76]	2.3.4
Manner of solemnization by prior marital status	Muslim, Sikh, other	England and Wales	Annual since 1969	OPCS	2.3.3
Fiance(e)s entering for marriage	Hindu, Muslim, Sikh; origin/destination by UK resident fiance(e)	UK	Oct.1978-Jan.1979	[QRL.53]	5.1.1
Interracial marriages	Response of woman, of parents, form of solemnization by Hindu, Muslim, Parsi, Sikh	London	Mid-1960's	[QRL.55]	5.1.2
Youth					
Religious adherence and practice	Hindu, Muslim, Sikh	Newcastle-on-Tyne	1962-67	[QRL.96]	5.2.3
Own and parents'views on school, social life, dress, women and employment	Hindu, Muslim, Sikh	Eight English towns and Glasgow	1975	[QRL.23]	5.2.4
Asian boys' leisure activities and needs	Hindu, Muslim, Sikh	Slough	1977	[QRL.59]	5.2.2
Male school leavers	Incl.Hindu, Muslim, Sikh	Glasgow	1972-1973	[QRL.27]	5.6
Single Religions					

Type of data	Breakdown	Area	Frequency	QRL Publication	Text Reference and Remarks
Buddhist					
Buddhist Society activities		UK	Annual	[QRL.17]	2.4.2.4
Hindu					
Local community size	Patidar caste only	Coventry, Rugby	1970	[QRL.95]	4.2.1
Regional origin, caste and organization	Population total	Leeds	1979	[QRL.56]	4.2.2
Local temples, cost and attendance		Bradford, Huddersfield, Coventry	1979-1980	[QRL.11]	4.2.2
Religious teaching; extent and attendance; extent of other activities	Brahma Kumaris World Spiritual University	UK	Annual since 1971	[QRL.12]	2.4.2.2
Membership, magazine circulation	Ramakrishna Vedanta Centre		Annual since 1949	[QRL.74]	2.4.2.2
Muslim					
Total population estimate		UK	Annual 1960-69	[QRL.20]	2.3.2
Total population	Ethnic composition	UK	1971-1975	[QRL.4]	4.1.1
Total population		UK	1975	[QRL.2]	4.1.1
Total population	Country of origin	UK	1980	[QRL.63]	4.1.1
Local community size		Glasgow	1967, 1972	[QRL.85]	4.1.2
Local community size		Birmingham	1971	[QRL.82]	4.1.2
Local community size		Birmingham	n.d.	[QRL.10]	4.1.3
Local community size	Ethnic origin	Birmingham	1971, 1974	[QRL.31]	4.1.3
Local community size, mosques' cost and attendance		Preston	1979	[QRL.34]	4.1.3
Local Pakistani community	Christian, Muslim	Bristol	1971-72	[QRL.50]	3.2.7
Turkish Cypriots		London	1975-76	[QRL.58]	3.2.8

Turkish Cypriots' professions and religious organizations		London	n.d.	[QRL.9]	3.2.8
Asians'age, education and employment	Indians, Pakistanis	Batley	Jan-April 1973	[QRL.60]	3.2.4
Attendance at prayer and festivals	Incl.Pakistanis	Birmingham Sparkbrook	1964	[QRL.80]	3.2.6
Shopping habits	Ethnic origin; (Muslim)	Bradford	Jan-March 1982	[QRL.92]	5.7
Observation of Ramadan fast		London	n.d.	[QRL.3]	3.2.8
Membership of Union of Muslim Organizations		UK	Annual since 1963	[QRL.100]	2.4.2.1
UK Islamic Mission staff and students, Library stocks	Male, female	GB	Annual since 1964	[QRL.99]	2.4.2.1
UK Islamic Mission membership correspondence, distribution of literature	Branch	GB	Annual since 1964	[QRL.99]	2.4.2.1
Local mosques		Birmingham	1980	[QRL.38]	5.5
Local mosques, attendance		Bradford	1972	[QRL.84]	4.1.2
Mosque construction costs and attendance		South shields	1972	[QRL.83]	4.1.2
Mosque construction cost and size		Birmingham	n.d.	[QRL.10]	4.1.3
Mosque construction costs and funding sources		Whitechapel, Liverpool, Nottingham, Leicester, London Central	n.d	[QRL.4]	4.1.1
Mosque construction cost, attendance		Birmingham	1978	[QRL.31]	4.1.3
Mosque school attendance and staffing		Rochdale	1975	[QRL.5]	3.2.3

Type of data	Breakdown	Area	Frequency	QRL Publication	Text Reference and Remarks
Pakistani children in Qur'an school	Male/female; place of instruction	Oxford	1980	[QRL.52]	5.4.2
Christian views of Muslims	Ministers, lay officers, members	Bradford	1966	[QRL.18]	5.9
Muslim images of Christians	Residence, social class	Birmingham	1978-79	[QRL.8]	5.9
Sikh					
Total population, number of temples		England, Wales, Scotland	n.d.	[QRL.22]	4.3.1
Local population residence, education, employment and language		Bradford by ward	1977-78	[QRL.91]	4.3.2
Local temple construction cost and attendance		Bradford	1977-78	[QRL.91]	4.3.2
Local population		Huddersfield Leamington Spa	1964,1969 1970	[QRL.48] [QRL.51]	4.3.1 3.2.5
Language and cultural identity	Bhattra Sikhs only	Cardiff	1979	[QRL.30]	4.3.2
Local population		Southall	n.d.	[QRL.19]	3.2.8
Number of temples, construction costs and management		GB	n.d.	[QRL.49]	4.3.3
Local temple construction cost, membership and attendance		Gravesend	n.d.	[QRL.36]	4.3.1
Children in school		Smethwick	1957	[QRL.25]	4.3.1
		Manchester	Nov.1965	[QRL.102]	5.2.1

Other

Bahai Spiritual Assemblies	UK by district	Annual	National Spiritual Assembly	2.4.2.4
Meditation Society income and expenditure	UK	Annual since 1961	Meditation Society [QRL.37]	2.4.2.4
Zoroastrians: numbers, religious practice, social composition, self-image	UK	1976		4.5

QUICK REFERENCE LIST KEY TO PUBLICATIONS

Reference	Author of Organization	Title	Publisher	Frequency or Date	Remarks
[QRL.1]	All Faiths for One Race	Elders of the Minority Ethnic Groups	AFFOR, Birmingham	1981	
[QRL.2]	Ahmad, Khurshid	Muslims in Europe: An Interim Report Presented to the Secretary General of the Islamic Council of Europe	Islamic Council of Europe, London	1976	
[QRL.3]	Alavi, Hamza A.	"Pakistanis in London", in Patterson, Sheila (Ed) Immigrants in London	National Council of Social Services, London	1963	
[QRL.4]	Ally, M.M.	History of Muslims in Britain, 1850-1980	MA thesis, Dept. of Theology, University of Birmingham	1981	
[QRL.5]	Anwar, Muhammad	The Myth of Return	Heinemann, London	1979	
[QRL.6]	Anwar, Muhammad	Who Tunes into What?	CRE, London	1978	
[QRL.7]	Barrett, David	World Christian Encyclopedia	Oxford University Press, Nairobi	1982	
[QRL.8]	Bhai, Paul	Image of Christian Life among Muslim Residents: A Study of Birmingham	Certificate dissertation, Selly Oak Colleges, Birmingham	1979	
[QRL.9]	Bhatti, F.M.	Turkish Cypriots in London	Research Papers: Muslims in Europe, 11	1981	
[QRL.10]	Birmingham Mosque Trust	A Story of Muslim Survival in Europe	Birmingham Mosque Trust, Birmingham	n.d.	
[QRL.11]	Bowen, David G. (ed.)	Hinduism in England	Faculty of Contemporary Studies, Bradford College, Bradford	1981	

[QRL.12]	Brahma Kumaris World Spiritual University	*UK Service Report*	Raja Yoga Centre, London	Annual since 1971
[QRL.13]	Brierly, Peter (ed.)	*UK Christian Handbook*	Bible Society, London	1982
[QRL.14]	Bristow, M., Adams, B.N. and Pereira, C.	*Ugandan Asians in Britain, Canada and India: Some Characteristics and Resources*	New Community, 4	1975
[QRL.15]	British Council	*Statistics of Overseas Students in the United Kingdom*	The British Council, London	Annual since 1956
[QRL.16]	Brown, John	*The Unmelting Pot: An English Town and its Immigrants*	Macmillan, London	1970
[QRL.17]	Buddhist Society	*The President's Report*	Buddhist Society, London	Annual
[QRL.18]	Butterworth, Eric	*A Muslim Community in England*	Church Information Office, London	1967
[QRL.19]	Campaign against Racism and Fascism	*Southall: The Birth of a Black Community*	Institute of Race Relations and Southall Rights, Southall	1981
[QRL.20]	Central Office of Information	*Britain: An Official Handbook*	HSMO, London	Annual
[QRL.21]	Christopher, E., Kellaher, L.A. and Koch, A von,	*A Survey of the Haringey domiciliary family planning service 1968–1975 Research Report 3*	Dept. of Applied Social Studies, Polytechnic of North London	1980
[QRL.22]	Cole, W. Owen, and Sambhi, P.S.	*The Sikhs*	Routledge, London	1978
[QRL.23]	Community Relations Commission	*Between Two Cultures*	CRC, London	1976
[QRL.24]	Department of Education and Science	*Statistics of Education*	HMSO, London	Annual
[QRL.25]	Desai, Rashmi	*Indian Immigrants in Britain*	Oxford University Press, London	1963

available from the Buddhist Society

Reference	Author of Organization	Title	Publisher	Frequency or Date	Remarks
[QRL.26]	Economist Intelligence Unit	*Studies on Immigration from the Commonwealth: 2, The Immigrant Communities*	Economist Intelligence Unit, London	n.d.	
[QRL.27]	Fowler, B. Littlewood, B. and Madigan, R.	*Immigrant school-leavers and the search for work*	Sociology, 11	1977	
[QRL.28]	General Register Office	*Census 1961: England and Wales*	HMSO, London		
[QRL.29]	General Register Office	*Sample Census 1966*	HMSO, London		
[QRL.30]	Ghuman, P.A.S.	*Bhattra Sikhs in Cardiff: Family and kinship organization*	New Community, 8	1980	
[QRL.31]	Gibson, Flora	*The Muslim Community in Birmingham*	Certificate dissertation, Selly Oak Colleges, Birmingham	1978	
[QRL.32]	Grudzinska, A.D.	*Planning for the Muslim Faith: A Study of the Provision of Mosques in the City of Birmingham*	Diploma dissertation, UWIST, Cardiff	1982	
[QRL.33]	Hahlo, K.G.	*Profile of a Gujarati community in Bolton*	New Community, 8	1980	
[QRL.34]	Harrison, S.W. and Shepherd, D.	*Islam in Preston*	2nd ed. Preston CRC, Preston	1979	
[QRL.35]	Hawkins, P.M.	*Pakistanis in Bradford*	Bradford CRC, Bradford	n.d.	
[QRL.36]	Helweg, A.W.	*Sikhs in England: The Development of a Migrant Community*	Oxford University Press, Delhi	1979	
[QRL.37]	Hinnels, J.R.	*Parsis in Britain*	The K.R. Cama Oriental Institute, London	n.d.	
[QRL.38]	Hodgins, Henry	*Planning permission for mosques: The Birmingham experience*	Research Papers: Muslims in Europe, 9	1981	
[QRL.39]	Home Office	*Commonwealth Immigrants Acts 1962 and 1968: Control of Immigration Statistics*	HMSO, London	Annual 1963-1972	

Key	Author	Title	Publisher	Date
[QRL.40]	Home Office	*Control of Immigration: Statistics*	United Kingdom, HMSO, London	Annual since 1975
[QRL.41]	Home Office	*Immigration Statistics*	HMSO, London	Annual 1973-1974
[QRL.42]	Home Office	*Report on the Work of the Prison Department*	HMSO, London	Annual
[QRL.43]	Home Office	*Statistics of Foreigners Entering and Leaving the United Kingdom*	HMSO, London	Annual 1967-1972
[QRL.44]	Home Office	*Statistics of Persons Acquiring Citizenship of the United Kingdom and Colonies*	HMSO, London	Annual till 1977
[QRL.45]	Home Office	*Tables of Persons Acquiring Citizenship of the United Kingdom and Colonies*	HMSO, London	Annual since 1978
[QRL.46]	Israel, W.H.	*Colour and Community: A Study of Coloured Immigrants and Race Relations in an Industrial Town*	Slough Council of Social Services, Slough	1964
[QRL.47]	Jabbal, Rajinder Singh	*Library services to ethnic minorities in Nottinghamshire, Serving All the Community: Library Services to the Disadvantaged*, Seminar, November 11-13, 1979.	Library Association, South Western Branch, Weston-super-Mare	1980
[QRL.48]	James, Alan G.	*Sikh Children in Britain*	Oxford University Press, London	1974
[QRL.49]	Janjua, H.S.	*Sikh Temples in the UK and the People behind their Management*	Jan Publications, London	1976
[QRL.50]	Jeffery, Patricia	*Migrants and Refugees: Muslim and Christian Families in Bristol*	Cambridge University Press, Cambridge	1976
[QRL.51]	Jenkins, Simon	*Here to Live: A Study of Race Relations in an English Town*	Runnymede Trust, London	1971
[QRL.52]	Johnstone, P.	*The Languages of Ethnic Minority Children: Pakistanis in Oxford*	MA thesis, University of Reading	1981
[QRL.53]	Jones, P.R. and Shah, S.	*Arranged marriages: A sample survey of the Asian case*	New Community, 8	1980
[QRL.54]	Kannan, C.T.	*Cultural Adaptation of Asian Immigrants: First and Second Generation*	C.T. Kannan, Greenford	1978

Reference	Author of Organization	Title	Publisher	Frequency or Date	Remarks
[QRL.55]	Kannan, C.T.	Inter-racial Marriages in London: A Comparative Study	C.T. Kannan, London	1972	
[QRL.56]	Knott, K.	Hinduism in England: The Hindu Population in Leeds	Religious Research Papers, 4	1981	
[QRL.57]	Knott, K. and Toon, R.	Muslims, Sikhs and Hindus in the UK: Problems in the estimation of religious statistics	Religious Research Papers, 6	1980	
[QRL.58]	Ladbury, Sarah	The Turkish Cypriots: Ethnic Relations in London and Cyprus	see [B.26]		
[QRL.59]	Livingstone, P.	The Leisure Needs of Asian Boys Aged 8-14 in Slough, Berkshire	The Scout Association, London	1978	
[QRL.60]	McGrath, Morag	The economic position of immigrants in Batley	New Community, 5	1976-77	
[QRL.61]	Morton-Williams, Jean, and Stowell, Richard	Small Heath, Birmingham: An Inner Area Study	SCPR, London	1974	
[QRL.62]	Nelson, G.K.	Religious groups in a changing social environment	Religion in the Birmingham Area, Dept. of Theology, University of Birmingham	1975	
[QRL.63]	Nielsen, Jorgen S.	Muslims in Europe: An overview	Bryman, A (ed.) Research Papers: Muslims in Europe, 12	1980	
[QRL.64]	Northern Ireland, General Register Office	Census of Population, 1971	County Reports, HMSO, Belfast		
[QRL.65]	Office of Population Censuses and Surveys	Birth Statistics	HMSO, London	Annual since 1974	
[QRL.66]	Office of Population Censuses and Surveys	Census 1971 England and Wales: County Reports	HMSO, London		

[QRL.67]	Office of Population Censuses and Surveys	*Census 1971 Great Britain: Country of Birth Supplementary Tables*	HMSO, London 1978
[QRL.68]	Office of Population Censuses and Surveys	*Census 1981: Country of Birth, Great Britain*	HMSO, London 1983
[QRL.69]	Office of Population Censuses and Surveys	*International Migration*	HMSO, London Annual since 1974
[QRL.70]	Office of Population Censuses and Surveys	*Labour Force Survey*	HMSO, London alternate years from 1973
[QRL.71]	Office of Population Censuses and Surveys	*Marriage and Divorce Statistics*	HMSO, London Annual since 1974
[QRL.72]	Office of Population Censuses and Surveys	*The Registrar-General's Statistical Review of England and Wales*	HMSO, London Annual till 1973
[QRL.73]	Phillips, D.	*The social and spatial segregation of Asians in Leicester*	See [B.12]
[QRL.74]	Ramakrishna Vedanta Centre	*Annual Report*	Ramakrishna Vedanta Centre, Bourne End, Bucks. Annual since 1969
[QRL.75]	Ratcliffe, Peter	*Racism and Reaction: A Profile of Handsworth*	Routledge and Kegan Paul, London 1981
[QRL.76]	Registrar General for Scotland	*Annual Report of the Registrar General for Scotland*	HMSO, Edinburgh Annual
[QRL.77]	Registrar General for Scotland	*Census 1971 Scotland*	HMSO, Edinburgh
[QRL.78]	Registrar General for Scotland	*Census 1971 Scotland: Usual Residence and Birthplace Tables*	HMSO, Edinburgh
[QRL.79]	Research Unit on Ethnic Relations	*Urban Institutions Survey*	Unpublished
[QRL.80]	Rex, John, and Moore, R.	*Race, Community and Conflict: A Study of Sparkbrook*	Oxford University Press, London 1969
[QRL.81]	Rex, John, and Tomlinson, S.	*Colonial Immigrants in a British City*	Routledge and Kegan Paul, London 1979

Reference	Author of Organization	Title	Publisher	Frequency or Date	Remarks
[QRL.82]	Ritchie, J.M.	*The Islamic community in the city of Birmingham*	Unpublished, available from the British Council of Churches, London		
[QRL.83]	Ritchie, J.M.	*Report on the Muslim community in South Shields*	Unpublished, available from the British Council of Churches, London		
[QRL.84]	Ritchie, J.M.	*A Survey of the Muslim community of Bradford*	Unpublished, available from the British Council of Churches, London	n.d.	
[QRL.85]	Ritchie, J.M.	*A survey of the Muslim community of the city of Glasgow*	Unpublished, available from the British Council of Churches, London		
[QRL.86]	Robinson, Vaughan	*The segregation of Asians within a British city: Theory and practice*	Research Paper 22, School of Geography, University of Oxford, Oxford, n.d.		
[QRL.87]	Robinson, Vaughan, and Flintoff, I.	*Asian retailing in Coventry*	New community, 10	1982	
[QRL.88]	Rose, E.J.B.	*Colour and Citizenship: A Report on British Race Relations*	Oxford University Press, London	1969	
[QRL.89]	Saifullah Khan, Verity	*The Pakistanis: Mirpuri villagers at home and in Bradford*	see [B.26]		

[QRL.90]	Sims, Ron	*Spatial separation between Asian religious minorities: An aid to explanation or obfuscation?*	see [B.12]
[QRL.91]	Singh, Ramindar	*The Sikh Community in Bradford*	Bradford College, Bradford, 1978
[QRL.92]	Singh, Ramindar, and Green, Sebastian	*Minorities in the Market Place: A Study of South Asian and West Indian Shoppers in Bradford*	National Consumer Council, 1982
[QRL.93]	Smith, David J.	*The Facts of Racial Disadvantage: A National Survey*	PEP, London, 1976
[QRL.94]	Social and Community Planning Research	*Ethnic residential choice*	SSRC Data Archive, study no.791
[QRL.95]	Tambs-Lyche, Harald	*A comparison of Gujarati communities in London and the Midlands*	New Community, 4, 1975
[QRL.96]	Taylor, J.H.	*The Half-Way Generation: A Study of Asian Youths in Newcastle-upon-Tyne*	National Foundation for Educational Research, London, 1976
[QRL.97]	Tayside CRC	*Ethnic Minority Groups in Tayside: A Brief Survey*	Tayside CRC, Dundee, 1979
[QRL.98]	Townsend, H.E.R.	*Immigrant Pupils in England: The LEA Response*	National Foundation for Educational Research, Slough, 1971
[QRL.99]	UK Islamic Mission	*Annual Report*	UK Islamic Mission, London, Annual since 1964
[QRL.100]	Union of Muslim Organizations of the UK and Eire	*Annual Conference*	Union of Muslim Organizations, London, Annual since 1971
[QRL.101]	Wade, Donald	*Yorkshire Survey: A Report on Community Relations in Yorkshire*	Yorkshire CRC, Leeds, 1971
[QRL.102]	Youth Development Trust	*Young and Coloured in Manchester*	Youth Development Trust, Manchester, 1967

BIBLIOGRAPHY

[B.1] Anwar, Muhammad, 'Pakistanis and Indians in the 1971 Census: some ambiguities', *New Community*, 3 (1974)

[B.2] Anwar, Muhammad, *Young Muslims in a Multi-Cultural Society: Their Education Needs and Policy Implications: The British Case.* The Islamic Foundation, Leicester, 1982

[B.3] Buddhist Society. *The Buddhist Directory.* The Buddhist Society, London, 1st ed. 1979, 2nd ed. 1981

[B.4] Buddhist Society, *Sixty Years of Buddhism in England.* The Buddhist Society, London, 1980

[B.5] Bulmer, Martin, 'On the feasibility of identifying 'race' and 'ethnicity' in censuses and surveys', *New Community*. 8 (1980)

[B.6] Catholic Commission for Racial Justice, *Rastafarians in Jamaica and Britain*, Notes and Reports, 10 (Jan.1982)

[B.7] Central Statistical Office, *Social Trends*, HMSO, London, annual

[B.8] Central Statistical Office, *Sources of Statistics on Religion*, HMSO, London, 1976

[B.9] Gay, John D., *The Geography of Religion in England*, Duckworth, London, 1971

[B.10] Hawkins, P.M. *Hinduism in Bradford*, Bradford Metropolitan District CRC, Bradford, n.d.

[B.11] Institute of Race Relations, *Facts Paper: Colour and Immigration in the United Kingdom.* Institute of Race Relations, London, 1st ed.1968

[B.12] Jackson, P. and Smith, S.J. (eds.), *Ethnic Segregation and Social Interaction.* Academic Press, London, 1981

[B.13] Knott, K. *Statistical Analysis of South Asians in the U.K. by Religion and Ethnicity*, CRP Research Paper, 8 (1981), Dept. of Theology, University of Leeds

[B.14] Knott, K. and Toon, R. *Considering Religious Statistics: Sikhs, Hindus and Muslims in the UK of South Asian Ethnic Origin*, CRP Research Paper, 7 (1980), Dept.of Theology, University of Leeds

[B.15] Mehta, G.M.T. 'Parsees in Britain: The Experience of a Religious Minority Group', *New Community*, 10 (1982)

[B.16] Office of Population Censuses and Surveys, The Registrar General, *The Official List: Part 3.* OPCS, London, 1981

[B.17] Office of Population Censuses and Surveys, *Population Trends*, 13, HMSO, London, 1978

[B.18] Office of Population Censuses and Surveys, *Population Trends*, 28, HMSO, London, 1982

[B.19] Peach, G.C.K. and Winchester, S.W.C. 'Birthplace, Ethnicity and the Under-Enumeration of West Indians, Indians and Pakistanis in the Censuses of 1966 and 1971', *New Community*, 3 (1974)

[B.20] Richmond, Anthony H. *Migration and Race Relations in an English City*. Oxford University Press, London, 1973

[B.21] Runnymede Trust and Radical Statistics Race Group, *Britain's Black Population*. Heinemann Educational Books, London, 1980

[B.22] Shaheen, Gulrez, *Ethnic Residential Choice: Methodological Report*. SCPR, London, 1975

[B.23] Sillitoe, Ken, *Ethnic Origins: An Experiment in the Use of a Direct Question about Ethnicity for the Census, 1-4*. OPCS Occasional Papers, 8 (1978), 9 (1978), 10 (1978), 24 (1981)

[B.24] Smith, Greg, *Locating Populations of Minority Language Speakers: An Example of Practice from the Coventry Language Project*, L.M.P. Working Paper, 1 (1982), Institute of Education, University of London

[B.25] Tiptaft, Norman (ed.), *Religion in Birmingham*, Norman Tiptaft Ltd, Warley, 1972

[B.26] Watson, James L.(ed.), *Between Two Cultures: Migrants and Minorities in Britain*. Basil Blackwell, Oxford, 1977

SUBJECT INDEX